GLORY
LOST
and
FOUND

GLORY
LOST
and
FOUND

How Delta Climbed from Despair to Dominance in the Post-9/11 Era

SETH KAPLAN   JAY SHABAT

First edition published in 2015 in the United States of America by
Airline Weekly Corp.
746 Northeast 7th Avenue
Fort Lauderdale, Florida 33304 USA
www.airlineweekly.com

ISBN: 978-0-9969901-0-3 (hardcover)
ISBN: 978-0-9969901-1-0 (paperback)
ISBN: 978-0-9969901-2-7 (eBook)

Library of Congress Control Number: 2015919030

First published in 2015 by Airline Weekly Corp.
Book design by Jera Publishing
Cover design by Jera Publishing

CONTENTS

9/11

"We're about to run out of money"

The weekly meeting of company executives had just begun. It was on a Tuesday morning this week, because Leo Mullin, the chief executive, had been giving a speech during the usual time on Monday.

Millions of Americans up and down the east coast, who were also settling in at their jobs that morning, know the next part of the story, because they experienced it too: Somebody got a phone call. Somebody turned on the nearest TV. People gathered around it.

"It looks like a small plane might have hit into the tower," Mullin, telling the story years later, would recall someone in the room saying. And for 17 minutes that Tuesday morning, Sept. 11, 2001, that seemed plausible. Most other Americans who had tuned in surely believed it too, because TV hosts scrambling to cover the story were guessing similarly and because the images from afar—of one World Trade Center tower with damage to some of its higher floors, smoke billowing—gave them no reason to believe otherwise. It could have been an accident. It could have been one lunatic with access to a private plane.

If anyone gathered around the TV in the executive offices of Delta Air Lines would have known better, that person would have been Fred Buttrell. Now he was a commercial man, Delta's head of strategic planning. But a decade earlier, he had been an Air Force fighter pilot, a commander of Operation Desert Storm missions and—before that—a Top Gun of his squadron. Buttrell knew airplanes. And Buttrell knew better.

"You know, that looks like a bigger plane," he said to Mullin.

Then at 9:03 a.m., what the world would later learn was United Airlines Flight 175 struck the other tower—the South Tower—and everybody quickly understood what was happening.

But at that moment, although air traffic controllers had received distress calls, nobody knew for sure which airline's planes had been lost or how many others might have been hijacked too. Mullin knew Delta operated roughly 20 percent of the flights in New York airspace, so it didn't take a Harvard-trained mathematician—although Mullin was one—to also realize Delta crew and passengers had likely fallen victim.

"But my heart was in my throat for a very personal reason," Mullin recalled.

He and his wife Leah, parents of a diabetic child, had for two decades actively supported the Juvenile Diabetes Research Foundation. Leah was a member of the organization's board and was traveling that morning on a Delta flight from Atlanta to New York, on her way to a foundation event.

"And I'm like, 'My God,' you know, 'could it possibly be her plane?'" Leo Mullin recalled thinking. "And I had no way of knowing."

A different Delta flight, meanwhile, looked even more likely to be a target.

Sandwiched right between American Airlines Flight 11, which took off from Boston at 7:59 a.m.—a Boeing 767 bound for Los Angeles but striking the North Tower at 8:46 a.m.—and United Airlines Flight 175, which took off from Boston at 8:14 a.m.—a 767 bound for Los Angeles but striking the South Tower at 9:03 a.m.—was another Boston-Los Angeles flight: Delta Flight 1989, a 767 scheduled, like the United flight, to push back from its gate at exactly 8 a.m. Mullin and his team feared the worst. Their fears only intensified as air traffic controllers couldn't immediately reach the pilots and then thought they heard someone in the cockpit send a distress signal, which had actually come from one of the hijacked flights.

Delta's Operations Control Center (OCC), a few hundred yards from the airline's executive offices and in full emergency mode, coordinating with the FAA, soon ascertained that Flight 1989 was safe. It was diverting to Cleveland. Still taking no chances, air traffic controllers told the pilots to increase cockpit security, and—as would later be detailed in the 9/11 Commission report—a SWAT team met the flight on the tarmac and held it at gunpoint for two hours.

Two other flights—American 77 from Dulles to Los Angeles and United 93 from Newark to San Francisco—had been hijacked and would end in disaster, crashing into the Pentagon near Washington, D.C., and in a field in Shanksville, Pa.

But within about a half hour after the South Tower was struck, the OCC team could assure Mullin, who by now had joined them in the OCC, that all Delta flights were accounted for and seemed to be safe. They were landing at airports everywhere, in almost no cases the ones for which they were supposed to be destined.

And Leah Mullin? Leo Mullin would later learn how close she had been to the carnage. The captain on her flight announced to passengers that if they looked out their windows, they could see smoke coming from a World Trade Center tower—a plane, he had been told, had struck it. But then she felt the plane she was on veer suddenly, and the captain spoke again: "Ladies and gentleman," she recalled him saying, "I don't know what's happening here, but there's some kind of a crisis going on in New York City, and we're going to Allentown, Pennsylvania." And that's where they went.

About six hours after the attacks, Mullin was in the OCC when his assistant ran to him. "Leo," she said. "Leah's on the phone!"

"I was so relieved," he recalled. He had known hours earlier that she was surely safe, but he hadn't yet heard her voice.

"And I remember she says, 'Well, when will a plane come to get us?' I said, 'Leah, you don't understand. The nation is shutting down its entire airspace.'" There would be no plane coming to get her—or anyone.

But he knew she wasn't alone. There was the flight's crew, after all, the pilots and flight attendants—they were stranded too. Most flights had other employees as well, either commuting or taking advantage of their flight benefits—non-revenue travelers, or "non-revs," as they are known in the industry.

"I said, 'You find somebody there and hook up and see if you can just drive back,'" Mullin recalled. "And she did. She found two Delta people and hooked on with them"—they had managed to rent a car—"and drove back to Atlanta. It took them 15 hours to drive back."

The next day, Wednesday, the FAA quietly allowed some flights that had diverted to continue to their destinations. By Thursday, U.S. airlines had begun operating a handful of new flights, and by Friday, they were running something that resembled a normal schedule of flights, albeit at reduced levels, which didn't matter too much to the flying public, because almost nobody wanted to fly. "But we were pretty proud to get going," Mullin recalled.

Mullin was responsible for the whole airline, which was now doing the most basic thing an airline needs to do. Delta was back in the air.

But Michelle Burns was responsible for one thing: the airline's finances. She, after all, was Delta's chief financial officer, and she approached Mullin that Friday morning.

"And I was kind of talking in a rather enthusiastic way about getting the system back up, although in a very limited way," he recalled. "And she says—she never calls me 'boss,' but she said, 'Hey, boss, you must feel pretty good about this?' I said, 'Yeah.' She said, 'Well, I've got another little problem I have to bring to your attention.'"

"What's that, Michelle?"

"We're about to run out of money."

Mullin's jaw dropped as Burns continued. "There's no revenue," the CFO said. "The costs are continuing with no prospect of any revenue coming back for some time. We really have a problem."

The airline business in 2001, after all, was largely what's called a fixed-cost business. Mortgages or leases on aircraft, leases on gates at airports, employee salaries... these were all payments Delta was obligated to continue making even if it had no customers, even if it was flying less than before. Sure, Delta didn't burn as much fuel while it was flying less—fuel was a variable rather than a fixed cost—but jet fuel, in September 2001, averaged (according to the U.S. Energy Information Administration) just 74 cents per gallon. The most important costs continued as if nothing had changed, even though everything had changed.

"And it was kind of a 'holy shit' moment," Mullin recalled of his conversation with Burns. "She and I got together shortly thereafter, and she ran me through our numbers. And I said, 'Oh, my God.' I mean, there was just no way Delta could survive, and I presume any airline could survive this financially, because we're all heavily levered organizations and therefore require enormous revenues to cover our costs. And here we are at zero and expected to be very low for a long period of time."

Mullin knew these weren't Delta-specific problems. If anything, Delta was healthier prior to 9/11 than most of its competitors, and unlike United and American, Delta hadn't lost any planes or people. Industrywide problems would require industrywide solutions.

Donald Carty was chairman of the Air Transport Association (ATA)—the U.S. airlines' lobby group—alongside his main role as CEO of American Airlines, which had indeed lost two planes and 17 crew members and 129 passengers.

"So I called him up," Mullin recalled, "and I said, 'Don, I don't know what you're doing, looking at your numbers, but I'm looking at mine, and we don't have much staying power here.'"

Carty, it seemed, had also had a "holy shit" moment—in his case while speaking with *his* CFO, Tom Horton.

"Leo," Carty said. "I'm in exactly the same spot."

Mullin and Carty decided during the same call to appoint a team of two: their two CFOs, Burns and Horton. "And they would go forward," Mullin recalled, "and obtain from all the airlines—all the large airlines, at least—some back-of-the-envelope calculations, some numbers that we could put together that somehow would give a sense of what the financial picture was for the airlines."

In normal times, competitors wouldn't have been allowed to discuss that sort of information—doing so would be collusion and could run afoul of antitrust laws. Everyone understood these weren't normal times. Still, it helped that Carty could call on ATA staff to help coordinate with airlines to ensure that however hastily these talks had to happen—there was no getting around that—they would happen legally.

"And they carried that out over that weekend," Mullin said. "And in about a four-day period, they put together a massive amount of data ... to show what the financial picture of the entire industry would be out, you know, five and six, seven months, and even a couple of years based on various assumptions that they would make." Financial forecasts can be dicey under far better circumstances. In this case? "Nobody really knew what the heck was going to happen."

That was true too of the country at large. Would the American economy recover from the shock? If so, how long would it take? Commerce was clearly disrupted. Residents of New York City were told to stay home from work. The U.S. dollar plunged in global markets. Wall Street in lower Manhattan, the site of two of the four aerial attacks and the heart of America's financial system, was closed for business. "When U.S. markets will reopen, and what will happen when trading resumes, is unclear, as officials sift through the physical damage and human carnage," *The Wall Street Journal* wrote.

***

Leo Mullin, then 58 years old, was not of the swashbuckling breed of glamorous aviators who had piloted the industry's early days. Mullin was an academic. To speak only of his master's degree in applied mathematics from Harvard, in fact, was to understate the case, because that was only one of three degrees he had earned at the institution. When Delta hired him as just the sixth CEO in the company's seven-decade history, its board of directors was looking for an industry outsider, someone who could modernize and professionalize a company famed for its southern charm and conservative finances but adjusting uncomfortably to massive industry changes. Mullin, the first outsider ever called upon to run Delta, had been a management consultant, a railroad executive and a banker before arriving in Atlanta in 1997.

On Monday, Sept. 17, 2001, six days after the attacks, he joined the CEOs of all ATA-member airlines—"every one of them," Mullin recalled—in Washington. The next day, they went to the White House to make their case that the industry needed help. They met in the Roosevelt Room, down the hall from the Oval Office, where President Bush worked. Mullin saw Dick Cheney, the vice president, and Tom Ridge, the future secretary of "homeland security," as the position would come to be known, rush by. In the room with the airline CEOs were Secretary of Transportation Norman Mineta and—because everyone understood the airlines would be asking for money—the heads of the U.S. Treasury and of the Office of Management and Budget. Carty, the tall, deep-voiced, snowy-haired Canadian who chaired the ATA, took the lead in explaining the gravity of the situation. The administration officials pledged their support to the CEOs. Following the meeting, Mineta and an industry representative—Carty was the logical choice—would address media members, who were waiting outside.

"And near the end of it," Mullin recalled, "Don Carty motioned to me for a moment and he said, 'Leo, look, I've got to get back to Dallas because my two planes were involved in this, and I've just got to go back.'" United CEO Jim Goodwin's predicament was similar. Mullin understood. He was the only CEO of one of the three giant U.S. airlines, United, American and Delta, who didn't bear the additional burden of having lost planes and people. Carty asked him to stand alongside Mineta and represent the industry.

"I said, 'Sure,'" Mullin recalled. "Little did I know what I was stepping into."

About 10 minutes later, Mineta motioned for Mullin to follow him. First they huddled in a corridor with one of Mineta's public relations people. Mineta, they decided, would speak first, followed by Mullin.

"And the two of us, after this five minute conversation, stood up and walked out of the West Wing to the largest number of cameras I have ever seen in my life," Mullin said. "I mean, you almost couldn't see how many cameras there were. It looked to me like there were a hundred yards of cameras staring at you. And, of course, what was happening was, the eyes of the world were on the White House. And they were starving for information."

Mineta spoke briefly of "positive exchanges" with the CEOs during the just-completed meeting. "We are talking about the safety, the security and the stability of an industry, not of one or two or three or four companies," Mineta said.

"And then," Mullin recalled, "he said, 'Now Leo Mullin will tell you what's going on.' I was thinking, 'You're the secretary!' And so I stepped in front and kind of addressed, I think, the world."

Speaking for about two minutes, he described, in his New England accent, how airlines and government officials had worked to safely ground all planes within an hour and a half of the attacks, and how they had created new security procedures and re-launched some operations within two days. "And now," he said, "with that immediate-term issue behind us, we have to turn to the financial stability of the industry."

Then came the questions, about five minutes' worth, some handled by Mullin and some by Mineta. Most dealt with the details of the planned stabilization efforts. Mineta, a Japanese American who was the only Democratic cabinet member in the Bush administration, made clear the administration was broadly supportive of the industry.

But that support wouldn't be enough, for it was Congress that would have to vote to allocate funds. And there was little time for the usual politicking between the White House and Capitol Hill. Carol Hallett, the ATA's top staff member, approached Mullin.

"Look, Leo," she said. "We've got to go up and talk to Tom Daschle"—the Senate majority leader—"so you'll have to repeat this conversation."

"So we went up there," Mullin recalled. "By this time, just by virtue of this, I was kind of slipping into a little bit of an unofficial role here." Mullin was the *de facto* industry spokesman.

Soon he was speaking in a committee room full of lawmakers and cameras. He had gone to Washington prepared to talk about Delta's situation, but now legislators were grilling him about the entire airline industry. How much did the industry want? Why that amount? How had the airlines come up with that figure? Mullin had just been appointed the unofficial industry spokesman and had no time, since Carty had deputized him a few hours earlier in the Roosevelt room, to fully synthesize the whole industry's figures. So "I didn't do too well on the numbers and I sort of stumbled my way through it," Mullin recalled.

The meeting ended. Mullin and some of the lawmakers spoke with media outside the room. "And then Tom Daschle motioned to me as I was going out," Mullin recalled, "and he says, 'Leo, I want to give you a bit of advice here,' he said. By this time, we had heard that there were going to be hearings for the next two days. And he says, 'Your people better be better on the numbers than you were today, because basically, you'll get killed.'"

Hours later, Mullin was in a conference room at the ATA's offices, eating a McDonald's hamburger. ATA staff had learned hearings had been scheduled at the

House of Representatives the following day—Wednesday—and at the Senate Thursday. "And the first thing that they said was, 'We have to decide on our principal witness,'" Mullin recalled. "And I was taking a bite out of my hamburger, and I looked up, and almost all the people were looking at me. And I said, 'Hey, wait a minute.'"

Again, Carty would have been the most logical choice. But as in the Roosevelt room, Mullin understood he was the one person in the world who had the stature to do what was necessary among those whose planes hadn't actually been hijacked.

This time, the pressure would be greater. Perhaps he could be forgiven, under the extraordinarily rushed circumstances, for today's sloppy performance. There would be no such excuse tomorrow.

"Well, at that point," Mullin recalled, "we had nothing. We had no testimony." He called his assistant Cindy Mullennix, who was in Atlanta. "And I told her to just grab some clothes and come on up to Washington and I'd meet her at the hotel."

At that time, flying to Washington didn't really mean flying to Washington—i.e., nearby Reagan National Airport—but to distant Dulles International Airport in Virginia, beyond most of the area's suburbs. National remained closed, and speculation was rampant about whether it would ever reopen—perhaps commercial flights there posed too much risk, being so close to so many of the world's most sensitive buildings? (It would ultimately reopen Oct. 4 with stringent new procedures in place.)

While he was waiting for Mullennix to arrive, Mullin met for about an hour and a half with Beverly Goulet, an executive in American's treasury who had helped its CFO Horton and Delta's CFO Burns gather all the airlines' financial figures—Bev Goulet, at this point, might have had a better grasp on the industry figures than anyone else in the world. Armed with everything he had gathered, Mullin began drafting an outline, about a page and a half of bulleted speaking points by the time Mullennix arrived at about 11 p.m. Mullin handed her his outline and asked her to—based on those—draft his remarks for the next day. He would get some overdue sleep and meet her in the lobby at 6 a.m.

He was pleased to awake to a "phenomenal" draft, one that didn't require too many of his own edits before he headed with Mullennix over to the ATA office. There, they passed out copies of the draft in a room that was "packed, largely with lawyers, all of whom wanted a piece of the action." More edits, and then it was time for Mullin to head over to Capitol Hill for the 11 a.m. hearing, prepared remarks in hand.

Or, what he thought were the remarks. As he was leaving, Mullennix realized she had handed him the wrong version. And there was no time to wait for the correct one. "And so I headed up to the Congress without any speech whatsoever," he recalled.

She stayed behind at the ATA office to fix it. Had Mullin's opening remarks truly opened the hearing, which did begin promptly at 11 a.m., it might have been yet another bad performance, and this time inexcusably so. But fortunately, congressmen first made their own opening remarks. And "just before my time was arriving," he recalled, "all of a sudden over my shoulder the printed remarks plop down. That's how much preparation I had."

The hearing—actually held by the House Commerce Committee, in a 55-seat room—lasted four hours. Mullin, although the key witness, was one of just six executives representing the industry. Among the others: Fred Smith, who one night in April 1973 had worked with a team to manually sort 186 packages on tables at the airport in Memphis and send them onward to their destinations, launching a company—Federal Express—that would become so ubiquitous that the company would later change its name to what Americans had decided it would be called. FedEx, of course, carried cargo, not people. The other four, in addition to Mullin, were John Kelly, the CEO of Alaska Airlines; Tom Horton, American's CFO; Doug Parker, a 39-year-old financial whiz, trained at both American and Northwest, who was now running a smallish airline called America West, having been elevated to the CEO role just 10 days before 9/11; and a bespectacled 45-year-old Texan named Richard Anderson, the chief executive of Minneapolis-based Northwest Airlines. Sitting behind Anderson, not among the six, was Northwest's No. 2 executive, a lawyer named Douglas Steenland. Everyone realized Delta's current plight was in Mullin's hands. No one realized then that not one but four of those men—Mullin, of course, but also Parker, Anderson and Steenland—would factor prominently in the history of Delta's forthcoming decade.

Mullin read his opening statement—the one he had outlined and his assistant had crafted overnight—which detailed the industry's "stunning" operational recovery, in just 13 days since the attacks, but contrasted that against its dire financial situation. U.S. airlines would lose $5 billion in September alone, he told them, and no one knew when consumer and corporate demand for air travel would begin recovering—airlines were guessing their total 9/11-related losses would be something like $24 billion. What everyone knew for sure, on the other hand, was that the cost of providing that air travel would increase thanks to dramatically heightened security procedures. "I am here to ask your help in the development and approval of a package of transition aid so that, as Transportation Secretary Mineta said recently, we do not allow the enemy to win this war by restricting our freedom of mobility," Mullin said.

And then he told them what airlines wanted from the federal government: a $5 billion immediate cash infusion plus $12.5 billion in loan guarantees—in other words, promises to cover shortfalls if airlines borrowed money and couldn't later repay it, because without such guarantees, no sensible bank would lend money to a U.S. airline right now. Mullin said airlines also wanted help covering their insurance premiums, which were already skyrocketing: The *increases* alone looked likely to top $1 billion, on top of the billions airlines had already been paying during better times. And airlines, Mullin said, wanted the federal government to bear the burden of increased security measures, because—the argument went—these were national security expenses, not airline expenses. Most of the people who had died on 9/11, after all, weren't even traveling that day.

Roughly three hours of questioning followed. Some congressmen were supportive, none more so than Atlanta-born Johnny Isakson, a longtime friend of Delta, which employed many of his constituents. Isakson, a Republican, told fellow committee members that airlines contributed a mammoth $30 billion in federal taxes annually, money that would disappear if the industry collapsed. Others were less supportive, including some who used the occasion to pontificate about corporate welfare, executive pay and worker rights.

Mullin took the lead in responding to most questions, including inquires about how the money would be divided up among individual carriers, the extent to which airlines would cut their own costs (this would be a condition for receiving some of the aid) and whether airline executives would share the pain that would be imposed on their workers. He acknowledged the possibility of 100,000 layoffs, although Delta itself hadn't dismissed anyone yet, and emphasized the need to act swiftly. How swiftly?

"Swift is like Friday," Mullin said. "I mean, that is the kind of time frame that we need."

Northwest's Richard Anderson handled questions about cargo, collective bargaining rights for workers, management compensation, serving small communities and one about whether airlines should cancel their aircraft orders with Airbus, the European aircraft manufacturer that competed against America's Boeing.

Anderson replied that not only would doing so be inappropriate and a breach of firm commitments, but in a globalized world where Toyotas are manufactured in Indiana and Fords in Mexico, what defined a U.S. aircraft, anyway?

"Those Airbus airplanes all have Pratt & Whitney and General Electric engines in them," Anderson said. "The day I cancel an order for an Airbus 320, I just canceled two engine orders for General Electric and a wheel and brake order for BF Goodrich and an avionics order for Honeywell," all U.S.-based manufacturers of aircraft parts.

That night, Mullin appeared on most network and cable television news programs, a rapid rise in prominence for a man whose name Mineta, the nation's top transportation official, had actually twice mispronounced (as "Mullins," adding an "s" at the end) during their first joint appearance at the White House two days earlier.

The next day, Thursday, Sept. 20, Mullin repeated the process for the Senate Commerce Committee, in a three-hour meeting that he handled mostly by himself—this time the only other airline executive testifying was Kerry Skeen, chief executive of Atlantic Coast Airlines, a regional airline contracted by large airlines to fly small aircraft, branded as "Delta Connection" or "United Express," on their behalf. Among the senators asking questions were the future presidential nominees John Kerry of Massachusetts and John McCain of Arizona, as well as the future presidential candidate and vice presidential nominee John Edwards.

Two days earlier, Tom Daschle had told Mullin he had to be better. This time, when a Senator—Ernest "Fritz" Hollings of South Carolina, who chaired the committee—commented about Mullin's performance, the review was starkly different.

"The industry sent the right man," Hollings said of Mullin.

His lobbying work done for the moment, and with so much to do back at Delta, he headed to the airport to catch a flight back to Atlanta. "And we were going through

Dulles," he recalled, "and all the employees came up, and it was—they just were all kind of cheering me on. The Delta team spirit was invigorating."

Late that night and into Friday's early hours, Leo and Leah Mullin were watching C-Span when the Senate approved the airline aid package 96-1. The House followed suit, 356-54; most of the "nay" votes were Democrats frustrated the legislation wouldn't do more to help the countless workers who were being furloughed.

The following day, Sept. 22, a Saturday, President Bush signed the Air Transportation Safety and System Stabilization Act, which included the $5 billion in grants to airlines that they had sought, with money allotted in proportion to each carrier's size as measured by available seat miles, or ASMs, a common industry measure of the number of seats an airline offers for sale multiplied by the distance those seats fly. Delta would receive $690 million.

The act also ensured airlines had affordable access to terrorism insurance at a time when providers withdrew from the market. And it authorized $10 billion in loan guarantees to airlines demonstrating an ability to restructure, which—far from the worker protection some Democratic congressmen wanted—often meant cutting labor costs. Labor costs were, after all, an airline's single largest expense: about 40 percent of Delta's total operating costs. If airlines were to survive the aftermath of 9/11, labor would have to sacrifice.

The government response to 9/11, however, was anything but uniformly positive for the airline industry. Even the cash infusion, for which most airlines were desperate, was not welcomed by cash-rich Southwest, which stood to gain if some of its competitors failed. Beyond that, Washington reinvented airport security in ways that were both expensive—airlines would have to pay for many of the changes—and greatly inconvenient to passengers, so much so that resulting hassles proved a major de-stimulant to air travel, especially on shorter routes where driving or taking the train were viable alternatives. In this area too, Southwest—with the shortest average flights, often between cities where driving was an option—was hardest hit. But Delta had some big-money shorthaul routes too, most notably in the country's densely populated northeast corridor. During the 1990s, in fact, the "shuttle" routes connecting New York with Boston and Washington had been among the most profitable in the nation. But that happy situation—happy for the airlines flying those routes, anyway, namely Delta and US Airways, if less so for their customers—would forever change after 9/11. As it happened, the new airport security hassles came just a year after Amtrak had debuted its new high-speed Acela rail service. Any business traveler who hadn't yet sampled Acela did so now.

The new approach to airport security involved federalizing a process for which airlines were previously responsible. Screeners employed by outsourced security firms with names like Globe Security and Argenbright were replaced with better-paid government employees, who were subject to more rigorous background checks. The 9/11 terrorists, after all, had carried their box-cutting knives through checkpoints staffed by contractors. (Lost in the debate: On that day, those knives were legal; federal workers, no matter how well paid or well trained, wouldn't have been expected to confiscate them either.) These new federal employees, moreover, were part of a new Department of Homeland Security, whose creation marked one of the largest expansions of the federal government since Franklin D. Roosevelt's New Deal.

Airlines argued they shouldn't be forced to pay for something that protected not just their employees and passengers but the entire country: Homeland security is a national defense priority, they said, which should be funded from general tax receipts. But general tax receipts were falling due to the post-dot-com-bubble recession and the fact that just three months before 9/11, President Bush had signed into law new legislation that significantly cut federal income taxes. So airlines lost the argument and faced what would eventually become a roughly $3.5 billion annual bill for aviation security.

And the headaches didn't end there. Also following 9/11 were terrorist watch lists, explosive detection machines, color-coded terror alert levels, body scanners, federal air marshals, fortified cockpit doors, random physical searches, comprehensive aircraft searches, advanced explosive detection systems and bans on box cutters and numerous other items.

Airlines were no happier about Washington's decision to tighten the nation's visa regime, making it far more difficult for foreigners to visit the U.S. In 2000, U.S. airlines had sold $20 billion worth of airline tickets to foreigners, a figure that dropped to $17 billion in 2001, $16 billion in 2002 and $15 billion in 2003, according to data from the U.S. Commerce Department. The U.S. issued 7.1 million non-immigrant visas in 2000, a number that dropped to just 4.9 million by 2003. Markets like Miami were especially hard hit. The country soon acquired an unwelcoming image abroad, especially among those whose visits were tainted by interminable waits in airport immigration halls and by demeaning searches.

"And then of course," recalled Fred Reid, Delta's president and its No. 2 executive behind Mullin, "even the smallest thing on a plane—anybody mumbling or praying—if it wasn't a Roman Catholic nun or a Jewish rabbi, everybody was like, 'What the hell?' I was traveling a lot, I remember, trying to calm everybody down, and I was literally preaching tolerance. I wrote letters to the staff saying, 'Look, you can't let this happen. This is what they intended.'" By "they," he meant the 9/11 terrorists.

(Cynthia McKinney, a Democratic Congresswoman from Atlanta, read aloud an excerpt of one such letter from Reid during a speech, in October, on the floor of the U.S. House of Representatives. "If only the rest of this nation's airline carriers could follow Delta's lead," she said.)

Worst off were Arab visitors and even Arab-Americans re-entering the country after a trip abroad. After 9/11, immigration officials had little choice but to view countries like Saudi Arabia as a source of anti-American fanaticism. But for airlines, that was only part of the reality. Lost in the fog of war were the many Saudis who routinely visited America and its many tourist sights. At one point, Saudi Arabian

Airlines had even operated flights from Jeddah to Orlando via New York, filling them with Saudi families eager to see Mickey Mouse.

Delta never flew to Saudi Arabia. But in the summer of 2001, it did fly to 54 cities abroad, mostly from New York and Atlanta. Many of the foreigners on these flights weren't really destined for New York or Atlanta but were merely stopping at airports in those cities en route to other places. And among these other places where Delta carried foreign visitors, Florida—and indeed Orlando—was near the top of the list. In 2001, during the peak month of March, Delta flew to 16 Florida cities and offered more than 100,000 weekly seats from Orlando, more than any other airline.

Now fewer foreigners could visit Orlando, not to mention New York and other big Delta markets. And citizens from Arab countries were hardly the only ones affected. Latin Americans suddenly had great difficulties obtaining visas to the U.S., not just for visiting the country but even for merely transiting it en route to somewhere else. Two of Delta's key Latin American routes—Atlanta-São Paulo and Atlanta-Lima—happened to be popular with ethnic Japanese citizens of Brazil and Perú, respectively, who would fly to Atlanta to pick up Delta's daily flight to Tokyo. Now connecting in Atlanta had become a huge hassle. Air Canada cleverly added a number of new Latin American routes after 9/11, taking advantage of the more restrictive U.S. visa regime and offering a hassle-free transit experience, in Toronto, for people who previously flew Delta. Fortunately, Delta's total international exposure wasn't as large as American's or United's or even—as a percentage of each airline's overall business—as large as the exposure smaller airlines like Northwest and Continental had. But the visa situation hurt.

The final three and a half months of 2001 were a time of jangled nerves in America. Some people found comfort in the nation's history and its record of recovery from previous crises and struggles: a battle to establish national independence, the burning of the White House by the British in 1812, a bloody civil war in the 1860s, the battle for civil rights, two world wars in the first half of the 20th century and a post-war generation gripped by fears of communism and nuclear devastation. Airline terrorism was nothing new either. Nor was the threat of religious extremism.

But the country had changed on 9/11. The attacks seemed less the latest in a mere string of national challenges than the end of a happier era, one that had been accompanied by a booming economy, America's status as the world's lone superpower, the thrilling advancement of digital technology and the global popularity of American cultural icons like Michael Jordan and Michael Jackson. The golden era of the 1990s might have begun to fade with the bursting of the dot-com bubble or the rise in oil prices at the start of the new millennium. But the final break with that era happened on Sept. 11, 2001.

The 9/11 attacks, of course, would have been reason enough for Americans to feel a new and uncertain era had begun. But the gloom and the fear were reinforced by a seemingly endless stream of awful news during the last three and a half months of 2001. Just a week after the attacks, letters laced with anthrax spores circulated through the mail, killing five Americans and sickening another 17; it was the largest biological attack in U.S. history. On Nov. 12, American Airlines flight 587 destined for Santo Domingo in the Dominican Republic crashed shortly after taking off from JFK in New York, killing 265 people, including five on the ground in Queens. Americans reflexively suspected terrorism; investigators subsequently blamed the deceased pilots. On Dec. 22, an Al Qaeda recruit named Richard Reid attempted to detonate a bomb, implanted in his shoe, aboard American Airlines flight 62 from Paris to Miami. The fuse would not light, and the would-be bomber was subdued by crew and passengers and arrested when the plane landed. Many Americans would never again be allowed to walk through security checkpoints wearing their shoes.

And America was now at war. On Oct. 7, the U.S. and its allies launched Operation Enduring Freedom to topple the Taliban government of Afghanistan and eradicate the terrorist groups it was sheltering, namely Osama bin Laden's Al Qaeda. In the realm of American business, meanwhile, the headlines were no more cheerful. On Dec. 2, Enron, a giant energy trading firm, filed for bankruptcy amid allegations of vast fraud. Its collapse would also take down one of America's largest accounting firms, Arthur Anderson.

Worldwide, the airline industry was experiencing one of its worst crises ever. Three days after the 9/11 attacks, Ansett, Australia's second largest airline, was forever grounded. Within weeks, Ansett's part owner Air New Zealand was re-nationalized to save it from a similar collapse. On Oct. 3, the Belgian national airline Sabena, 78 years old at the time, filed for bankruptcy; on Nov. 7, it would operate its last flight. To be sure, these airlines were troubled before 9/11. But the fallout from the attacks hastened their demise.

Thankfully, the closing months of 2001, morose as they were, did produce signs of recovery. Planes were at least flying again, and they weren't empty: Delta filled 61 percent of its seats in October, even if it had to deeply discount its fares to achieve that. Airlines had recovery plans in place. There was also early evidence—difficult to see at the time but clear in retrospect—of world-changing mega-trends that would shape and define the decade. On Oct. 23, Apple released a new music player called the iPod. Another Silicon Valley company with the strange name Google managed $86 million in annual revenue, on its way to $38 billion a decade later. On Dec. 11, China became the 143rd member of the World Trade Organization, a milestone along its rise to become the world's second largest economy—and second largest domestic airline market. On Dec. 2, a little-known Malaysian music executive bought a defunct airline for a symbolic one Malaysian ringgit, about 25 cents. Soon, Tony Fernandes would turn AirAsia into another Southwest Airlines, advancing a worldwide trend toward low-cost air travel. Other Southwest-inspired low-cost airlines that would come to greatly influence their regional economies were also still in their relative infancy. Among them: Ryanair and easyJet in Europe, WestJet in Canada and Gol in Brazil. And in the U.S., two young low-cost airlines called AirTran and JetBlue, based at Delta's two largest hubs, were planting the seeds of rapid growth, growth that would prove extremely vexing for Delta in the post-9/11 years.

In those final weeks of 2001, Delta too had a premonition of big things to come. On Oct. 19, the U.S. and France announced what's called an open skies agreement, meaning airlines from either country could essentially offer as many flights as they wanted to the other country without having to ask for in-depth regulatory reviews. That paved the way for a close alliance between Delta and Air France, an alliance that would later form a crucial part of Delta's business strategy. The year before, in fact, Delta and Air France had joined with Korean Air and Aeroméxico to form a new global alliance called SkyTeam.

One seemingly happy development in late 2001 was—unhappily—less indicative of the future. By December, global oil prices had fallen to just $19 per barrel. In the U.S., jet fuel was selling for an average of just 52 cents per gallon. Incredible as this would later seem, airlines viewed those prices as mercifully down from levels earlier that year ($30 per barrel and 87 cents per gallon) but rather pricey compared to a few years earlier.

Little did they know what awaited them.

THE EARLY YEARS

"The best anti-freeze you can buy"

It wasn't just a new year. Or even just a new decade. This was a new century. And like many milestones in the passage of time, this one triggered hope for better times ahead. The second half of the previous century, especially the post-war period, had brought wealth creation on a scale that dwarfed all preceding periods of economic development. And there was every reason to believe the trajectory would continue.

That could have likewise been said of the year 2000. But this was the year 1900, not even four decades after the Civil War. The United States was already the richest nation on earth, just 12 decades after its people—now numbering almost 80 million—had declared independence from England. Restless from the outset, the Americans had used their humble Conestoga wagons to move westward, and then farther westward, all the way to the shores of the Pacific Ocean. And as they moved, they produced and traded across the immense distances they covered.

Movement over land was slow. But water travel was quicker. And did the United States ever have water! There was the mighty Mississippi, with all the young seaport cities that developed along it: Minneapolis, St. Louis, Memphis, New Orleans and so on. There was the Ohio River and the Great Lakes, so crucial to the settlement of the Midwest. From its earliest days, New England's economy depended upon the Atlantic Ocean. And where there wasn't a waterway, the Americans built one. They built the Erie Canal, certainly not the only example but the grandest one of all, which, when it opened in 1825, linked Midwestern producers to east coast consumers and solidified New York City as the nation's largest economic center, a position it would never relinquish.

Then the Americans discovered a way to move and trade quickly over land. They built railroads. And with these railroads came more new cities, cities no longer required to be located along key oceans or rivers or lakes. Among these cities: one in the agricultural south that would eventually take the name Atlanta.

Nevertheless, as the 19th century gave way to the 20th, even with all the bustling sea and rail links; even with streetcars within cities, powered first by animals and, by the turn of the century, by motors; even with America's first subway line having opened in Boston two years earlier; America was still a place where most people got around with their own two feet. Many still worked and lived on farms, and those who worked in the newly sprouting factories often lived steps from where they worked. Little did they know that in the new century their lives would radically change thanks to two new transportation developments—developments that would lead to new cities, new forms of commerce, new ways of connecting people and new heights of national affluence. One was another form of land transport, the automobile. The other? An invention even more daring: a machine that flew like a bird.

When the Wright Brothers made history Dec. 17, 1903, their flight, which lasted just seconds, gave little indication of the revolution to come. But aircraft technology improved rapidly, and by 1914, the world had its first scheduled passenger air service, linking Tampa and St. Petersburg in Florida. That service, however—which was designed for tourists—did not last long. Besides, its aircraft had accommodated just one passenger. A humble beginning indeed.

World War I disrupted the evolution of commercial aviation in America. But it also produced trained pilots who returned home when the war ended. Some found jobs as swashbuckling aviation acrobats, dazzling the public as they barnstormed across small-town America. Others would fly for the U.S. post office, which operated its own aircraft fleet, on big "trunk routes" connecting New York and San Francisco, with stops along the way. Still others worked for a new breed of private operators with government contracts to feed these big trunk routes with mail from smaller cities.

Another invention, the telephone, further deepened links across the sprawling nation. Some people predicted—as others would later predict with every subsequent communication advancement—that the telephone would reduce the need to communicate by airmail and reduce the need to travel in order to communicate in person. But just the opposite happened. The telephone—just like fax machines, email and video-conferencing in later generations—meant more people, not fewer, doing business with other people. And as more people engaged in long-distance commerce, the demand for long-distance travel didn't shrink. It expanded.

The impact of even the telephone, however, was perhaps surpassed by another world-changing development. In 1901, at a place called Spindletop Hill in a town called Beaumont, not far from Houston, drillers struck the largest oil well the world had ever known. The entire vast state of Texas, at the time, had fewer residents than Missouri, and fewer than half as many residents of Pennsylvania. All of Texas, in fact, had fewer residents than one city—New York City—not to mention far fewer residents than all of New York state, counting other big cities like Buffalo, which was then the eighth most populous city in the country. But that changed quickly as

Spindeltop ushered in an age of cheap oil, which happened to be an ideal fuel source for both automobiles and airplanes, not to mention farm machines that helped expand food production, factory machines that helped expand industrial output and war machines that would prove vital in both World Wars.

The Roaring Twenties, with the U.S. awash in capital, created a fertile environment for entrepreneurs experimenting with new aircraft technologies and new airline business models. In 1924, a forerunner of Eastern Airlines began selling passenger sightseeing flights in New York. The next year saw the privatization of airmail services for the post office. And in 1927, Charles Lindbergh piloted a flight across the Atlantic, kindling even wilder dreams of how aviation might shrink the globe.

Still, flying was a rather dangerous affair. As the industry entered the 1930s, the airline business was still dominated by mail carriage rather than passenger carriage, in part because flight was still perceived as risky. The Great Depression, of course, was further deflating passenger demand. Still, the young industry developed. In 1930, the government under President Herbert Hoover, seeking a stronger, more consolidated and more profitable airline sector, altered mail carriage contracts to incentivize airlines to buy larger and more sophisticated airplanes. It further granted long-term route certificates to individual carriers, limiting competition and giving birth to the forerunners of four major airlines: United, TWA, American and Eastern. A fifth, Pan Am, established itself on international routes. The Hoover Administration—a White House so otherwise noninterventionist that it would draw criticism for doing little to prevent even the Great Depression—was not only involving itself in aviation but even, in retrospect, picking early winners and losers that would dominate the industry for a century to come. So began an inextricable link between government and the airline industry.

A few years later, Franklin Roosevelt's administration renationalized airmail, bemoaning the previous administration's "spoils conference" that had doled out lucrative route monopolies to favored players. But FDR quickly reversed the decision after crashes killed several pilots—perhaps the government was unfit for the task.

Other laws to regulate aviation followed. One prevented plane makers from owning airlines—Boeing owned United at the time. Washington also created a new agency to decide which airlines could fly which routes and—at least as importantly—how much they could charge. A decade earlier, nobody had known exactly what role the federal government would play in the airline business. By the 1930s, the essential nature of that involvement was in place. It would last for nearly another half century.

Despite the Depression, the 1930s marked an era of rapid growth for the airline industry. At the start of the decade, airlines were carrying 418,000 passengers annually, according to the newly formed Air Transport Association of America, a lobby group. Six years later, they were carrying more than a million. In 1939, passenger counts crossed the 2 million mark. The very next year: *3 million*. By this time, mail—although still critical to airline revenues—accounted for just 30 percent of those revenues. Passengers provided most of the remainder.

The mid-to-late 1930s also saw the advent of two new airplanes with great advancements in comfort, safety and efficiency: the Boeing 247 and the even more popular DC-3—"DC" stood for Douglas Corporation. In the meantime, cities built airports, and the federal government built air navigation facilities to accommodate all the new flying. Small communities without good rail or road access became especially reliant on air travel. Still, activity centered on the great metropolises of the northeast, the Midwest and the fast-growing state of California. In the 1930s, New York, Chicago and Philadelphia were the nation's largest cities, followed by Detroit, Los Angeles, Boston and San Francisco. Also boasting busy skies, though, were the young cities born of the new oil trade. In his 1996 book "Hard Landing," Thomas Petzinger noted that the world's single busiest airport of all in 1930 was in booming Tulsa. It "served more passengers than London, Paris and Berlin combined."

In 1920, less than three generations removed from the Civil War, the American South featured just one of America's 20 largest cities: No. 18 New Orleans. The region was still far less industrialized and far more agricultural than the north, and most of its towns and communities looked less like New Orleans than another city in the same state, Louisiana, about 280 miles to the north. Monroe featured little of the cosmopolitanism of the bustling Big Easy, with its Mardi Gras parades and jazz musicians. Monroe was perhaps best known for the sleepy cotton fields symbolic of the South's economy.

But the cotton crop was in crisis during the 1920s, which were not roaring in Monroe. When residents there looked to the sky, they saw not the new man-made flying machines that were electrifying the imagination of people elsewhere but a far less welcome flying phenomenon. In the latter 19th century, an invasion of beetles with an appetite for cotton plants arrived from Mexico, devastating the livelihoods of cotton farmers. Among the victims were many African-American farmers—"Negroes" was the most polite term for them then and for decades to come—now struggling to earn a living in a land still thick with bigotry. Like rural blacks in Mississippi, who left for a better life in the cities of the Midwest, and blacks in Florida and Georgia, who moved to the northeast, those of Monroe, La., moved to California in droves, as personified by Robert Joseph Pershing Foster in Isabel Wilkerson's "The Warmth of Other Suns."

It was during this crisis that a man named Collett Everman Woolman had an idea. A trained pilot from Indiana with a degree in agriculture from the University of Illinois, C.E. Woolman envisioned an air war pitting man against bug. If the boll weevil was vulnerable to pesticide, and if the challenge was spreading that pesticide over large distances, then why not have airplanes fly across the cotton fields, dusting the crops with calcium arsenate? Woolman understood the problem well: He had managed a plantation in Mississippi and served as an agricultural advisor in Louisiana. His idea proved so successful that he and a colleague convinced a New York manufacturing firm to launch the Macon, Ga.,-based Huff Daland Dusters, the country's first crop dusting company. The year was 1924.

Once established, the new airline learned what every airline would come to learn, whether it was dusting crops, hauling mail or carrying passengers: that the business is seasonal. There was no need for crop dusting in the winter, so Woolman took his planes south of the equator—until, that is, revolutions in South America forced an abrupt departure. By then the company had moved from Macon to Monroe and was equipped with 18 planes—"the largest unsubsidized air fleet in the world," it boasted.

In 1928, the owners of the Huff Daland Dusters wanted to sell, so Woolman teamed with three local Monroe investors to buy the company. One was Malcolm S. Biedenharn, son of the first-ever Coca-Cola bottler. The airline would serve the Mississippi Delta region, so they renamed the company Delta Air Service, which soon became Delta Air Corporation. Its first passenger flight came in June 1929, connecting Dallas and Jackson, Miss., via Shreveport and Monroe, with Atlanta and Charleston added to the network shortly thereafter. The Travel Air S-6000B aircraft Delta used carried one pilot and five passengers.

Nearly a century later, after hundreds of others had come and gone, American, United and Delta would again, along with just a few others, dominate the U.S. passenger airline industry. But by beginning its life in the 1920s as a crop duster rather than as a mail carrier, Delta's very roots, in retrospect, already foreshadowed that it would always be different from its peers.

The Great Depression and a failure to win government airmail business forced Delta to suspend passenger operations in 1930. But it won an airmail contract in 1934 and was now using a third variation of its name: Delta Air *Lines*. In 1940, Delta introduced its first flight attendants—then and for several decades to come called "stewardesses"—and in 1941 moved its headquarters to the fastest growing city in the south.

Atlanta wasn't exactly a new city. It got its name in 1845 and began as a terminus for the rail line running between Chattanooga, Tenn., and Georgia. The town spread outward from the rail depot, becoming, by the time the Civil War began, a major transportation hub and cotton distribution center for the southeast. Because of Atlanta's economic importance, General William T. Sherman burned it down before his march to the sea. But the city recovered, becoming Georgia's state capital in 1868 and surpassing Savannah as the state's largest city in the 1880s. By the turn of the century, Atlanta's most famous company was one founded in 1886 by an Atlanta pharmacist: The Coca-Cola Company, it was called. And by 1924, the U.S. Post Office had identified Atlanta as a well-placed stop on the New York City-to-Miami airmail route, assuming the city would build an adequate airport—if it didn't, nearby Birmingham was ready to grab the opportunity. Under the leadership of a future mayor named William Hartsfield, Atlanta built the airport, and the city's financial sector suddenly enjoyed a giant advantage: air access to New York. Smack in the center of eight southern states, Atlanta proved central along the paths between so many pairs of cities that even as early as 1930, the city's airport was the third busiest in the nation, behind only New York and Chicago, even though Atlanta wasn't even among the country's 30 largest cities, according to that year's U.S. census. Already, the city was vastly outpunching its weight in air service.

"The skies would be to the 20th century what the seas had been in centuries past," Frederick Allen wrote of Hartsfield's vision in "Atlanta Rising: The Invention of an International City." He quoted Hartsfield: "The city that makes its port on this new ocean [will] be the city of the future." C.E Woolman, according to his biographical sketch in the National Aviation Hall of Fame, "persuaded the Board of Directors to move Delta's national headquarters to Atlanta, foreseeing that the location, population and financial resources of that city were all pointing to a prosperous future."

World War II meant another pause for the country's civilian aviation sector. Like other airlines, Delta dedicated its resources to the war effort, training pilots, maintaining planes and transporting troops. In fact, Atlanta's airport, then called Candler Field, became a military air base and doubled in size. Civilian aviation growth resumed in earnest after the war. By 1950, America's scheduled airlines, operating more than a thousand planes, were carrying more than 16 million domestic passengers, compared to less than 4 million when the war began. Measured by miles flown, American, Eastern, TWA and United still represented the Big Four, flying more than half of the domestic "trunk" lines connecting major cities. Not far behind was Northwest Airlines. Now ranking No. 6 was Delta, which in 1946 had flown its millionth passenger. It also happened to be the 12th largest airline in the world.

As Delta rose through the ranks, it did so with admirable financial success, doing something that would later become even more unusual in the airline industry: growing not only quickly but also profitably. Delta suffered a rare financial loss for 1947, a year in which several accidents throughout the industry deterred people from flying. Even so, its losses that year were well below the industry average, and incredibly, 1947 would be Delta's last lossmaking year until 1983.

In 1948, Delta flew its first pressurized airplane, the DC-6, which could soar above most inclement weather. That same year, Delta launched the industry's first "interchange" agreements with TWA and later American. These arrangements—devised to sell tickets to places carriers didn't serve—involved a Delta crew flying a plane full of passengers to Dallas, for example, at which point an American crew would take over, flying the same plane to some destination beyond—say, Los Angeles. The era of competing airlines partnering for their mutual benefit had begun. And it had done so with something that was in some ways more extreme—one airline's pilots actually flying another airline's airplanes—than the global alliances that would emerge a half century later.

Delta's own network in the early 1950s stretched east-west across the south from Charleston to Fort Worth, and also north-south from Chicago to Miami, with the two lines meeting in Atlanta. This meant that passengers could easily get to a large number of cities by first going to Atlanta and then onward, a hub-and-spoke network model that Delta pioneered. People had already begun to joke, as their children and grandchildren would likewise do generations later, that whether you went to heaven or hell when you died, either way, you would have to stop in Atlanta.

Gradually, Delta won the rights to serve more and more routes, including many connecting the South to cities in other areas of the country, including—in 1956—the great metropolis New York. Other northeast business centers followed, and as Delta then touted, it was now connecting the South to the "main street of the nation." Another Delta advertisement showed a business passenger returning from outside the region with the tagline: "Back to his Southland." Yet another, this one targeting people for whom the southern U.S. was a destination rather than an origin, implored: "Fly south with Delta to prosperous Dixie."

At the time, all service was first-class service. But some exceptions began emerging as Delta and other airlines experimented with "coach" flights that often operated at off-peak hours. The seats were more numerous, the service less bountiful and the airfares less expensive. Airlines also experimented with discounts for military personnel and group travel. In the early 1950s, Delta, recognizing the surge in northerners traveling to Florida for their winter vacations, began offering vacation packages too. The big boom was in Miami, which a half century earlier had been a remote town with a few hundred people. "The best anti-freeze you can buy," one Delta ad proclaimed.

America in the 1950s wasn't entirely the age of bliss that some would later come to imagine. It was, after all, the start of the Cold War. A war in Korea, the Suez crisis in the Middle East, the rise of Fidel Castro in neighboring Cuba and fear of nuclear annihilation never let Americans forget about the world beyond their shores. At home, meanwhile, were Senator Joseph McCarthy's demagoguery and the early struggles of the civil rights movement. Nevertheless, the 1950s were indeed golden in many ways. By now Americans had come to understand that the abundance of cheap oil had powered the planes and the ships and the tanks that helped win the Second World War. Cheap oil was what ran the factories that built these planes, ships and tanks, and it was what transported soldiers to the front lines and moved supplies to these lines. Simply put, America had access to cheap and abundant oil, and its enemies didn't—not Germany, drawn to invade Russia for its oil, nor Japan, drawn for the same reason to Indonesia.

America's destiny would become intertwined with the price of oil to an even greater extent after the war, for cheap oil was instrumental not merely to modern warfare but also to a modern economy and to a modern society. It was cheap oil that built Detroit and made it the paragon of industrial might. It was cheap oil that made Detroit's vehicles affordable to nearly everyone, making America's labor force more mobile, making goldmines of opportunity like California suddenly accessible and enabling people and companies to move away from densely packed cities to where they could find something else cheap and abundant: land. So Americans could have large homes in suburbia, and in those homes they could have air conditioning and heat, which were also made possible by cheap energy. There was, of course, the need for people to build these cars and homes. But getting workers to where they were needed was hardly a problem in an unprecedented age of mobility.

Americans, of course, were mobile not just on land. They were mobile too in the air thanks to airplanes that were becoming ever faster, lighter, more comfortable, more economical and capable of flying greater distances—powered by fuel refined from oil. Although only a small minority of Americans would actually take to the skies in the opening decades of the new post-war era—true airline travel for the masses wouldn't happen until the 1980s—people were flying to an extent unknown in prior generations. They took long-distance vacations, triggering the creation of a giant tourism industry. And they flew even more often for business, taking advantage of new trading opportunities made possible by quick access to distant markets. In 1950, Americans were taking 19 million annual airline trips, including international trips. By 1960, the figure had more than tripled to 62 million. By 1970, it had nearly tripled again.

David Halberstam noted (in "The Reckoning," a book about America's auto industry) that "in 1950, the price of a gallon of gas at the pump had been 27 cents, 20 cents of it for the gas itself and the rest for taxes. Twenty years later, the price of virtually every other basic consumer commodity had approximately doubled, but the price of gas had remained, tantalizingly, almost the same." It was cheap oil that fueled the planes and the cars, and the planes and the cars that fueled the American Dream.

Delta, all the while, made money year in, year out, advertising nationally and establishing a sterling reputation for southern hospitality. C.E. Woolman remained in charge, as he would until the mid-1960s, cementing his place among the industry's great leaders. Delta was growing rapidly too, and not only organically. What it really wanted was a bigger presence in the bustling northeast. But after failing in 1950 to get the merger it wanted with Northeast Airlines, it merged three years later with its Memphis-based rival Chicago and Southern, or C&S. With C&S's handful of Caribbean routes from New Orleans, the deal, for the first time, made the re-named Delta C&S Air Lines an international carrier. Delta dropped C&S from its name two years later, in 1955. Two years after that, it became a publicly traded company, listing its shares on the New York Stock Exchange.

The C&S merger also brought Delta closer in size—and closer in competition—to one of the all-stars of the airline industry. In 1935, a famed World War I pilot named Eddie Rickenbacker took control of Eastern Airlines, quickly growing and transforming it into one of the sector's most profitable companies. Eastern was headquartered in New York and had a major corporate presence in Miami. It competed head-to-head against Delta for Florida vacation traffic. But that was not the only place they overlapped. Eastern, like Delta, operated a major Atlanta hub, implying a looming competitive war between the two fast-growing carriers as the jet age beckoned.

For Delta, that age arrived Sept. 18, 1959, when it became the first carrier to fly the Douglas Corporation's DC-8, a plane that would prove among the most successful of all time. On May 15, 1960, Delta began flying the Convair 880, a jet that would prove less enduring. Whatever the model, jet-engined airplanes were the latest example of rapid technological progress, making air travel faster, safer, more comfortable and more economical. And Delta was doing something different now. For the first time, it was offering premium and economy seats not on separate flights but in separate cabins on the same flight: DC-8 passengers could choose "deluxe Deltaliner" first class seats toward the front or "thrifty 'Flying Scot' Aircoach" seats in the back. The experiment worked well. By early 1961, for the first time, more U.S. passengers flew coach than first class.

The 1960s brought a number of changes to Delta beyond the introduction of its now-famous "widget" logo. In 1961 it began flying to California, mostly via Dallas. It also introduced boarding jetways, enabling passengers to walk from the terminal to the airplane without being exposed to the elements. In 1962 it introduced its first computerized reservation system, an early indication of how important information technology would become. In 1964 a system called Deltamatic began handling the ever-greater volume of reservations, a task made more complex by the split between first and coach class tickets at different prices. In 1965 Delta's annual passenger counts crossed the 6 million mark. A new way to pay for tickets—credit cards—also became popular. Who would have known, when Delta processed its first American Express charge that year, how important the two companies would later become to each other? Who would have known Deltamatic—in name, at least, even if the technology would change dramatically—would endure for at least another half century? Importantly, Delta also recognized that the new computer systems provided valuable advance booking and travel history data, greatly enhancing the airline's ability to forecast future demand and adjust its pricing and staffing accordingly. In its advertisements, though, Delta was at pains to emphasize that a human reservation agent would still be there providing service on the phone or at the city ticket office: Computerization did not mean impersonalization, it assured customers.

In 1963, Delta ordered another more advanced jet airplane called the DC-9, a model it would fly—remarkably—until 2013. And in 1964, it placed a $300,000 deposit with the FAA for three "Supersonic Transport" planes that Washington was encouraging plane-makers to develop: Supersonic air travel would surely be the next advancement after jet travel, just the next big thing in a steady string of advancements. By 1969, after all, a man was due to walk on the moon. Would Atlanta be a stop along the lunar route that would surely be welcoming space tourists by the year 2000? The future, in the eyes of many Americans at the time, looked something like how it was portrayed in an animated television show, "The Jetsons," which debuted in 1962.

The DC-9 arrived in 1966, just as Delta was doing its best to outduel Eastern with off-peak "Early Bird" and "Owly Bird" fares and flight schedules that enabled business travelers to leave for their destinations in the morning and get back to Atlanta that same day. The year 1966, however, also marked the death of C.E. Woolman, who was replaced by C.H. Dolson. Like all senior Delta executives, Dolson was promoted from within the company ranks, ensuring preservation of the company's unique southern culture. Woolman, who kept executive salaries modest and published his home telephone number in the white-page directory for customers to call, had built Delta into the fifth largest U.S. airline and the seventh largest airline in the world, with $260 million in annual revenues.

More impressive yet, Woolman had built a company that almost never lost money. In its fiscal year that ended in mid-1960, Delta's net profit was just short of $3 million. The next year it was $4 million. Then $7 million, followed by $14 million, $16 million, $23 million, $35 million and $49 million. This phenomenal streak of improvement stood in stark contrast against an entirely opposite trajectory for Delta's closest rival. For Eastern, the 1960s marked the onset of three decades of decline, a decline primarily of its own making. Rickenbacker himself, the legendary aviator who made Eastern what it was, increasingly seemed imperial and out of touch with the times, emphasizing cost control and operational integrity, for example, but with shocking disregard for customer service. A group of Eastern's regular passengers became so upset, in fact, that they formed a group called WHEAL: We Hate Eastern Airlines.

Eastern, to be sure, created a few brilliant innovations, including the Eastern Shuttle in 1961. But these were the exceptions. A management split between executives working in Eastern's New York and Miami offices created serious governance issues. The airline failed to modernize its fleet in preparation for the jet age. Rickenbacker's rants against regulators failed to win Eastern any friends at the Civil Aeronautics Board (CAB), which rejected a proposed Eastern merger with American in 1962—this would have given the combined carrier more than 35 percent of the domestic market. The CAB also tended to favor Delta when awarding route rights, demonstrated by Eastern's failure to win any transcontinental routes. More generally, the jet age, for all the technological advancement it represented, left the industry with too many seats chasing not enough passengers, a case of overcapacity made even worse because raising or lowering airfares required approval from the slow-moving CAB bureaucracy.

None of these problems, however, matched the severity of Eastern's labor unrest. Delta, whose pilots had joined the Air Line Pilots Association back in 1940, was otherwise a non-union company. Eastern, by contrast, was heavily unionized. And, more to the point, its unions repeatedly adopted a militant approach to contract negotiations—an approach sometimes triggered by management's unresponsiveness. Once in a while, Eastern was lucky enough to resolve strikes within a day or so after they began—it managed that with its mechanics twice in 1958—although even these scared away customers who might have otherwise booked with Eastern as the strike deadlines approached. Other times the damage was more severe: Its flight engineers alone (at a time when every flight required a third person in the cockpit), never mind all the other unions, struck for 38 days in 1958, a week in 1961 and 83 *days* in 1962, according to a National Mediation Board history of airline strikes. Between the late 1950s and mid-1960s, Eastern's machinists twice struck for more than a month at a time. Pilots walked off the job for a week and a half. Other Delta competitors like United, American, Pan Am, TWA and National likewise, to varying degrees, suffered debilitating strikes. Northwest's flight engineers struck for *137 days* in 1960 and 1961. But Delta? Not a single day lost to a strike.

The 1960s also brought great cultural changes to the South—and to Delta. Atlanta was home to the civil rights leader Martin Luther King, Jr. In a sign of the times, Delta's 1967 annual report featured, for the first time, a photo of an African-American flight attendant. That same year, by the way, Delta began permitting flight attendants—then still called stewardesses—to continue working after they married. African Americans began appearing in Delta advertisements too, and the company began actively recruiting minorities. Consciously or not, Delta actually had played an important role in the civil rights struggle by providing essential transport links to otherwise-isolated areas. This contribution was cited by none other than Andrew Young, the civil rights leader who had served as Atlanta's mayor throughout much of the 1980s before eventually serving on Delta's board of directors, when he helped it win flight rights to Africa at about the same time its rival Continental was denied access.

Corporate America, indeed, was moving more quickly than local politicians to normalize race relations, especially in rural states like Georgia, which had an illiteracy rate twice the national average. But Atlanta was a relative oasis of calm during the worst of the civil rights era violence, in part because the city was so keen to advance economically. While the country's powerful corporations stayed away from cities like Little Rock after the "Little Rock Nine" desegregation struggle in 1957, General Motors, Ford, Lockheed and others were firmly implanted in Atlanta, enjoying integrated workforces, a large middle-class African-American population, excellent African-American universities and lots of trained workers—whites and blacks alike—who had been stationed in the area during World War II. Relatively successful Atlanta, although it certainly had its own racial issues, had largely become "a city too busy to hate."

Atlanta was home to one of the 12 Federal Reserve branches, covering six southern states. It became a popular spot for business and political conventions. And of course it had its airport, which in 1961 opened the largest passenger terminal in the country. Although many of the most racially divisive areas of the South would lose population and remain economically underdeveloped for decades, the wider southern half of the U.S. became the epicenter of population growth for the next half century. From 1960 through 2010, the 19 fastest growing counties in the U.S. by absolute population gains were all "Sun Belt" areas, stretching from Florida to California. Growth in the Atlanta metropolitan area was every bit as explosive, soaring from fewer than a million residents in 1950 to three million by 1990. The southern surge had immense political implications too: John F. Kennedy of Massachusetts would be the last elected U.S. president from the north until Barack Obama of Illinois in 2008.

Back in the air, Delta used its expanding financial muscle to buy Boeing's giant new 747, which made its debut with Pan Am, a carrier that was then still confined to international service, competing against Northwest across the Pacific, TWA across the Atlantic and Braniff and later Eastern to Latin America. In 1968, the same year Delta unveiled its "Delta is ready when you are" campaign, the airline ordered another large widebody plane that—unlike the 747—would remain a staple of its fleet for decades to come. This was the tri-engined Lockheed 1011. The 1960s were turbulent years for America, with the civil rights struggle, the Cold War, the assassinations of JFK, RFK and MLK, the Cuban Missile Crisis and the Vietnam War. But it was a triumphant decade for Delta, which finished 1969 with more than a half billion dollars in revenue.

The 1970s would prove more challenging but no less successful. Inflation soared, scandal rocked the White House, unemployment spiked, urban communities decayed and—most distressingly of all for an airline—fuel prices spiked. From 1973 through 1979, fuel prices per gallon ballooned by 264 percent. In 1970 alone, the industry as a whole, never mind that routes and fares were regulated to ensure profits, lost more than $200 million. Labor unrest was one reason for the decade-long torpor. Economic distress and higher fuel prices were others. Airlines also faced huge capital outlays. A hijacking epidemic led to costly security procedures. And although regulation protected airlines from competition, it also came with the frustrations of bureaucracy. Route awards and requests for fare changes were often handled arbitrarily, and decisions were anything but swift. Charter or "supplemental" carriers, moreover, began slipping through the regulatory cracks, skirting the CAB's fare restrictions by agreeing to certain practices like offering only advance-purchase tickets or selling only through travel agencies. Service overall, meanwhile, declined as carriers saved money by cutting back on everything from inflight meals and movies to freshly cut flowers and linen napkins.

Amazingly, throughout this stormy decade, Delta, with its 20,000-plus workers, kept on printing money, earning $45 million in fiscal year 1970 and then $30 million the next year, then $42 million, $66 million, $91 million, $52 million, $70 million, $92 million, $131 million and $137 million in the decade's final year. But how?

A beneficial merger in 1972 was one reason. Delta purchased Northeast Airlines, giving Delta a big presence in Boston and New York and nonstop access from the northeast to Florida, a big boost in competing against its archrival Eastern. Delta was now the No. 3 airline in the nation by passengers carried, behind United and Eastern, although it was still No. 6 by revenues. In an industry in which mergers would often come to be viewed as, at best, merely bad—and those were the mergers that didn't actually destroy companies—Delta had just executed what would be the first of three highly successful mergers during a four-decade period. Eastern, as it happened, executed a much smaller takeover of a Caribbean carrier but abandoned a proposed deal with National Airlines. American, for its part, saw its proposed merger with Western Airlines rejected by regulators.

Eastern itself continued to implode, further contributing to Delta's success. Now run by the former astronaut Frank Borman, it fought incessantly with unions, suffered multiple accidents and became increasingly dependent on low-fare leisure traffic. A non-union Delta mechanic could help expedite a flight's dispatch by loading bags; his highly unionized Eastern counterparts could not. In a contest for reliability and service, Delta won every time. In 1971 Eastern did, at least, manage to become the official airline of the new Walt Disney World Magic Kingdom in Orlando—a Tomorrowland ride called "If You Had Wings" opened a year later and would carry Eastern's sponsorship for a decade and a half. (Eastern would eventually lose even that claim to Delta, which in 1987 took over as the theme park's official airline.)

The South, for its part, was still growing. So was Dallas, another big base for Delta. So was Florida. And Atlanta, with a giant new terminal under construction, was now the country's second busiest airport after Chicago O'Hare. Atlanta was an international airport now too, with Eastern launching flights to Mexico and Jamaica in 1971. The airport's first foreign carrier, Belgium's Sabena, arrived in 1978. And that same year, Delta became a longhaul international airline by adding London flights. In 1979, it added Frankfurt. Before flying overseas itself, Delta had an interchange agreement with Pan Am, which enabled Delta to sell tickets to Europe.

By 1970, Delta had an all-jet fleet, which in 1973 it supplemented with the 727. Two years earlier, a new CEO—another insider named W.T. Beebe—had taken the helm. Rising through the management ranks all the while was an ambitious young executive named Ron Allen, who could barely have noticed another ambitious young airline mind relentlessly pushing to launch flights in Dallas. In 1971, a lawyer from New Jersey named Herb Kelleher, who wasn't interested in playing the CAB-regulated airline game, finally triumphed in the courtroom and launched Southwest Airlines, which—this was the loophole that enabled Kelleher to do this—could only, for now, fly within the state of Texas.

In 1972, the first year all passengers had to pass through airport security screenings, Delta updated its computerized ticketing system. In fiscal year 1973, the company's revenues, for the first time, exceeded a billion dollars. Delta earned a record profit too, despite a DC-9 crash near Boston that killed 89 people and despite filling just 52 percent of its seats, a "load factor" that in subsequent decades would have been considered extraordinarily low. Another 1973 highlight: Delta's introduction of those three-engined Lockheed 1011 widebody planes it had ordered a few years earlier. Delta's 1974 profit of $91 million was the most ever by a single airline in a single year, never mind outside forces like double-digit inflation, extremely high interest rates and the Arab oil embargo. Counterintuitively, the oil crisis actually *helped* airline earnings for a while, because jet fuel shortages forced carriers to reduce capacity—and convinced the CAB to permit fare increases.

The 86 percent increase in fuel prices that year had another major impact on the future of commercial aviation: It buried once and for all Boeing's supersonic aircraft project and doomed the European version, the Concorde, to economic failure, never mind the engineering marvel that it was. Even more consequentially, upward spiraling fuel prices and inflation more broadly caused policy makers in Washington to consider initiatives that would lower prices for consumers. One idea gaining momentum in the 1970s was deregulation, the idea that removing government controls on industry would foster more competition. Led by economists from the University of Chicago, the deregulation movement reached the corridors of Capitol Hill by way of Senator Ted Kennedy, who needed an issue to champion as he prepared to run for president in 1976. Alfred Kahn, one of the economists championing deregulation, focused his efforts on transportation, and the regulated airline business seemed a perfect test case. It was a cause politicians could embrace, one that would give the public tangible benefits.

The airlines themselves, however, felt differently. For all their frustrations with the CAB, it was an agency tasked, after all, with ensuring that those very airlines generated reasonable returns on investment. And although that result wasn't guaranteed and didn't always happen, the protection it offered from excessive competition was invaluable. United actually broke with its peers and supported airline deregulation. But Delta was adamantly opposed: "Some of these proposals reveal a frightening lack of understanding of our nation's air transportation system," one company dossier argued. Delta said deregulation would favor smaller carriers, new entrants and the supplemental/charter carriers. It said costs and fares, in the absence of regulation, would rise. Fuel would be wasted. And competition would become excessive on many routes. "If you put two cows in a pasture that's fit for two cows," W.T. Beebe said, "you have two fine, fat cows. But if you put three cows in the same pasture, you have three bags of bones." In 1978, Beebe was replaced as CEO by David C. Garrett, a South Carolina native who had joined Delta in 1946 as a reservations agent.

Ted Kennedy never did become president. His primary opponent Jimmy Carter, from Delta's home state of Georgia, won the 1976 election. But his hometown sympathies for Delta notwithstanding, Carter too supported airline deregulation, as he made clear in a message to Congress in 1977: "As a first step toward our shared goal of a more efficient, less burdensome federal government, I urge [you] to reduce Federal regulation of the domestic commercial airline industry."

On Oct. 24, 1978, Carter signed the airline deregulation act into law. Gone were restrictions on where an airline could fly and what an airline could charge, for domestic routes anyway. And new airlines, as long as they met the FAA's safety standards, could join the competitive fray.

And so it had come full circle. Economic regulation of the airline industry and protection of incumbents, which had come of age under a Hoover White House that would otherwise come to be viewed historically as a symbol of economic nonintervention, was largely ending under President Carter, of the more pro-government Democratic Party. Carter, his pro-business rhetoric notwithstanding, would lose his re-election bid to a successor, Ronald Reagan, who accused Carter of not doing enough to deregulate. Only Nixon, went the fashionable argument a half decade earlier—only a president with such solid anti-Communist credentials—could visit China. Perhaps only a Democrat like Carter, one with at least some skepticism of the power of unfettered free markets, could deregulate the airline industry.

But the new law, passed 75 years after the first Wright Brothers flight and 49 years after Delta's first passenger flight, didn't have a big impact right away. Another oil crisis in 1979, followed by a deep recession and efforts by the Federal Reserve to use extremely high interest rates to break inflation, actually caused, in 1980, a rare annual decline in air traffic, to just 297 million passengers from 317 million the year prior. As Delta observed in its 1979 annual report: "The national economy is largely at the mercy of the oil-exporting nations and the oil companies." In 1981 traffic fell again, this time due to an illegal air traffic controller strike, which the new President Reagan addressed by firing all the strikers. American, Braniff, Continental, Eastern, Republic, TWA, United, Western and especially Pan Am all fell into the red. But it was nothing Delta couldn't handle. As always, it went right on making money, posting a $93 million net profit in 1980 and then a $146 million net profit in 1981. It also pulled the trigger on an order for Boeing's latest widebody plane, the 767.

Delta markets were now entirely open to new entrants. But "those carriers that have chosen to enter many of Delta's markets" it brashly stated, "have discovered that our reputation as a strong competitor is no myth." Delta did, however, have to confront lower fares. In the first year after deregulation, 26 percent of its passengers flew on discounted tickets, up from 11 percent in 1975. By 1980, the figure had risen to 45 percent. First-class travel, meanwhile, represented only 9 percent of revenues by the start of the new decade, while international revenues were just 4 percent, having fallen after Delta dropped flights to Caracas and Maracaibo in Venezuela.

The CAB remained in place for several years after deregulation, phasing out completely in 1984 but still empowered to block a proposed Eastern Airlines-National Airlines merger in 1979. Again, Delta got a break. In 1980, it moved into its giant new terminal in Atlanta, which could handle 50 million annual passengers. With its excellent credit rating, fiscally conservative Delta, for the first time, issued "commercial paper," a common way for U.S. companies to borrow money for the short term without putting up any collateral. Delta placed the largest order in aviation history, for Boeing's new single-aisle narrowbody 757s. It used the opportunities afforded by deregulation to greatly expand its Dallas hub and to open a new hub in Cincinnati. In fiscal year 1981 alone it launched 39 new routes. Following American's lead, it experimented with a new scheme in which passengers received award miles every time they flew and could later redeem these miles for free trips—the Delta Air Lines Frequent Flyer Program, it was called. And Delta introduced a new computer reservation system, DATAS II, for travel agents.

But fares continued falling as rivals relentlessly attacked Delta's Florida routes from the Northeast and Midwest, in particular. Delta had little choice but to match the fares, and before long, 92 percent of its passengers were flying on discounted fares. Rivals struggling for survival during the dark days of the early 1980s started "pricing for cash," as the practice is known, rather than for profitability, charging just enough to get enough money to live another day. Delta complained bitterly about this "irrational pricing" and also lamented the growing complexity of airfare shopping, which caused more passengers to rely on travel agencies, to which Delta paid commissions. Delta agents too were forced to spend more time helping customers shop for tickets. The airline also said the proliferation of so many discounted fares was unfair to passengers paying full fares. Delta was voicing a common post-deregulation frustration that Gordon Bethune, the future CEO of Continental Airlines, would two decades later express (to *Texas Monthly* magazine) more bluntly: "You're only as good as your dumbest competitor."

The industry situation was so bad that one giant, Braniff, collapsed in 1982. There were new airlines too with names like New York Air, a non-union airline launched by a hard-charging financier named Frank Lorenzo. It was Lorenzo who in 1978 had launched the first hostile takeover attempt of an airline, against National Airlines, which Pan Am ultimately bought out of desperation for a domestic network (a merger often viewed as ill-advised and perhaps the beginning of Pan Am's decade-long demise). Lorenzo did manage to buy Continental in 1981, taking it into bankruptcy and breaking its unions. Other startups included People Express and America West. And Southwest was now free to move about the country.

Alas, all this tumultuousness eventually caught up with Delta. For the first time since 1947, the company reported a loss in the 12 months to June 1983. Traffic was also declining for the first time since the 1940s. This was the worst crisis in Delta's history, an $87 million net loss that forced management to reduce staff through early retirement programs, worker reassignments and the reduced use of seasonal hires. Delta did not, however, lay anyone off involuntarily, maintaining the family-like culture Woolman had worked so hard to cultivate. In a stunning display of gratitude, employees themselves agreed to voluntary pay cuts to fund the purchase of Delta's first 767. In all the world, had airline employees ever before, and would they ever again, *buy an airplane for their employer?* "The Spirit of Delta," employees christened the plane when they presented it to the airline. This was a plane destined to revolutionize Delta's international route network in later years, although for now its mission was Florida—Delta's first 767 route was Atlanta-Tampa.

Delta had to defer some plane deliveries too, although it didn't cancel any of the 84 it had on order. And it added additional seats to many of its airplanes, recognizing that people increasingly valued low fares above all else, including comfort—with more passengers aboard, it could charge lower average fares. But it also installed "sleeperette" seats on some of its L-1011s and opened a new airport terminal at New York's LaGuardia Airport. It was able to pay for these things despite the current crisis thanks to the excellent balance sheet it had built during year after year of profitability. In late 1982, Delta added to its aircraft order book by purchasing 737-200s with 107 seats, urging Boeing all the while to build what it called the "Delta III," a 150-seat prototype it hoped would replace its DC-9s. As of Dec. 31, 1983, Delta had no fewer than 226 planes on order: 115 727s, 43 L-1011s, 36 DC-9s, 13 767s, 13 DC-8s and six 737s.

Moves like these suggested confidence. But considering the turbulence of the early 1980s, and 1983's heavy loss, was Delta's era of perennial success a thing of the past? Was Delta, like so many of its rivals, becoming a loss-making airline?

It was a reasonable question. The answer, as history would reveal?

No.

Trends had, in retrospect, reached their low points. This was, as cheerful television advertisements would likewise soon proclaim, in their case encouraging Americans to re-elect President Reagan, "morning again in America." The economy was perking up with almost precise correlation to a sharp fall in oil prices. In 1972, the average per-gallon cost of jet fuel was 13 cents. A decade later, Delta was paying $1. But then it paid 92 cents in fiscal year 1983. And then only 84 cents in 1984. Then 80 cents, then 72 and just 47 cents by 1987. The effect: a massive transfer of wealth from oil producers back to American consumers, with airlines along for the ride.

At the same time, established airlines, led by American, developed an important weapon against prolific discounting by upstarts. Instead of matching discounts across the board, they matched them selectively, selling some seats at bargain fares but making them unavailable on busy flights, flights during peak seasons, flights on routes with no competition and flights with a lot of business passengers unwilling to accept the conditions attached to bargain fares: advance-purchase requirements, Saturday night stays, no refunds, no date changes and so forth. This new science of "yield management," also sometimes called "revenue management" or "inventory management," made possible by ever more powerful computing muscle, helped Delta's yield—that's the money it collects for flying one passenger one mile—increase fully 18 percent in fiscal year 1984.

And thus the gloom was gone. Fiscal year 1984 was one of Delta's best years ever, highlighted by $176 million in net profits on $4.3 billion in revenue. The year also marked a major evolution of its network: the first-ever addition of Hawaii flights, plus Frankfurt flights from Dallas-Fort Worth. Delta expanded its reach not only to big global destinations but—just as importantly for feeding those global flights—also into smaller markets by establishing what it called Delta Connection, a partnership with several "commuter airlines" operating under Delta's brand, piping passengers into its Atlanta, Dallas-Fort Worth and Cincinnati hubs. Chief among the commuters were Comair and Atlantic Southeast Airlines. Other Delta moves that year: ordering a longer version of the 767 called the 767-300, accelerating 757 deliveries, getting its first 737s, introducing seat assignments and boarding passes before passengers arrived at the airport, applying computer power to everything from bag handling to crew scheduling, adopting an employee stock ownership plan and developing a database for the frequent flier program, which now had more than a million members. In the executive suite, Ron Allen became president and chief operating officer under CEO David Garrett. And to keep employee costs in check,

Delta, while not taking anything away from current employees, instituted lower pay scales for future hires—a tactic, incidentally, that encountered heavy union resistance at other airlines.

On Aug. 2, 1985, Delta's flight 191, a Lockheed 1011 flying from Fort Lauderdale, crashed just before landing at Dallas-Fort Worth, killing 137 people, including a motorist on the ground. The tragedy introduced to the masses the meteorological term "wind shear"—lessons from the incident would, at least, contribute to the development of wind shear detection systems, which would dramatically reduce the frequency of such crashes in the future. But 1985—underpinned by a strong economy, falling fuel prices, a strike at United, mounting troubles at Eastern, the arrival of Delta's 757s and the expansion of its Atlanta international network to Paris, Shannon, Munich and Stuttgart—was otherwise another great year for the airline. Georgia's state capital, although not immune to the urban violence afflicting many U.S. cities in the 1980s, now had a highly developed economy, with affluent suburbs tied together via a spaghetti bowl of highways and an urban heavy rail system, MARTA, that—however inferior it was to systems in northern cities—at least existed, unlike in most other Sun Belt cities. Atlanta had major league sports teams, a major league convention center and major league corporations: not just Coca-Cola anymore but also Home Depot, Trust Company Bank (later SunTrust, following a merger) and CNN, the brainchild of an eccentric Atlanta resident named Ted Turner—who had ever heard of such a crazy thing as an all-news network? (The cargo airline UPS would in 1991 move its headquarters, although not most of its operations, to the Atlanta metro area too.) Delta, meanwhile, stepped up its marketing activities with nationally televised commercials featuring its "Signature Service" and a new tagline: "Delta Gets You There." In one spot, hundreds of employees stood around an L-1011 singing a feel-good melody typical of 1980s advertising: "We love the things we do, and we do them all to please you..."

Delta earned profits in every subsequent year of the 1980s, ending fiscal year 1989 with its highest earnings yet: nearly a half billion dollars on $8 billion in revenue. But the nervousness that characterized Delta's money-making days in the late 1970s was back. As the 1980s rolled on, Delta was an emperor peering into the distance only to spot barbarians at the gate—still a champion, yes, but one that now faced legitimate challengers. Forget sickly Eastern. The new threat came from increasingly competitive low-fare airlines. "We know that we will continue to be challenged by airlines who view their product as a commodity rather than Delta's view that our product is a service," Delta wrote in 1986. "We know too that we will have to grow and become increasingly more efficient to compete successfully with airlines which offer a low level of service and are able to achieve low costs and low fares. More and more of our route system is being exposed to that kind of competitive threat."

The second half of the 1980s brought other great changes, including a bevy of airline mergers—USAir merged with Piedmont and Pacific Southwest, Northwest merged with Republic, TWA with Ozark, American with Air Cal and Southwest with

Muse Air. Frank Lorenzo's Texas International Airlines amassed a motley collection of other airlines including Continental, People Express, Frontier and—ultimately—the barely-breathing Eastern. The post-deregulation era also brought a scramble among the established full-service carriers—which realized most international markets were still governed by restrictive bilateral treaties that kept competition to a minimum—to plant their flags abroad. This didn't bode well for Delta, whose three hubs, as good as they might be for transferring domestic traffic, were hardly ideal international gateways. Pan Am and TWA still had the New York-Europe market; their London routes would soon transfer to United and American. United would buy Pan Am's Pacific and Latin American routes too, and American would buy Eastern's even more impressive Miami-based Latin American network, a network Eastern itself had acquired in 1982 from Braniff. Northwest was still strong in the Pacific, and even back in the domestic market, Delta watched fretfully as American invaded Delta's southeastern stronghold with hubs in Raleigh-Durham and Nashville, all while outpunching Delta in Dallas-Fort Worth. United was right behind American, having become the No. 2 airline by revenues.

With its yields plummeting and profits sustained only thanks to cheaper fuel, Delta felt a need to act boldly and decisively. It doubled its Cincinnati capacity and grew almost as much in Dallas-Fort Worth, itself an aviation-heavy Sun Belt boom city like Atlanta. Delta ordered 30 MD-88s, an advanced version of its DC-9s, plus nine MD-11s, a new version of the longhaul widebody DC-10. It launched its first Pacific service with nonstop Tokyo flights from Portland, Ore. It began its first Cincinnati flights to Europe. It fortified its Delta Connection program by adding Business Express as a partner in the northeast and by buying 20 percent of Atlantic Southeast and 19 percent of Comair. It introduced a new "Medallion" status for the top 2 percent of its frequent fliers. It launched what would become perhaps its most famous ad campaign ever: "We Love to Fly and It Shows." After grabbing the Disney sponsorship from Eastern, it launched an Orlando hub, for a time even flying from the Florida city nonstop to Frankfurt. It also won sponsorships of both 1988 political conventions, including the Democratic one in Atlanta. And it retained its service reputation, demonstrated by a No. 1 ranking for fewest customer complaints year after year.

On the other hand, its reputation for placid labor relations began to fray. Convinced of the need to lower pilot costs as its yields fell, Delta engaged in tough negotiations with the Air Line Pilots Association (ALPA), finally clinching a contract deal that included lower pay rates for new hires. Delta did continue to honor its no-layoff policy but made more use of part-time staff. More generally, it expanded its staffing levels at a much slower pace than it expanded its network, a tactic that enhanced productivity but not labor relations.

Delta's actions to address the changing times didn't stop there. On Sept. 9, 1986, for the third time in its illustrious history, Delta announced a major merger. This one was with Western Airlines, the country's ninth largest airline, which was itself feeling pressure to upsize. Run by a Harvard Law graduate named Gerald Grinstein, Western ended 1986 with 93 planes, 44 destinations, nearly 12,000 employees, 12 million passengers, $1.2 billion in revenues and a modest profit. "This merger represents an ideal culmination of all of our efforts in recent years," Grinstein said at the time. "We managed to survive the most threatening days in the company's history, and we were able to rebuild, restructure our finances and restore Western to a position of financial health and profitability."

Merging with Western cemented Delta's spot as the industry's third largest airline behind American and United, now comfortably ahead of Northwest, Continental, TWA and the newly bulked-up east coast powerhouse USAir. Only there, after USAir, did the withering Pan Am and Eastern appear on the list. More importantly for Delta, its $860 million acquisition gave it the western U.S. presence it never had, with hubs in Salt Lake City and even Los Angeles, which had long ago passed Chicago to become the nation's second largest city. To amplify the Salt Lake City hub, Delta promptly bought 20 percent of a newly added Delta Connection carrier called SkyWest. Adding Western increased Delta's revenues some 25 percent and expanded its workforce to more than 50,000 people. The integration proved uncharacteristically smooth and free of financial distress, unlike nearly every other post-deregulation airline merger. US Air, to cite one example, practically ignited a civil war when trying to meld Charlotte-based Piedmont employees with the grizzled union veterans from rust belt cities like Pittsburgh.

On July 23, 1987, the longtime heir apparent to the Delta throne was crowned. Ron Allen was the CEO who would lead Delta into the 1990s. During the 1980s, air travel had boomed as low fares triggered by deregulation and cheaper fuel brought more and more first-time fliers onto airplanes. In 1988, U.S. airline passenger counts crossed the 450 million mark—that equated to roughly one annual round trip for every American man, woman and child. Flying had become unprecedentedly safe too, with just three fatal accidents that year (including one involving Delta) from among 6.7 million departures—a safety record that would be easily surpassed in future decades but that was, at the time, remarkable. Delta had 7 million frequent flier club members, a domestic route network that stretched from coast to coast and an international network that was now contributing 9 percent of total revenues. It would soon head to Seoul and Hamburg and Taipei, Dublin, Amsterdam and Bangkok and six points in Mexico. In 1989, Allen further internationalized Delta with two novel deals abroad. Delta and Swissair each took a 5 percent equity stake in the other, while Delta and Singapore Airlines did the same with 3 percent stakes. These were early examples of global airline alliances, in which one carrier sells another's flights, and the two (or more) cooperate in marketing and other areas. The value of such cooperation was increasing as frequent flier programs and bookings through computer reservation systems became commonplace. Those systems made it easier for carriers to sell each other's flights simply by listing one carrier's flights under another carrier's two-letter code—"DL" for Delta, "SR" for Swissair or

"SQ" for Singapore Airlines. Some consumer advocates, and even American's CEO Robert Crandall, questioned the integrity of such maneuvers—advertising a Swissair flight as a Delta flight was deceptive and unfair to consumers, they charged. But this practice of "codesharing" would become a staple of airline marketing.

The Delta alliances with Swissair and Singapore Airlines—which both, incidentally, had impeccable service reputations—weren't entirely unique. United was now working with British Airways, and USAir with Alitalia. SAS had invested in Continental, and KLM in Northwest. But Delta's move had an ulterior motive: to enlist two friendly shareholders that could help block any attempted takeover—this was, after all, the late 1980s, when Wall Street raiders were hunting for deals. The same concerns motivated a new employee stock ownership plan, or ESOP: The more shares in the hands of owners with more than just purely financial interests in Delta, the harder it would be for a raider to accumulate enough shares to take over.

In 1989, Delta's longtime rival Eastern filed for bankruptcy and temporarily suspended its operations while unions struck. Some observers at the time criticized Ron Allen for not doing enough to take advantage and for thus enabling Eastern to get back in the air, albeit as a shadow of its former more formidable self. Other analysts criticized Delta for an expensive triple-mileage frequent flier promotion that the whole industry reluctantly matched. One analyst, speaking to the *Dallas Morning News*, used terms that reflected a wider sentiment taking hold: "What do I think of Delta?" the analyst asked. "They're a boring company... Delta is a stodgy, follow-the-leader company that prefers imitation to innovation. In the frenetic airline industry of the 1990s, Delta has a quaint, old-fashioned feel about it."

Fair or unfair, given all the steps Delta had indeed taken—the Western merger, the Swissair and Singapore deals, the new pilot contract—a sense of urgency prevailed as the 1990s approached. Delta was still not international enough in a world that was changing beyond recognition. The Berlin Wall had come down and the Cold War was suddenly over, leading at least one scholar to proclaim the "end of history." The Soviet Union collapsed for many reasons: The U.S. policy of containment, an expensive arms race with the U.S., the USSR's own disastrous war in Afghanistan and fundamental flaws with the communist economic system. But what had pressured the Soviets most in the USSR's final decade was the dramatic decline in the price of oil, its chief export.

Ron Allen took the hint. In a spasm of international expansion, Delta applied to serve Berlin, Milan, Rome, Barcelona, Madrid, Manchester, Copenhagen, Hong Kong and—in a rush of premature post-Cold War enthusiasm—Moscow, St. Petersburg and even Tbilisi in the newly independent nation of Georgia—a Georgia-to-Georgia connection, its backers would say. Delta announced an Asian hub in Taipei. It applied to fly to Tokyo from Los Angeles, Nagoya from Portland, London Gatwick from Detroit, London Stansted from New York and Atlanta, São Paulo and Rio de Janeiro from Atlanta, Frankfurt from Newark and Los Angeles, Paris from Orlando and Los Angeles and Mexico City from New York. At home, Allen began cross-country

Newark-Los Angeles flights and expanded within California by increasing frequencies between Los Angeles and San Francisco. In fiscal year 1991 alone, Delta would add 13 new cities and 22 new markets. Separately, it cut the cord on DATAS II, its computer reservation system (CRS), which had become a perennial money loser. As an alternative, Delta agreed to a CRS joint venture with American's Sabre, but antitrust regulators rejected that plan. So it joined with Northwest and TWA to form an all-new CRS called Worldspan.

Just as Delta was increasing capacity a stunning 19 percent annually, however, and pursuing quixotic overseas markets, cracks began appearing in both the U.S. economy and the geopolitical arena. The culprit again: an oil spike.

In fiscal year 1990, Delta's average cost per gallon of fuel jumped 18 percent. The next year it rose another 24 percent. The underlying barrel of oil, just $16 in 1988, rose to $25 in 1990 and stayed above $20 for the next two years. The cause: Iraqi dictator Saddam Hussein's invasion of Kuwait in the summer of 1990. This gave Iraq control of a key oil producer and better positioned it to threaten *the* key oil producer, Saudi Arabia. Alarmed at the prospect, the U.S. and other countries assembled a force to drive Hussein's army out of Kuwait and to fortify Saudi Arabia's defenses. The military operation was a quick success, but the higher oil prices dragged the U.S. economy into recession, a double dose of poison that devastated the fragile airline industry.

No carrier was spared. The weak among them began pricing for cash, slashing fares when exactly the opposite was needed to offset the higher fuel bill. It was the greatest industry crisis of the deregulated era, perhaps the greatest industry crisis ever, causing $4 billion in industry losses in 1990, nearly $2 billion in 1991, $4 billion again in 1992 and $2 billion again in 1993. More broadly, the U.S. economy shrank from 1990 to 1991, burdened not just by high oil prices but also by the cost of cleaning up the savings and loan (or S&L) crisis, one that presaged a much larger real estate crisis the following decade. High unemployment followed. Americans sank into despair, lamenting the strength of the Japanese economic model and convinced that many of the country's best jobs were moving to Mexico. Looking for a white knight, they made Bill Clinton their president. One of his early acts: forming a commission to address the problems of the airline industry.

The problems were certainly too much for Eastern, which in 1991 disappeared once and for all. Delta grabbed 18 of its airport gates in Atlanta, although it fought bitterly against city politicians trying hard to recruit an Eastern replacement—Northwest, for one, considered the offer. Maynard Jackson, Atlanta's mayor at the time, told *The Wall Street Journal* of a telephone call with Ron Allen, who "went ballistic" when Jackson said he wanted to attract a rival airline. The *Journal* recounted: "[Jackson] says Mr. Allen angrily asked whether the mayor would tell Coca-Cola he was trying to attract Pepsi." There was only one notable exception to the carnage, in fact. While most airlines lucky enough to stay in business were at least spilling red ink, Herb Kelleher's Southwest earned a stunning 7 percent operating profit margin in 1990, a 5 percent margin in 1991 and an unbelievable 11 percent margin in 1992.

(Profit margin is, essentially, how many cents of profit an airline keeps, after paying for most of its expenses like fuel, employee salaries and so forth, for each dollar of revenue it collects—so a 7 percent margin is equivalent to 7 cents of operating profit for each dollar of revenue.)

As for Delta, the realities of previous industry meltdowns, during which it had always fared far better than its competitors, no longer applied. Financially, at least, Delta looked more and more like just another airline.

Fiscal year 1991 was a bloodbath, blighted by a mammoth $324 million net loss. The next year was even worse: a $506 million net loss, then $370 million in 1993 (adjusting for some extraneous accounting items) and another $77 million in 1994, by which time a recovery began to take hold. The collective $1.3 billion loss in those four years wiped out nearly every penny of profits from the previous four years and eroded what had been a sterling balance sheet. In the spring of 1991, Delta felt compelled to fortify its cash reserves by, for the first time since 1962, selling new shares of stock, which diluted the stakes of existing shareholders and thus made Delta, in that regard, a less attractive investment.

The pressure on Allen was immense. The losses, the falling fares, the rising fuel prices, the weak economy, the intense cost cutting by rivals, the Southwest menace, the transactions that globalized American and United, the outside pressure for Delta to globalize itself... This was unlike anything any Delta CEO had faced before. Delta needed to do something. But what?

There was a time when Pan American World Airways represented everything that was glamorous about America in the jet age. Its logo was a worldwide icon. Its New York City headquarters sat imposingly atop Grand Central Station. Its pilots and flight attendants strutted through airports like rock stars. When the Beatles went to the United States for the first time, they flew Pan Am.

But when the glory began to fade, it did so quickly. Already financially distressed throughout the 1970s, Pan Am entered the brave new world of deregulation without any domestic routes, forcing it to rely on "local" point-to-point traffic—passengers, for example, beginning or ending their trips in New York, without the benefit of those connecting to or from smaller cities. Rivals, meanwhile, were developing sophisticated hub-and-spoke networks to facilitate domestic-to-international traffic flows. In 1980, Pan Am expensively acquired National Airlines after Frank Lorenzo drove up its price, and the subsequent integration proved a case study in corporate culture clashes. The red ink kept pouring throughout the 1980s. Then, just before Christmas in 1988, Libyan terrorists bombed one of the airline's 747s over Lockerbie, Scotland, killing 270 people, including 11 on the ground. Pan Am would never recover.

Shortly thereafter, the rest of the industry engaged in a mad scramble for Pan Am's lucrative overseas route portfolios. At various times, United, TWA, American and Northwest offered to buy all or part of the dying carrier, which in 1990 announced major layoffs, fleet restructurings and route suspensions. Delta, quiet at first, protested vigorously when United agreed to buy Pan Am's lucrative London Heathrow routes—the Department of Transportation, Delta argued, should block the deal. "While American and United... spent over a billion dollars buying up the routes of Pan Am, TWA, Continental and Eastern, Delta held back," Robert Gandt wrote in the book "SkyGods." Gandt quoted Delta's president Whitley Hawkins: "We sit around quietly doing our thing while the rest of them go around killing each other."

In January 1991, Pan Am filed for bankruptcy, with Delta among those bidding to pick at its carcass. By April, Delta and Pan Am confirmed merger talks. One idea: for Delta and United to bid jointly, with the two sharing the spoils, if they won, instead of bidding each other into oblivion. But that plan fell through. So Delta kept bidding higher and higher until it won. In August, Pan Am's creditors selected Delta's most recent offer, worth close to $1.4 billion. Delta also offered financing to keep Pan Am flying until the deal closed. And importantly, it offered to re-launch Pan Am as a new Miami-based airline focused on Latin America, one in which Delta would own 45 percent and the Pan Am creditors the rest.

But it wasn't to be. By December, with Pan Am's advance bookings almost non-existent, Delta got cold feet and withdrew the financing and re-launch offer. It was now interested only in Pan Am's assets. "They love to lie, and it shows," an attorney for Pan Am's creditors told the *Atlanta Journal-Constitution*. On Dec. 4, 1991, Pan Am suspended operations, the highest-profile casualty yet of airline deregulation.

Despite not saving Pan Am as a functioning airline, Delta walked away with 7,800 Pan Am workers, 45 planes, the Pan Am Shuttle (linking New York, Boston and Washington), a Frankfurt hub with nonstop service to nine cities in Europe and most of Pan Am's mostly New York JFK-based transatlantic routes (but not the most valuable ones of all: the Heathrow routes United had grabbed). Delta took over the "Worldport," Pan Am's iconic JFK terminal (which would two decades later feature prominently in an historical fiction ABC television series about Pan Am). For $416 million plus the assumption of another $400 million or so in debt, Delta became an overnight global powerhouse with 500-plus planes, nearly 80,000 employees and more than $10 billion in annual revenues. By most measures it was still the No. 3 airline behind American and United. But by 1993, Delta was flying more passengers and operating more daily departures than anyone else.

Bigger, however, didn't mean better. Almost from the outset, the Pan Am asset takeover proved disastrous. As the recession trudged along, routes to Europe lost vast sums of money. The Delta brand was almost completely unknown outside the U.S., and Delta's management was almost completely unfamiliar with the unique aspects of marketing international routes—complicated, as they were, by language, culture, currency differences and the need for relationships with over-seas travel distributors. The Frankfurt hub was perhaps the biggest black hole, although Delta wouldn't finally close it and redeploy the 727s based there until 1997. Culturally, the integration of Pan Am's workforce proved difficult too. In the first three years after the transaction, Delta's new European network amassed more than $1 billion in losses.

Such bloodletting led to an immediate need for restructuring. Having over-expanded, Delta now reversed course and slashed transatlantic capacity by 15 percent. It took to shedding Pan Am's Airbus 310 widebody aircraft, deferring capital expenditures, reducing its dividend payout to shareholders, outsourcing more domestic routes to Delta Connection partners and—in a move that tested its corporate culture—reducing management staffing and imposing a 5 percent pay cut on all non-union employees (i.e., almost everyone except its pilots).

But in Allen's estimation, this would hardly be enough. By 1994, the economy had begun to improve, and oil prices had begun falling. The problem was, yields continued falling too. In late 1993 a new low-fare airline, recognizing the vacuum left by Eastern, launched operations from Atlanta, immediately eating into Delta's Florida franchise. This new airline, called ValuJet, had a cost base far lower than that of Delta, which estimated that about half of its traffic now overlapped with one low-fare airline or another. It didn't help when earlier that year, American attempted to radically overhaul airline pricing with a disastrous initiative called Value Pricing—the idea was to simplify complex fare structures, but instead it simply bled the industry of untold sums of money.

So in April 1994, Allen announced his boldest and most controversial initiative yet. "Leadership 7.5," as the plan was called, targeted unit costs of 7.5 cents per mile by mid-1997 (down from 9.3 cents at the time), realized through a series of draconian measures that included 12,000 to 15,000 job cuts. The massive $2 billion cost-cutting program also envisioned up to $340 million in concessions from pilots, whose contract became amendable at the start of 1995. On the other hand, Allen, after studying the idea, abandoned the thought of launching a separate low-fare unit within Delta.

On the network front, Delta added more domestic flying at New York JFK to feed international flights, increased flying at its Atlanta, Cincinnati and Salt Lake City hubs and restructured its Dallas Fort-Worth hub to focus on east-west connections. It also added more European flying from Cincinnati and some new routes like Atlanta-Nice, New York-Hamburg and—very briefly—San Francisco-Frankfurt. Still, the overwhelming momentum was toward downsizing, exemplified by exits from Cincinnati-Munich, Miami-London, Detroit-London, Dallas-Frankfurt, Frankfurt-Delhi, Los Angeles-Hong Kong, Paris-Tel Aviv and New York flights to Oslo, Stockholm, Lisbon and Hamburg. Delta soon pulled out of Bangkok and Taipei too, while trimming its presence in Boston, Los Angeles and Orlando.

The efforts began paying off. In fiscal year 1994, Delta finally showed a small operating profit, excluding special accounting items, although it was its fifth straight year of net losses (net results, unlike operating results, are dragged down by items like interest costs). In 1995, the Delta frequent flier program changed (Delta, for example, became the last major airline to adopt the industry-standard 25,000-mile award ticket) and got a new name: SkyMiles, whose membership was fast approaching 20 million. Somewhat daringly, Delta imposed caps on how much commission it would pay travel agents for booking domestic tickets—the airline was betting a new development called the Internet, although at this time still unfamiliar to much of the population, might reduce its reliance on agents. The Pan Am Shuttle routes, always profitable, were doing as well as ever. And Atlanta was preparing to host 1996's Summer Olympics. Delta was now holding its annual shareholders meeting in Atlanta, after years of clinging to tradition and holding it back in its Monroe, La., birthplace. Delta became the first airline to ban inflight smoking worldwide and continued to forge new codeshare partnerships, including one with Virgin Atlantic. This gave Delta indirect access to London Heathrow—a restrictive treaty between the United States and United Kingdom prevented all but American and United, among U.S. airlines, from actually flying to Heathrow with their own jets. Best of all, net profits were back, amounting to almost $300 million in fiscal year 1995.

Allen wasn't quite done. In 1996, he achieved the new ALPA contract he demanded, one that would lock in pay and benefit concessions through May 2000. Excluding any profit sharing pilots might earn, this meant roughly $100 million in savings for Delta during fiscal year 1997, another $200 million for 1998 and yet another $230 million for both 1999 and 2000. It also permitted Delta to launch a new low-fare unit after all. "Delta Express," which first flew in October 1996, used a dedicated fleet of 12 737-200s deployed on highly competitive domestic routes between the Northeast/Midwest and Florida, using lower-paid crews and efficient operating procedures characteristic of airlines like Southwest: quick aircraft "turn times" between flights, for example, to ensure that the airplane spent less idle time at the gate and more revenue-producing time in the air. By 1999, Delta Express would have 37 planes flying to 22 cities.

In the spring of 1996, Delta received antitrust immunity—in other words, clearance from regulators to do things like coordinating schedules and prices, which competitors are normally prohibited from doing—to cooperate with Swissair, Austrian Airlines and Belgium's Sabena. That fall, Allen also inked a marketing pact—this one with Air France—that would provide a stronger European hub and prove more lasting. This was partly in response to a new mega-alliance proposed by American and British Airways, the latter now abandoning a more modest existing alliance with USAir. Air France, as it happened, simultaneously agreed to an alliance with Continental, which coincided with another major Ron Allen initiative: a proposed merger with Continental. Toward the end of 1996, a deal looked possible.

None of this, however, was enough to save Ron Allen's job. In the spring of 1997, amid disputes with his board of directors, the man who had never spent a day of his professional life working for another company announced his departure. Allen, who once told *The Wall Street Journal*, "We'll still be a slow, methodical, southern-based airline that serves a lot of fried chicken," would make way for a new CEO.

Why did the board fire Ron Allen? Without a doubt, his controversial Leadership 7.5 program gave Delta a more competitive cost base. But the Pan Am acquisition was a major blot on his record, and Leadership 7.5 itself proved to be a medicine with harsh side effects. Delta's fabled family-like culture was shattered. Employee morale had perhaps never been worse. Executives were fleeing, and the company's CFO—a Western holdover who had worked under Gerald Grinstein—had openly broken with Allen, who seemed unaccustomed to dissent. Customer service suffered from inadequate staffing. Atlantans developed a love-hate relationship with their hometown airline, recognizing its importance to their economy, yes, but feeling frustrated with its high fares and declining levels of service. Firing so many mechanics meant more delays and longer delays. Firing aircraft cleaners meant dirtier planes. Firing airport customer service agents meant longer lines at the ticket counter. Besides, "we never got to 7.5 [cents per mile] because we realized in doing so, we'd do stupid things," Joe Kolshak, a Delta pilot and its future operations chief, recalled. "Dumb, dumb things" like "taking the lettuce off the tray" for first-class meals, which saved little money and made Delta less appealing.

What Delta needed, it was clear to the board, which had appointed former Western Airlines CEO Gerald Grinstein to head a search committee, was an outsider to modernize the company's culture and restore morale—an outsider, perhaps, who was unaccustomed to eating a lot of fried chicken.

The board's answer: Leo Mullin, a senior executive at a giant Chicago-based electric utility company, who took Delta's reins on Aug. 14, 1997.

Mullin's wife Leah had been in the room when Grinstein called to offer him the job. Mullin, chosen from a field of qualified executives from across a wide swath of industries, would soon feel flattered and excited. But at that first moment when he got the call?

"I hung up," he recalled years later, "and my wife looked at me, and she said, 'Did somebody die?' I mean, I thought, 'I can't believe it!'"

Another problem was that Mullin and his family were, that Friday, due to head to Africa for two weeks for a long-anticipated safari. Delta wanted him to start immediately.

The compromise, to disappoint neither his new employer nor his family: They would head to Africa first, and he, after "one week in a whirlwind of activity with Delta," would join them for the second week. Then it would be time to really get to work.

Mullin set about learning the company and assessing its strengths and weaknesses, working 16-hour days and interviewing countless Delta employees. Was he ready to lead one of the biggest companies in an industry in which he had never worked at any level? "It would be absurd for me to say that I had an in-depth knowledge of the airline industry," he reflected. "But from a CEO perspective, I felt like I knew what I needed to do."

He was impressed, to be sure, by "a number of things that I just found extremely positive. There was the Delta brand, the commitment to the people—and their belief in Delta as an organization. These were all very positive. The attachment to the community of Atlanta. I think all of that was very, very positive."

There was also the key fact that most of Delta's workers—almost everyone except pilots—were not represented by unions. Mullin understood the tacit deal: "You will be treated fairly with respect to your wages and benefits, relative to anything that anybody could achieve under unionization. Basically," he explained, "the pay rates and benefits at Delta were slightly better than elsewhere." But because Delta employees could work more flexibly than those at other airlines, add it all up—the better pay and benefits but the greater flexibility—and "Delta had an efficiency advantage over a number of the other airlines."

Of course, the whole reason Mullin was there—the reason the board had, for the first time, brought in an outsider to run the company—was that not all was right at Delta. And not only did Delta have problems. Mullin himself detected "a lack of urgency and a lack of true appreciation for the depth of the problems that they had."

One problem: Delta's technology. The "technological systems, computerization and data processing and so on, was just plain awful," he said. "I mean, American Airlines"—which had essentially invented not only frequent flier programs but also computerized reservation systems and revenue management science and technology—"was way, way out ahead in terms of anything that was going on at Delta."

Even more core to an airline's fortunes, Delta's route network, in Mullin's estimation, was a laggard, especially (compared to American and United) in growing and relatively nearby Latin America. So Delta quickly expanded its network there. But that was too little, too late, to address Delta's overall global clout, a point driven home to Mullin by none other than the CEO of an airline based 9,962 miles from Atlanta—so far that no passenger aircraft could have flown nonstop between the two cities, even if an airline wanted to do so. That airline: Singapore Airlines, which, along with Swissair and Delta, had formed the "Global Excellence" alliance.

"Not more than three weeks into my time," Mullin recalled, "I received a call from [Singapore Airlines CEO Cheong Choong Kong] to say that they were dropping out of the alliance and severing their relationship—the codeshare relationship—with Delta, despite the fact that we're a great airline and all that." Delta wasn't a big enough player in international markets.

"They thought they'd do better elsewhere," Mullin said, "and that was incredibly disappointing to me, because everybody knows what a great airline Singapore Airlines is."

On Nov. 27, 1997, Global Excellence dissolved. Singapore Airlines instead joined United in the Star Alliance.

Another shortcoming closer to home: Delta's position at Los Angeles International, known by its three letter code LAX, and Dallas-Fort Worth, or DFW. "Pretty early on, both of those—I'm talking about within the first year, year and a half or so—I mean, we recognized that neither one of those had the staying power of Atlanta or, for that matter, Cincinnati and Salt Lake City, which were not that great."

Delta's positon in New York, on the other hand, was "relatively strong," in Mullin's estimation. And "very, very important for us [was] our position in Florida. I mean, very few people recognized that 25 percent of all of Delta's traffic either originated or had destinations in Florida."

Mullin went about modernizing Delta's information technology, improving service, granting benefits to partners of gay employees and revamping the senior executive team with outside talent. "It was kind of cool," Joe Kolshak remembered, "to get somebody from outside the industry with a different perspective that really knew nothing about airlines. But he was a very, very bright guy. He was down to earth, even though he was a very cerebral guy."

One new hire: Fred Reid, whom Mullin poached from Lufthansa to serve as Delta's marketing chief and later its president and chief operating officer. Another was Warren Jenson, the chief financial officer of NBC television. To improve and internationalize Delta's image, Mullin ordered a new paint job for the fleet and ran ads with the tagline, "On Top of the World." Delta was now flying to Tokyo nonstop from Atlanta, eying more Asian flights from Portland and Los Angeles and planning a big offensive to Latin America from Miami. Delta also negotiated a major contract with Boeing, making the U.S. manufacturer its exclusive plane supplier for 20 years.

At least as importantly, it invested in a new dot-com travel startup called Priceline, a move that would later reap an enormous windfall.

Richard Braddock, then head of Priceline, had previously served as chief operating officer at the giant Citibank at a time when Mullin was an executive with First Chicago Bank. The two, who were both on the Visa credit card association's board of directors, knew each other well. Braddock was contacting all the big airlines, looking for unwanted airline seats he might be able to sell at low prices, hoping the airlines would see Priceline as a useful channel to shed seats that would otherwise fly empty. He would accomplish this by allowing Priceline customers to blindly bid for seats without knowing the airline they'd fly or exactly when they'd be flying until their bids were successful. The idea was to cater to very price-sensitive travelers who wouldn't otherwise pay much money anyway, but to do so without cannibalizing airlines' published fare structures, because most passengers would never accept terms like those.

But airlines were nonetheless reluctant. "There was an enormous amount of concern throughout the industry with respect to this intermediation—that somehow by offering inventory to a Priceline, that you would undercut your own sales, which would be much higher margin. The industry as a whole was very reluctant to engage," Mullin recalled.

"The question really," he continued, "was whether this was a seismic strategic shift in the way that the airline sales were going to take place, or was this something that was just going to come and go? It wasn't real clear at that point."

Braddock soon enough contacted Mullin. "He came down and he talked to me for two hours, just the two of us in our office," Mullin recalled. "He took me through the whole Priceline model and the way that the airlines would do it. I asked him a ton of questions. At the end of it he walked out the door and I said, 'This is true. This is going to happen. We ought to be at the front of this, not at the back.'"

Delta would ultimately not only offer Priceline some of its seats but do so in exchange for—this, history would reveal, was the more important part—shares in Priceline. Delta would become a part owner of the fledgling company.

Mullin actually agreed with Braddock on the deal's final terms while Mullin was meeting with his counterparts at Air France in a hotel in the French town of Versailles. His assistant called his mobile phone: Braddock was on the line. It was a "beautiful day," so Mullin walked outside the hotel to take the call and ended up sitting on a park bench near a statue of Louis XIV by the time he told Braddock they had a deal. "I kept looking up at Louis the Fourteenth wondering if he'd believe this!" Mullin recalled. "It was really a moment."

In 1997, meanwhile, Delta became the first airline in the world to carry more than 100 million passengers in a single year, helping Atlanta reclaim the title of world's busiest airport.

Addressing disaffection throughout the employee ranks wasn't easy. Workers were angry about the pay and benefit cuts Allen had imposed. With profits improving, pilots thought it fair to re-open contract talks and reverse the concessions they reluctantly surrendered when times were tough. At the same time, the Transport Workers Union filed an application with the government to try to represent Delta's 8,000 fleet workers. Also rankling the Delta workforce was the big payout Ron Allen had received when he left the company, including a $4.5 million lump-sum severance payment, lucrative retirement benefits and a $500,000-per-year consulting contract.

Mullin negotiated a potentially powerful domestic alliance with United. But his pilots nixed the idea, fearing the result would be more outsourced flying and less organic growth.

Nevertheless, Mullin's first three years, the final three of the 1990s, were three of Delta's best years ever. In 1996 ValuJet, Delta's greatest low-fare threat, disappeared—for the time being, anyway. It was victimized not by a lack of commercial success—it had plenty of that—but by a gruesome crash in Florida's Everglades, which killed all 110 people aboard and for which the airline and one of its suppliers were blamed. So federal regulators stepped up their scrutiny of low-fare airlines, making it more difficult for new startups to launch and causing would-be passengers to think twice about booking those that were already flying, thus further easing pressure on Delta. The late 1990s, in any event, were a golden era for the U.S., with the economy booming, an information technology revolution underway, a booming stock market, low interest rates and dramatically improved government finances. This was the age of Michael Jordan and Jerry Seinfeld and *Titanic*—not the tragedy itself but the wildly successful movie about it. Scientists were mapping the human genome. The U.S. was the lone superpower. Young and educated people moved back into city centers; some even gave up their cars. Sure, the president was impeached. But as Democrats would say a few years later, when the next president was accused of being less than truthful about more serious matters: When Clinton lied, nobody died. The fact that the country found time to be gripped by a scandal about the president's sexual dalliances meant not that things were bad, but that they were good.

Most importantly of all for America's airlines, and maybe even for America more generally, was the collapse in oil prices that characterized the end of the 1990s. The decade started with crude oil prices close to $25 per barrel, swollen by conflict in the Middle East. In 1998, they dropped to less than $11 late in the year, depressed by an Asian financial crisis that shrank demand just as OPEC was boosting supply.

Delta, to be clear, wasn't just along for the ride. Its profits and profit margins were better than those of almost any other carrier, and its balance sheet was the industry's strongest. Its operating profit in 1997 alone was a monstrous $1.5 billion. That figure rose again in 1998, to $1.7 billion, and yet again in 1999, to $1.8 billion. Operating margin for these three years: 11 percent, 12 percent and 12 percent, all this is an industry where companies are often happy just to break even and where anything above 10 percent can seem downright heroic. American and United, for their part, posted solid profits too—it was hard not to do so with fuel prices so low. But neither ever bested Delta. Between the two of them, they reached a double-digit operating profit margin only once, with American's 11 percent showing in 1998. And as if to symbolize the resurgence of all things Atlanta, baseball's Braves—"America's Team," they called themselves—dominated Major League Baseball's National League throughout the 1990s, winning the World Series in 1995 and also getting there (but falling short of a championship) in 1991, 1992, 1996 and 1999.

In the late 1990s, just about everything in Delta's route network—led, of course, by the Atlanta hub—was profitable. Cincinnati, with the advent of new 50-seat regional jets that offered more capacity and comfort than the turboprops that connected smaller cities to most other airline hubs, was nearly as good. Salt Lake City, even with Southwest in the market, was next best. Dallas Fort-Worth remained the laggard, losing money against American on California routes, most notably, but still breaking even overall—not bad for an airline's worst hub. International markets boomed once the Frankfurt hub closed, with Latin American and Caribbean routes exceptionally profitable. New York nonstops to Europe were tougher, but transatlantic flying from Atlanta showed great potential. Cincinnati, remember, had a few routes to Europe too, with Cincinnati-Zurich at one point running the highest profit margin of any route in the entire international network.

The good times kept rolling right into the new millennium. The year 2000 never did bring the computer chaos that the "Y2K" scare heralded. What it brought instead was another hefty operating profit for Delta, amounting to $1.7 billion, excluding special accounting items. Operating margin was an excellent 10 percent. And that $1.7 billion profit didn't even include a $300 million windfall from the sale of some of the Priceline stock that Mullin had agreed—on that park bench in Versailles—to accept.

Together with Air France, Korean Air and Aeroméxico, Delta announced the formation of SkyTeam, a global alliance to compete against the three-year-old Star Alliance (founded by United, Air Canada, Lufthansa and others) one-year-old oneworld (American, British Airways and others). Delta simultaneously deepened its bilateral relationship with Air France and did the same with its business partner American Express. More generally, it began the new decade with a strong international presence, a budding network of alliance partners, a competitive advantage on regional jet flying, its low-fare Delta Express unit to combat low fare competitors and the best hub in the industry, almighty Atlanta—which, incidentally, hosted the 2000 Super Bowl.

On the other hand, the year 2000, much more so than the 1997-to-1999 period, contained signs of trouble—signs that, in retrospect, were rather clear even if they were subtle at the time, like the first coughs of an otherwise healthy child who will later be diagnosed with the flu. The dot-com boom was over, culminating in a stock market crash. The wider economy softened too, in tandem with an uptick in oil prices—all this helped George W. Bush defeat the incumbent vice president Al Gore in a disputed presidential election. With annual passenger traffic reaching a record 666 million, airports and air traffic navigation infrastructure became increasingly overwhelmed, resulting in severe flight delays that received widespread media coverage. Air traffic control delays alone, according to the Air Transport Association, had risen 84 percent since 1997.

With the U.S. west coast hurt most by the dot-com implosion, and with Asia still embroiled in a financial crisis, Delta was left with little choice but to shutter its Portland gateway, seriously impairing its coverage of the Far East. The dawn of e-commerce had its upside, including lower commission payments to travel agents. But it also empowered consumers to self-shop for low fares while removing one additional cost barrier for would-be startup airlines. Southwest, with an unblemished record of profitability dating back to its earliest days in the 1970s, was invading the eastern seaboard, assaulting Delta's Florida markets in the process.

In May 2000, Mullin was vacationing with his family in southeast Asia when he received unnerving news: United planned to merge with US Airways. The two would create a goliath heavily overlapping Delta's east coast markets.

It was the middle of the night in lodging "way worse than a Motel 6" in a "very remote part of Thailand." Somehow, someone from back home managed to reach not Mullin's room but the room of his daughter and son-in-law. His daughter came down the hall and knocked on his door, waking him up.

"There's some guy named Don Carty," she said. "Do you know anybody named Don Carty?"

"Well, yeah," Mullin replied.

"Well, he really wants to talk to you."

Don Carty was the CEO of American Airlines.

Carty excitedly asked Mullin if he had seen the news about United and US Airways. "You know," Carty said, "maybe we ought to explore things." American and Delta were probably too big to merge with each other—even United and smaller

US Airways would raise antitrust fears—but maybe American and Delta could join forces in some way short of a merger, such as a codeshare alliance.

So Mullin began flirting with American and—even more seriously—with both Northwest and Continental together, discussing what might be a three-way merger. Ultimately, the Justice Department objected to the United-US Airways proposal, and the two carriers, instead of fighting the government, voluntarily called off the deal. Soon after that, American bought the withering TWA, which, although a shadow of its former globetrotting self, still added enough to American to cement its position as the country's largest airline.

Even the weaker economy and higher fuel prices, however, paled in comparison to the challenges from Delta's own workforce. Still smarting from their concessions in 1996 and emboldened by a rich new contract that United had given its pilots, Delta's pilots refused to work overtime during the busy Christmas 2000 travel season, causing an estimated $100 million in lost revenue as Delta pared its schedule. Earlier, pilot demands for a new contract—demands Mullin felt were unaffordable—had led Delta to defer deliveries of Boeing's new 777, the manufacturer's most efficient long-range widebody yet. And that wasn't all. Delta had in late 1999 paid a princely $1.8 billion to purchase the rest of its Delta Connection partner Comair—it had earlier bought just part of it. But now Comair was experiencing even more disruptive labor strife than Delta itself—its pilots struck for 89 days in the spring of 2001.

Alas, Delta, in March 2001, warned it would lose money for all of 2001. If that forecast proved accurate, it would mean red ink for the first time in six years. One month later, Delta reached an agreement with its pilots. They would receive the most lucrative contract in the history of the U.S. airline industry if they ratified the deal, which they indeed did June 20, just two and a half months before 9/11.

2002

"The greatest competitive threat to Delta"

Had Steve Jobs been bitten by the airline bug rather than the computer bug, he would have been David Neeleman. Neeleman—just as Jobs was—is tall, thin, brash, charismatic, unconventional and sometimes difficult to work for. Like Jobs, Neeleman was an undistinguished student, in his case afflicted, he would later learn, by attention deficit disorder. Like Jobs, he became a multi-millionaire in his 20s by innovating and upending an industry. While studying at the University of Utah after returning from a two-year Mormon mission to Brazil, Neeleman started selling package tours to Hawaii. He amassed a small fortune. But then the airline carrying his passengers went bankrupt. Soon, so too did Neeleman. Like Jobs and so many other impatient entrepreneurs, Neeleman had dropped out of school. Out of money and with a young family to support, he went back to working the cash register and stocking shelves at the place where, as a child, he had first developed his work ethic: his grandfather's grocery store.

But his remarkable if brief success as a travel salesman didn't go unnoticed by a family friend named June Morris, who offered him a job at her travel agency. Soon, Neeleman was running a small Salt Lake City-based low-cost airline called Morris Air. Under Neeleman, Morris air started to become not so small and rather successful—big and successful enough, in fact, to get the attention of the biggest and most successful low-cost airline of them all, Southwest, which bought Morris Air for nearly $130 million. Part of the idea was that Neeleman might eventually succeed the king himself, Herb Kelleher.

Alas, Neeleman's hyperactive management style quickly clashed with Southwest's long-established culture—a clash so irreconcilable that Kelleher, who famously had never laid off any employees, showed his would-be protégé the door.

Yet Kelleher hadn't become a billionaire by being a fool. He might have doubted Neeleman's style as a good fit for Southwest, but he sure didn't doubt his substance—and the threat it could present once he was gone.

"He convinced me to sign a five-year non-compete [agreement] before he fired me," Neeleman would recall years later. "I tried to get him to modify it, and he said, 'No way. You're the last person I want to see in the airline business.'"

So Neeleman didn't compete. But he kept plenty busy. He helped launch a new airline technology company, Open Skies, that would later power reservation systems for dozens of low-cost airlines around the world. And he did, sure enough, help launch a new low-cost airline—but one called WestJet that was based in Canada and thus didn't compete directly against all-domestic Southwest. "I was working on it for a couple of years before the non-compete was over," Neeleman would say of WestJet years later, "just trying to figure out what I wanted to do."

Only a serial entrepreneur could view co-founding WestJet, which would later become one of the world's most profitable airlines, as a mere hobby to pass the time before he became completely unshackled.

The moment his five-year non-compete clause expired in 1999, he was back in the U.S., ready—like Steve Jobs—to redeem himself with a second act.

New York's John F. Kennedy International Airport, or JFK, was unusual in that most of its flights were international, operated by airlines like Delta, American and countless foreign airlines from all corners of the earth. It was a congested airport too—so congested, in fact, that an airline couldn't just add flights when it wanted, even if it had an available airplane and a gate. Instead, it needed to acquire special rights called "slots" to take off and land. Under these conditions, launching an all-new airline at JFK was virtually impossible—if adding even one flight was challenging, how could enough slots be found for a whole new airline? But certain less obvious realities simmered in Neeleman's mind. One: that domestic traffic growth in New York simply hadn't kept pace with traffic growth in the rest of the country. And every time he would fly from JFK, he would note that despite its overall congestion, there were periods during the day that were eerily quiet, times when it didn't make sense to operate flights to or from Europe or Asia—most people, for example, want to leave the U.S. in the early evening for an early morning arrival in Europe, so almost all 75 or so flights from JFK to Europe each day left within a few hours of each other. Neeleman talked to Don Burr, the founder of People Express, and learned more about operating a low-fare airline in the New York market. And Neeleman knew communities throughout the northeast and beyond yearned for affordably priced nonstop air service to the country's largest city.

Nearly a decade later, in 2007, an airline called Virgin America would launch, with great fanfare, in San Francisco. But it was actually supposed to launch much earlier—and along a different U.S. coast.

While Neeleman's thoughts were churning in 1999, another even wealthier and more famous serial airline entrepreneur also happened to be thinking of starting an airline in New York City. The problem for this other serial airline entrepreneur was that he was from the United Kingdom, and U.S. airline investment rules prohibited foreigners from controlling U.S. airlines. So the brash British billionaire Richard Branson, founder and owner of Virgin Atlantic, was ready to settle for the next best option: start a new airline with an American partner. Branson knew U.S. law would, showing some mercy, at least allow him to own up to a quarter of a U.S. airline's voting shares as long as U.S. citizens owned the rest and controlled the airline. And Branson's brain trust had told him the U.S. east coast was ripe for an attack given the vulnerabilities, in particular, of high-cost US Airways. That was something Neeleman had recognized too.

David Neeleman, in fact, had first approached Branson. He did so shortly after he left Southwest, while he still hoped Herb Kelleher might waive or at least modify the non-compete clause, before realizing Kelleher would not even consider such a thing. Neeleman's lawyers had actually told him the clause was legally unenforceable, and he could ignore it. But as lousy of a deal as it was for him, it was a deal, and he planned to abide by it, however impatiently, those five long years while waiting to pursue his Big Apple dreams. Determined to start his new airline with ample capital, Neeleman saw Branson as an ideal partner, and—with the non-compete now having expired—the two iconoclastic business figures moved closer to launching a new JFK-based airline called Virgin America.

But it wasn't to be.

"We were pretty close to getting a deal," Neeleman would recall years later. "And then he kind of decided, at that point in time, that he wanted to go to Washington to try to change the rules."

Some of Branson's advisors had urged him to hold out for the right to control a U.S. airline himself. It wasn't such a crazy idea. The Virgin Group, in fact, was making some headway in its lobbying efforts, eliciting great interest among U.S. congressmen from districts that were saddled with high airfares because of limited competition. Tear down this regulatory barrier against foreign-owned airlines, Branson would say, and all your high-fare problems will be solved.

Hedging his bets, Branson did continue talking with Neeleman. But the two disagreed on a number of items, such as how much Virgin America would pay Branson to license the Virgin name and how much influence Branson would actually have. During their negotiations, Neeleman didn't hide his thoughts regarding this matter. And he was even more blunt years later in describing his position: "I didn't want his interference with the company. I just wanted his name."

So the talks eventually fell apart. Branson ultimately failed to change the foreign ownership rules. He would have to wait another eight years to break into the U.S. market. And even then, with just a partly owned airline, because the law never did change. *And even then*, with an airline that would never, in nearly its first decade of life, anyway, attain nearly the degree of commercial success quickly attained by the airline Neeleman managed to launch without Branson.

Neeleman, for his part, had turned to some of the same politicians representing the communities hungry for low airfares, including members of New York's congressional delegation. Among them was a Brooklyn congressman named Charles Schumer, better known to friends and voters alike as "Chuck," who had run for a U.S. Senate seat in 1998 with a campaign promise: he would help secure low-fare air service to cities in upstate New York to help revitalize their deteriorating economies. A 2006 book called "Flying High," which profiled Neeleman, recounted that he donated to Schumer's campaign—and that three weeks after Schumer won, the entrepreneur met the new senator for breakfast. There Neeleman agreed his new airline would serve cities like Buffalo, Syracuse and Rochester—not the high-growth cities an ambitious upstart airline might typically select—in exchange for Schumer's pledge to help secure slots at JFK.

Neeleman ended up having no trouble securing capital. This was, after all, the late 1990s. The U.S. economy was healthy and prosperous. Neeleman turned to Michael P. Lazarus, a private equity investor who had made money with Neeleman once before by investing in Morris Air before Southwest bought it. Another investor: the famed currency trader George Soros. All told, Neeleman raised $130 million, more than any other startup airline in history had ever raised.

With Virgin out of the picture, the next question was what to name the new airline. Brand consultants came up with a litany of possibilities. "Taxi" and even "Chocolate" got serious consideration. The winner: "TrueBlue." Or at least, that *was* the winner until about a week before a press conference to unveil the new airline. "TrueBlue" sounded more like a frequent flier program than an airline, Neeleman suddenly thought. So years later, it would become just that: the name of the airline's loyalty program. As for the name of the airline itself, Neeleman liked an idea from the airline's soon-to-be marketing chief, Amy Curtis-McIntyre, herself recruited from Virgin Atlantic. "JetBlue," she had suggested.

But there was one problem. The name was already taken—by a Midwestern tractor distributor. It didn't have a website, so the internet domain was available. But it did have the 1-800-JetBlue phone number. Fortunately, a few thousand dollars made the problem go away, and JetBlue began life on Feb. 11, 2000, with flights from New York JFK to both Buffalo and Fort Lauderdale.

Florida was where the new airline would make most of its money. And make money it did, almost right from the start. As any successful low-cost airline should do, JetBlue established substantial cost advantages. It shunned expensive amenities like plush first-class cabins, airport lounges and inflight meals. It kept things simple—no alliances with other airlines, no complex flight schedules designed to foster connecting traffic, no sales forces negotiating travel contracts with big corporations. None of its workers were unionized. JetBlue took advantage of new technologies like internet distribution, electronic ticketing and self-service airport check-in counters, all unavailable to the previous generation of low-cost airlines. And operating a low-cost carrier was becoming easier because the labor-intensive airline business was becoming less labor intensive at the turn of the millennium. Internet distribution meant fewer call centers. Do-it-yourself check-in kiosks meant fewer airport agents. In addition, all of JetBlue's modern Airbus 320s required just two pilots, not the three some of the aging Boeing 727s that Delta and others were still flying required.

But Neeleman didn't stop with just cost and labor productivity advantages. He was determined to make JetBlue an enjoyable airline to fly. So he offered generous legroom and outfitted all seatbacks with television screens featuring complimentary live satellite TV. An unintended benefit: flight attendants loved the TVs just as much as the passengers, who were so blissfully preoccupied watching Regis Philbin host "Who Wants to Be a Millionaire?" that they didn't ask much of the cabin crews. Unlike other airlines, JetBlue did not overbook its flights, knowing nearly all of its passengers would show up for their flights because all tickets were nonrefundable—most carriers made some of their tickets refundable to attract business travelers, whose schedules might change. But this meant people would inevitably not show up for flights, leaving empty seats that could have otherwise been sold and thus requiring overselling and complex revenue management techniques to optimize it all.

JetBlue's innovative inflight product enabled it to achieve something that not even perennially successful Southwest had managed to achieve. For probably the first time in the history of the world, passengers were actually willing to pay more to fly a low-cost airline rather than its legacy competitors. Airlines call this a "revenue premium." Low costs and high revenues are a great recipe for profits.

So JetBlue managed to produce an operating profit not only in its very first year of operation, something few airlines have ever managed, but also in hellish 2001. It never furloughed anyone—the unusually large sum of capital it had raised before launching, which seemed like a luxurious cushion, instead proved vital. It made money even during the very *quarter* in which 9/11 happened. And it made its money by stealing more than a few passengers from Delta.

***

Making money after 9/11, of course, was the exception, not the rule. America's airlines were, to say the least, happy to put 2001 behind them. The year started with economic malaise, enough of a challenge by most standards. It ended with war and terror, when civilian airplanes became weapons of mass destruction.

But the symbolism of the calendar turning to a new year spoke little about what might really happen next. Would 2002 bring quick recovery? Or would the fallout from 9/11 linger for years? Was this a harsh but temporary shock? Or had the airline business changed forever?

When the accountants finished tallying all the red numbers, U.S. airlines revealed they had lost nearly $8 billion in 2001, even including the benefit of $4 billion in federal government grant revenue. For only the second time in industry history, annual revenue declined—and not by a token amount, but by fully 12 percent compared to 2000. The only other year in which U.S. airline revenue fell was 10 years earlier, in 1991, when the industry was hit by a war in Iraq, a fuel spike and a weak economy. This time, even with all the panicked cost cutting and job cutting after 9/11, operating expenses still *increased* 1 percent from 2000 levels—these rising costs, coupled with the plummeting revenues, explained the unprecedented losses. Unsurprisingly, airline credit ratings were shot. Aircraft values were depressed. The survival of many carriers depended on government aid. And even that aid came with a huge catch: a new regime of government taxation and airport security procedures that not only inflated airline costs but also depressed demand. All the added time travelers needed to spend at airports because of new security procedures, for example, caused even time-sensitive business travelers to begin driving between cities a couple hundred miles apart. Other people, especially more occasional leisure travelers, shunned flying out of fear.

As 2002 began in this upside-down world, Delta was contemplating its own fate. And the very first week of the year didn't augur well. A giant winter storm blanketed much of the south, severely disrupting operations at Delta's Atlanta hub, the busiest airport in the nation. At the time, Delta was despondently surveying the damage from 2001, which included a $1.1 billion net loss on $13.2 billion in revenue. Delta's first loss at all in six years had been massive, not modest. Delta was still, however, the nation's second largest airline by passengers carried after American, which had purchased the bankrupt TWA months before. And Delta was the third largest by revenue after American, which dominated Latin America, and United, the top U.S. airline to Asia. Well behind Delta in the revenue rankings were Northwest, US Airways, Continental, Southwest, America West, Alaska Airlines, ATA and a small low-cost carrier ("LCCs," people in the industry were now calling them) named AirTran, a reincarnation of the old ValuJet. Even tinier carriers on the industry's fringes included the young JetBlue.

All these airlines faced significant challenges in the aftermath of 9/11, although some were better off than others. Delta, in fact, was among the better off, less in tatters than many of its peers, including American and United. For starters, they had lost planes and people on 9/11; Delta had not. In addition, they had higher labor costs than Delta, partly because all their major work groups were unionized; at Delta, flight attendants, mechanics and airport ground staff—all large groups of employees except pilots, in fact—were not. Delta's route network wasn't as international. That meant Delta stood to gain less than its peers from a rapidly globalizing world. But less international exposure turned out to be a *good* thing at a time when international revenues were now falling faster than domestic revenues. Delta's domestic network, meanwhile, was less dependent than those of its peers on corporate travel, which the crisis also hit disproportionately. And Delta, thanks to visionary thinking at its now-wholly owned Comair subsidiary—Comair's recent labor woes notwithstanding—had the largest fleet of 50-seat regional jets, planes that passengers greatly preferred on routes Delta had previously served, and its competitors still served, with noisy, bumpy propeller planes. Regional jets could also fly greater distances than propeller planes. Their fuel efficiency wasn't great: A turboprop was more economical than a similarly sized regional jet. But this wasn't a major concern, because fuel, although not quite the bargain it had been in the late 1990s, was still rather cheap. These 50-seat jets, it's fair to say, had single-handedly powered the striking late-1990s success of Delta's Cincinnati hub, which robbed passengers from competing hubs like Cleveland and Pittsburgh that still relied more on turboprops. It's also fair to say, for reasons including geography and infrastructure, that Atlanta was still the nation's most powerful hub, a hub Delta had more or less to itself.

But most comforting of all for Delta was its balance sheet, which at the start of 2002 was among the industry's best. In the boom years of the late 1990s, remember, Delta was practically printing money thanks to its Florida flights, its European flights and its flights from Atlanta to all major U.S. business centers. On top of that, it had reaped giant windfalls from its Priceline investment. Delta, in other words, had built a sturdy war chest as it entered the new decade. And even after 9/11, on Jan. 1, 2002, Delta was still sitting on more than $2 billion in cash, helped by its investment-grade credit rating, which was still intact six days after the attacks, when it borrowed $1.3 billion by using its aircraft as collateral to issue bonds. American and especially United were in far worse shape.

Delta enjoyed some competitive tailwinds too. US Airways, for example, a close competitor along the east coast, closed its ostensibly low-cost Metrojet unit just before the start of 2002. In late January, for the second time in six years, American failed to get permission from regulators to form a close alliance with British Airways, one that might have dominated travel between the U.S. and London, which was by far the busiest transatlantic market. In stark contrast, Delta did, just days earlier, get antitrust immunity—that is, the right to jointly set transatlantic fares and schedules, or in other words, to legally "collude"—with its SkyTeam partners Air France, Alitalia and CSA Czech Airlines. It was also cooperating anew with SkyTeam's Korean Air after one of Delta's executives helped the carrier improve its safety practices following several deadly crashes, a chapter in Delta's history that would later be made modestly famous by Malcolm Gladwell in his 2008 bestselling pop economics book "Outliers."

And speaking of outliers, Delta was certainly that regarding labor relations in the immediate post-9/11 period. Unlike United and US Airways, in particular, it was not asking its employees for wage cuts—not at the start of the year, anyway. And not being highly unionized—only 18 percent of its workers were union members—gave it greater flexibility than its competitors to, for example, schedule its crews efficiently. Distribution costs for all airlines were also falling as the internet shifted the balance of power from travel agents to airlines. For leisure travelers, at least—business travelers would long remain another matter—booking tickets on delta.com could be easier and more convenient than visiting an agency. And it could be more rewarding too, because Delta offered frequent flier mileage bonuses for booking online. People who wanted to comparison shop, meanwhile, had shifted to a new breed of "online travel agencies" like Expedia, which Microsoft launched in 1996. These agencies charged airlines much lower commission rates than their disappearing "bricks-and-mortar" predecessors had charged. One rare piece of bright news during 2001 had been that Delta sold more than 4.2 million tickets through its own website that year, a 60 percent increase compared to 2000.

Delta, in other words, had at least some causes for optimism at the start of 2002. And its spirits certainly weren't dampened in February, when the Winter Olympics were held in Salt Lake City, one of Delta's five hubs. Indeed, Delta was a top-tier sponsor of the games. It painted one of its 757s in an Olympic-themed design and worked closely with the event's chief organizer, a man named Willard Romney, who was better known as "Mitt" and whom 10 years later the Republican party would nominate to run for the U.S. presidency.

By April, it was time for Delta to report first-quarter earnings, which, to be sure, were not good—a $400 million net loss in just three months, with year-over-year revenues plummeting by nearly a fifth. But Leo Mullin, choosing to emphasize the positive, noted a small operating profit for the month of March, the first such operating profit in eight months, along with improving macroeconomic forecasts. "As a result of our consistent focus on disciplined capacity control, a competitive network, strong capital infrastructure and a motivated, primarily non-union employee base," he told Wall Street analysts April 16, "Delta is extremely well positioned to respond quickly and fully to the coming economic recovery."

For all the optimism, however, and for all the strengths that Delta had relative to peers like United, American and US Airways, the giant airline had alarming vulnerabilities too, some of which were magnified and exacerbated by new post-9/11 realities.

Two of these— a growing exposure to low-cost airlines and an expensive pilot contract—were especially troubling. Since the dawn of deregulation in 1978, Herb Kelleher's Southwest Airlines had terrorized competitors with low fares made possible by a workforce that, although actually highly unionized, was ultra-productive and famously committed to caring for customers. And to be sure, Delta felt Southwest's growing presence, from cities like Baltimore and Orlando to Salt Lake City and Dallas. The fact that a large proportion of Delta's traffic was connecting through hubs also made it particularly vulnerable to Southwest's constantly growing menu of nonstop flights—more travelers could fly from, say, Baltimore to Tampa on Southwest without bothering to stop in Atlanta. Delta, after all, relied more on connecting traffic than most of its rivals.

There had been ValuJet in the 1990s. And Continental Lite and Shuttle by United and Metrojet and an endless succession of low-fare Southwest wannabes with names like Eastwind, ProAir, Carnival, Western Pacific, Vanguard, Kiwi, National, the "new Pan Am," Tower Air and Midway. So Delta was no stranger to low-fare competition entering the 2000s and had itself in 1996 launched Delta Express as a defense mechanism. But in a way, Delta was lucky as it began the new millennium.

Southwest mercifully stayed out of Atlanta, New York and Cincinnati. ValuJet had nearly disappeared after a deadly crash in 1996. Competitors' low-fare offshoots like US Airways Metrojet unit failed to take hold. And a host of barriers limited the advancement of LCCs other than giant Southwest.

One of these barriers was extremely aggressive pricing tactics by established players, which had the staying power to dump a lot of extra seats and extremely low fares into a market contested by an upstart, knowing full well that temporary losses would be offset in the long run by the benefit of running a new rival out of town. In 1999, the Clinton administration's Justice Department, pressured by politicians representing communities eager for low-fare air service, had accused American Airlines of predatory pricing to drive three low-cost carriers—Vanguard, Western Pacific and Sun Jet—from American's Dallas-Fort Worth hub. For most of the late 1990s, though, full-service legacy carriers like American, United, Delta, Northwest and Continental commanded a strong degree of pricing power, boosted by a booming economy and checked by the growth of just one airline: Southwest. Where Southwest wasn't, fares skyrocketed, especially the highest-tier fares favored by business travelers, because these fares were for tickets that could be changed or refunded or even accepted by other airlines.

All this began to change abruptly by the turn of the millennium, as a weakening economy disrupted the ability of incumbent carriers to repeatedly raise business travel fares. At the same time, the internet enhanced the ability of low-cost carriers to drop their fares.

The fast expansion of Southwest, the rise of new LCCs like AirTran and the quick emergence of JetBlue naturally put revenue pressure on Delta. But back on the cost side, there was another critical reason Delta was becoming so vulnerable to these new LCC challenges. The reality is, all newly launched airlines enjoy a key structural advantage with respect to labor costs. Why? Because in the airline business, flight crews, mechanics and airport workers are paid according to seniority, with vastly different levels of pay linked to tenure. So a flight attendant working for an airline for 20 years, for example, will earn a lot more than one with just two years of tenure who's doing the same job. Well, for a young airline like AirTran or JetBlue, one thing is certain: No workers on the payroll have 20 years of tenure. At an old airline like Delta, especially one that now wasn't growing its workforce (and thus wasn't hiring young, low-seniority workers), average seniority was much higher, implying much higher labor costs and creating a vicious cycle: Delta and its legacy peers weren't growing, partly because of their labor cost issues, but the lack of growth pushed average labor costs even higher. And that's to say nothing of the less risky pensions new airlines offered their workers, ones whose value when a worker retired depended on the stock market. Delta and its legacy peers still offered traditional pensions with guaranteed benefits and thus much more risk for employers, which would have to make up any shortfalls at retirement relative to what they had promised workers.

Which raises the second of Delta's two major challenges at the dawn of the post-9/11 era: its expensive pilot contract. Just as AirTran and JetBlue were slicing away at Delta's markets, the wages, benefits and work rules of Delta's new pilot contract were kicking in. Just six months before 9/11, Leo Mullin, wary of more labor unrest and feeling cornered by a princely new pilot contract agreed to by United, had reluctantly agreed to one for Delta's pilots that—once ratified by pilots that summer—locked in pay increases of up to 34 percent between 2001 and 2005. Pilots at Delta Express, the low-cost offshoot created by Mullin's predecessor to defend against Southwest and others, would see pay increases of closer to 60 percent. The new contract also provided enhanced retirement benefits, limits on further regional jet outsourcing and more vacation time.

Although most of Delta's workers weren't unionized, the most expensive group of all was unionized. Pilots belonged to the Air Line Pilots Association, or ALPA, which also represented pilots at other carriers. Determined to win back concessions surrendered in the early 1990s, ALPA secured new contracts for US Airways pilots in 1997, Northwest pilots in 1998 and United pilots in 2000—the United contract was particularly rich. Naturally, Delta pilots wanted at least what their colleagues at United got and used the same hardball tactics to get it. During the peak winter holiday travel season in 2000, they had engaged in what the company alleged was a work slowdown—refusing to fly because of minor maintenance issues, for example, ostensibly on safety grounds—as well as a refusal to work overtime. This cost the company millions of dollars and lots of customer goodwill. And it handed a golden opportunity to JetBlue and especially AirTran, which—because it was running a hub of its own in Atlanta—competed even more directly against Delta. Relations became even tenser when management sued the union, asking for a restraining order.

"After a judge—a very liberal judge, by the way—threatened to fine them," Mullin recalled, "all of a sudden everybody went back and was accepting overtime again. In one day. For heaven's sake, come on."

Mullin, meanwhile, thought pilots were asking for too much. "They came in right off the bat and the wanted 'United plus 10 percent,'" he said. "That would have just cratered the company. But they were serious."

The feud lingered through the start of 2001 until the April agreement, which essentially gave the pilots not United plus 10 percent or even five percent but "United plus one."

On the heels of this bloody confrontation, Delta was in no mood to reignite conflict by asking to re-work the terms of the new contract, as other airlines were desperately doing after 9/11. The airline did furlough pilots in conjunction with its heavy reduction in flying, invoking a *force majeure* clause in the contract—in other words, a provision covering extremely adverse circumstances beyond anyone's control, which the 9/11 attacks certainly were. But again, Delta did not initially call for a renegotiation of the contract, taking comfort—perhaps too much comfort—in the company's relatively strong balance sheet and Leo Mullin's optimism about returning to profitability. One fact, however, was inescapable: Delta's total outlay for salaries, wages and benefits reached $6 billion in 2002, this for a company whose total revenues were just $13 billion. Labor costs, in fact, accounted for fully 45 percent of the airline's operating costs. At JetBlue, the figure was 31 percent. At AirTran, it was 29 percent. Even at United, it was just 41 percent. Indeed, Delta in 2002 had a labor cost problem, which was tied to having the industry's richest pilot contract.

Optimistic though he was about a near-term recovery, Mullin understood these twin threats of low-cost carriers and Delta's pilot contract. As early as the first quarter, Delta sold more Priceline stock and issued another $731 million in aircraft-backed bonds—money, in other words, investors didn't mind lending because they could always repossess airplanes if Delta didn't pay. Delta delayed delivery of 39 airplanes and began retiring aging Boeing 727s even more quickly than it had planned— these were planes that weren't all that big, roughly the size of a 737, but had three fuel-guzzling engines and required three pilots, not the two engines and two pilots of newer airplanes of a similar size. All this helped fortify a deteriorating balance sheet, and the bond issuance in particular marked another big difference between Delta and some of its peers: It could still borrow from the capital markets. In fact, it issued yet *another* $1.1 billion in aircraft-backed bonds in April. But all this borrowing, while boosting the company's cash cushion, piled on more long-term debt.

At least as importantly, Delta cut its labor costs. In March, it suspended pay raises for about 40,000 employees, most of them flight attendants and customer service agents. Pilot pay, of course, could not be cut without a negotiated contract change. Mechanics were due for a big pay raise just after 9/11, but management postponed that until March 2002. Mullin, meanwhile, cut his own pay after 9/11, dropping his income by 72 percent from $2.1 million in 2000 to $596,000 in 2001. At the same time, technology was making ground operations less labor intensive. To save money on airport staffing while improving the customer experience, Delta aggressively expanded the availability of airport kiosks, which enabled passengers to check in for their flights and select their seats on their own.

Mullin and his team also saw the area of ticket distribution as a lever to lower costs. In March, Delta became the first major airline to eliminate standard commission payments to North American travel agents. Airlines, to be sure, relied on these agents in fiercely competitive markets. But Delta relied on them less than some of its competitors did, because it dominated many markets in the southeast, had few battles against foreign carriers (because of its limited international network) and competed closely against low-cost carriers—airlines that already avoided paying commissions. Delta did, however, continue to pay agencies that met certain performance targets, such as booking a certain volume of tickets with the airline. In May, it stopped issuing paper tickets for most itineraries and started charging a $10 fee if passengers insisted on paper tickets. And it continued to develop delta.com, dangling frequent flier bonuses to passengers who booked their tickets there. This would help lower labor costs too, because more website bookings diminished the need for call center employees.

By the summer, however, it was becoming painfully clear that these measures weren't enough. As late as April, Mullin and Reid were telling investors Delta could profit in the second half of the year as cost-cutting efforts kicked in and demand gradually improved. Instead, Delta lost more than $300 million in the third quarter, which is normally the time of year when airlines earn most of their money. In the off-peak fourth quarter, losses grew to $363 million. By mid-year, losses, debt, taxes and fuel prices had been rising even as demand and average fares were falling. In addition, Delta started getting uncomfortably close to violating its bank loan covenants—in other words, losing so much money and accumulating so much debt that its lenders were getting nervous. At one point, in fact, Delta's bankers forced it to have at least $1 billion in cash on hand at the end of every month.

In the simplest sense, profiting in any business means keeping your revenues above your costs—selling a hamburger, say, for more than it costs to produce. But in late 2002, profiting was becoming harder than ever for Delta. Fuel costs were rising. So was the cost of insurance. Suddenly, airlines faced much higher taxes to pay for the new federal Department of Homeland Security. Lower interest rates, although a blessing when borrowing money, were a curse when it came to funding pension liabilities. Older airlines like Delta promised their workers clearly defined benefits upon retirement, and the ability to fulfill those promises depended on how much their pension funds grew. Well, with interest rates low, they grew less, so airlines had to pour in even more cash to make up for the shortfall. In Delta's case, this meant hundreds of millions of dollars.

If costs were a concern, the revenue picture was even more alarming. As early as January, President George W. Bush was laying the rhetorical groundwork for an invasion of Iraq, telling congress the Middle Eastern country was part of an "axis of evil." By autumn, another war seemed all but inevitable. Oil prices surged to nearly $30 per barrel in September, up from just $20 at the start of the year and as low as $11 a few years earlier. Worse, the prospect of war in Iraq was weighing on an already weak economic recovery—and weighing even more heavily on an already weak air travel recovery. On top of this, new airport security hassles continued to depress demand, especially in the shorthaul business markets like those in the northeast, markets on which Delta depended heavily. In the biggest northeast shorthaul markets of all, the "shuttles" between New York and both Washington and Boston that Delta duopoloized with US Airways, this was all happening even as Amtrak's city center-to-city center rail service, called Acela, was becoming faster than ever. The "hassle factor," Mullin told investors in October, had cost the industry some $2.5 billion in revenue since 9/11 on top of the $4 billion cost burden from new government mandates, taxation, prohibitions and regulations. At the same time, LCCs like Southwest, AirTran and JetBlue kept growing, hitting Delta's Florida franchise especially hard. This hurt because roughly a quarter of all

Delta's passengers were flying to or from Florida. These LCCs now had the added benefit of fare transparency too—in the age of the internet, consumers could more easily than ever find low-fare options on their own without depending on a travel agent. By late 2002, 40 percent of Delta's passengers had low-fare carrier alternatives. AirTran, for its part, was escalating the pressure by putting regional jets into Atlanta, penetrating deeper and deeper into even Delta's smaller markets, while also targeting new west coast routes from Atlanta and launching a frequent flier plan. Here, in other words, was an airline that increasingly could do a lot of what Delta could do in Atlanta. But it could do it all at a far lower production cost than Delta could ever imagine.

Competition against high-cost incumbent carriers wasn't getting easier either. Price wars proliferated as too many airline seats chased too little consumer demand for them. And what should have been a blessing—the bankruptcy of rival competitors—turned out to be a curse. In August, US Airways, with no money left to pay its bills, filed for bankruptcy. In December, much larger United did the same.

By the time he got home that day—Dec. 9, 2002—Mullin's wife Leah had heard the news. Her quick analysis was the same as that of a lot of other people: "Well," she said to Leo Mullin, "maybe that will be good for Delta, because you'll be able to compete with a bankrupt carrier."

"Leah, you don't understand," Mullin recalled replying to her. "A bankrupt airline reduces its costs and does not go away. They're here. Their planes will continue to fly. And all of a sudden, due to their lower cost structure, they're going to be charging less. And believe me, people will flock to them if their prices are lower than ours."

As early as 1970, Mullin, then a railroad executive, had witnessed what happens when a company's key competitor files for bankruptcy—in that case, the bankruptcy of the Penn Central railroad was the largest in U.S. history. "All of a sudden," Mullin said, "the bankrupt carrier starts to price in a very different way and basically destroys the economics of all its otherwise healthy competitors."

In Delta's case, in 2002, it was one thing to compete against low-cost upstarts like AirTran and JetBlue. But "it's another thing," Mullin said, "to have United all of a sudden become a low-cost carrier."

American's costs, meanwhile, remained relatively low too, because unlike United and Delta, it hadn't agreed before 9/11 to give its pilots big raises. And it wasn't about to do so now.

Bankruptcy in the U.S. is unusual compared with some parts of the world, where "bankruptcy" and "liquidation" can be practically synonymous—where going bankrupt means going out of business. In the U.S., in the name of sustaining employment and giving troubled companies a chance to reorganize, bankrupt companies are allowed to stop paying many of their bills while they revamp their business plans. In the airline business, this meant benefits like the right to stop making aircraft lease payments for two months without worrying about the planes being repossessed. It also meant enormous leverage for airlines to break contracts and secure heavy cost savings from workers and suppliers. What's more, companies that at first glance might appear to have nothing to do with aviation feel compelled to prevent bankrupt airlines from collapsing, even if that means extending a risky loan to keep them alive. Credit card-issuing banks, for example, whose most valuable credit cards are often the ones that offer frequent flier miles, have played an instrumental role in rescuing bankrupt airlines, because those cards would have become worthless had the airlines disappeared.

All of this made it tough to be the "healthy carrier," so to speak—which Delta still was in late 2002, relative to its legacy peers, anyway. Even American, despite having the least expensive pilot contract among the big carriers, had a weaker balance sheet than Delta. United and US Airways, although much weaker, were not disappearing as they surely would have had U.S. bankruptcy laws looked more like laws elsewhere in the world—in the wake of 9/11, Belgium's Sabena Airlines had gone bankrupt and actually stopped flying, for example, as did Australia's second largest airline Ansett. Instead, United and US Airways had new powers to drastically improve their cost competiveness. In addition, US Airways won a loan guarantee from the U.S. government, a lifeline that—from Delta's perspective—merely prevented uneconomical airline seats from disappearing. Creative destruction? Not in the airline industry. Eventually, 16 carriers would apply for federal loan guarantees, with seven of these applications accepted and nine (including United's) rejected. A few airlines, including Midway and Vanguard, did actually liquidate in 2002. But these were small. Excess capacity was rife. And airfares, by extension, stayed low.

Nor was the world looking any safer for would-be global travelers. In October 2002, 202 people, many of them foreign tourists, died in terrorist attacks on the Indonesian resort island of Bali. That same month, terrorists seized a Moscow theater, where 129 hostages ultimately died. The U.S. itself was on edge when two "Beltway snipers," also in October, killed 10 innocent people in the Washington, D.C., area, creating widespread fear in the process. During the course of the year, terrorists also killed people in Israel, Pakistan, Tunisia, Kenya and the Philippines.

The U.S. economy, meanwhile, was under pressure. And not just because of the impending Iraq war. And not just because of energy prices, which were rising due to the impending Iraq war. Political disruptions and labor strikes at oil installations in Venezuela were also putting upward pressure on energy prices, a fact that led Boeing to abandon plans for what it called the Sonic Cruiser, a next-generation aircraft that would be somewhat faster than existing airplanes. The Sonic Cruiser would have been far more economical (albeit slower) than the recently retired supersonic Concorde. But even the Sonic Cruiser could only work well in a cheap-fuel world—a world that was rapidly disappearing. At the same time, United and US Airways were hardly the only U.S. companies filing for bankruptcy. So did major corporations like the retailer Kmart and the telecom provider Worldcom, the latter due to fraud that exceeded even Enron in the damage it did to shareholders. As a consequence of these many economic headwinds, stock markets unsurprisingly plummeted, with the Dow Jones falling 17 percent for the year. That marked the third straight declining year for the Dow, the first time that had happened since the 1939-to-1941 downturn.

Mullin and his team understood Delta needed more drastic measures. After assuring employees as recently as August that no additional job or pay cuts would be necessary, Delta announced up to 8,000 job cuts in October, nearly as many as the 10,000 it cut immediately after 9/11. Many of these would be voluntary—workers agreeing to leave in exchange for a severance package and other benefits like free travel. But a few thousand would lose their jobs involuntarily too. Delta closed flight attendant bases in New Orleans, Chicago, Houston, Portland and Seattle. It outsourced some call center work to India and the Philippines. It altered its employee health care plans. It moved everyone except pilots away from traditional defined-benefit pensions and toward defined-contribution, or 401(k) plans, with the company (like many other American companies that had made similar changes) promising to make contributions but making no guarantees about what employees would collect when they retire: The employee, not the company, would bear the risk. Not stopping there, Delta grounded its MD-11s. Like the 727s, these were three-engined dinousaurs, in the MD-11's case a dinosaur that had been flying longhaul international routes. Its replacement? The smaller and more modern Boeing 767, which had been flying a lot of domestic routes. Replacing 767s with even smaller planes for domestic routes would have the added benefit of reducing seat supply on those routes and thus hopefully forcing fares to rise a bit. Delta also deferred 29 aircraft scheduled for delivery in 2003 and 2004, holding onto $1.3 billion that it would have spent for those planes.

So Delta did a lot. But one thing it didn't do was perhaps the single biggest thing it could have done to address its increasingly uncompetitive cost base: ask its pilots for concessions. "Have you been talking with the pilots with respect to any midstream opening of their contract with respect to productivity or wages?" one Wall Street analyst asked during the airline's fourth-quarter earnings presentation. "No, we have not," Fred Reid answered. "As of this date, we have not held such discussions."

Just cutting costs wouldn't have been enough anyway. Mullin needed to find ways to raise revenue too. Fortunately, the new alliance with Air France was off to a strong start, enabling new international Delta routes like one to Mumbai from Air France's Paris hub. In the summer, Delta also added a second daily New York flight to Paris. And it started flying from Atlanta to Milan thanks to a new marketing pact with Italy's Alitalia. At least as importantly, Delta since 9/11 had suspended loss-making flights from New York to Tokyo, Shannon, Dublin, Zurich, Cairo, Lyon, Tel Aviv, Munich and Stockholm. Also gone: Nagoya flights from Los Angeles, London flights from Boston and Mumbai flights from the old Pan Am Frankfurt hub. By the end of the year, Atlanta service to Buenos Aires was gone too, a casualty of Argentina's latest financial crisis, with Atlanta-Rio de Janeiro also withdrawn for good measure.

Back on the domestic front, Delta was replacing "mainline" service—Delta's own jets flown by Delta's own pilots—with smaller regional planes. In Salt Lake City, for example, Delta's regional partner SkyWest was now operating more flights, painted in Delta's colors, than Delta itself was operating. Why? In large part because this meant less flying performed by Delta's expensive mainline pilots. In Orlando, Delta hired another independent regional carrier called Chautauqua, which replaced Delta's wholly owned Comair unit there. Here too, Delta was saving on pilot costs, which rose at Comair after the 89-day pilot strike there the year before—Comair pilots earned less than Delta mainline pilots but more than other regional airline pilots, including those at Chautauqua.

But moving more service to smaller planes was about more than just pilot cost management. It was also about sizing planes to the new reality of lower demand. Delta's Atlantic Southeast regional unit, in fact, also wholly owned by the airline, grew capacity some 20 percent in 2002, in part by deploying some larger 70-seat regional jets for the first time to supplement the 50-seaters that had become so common.

Nowhere was this move to replace mainline flying with regional flying more evident than at Delta's Dallas-Fort Worth hub, or DFW. For as long as anyone could remember, DFW was a winless battle for Delta. Delta was up against American, which dominated the market. Unwilling to completely retreat, however, Mullin in late 2002 removed most of the hub's mainline planes, adding regional jets that, in effect, led to more daily departures but fewer seats overall. Ultimately, though, this only gave American an even greater competitive revenue advantage at DFW, where its full-sized mainline planes were more comfortable and offered first-class seating.

But all this maneuvering—the new international flying, the retreat from some markets and the swapping of regional planes for mainline planes—was a sideshow to two more consequential strategic moves, one (a new alliance) announced in August and another (a new low-cost airline-within-an-airline) announced in November.

Delta's late 1990s failure to merge with Continental did not dampen its enthusiasm for consolidation. At one point, also during that period, Mullin briefly spoke with American. Next, in 1998, he was close to a deal to cooperate with United in a way similar to how Northwest was now cooperating with Continental. Unlike the Northwest-Continental deal, no equity would change hands. But like the Northwest-Continental deal, Delta and United would similarly retain their own brands, allow their passengers to earn and burn frequent flier miles on each other's flights and actually sell each other's flights by way of codesharing. So Delta's "DL" flight code would be assigned to United's flights and United's "UA" code to Delta's flights, giving each carrier more flights to sell and passengers more flights from which to choose. American had long called codesharing deceptive. But deceptive or not, it was a practice that had become a widespread revenue-boosting tool. Business travelers value frequent flights above all else. So an airline that could offer more flights in a market, whether or not all of the flights were really on its own "metal"—the term airlines use to refer to whose plane actually flies—would be at a big advantage over a competitor that, when a travel agent went to book a flight for an important corporate traveler, appeared to have fewer flights.

But the Delta-United codeshare was not to be. It fell victim to pilot mistrust. Delta pilots, still fuming over a contract they had signed with Ron Allen in 1996—still rather recently at that point—were in no mood to allow their airline to sell flights operated by other airlines with other pilots. So they refused to go along. Delta and United did agree to a far more limited frequent flier reciprocity arrangement so that a United loyalist, for example, could at least earn miles when flying Delta "to offer new opportunities for our 23 million members" of SkyMiles, Delta said, while emphasizing, in the same press release: "Delta and United have no plans to merge, however, and will remain independent companies and competitors." The emphasis on competition was a nod to the regulatory mood at the time. Soon came 2000, when United announced a full merger with US Airways, only to have its plans fall apart when the Justice Department under President Clinton, citing antitrust concerns, refused to go along.

That cooled industry merger talk for a while. But by mid-2002, United was talking to US Airways again, this time about a codeshare alliance rather than a full merger. And that's indeed what happened: a new United-US Airways alliance announced on the eve of the latter's bankruptcy filing. Mullin was alarmed. So was Richard Anderson at Northwest, which competed directly against United on many routes, including to, from and within Asia. Northwest itself was no stranger to alliances. It had practically invented the concept when it pioneered a groundbreaking joint venture with KLM in the 1990s, one that essentially merged the transatlantic businesses of the American and Dutch airlines. This went far beyond codesharing and frequent flier reciprocity. In a global first, the airlines coordinated their schedules, priced their seats jointly, standardized their products and shared the profits. The Netherlands, in fact, in 1992 became the first country in the world to sign an aviation free trade agreement with the U.S.—an "open skies" agreement, in industry parlance—in exchange for U.S. antitrust immunity for the new Northwest-KLM alliance. The relationship proved so profitable and so capable of stealing traffic from other airlines that Lufthansa urged its government to sign an open skies deal with the U.S. so that it could form an antitrust-immune joint venture with United. And Air France urged its country to do the same for the sake of an alliance with Delta.

But by 2002, although Northwest had a strong transatlantic partner in KLM and a strong domestic partner in Continental, it was not part of Star, oneworld or SkyTeam, the three young global alliances that offered customers benefits such as airport lounge access and frequent flier accrual on airlines near and far throughout the world. Anderson began thinking about joining an alliance—specifically, SkyTeam.

Across the Atlantic, meanwhile, KLM was doing its own strategic thinking. As successful as its transatlantic business was thanks to the Northwest partnership, the fact remained that the Netherlands was a relatively small country and Amsterdam a relatively small hub compared to what British Airways could offer in London, Lufthansa could offer in Frankfurt or Air France could offer in Paris. At the same, the post-9/11 downturn was doing substantial damage to KLM's own balance sheet.

By 2002, it had $4 billion in long-term debt and many a sleepless night wondering about its ability to maintain itself as an independent airline in the age of large airlines getting larger. In its annual report that year, its worries were transparent: "Continued consolidation may increase the competitive pressures on us, reduce revenues and threaten our strategic position. The impact of any future consolidation within the U.S. or European sectors of the airline industry cannot be predicted at this time but could adversely affect our financial results and condition." Low-cost carriers with names like Ryanair and easyJet were a growing threat in Europe too. KLM even tried launching its own low-cost airline-within-an-airline, "Buzz," which struggled. Ryanair eventually bought it.

So KLM concluded its only path to a strong future was through merging. As early as 2000, it neared a deal to combine with British Airways, a deal that succumbed to the same fate as the United-US Airways merger that same year: Regulators killed it. About the same time, KLM also neared a deal to merge with Alitalia, a plan that died partly because of Italy's unwillingness to privatize its national airline and partly because a new airport in Milan proved poorly designed to serve as a connecting hub. In 2002, discouraged but still determined, KLM started speaking with Air France, which itself had just completed one of the industry's greatest-ever turnarounds, evolving from a strike-prone basket case to an airline that withstood the impact of 9/11 better than just about any other major airline on either side of the Atlantic. It too, however, saw the value in size, understanding that business travelers wanted the largest networks with the broadest menus of destinations. And however well it was doing at the moment, sitting on the sidelines as rivals merged and enhanced their clout was a bad idea.

If it were to buy KLM, Air France would need to get Delta's consent to allow the Dutch carrier into SkyTeam. But doing so would be easy. Delta would be happy to have another European partner with another European hub through which to flow its traffic. Delta could fill a flight from Atlanta to Amsterdam not only with passengers from places "behind" Atlanta, as airlines call them—places like, say, New Orleans—but also passengers going to places in Europe "beyond" Amsterdam—say, Berlin. But KLM's ironclad joint venture with Northwest meant Northwest too would have to join, as would Northwest's partner Continental. And Delta was less convinced of the benefits of allowing *these* two to join. Sure, Northwest and Continental might provide some feed traffic for Delta hubs like Atlanta. But Delta might also be aiding an enemy, Continental, whose powerful Newark hub would compete for connecting traffic—especially transatlantic connecting traffic—against Delta's New York JFK hub.

In February, Leo Mullin and Fred Reid had invited their Air France counterparts to the Salt Lake City Olympics to discuss the matter. Back in Atlanta, analysts were hard at work weighing the pros and cons of welcoming Northwest, Continental and KLM into SkyTeam. In the end, the pros were more compelling, all the more so as Delta observed United and US Airways growing closer—and as market conditions badly deteriorated, rather than improving, as Mullin had hoped, as 2002 progressed.

By the summer, not only was Delta willing to allow Northwest and Continental into SkyTeam. It even wanted to codeshare with them on domestic routes. And so, in a major development attracting widespread mainstream news coverage, Delta, Northwest and Continental, on Aug. 23, announced a three-way alliance.

There was, of course, the matter of getting Delta's pilots to agree. But this time they did. That reaction was far different from their reaction to the proposed Delta-United codeshare alliance four years earlier, because the context was far different. In the late 1990s, after all, the industry was booming, Delta was growing and pilots were still steaming about the concession-laden contract they had signed with Ron Allen. This time, they had the best contract in the industry, and Delta clearly needed partners to navigate the extremely harsh post-9/11 market conditions. Reid, for his part, frequently reminded pilots that the real risk to their jobs wasn't alliance partners but competitors.

One other big hurdle for the new alliance: antitrust clearance. Some consumer groups were upset. So were some competitors. US Airways CEO David Siegel, borrowing from the George W. Bush lexicon of the era, called Delta, Northwest and Continental the "axis of evil." He even called Leo Mullin "Dr. Evil." But the Bush administration's Justice Department seemed more relaxed about consolidation than the Clinton team had been, and this wasn't a full merger anyway. And regulators too understood the world had changed: Airlines were now trying to play defense to survive, not offense to conquer the world. Mullin got to work trying to convince them, while speaking several times per week with his counterpart Richard Anderson. He and Anderson engaged in what Mullin later described as a "massive regulatory education effort with the DOT," the Department of Transporation. It helped that Mullin, after his post-9/11 role as airline industry spokesperson, had, in his estimation, good "standing in Washington and a good relationship with the DOT." Regulators approved the deal.

Delta, however, wasn't done. Along with its new three-way alliance plans, Mullin and Reid felt compelled to address the low-cost carrier threat head on. Not only were AirTran, JetBlue and Southwest all growing. High-cost rivals like US Airways and United were also lowering their costs dramatically. By the end of the year, both carriers managed to secure deep labor concessions.

In July, Delta made clear that it was mobilizing for battle against the LCCs. That next month, Delta Express increased capacity between New York and Florida. But Delta Express was not the real weapon Mullin had in mind. Behind the scenes, a team of executives and consultants, including some from the consultancy McKinsey, were working on the creation of an all-new airline-within-an-airline, one that would mimic the style and pizzazz of JetBlue. Project Fresh Air, as the effort was known, would use planes—Boeing 757s plucked from underperforming hubs like Dallas and Salt Lake City—which would, if all went according to plan, have costs 20 percent lower than those at mainline Delta. The low-cost unit would achieve this savings by flying the planes more intensively—in other words, keeping them in the air more hours each day—and by configuring them with nothing but economy class seats, using just four flight attendants rather than five or six, demanding more productivity from non-pilot workers, distributing tickets directly to consumers rather than via agencies, using customer self-service tools like automated check-in, getting rid of corporate contracts that required salespeople to negotiate and manage and charging for inflight meals. Flight attendants, who would "audition" (rather than interview) for jobs, would work more hours per month than mainline Delta flight attendants for about the same pay. Unionized pilots, with their untouchable contract guarantees, would not see any salary or work rule changes.

On the revenue side, the new airline would practice simplified pricing. It would offer just a few different fares for each flight. Customers would get inflight satellite TV, like on JetBlue. Importantly, they would also receive Delta SkyMiles, redeemable for dream vacations anywhere in the world, a big advantage LCCs like JetBlue couldn't match. And Project Fresh Air, with a total launch budget of $75 million, was prepared to spend heavily on advertising and promotion.

On Nov. 21, Delta went public with its plan. At a conference with Wall Street analysts, Mullin noted "low-fare carriers represent the greatest competitive threat to Delta, substantially more than that from our other hub-and-spoke competition."

Delta, like its nation, was declaring war.

2003

"I don't know how Delta could have done any more than they did"

On the morning of Sept. 11, 2001, Joe Leonard was in his office near Orlando International Airport when the phone rang. On the other end was one of his airline's top shareholders.

"Could that possibly be one of *our* birds?" the shareholder asked.

Leonard had yet to see the news. "What the hell are you talking about?"

He turned on his television and saw the World Trade Center billowing smoke. The shareholder continued: "An airplane just flew into the tower."

"That's gotta be a general aviation airplane," Leonard said, echoing what many people thought at first.

He hung up the phone and went to a nearby conference room, where people were gathering around a television. There, as everywhere in America—for the 17 minutes, anyway, after only the first tower had been struck—speculation continued.

"That's gotta be like a Cessna 150 or something," Leonard continued to believe, perhaps wishfully.

"I don't think so," he heard someone else in the room say. "I think that's a transport-sized airplane."

Then United Airlines flight 175 crashed into the south tower, and the guessing was over.

Shock set in. For some reason—"I don't even know why I did it," he would recall years later—Leonard soon left the building, got in his car and drove the six miles from his office around Orlando's runways to the terminal, which was located just opposite his building but on the other side of the long runways.

The terminal was empty—no passengers at what was then the 15th busiest airport in the U.S. No planes overhead: "You talk about an eerie feeling…"

Of course, that was just a microcosm of what was going on. "It dawned on me," he would recall, "that there wasn't a single airplane in the sky over the United States of America."

Leonard was no stranger to drama in the airline business. As president of Eastern Airlines, competing against Delta at a time when Eastern faced extreme labor unrest, he was often on the front lines of battles against unions, including battles waged by labor's nemesis, Frank Lorenzo. In the book "Grounded: Frank Lorenzo and the Destruction of Eastern Airlines," Leonard is described as "purple with rage" in a confrontation with his pilot union counterpart Larry Schulte. As pilots were threatening to strike, Lorenzo was negotiating to buy the airline, which he did. "You son of a bitch," Leonard screamed at Schulte, according to the book. "You wanted new management. Now you got it."

Next, Leonard would move to a calmer arena, securing a top executive job at the aerospace conglomerate Allied Signal. While at that job, three years before 9/11, he was attending the 25th wedding anniversary of an industry colleague named Lewis Jordan. But this would prove more than just a social affair. Jordan, who had previously asked Leonard to run his airline, was asking again. Trying to distance itself from a devastating 1996 crash in Florida's Everglades, the old ValuJet was rebuilding itself under a new name, AirTran. And it needed a new CEO. Leonard was Jordan's man, and this time, after meeting ValuJet's founder and chairman Robert Priddy for breakfast the next morning, Leonard accepted. He was enticed by three alluring realities about AirTran that other people were perhaps overlooking.

First, the carrier's 18 gates in Atlanta, with the opportunity to expand that to 21—"a huge real estate holding in the busiest airport in the world." Second, AirTran had gotten a great deal on a large number of attractively priced Boeings. "I saw a hundred really good airplanes coming into the fleet," he said, "and I thought you could really do something with that." And third, he sensed vulnerability at Delta, particularly in the area of employee morale: "It's been my experience over the years that when employees are tested and stressed, they either fold and give up, or they get stronger," he said, "and I put Delta in that first category." Some Delta employees didn't even stick around following mid-1990s cost-cutting measures. "They just quit," recalled Leonard. "I don't know what they expected [then-CEO Ron Allen] to do with the expenses going up and revenue going down. He had to do something."

AirTran's people, he felt, were different. "After the crash, these people really believed in themselves. They wanted to win," he said. "They *really* wanted to win."

Leonard, a mechanic by training, began his career at Boeing, working on its 747 jumbo jet. When Northwest ordered the plane, he went with it, falling under the tutelage of the airline's famously tightfisted boss Donald Nyrop. "I used to think he hated me with a passion," Leonard remembered years later of the boss who never complimented him. "But it turns out I was one of his favorites! Praise was the absence of criticism."

Leonard then moved to American, where he worked for Robert Crandall, the legendary CEO who also had his share of labor pains but was just as well known for introducing the world to frequent flier programs, revenue management systems and computerized reservation systems. Next was the Eastern stint, where the former astronaut Frank Borman was determined to keep the embattled company alive while "employees were burning the place down," as Leonard described it. At Eastern, whose main hub was in Atlanta, where it shared an airport with Delta's even larger hub there, Leonard learned a thing or two about competing against Delta. After living through the tumultuous tenure of Frank Lorenzo, Leonard returned to Northwest, where he worked alongside a fellow executive, Richard Anderson, who had also previously toiled for Lorenzo, in his case at Continental. At Northwest, Leonard recalled, "Richard and I spent a lot of time together sitting around and talking about how you run the airline business."

But Joe Leonard, the man who learned cost cutting under Nyrop and Crandall, crisis management under Borman, deal making under Lorenzo and a host of other leadership skills at Boeing and Allied Signal, was now running tiny AirTran, which had lost $97 million in 1997 and another $41 million in 1998 at a time when almost every other airline was profiting. Nor was its balance sheet a paragon of health. "If I had done a proper job of due diligence, I never would have gone" to AirTran, Leonard remembered with a chuckle years later. "The company was in much worse shape than I had been led to believe."

In the film "Star Wars Episode III: Revenge of the Sith," Anakin Skywalker is left for dead. But he never quite dies. Instead, his broken body is salvaged and rebuilt to become the powerful Darth Vader. For Delta, ValuJet was Anakin Skywalker. ValuJet flight 592, which crashed May 11, 1996, in Florida's Everglades, killing all 110 passengers and crew in an accident that was partly the airline's fault, seemed to be the end of a company that was the sort of upstart whose safety many passengers, in those days, didn't fully trust to begin with. But ValuJet never quite died. Instead, it acquired a small Orlando-based airline, with roots in Minneapolis, called AirTran. It shrewdly adopted the lesser known but untarnished AirTran name for the merged airline. It then got a huge break when Boeing, after acquiring its rival McDonnell Douglas and inheriting a plane called the MD-95, wanted to keep the production line going. But most airlines were unenthusiastic. So Boeing gave AirTran, which in the late 1990s needed new aircraft about the size of an MD-95, an extremely attractive deal for the plane, which Boeing renamed the 717. AirTran used its 717s to quietly rebuild ValuJet's old Atlanta franchise, with nonstop service to a few dozen cities by 2002. AirTran even offered business class seats.

Delta might have seemed to let AirTran expand without much of a fight, at least compared to the ruthless pricing tactics of American and Northwest, the latter run by the hard-nosed former lawyer from Galveston, Texas, Richard Anderson. Was Delta merely complacent? Or was it spooked by the thought the Justice Department, even now under a Republican administration, might punish Delta for anything smacking of predatory pricing as the department had, under Clinton, punished American for getting aggressive against new entrants?

Whether Delta could have or should have done more to fight AirTran, Leo Mullin was well aware of what he faced. In fact, he was incredulous that not only had Boeing offered great pricing to AirTran: It had even financed the planes itself for an airline that might not have gotten financing from the places airlines usually turn for credit. "And in one fell swoop," Mullin said of Boeing, "they converted AirTran from a company that was on the ropes to one that had the financial capacity to be a strong competitor."

So strengthen AirTran did, attacking Delta's key Florida markets too. It actually increased revenues 7 percent in 2001, a year in which Delta's revenues, remember, fell 12 percent. AirTran started flying 14 new planes that year too. But most uncomfortably of all for Delta, AirTran was making money. In 2000, its breakout year, the low-cost carrier earned an excellent 13 percent operating profit margin. (That same year, another upstart company calling itself "Google" had far less revenue than AirTran and had not yet managed to turn a profit at all.) Even more remarkably, like Southwest and JetBlue but unlike almost every other airline, AirTran managed a solid operating profit in 2001, the industry's worst year ever. After a Delta pilot work slowdown, which disrupted holiday travel, and an 89-day strike at Comair, some travelers—especially those less concerned with high-frequency schedules and frequent flier miles—were defecting to AirTran. "Every single flight that I've been on in the last six months," Leonard said during a 2002 conference call with analysts, "I've had people come up to me and say, 'I used to fly the other guys and now... you are my carrier of choice.'" He added: "Delta is doing everything they can possibly do to drive us out of business, and they're losing $325 million a quarter and we're making money."

Route by route, AirTran was attacking Delta's best markets. "And every time AirTran entered and was able to put a couple or three flights per day on the route," Mullin recalled, "you immediately had to adjust to meet the price. And this was a period too where the internet was just starting to be available to people in terms of online price comparison so readily."

Sept. 11, 2001, to be sure, created a scare at AirTran. A big scare. In the 30 days after 9/11, AirTran's cash balance fell below $5 million. "I'm not sure we'll survive this one," Leonard thought, wondering not just how the company could survive but also why he even took the AirTran job in the first place.

"You just left the most admired aerospace company in the world to come here and file bankruptcy," he recalled saying to himself. "You're a pretty dumb guy!"

But that turned out to be the low point.

In the days after the terrorist attacks, Leonard had actually called his foe Leo Mullin to ask for updates on Mullin's Washington lobbying efforts. AirTran was not a member of the Air Transport Association, so Leonard didn't have the same access to information that Mullin had.

"Leo," Mullin recalled Leonard saying. "Can you just tell me what's going on?"

Mullin graciously complied. "I actually took time fairly frequently throughout this to just keep Joe posted on it all," Mullin said. It was a courtesy Leonard would still recall and appreciate years after both men were no longer running airlines. The two were like opposing football coaches momentarily putting their rivalry aside when a player is severely injured.

"And it was just an informational briefing," Mullin said. "But I think he appreciated it, and I certainly felt he needed to know it."

"I thought he was very gentlemanly to do that," Leonard confirmed, "which he didn't have to do."

Of course, the graciousness did not continue when the whistle blew and play resumed. As the industry regained some sense of normalcy, AirTran was back to making life miserable for Delta. And Delta, by then, had shed its initial reservations about competing vigorously against its low-cost rival. At one point Delta dumped nearly 500 extra seats each day into tiny Fort Walton Beach, one of AirTran's many bread-and-butter secondary markets. Other battlegrounds included Newport News in Virginia and Akron-Canton in Ohio, small markets where, at first, AirTran was content to make its living. But when Delta came at these markets hard, AirTran had little choice but to revise its strategy and make a play for much larger markets. And with its huge cost advantage, it could beat Delta on these routes too, even if Delta could still get somewhat higher fares—a revenue premium—from business travelers. One of AirTran's most profitable routes, in fact, would be Atlanta-New York.

"They tried every day to put us out of business," Leonard would recall. "It was kind of silly because we had a 40 percent cost advantage, and when you have a 40 percent cost advantage, you could pretty much do what the hell you want. There's not really much the other guy could do about it."

So was there, in Leonard's own post-game analysis, anything more Delta could have done to defeat his airline? "I don't know how Delta could have done any more than they did," he said.

And so AirTran made money again in 2002. So did Southwest and JetBlue. But for just about everyone else, as bad as 2001 had been, 2002 proved even worse. U.S. airlines collectively amassed a record $11.3 billion in net losses for the first full year after 9/11. Traffic, measured by revenue passenger miles, or RPMs—that's how many passengers are flying multiplied by how far they fly—shrank 2 percent. Passenger revenue shrank 10 percent. And 80,000 fewer people were working in the industry than had been working just two years earlier. United and US Airways were bankrupt. American was headed in that direction too.

Delta itself lost $1.3 billion in 2002. Of little comfort was the fact that its loss margins were less awful than those posted by United, American and US Airways. The reality was that due to bankruptcy laws designed to prevent big companies from liquidating, two giant rivals that might have disappeared instead stuck around—and, moreover, with new powers to restructure their costs and become more competitive. US Airways, in its case, was also propped up by a government-backed loan, and advantages like these encouraged bankrupt carriers to slash fares in a bid to generate quick cash and steal market share from healthier carriers. The absence of creative destruction, in other words, created excess capacity. At one point, about 30 percent of all people flying within the U.S. were flying on bankrupt airlines.

"Liquidation is what takes capacity out," Mullin said. But liquidation wasn't happening.

Bankruptcy gave United and US Airways enormous negotiating power over their unions. Agree to lower pay, fewer benefits, more flexible work rules and more outsourcing of small jets to third-party regional partners, the airlines could threaten, or we will liquidate and you'll lose everything. On top of this, the Bush administration's Air Transportation Stabilization Board, or ATSB, made labor concessions a prerequisite to qualifying for post-9/11 federal loan guarantees. To protect taxpayers, the thinking went, guarantees would go to only those airlines with credible turnaround plans, which inevitably involved deep labor cuts. United's application, in fact, was rejected because of what the ATSB considered an insufficient cost-cutting plan. The board would go on to reject bids by Vanguard Airlines, Spirit Airlines, National Airlines and others, as well as United—a second time—in 2004. Ultimately, the ATSB approved less than $2 billion of the $10 billion Congress had authorized, almost all of it to US Airways plus some to America West, which itself would later become part of US Airways. Taxpayers would actually end up earning a healthy profit from the airline ownership stakes Washington demanded in exchange for the guarantees. A "charade," Mullin called the underutilized program years later.

American, meanwhile, having forked out $742 million to buy TWA five months before 9/11—and having spent then-surplus cash buying back its own stock—was now hurtling toward bankruptcy too. In April 2003, on the verge of filing, its three largest unions reluctantly agreed to almost $2 billion in concessions. American's pilots, who never did get the rich contracts given to their counterparts at United and Delta, were now working for even less money than before despite a union with hardline factions considered so adversarial that they came to be known in airline management circles as "the Taliban."

The result: Delta was losing its cost advantages against American, United and US Airways. At the same time, rivals like Continental and Northwest were obtaining more regional jets, eroding Delta's advantage at a hub like Cincinnati. Nearby hubs like Cleveland and Detroit, which competed for the same connecting passengers—say, someone flying from Buffalo to St. Louis—now had similar planes. And perhaps worst of all, LCCs like AirTran were still expanding rapidly. JetBlue, for its part, announced in January it planned to grow capacity 50 percent in 2003. One month later, it aimed straight for Delta's heart by proclaiming its intention to enter Atlanta, starting with service to Long Beach near Los Angeles. Soon AirTran, reacting to Mullin's assault on its niche small markets, said it too would also head to Los Angeles, in its case, competing even more directly between Atlanta and the main airport that's often known simply by its code "LAX." For good measure, it also added Atlanta-Las Vegas.

It was the last thing Delta needed at a time when its fuel, pension, insurance, security and interest costs were rising, its credit rating and borrowing capacity worsening, the value of its aircraft collateral declining, its debt reaching uncomfortable levels, its cash pile thinning and its Dallas hub still bleeding. The economy and stock markets were still languishing. And Delta's pilots were due for another raise. Employee morale was suffering. Announcement after announcement of layoffs and pay cuts created a sour mood. Even pilots, contractually protected from pay cuts, suffered from working at an airline that was shrinking rather than expanding, which meant less frequent opportunities for first officers to become captains or for pilots of smaller jets to advance to larger ones. At Southwest, AirTran and JetBlue, meanwhile, pay rates were often lower, benefits less generous and work schedules more demanding. But at least workers there were seeing their incomes and career opportunities grow, a fact that engendered enthusiasm and job satisfaction. Back at Delta—and at other legacy carriers too—the mood was growing gloomier, and not just among the rank and file. Executives too, also taking pay cuts and no less dejected by the constant need to cut and shrink, began sending out résumés.

It was hardly a comforting state of affairs as yet another new headwind approached. But there it was: another war. On March 20, 2003, the United States, together with the United Kingdom and some less geopolitically significant allies, invaded Iraq, ostensibly to preempt it from using nuclear weapons and harboring terrorists but more broadly to transform it into a stable, democratic ally in the heart of the tumultuous Middle East, a region that provided a large amount of the oil essential to run the American economy.

The American economy, though, suffered as the nation mobilized for war, and few aspects of the American economy suffered more than the air transport sector. Business plummeted as fearful would-be travelers avoided flying. Delta's revenues alone dropped by $125 million during the first quarter of 2003, which roughly corresponded to the three months leading up to the start of the war, compared to the same period a year earlier. This was a time, with the 9/11 attacks a year more distant in the rear-view mirror and with the economy at least growing, however tepidly, when things should have been improving, not further deteriorating. During those first three months of 2003, Delta lost another $466 million, burning through about $2.7 million of cash each day. Starting in early February, when the war looked increasingly imminent, bookings fell significantly, especially for flights to Europe. Making matters even worse, the uncertainties of war rattled energy markets, causing fuel prices to spike 51 percent in the first quarter of 2003 compared to the same period a year earlier. Costs were surging just as revenues were plummeting.

So Mullin and his team once again cut capacity, reducing mainline flying by another 12 percent. Delta suspended no fewer than 14 of its 18 transatlantic routes from New York. From Atlanta, which it dominated and where things were thus always somewhat better, it stopped four of 18. Delta's lone route to Asia, meanwhile—a flight between Atlanta and Tokyo—was flying virtually empty for a different reason. By early 2003, a virus called severe acute respiratory syndrome, or SARS, was spreading, via air travel, from its origins in southwestern China to much of East Asia and all the way to Toronto, leading health officials to advise travelers not to visit affected cities. In the end, SARS never became the widespread epidemic travelers and some experts had feared. But the fear itself, and the resulting drop in demand, was enough to cause Air Canada, with its busiest hub in Toronto and a large network of flights to Asia from both there and its Vancouver hub, to catch another increasingly contagious condition: bankruptcy. Hawaiian Airlines filed for bankruptcy too.

***

A few years earlier, Delta had replaced the hot inflight meals economy passengers had long loved to hate with cheaper "Delta Deli" bags, which they collected as they boarded and which contained cold sandwiches and chips. Frequent fliers on early internet message boards debated, as the new millennium dawned, which was less bad: the "Delta Deli" or the competing "American Bistro?" So Delta had replaced hot meals with cold meals. And then it took this a step further. Following the lead of America West, Delta began *charging* passengers on some domestic flights for even these Spartan inflight meals. It also raised fees for passengers checking over-weight bags. It set out to cut non-fuel unit costs 15 percent by the end of 2005. It furloughed 250 pilots and sought ground worker and flight attendant volunteers to take two months of unpaid leave. It began testing cheaper walk-up fares—in other words, the last-minute unrestricted fares that business travelers tended to buy. It restructured its struggling Salt Lake City hub, adding more regional jets. It retired its last 727 in April. It suspended dividend payments in July. It raised $285 million by selling a stake in Worldspan, a technology company that powered its reservation system. It later sold stakes in the online travel websites Orbitz and Hotwire. And it piled on more debt.

On Jan. 30, it borrowed $392 million using 10 767s and two 737s as collateral. Then on April 15, it turned to General Electric for another $761 million. By the 2000s, GE's business was heavily exposed to the airline sector in two ways: through its aircraft engine business and through GECAS, its aircraft leasing business. So naturally, it was eager to do what it could to keep some of its best customers from disappearing. And the loans it gave to United, US Airways, Delta and others were well collateralized and ultimately proved profitable for GE in their own right. The larger point was that here again, just as with the credit card companies that had done what they could to keep airlines in business because of the lucrative airline-branded credit cards, which would be worthless without the airlines, an industry supplier was keeping an otherwise-doomed airline from going away—and by extension keeping industry fares artificially low, thanks to excess seat supply. But this time, Delta was at least a beneficiary of the new capital rather than just a bystander watching others spoil the revenue environment.

Fortunately for the distressed airline industry, Iraq's military forces didn't last long. Less than two months after the invasion, on May 1, 2003, in a brash speech delivered aboard an aircraft carrier called the USS Abraham Lincoln, President Bush declared "mission accomplished." The flying public was relieved. Air traffic volumes began to rebound by summer, boosted further by some modest signs of economic expansion. Shares of Delta stock rose sharply in late May as some investors viewed the end of the war as the start of an industry recovery, one in which Delta would have an edge over its more financially troubled rivals. Overall optimism was so flush that spring that Northwest even applied for the right to fly to Baghdad.

It certainly didn't hurt that President Bush had, on April 16, signed the Emergency Wartime Supplemental Appropriations Act, providing airlines with $2.3 billion for airport security costs and another $100 million to fortify their cockpit doors to prevent future 9/11-style attacks. Delta's portion of the aid amounted to about $400 million. The law also suspended the collection of passenger security fees from June through September and extended, for one more year, government financial support for wartime aviation insurance. Separately, airlines earned charter revenues by using their planes and crews to ferry troops and supplies to the Middle East. Delta, for its part, flew 245 military charter missions during the first six months of 2003, transporting more than 47,000 soldiers and other military personnel.

Delta was also lucky that with less international exposure than United, American, Continental and Northwest, the Iraq war impacted Delta's revenues less than those of its peers. And although Delta's routes to Europe and Tokyo certainly suffered, routes to Latin America held up rather well. On the domestic front, Delta scored some tactical wins by, for example, enhancing its presence in Columbus, Ohio, after America West abandoned its hub there.

More significantly, regulators approved Delta's proposed alliance with Northwest and Continental. This meant the three carriers—although still prohibited from colluding on prices and schedules—could sell each other's flights through the practice of codesharing, while also offering each other's customers frequent flier benefits and airport lounge access. For Delta, according to its estimates, the new arrangement would generate between $150 million and $200 million in revenue gains—less than 2 percent of its total revenues but potentially the difference between profit and loss in a thin-margin business. And that was just the start. Delta also agreed to allow Northwest, with notable strength in the Pacific, and Continental, strong to Europe and Latin America, into SkyTeam, clearing the way for Northwest's Dutch partner KLM to join too. And in September, Air France and KLM formally announced their intention to merge and create the world's largest airline, measured by revenue.

Air France, as it happened, had become increasingly convinced that inviting Continental into SkyTeam was more than just a necessary evil to enable the Air France/KLM merger. Continental's blunt CEO Gordon Bethune had seen to that when Air France's Chairman Jean-Cyril Spinetta flew to New York to learn more about Continental's increasingly global Newark hub—an airport that was actually closer to much of Manhattan than the more globally famous JFK. "We picked him up off the Concorde with a helicopter we had rented," Bethune recalled, "and flew him down Manhattan, across Central Park, made a right turn and landed in Newark. And he was amazed we had built Newark as this huge international gateway—and its proximity to Manhattan."

Spinetta was sold. "He turns to his alliance guy," Bethune recalled, "and says, 'We're going to do this deal.'" Suddenly SkyTeam, the alliance Delta had co-founded, was looking a lot more powerful, especially on routes between the U.S. and Europe.

Delta's finance department, all the while, continued to come up with new ways to raise cash, like issuing $300 million in convertible notes in May. These instruments, which companies in trouble often use, offer lenders the option to be repaid in stock if the company's business plan proves successful. Not long after, Delta was able to restructure the terms of some of its existing debt. It managed to push repayment deadlines further into the future. In the second quarter of 2003, April through June, Delta officially posted a net profit, but only thanks to a one-time jolt from its sale of Worldspan stock and the $400 million from Washington's emergency wartime act. Strip those items out, and the airline was still losing money—$237 million, to be exact, in what was typically the second best quarter of the year.

In the meantime, even as traffic was recovering from the extreme depths seen during the run-up to the war, revenue still suffered from overcapacity and low-cost competition—fuller planes don't equate to profits if the people occupying the seats aren't paying very much. In May, AirTran, its shares soaring, continued its westward advance with new flights from Atlanta to Denver. And then, on the first of July, it stunned Delta by announcing an order for up to 110 more new Boeings, this time mostly larger 737-700s with the range to fly anywhere within the U.S. What's more, AirTran again got a great deal, just as it had when it bought 717s several years earlier, because Boeing was desperate to keep its production lines running at a time when, once again, most other airlines—including Delta—were canceling and deferring orders. In Europe at this same time, an LCC called Ryanair was well on its way to becoming one of the world's most profitable airlines after placing a giant 737 order just four months after 9/11, securing rock-bottom prices that gave it an unbeatable competitive advantage for years. Similarly, not only would AirTran have lots more airplanes to fly against Delta. It would also continue to have a cost structure that would enable it to charge low fares at which it could profit—fares that would cause Delta, if it had to match them, to spill ever more red ink.

Unreported at the time was the fact that AirTran, on its way to becoming one of Boeing's most important customers, nearly got its planes from Airbus instead.

Leonard had sensed Boeing wasn't taking his airline's negotiating ultimatums seriously. With help from GECAS, which would lease some of the planes to AirTran, Boeing won the deal after a late scramble—but not without a hard-fought negotiation with Joe Leonard. He recalled hearing too many times that airlines and aircraft manufacturer salespeople would reach a deal in principle, but then the real terms, once the lawyers had drafted the detailed contracts, would skew more to the advantage of the manufacturers.

"I said, 'I'm not going to let that happen. We're going to do this the way we do labor negotiations,'" Leonard affirmed. "And that is, once we agreed to something, we're going to walk down the hall and put it in contract language, and we're going to come back and we're going to sign the page.

"So," he continued, "we told Boeing and Airbus and [their leasing partners] GE and ILFC that we'd like to see their best and final offers on Friday, and then we would take those and begin discussions on Monday, and we would continue until we had a signed contract at the end of that process. So we did, and Boeing didn't take it seriously. They thought we were just kidding." Neither manufacturer had ever been through a negotiation like this one.

"And so by about Thursday of that week," Leonard continued, "they realized we were deadly serious and they were way behind, so they had to put teams together in Seattle working around the clock to get caught up."

Boeing did catch up, and on the following Monday night, the two parties signed the contract, which included a 20-year maintenance agreement on both the airframes and the engines. Boeing, although victorious, had done a deal on AirTran's terms. "They didn't like the process," Leonard said, "and I'm told that Boeing has never agreed to do that again."

Shortly thereafter, the manufacturer's head of commercial airplanes, Alan Mulally, who would years later become known as the man who saved the Ford Motor Company, flew to Atlanta for a signing ceremony with Leonard. Shirley Franklin, the mayor of Atlanta, was also there. AirTran would thus start receiving the planes that would underpin eight straight years of 20 percent-per-year capacity growth, while also, like JetBlue, helping to change traveler perceptions about LCCs. No longer were they flying ratty old airplanes. Instead, they were flying newer, cleaner airplanes than airlines like Delta were flying. Unlike JetBlue, AirTran didn't offer satellite TV. But it did offer satellite radio, which likewise became a flier favorite.

And there was more to Delta's nightmare. As AirTran was ordering larger aircraft—lots of them—David Neeleman's JetBlue was doing the opposite. Just weeks before the AirTran announcement, the immensely successful New York upstart unveiled an order for 100 new Brazilian-built Embraer 190 jets, with options for another 100. These were 100-seat airplanes that, in theory, would enable JetBlue to bring its low-fare, high-quality business model to many more markets throughout the U.S., cities that didn't have quite enough demand to fill JetBlue's 162-seat Airbus 320s. Of course, it also had more than 100 of those on order too.

So Delta felt justified in its decision to play copycat, to start another low-cost airline unit of its own, replacing its stale Delta Express product with a savvier, sexier one modeled after JetBlue. "Song," as it would be called, took flight April 15, 2003—smack in the middle of the Iraq war. The timing was bad, but with a big cost advantage over mainline flights that used the same planes—757s—Delta was hopeful. The initial 36 aircraft were painted lime green—the "Skittles planes," JetBlue founder and CEO David Neeleman mocked them internally, a reference to multi-colored candies sold in the U.S., of which one of the colors was roughly the same as Song's livery. On all seatbacks were television screens, like on JetBlue, although these screens at first offered only pre-recorded content rather than live satellite TV, which would come later. Hoping to lure female New Yorkers yearning for some Florida sun—Delta considered these women a key target demographic—it hired the famous designer Kate Spade to design the flight attendant uniforms. It opened a Song-themed storefront in New York's posh Soho district. It sold apple martinis on board.

Song, of course, would need to grapple with the fact that its pilots were Delta pilots, making no less money and working no more productively than their counterparts back at mainline Delta. This further highlighted the larger point: Delta's impossibly expensive pilot contract was becoming all the more crippling as rivals cut labor costs.

Mullin had no choice. He had to ask pilots to renegotiate their deal.

So in May, he proposed a 22 percent wage cut. In July, ALPA rejected the proposal, saying "Delta's current approach is inconsistent with ALPA's perspectives" and—lest management think the proposal was only slightly off the mark—"Delta's concepts do not furnish a basis for continued negotiations regarding reducing pilot employment costs." Not stopping there, ALPA filed a grievance, arguing that even prior furloughs had violated the current contract. An arbitrator, accepting the pilots' argument that these furloughs were motivated by a bad economy and not the 9/11 attacks—and thus were not a result of *force majeure*—agreed. By autumn, Delta was perhaps further than ever from addressing its most critical cost problem. Comair pilots, for their part, also rejected company requests to renegotiate their own contract.

Management gradually escalated its rhetoric. In April, Mullin said Delta would do everything it could to avoid bankruptcy. Just mentioning the "b" word, even if only to say what he hoped to avoid, had an underlying message of urgency directed, no doubt, at ALPA. In the company's third-quarter results presentation, Mullin told Wall Street analysts plainly and simply that "Delta has not yet achieved a competitive cost structure, a problem which is primarily related to our pilot costs." He continued: "Delta's unit cost has, for a number of years, been among the lowest of any network carrier. Now, however, it has catapulted to one of the highest. Based on the terms of our 2001 contract, Delta's total pilot costs—including pay, benefits and work rules—are now running 80 percent higher than American Airlines."

"Now let me make a continuing point here," he added, "which is that no blame can be placed on Delta's pilots based on how this situation develops. The current contract was achieved through the collective bargaining process, and at the time of its conclusion in 2001, it was an appropriate arrangement. However, the aviation industry has been significantly and permanently altered since then."

Delta's CFO Michelle Burns, later in that same third-quarter earnings presentation, again revived the comparison with American: "We recognize [our] cost performance is very different from our peers. The largest difference is driven by approximately $1 billion in annual cost disadvantages from the pilot cost structure. Leo has said that this is not the fault of Delta pilots. But improving this financial differential is crucial to our recovery. If Delta had the estimated pilot cost structure of American Airlines, we would have reported a [Q3] loss of $46 million versus the current net loss of $172 million."

Another year, another huge peak-season loss.

The crusade to lower pilot costs had also encountered a major problem of Delta's own making. On March 25, 2003, five days after the Iraq war started, Delta, in a lengthy filing with the Securities and Exchange Commission, disclosed a $42 million executive compensation plan covering 33 senior officers that—most controversially—offered rich pension plans that were immune from any future bankruptcy filing. Just as executives were cutting pensions for the rank and file—pensions at risk of being greatly reduced if the company went bankrupt—their own retirement plans were becoming more secure. Employee pensions, moreover, were underfunded by almost $5 billion, meaning the money in the plans was far short of the expected need. It didn't help that Mullin, despite Delta's dismal financial results in 2002, took home a $1.4 million bonus for the year, bringing his official total compensation for the year to more than $13 million (although that included stock options he might never get to cash in). Michelle Burns, for her part, got a pay raise and was also among 60 top executives that received a combined total of $17 million in bonuses.

Mullin called Joe Kolshak into his office. Kolshak was Delta's head of operations, yes, but he was also still a pilot—still paid his union dues, even though he didn't fly much anymore. If anyone in management knew how the rank and file would react to the pension disclosure, Kolshak would know.

"Is this going to be a big deal with the pilots?" Mullin asked Kolshak, who hadn't been included in the pension insurance plan.

"Leo," Kolshak replied. "It's going to be a huge deal." (Kolshak, reflecting years later, remembered the situation as not "one of [Mullin's] shining moments" but allowed that "I think Leo got sold down the road a little bit by some of the HR consultants that came in. Common practice.")

Delta's board of directors—excluding its chairman Mullin, because of what would have been a conflict of interest, but including its lead non-executive director Gerald Grinstein—having acted on the advice of those consultants, argued such compensation was necessary due to "significant concern for retention of management personnel." In other words, it worried its top executives would leave the company. Besides, the board said, Mullin hadn't even accepted his $795,000 salary during the final quarter of 2001 and had agreed to cut his salary by 10 percent starting in 2003. So had President Fred Reid, while all other senior officers had taken an 8 percent pay cut.

A board member had pointed out to Mullin that without some kind of pension insurance plan, executive pensions were actually more vulnerable than rank-and-file employee pensions, which would at least be partly covered—or nearly entirely covered, in the case of some of the lowest-paid employees—by the federal government pension insurance in the event of bankruptcy. Some executive pensions, as opposed to the rank-and-file pensions, could essentially vanish.

Moreover, roughly 80 percent of Mullin's Delta pension wasn't really a Delta pension at all. As is common when companies recruit outside executives, Delta's board had agreed to roll over and guarantee the benefits Mullin had earned at his previous employers (First Chicago, a bank, and Commonwealth Edison, an electric utility). The pension insurance had protected those benefits too. "I could never have come to [Delta] without that," Mullin said.

Reid, speaking years later, said he and other executives—Michelle Burns, for one—were being recruited by companies in other industries, which could afford to pay far more than what Delta could pay to retain them.

Reid recalled holding meetings with employees. "I would tell them, 'Look, with this package, I am in the bottom 25 percent of similar executives with similar responsibilities.... And before this program, I was in the bottom 8 percent of relevant executives.' So I said, 'Look, the comparison is not you and me. It's not a flight attendant versus a chief operating officer. We have to pay flight attendants what the flight attendant market says we do, and the company has to pay executives what the market says executives make. Nobody's inventing this stuff. These are real numbers.' I said to them, 'I am willing to work permanently in the bottom 25 percent here, but I am not willing to work in the bottom 8 percent. I'm not willing to do that.'"

According to Reid's recollection, some employees sympathized and even applauded. But others would hear none of it. Neither, for that matter, would a group of former Delta executives, who wrote a blistering letter to the company, calling the plan to spend millions of dollars to insulate top executive pensions from potential bankruptcy claims "morally wrong."

The story hit newspapers throughout the country. "Delta boss is paid $13.5 million as airlines beg for aid," screamed one headline. "Delta dealing out bonuses that would make Enron blush," blared another. "Bonuses don't fly with Delta employees." "Pilot union chief blasts Delta bonuses—$42 million package for airline's executives also labeled 'insulting' by Arizona Sen. John McCain."

Those last two points were especially troubling. Whatever the merits of the talent retention scheme, the reaction to its disclosure took a giant toll on management's negotiating leverage with both Washington and, most importantly, ALPA. McCain, who had run for president in 2000 and eyed another bid in 2008, was the chairman of the Senate's aviation subcommittee at the time, making him a key figure in the airline industry's efforts to reduce taxation and regulatory burdens. But with the Enron, Worldcom and other scandals fresh in the public's mind, McCain made sure to get on the right side of resentment against exorbitant executive pay. "It's insulting when they lay off thousands of people and then pay top executives millions of dollars in bonuses," McCain, a pro-business Republican who, at another moment in time, might not have seen fit to tell a company what to pay its executives, told Bloomberg News. "I'm not the only person that's angry. Everybody's angry." In the wartime supplemental appropriations act that passed not long after Delta's pension disclosure, Congress included limits on executive pay.

But Delta's much larger problem was the outrage stewing among pilots, who were now even less eager to surrender hard-fought pay and benefits. If the company had money to pay top management untold millions, the thinking went, why should we be the ones to bear the burden of rescuing the company from financial ruin? William Buergey, who was chairman of Delta's ALPA unit when news about the bankruptcy-proof executive pensions first broke, said publicly he understood the math: Delta couldn't survive without pilot concessions. At the same time, he was also alarmed that the firm's financial distress was leaving it no choice but to cancel, defer and sell its aircraft orders, which implied fewer future pilot jobs. But he also knew any cuts the union accepted would require approval from the rank and file, whose blood was boiling. And that approval, sure enough, never came.

Kolshak's fears had been realized.

The extent of the outrage surprised Mullin. "Not the fact that it was brought up," he said. "But I thought, like, we could explain it."

"I didn't handle it as well as I should have," he allowed. "That's for sure. But it was certainly done with perfectly good intentions in mind."

If misery loves company, Delta could take comfort knowing it wasn't alone in facing executive compensation backlash. American, also worried about executive flight, had similarly devised rich compensation packages for top managers. But it kept them from public view until *after* employees had voted on steep pay cuts for themselves, leading to outrage and animosity. His trust with employees in tatters, American's CEO had little choice but to resign, even after agreeing to cancel some bonuses. "What was Don Carty thinking?" asked a headline in *BusinessWeek*.

Delta too, on Aug. 12, canceled many of the executive compensation benefits. Mullin delivered the news to his executive team. "I said, 'You're going to make your own decision about what you do, now that it's rescinded,'" he recalled. In other words, he couldn't blame them if they decided to seek more stable employment. "It didn't mean you don't have a pension. But under the circumstances that Delta is facing, you're not protected, and that's the way it's going to be."

Despite the U-turn on the program, the public relations damage—and even more importantly, the *employee* relations damage—was irreversible. Management's plea for a big pilot pay cut was going nowhere. In October, a fiery pilot named John Malone replaced the more mild-mannered Buergey as ALPA chief at Delta. By then, members of Delta's board of directors were worried. Among them: Gerald Grinstein, the former CEO of Western Airlines.

***

Recollections later would vary somewhat. Was it Mullin's decision to leave? Was he coaxed out? Pushed out? Either way, by late 2003, Mullin knew it was time to go. "I felt like we were making some progress," he recalled, "but not enough to the point where I felt that somebody might not be able to do it better." On Nov. 24, despite—he said in a statement at the time—"a warm regard for this company and its people," he announced his resignation, saying he would step down as CEO Jan. 1, 2004, and remain as board chairman until the company's annual shareholders meeting April 23.

It was the beginning of a difficult farewell tour for a CEO whose six years at Delta were split into two starkly different halves. The first half featured three of the company's greatest years ever; the latter, its worst three years ever. From 1997 through 2000, Mullin modernized Delta—longtime employees today can still point to technological advances that began during his tenure. He internationalized Delta and—demonstrating it would be a cosmopolitan airline at home too—appointed the company's first vice president of diversity and granted health benefits to same-sex partners of Delta employees, at a time when moves like these were still unusual for a company headquartered in the American South. He gave Delta a rock-solid balance sheet and restored its place as one of the industry's most profitable airlines. But the next three years saw its fortunes fall just as quickly as the economy weakened, low-fare competition intensified, war and terror decimated demand and distressed rivals slashed their costs. As it happened, Mullin had agreed to the most expensive pilot contract in industry history not long after reaching the apex of profitability and just months before the 9/11 attacks. This created a suddenly unaffordable financial obligation, made harder to fix by an executive compensation scheme that alienated pilots just as their consent for concessions was required. Mullin would leave with retirement benefits worth $16 million.

The closing months of 2003, meanwhile, brought a few small victories during Mullin's final months in charge. JetBlue, for example, just six months after invading Atlanta, raised the white flag and left. Competing against Delta to the west coast was difficult enough, but the challenge became nearly impossible when AirTran also jumped into the fray. Mullin also won a victory on Capitol Hill by successfully urging Congress to pass an airline pension relief bill that eased federal rules regarding how much cash airlines had to contribute to their underfunded plans. With interest rates low, stock markets weak and retirees simply living longer, airline pension plans were indeed underfunded, in Delta's case by billions of dollars—billions of dollars it didn't have. So now, with the new law, airlines could hold their cash and deal with the pension problem later. Truly dealing with the pension problem, of course, often meant terminating the plans altogether.

At about this time, Delta also announced the first route—Atlanta-Tokyo—for the first Boeing 777 it would soon receive. It expanded inflight meal charges, announced further work rule changes to boost flight attendant productivity and sold 11 Boeing 737-800s that were supposed to be delivered in 2005. It also stepped up pressure on AirTran by forcing it to pay more money whenever it canceled a flight and had to re-accommodate passengers on Delta.

But these modest victories paled in comparison to a sea of additional troubles and challenges surfacing in the final months and weeks of 2003. Pricing competition was growing so intense that Delta felt compelled to relax restrictions on the nonrefund-able fares that price-sensitive leisure travelers typically purchased—otherwise they might flee to less restrictive LCCs. But with more flexibility to change travel dates and make other adjustments, business travelers began to find these fares acceptable too. So they reduced their dependence on the more expensive fares that carriers like Delta counted on to cover their costs. In August, a power blackout crippled flight schedules in New York City and elsewhere in the Northeast. In October, AirTran began flying to Reagan National Airport, the high-fare gateway to Washington D.C. Even more disturbingly, it announced plans to quadruple its flights at Delta's struggling Dallas-Fort Worth hub. In November, Atlantic Coast Airlines, a regional carrier, said it would turn itself into an independent low-fare airline based at Washington Dulles. That same month, United unveiled a new Song-like low-cost carrier called Ted. Richard Branson, the British billionaire, was still planning a new U.S.-based low-cost carrier. Beset by high fuel prices and a recent crash, Air France and British Airways flew the supersonic Concorde for the last time.

All this, meanwhile, in the context of a world that wasn't feeling any safer for travel. Saudi Arabia, Morocco, Israel, Turkey, Russia and India all suffered gruesome terrorist attacks. What seemed like a quick end to the Iraq war wasn't an end after all but merely the beginning of a fiasco that would kill 5,000 U.S. troops and cost U.S. taxpayers more than $1 trillion. Ongoing instability contributed to high oil prices, while there was no evidence of the nuclear or chemical weapons that had ostensibly justified the war. What there *was* was an endless string of attacks against civilians, a bloody civil war between various ethnic groups, major strategic gains for America's enemy Iran and actual degradation rather than enhancement of America's geopolitical influence in the Middle East at large. The mood brightened briefly when, on Dec. 14, U.S. forces captured Saddam Hussein. But it was difficult for Americans to celebrate with the mastermind of the 9/11 attacks, Osama bin Laden, still at large.

On the home front, Jennifer Lopez and 50 Cent were entertaining while Arnold Schwarzenegger was making news both on screen and off, starring in another "Terminator" movie and triumphing in an election to govern the state of California. Scientists finished mapping the human genome, Apple introduced an online music store called iTunes and the low-cost Florida Marlins improbably defeated the legacy New York Yankees in 2003's World Series.

None of this distracted Delta, whose situation was deteriorating as 2003 wound down. On top of all the additional worries, staffing shortages were starting to become a problem, with some flight attendants failing to show up for work on Christmas and pilots retiring early, given incentives to do so under their contract.

These were now problems for a new chief to solve.

2004

"And it was logical, and it was plausible, and it was appealing. And it was wrong."

Unlike Leo Mullin and Joe Leonard, Gerald Grinstein—"Jerry," most everyone called him—wasn't in an office on the morning of Sept. 11, 2001. He was at home in Seattle, a 71-year old Yale undergrad and Harvard law graduate retired from a career running airlines and railroads, when American Airlines Flight 11 crashed into the World Trade Center's north tower at 5:46 a.m. Pacific time. A phone call from a friend in Texas alerted him to what was happening: "Turn on your TV," the voice on the other end of the line said.

Before long, amid all the uncertainty, Grinstein was sure of one thing: No Delta planes had been involved in the attacks. Because if they had been involved, Grinstein would have been among the first to know. He was retired, yes, but he was no ordinary retiree. Grinstein was a member of Delta's board of directors, as he had been since 1987, the year in which Delta acquired the airline he was then running: Salt Lake City-based Western Airlines, the country's ninth largest at the time. So he would have known. And before long "I was certain Delta wasn't involved."

What he was less certain about, he would claim years later, was Leo Mullin's judgment in signing the industry's richest pilot contract in mid-2001. Terrorists had just attacked the country using four commercial airplanes, and the U.S. airline industry was on its knees—a surprising and catastrophic event, no doubt. But even before 9/11, Grinstein—he said later—detected what felt like more than just the bad end of a business cycle. The end of the 1990s was perhaps the start of a structural shift in the way businesses and consumers were buying airline tickets, saving money by shopping online and flying low-fare airlines. Indeed Delta began losing money before 9/11—losing, for example, $133 million in the first quarter of 2001. Was it just a downturn that would eventually give way to a restoration of better times? Or was it a fundamental change in the economics of the industry?

"You should not sign a pilot contract in the spring of 2001 when you don't know the answer to that," Grinstein said later.

Reasonable people can, and do, differ on the question of whether Mullin, at the time, could have really gotten a better deal for the airline. He had already endured a debilitating pilot work slowdown the previous Christmas season, causing flight cancellations and leading passengers to avoid Delta—and a dollar of lost revenue is just as bad as a dollar of increased costs. And Mullin had only done what all major airline CEOs found themselves doing in times of non-crisis: He agreed to a contract a bit richer than the last one signed by a major airline, the "parity plus one" that pilots usually demanded. American, had 9/11 not happened, might have given its pilots even more. And Grinstein himself was on Delta's board—he was, in fact, probably the board member with the most experience negotiating airline labor contracts. If he was unsure at the time about the contract, perhaps he could have used his position to try to block the deal.

But in retrospect, at least, Grinstein was correct. The industry's economics had indeed changed, and Delta was saddled with a pilot contract it couldn't afford given the new realities: the low-fare carriers, the cost cutting by rival legacy carriers, the higher fuel costs, the new security hassles, the easy-to-find low fares proliferating on the internet and so on. "When businesses get in trouble, they frequently miss an inflection point," Grinstein said later. "At these points you want to know what's going on before committing yourself to such a big contract." Mullin, Grinstein was saying, had missed an inflection point.

Still, it wasn't until mid-2003, amid the fallout from the executive compensation controversy, that the board of directors began to question Mullin's ability to remain effective. "Employees were just furious, just angry," remembers Grinstein. "You can't explain to people that we're in the same boat, and we're going to fight together to do this, if you're in another economic situation and your future is secured and theirs is at risk."

Mullin wasn't the first Delta CEO to feel backlash like that. Grinstein recalled the time when former CEO Ron Allen, asked by *The Wall Street Journal* about the impact of his cost-cutting plan on employee morale, tersely replied, "So be it," prompting workers, in passive protest, to wear "so be it" buttons on the backs of their lapels.

In the fall of 2003, non-executives on the board—a former General Motors CEO, a former mayor of Atlanta, Grinstein and others—convened with Carl S. Sloane, a Harvard business school professor who specialized in corporate leadership, to discuss who would be Delta's next CEO. The rest of the group asked Grinstein to leave the room. A short time later, they called him back in and asked him if he would take the CEO job. His first reaction? "The usual chicken-shit way: 'I'd better call my wife.'"

So he did. And she had no desire to move to Atlanta. The couple had just settled into a new house in Seattle. They had grandchildren there, with another grandchild on the way. But she consented, and so he agreed to take the job, expecting to stay for four to six months as a transition figure. In the meantime, Leo Mullin completed his last few weeks on the job, surrendering the reins to Grinstein Jan. 1, 2004.

Still living in Seattle for the moment, Grinstein began commuting to Atlanta in the final weeks of 2003. Soon enough, he learned the gravity of the situation: His job was to save Delta. And that would take a lot longer than four to six months. What he found was a company whose balance sheet, so potent just two years earlier, was now in tatters, exhausted by a furious run of borrowing. In 2003, Delta's interest costs alone reached $732 million, up from just $69 million in 1998. It now had $20 billion in debt, including nearly $5 billion in pension liabilities. To ensure the assets of these pension plans didn't fall too far below the company's anticipated retirement obligations, management felt compelled to inject $177 million in cash, representing yet another huge drain on Delta's increasingly strained cash flows. By the start of 2004, most of the airline's aircraft collateral was already pledged, squeezing its future ability to borrow. And if anyone would even lend Delta money, they would be sure to charge an uncomfortably high interest rate, because by now, Delta's credit rating was junk. Making matters worse, for the third straight year, Delta lost money in 2003—this time $773 million, or really more like $1 billion without a one-time boost from government aid and the sale of Worldspan stock. While JetBlue, AirTran and Southwest grew capacity 66 percent, 22 percent and 5 percent, respectively, Delta shrank its capacity 7 percent—and remember, a shrinking airline actually pays *more* to carry each passenger because of factors like higher average worker seniority after furloughing the most junior employees. So Delta, already with huge labor cost problems, was caught in a vicious cycle compared to its younger, nimbler peers, who you might say were "growing down" their average costs. All the while, the average jet fuel prices Delta paid rose 22 percent in 2013, to 82 cents a gallon. Oil was now above $30 per barrel, a far cry from the time it hovered as low as $11 in the late 1990s. Setting aside fuel and looking at all the other costs—labor, aircraft and so forth—Delta, the lowest-cost carrier among its closest peers two years earlier, was now the highest-cost carrier.

This was hardly the way to start what was supposed to have been a festive year. Delta was celebrating its 75th anniversary in 2004. It had survived World War II, the fuel shocks of the 1970s, the turbulent aftermath of deregulation in the 1980s and the first Gulf war of the 1990s. But would it live to see 76? The question was gaining a measure of seriousness, especially with the dreaded "b" word heard more and more as the year progressed. The threat of bankruptcy was now very much in the air.

Some of Delta's problems were obvious. Not only was the pilot contract utterly unaffordable in the context of new market realities; it was about to get more expensive still, with another wage hike scheduled for May. Rising fuel prices were a vexing cost problem too, one with even fewer obvious solutions. And pension and interest costs were stinging. But at least costs were falling in the areas of non-pilot compensation, distribution, crew scheduling and maintenance.

Unfortunately, Grinstein quickly learned that even were he to strike a rapid deal with ALPA and enjoy a sudden drop in fuel prices—either one was unlikely, and the chance of both happening was even more remote—even *if* the nearly unimaginable happened, Delta's problems wouldn't be solved. On the contrary, Delta didn't just have a severe cost problem. By the start of 2004, it had a severe revenue problem too.

A few very profitable airlines in the world have both higher revenues and lower costs than their competitors. Most other successful airlines win by running up the score on one half of the ledger: Southwest had long been so efficient—spending so little money transporting each passenger—that it could be among the world's most profitable airlines even with the mediocre revenue of a budget airline. But no airline can profit with both higher costs and less revenue than its competition. And Delta, sure enough, had both cost and revenue problems.

Nothing is more important to an airline's revenue-generating capability than its real estate, or more precisely, the hubs and markets it dominates. For most of Delta's history, that meant first and foremost Atlanta, one of America's great economic success stories of the late 20th century. Atlanta's unofficial slogan, the "city too busy to hate," distinguished itself from the Old South's image of racial intolerance. Atlanta attracted job seekers with its low cost of living, including an abundance of cheap land for large suburban homes with manicured lawns. It became a prototypical suburban paradise of Olive Gardens, Walmarts, sport-utility vehicles and a downtown that almost nobody visited after dark. Businesses were attracted by a relatively high-skilled, low-cost labor pool, for sure, but also by an incredibly convenient airport with nonstop links to just about anywhere anyone needed to go. Atlanta was home to CNN, Home Depot, UPS and, most notably, the world's most recognizable brand: Coca-Cola. To this day, all these Atlanta-based companies and many more consider the city's airport a key competitive advantage. In the 1990s, Atlanta's population grew an astounding 38 percent, more than even Dallas, Houston, Orlando and other Sun Belt boomtowns. In the 2000s, Atlanta's population would grow another 24 percent, reaching 5.3 million people and counting by 2010, making it the nation's ninth largest metro area.

As early as 1998, the airport that would later be renamed Hartsfield-Jackson International Airport (adding "Jackson" for Maynard Jackson, Atlanta's first African-American mayor and a man credited with supporting much of the airport's modern growth to "Hartsfield," the mayor credited with its earlier growth) had surpassed Chicago O'Hare to become the busiest airport in not only the nation but also the world. And Atlanta's airport remains atop the list, testament to its extraordinary advantages as an airline hub. Not only is it located in a fast-growing, economically dynamic city with a large population. It's also located roughly midway between the U.S. northeast and Florida, one of the busiest air travel corridors in the world. Like birds migrating south for the winter, residents from New England through the mid-Atlantic states flock to Florida when the weather is cold, joined by residents of Midwestern states like Illinois, Ohio, Indiana and Wisconsin too. And especially for people living in secondary cities without a lot of nonstop flights to Florida, there's often no more convenient way to get there than via Atlanta. And that's just the start of it. Atlanta lies far enough north to be a good connecting point between New York and California. It's well situated to bring people from the giant population centers of Texas to Europe. It's a great hub for northeasterners and Midwesterners traveling to Latin America. As it happens, the southern U.S. is replete with smallish cities unable to support global airports of their own—think Savannah, Ga.; Jacksonville, Fla.; Jackson, Miss.; Huntsville, Ala., and so on. Atlanta is their default gateway to the world, in some cases the only way for them to get to points in Europe, Asia or Latin America with only one stop along the way. And Atlanta doesn't have much hub competition—only Charlotte, hubbed by American, has similar geographic endowments but a smaller local population that can't support as much air service as Atlanta.

And there's more to Atlanta's preeminence. The main airport happens to be the *only* commercial airport serving the city, which means Delta can aggregate all of the market's traffic in one place, a huge advantage relative to cities with traffic splintered among multiple airports where many flights are of no use in terms of providing connecting passengers to other flights, killing the powerful "network effects"—the idea that the whole network is much greater than the sum of its connecting parts—of a hub. New York, for example, is a much larger airline market than Atlanta, but its more than 100 million annual passengers are split across three major airports. Chicago, Dallas and Houston each have two major airports. If that weren't enough, Atlanta's airport was masterfully designed for connecting traffic, with multiple rectangular concourses lying parallel to one another, all connected by an underground train that runs, like a spine, straight through the middle of them. Other hubs like Chicago O'Hare and Dallas-Fort Worth, by contrast, are far more difficult to navigate. At the same time, Atlanta is one of the cheapest big hubs to serve, with costs-per-enplanement—in other words, what an airline pays to handle each departing passenger—well below those of most other big hubs.

No surprise, therefore, that Atlanta was still the jewel in Delta's crown. But the crown's luster was fading. And the jewel had some scratches. AirTran's growth, of course, was increasingly problematic. Although Delta had the much larger and more powerful frequent flier plan, the greater network coverage and the perks like lounges and overseas alliance partners that high-flying corporate travelers demanded, AirTran, as Joe Leonard liked to say, attracted folks that flew Delta during the week and AirTran on the weekends—business travelers when they were spending their own money. Unlike Southwest and JetBlue, moreover, AirTran offered business class seats, something Leonard originally planned to scrap until his lieutenant Bob Fornaro told him that no, business class is profitable: "You're producing 19 percent of your revenue with only 15 percent of your real estate," Fornaro told Leonard, referring to the "real estate" aboard an aircraft occupied by the larger seats. In addition, AirTran, in 2004, had begun receiving its new 737s and equipping them with satellite radio.

Its product and planes, in other words, were getting better and newer just as Delta's deteriorated and aged. Atlanta was also losing connecting traffic as airlines scheduled more nonstop flights between northern cities and Florida. AirTran itself was doing this from places like Baltimore and Akron-Canton. JetBlue was doing it from New York, Boston and Washington's Dulles International Airport, while also stepping up nonstop New York flying to the Caribbean, similarly bypassing Atlanta. Southwest was doing it. United was preparing its new low-cost Ted unit to do it. And even Delta itself was doing it with Song, in a sense competing against itself.

This naturally created immense downward pressure on fares to Florida and elsewhere in the southeast, hurting Delta most because it had both 1) the highest concentration of flying in that region and 2) the highest costs. But if only the heartache ended there.

About 500 miles to the northeast, back at Washington Dulles, a regional airline called Atlantic Coast Airlines, which made a living flying small planes painted in the colors of big airlines under contract for those airlines, faced an existential crisis. Atlantic Coast's biggest partner United, in bankruptcy, wanted to renegotiate its regional flying contracts and pay its regional partners less to carry its passengers. Daringly, Atlantic Coast walked away from United and converted itself into—ostensibly, anyway—an independent low-cost carrier, "Independence Air," using its fleet of 50-seat regional jets. By the logic of airline economics, this was absolute madness. There's no such thing as low-cost 50-seat service. Small jets inherently have *high* costs per unit, simply because there aren't so many units. Like a 150-seat jet, they have two pilots and two fuel-burning engines and require roughly as much maintenance, but these costs can only be spread among a third as many passengers. Sure, they require fewer flight attendants, and they don't burn quite as much fuel. But they burn far more than just a third as much. Their *trip* costs are lower, but their *unit* costs—what it costs to carry each passenger—are far higher. Regional jets were good for luring people away from turboprops or competing in markets that bigger jets couldn't support—an airline could cover the higher unit costs with higher fares on certain routes. They were useful for taking passengers from small cities to a hub, where those passengers would connect to larger planes and thereby reduce the average unit cost of the whole journey. But using them to offer low fares to points throughout the U.S. east coast, up against airlines with more appropriate aircraft? This was a low-*fare* carrier, not a low-*cost* carrier. Low fares and high costs are a toxic mix for an airline.

Competitors soon began calling Independence Air a "suicide bomber," bleeding itself to death by charging irrationally low prices, while forcing everyone else to match these prices. "I think Independence Air has shown that it's hard to make the economics work without a hybrid model that includes the mainline planes," Jim Whitehurst, Delta's chief operating officer, said in a conference call with investors later that year. But Delta could take little solace in that. "We have a lot of east-to-east connections that have been hit hard by Independence Air," Joe Kolshak, Delta's chief of operations, said during the same call.

AirTran showed its own frustration before the project even launched. "You've got Independence Air coming online," Joe Leonard said during an April 2004 conference call with Wall Street analysts. "United's going to fight with them.... Who knows what Virgin's [the then-soon-to-launch Virgin America] going to do. We just view this as a pretty hostile environment." Bob Fornaro, in an accent and lack of subtlety characteristic of his native Long Island, was even more blunt: "Independence Air is having a pretty big impact on pricing, and the East Coast... it's very, very competitive. You have an RJ operator who has walk-up fares anywhere from 50 to 70 percent below AirTran and everybody else. And those fares, we don't believe, are sustainable. But they're going to create a considerable amount of pain in the upcoming months." Five months later, he was even less charitable: "To be flying [a regional jet] with $59 fares is one the silliest things that I have ever seen, because RJs are high-cost airplanes." JetBlue's David Neeleman, the competitive but polite Mormon missionary, was, in his airline's conference call with Wall Street, more restrained, even if it didn't take much to read between the lines and realize he probably shared Fornaro's sentiments: "From what I can see, just kind of cruising around the website, and the average fares that they're charging during the peak of the peak here in July and August, I am a little surprised at the fares that are still out there. Based on the size of the airplanes, relative to the size of the airplanes—it's a very difficult position that they find themselves in."

Those 50-seat regional jets that were so ill-suited for Independence Air, however, seemed perfectly suited for Delta's Cincinnati hub. To be sure, Cincinnati was no Atlanta in terms of hub power—not even close. But it earned good money for Delta throughout most of the 1990s thanks in large part to Comair's successful gamble on Bombardier's CRJ regional jets at a time when airlines at neighboring hubs like Detroit, Cleveland and even mighty Chicago relied on older turboprops to bring people in from secondary markets throughout the region. The CRJs could fly farther, reaching more markets. They were more comfortable than propeller planes, meaning travelers were willing to pay more to fly them. And although their fuel burn-per-passenger economics weren't great, that didn't really matter when oil was $11 per barrel. By the late 1990s, regional jets had been pulling in so much traffic that Delta could schedule widebody flights from Cincinnati to Europe—and make a nice profit doing so. There was service not only to Europe's big three hub cities, London, Paris and Frankfurt, but also to Amsterdam, Rome and Zurich. In 2000, Delta even applied for rights to fly from Cincinnati to Beijing.

The Cincinnati metro area, although smaller than Atlanta, had its share of giant companies too—companies like Proctor & Gamble, Toyota's North American headquarters, GE's engine division and Kroger, the nation's largest standalone supermarket chain (only Walmart, if counted as a grocer, was larger). It was well placed for east-west traffic flows within the northern half of the U.S. And the airport was well designed, liked by travelers and had ample runway capacity. By 2004, however, Delta's Cincinnati machine was starting to show major cracks. Other airlines with hubs in the area, including Continental and Northwest, were catching up on regional jet deployment—Cincinnati lost its advantage, in that regard, over Cleveland and especially Detroit, which had a far larger local population too. At the same time, although Southwest and AirTran didn't serve Cincinnati itself, they increasingly did serve the city indirectly via airports like Indianapolis, Columbus and Louisville that weren't far from parts of Cincinnati's "catchment area," as airlines and airports call the swath on a map within which people might consider using a particular airport. Dayton, where AirTran was building service rapidly, was even more problematic from that perspective—it was *closer* to some of Cincinnati's northern suburbs than those areas were to Cincinnati's main airport, which is actually across the Ohio River from Cincinnati in northern Kentucky (the airport's three-letter code, CVG, stands for CoVinGton County, Ky.) Not helping matters: Cincinnati's metro area population ranked just 23rd in the nation, smaller than Pittsburgh, where US Airways was dismantling a once-formidable hub, and St. Louis, where American was doing the same. And Cincinnati, moreover, was dropping down the list. In the 1990s, it grew just 9 percent, followed by a paltry 6 percent growth in the 2000s, well below the national average.

Delta's Salt Lake City hub, by contrast, was serving a fast-growing metro area, underpinned by many of the same Sun Belt amenities that Atlanta offered. In the 1990s and 2000s, the city and its surroundings grew 26 percent and 16 percent, respectively, attracting residents and companies from high-priced California, in particular. It had some notable advantages as a hub too, being one of just two major gateways, alongside larger Denver, for the U.S. mountain region—not its region's Atlanta, in other words, but perhaps its Charlotte, which is not a bad thing to be. And unlike Atlanta and Cincinnati too, Utah attracts many tourists—only Alaska and California have more national parks. The Mormon Salt Lake Temple, the Sundance Film Festival and Great Salt Lake itself are big draws too.

Nevertheless, Salt Lake City was hardly a profit gusher for Delta. The metro area was far smaller, after all, than even Cincinnati, with only half as many people. Even if it continued growing more rapidly, it would long be smaller. Just as troubling, Southwest served 14 routes from Salt Lake City at the start of 2004, including many of the busiest markets like Los Angeles, Las Vegas and Houston.

The worst of all the hubs, as Grinstein quickly learned, was Dallas-Fort Worth. Even in good times, Delta was fighting an uphill battle there against American, which called the Dallas-Fort Worth region home and for which the airport was its biggest, busiest and most profitable hub. What Delta was to Atlanta, American was to Dallas-Fort Worth. It was a dominance no airline—not Delta, not even mighty Southwest from nearby Dallas Love Field—could successfully challenge.

Delta thus had no easy answers to its Dallas dilemma. "Now there were people inside the company that wanted to keep Dallas-Fort Worth and had an explanation for it," Grinstein recalled. "And it was logical, and it was plausible, and it was appealing. And it was wrong."

Why?

"We were losing $250 million trying to put a hub there," Grinstein said. For Delta, Dallas-Fort Worth was "Afghanistan," in his view. "And you sure as hell hate to roll over and get kicked in the ass by the Taliban—American—but you've got to get out. There's no way you're going to ever win there. You cannot put in enough resources to turn that into an effective winning place."

And then there was New York, the world's second busiest airline market after London, but one no single airline—most certainly not Delta—dominated. Throughout 2004, Continental repeatedly told investors that through aggressive marketing efforts, it had captured 25 percent of the New York City metro air travel market by luring Wall Street firms, for example, to use its Newark hub just across the Hudson River in New Jersey rather than a combination of LaGuardia and JFK airports. Newark, indeed, had a huge advantage over LaGuardia and JFK, offering a large menu of domestic and international flights all under one roof. It could support, for example, a flight to Indianapolis in its own right, which in turn could also help it support a flight to say, Madrid, meaning Continental could sell both the nonstop journeys to these places, as well as connecting itineraries such as Indianapolis to Madrid via Newark.

These economies of scale were more difficult to achieve at JFK because for shorthaul flights, business travelers preferred to use LaGuardia, which is much closer to Manhattan but where longhaul flights are prohibited. So the ideal shorthaul flight from Indianapolis to LaGuardia didn't connect to longhaul flights from Madrid. Even worse, Delta's JFK airport terminal, which began life in 1960 as Pan Am's then-futuristic "Worldport," was now, as one of Delta's own executives conceded, a "third-world facility." And if there was one thing Delta didn't have, it was extra money to spend on sprucing up airports.

By the summer of 2004, Continental was offering 18 routes to Europe from its all-purpose Newark hub, compared to Delta's 13 from mostly longhaul JFK. More than 10 years after Delta established a JFK foothold by buying Pan Am's transatlantic network, it still had just 15 percent of the New York market, five points behind even American, which offered just five European destinations from JFK. But one of those American destinations was London Heathrow, which was by far the most important business travel destination from New York. American served Heathrow with no fewer than six flights each way, each day, while Delta did not have the right to serve it at all. Delta also had to contend with a lot more competition from foreign airlines at JFK than Continental did at Newark, which Continental dominated in a way no single airline could ever dominate JFK. And then there was JetBlue, able to survive domestically at JFK by shunning business travelers and targeting vacationers and family-visit traffic, picking off Delta's passengers to Florida and the west coast one by one—and profiting all the while thanks to its rather nice inflight product and rather low operating costs.

As Grinstein further observed, Delta's grand scheme to take back share from JetBlue—its new airline Song—was off to a terrible start. "It was a clever idea, sort of, and beautifully executed," he recalled years later. "But never in a million years would I have started Song, because no American airline had ever been successful in creating a low-cost subsidiary." (Recall that Grinstein was, however, on Delta's board when Song launched.)

Indeed Delta itself had tried and failed with Delta Express. United, after failing with Shuttle by United, was likewise trying a second time with Ted, which would likewise fail. US Airways Metrojet and Continental Lite before it had failed. Air Canada was at the time, in early 2004, getting ready to fold up the tent on its Tango failure. And those were just the low-cost-unit-within-a-legacy-airline failures in North America, to speak nothing of Go (British Airways), Buzz (KLM), Snowflake (SAS) and so many others.

"What the hell were we doing that for?" Grinstein concluded rhetorically. But it was his problem now, a problem he had to figure out how the hell to solve.

For starters, "We were locking out the 757s from Atlanta, giving up one of the most efficient airplanes [we] had in the whole cockamamie fleet." And they had the opposite problem from Delta's 50-seat regional jets: low unit costs but 199 seats to fill. And the only way to fill so many seats? Extremely low average fares, of course, in leisure markets where fares were low to begin with, far below Delta's average costs. So Delta was taking passengers that might have connected through Atlanta and moving them to Song, where it was forced to charge, well, just a song. Novelties like a for-hire inflight exercise kit (featuring an elastic band and a squeezable ball) didn't do much to close the profitability gap.

The 757s were also long, thin planes with just one aisle, making them one of the slowest planes to board and de-plane. This meant they had to spend a long time on the ground, where they weren't generating any revenue. Herb Kelleher at Southwest, all those decades earlier, had invented the low-cost airline model based on his realization that the airplane doesn't make money on the ground. To ensure the 757s did get sufficient air time, Delta flew them an average of 13 ½ hours per day, which inevitably meant flights in the early morning and late night—times, in other words, when few people want to fly. So again, Song had to lower its fares to fill seats.

Joe Leonard of AirTran summed it up in his quarterly earnings call with Wall Street: "The notion that Delta or any of these legacy carriers can get their costs down in the neighborhood of ours is really just not in the cards. The thought process, from the time we get up in the morning to the time we go to bed at night, is so much different than the way these other guys think that they just can't get there.

"I will give you an example," he continued. "I read in the clips on Friday"—relevant newspaper clippings commonly compiled and photocopied by staff at companies to keep managers informed—"that Song and Delta had installed these [special] bag bins so that they could get the turn time down from 90 minutes to 50 minutes on a 757. And our approach would be to get it down to 30 minutes without making the investment in these heavy, troublesome systems. And we would [accomplish] that.

So that's just one example, and there are hundreds and hundreds and hundreds a day in the thought process of these legacy carriers and the way we think.

"They may make progress in getting their costs down, but they will never get their costs as low as ours because they approach the business differently," Leonard concluded. "And I will just reiterate what Bob [Fornaro] said: They already compete with us as though they had our costs; they just lose a billion or two a year in the process."

In *his* earnings call, David Neeleman of JetBlue—with costs not quite as low as AirTran but much lower than Delta and which, remember, had become probably the first low-cost airline to actually take revenue premiums over legacy competitors—said, with his tongue firmly in cheek: "I've been very uncomfortable, to be honest with you, with the extent of our average fare difference. When they [Song] were trying to get established and they were out there with some really low fares, and we were full, it was really difficult for us to match the fares. I told our people I don't want to have a $20 fare premium, a $20 average fare premium. I don't think that's good for the long-term success of our business. And the only way you can counteract that is to add more frequency. And so I would rather have a unit revenue premium because of load factor. And we certainly have a lot easier time doing that. If we're both flying around 135 people on an airplane—Song, I'm talking about particularly—we're flying in the mid-80 percent load factors, and they're flying the mid-60s." Song, he was saying, wasn't filling its flights despite very low fares; JetBlue was filling its flights despite higher fares. And Song was actually encouraging JetBlue to add more capacity, which was exactly what Song was designed to prevent.

Song was also confusing customers who had no idea what it was. (Over at United, where the same was happening with its "low-cost" Ted unit, a confused passenger who booked with United and ended up on a Ted flight from Fort Lauderdale to Washington Dulles was overheard asking a flight attendant: "What is 'Ted?'" The flight attendant shrugged: "*We* don't know either.") While Delta's decrepit JFK airport terminal was starved of funding, the airline spent millions promoting Song in the most expensive media market in the world. Song would, in time, diversify away from JFK somewhat, launching service from Boston and quixotic flying between California and Florida, robbing Atlanta of connecting traffic in the process, especially in marginal markets like Hartford-Los Angeles, which before Song had no nonstop options. Song's unit costs really were 20 percent lower than mainline. The problem was, its unit revenues were down even more steeply.

Grinstein also recognized that Song or no Song, Delta had just 20 percent of its capacity flying international routes, measured by the industry standard available seat miles, or ASMs—the number of seats times the number of miles they fly. Continental, United, Northwest and American were all 30 to 40 percent international by that measure. This had a lot to do with so much of Delta's capacity flying into and out of Florida, where prevailing fares were now so low that Delta—with its high costs—had little chance of ever making any money, at least outside peak travel months like March, when university students on their spring break and winter-worn families headed south.

In March 2004, while Delta was burning dollar bills every time one of its aircraft took off, it was sending 812 flights and 91,000 seats per week to Orlando alone, from not just its five main hubs but from 29 other cities too. Even during the sweltering summer, when the only break from the heat and humidity is when a devastating hurricane strikes, and thus when few people want to visit Florida, Delta was sending planes to Orlando from 12 different cities. Worse yet, many of the Atlanta, Dallas and Cincinnati flights were operated with 200-plus seat widebody Boeing 767s, "a total misuse of a widebody, a misallocation of resources," an incredulous Grinstein said years later of the situation he inherited. "It's just not efficient on a shorthaul market like that. You're dumping all those seats, and you need an ass in every one of those seats and need to cut prices to do it. And once you start cutting, there's no end to it. You're competing against yourself."

Nor was Delta's fleet anything close to ideal. The airline entered the 2000s with a motley collection of 15 different aircraft types, each with its own set of trained pilots and mechanics. The upside of having different plane types is being better able to assign the right plane with the right economics to the right routes. Southwest, flying just 737s, was essentially forfeiting opportunities to serve markets where that plane was too big (a metro area with fewer than a million residents, for example) or didn't have enough range (i.e., overseas markets). A legacy airline would never want quite the simplicity of a low-cost airline's fleet, because it would give up too many revenue opportunities. But the downsides of having *so many* fleet types—some of which, in Delta's case, served roughly the same purposes—are extreme scheduling complexity, diseconomies of scale and a diminished ability to manage irregular operations. Imagine a 737 flight cancels because of a mechanical problem, and there's a similarly sized spare MD-88 at the airport. Problem is, the 737's pilots can't fly the MD-88. And fleet complexity means enormous time and money spent training pilots.

"One of the arcane arts of the airline business is getting your fleet plan right," Grinstein said. "If you get your fleet plan right, you can make a dozen other mistakes and still be able to survive." Delta, alas, didn't have its fleet plan right.

But never mind that it didn't have any money left to revitalize and rightsize its fleet. Because even if it did, the airline seemed to be mismanaging something even more basic. As Grinstein was assessing the mess on his hands, a visitor told him Delta's flight operations were unusually messy by industry standards—"sloppy," was the word. But it wasn't just any visitor. It was Rakesh Gangwal, the former CEO of US Airways who now worked closely with Delta as the CEO of Worldspan, which ran the airline's reservation system and sold many of its tickets through travel agencies. Back at US Airways, Gangwal had held weekly quality review meetings. He told Grinstein bluntly, "You have a really undisciplined airline."

Grinstein saw chronically late flights, often starting with a flight early in the day delayed by a few minutes, causing the next flight to be delayed and the next flight and "before you knew it, late flights would cascade through the system." He saw declining morale, notably among flight attendants outfitted in uniforms that some people said made them look like prison wardens. He saw declining service standards. He saw dirty planes. And he saw an airline briefly but embarrassingly humiliated in March, when the national media jumped on Delta for losing an 80-year-old Alzheimer's patient whom the airline was supposed to escort as he connected between flights in Atlanta. He was found 24 hours later at a bus station downtown.

It was this long list of network, fleet, product, operational and financial deficiencies that greeted Delta's new chief executive officer. Two years earlier, Delta had been a rare airline with an investment-grade credit rating. Now it was on the brink of bankruptcy. It was time, Grinstein concluded, for a "complete strategic reassessment," one with "no sacred cows."

Crafting a comprehensive turnaround plan, however, would take time—time to fully assess the details of the company's problems, time to discuss these problems with employees, time to prepare the employees for big changes to come and time to discuss inevitable cost cutting with suppliers, aircraft lessors, bankers and, most importantly, ALPA.

Grinstein called ALPA's John Malone to begin a dialogue. But the two were far apart. The company called for 30 percent wage cuts. Malone offered just 9 percent plus giving up the 4 percent increase scheduled for May. Grinstein found the offer grossly inadequate. Four weeks into the new year, Malone distributed a letter to his members that presaged a stalemate. "Until today's proposal from management," he wrote, "I was hopeful that we could reach a settlement... [but] optimism is fading." He also advised his members to prepare for a possible bankruptcy or even a strike. There was, at least, now some union recognition that the 2001 pilot contract needed to be renegotiated. But months would pass with little negotiating progress.

Events were moving more quickly on other fronts. Also in January, Grinstein and his team—at this point still comprised mostly of holdovers from Mullin's administration—announced their first major strategic initiative: Delta would greatly escalate its battle against JetBlue, American, Continental and others in New York City. JFK capacity would spike nearly 40 percent, with new mainline service to Denver, San Juan, Santo Domingo and San Diego and more frequencies on existing routes to Los Angeles, San Francisco, Seattle and Las Vegas. These routes to the west coast, incidentally, did not suffer the JFK/LaGuardia split dilemma thanks to a federal perimeter rule that prohibited flights from LaGuardia to all those destinations except Denver. So most of the JFK additions were not at a competitive disadvantage, in terms of attracting "local" rather than connecting passengers, versus anything at LaGuardia. As a result, hundreds of furloughed flight attendants and airport agents were getting their jobs back. Not stopping there, Delta hired regional partners to introduce new JFK service to smaller markets like Savannah, Greensboro and Charleston, attempting to build critical mass for connecting traffic, never mind the LaGuardia preference problem in those markets.

Perhaps more conspicuous than what Delta was adding in New York was what Delta *wasn't* adding in New York. It wasn't adding any additional Song flights, aside from two new daily flights to Fort Myers. In fact, it was simultaneously canceling some Song service to Orlando from Washington.

Separately, Delta decided to move ahead with a "reconditioning program" for domestic aircraft interiors. That this would cost $20 million at a time of intense cost cutting demonstrated with no uncertainty—to both Wall Street and employees— that Grinstein believed strongly that good customer service was a prerequisite to reform. Delta also, incidentally, redesigned its airport boarding procedures, boarding by "zones" rather than rows in an attempt to slice precious minutes from aircraft turnaround times.

Grinstein also adopted an almost politician-like management style, spending time on the front lines and actively soliciting rank-and-file employee input. "I mean, it's the easiest thing to stay in the office and work on things that the CEOs work on," he said. "On the other hand, you're in a company with 50,000 people and you've got to keep them motivated, and execution is a huge part of your project. And if they're not motivated, you're not going to have a satisfactory passenger experience.

"They call it 'management by walking around,'" he continued. "But you can abuse that by just walking around and tipping your hat and saying 'howdy.' But that isn't really what it's about. It's about having meetings with people and letting them talk."

In February, Delta liquidated its fuel hedge position, booking a profit of $82 million. Airlines purchase fuel hedge contracts, usually from investment banks, as an insurance policy against a sudden spike in prices. If the actual fuel prices rise later, the airline saves money. Delta was indeed an active fuel hedger, saving millions when fuel prices began to rise in the early part of the 2000s. But now it was liquidating its contracts—giving up that future protection—because it badly needed cash. And as for buying new contracts? That was the last thing Delta could afford. Premiums were growing significantly more expensive as fuel prices kept rising—just as insurance for a home gets pricier if hurricanes seem more likely, fuel price insurance, as you might call it, gets pricier with an increased risk of a fuel price spike. Delta was now completely exposed to a future fuel shock. Just as troubling, many of its rivals were protected. Southwest, in particular, was in very much an opposite position: Southwest had more cash than it knew what to do with. With jet fuel now selling for what seemed like a rather pricey 95 cents per gallon, Southwest was still *buying* hedges for the future, not liquidating them, while simultaneously benefiting from hedge protection it bought back when jet fuel cost as little as 30 cents per gallon in 1998.

Also in February, Delta borrowed more money. It issued more of that debt that lenders, if things went well, could later convert to shares of Delta stock—and it used the $300 million it raised from that to shore up its still badly underfunded pension plans. It also canceled plans to take five Boeing 777 widebodies scheduled for delivery in 2005 and 2006, despite the plane's excellent economic credentials for making money on international routes—Delta simply didn't have the money to pay for them.

And it ended a contract with Atlantic Coast Airlines, which was still doing some regional flying for Delta even as it prepared to launch Independence Air. At the same time, Grinstein decided to invest in new uniforms for front-line employees. He hired Richard Tyler of Los Angeles, a designer better known for outfitting Hollywood stars like Julia Roberts. "What the hell are you doing that for?" Grinstein, speaking years later about the decision, recalled being asked. How, in other words, could he on one hand be desperately borrowing money while on the other hand spending precious cash on what seemed like a luxury? "But flight attendants are the face of the airline in so many different ways, and they felt like they were in burlap sacks," he reasoned. New uniforms were core to Delta's turnaround, not a luxury.

Grinstein also organized two-day training sessions for all flight attendants, in which management thundered home the message that "We're going to make it. Don't give up."

"I don't want to call it 're-education,'" he recalled, "but..."

And everything he did, he did it realizing it had to be done a little bit differently at Delta, because Delta was a little bit of a different airline. "There was sort of a social contract at Delta, I thought," he recalled, "that 'you take care of the passengers, and we'll take care of you.' And that, to me, was always a hangover of its history. And it may be part of its religious fundamentalist or Baptist base—I don't know what the hell it was. But it was something that existed, I think, inside Delta."

In March, Fred Reid, Mullin's No. 2, resigned to become Richard Branson's CEO for the new Virgin America he hoped to launch. He had clearly wanted the job Grinstein now had and, after getting passed over, saw his Delta days as numbered. In April, CFO Michelle Burns resigned too. Replacing her in May was Michael Palumbo, a former TWA CFO and one-time finance executive under Jerry Grinstein at Western Airlines. Delta's vice president of human resources under Mullin, Robert Colman, also left. For the most part, Grinstein had his new team in place, although he still felt uncomfortable about having one vice president charged with all marketing functions, which in the airline business encompasses a lot. He wanted to find a high-level executive dedicated specifically to managing network planning and flight scheduling. For that person, he was determined to look outside the company.

But that would have to wait. As summer approached, pilot negotiations were still going nowhere, all while oil prices rose from $34 per barrel in January to $37 in March and $40 in May. Average jet fuel prices per gallon were now solidly above $1, a level below which they would never again dip. The U.S. economy, fortuitously, was nevertheless showing signs of improvement, as Americans increasingly took advantage of low interest rates to buy new homes on credit. They were borrowing plenty with credit cards too. And why not, with capital pouring in from China, soon to become America's largest foreign lender? This, after all, was a major reason why the price of money was so low. The federal government was borrowing no less enthusiastically, demonstrated by a sharp reversal in its fiscal position. In 2001, Uncle Sam had posted a budget surplus of $128 billion. By 2004, that had become a

$413 billion deficit, the result of two expensive wars and a massive new homeland security bureaucracy combined with two large tax cuts. These deficits, moreover, were contributing to a weaker U.S. dollar, which was yet another factor fueling higher oil prices—the dollar tends to be weak when oil prices are strong, although economists debate which factor is the cause and which is the effect. Even worse for America's global airlines like Delta, this weaker U.S. dollar handed a natural cost advantage to foreign rivals, who were now earning revenues in strong currencies and paying for their fuel—not to mention their aircraft leases—in depreciated dollars. When fuel prices double, in other words, a non-U.S. carrier might not really pay double if its currency has risen too—that stronger currency gives it a discount on fuel, which is priced in weakening U.S. dollars. For Delta and other U.S. carriers, double meant double, unless they had hedge protection, which Delta now did not.

It was time to step up the pressure on pilots. On July 30, 2004, still making no progress with ALPA, Grinstein wrote an open letter appealing directly to the company's 7,000 mainline pilots:

Dear Delta Pilot:

Today, Delta responded to ALPA's proposal and provided ALPA its proposal to achieve the pilot cost savings needed to help ensure we have the best chance possible to restructure outside of bankruptcy court and avoid the additional sacrifices that an alternative course of action would demand. While I respect the negotiating process and believe details are best resolved privately at the table, the sheer life-altering magnitude of the need—approximately $1 billion in annual savings—deserves acknowledgement, hard truths and assurances from me personally.

First, the hard truths. As the financial data and modeling we have shared with ALPA over time demonstrates, the $1 billion in annual savings represents the minimum amount, in combination with reductions from other stakeholders, required for our company to regain long-term viability. So unlike traditional talks where a company's opening proposal represents a ceiling from which it can afford to lower its target, this level of savings must be achieved.

Importantly, how we get there—i.e., the combination of changes in benefits, wages and work rules required to deliver the permanent, steady-state savings the company must have—is something best determined through a collaborative effort with ALPA. We look forward to receiving ALPA's input and suggestions on how to best achieve the objective. We will be as open to solutions as market realities and developments allow. To be clear, the marketplace is dictating our level of need.

Because of the current situation we are in, the limited amount of time we have to do this together, and what we are trying to avoid, it would be irresponsible for us to be unprepared. We therefore have proposed certain pension plan changes for ALPA's consideration and input which, unlike United, are designed to achieve viability, preserve accrued benefits and provide a sustainable pension plan going forward. Appreciating how important this issue is to you and to all of us, I wanted you to hear about this directly from me and understand the very real and meaningful differences between our position and United's actions.

We are watching United closely, as I am sure you are, because what happens there could have far-reaching effects throughout our industry. Our options are limited by the marketplace and the requirement of viability. However, our goal in this proposal with respect to the pension plan is to preserve and protect your accrued benefits (including your ability to receive money in a lump sum). Delta's objective is to maintain the ability to fund the existing plans and provide a secure, sustainable new retirement plan for the future, within the boundaries of viability for Delta.

Second, the assurances. To consider making the level of sacrifice needed, you must believe your sacrifice will be worth it. Is the need real? Does the company have an innovative, strategic plan? Are other stakeholders being called upon to be a part of the solution? Will sacrifices be shared fairly and equitably? Will there be an upside? These are legitimate questions that deserve direct answers.

The need is real. We have opened our books to ALPA and its independent advisors for verification, so they could ensure that the numbers are accurate. Seven credit downgrades and the worst second-quarter performance in the industry further confirm the severity and precariousness of our situation.

Delta has a plan. After months of intensive planning, we are poised to roll out at the end of August decisive, strategic initiatives that will transform Delta and the way we do business. Our plan is not to simply mimic low-cost carriers, nor is it to continue to struggle for another few years as a traditional legacy carrier. We are instead pursuing a Delta Solution, using the tools and resources unique to us to carve out new and previously uncharted airline territory. Make no mistake: this is designed as an out-of-court solution. And, as we implement it, the Company must and will generate significantly more savings than the $1.8 billion achieved to date through our Profit Improvement Initiative.

Other stakeholders will be a part of the solution. Though significant, pilot costs alone are not the problem, and they alone are not the solution. We are working hard to restructure debt, renegotiate aircraft leases, and reconstruct our relationship with vendors and suppliers. Everyone must participate, or we cannot transform this Company without court supervision. Our goal is to do it once and do it right.

Sacrifices will be shared fairly and equitably. Our circumstances do not permit us to enjoy the benefits of being at the top of the industry compensation ladder. Our goal is for Delta's compensation packages to be market-competitive against legacy and low-cost carriers —not the highest, not the lowest, but mid-range. Though our non-contract employees are generally at market, and management is below, the need for greater savings through PII will require even more change.

There will be an upside. I am committed to the principle that the people of Delta must have an opportunity to share in any success their sacrifice helps make possible. If we are able to restructure consensually, rather than through the courts, this principle will be a meaningful component of our ongoing relationships with all of our people. We already are working on a combination of equity, profit sharing and some type of incentives tied to productivity as we move forward.

I appreciate ALPA's willingness to work constructively with the company. As we tackle together painful and difficult issues, there are few good options and no easy choices. Delta's work to transform itself into a viable company that can provide stable and rewarding career opportunities for its people over the long term will require enormous change and sacrifice from its people now. And, while there are no guarantees in life, and particularly in this industry, I do believe all of us would be better off if we could avoid a court-supervised restructuring. We have a window of opportunity and it is my view we should take advantage of it.

Thank you very much for your continued dedication and commitment—particularly in the face of almost unimaginable change. I appreciate your contributions and am proud of the dignified and professional manner in which you and all of Delta's people are serving our company and our customers.

Sincerely,
Jerry Grinstein

As management awaited a response, the competitive battleground wasn't getting easier. Independence Air continued to bloody the marketplace with cut-rate airfares by flying for example, 17 times a day from Washington Dulles to New York JFK, 14 times a day to Atlanta and 13 times a day to Raleigh-Durham, N.C. It also ordered narrowbody Airbus 319s to go along with its inappropriately sized 50-seaters, meaning even more low-fare seats were coming. In May, Southwest, smelling blood, moved planes into Philadelphia, a major stronghold for still-struggling US Airways. By year's end, Southwest would also outmaneuver AirTran to improve its position in Chicago, where bankrupt ATA was selling pieces of itself. Southwest won a bidding war to establish what would later become a major hub at Midway International, an alternative to busier O'Hare International.

JetBlue, for its part, laughing off the Song challenge, managed to make its way into high-yield LaGuardia Airport—launching markets like LaGuardia-Fort Lauderdale, in direct competition against Delta—while establishing a foothold in Boston and adding points in the Caribbean. It also, for good measure, exercised options to buy another 30 Airbus 320s. Doug Parker's America West, kept alive like US Airways by a federal loan guarantee, launched an assault on transcontinental routes including New York JFK-Los Angeles, depressing fares there. Overall, the Big Six U.S. legacy airlines—United, American, Delta, Northwest, Continental and US Airways—had cut seat capacity 13 percent between 9/11 and the beginning of 2004, all while low-cost airlines *increased* their seat capacity 26 percent during the same period, according to an analysis for Congress by the U.S. Government Accountability Office. A major shift in the balance of U.S. airline industry power was accelerating—a shift away from airlines like Delta.

In July United, still wallowing in bankruptcy, had abruptly stopped contributing to its pension plans—hence Grinstein's statement in the letter to pilots that "we are watching United closely"—saving the airline hundreds of millions of dollars, never mind its investment in its new low-cost Ted unit, which would suffer many of the same shortcomings as Song. The new alliance involving Continental and Northwest, meanwhile, was working reasonably well for Delta. And by the third quarter of 2004, both were fellow members of SkyTeam. But Continental was at least as much a foe as a friend. In January, its legendary CEO Gordon Bethune, the mastermind of an epic turnaround, announced his retirement. His successors, however, were no less ruthless in their pursuit of New York international traffic. Under the guidance of network planning executives named Glen Hauenstein and Bob Cortelyou, Continental expanded transatlantic capacity from Newark 17 percent and placed orders for a revolutionary new plane that Boeing was building—the 7E7, the manufacturer was calling the project for now—capable of reaching nearly any point in the world from the U.S. and with much greater fuel efficiency. Airlines had told Boeing that if the Sonic Cruiser it pondered could have flown faster while burning about the same amount of fuel as current models, then surely Boeing could instead build a plane that could fly the same speed but burn less fuel. Boeing listened; the 7E7 was its answer. Connecting traffic flowing through Newark to Europe, furthermore, was connecting traffic that might have flowed "over" JFK or Atlanta, as airline planners describe connections—passengers connect "over" one hub or another. Was inviting Continental into SkyTeam such a great idea after all?

All the Big Six, in any event, were running well behind their revenue and expense forecasts. At the start of 2004, all had expected higher fares and cheaper fuel than what they ended up getting and buying. The peak summer season came and went with little relief as Delta continued to work on its grand turnaround plan. August proved especially troubling for carriers with a big Florida presence: Two severe hurricanes, first Charlie and then Frances, caused mass flight cancellations. In September, two more—Ivan and Jeanne—followed.

As summer turned to autumn, Delta also began seeing an alarming uptick in the number of pilots opting to retire early. Their contract gave those over the age of 50 the right to do so and instantaneously receive half their pension benefits—sometimes as much as $1 million—as a lump sum, with the other 50 percent distributed as an annuity for the rest of their lives. Any pilot who lived long enough would theoretically receive less this way, over the remainder of his life, than had he taken it all as an annuity. But the lump-sum option was looking more and more attractive with Delta's increased risk of bankruptcy, for pilots knew all too well pension plans were being terminated altogether at bankrupt United and US Airways—and pilots whose pensions are terminated end up receiving just pennies on the dollar through a government pension insurance scheme. So it could be better to snatch at least some of the money now from the hands of a troubled company. Effective Sept. 1, 2004, 100 Delta pilots retired, 71 of them early. On Oct. 1, 99 more followed, of whom 71 were again leaving early. This was causing strains for two reasons: One, the lump-sum payouts were a drain on dwindling cash, and two, the airline found itself without enough pilots to fly its schedule. Making matters worse, pilots retiring early tended to be senior captains flying widebody planes, often to high-revenue international destinations. Mid-career pilots would need to be quickly promoted and trained to fly those aircraft.

Finally, after more than eight months of diagnosing Delta's escalating problems, Grinstein and his team, on Sept. 8, 2004, unveiled their long-awaited plan to create "the right airline for the new era." It included, uncomfortably, more pay and benefit reductions for non-pilot employees, the details of which were announced Sept. 28. Salaries, executive salaries included, would be cut by another 10 percent. Workers would pay a greater share of their health insurance premiums. Maximum vacation accrual would fall from six weeks to five. Company funding for retiree health plans would be reduced.

In addition, as Grinstein had said back on Sept. 8, another 6,000 to 7,000 jobs would go.

"My hope," Grinstein wrote, "was that increases in productivity, the lack of general pay increases since 2000 and the reduction of 16,000 jobs would be sufficient. I did not want nor intend to ask everyone for more sacrifice. But regrettably, the industry environment and our company's worsening financial situation have deepened the gap between where we are and where we must be to survive and succeed over the long term. Now, the marketplace and other factors are demanding even more from all of us. Fuel costs have skyrocketed, and our fuel bill this year will be $680 million more than last year. Unrelenting pricing pressures brought on by the onslaught of low-cost carriers and growth in internet fare shopping have further worsened our situation, requiring an even greater level of savings than we had originally anticipated.

As demonstrated by what is happening at other legacy carriers, the harsh reality is that our world has permanently changed, and we must change with it if we are to protect and preserve Delta today and in the future." To minimize layoffs, new voluntary schemes emerged: Senior employees who agreed to leave would get certain future medical or travel benefits.

Grinstein tried to be more careful than Mullin had been to demonstrate management was sacrificing too. Delta's officer ranks, he explained, were 20 percent smaller than they had been in 2003, and executives had already swallowed an 8 percent pay cut in March, in addition to the 10 percent reduction that would take effect Jan. 1, 2005. "In distressed times like these, when everyone must sacrifice, it is especially important that leadership participates, and they have," he wrote. Mindful of 2003's executive bonus and pension fiasco, Grinstein went one step further: "It is also necessary for me to lead the way. I have declined my salary and will not be paid for the remainder of the year." (Leo Mullin had similarly, in late 2001 and 2003, declined his salary for the remainder of those years.)

The transformation plan next turned to addressing Delta's network woes. Finally, Delta was pulling out of Afghanistan, so to speak, by closing its money-bleeding hub at Dallas-Fort Worth. That meant it would no longer serve small Texas cities like Amarillo and Lubbock, which Southwest and American dominated. In turn, DFW-based aircraft would go to other hubs like Atlanta, where Delta would redesign its flight schedules to boost aircraft utilization.

For Grinstein, the decision to close the DFW hub was "a no-brainer." For Delta's employees there and for the airport itself, it was heartbreaking.

"It was a very, very difficult day," Jeff Fegan, the head of the airport at the time, recalled of the announcement, which Delta made public Sept. 8. Difficult—but not incomprehensible.

"I mean, we're all big boys in this business," he said. "We all have to understand people have to make decisions." And Delta "always treated me with a great deal of respect."

In a legacy airline hub-and-spoke system—the "spokes" are like the literal spokes on a bicycle wheel that radiate from the axle in the middle out to the rim—almost all airline hubs have "banks" or "waves" of flights optimized to offer as many convenient connecting itineraries as possible. At about the same time, flights from numerous "outstations," as airlines call non-hub airports, arrive at the hub. Those airplanes sit on the ground for 45 minutes to an hour or more while passengers rush through the terminal to make their connecting flights, perhaps stopping briefly to shop or eat if they have time. Then with everyone on board and the terminal markedly more empty of passengers—as workers at airport restaurants and stores catch their breath after a particularly busy half hour—all the same airplanes push back from their gates, at about the same time, to carry the connecting passengers to their final destinations. A plot of daily flight activity at a typical hub looks like an electrocardiogram, with noticeable peaks and valleys—three or four peaks, representing the banks of flights, at a less busy hub, or more like six or seven at a busier hub. Hubs generally have to be scheduled in banks, because if flights just came and went randomly, passengers would have to wait many hours for their connections—and would instead opt for a more convenient itinerary using another airline's better-timed hub. The downside to "banked" hubs: To ensure that people on the incoming wave of flights have time to walk to their new gates and board the outgoing wave of flights, an airline must keep all those airplanes on the ground longer than would be necessary to just clean them and immediately board a new group of passengers, who might already be waiting at the gate. Airplanes often spend a lot of time on the ground at outstations too, because the flights back to a hub are timed based not on how quickly the airplane can be deplaned, cleaned and boarded at the outstation—but based on when it should leave to arrive at a hub with the next bank of flights. Although all of this is helpful for creating revenue-rich connecting itineraries, airplanes on the ground longer than operationally necessary are one reason legacy airline costs are higher than those of LCCs.

But Delta realized Atlanta was different from almost every other hub in the world because it had *so many* flights to *so many* destinations—and would soon have even more, with aircraft being brought over from DFW—that passengers actually wouldn't have to wait all that long for their connections even if flights just came and went not in waves, but more randomly, as part of a "rolling hub." Picture a Delta outstation like Kansas City, from which (after the demise of its DFW hub) Delta would fly to its Atlanta, Cincinnati and Salt Lake City hubs. Cincinnati and Salt Lake City would get seven and five daily flights, respectively, necessitating traditional banks—with a domestic network flying from roughly 6 a.m. to midnight, imagine how many hours a passenger might have to wait to connect in Salt Lake City if the five flights from Kansas City weren't well timed to meet connecting flights to other places. Ditto, to only a slightly lesser degree, for Cincinnati. But Atlanta? Atlanta would soon have 11 daily Kansas City flights. With that many flights to Kansas City—and with 37 to New York's three airports and 15 to Philadelphia and a dozen to Boston and 10 or more even to smaller cities like Richmond and Savannah and Fort Myers and Norfolk and so many others—passengers just wouldn't have to wait all that long for their connections, even if flights just came and went without being scheduled in banks so that the airplanes would spend less time sitting at gates and more revenue-producing time in the air. Precisely because Delta's Atlanta hub was *so* robust, in other words, it might get the revenue benefits of the world's busiest hub but also the cost-saving high aircraft utilization of a low-cost airline.

An added benefit would be less congestion, not only of passengers in the terminal at peak times but also of aircraft at gates. Flights spread more evenly throughout the day rather than bunched together meant each gate—and by extension, the whole hub—could handle more flights.

The concept was rare but not entirely new: American had already done something similar, during its 2003 restructuring, at DFW. American's DFW hub, although not quite as busy as Delta's in Atlanta, was one of the few other hubs in the world just busy enough that such a thing might work.

Away from Atlanta, Delta's new turnaround plan featured more JFK flying, including new service to Charlotte and three Florida cities: Melbourne, Pensacola and Tallahassee. But Delta would also, perhaps not knowing what else to do with all the surplus aircraft it was removing from DFW, ramp up flying from non-hub cities like Boston, where it ranked third in flights offered, behind American and US Airways. To pressure AirTran, it would build new nonstop links from secondary cities like Dayton, Columbus, Hartford, Norfolk, Charleston, Richmond, Knoxville, Pensacola and Greensboro to key Florida destinations like Orlando, Fort Lauderdale and Tampa. To enhance its presence in the western U.S., it created a new alliance with Seattle-based Alaska Airlines—either airline's frequent fliers could earn and redeem miles on the other. Internationally, it applied for new flying rights to China, whose economy began surging not long after the SARS crisis. To nearly everyone's surprise, Delta even reversed course and began expanding Song again, by 12 additional 757s deployed on transcontinental routes—Grinstein might have quickly realized how badly Song was performing, but rather than cutting his losses, he first doubled down on Mullin's bet. In all, Delta would add 31 new nonstop flights to 19 new destinations on Jan. 31, 2005—a "big bang," some people called the initiative, officially known as "Operation Clockwork," which the airline heralded as "the largest single-day schedule transformation in Delta's history."

That wasn't the end of it. The "comprehensive, 360-degree" turnaround plan also set out to retire at least four fleet types by 2008, cut management overhead costs by 15 percent and ensure employees would benefit—through performance-based incentives, stock rewards and profit sharing—if the harsh measures worked and Delta became profitable again. The plan called for continued investments in better products and services including leather seats, planes with better lighting, a better website and more airport kiosks. Two reservation call centers would close. The airline's SkyMiles frequent flier plan, a cash cow courtesy of miles sold to credit card issuers, retailers and other partners like hotels and rental car agencies, would become easier for customers to understand, with award trips easier to redeem. "We are going to take the fine print out of the way we do business to make it easier for customers to do business with us," a Delta press release said. The plan did not, on the other hand, call for removing first class cabins from any mainline domestic planes—in fact, Delta abandoned a short-lived experiment to do just that in a few markets like Houston and Kansas City.

Delta was also redesigning the way it priced its seats. Airlines had learned long ago that different travelers will pay different prices depending on when and where the flight was going, whether or not the journey was nonstop or double-legged, how far in advance the ticket was purchased and the fare rules attached to the ticket: Was it refundable? Could the dates be changed without a fee?

What evolved was a hierarchy of many fare options for the same flight, some available only at certain times, some available only with a litany of restrictions. Low-cost carriers, to be sure, were practicing this same art of revenue management but with less of a spread between their cheapest restricted fares and the most expensive "walk-up" fares favored by business travelers. Discount carriers also tended to have fewer rules like Saturday night-stay requirements, which were designed to discourage weekday business travelers from grabbing them—the biggest distinction between time-sensitive business travelers and price-sensitive leisure travelers was whether they wanted to be home or away on a Saturday night. Low-cost airlines also didn't have an entirely separate set of unpublished fares individually negotiated with corporations, fares that promised discounts and perks in exchange for hitting volume, revenue or market share targets. Delta had such contracts with thousands of companies, including many of America's largest.

All this complexity produced revenue benefits, yes, but it was complicated to manage and confusing for customers. And its effectiveness was eroding anyway as low-cost carriers tore down what airlines like Delta called "fences"—to keep high-budget travelers away from low fares—such as the Saturday night-stay requirements.

So Delta began experimenting. In Cincinnati it converted to more of an LCC-type fare structure, "SimpliFares," understanding it would lose some revenue from its highest-paying customers but hoping it might make up for that by stimulating volume and winning back some customers from nearby airports like Dayton, where AirTran was expanding. As Grinstein recalled years later, explaining the decision: "Every focus group, every analytic group, every significant advisor you talk to will tell you: Why do people pick a certain airline? Price. You want evidence of it? Southwest."

The whole plan, from the pay cuts to the big bang at Atlanta and SimpliFares at Cincinnati and everything in between, targeted $5 billion in annual cash savings by 2006, including some previously announced revenue and cost initiatives. The plan had a name too: ACES. That stood for 1) achieve viability, 2) create a customer-focused culture, 3) excel in operational performance and 4) sustain profitable growth. But while using the plan as a foundation to generate hope and optimism, Grinstein simultaneously warned that "bankruptcy is a real possibility. We're working hard and fast to avoid it, but if the pilot early retirement issue is not resolved before the end of the month, or if all of the pieces don't come together in the near term, we will have to restructure through the courts."

Cognizant of the bankruptcy threat, ALPA on Sept. 20 accepted an "interim agreement" that enabled pilots who elected early retirement to return to work, essentially as temporary private contractors. In exchange, Delta agreed to limits, valid until Feb. 1, 2005, on its ability to terminate pensions should it enter bankruptcy.

And entering bankruptcy was still very much a possibility, one that gripped Delta's employees, customers, suppliers and hub cities with apprehension and uncertainty. Back in May, management had taken a major step toward preparing for the worst by hiring the Blackstone Group, a high-powered Wall Street firm, as a bankruptcy advisor. Then a group of Delta's creditors formed a committee to negotiate with the airline in the event it filed for Chapter 11 court protection. By autumn, the airline's auditors began to question its ability to survive. Many pilots were worried, with some urging their union to offer deeper concessions. By autumn, ALPA was offering roughly $700 million in givebacks, still well below the $1 billion Grinstein was demanding. Reuters reported Delta had the sixth most short-sold stock on the entire New York stock exchange. Traders, in other words, were betting on bankruptcy.

As September gave way to October, with Delta burning through $4 million of cash each day, oil prices crossed the psychologically terrifying $50 mark, a level that had been unthinkable just months earlier. And it wasn't just the extreme level that hurt but also the volatility, which made planning for the future impossible. Draconian as a $5 billion restructuring plan might have seemed, would it even be enough? That depended entirely on the future price of oil. Making matters worse, Delta and Northwest were the only completely unhedged U.S. airlines. ALPA, meanwhile, was equally at the mercy of oil markets. Deregulation after 1978 had caused a huge transfer of wealth from airline workers to airline consumers, highlighted by endless labor concessions and falling fares. Now, falling fares were still pressuring airlines to reduce their labor costs even as high oil prices were adding to the pressure. Money was shifting from the pockets of pilots to not only the pockets of American consumers, as had been the case for 25 years, but also now to the coffers of companies like Aramco and ExxonMobil and countries like Russia, Iran, Venezuela and Saudi Arabia.

ALPA chief John Malone was conflicted. As the head of the union's negotiating committee, he had won his members the lucrative 2001 contract. He knew what had happened to Delta's close rival Eastern, which was relegated to the dustbin of history when its mechanics staged a strike at the carrier's most vulnerable hour. He also understood as well as anyone that his job was an elected position—and that presiding over major concessions was a sure recipe for losing support among the rank and file. United's pilot union leader Paul Whiteford had failed to win reelection in 2003 after presiding over steep pay cuts. With George W. Bush in the White House, Malone also didn't have a man in the White House to whom he could turn for possible support, less so because Delta was based in Georgia, a state Bush was guaranteed to win in the upcoming presidential election (whereas he might, some analysts believed, help US Airways in order to help himself win votes in more closely contested Pennsylvania, where that airline had two hubs). In the meantime, ALPA's own finances, dependent on member dues, were themselves deteriorating as the industry's pilot workforce shrank.

Whatever his reservations, Malone was telegraphing a willingness to deal. On Oct. 3, he told the *Atlanta Journal-Constitution* management was "doing things they should have done three years ago... I'm glad the company is taking a hard look at its revenue and coming up with a business plan to make the corporation financially viable," he said. Seven days later, incidentally, another *AJC* article quoted Dick Bressler, a former Burlington Northern chairman who had recruited Grinstein to the railroad's board in the 1980s, questioning why Grinstein took the Delta CEO job. "I told him early on I thought he ought to have his head examined for taking it on," Bressler told the newspaper. "He is spending some of the best years of his life in what I would regard as a thankless task."

Finally, on Oct. 28, 2004, a pilot union whose members were earning more than its industry colleagues and a CEO who was earning less than his industry colleagues announced the news that everyone was awaiting: They had reached a long-elusive $1 billion concession deal. About two thirds of the savings would come from lower pay, with the rest coming from medical benefit givebacks, a switch to defined-contribution pension plans for newly hired pilots, longer work hours and less sick pay. Delta also won the right to outsource more regional flying and use larger 70-seat regional jets to complement the 50-seaters. These 70-seaters, importantly, offered better economics (still two pilots and two engines, and just one more flight attendant, but 20 more revenue-producing passengers) at a time of rising fuel prices. Pilots did, however, win stock options, although they failed to get a seat on Delta's board of directors.

Grinstein was naturally pleased at having finally struck a deal. But "we weren't spiking the ball in the end zone," he recalled. "This was not the time to do the rooster strut or anything. I was not celebratory at all. I can't even say it was a relief, in the sense that we were looking at as, 'Oh my God, do you realize we still have to climb Everest?'"

Once pilots ratified the deal in early November, the centerpiece of Delta's turn-around effort was in place. But Delta hadn't yet escaped the jaws of bankruptcy. The company still needed an immediate injection of capital, which it got, and not from a traditional bank nor by issuing new bonds. Instead, it turned to a business partner that was terrified of seeing Delta disappear. American Express, best known for its credit cards, earned money from Delta in many ways, including millions of dollars in commissions when it sold Delta flights to business travelers—Amex, as it happens, operated the largest corporate travel agency in the world. But credit cards are indeed its biggest business, and its most profitable cards are those that award Delta SkyMiles to Amex "members" who hold the cards. With "co-branded" credit cards (whether an Amex card that awards Delta SkyMiles or a Citibank Visa or MasterCard that awards American AAdvangtage miles), the card-issuing bank actually purchases the miles—billions of miles, a penny or so at a time—from the airline and passes those miles along to the cardholders. The banks are happy to do that because they earn far more than they spend thanks to merchant fees of several pennies on the dollar every time a cardholder buys something, not to mention annual fees, interest charges and so forth. If Delta collapsed, so would the popularity of Amex's most lucrative credit cards.

So Amex essentially gave Delta $600 million as advance payment for future SkyMiles, a gamble it was willing to take now that pilot concessions were in place. General Electric, which provided Delta with $761 million in capital in early 2003, also came back with additional financing help—GE too, recall, is not only a financier but also an important supplier, in its case of jet engines. For good measure, Delta also pulled off a "debt swap" with bondholders and sold Orbitz shares.

By then more of Delta's top executives were gone, including its customer service chief Vicky Escarra and the man behind Song, John Selvaggio. Mullin, incidentally, was now working as an advisor to Goldman Sachs, the esteemed and highly profitable Wall Street investment bank. (Northwest's CEO Richard Anderson, meanwhile, had left the airline for a more lucrative job running United Healthcare.) In Europe, Greece had enjoyed a successful Olympics during the summer, even if it did borrow gargantuan sums of money to pull it off. Back in the U.S., meanwhile, the Boston Red Sox, of all teams, won baseball's World Series for the first time in 86 years.

President Bush, in the end, won his hard-fought reelection against a Massachusetts senator. Not the one who spearheaded airline deregulation in the 1970s—that was Ted Kennedy—but John Kerry, who might have lost partly because... well... he didn't look like a guy who would fly economy. More substantively, he had also initially voted to support Bush's increasingly unpopular and chaotic war in Iraq. Because of that, criticizing the war's execution proved a difficult rhetorical line to walk. In any event, Kerry's campaign had gotten a bit of a boost when a little-known young senator from Illinois named Barack Obama delivered an energetic keynote address at the Democratic National Convention in Boston.

On the airline battlefield, the final weeks of 2004 failed to bring much relief from intense price competition and high fuel prices. And on Christmas Day, Delta was hit with a computer outage that badly disrupted Comair's flights. Grinstein took another pay cut, but other top Delta brass received a dollop of new stock options just days after pilots ratified their concessions. Naturally, ALPA howled.

There were, however, some encouraging signs that the oversupply of seats might ease. Independence Air, after losing $83 million from July through September—the only quarter when it might have hoped to break even—was already on the verge of bankruptcy and didn't appear long for the world. More reputable low-cost carriers, other than well-hedged Southwest, were no less welcoming of high fuel prices than their legacy peers. AirTran, in fact, was losing money on its new California routes and abandoned a plan to feed traffic into Atlanta with 50-seat regional jets operated by a regional partner. Its initial returns in Dallas weren't terribly promising, and it slowed capacity growth overall. JetBlue too complained of an extremely tough fare environment, even as it continued to collect fares well above what Song was getting on the same routes. JetBlue had the added worry of finding homes for a large number of its newly ordered 100-seat Embraer jets, the economics of which were already looking less attractive in a world of $50-per-barrel oil.

As troubled as Delta was, if misery loves company, Delta could take some solace in knowing *every* legacy airline was doing worse than forecast. They were all similarly asking for worker concessions while uncomfortably adjusting to a new world of extreme fuel prices and ubiquitous low-fare competition. Northwest, in fact, clinched pilot concessions in November, just as Delta did.

Then there was the curious case of US Airways. After filing for bankruptcy protection in 2002, it cut costs, terminated pension plans, secured new capital with the help of a federal loan guarantee and emerged, in March 2003, a slimmed-down version of its former self. But relentless attacks by Southwest, in particular, left it no better off, and on September 12, 2004, it was back in the bankruptcy court—"Chapter 22" (i.e., 11 times two), went the macabre joke in bankruptcy lawyer circles—this time with far less hope of emerging alive. That, naturally, presented an enticing prospect for Delta: One of its closest rivals, one with a major presence in many of its key east coast markets, could liquidate. If nothing else, it might dismantle itself piece by piece, with stronger carriers circling like buzzards overhead as it contemplated divestiture of valuable real estate at airports like Reagan National in Washington and LaGuardia in New York. For the time being, US Airways—whose new CEO Bruce Lakefield was a former Lehman Brothers executive—was flooding the market with cheap "GoFares," adding flights to Europe from Philadelphia, winning yet another round of concessions from pilots, obtaining more financial assistance from General Electric and building a small Caribbean hub in Fort Lauderdale, the brainchild of its marketing chief Ben Baldanza.

US Airways was, in other words, still part of the problem as the calendar turned to 2005. But if it really were to disappear, its absence could very well be part of the solution.

2005

"They were competing for 'Who's the dumbest airline in America?'"

D oug Parker was riding high on Sept. 1, 2001. Not yet 40 years old, that day he became chief executive officer of America West Airlines, the eighth largest airline in the United Sates, behind only the Big Six (American, United, Delta, Northwest, Continental and US Airways) and Southwest. America West had 146 airplanes, 12,000 workers and $2 billion in annual revenue. Parker, the son of a supermarket executive, had an impressive airline resume. He had, since 1995, already served as America West's CFO under its CEO William Franke (who would later become a legend in "ultra-low-cost" airline investment and management) following five years as a vice president at Northwest Airlines and—first—a job at Robert Crandall's American Airlines after completing his MBA at Vanderbilt University in 1986.

Nothing, however, could have fully prepared him for what happened 10 days later. Doug Parker's job after the 9/11 terrorist attacks became a fight for survival. Up to that point, America West had indeed been a survivor. The brainchild of an entrepreneur named Ed Beauvais, it launched in 1983, five years after deregulation, from the fast-growing Sun Belt city of Phoenix. The early days were promising: America West was making money by 1985, becoming the second largest post-deregulation startup behind only People Express. But like People Express, it wildly over-expanded. After selling 20 percent of itself to an Australian airline in 1987, it applied to serve Sydney and Tokyo, failing to secure flight rights but still determined to reach Asia. So it flew to Nagoya instead, just as the Japanese economy was deflating. It flew to Honolulu too, ordered giant 747s and a large number of Airbus 320 shorthaul airplanes while buying some 757s from a withering Eastern. America West started a hub in Las Vegas, formed alliances with Continental and Mesa, tried to buy the Eastern Shuttle (but was outbid by Donald Trump), toyed with the idea of taking control of American's San Jose hub and expanded into the northeast.

Such frenetic growth, as well as head-to-head competition against Southwest, caused America West to lose money in six of its first nine years, culminating with bankruptcy in 1991 after fuel prices spiked and the economy tanked. But it managed to stay alive with support from aircraft lessors and several Phoenix institutions, including the Arizona Cardinals football team. America West eventually got out of bankruptcy with financing from the investor David Bonderman and his Texas Pacific Group, which also controlled Continental.

The rest of the 1990s saw construction of a hub in Columbus, Ohio; heavy use of overnight "red-eye" flying; and decent profits during boom years like 1997 and 1998, mixed with episodes of labor unrest and a less-than-stellar reputation for operational integrity. In 1999, United offered to buy America West, and Delta and American looked at buying it too, according to a *Wall Street Journal* account at the time. But it remained independent.

It was in 1995 that America West made arguably its most fateful move: It hired Doug Parker, then 35, to be its CFO. In an interview a few years later with the *Arizona Republic*, Parker described his days as a football player at Albion College, his experience running with the bulls in Pamplona and his penchant for baseball statistics when he was a child rooting for Pete Rose and the Reds in Cincinnati—giant Kroger, based there, was the grocery chain where Parker's father had risen up the ranks from meat cutter to executive.

That same year, America West also hired Scott Kirby, a numbers-crunching Air Force Academy graduate with an MBA (from George Washington University) in operations research. After 9/11, it was Kirby who Parker, now CEO, tapped to oversee many aspects of America West's corporate strategy, including its pricing and revenue management. Parker, meanwhile, had a more immediate task after the attacks: fly to Washington and convince Congress to authorize federal loan guarantees—and then the new Air Transportation Stabilization Board to agree to one. America West was the first airline to apply, in fact, with support from Senator John McCain of Arizona. The effort worked. In December, the ATSB granted a $380 million loan guarantee. America West avoided bankruptcy. Parker had made his case by convincing the Feds of his seriousness about turning the carrier around, citing concessions from Airbus and GE as evidence they had faith too. In exchange for the support, though, the ATSB demanded he control labor costs. It also got the option to buy a third of the airline, giving taxpayers a lot of upside if the airline did manage to turn itself around.

"I think," Parker said in a conference call shortly before getting the government aid, "we are in as difficult a time in our industry as we've ever faced. And in that environment, America West is outperforming.... Our load factors are well ahead of the industry average. While we're seeing declines, they are lower than the industry is seeing in aggregate. Our [profit] margins are... higher than the industry average, and we are running as good of an operation as we have ever run."

With fares down approximately 20 percent, America West slashed its flight schedule by 20 percent and cut 2,000 of its 14,000 jobs. Still, a lot more work remained. Parker and Kirby closed the Columbus hub, among other strategic retreats. And they experimented with two bold moves: charging for inflight meals—something that would, years later, become commonplace throughout the industry but that, among U.S. airlines, started at America West—and simplifying fares, not unlike Delta's later 2004 SimpliFares experiment, but in America West's case in a way that proved smart for a low-cost carrier in its position. Now, no economy fare was more than $299 each way, which helped America West poach price-sensitive small business travelers from rivals—a business class cabin, like AirTran but unlike most LCCs, helped in that regard too. Kirby would later (in January 2005) tell Dow Jones that if other airlines had matched these fares back in 2003, he would have reversed course and reverted back to the higher, more complicated fare structure. "Our worst-case scenario," he said, "was that everyone matched us."

"Our goal, frankly, was to shift market share," he added. "We made a calculated gamble that the Big Six carriers could not afford to match our fare structure and, as a result, we would be able to steal market share from the Big Six carriers. And that is in fact what happened."

But America West nonetheless lost $148 million in 2001, $377 million in 2002, $10 million in 2003 (excluding federal government grant money) and $106 million in 2004. Its staying power remained questionable—compared to larger airlines, it had less collateral for borrowing, less clout with suppliers and no giant frequent flier plan that a giant credit card-issuing global bank would go to great lengths to save. What it did have, at the end of 2004, was almost $800 million in debt.

This hardly seems the profile of an airline seeking to buy another airline. Still, America West carefully considered buying ATA, mostly for its valuable Chicago Midway airport gates. But in late 2004, ATA filed for bankruptcy, and Southwest outmaneuvered AirTran for its Midway gates, with America West on the sidelines. Parker and Kirby believed their airline was dangerously small. To survive, it would somehow need to get bigger.

For Delta, on the other hand, size was the least of its problems. At the start of 2005, even after three years of shrinking, it still had more than 500 airplanes, more than any of its rivals except American. It still had its mighty Atlanta hub too and its highly profitable SkyMiles frequent flier plan. The SkyTeam alliance was stronger than ever, fortified by the entry of Continental and Northwest and by Air France's giant merger with KLM. And now, for a change, there was a sense of optimism in the air—not euphoria, by any means, but a sense that a hellish chapter in Delta's long and illustrious history might be closing.

The wounded giant did, after all, have a new transformation plan in place, with bold new initiatives like quitting its hopeless struggle in Dallas and, finally, a new pilot contract that promised $1 billion in annual savings. Non-fuel unit costs in the final quarter of 2004, in fact, had fallen by no less than 13 percent. Delta was—to be perfectly clear—still no AirTran or Southwest or JetBlue. But it didn't need to be. It just had to ensure the cost gap wasn't too wide, because it did, after all, have a revenue advantage thanks to everything the low-cost airlines lacked: the global network, the giant frequent flier plan, the premium amenities and so on.

At the start of 2005, Delta's balance sheet was plump with $1.8 billion in unrestricted cash, boosted by the major financing deals it had struck with GE and American Express during its escape a few months earlier from the jaws of bankruptcy. Airplanes were getting new interiors. Flight attendants were getting new uniforms. And there was reason to hope the bloody fare war raging up and down the U.S. east coast, the consequence of excess capacity and irrational pricing, might be on the verge of easing. Independence Air, with its nutty business plan, had filled an astonishingly low 54 percent of its seats during 2004's peak summer quarter despite its bargain fares—it almost literally, in other words, couldn't give away seats—and was, by autumn, already flirting with bankruptcy. Also in the autumn, United said it would cut domestic capacity 12 percent, which followed America West's raising of the white flag on transcontinental routes. Virgin America's launch efforts, led by Fred Reid, were bogged down by protests that Richard Branson's involvement would violate U.S. airline foreign ownership restrictions—he could, remember, own up to a quarter of a U.S. airline's voting shares, but he couldn't "control" it, a term whose definition was a matter of debate. And most enticingly, giant US Airways, Delta's closest competitor in terms of route map overlap, was mired in its second bankruptcy and heading toward liquidation. This seemed even more probable after Southwest said it would challenge US Airways at its already-struggling Pittsburgh hub.

Delta, furthermore, was encouraged by the early results of its new SimpliFares pricing experiment in Cincinnati, where it was winning traffic back from nearby airports, most notably Dayton. As a result, on Jan. 5, 2005, the airline said it would expand the concept to all its domestic routes. This was "not a fare sale," it explained, but a means to compete more effectively against low-cost airlines by capping even Delta's most expensive, fully flexible economy fares at $499 each way. Domestic first class would be capped at $599. This meant a price cut of as much as 50 percent on some routes. Never would Delta charge more than that on any domestic route, even if supply and demand conditions supported charging something higher. Gone was the Saturday night-stay requirement, the longstanding poison pill to prevent business travelers from grabbing cheap seats—few companies would force their employees to spend a weekend away from home just for a cheap ticket.

Negotiated discounts for corporations would be scaled back. The simpler approach would be easier for Delta's staff to manage and communicate, and it would foster more online bookings.

America West, remember, had converted its traditional fare structure to a SimpliFares-type approach in 2003, and the results were encouraging. More recently,

American had begun experimenting with the idea at its Miami hub. Alaska Airlines, Air Canada and even Aer Lingus in Ireland were now using simplified fare structures. Delta, meanwhile, reminded investors it was doing this despite scoffs and eye-rolls from competitors like Continental because Delta was most exposed, among legacy airlines, to LCCs. By Delta's count, 70 percent of its passengers already had access to LCC-style pricing anyway. And its average domestic flight was relatively short—66 percent of its revenues came from short- and medium-haul routes for which a top one-way economy-class fare of $499 isn't all that low—imagine $998 roundtrip for a 260-mile trip between Atlanta and Charleston, a fare that would more than cover Delta's costs.

A leaner cost structure, a reinforced cash stash, the prospect of key rivals disappearing and early success with its new fare structure were reasons enough to think Delta's outlook was brightening. And there was more. The U.S. economy was suddenly as perky as the Gwen Stefani song "Hollaback Girl" that was then permeating the airwaves. The residential real estate market was now downright bullish, with home prices rising faster than the books about a boy named Harry Potter were selling. Forget the internet bubble of the late 1990s. This was more like the even more extreme roaring 1920s, with people now voraciously buying houses like they bought shares of stock back then. With the prices of their homes continuously rising, Americans were in a spending mood, with no shortage of cheaply imported Chinese goods from which to choose. They spent, naturally, on air travel too, with America's airline traffic, sure enough, returning to pre-9/11 levels in 2004 and in fact setting an all-time annual record. Average fares per mile, or yields, remained 13 percent lower than they were before 9/11. But then again, the price of just about everything was falling, the big exception being commodities like oil.

Falling prices for goods signaled to the Federal Reserve, the keeper of America's money supply—whose chief concern was *rising* prices—that it could keep interest rates low, which it did. But America's money supply was growing enormously. In effect, the giant sums of money that Americans were sending to China in exchange for cheap goods—and to Saudi Arabia and elsewhere in exchange for expensive oil—were being recycled back into the U.S. financial system. How? By China buying U.S. treasury bonds, which it did to keep its own currency weak and hence its exports cheap. And by Saudi Arabia and other oil producers similarly re-investing their suddenly surging wealth in the U.S. by, for example, depositing their money in U.S. bank accounts. When a financial system is awash in capital, the price of borrowing money plummets—all the more so with the central bank, in the U.S.'s case its Federal Reserve, not raising interest rates. And the pressure to compete for new borrowers intensifies.

This was not an entirely new story. During the oil boom of the 1970s, U.S. banks were similarly awash in capital reinvested by countries like Saudi Arabia—and those banks felt similar pressure to find new borrowers to whom they could loan all that money and charge interest. The answer then? Emerging market governments in

Latin America, which in the end borrowed way too much and couldn't repay their debts. The answer this time? American homebuyers, even those with "subprime" credit histories, as the euphemism described them. But this time would be different, the thinking went, because large numbers of these subprime loans could be packaged together, and the risk of 100 borrowers all simultaneously defaulting was not as likely as any one individual borrower defaulting. With the subprime borrowers paying higher interest rates than prime borrowers, the whole "tranche," or package of loans, could still be profitable even if one or two borrowers indeed defaulted. So banks made the loans, and Wall Street sold packages of loans to investors—sold them extremely well thanks to the triple-A credit ratings they were given by the same ratings agencies that since 9/11 had been rapidly downgrading Delta's credit rating.

In any event, all this lending and borrowing seemed, for the time being, like productive lending and borrowing. A booming housing market meant lots of new domestic jobs—you can't build a single-family house in China and ship it across the ocean. And it meant lots of new consumer spending, the sort of spending that's responsible for roughly 70 percent of U.S. economic production. So there it was: an economic boom in full bloom by 2005.

For airlines like Delta, there was another important angle to this boom. Driven in large part by America's spending boom, China, the oil-producing nations and other emerging markets were themselves booming. China's story perhaps mattered most. It had spent the first half of the 20th century literally dominated by foreign powers, including the U.S., Europe and most notably Japan. That ended with Japan's defeat in World War II and Chairman Mao's victory in the Chinese civil war, which ushered in a second half of the 20th century characterized by self-imposed famines and social chaos. By the time of Mao's death in 1976, China's economy was as primitive as ever, dominated by rural farmers living in medieval conditions. Everything started to change with Deng Xiaoping's decision to open the country to foreign trade and remove its suffocating laws against free enterprise, if not against other freedoms. In the ensuing quarter century, China would see the greatest and fastest advancement of wealth in the history of humanity. By 2005, it was on its way to passing Japan to become the world's second largest economy, and it was obtaining enormous geopolitical influence in the process. It also, not trivially, had established a thriving airline industry of its own, not to mention a host of airline markets that foreign airlines were eager to serve.

China's boom was most spectacular, but it was hardly alone. By the mid-2000s, India—the world's second most populous country after China—was booming too, not so much by exporting cheaply made manufactured goods to Americans but by selling them services like help with computer software, accounting and customer service. Whatever they might have thought of it, Americans became familiar with this when they called their airlines to change their flights, only to be greeted by an accented agent in Chennai. Southeast Asia was booming too, led by the dynamism of new low-cost airlines like Malaysia-based AirAsia. The boom was equally robust in commodity-rich places like the Arabian Peninsula and Russia with their oil, Latin America with its soybeans and copper and Australia with its iron ore and coal—China needed these commodities to manufacture its cheap goods. Even Europe was enjoying a measure of prosperity, its growth rates a bit sluggish but its real estate booming in Spain and Ireland, its financial institutions booming in the U.K., its exports booming in Germany and so on. The world economy was more globalized than ever, and people were benefiting worldwide.

All this was enticing but frustrating for Delta. It was still, after all, the least global of America's global airlines.

Grinstein was determined to take advantage of the international boom somehow, not least because in international markets, low-cost carrier exposure would nearly disappear—Southwest, for example, had never set foot outside the U.S., even to the near abroad. One of Grinstein's chief priorities, therefore, was finding a network planning executive who understood international markets.

And so it was: a refreshingly optimistic start to 2005—but one with a catch. When Grinstein and his team devised their turnaround plan, the goal was to boost revenues and lower costs enough so the airline could comfortably make money at $40-per-barrel oil. This seemed a conservative enough estimate: If anything, $40 was high by recent standards, well above oil's $30 average in 2000, $26 in 2001, $26 again in 2002 and $31 in 2003. In 2004, the price had jumped to an average of $42, but futures markets, where commodity traders bet on such things, suggested $40 oil for 2005 was a sound assumption.

That assumption, however, was already looking dubious just one quarter into 2005. In January, oil prices averaged $47. In February, they rose to $48. Then in March, they jumped to $54, the highest they had ever been in nominal terms (i.e., not adjusting for inflation). Even adjusting for inflation, crude oil was pricier than at any time since the early 1980s. The result: another colossal net loss, this time $684 million, excluding special items. These losses, moreover, were especially painful for a company with $7 billion in operating losses from 2001 through 2004, $21 billion in debt, no more collateral to pledge for new loans and outstanding loans from Amex and GE that came with strict conditions: If Delta's cash balance or core operating earnings fell below certain levels, the lenders could demand immediate repayment in full, an impossibility thanks to all the debt.

Oil, indeed, was the killer in the first quarter of 2005. Delta's labor costs actually fell 12 percent even as capacity increased 6 percent. In that regard, the airline was, in other words, producing more for less, the very definition of economic progress. But it was producing more for more—a lot more—in terms of what it was now paying for jet fuel. Fuel outlays in the quarter skyrocketed 54 percent compared to the same period a year earlier, with average prices spiking from 95 cents to $1.42 per gallon. "Today's financial results clearly are disappointing," Grinstein said in an April 21 conference call with Wall Street. "Record-breaking fuel prices are masking the many crucial, large-scale, core initiatives our airline implemented during the quarter. The issue is simple: Including fuel, Delta is not on plan, but excluding fuel, we are better than plan."

Fuel, however, wasn't the only killer. Even setting fuel aside, the rest of Delta's optimism wasn't so justified after all. The SimpliFares campaign, as was fast becoming evident, wasn't off to a good start. On the contrary, it was costing Delta millions in lost revenue as share shift—in other words, traffic it expected to steal from others— never materialized nationwide to nearly the degree it had in the Cincinnati petri dish. For LCC competitors, it was mostly a non-event: Delta had always matched their fares. As AirTran's Joe Leonard recalled years later: "That was a frontal assault designed to take us out, [but] it was a disaster for Delta and, for that matter, the rest of the industry. It cost the industry billions of dollars."

Delta's legacy rivals—United, American, Continental, Northwest and US Airways—all felt compelled to match Delta's new pricing structure, obliterating any chance of Delta winning share from them. Worse yet, the new fare caps prevented airlines from raising the only prices they could have raised to help offset fuel inflation. Business travel fares, after all, were purchased by travelers with inelastic demand—they needed to go and were ready to pay what was necessary. Northwest was least exposed to LCCs, among the most exposed to high labor costs and blessed with an unmatched degree of pricing power in markets like the Dakotas ignored by most airlines—"it's cold, it's dark and it's all ours," managers at the airline's headquarters in Eagan, near Minneapolis, would say to each other, describing the U.S. region known as the Upper Midwest. Northwest didn't match the new fare structure everywhere—or *anywhere*, where it could avoid doing so. But in a competitive industry, it had no choice but to match it for connecting itineraries (i.e., a customer flying from Indianapolis to Buffalo, who could choose to connect on Northwest in Detroit or Delta in Cincinnati) and nonstop itineraries where it overlapped with Delta, such as flights from Cincinnati to Detroit—if Northwest didn't match, its planes would fly empty. Customers got the benefit. "There are many things that may make people happy," Tim Griffin, a Northwest executive vice president, said dryly during an earnings conference call with analysts, "but may not produce more revenue or be sustainable." Northwest agreed with an assessment from Continental that SimpliFares was costing the industry "a couple hundred million dollars."

Continental, estimating the impact of SimpliFares (which it called "Simply Stupid Fares") on its own income, said in late January it was losing about $10 million to $12 million monthly because of the move. "They misread the competition" Gordon Bethune remarked years later. "They were competing for 'Who's the dumbest airline in America?'"

He continued: "These guys were acting stupid.... Here's a company based in Atlanta, which had one of the strongest balance sheets in the history of aviation.... And they took that thing and threw it in the crapper."

Shortly after Delta's announcement, the wire service Dow Jones quoted Scott Kirby, who would soon be president of US Airways: "My first thought is, it's going to be extremely expensive for the major carriers.... It's going to significantly impact their revenue in 2005." America West's decision to offer simplified pricing, by contrast, had worked because it was a smallish airline that bigger players didn't feel the need to match. "Kirby," Dow Jones continued, "also said he thinks the risk of revenue reduction for Delta is greater than it was for his airline. America West only derived about 5 percent of its revenue from the top fare classes before the airline cut those fares. Delta derived 10 percent of its revenue from the top fare classes." Delta, in other words, was hurting its competitors. But it was hurting itself more.

Sure enough, Delta's passenger yields—how many cents passengers paid, on average, to fly one mile—dropped 8 percent during the first quarter. Flights were indeed fuller, as Delta had hoped. But not full enough to make up for the dramatic drop in fares. So the most important revenue measure of all, unit revenue—in other words, the amount Delta earned, on average, every time one seat flew one mile, averaging both occupied and vacant seats—was down 3 percent.

Looking back years later, Grinstein acknowledged the error, which he would recall as one of his biggest while running Delta.

"It worked in Cincinnati," he said. "So then we thought if it works there, maybe we should expand it. Mistake. It didn't, and it became expensive.... When you're running a major airline, you take chances, and some of them you're gonna screw up, and that was one of them." The episode was reminiscent of American's Value Pricing in the early 1990s, a similar move to simplify fares that similarly flopped. But for now, Delta's new fares were in place, and they were depriving Delta and its competition of badly needed revenue.

Delta had other problems too. It was glad to be out of Dallas, but now it had to reposition all the planes that had been based there. It had to make mortgage or lease payments regardless of what it did with them—better to fly them somewhere and earn some revenue rather than just ground them. So now Atlanta had more than 1,000 daily flights, more than any other hub in the history of commercial aviation. Other planes went to Salt Lake City and Cincinnati, which probably had too much capacity to begin with, relative to demand—and excess capacity relative to demand leads to low fares. Still others were assigned to non-hub, point-to-point routes, which by nature are tougher markets to crack because companies in these cities generally don't have corporate contracts with Delta, because travelers in these cities aren't generally loyal to Delta and because the flights can't be filled with connecting traffic from across a broad network. The result: further downward pressure on fares throughout Delta's network.

Back on Jan. 31, Operation Clockwork (the "big bang") had, among other things, de-banked the Atlanta hub to keep airplanes in the air more hours per day, even if average connecting times in Atlanta were a bit longer than they had been when the hub had more traditional "banks" or "waves" of flights. That made Delta's itineraries a bit less attractive, which meant lower airfares. It also meant even more capacity growth—and, by extension, even *more* downward pressure on airfares. Worse yet, the unit cost benefits associated with more intense aircraft usage were now decreasing, because fuel prices made all flights more costly. When fuel was cheap, most of a flight's costs were fixed—you paid them whether the plane was in the air or on the ground, so might as well fly it and collect some revenue. The intense utilization model was what had made Southwest the most successful airline in the history of the world: If it got more use out of its aircraft than its competitors, its cost of carrying each passenger one mile was lower than its competitors' costs of doing the same thing and so, as a result, it was more profitable. But not anymore. Now a big chunk of a flight's costs—fuel—was a *variable* rather than fixed expense. Now, flying a plane more actually did cost a lot more money. Delta, as was becoming obvious, had too many planes flying too many flights. And Atlanta's airport, not incidentally, simply couldn't handle the volume, causing terrible delays. "Everyone internally loved [operation Clockwork]," Joe Kolshak, Delta's operations chief at the time, recalled. "But the problem was, we're pretty much telling the passengers, 'This is when you're traveling, because this is good for us'" rather than trying to match schedules with what passengers really wanted.

There was yet another problem, this one also linked to fuel's impact on the basic tenets of airline economics: Delta had too many 50-seat jets. As late as February 2004, with fuel prices already on the rise, Delta was still buying Canadair regional jets, ordering 32 CRJ-200s for delivery in 2005. By the start of 2005, it had no fewer than 229 50-seat regional jets. Once upon a time, these planes had been all-star performers for Delta. Now they were liabilities.

Delta's pension obligations, in the meantime, continued to drain enormous sums of cash, with funding requirements for 2005 expected to reach nearly a half billion dollars. Competition, meanwhile, wasn't easing quite as Delta had hoped, with Independence Air—however obvious its ultimate fate might have been—now deploying larger Airbus 319s on transcontinental routes, JetBlue expanding in Boston, AirTran entering Charlotte and US Airways extending its life with new financing from its regional partners. Early pilot retirements remained vexing. When customers purchased Delta tickets with credit cards in advance of their flights, the credit card processing companies involved in the transaction refused to give Delta the cash until after it operated the flights, because the processors worried about Delta's ability to stay in business. This created a vicious cycle: The worried processing companies withheld cash, which hurt Delta's cash position even more—a self-fulfilling prophesy. And sure enough, Delta, its optimism now vanished, was using the "b" word again.

Bankruptcy, though, was not going to happen without a fight. Going to the courts might be good medicine for eradicating debt and undesirable contracts. But bankruptcy also usually means wiping out shareholders, to whom management is ultimately responsible. So at any company, management's job is to do everything possible to keep a company out of bankruptcy until it enters what lawyers call a "zone of insolvency"—a situation where bankruptcy is practically unavoidable. Bankruptcy creates great hardship for employees too. And the fate of a bankrupt company falls into the hands of high-priced consultants, lawyers and a bankruptcy judge listening to the demands of creditors—in other words, those to whom the company owed money before determining it couldn't pay its bills.

The spring brought no relief from fuel prices, although a few new tactical offensives had begun. Delta unveiled a new advertising campaign with the tagline "Good Goes Around," a feel-good what-goes-around-comes-around theme. Delta closed reservation centers in Boston and Los Angeles. And it installed new revenue management software that could forecast demand not just for individual flights but for total journeys, an important upgrade for an airline that handled more connecting passengers than most.

The idea of airline revenue management is to fill a flight with people paying as much as they, individually, are willing to pay (or for the ones who pay the most of all, how much their *employers* are willing to pay on their behalf). A business traveler who needs to rush to Chicago for a last-minute meeting might be willing to pay $1,000 for the flight, because the meeting might seal a million-dollar deal. Airlines would love to fill flights with only travelers like that. But there aren't enough of those people to go around. So airlines have to take what they can get from everyone else. And sometimes they might be willing to take not very much at all, because almost any revenue is better than an empty seat, which airlines consider "spoilage"—just as a bakery might be willing to discount day-old bread rather than throwing it away and getting no money at all for it, an airline might be willing to sell the last few seats on a flight for very little rather than getting no money at all for them. Once a flight departs with empty seats, those seats have "spoiled."

So ideally, from their perspective, airlines would love to auction all the seats on a flight, ensuring all seats are filled with people paying as much as they are willing to pay. In reality, that's impossible for many reasons, including the fact that the people who are willing to pay the very most don't even know they'll be traveling until long after most other people have bought their tickets.

The next best solution is revenue management. Based on a number of factors, such as what happened on the same flight a year earlier, revenue management software, aided by human revenue management analysts, forecasts what the results of such an auction might be—one or two executives willing to pay a fortune to attend the million-dollar meeting, some other business travelers willing to pay quite a bit, someone going to a funeral willing to pay more than usual and so on down to the most discretionary leisure travelers, who won't travel at all unless the tickets are cheap. Based on that forecast, revenue managers allocate seats into various fare "buckets," as they call them. They'll sell some seats at deep discounts long before a flight—these are the day-old bread that they otherwise would never sell at all. But they'll resist the temptation to fill the flight with customers too soon. Instead, they'll hold aside a couple of very expensive seats for the executives, a few more rather expensive seats for the other business travelers and a few somewhat pricey seats for the funeral-goers. By the time these people book, either the cheap seats will be gone, or "fences" like Saturday night-stay requirements will prevent them from being sold, and the last-minute travelers will have little alternative but to pay more.

Airlines had, decades earlier, figured out how to revenue manage individual flights by using early-generation "segment-based" revenue management. But at Delta, where the majority of passengers are connecting through giant hubs like Atlanta, passengers aren't really booking individual segments. They're booking complex itineraries involving two or more segments in each direction. And what might seem to make sense for one flight might not make sense for an entire itinerary. Imagine a rather full flight from Savannah, Ga., to Atlanta. On a segment basis, Delta might be best served only accepting a very high fare for the few remaining seats. But what if someone from Savannah really wants to go not to Atlanta but to Tokyo—and that person is only willing to pay a discounted fare to Tokyo, but the discounted fare to Tokyo is much higher than the full fare to only Atlanta? In that case, Delta should probably accept the Tokyo passenger, even though the pro-rated Savannah-Atlanta fare for that trip might look rather low. This new "origin-and-destination-based" revenue management system, which replaced the old segment-based system, could properly do that math.

Back on the debt management front, Delta negotiated some relief from Amex and GE, which relaxed the covenants attached to their loans. It separately sold some Boeing 767s, removed spare planes on its corporate travel-rich shuttle routes in the northeast corridor (it had previously promised shuttle passengers a seat would always be available, even if it had to roll out a new airplane for just one extra passenger) and outsourced some maintenance jobs. Grinstein told senior executives they wouldn't be getting any bonuses for 2004. Delta's regional airline partner Republic Airways ordered new 70-seat jets to fly in Delta's network. Comair's pilots accepted a pay freeze in exchange for promises of future growth, although its mechanics rejected concessions. And speaking of Delta's wholly owned regional carriers, Grinstein now viewed Comair and Atlantic Southeast as potential sources of liquidity—if no one would lend the company any more money at tolerable interest rates, if nobody wanted to buy its stock and if it wasn't generating any profits from operations, then selling assets had to be on the table. Of course, nobody would pay anything close to what Delta originally paid for these two regional airlines—Comair's Christmas Day 2004 computer meltdown wasn't the reason for this, although it didn't help—but selling at a loss could make sense anyway given Delta's desperate need for cash to avoid bankruptcy.

If it was going to do that, the airline also needed to revitalize its route network. Song was still losing money and was still viewed skeptically by Grinstein, but closing it would take some effort—re-painting and reconfiguring planes, reassigning people, rewriting marketing budgets and so on. And by the spring of 2005, management had more immediate priorities. So Song lived on, moving into and out of routes haphazardly, with its increasingly uneconomical 757s pitted against JetBlue's newer, more fuel-efficient Airbus 320s. Most significantly, Song was retreating from Florida routes like Newark-Orlando and JFK-Fort Myers. Instead, it was competing against JetBlue on big-money transcontinental routes between the northeast corridor and California, the idea being that its product—which was in many ways better than what Delta mainline offered—would give it an edge on longer routes where things like inflight television mattered more. Song was, incidentally, still engaged in some bizarre and wasteful marketing campaigns, including one in which it teamed with the designer Henri Bendel to sell limited-edition Song blue jeans. It even started a Song record label "to create a unique platform for showcasing a diverse collection of recording artists," which some people joked would produce music that passengers could listen to while flying to Florida on JetBlue.

Although it was closing its reservation center in Boston, Delta remained committed to beating American, US Airways and JetBlue in that highly fragmented market. On March 23, Grinstein traveled to Boston's Logan International Airport, where he and Mitt Romney, the governor of Massachusetts, held a ceremony to inaugurate a new Delta terminal. Elsewhere, as a result of Operation Clockwork, Delta's summer schedule now featured 92 new routes, many from Atlanta, Cincinnati, Salt Lake City and New York JFK and others connecting various non-hub cities to Florida's key tourist markets, namely Orlando, Tampa and Fort Lauderdale. The planes for these new routes became available by flying each aircraft more hours per day and—more importantly—by closing 81 routes, all but 14 from Dallas-Fort Worth.

In the meantime, a far more important change was taking place, one that would have profound consequences for Delta in the years ahead. Recognizing the boom in international travel, and enticed by competing in a market where low-cost carriers weren't a factor, Delta grew its international capacity 20 percent in the first quarter of 2005, relative to the same quarter one year earlier, driven by new Atlanta and New York JFK routes to the Caribbean, Salt Lake City routes to Mexico, new Cincinnati flights to Amsterdam and Rome and a return to Buenos Aires from Atlanta. It also added Atlanta frequencies to Frankfurt, London's Gatwick Airport (it still wasn't allowed to serve Heathrow), São Paulo, Cancún and elsewhere. And Delta began applying for new routes like Atlanta-Moscow and Atlanta-Beijing, although it failed to win the latter following the U.S. DOT's decision to accept competing plans from American and Continental. All this was nothing terribly radical. But it was an important shift for an airline that got just 14 percent of its revenues from European routes, 4 percent from Latin America and the Caribbean and 1 percent from Asia.

Back at home, the industry was abuzz with rumors about something else. US Airways, still clinging to life thanks to $250 million in loans from its regional partners Air Wisconsin and Republic, was close to skirting liquidation once and for all by selling itself. But who would buy a dying carrier? On April 20, *The Wall Street Journal* reported "advance merger talks" between US Airways and America West, which was suddenly enjoying some of the strongest revenue gains in the industry, highlighted by an impressive 8 percent year-over-year unit revenue increase thanks to its deft new pricing and revenue management tactics; a more benign fare environment in its core western U.S. markets (and more specifically, a big pull-down by United in the western U.S.); strong performance in Mexico, where it didn't have to compete against its close rival Southwest; a casino-building boom in Las Vegas, where it had a hub; an enormous population boom in Phoenix, where it had an even bigger hub; housing booms in both of these cities; and—critically—a decision to buck the industry trend and *cut* capacity rather than growing it. In the first quarter, in fact, it was one of only three airlines to shrink compared to the same period a year earlier, the others being bankrupt United and ATA, the latter now controlled by Southwest. America West, recall, had itself considered buying ATA. What Doug Parker and his lieutenant Scott Kirby learned as they went through the exercise, however, was that buying a bankrupt airline had many advantages, including unusual flexibility in shedding unwanted assets. A significant change was taking place too: Aircraft lessors like GE were suddenly eager to take their planes out of the U.S., partly to reduce their exposure to the battered industry there but—just as importantly—to increase their exposure to airlines abroad, which needed more seats to address a surge in demand. Why not take planes from deadbeats like US Airways and find homes for them in China or Brazil?

This was little America West though, an airline with just $2 billion in annual revenues and 12,000 workers. How could it possibly buy US Airways, a $7 billion behemoth with 30,000 workers? It certainly didn't have the balance sheet muscle to do it on its own. There were other concerns too. In the first quarter, US Airways posted another mountain of losses, this time exceeding $100 million. More generally, airline mergers are inherently complex—in the past, more had gone wrong than right. Integrating unionized work groups, combining two different fleets and meshing highly intricate IT platforms had caused giant headaches for none other than US Airways itself, which was the product of messy past mergers with Piedmont Airlines and Pacific Southwest Airlines. Through the years, American purchased Air California, Reno Air and TWA—and regretted all three deals. Frank Lorenzo's airline empire collapsed after a succession of acquisitions. Pan Am's purchase of National Airlines was a colossal mistake. And so on. One of the very few successful mergers, in fact, was Delta's acquisition of Western Airlines, a success story written in part by Jerry Grinstein.

On April 21, one day after *The Wall Street Journal* reported America West's flirtations with US Airways, Grinstein told Wall Street analysts, "It may take a longer period of time, but I do think you're going to see consolidation." But as for America West and US Airways specifically, he warned, "If you are picking up a whole airline you've got all of the labor issues, the integration of the seniority systems and all of those barriers that in the past have caused costs to go up. Even though you may get rid of some overhead costs, your frontline costs tend to go up.

"Doug Parker," Grinstein continued, "is a smart, seasoned CEO, and he has tested this [with ATA], and I think he is also doing the same thing at US Airways. And I think he knows when to hold them and when to fold them. And so he is taking a look at what their business opportunities are. But in the immediate term, I think it is going to really be hard to put these companies together."

That wasn't how Parker saw it, other than perhaps the part about him being smart. Sure enough, on the evening of May 19, America West and US Airways announced their intention to join forces.

America West bought US Airways for several reasons, including the opportunity to join the Star Alliance; the synergies that would come from moving certain planes like 90-seat regional jets to the east coast, where they would generate more value; the fruits of cutting overhead; the immediate benefit of travelers feeling more confident about booking with US Airways, knowing it would actually still be flying by the time they traveled; the prospect of replacing money-losing transcontinental flying with inherently stronger hub-to-hub east-west flying; two bankruptcies' worth of cost cutting at US Airways—its labor costs had plummeted 26 percent year-over-year in the first quarter; and the opportunity to enhance the airlines' relevance in non-hub cities. "There is some value in here in what is commonly called the S-curve effect," Scott Kirby explained to analysts during a conference call to explain the deal. "A city like Dallas, where America West is No. 8 and US Airways is No. 7... We only serve the West Coast; they only serve the East Coast. When we combine and become the third largest carrier in Dallas with service to both the East and West Coasts, all of a sudden we can go in and make headway with corporate accounts."

Kirby also saw a chance to correct what he saw as flaws in the US Airways network plan. "US Airways, while they have shrunk some through the bankruptcy process, in January and February had a significant increase in ASMs," he said. This ill-advised growth stemmed from transforming Philadelphia into a rolling rather than a banked hub, as Delta had done in Atlanta (smaller Philadelphia would face all the same disadvantages and fewer advantages of such an operation) and from launching a Caribbean offensive from various cities including New York, Washington and Philadelphia. In addition, America West was clearly concerned about Southwest, whose two busiest airports were America West's Phoenix and Las Vegas hubs. Competing against Southwest would have been difficult enough even without Southwest's remarkably advantageous fuel hedge position. In all, America West identified more than $600 million in potential merger synergies.

But the two most important motivations for Parker: the opportunity to shrink the combined airline and the opportunity to greatly reduce the likelihood of America West itself having to file for bankruptcy. As it happened, America West, having witnessed the power of capacity cutting on revenue growth, wanted to shed planes but couldn't—GE, for one, had profitable long-term leasing deals with America West that it had no incentive to break. But GE was worried about its heavy exposure to US Airways, enabling Parker to present an enticing offer: We keep US Airways alive by buying it if you agree to break some leases from both the America West and US Airways fleets. The move worked, and the combined airline managed to shed no fewer than 60 airplanes, including Boeing 737s and Airbus 319s and 320s.

Just as importantly, America West, highly vulnerable as a smallish carrier with a dicey balance sheet and dependence on one region of the U.S., was buying staying power. Combined with US Airways, it was now a company on which airports, distributors, local economies, business travelers, aircraft suppliers and other stakeholders depended to a greater degree than most of them depended on either airline individually. The U.S. government too was an important creditor for both airlines, having provided both of them, and no other airline, with loan guarantees. The importance of all this was made crystal clear by the number of times desperate partners had bailed out US Airways, not to mention the Delta/Amex example. GE alone—remember, a huge engine maker and servicer as well as a financier—provided financial help to US Airways, Delta, United, Air Canada, Independence Air and even America West itself.

The merged airline would have a stronger frequent flier plan too, implying more value for customers—a US Airways traveler in Philadelphia could now more easily use her miles to reach Hawaii, for example—which, in turn, implied more value for the credit card companies, hotel chains and retailers ready to dole out millions of dollars to buy miles that they would pass along to their customers. The deal would surely face little resistance from antitrust officials, not only because the Bush administration was more relaxed about such matters than the Clinton administration, which was prepared to block a United-US Airways merger five years earlier, but also because there was little route overlap between the two airlines—their fusion, in other words, would create few new monopoly routes. On top of that, Parker could also sell the deal to Washington as a transaction that would save jobs, never mind the thousands of layoffs he made no secret would happen as a result of the merger. During Capitol Hill testimony, one legislator pressed Parker on the matter. His response: "What I think is happening here is we're saving 37,000 jobs, [not] eliminating 5,000 jobs." US Airways, in other words, was a stone's throw from liquidating. Saving every job wasn't an option. The choice was between saving most jobs and saving no jobs at all.

Skeptics certainly existed. One Wall Street analyst asked: "It is usually hard to bring your unit costs down when you're shrinking, so are we going to see unit costs go up before they go down at US Airways?"

Parker's response: "The reason unit costs go down when you are shrinking in the airline business is because in general, you end up not being able to get out of all the costs. That again is the value of bankruptcy. Indeed, the shrinking will occur before the airline comes out and not after. So the cost structure that it emerges with should actually decline.... We certainly don't expect to see unit costs increasing at Airways. We expect to see them declining over time." ("Airways" is how people in the industry often referred to US Airways ever since, in 1997, it had changed its name from USAir.)

Others criticized the lack of route overlap, questioning the synergies from a combined network that was shaped like a "barbell"—America West's own term for it—that didn't feature a mid-continent hub. Picture Phoenix and Las Vegas as one "weight" on the barbell and Charlotte and Philadelphia as the other, connected by a few trunk routes between them. In other words, the very selling point as to why regulators shouldn't worry too much was—perhaps—also a reason why America West investors and US Airways creditors shouldn't get too excited.

In any event, the upside was convincing enough for Parker and Kirby to do the deal, assuming, that is, they could secure enough third-party financing—America West, remember, couldn't fund this itself. Luckily, this was 2005, with oceans of capital looking for investment returns. PAR Capital, for example, an investor in Independence Air, agreed to provide $100 million in equity. Peninsula Investment Partners, another equity investor, pledged another $50 million. Then there was Air Canada. The Canadian airline, which itself had just exited bankruptcy in late 2004, was now earning solid profits thanks to lower costs and international revenue growth. It wasn't done restructuring, however, with its parent company looking to spin off the airline's frequent flier plan, regional carrier and maintenance unit. Naturally, the more customers these units had, the more money they could fetch. So the group's CEO Robert Milton thought it wise to invest $75 million in the new US Airways, in exchange for commitments to use Air Canada's maintenance services. This was an immediate example of how growing bigger could open opportunities: Nobody cared quite that much about either airline, US Airways or America West, individually. Including some deals struck shortly thereafter, the new US Airways was able to muster $678 million in new equity financing, a testament to the market's confidence in Parker's plan.

And there was more. In the late 1990s, US Airways, under its former CEO Stephen Wolf, had placed a giant Airbus order, making it one of the European manufacturer's largest customers worldwide. So naturally, Airbus was nervous about the airline's potential liquidation. The manufacturer readily lent the airline $250 million while agreeing to push back the delivery dates of eight 320s (shorthaul planes that hold roughly 150 passengers) and three 319s (which hold roughly 125) that were originally scheduled to arrive in 2006, further reducing the airline's planned capacity growth, not to mention capital commitments, for the year ahead. Airbus let US Airways push back deliveries for 10 widebody 330s too. In turn, US Airways agreed to buy 20 Airbus 350s, the new midsized longhaul plane Airbus was building to compete against Boeing's new 7E7, which would soon be renamed the 787 Dreamliner.

In the end, America West shareholders got a 39 percent stake in the new US Airways. Shareholders of the old US Airways, as typically happens when a company goes bankrupt, got nothing. US Airways creditors (companies to which it owed money when it filed) got 12 percent of the new company. The outside investors, including Airbus, Air Canada and the rest, took the remaining 49 percent. Wellington Management, Air Wisconsin and none other than the federal government, via its airline loan board, had the largest stakes.

The new US Airways would go on to restructure its U.S. government loan guarantees, its co-branded credit card deals and its credit card processing agreements.

And it would sell $100 million worth of Embraer jets and airport slots to its regional partner Republic, with other liquidity-stretched airlines looking on with no small measure of envy.

"We are particularly excited about the amount of interest we've had in financing this transaction," Parker told analysts on a conference call the day after the airlines announced the deal. "That clearly, as we started, was one of our major concerns that we needed to address and one of the criteria of America West in order to announce this. We wanted to be highly confident that we had sufficient liquidity to weather any sort of downturn. We have accomplished that and indeed, I think, exceeded even our own expectations."

More importantly, Parker was telling the world that with his new airline, "We have created a competitive business that is profitable even with oil prices at $50 per barrel." He said this, incidentally, just weeks after Michael Palumbo, Delta's chief financial officer, had said: "No commercial airline's business works at $50 to $60 a barrel for oil." Maybe that was true in June 2005. But Parker was ready to alter that truth.

"This [merger]," Parker said, "is the beginning of something that can change our industry."

***

Back in Atlanta, Grinstein certainly felt some frustration that US Airways was not going to disappear after all. But he took some solace in knowing the new US Airways would, at least, significantly decrease capacity, most importantly along the east coast. Trouble was, that wasn't going to happen fast enough—not with Delta now gasping for breath. In the second quarter, Delta spilled another $300 million in red ink, even as most other major U.S. carriers reported profits. Internally, management debated whether there was any chance the airline could avoid bankruptcy.

On June 7, Grinstein traveled to Washington for a Senate finance committee hearing on pending legislation to relax the payment schedule for airlines with underfunded pension plans. "The current pension funding rules are not workable in the current airline environment," he said, delivering prepared remarks, "and they need to be fixed.... One of the two biggest factors [the other being fuel prices] that will determine whether we can successfully complete our transformation outside of bankruptcy is the pension cloud now hanging over our company and many other traditional legacy carriers." The problem was that Delta, when it looked at its retirement plan assets and future retirement liabilities, saw a gaping $2.6 billion deficit. That figure could change based on factors ranging from interest rate movements to stock market performance to how long retirees lived. But federal law said companies must patch their pension deficits with cash contributions, which in Delta's case amounted to hundreds of millions of dollars per year, according to the legal funding schedule. Delta, with the help of Johnny Isakson, a Republican

U.S. senator from Georgia, was now asking if it could spread those payments over 25 years. In 2004, Congress had granted pension payment relief—but only on a temporary basis.

Northwest was in a similar position, threatened not just by its own hefty funding obligations but the fact that rivals United and US Airways had, by this time, nullified their defined-benefit pension plans and dumped their obligations on the federal government's pension insurance plan, the Pension Benefit Guarantee Corporation, or PBGC. Naturally, senators were concerned about two more airlines following the lead of United and US Airways, which would greatly multiply the already-strained resources of the PBGC, with taxpayers potentially at risk. Airline employees were greatly concerned too, because the PBGC would pay only a portion of their promised pensions. Pilots, in particular, stood to lose the most. That's because much like government unemployment insurance, the PBGC capped its payments at a certain salary. So whereas a low-paid flight attendant's monthly pension check might come from a different place but be for about the same amount she expected, a pilot's check would not only come from the government rather than from the airline—but would, more significantly for the pilot, be for far less money than it would have been had the airline not defaulted on its pension obligations.

Grinstein told senators about Delta's four straight years of massive losses, the latest being a $5.2 billion bloodbath for all of 2004, despite a U.S. economy that grew a healthy 4 percent. He explained how the company and its pilots agreed to freeze the plan, meaning all future pilot hires would switch to a more modern defined-contribution plan—the company would promise only what it would contribute each month, not how much it would provide for retirement. He discussed the industry's challenges as well as Delta's specific challenges and its plans to address them. To Sen. Ron Wyden of Oregon, he defended himself against broad criticism of excessive management pay. "I do not want to pretend to be a goody two-shoes," he said, "but none of our senior executives have contracts. I do not have a contract. I have no retirement plan. I have no bonus plan. I have no pension plan." To the ranking Democrat on the committee, Sen. Max Baucus of Montana, he responded to questions about the peculiar right for pilots to retire early in exchange for big lump sums and smaller payments later. Suspending these, Grinstein explained, would create a "run on the bank," meaning pilots would rush to this option in even greater numbers if they knew the option would soon be made unavailable.

Grinstein had a testier exchange with Sen. Jim Bunning, whose state happened to be home to Cincinnati's airport and many of the people who worked there—the airport is actually located across the Ohio River from Cincinnati, not in Ohio but in Kentucky.

> *Bunning:* But if you want to really get your financial house in order, can you tell me, sir, in the last two and a half years, how many dollars has Delta Air Lines lost?

Grinstein: Yes, I can tell you how much Delta Air Lines has lost in the last several years.

Bunning: Would you like to bring it out?

Grinstein: Well, we lost $5 billion last year.

Bunning: Five billion?

Grinstein: Yes.

Bunning: And how long can a company operate, bleeding $5 billion out the front door? How long?

Grinstein: Senator, obviously, bleeding only stops—I am sure Dr. Frist [another Republican senator who happened to be a physician and was at the hearing] would understand that—

Bunning: I am not sure anybody would understand how bad management—

Grinstein: But the point is—

Bunning: No. You are going to listen.

Grinstein: Alright.

Bunning: How bad management at Delta Air Lines has cost the employees of Delta not only their pensions, but reduced pensions, reduced pay, and reduced everything. You blame it on everybody but your own management group. Now, I know you have not been there very long, but I knew your past management group pretty well. I knew when you bought Comair and Comair was operating completely profitably, to the point where you paid—I never have figured that one out—cash for their stock. Now you are coming to us and you want us to allow you to do something that I do not think is in the best interests of Delta Air Lines. We want to freeze or reduce your costs, and we want you to do it on your own, because we do not want to force the federal government down your throat. You are going to come to us with your pension program, like United Airlines did, and add $6.6 billion in losses to the PBGC. We do not want Delta to have to do that. Now, I know you have taken some remedy steps to avoid that, but we do not think you have taken enough.

Grinstein: Let me try to answer it this way. There are certain things that we can move and certain things that we can change, and we are working on that. As I mentioned in my direct statement, in the last 10 months we have taken $2 billion of costs out of the company, which is an enormous amount.

Bunning: Thanks to your employees.

Grinstein: Thanks to all of us, every employee and every person at every level in the company. That was one source of it. Being smarter, more efficient and utilizing technology better is another piece of it. Changing the business processes was another piece of it. It is not just one level or one attack. It is going at the problem from every possible angle, including the way you run your system. We had to make some very tough choices. We had to end our hub at Dallas-Fort Worth, which was not an easy thing to do. We had to completely reschedule the way we flew Atlanta. We, in one day, rescheduled 51 percent of the airline and dramatically improved customer satisfaction. So at the same time that we are cutting the costs, we are making significant improvements in the way we take care of our passengers. But at the same time, fuel has moved up dramatically and has spiked, as you know, at about $58. That was something that was not possible for us to anticipate. If we had 1999 fuel levels, we would have been a profitable company. But we do not have that. So, that is something that neither you nor I, I guess, can do anything about. But we can attack the problems that we can move. We can come to you and say, not looking at past mistakes, but what does it take to keep you going and make it a viable airline and continue to operate? What we want to do is be able to honor the promises that we have made through our pension plans by having this legislation spread those payments out over a longer period of time. But there is probably a lot of blame that can go around for the past. The truth of the matter is, our job—my job, our collective job—is to focus on what we can do to make this company operate in the future.

Bunning: Well, I hope so, because I have 8,000 constituents who work for your company, and their livelihood depends on whether you survive or whether you do not survive, and I see them on a daily basis. I hope that your airline is able to avoid Chapter 11, but at the rate of losses, I do not know how that is going to be possible. I am worried about the employees' pension and the suggestions that all of you, and everybody here, have made to make our laws better so what has happened cannot happen again. That is the main thing that this committee is holding these hearings for. My God, it does not do any good to promise a pilot, an attendant, a mechanic or anybody in management a certain amount of money if you cannot deliver it in the future. If you cannot stay current with your benefit plans, then you have over-committed somehow. I can give you chapter and verse on other pensions that are doing quite well, in spite of the fact that fuel costs are very high—not necessarily airlines, but certain other things. Thank you for your time.

Also testifying at the committee was Northwest's CEO Doug Steenland, an all-business cost-cutter trying to navigate a predicament that was no less dire than Delta's: Northwest's revenues were better, but its costs were even higher, aggravated by a management-union relationship ravaged by years of mistrust. United's CEO Glenn Tilton was also there and took a grilling from senators upset by his decision to terminate pensions. Union executives were there too. And although he wasn't a member of the finance committee and was thus not there in person, Sen. Barack Obama of Illinois weighed in with a letter expressing concern for his hometown airline United and its employees. Eventually, Grinstein and Steenland were successful in their pleas, despite opposition to pension relief by American and Continental, which weren't going bankrupt and whose plans weren't quite so underfunded—and which were thus not happy to see their more desperate rivals Delta and Northwest get a break from Washington.

Back in the trenches, airlines by the summer of 2005 were doing their best to raise fares in reaction to surging fuel prices. One barrier was partly removed when Delta, in July, backtracked on its SimpliFares pledge and raised its economy class fare cap for domestic routes by $100, to $599, and its first class cap by $100 as well, to $699. "When Delta launched SimpliFares in January, crude oil was selling at $43 per barrel compared to as much as $61 per barrel in recent weeks," Paul Matsen, the airline's marketing chief, told *Business Travel News*. "Despite our best intentions to keep the current fare caps in place, we have been forced to find ways to offset this dramatic spike in costs." Soon, Delta went a step further and began breaking its self-imposed caps for tickets it sold for seats on other airlines with which it codeshared, notably Northwest and Continental.

Competitive pressures were, in fact, easing by summer, as big airlines like American and United—although not Delta—were shrinking their domestic capacity. The east coast was still the hardest hit by fare wars, but even here, yields were rising somewhat. Nevertheless, the industry's effectiveness in raising fares was stymied by Southwest, which could afford to keep prices low thanks not so much to anything it was doing now but to the highly fortuitous decision it had made to load up on fuel hedges, or essentially pre-purchase years' worth of fuel, back when fuel was cheap. So Southwest was operating in a different universe from every other airline, paying just $26 per barrel for 85 percent of its fuel, while everyone else was paying more than $50. In 2004, it had saved nearly a half billion dollars thanks to this golden armor. This year, in 2005, it would save nearly $1 billion.

In the meantime, Independence Air remained in dire financial straits. But that didn't stop it from nonetheless flying twice as many seats this summer than last. Yet another new low-cost airline named Skybus was preparing to launch in Columbus, Ohio. American opened a gleaming new terminal at New York JFK, further disadvantaging Delta and its dumpy digs there. United was moving on from its labor strife and heading toward a bankruptcy exit. Northwest was preparing to break a planned mechanics' strike by organizing third-party providers to do the work, part of a long-term plan to outsource a large part of its maintenance. Southwest was waging a legislative war to repeal the Wright Amendment, which restricted its operations at its Dallas airport of choice, not big Dallas Fort-Worth International but old Love Field—it wasn't allowed, for example, to fly from there to Atlanta. JetBlue, growing capacity more than 20 percent, expanded its presence in the New York area with flights from Newark. AirTran was still growing at a remarkable 30 percent clip—one of its new markets was the Delta stronghold Richmond—but was no less welcoming of high fuel prices. Fuel jumped from a quarter of its total operating costs in the summer of 2004 to more than a third one year later, which meant the parts of its cost base where it had big advantages—labor and ticket distribution, for example—were becoming an ever-shrinking portion of its overall cost base and simply didn't "matter" as much, so to speak, in terms of giving it a big advantage over its higher-cost competitors. That's because hedging differentials aside, AirTran paid no more or less for jet fuel than anyone else, and jet fuel was now what mattered most. AirTran was also feeling pressured by Delta's Atlanta buildup as well as by some of its own newly signed labor contracts.

The continued low-cost airline growth at home gave the Big Six legacy carriers all the more reason to venture abroad. Delta and Continental both added new service to Berlin. Continental also added Newark flights to Beijing, Hamburg, Stockholm, Belfast and Bristol. American connected Chicago with Nagoya and Dublin and announced Chicago-Delhi service. United started Chicago-Shanghai, Chicago-Munich and San Francisco-Nagoya. US Airways launched Venice and Barcelona service from Philadelphia. The world was globalizing at the fastest pace ever, and the Big Six were jumping on the bandwagon, aggressively raising fares all the while. Delta's SimpliFares, happily for its competitors—and, as was becoming increasingly apparent, for Delta itself—only applied to domestic routes. Indeed, Delta itself was hiking international fares and fuel surcharges with as much enthusiasm as everyone else.

Grinstein was still looking for the right man to lead Delta abroad when he happened to come across an *Aviation Daily* article that mentioned an Alitalia network planning executive named Glen Hauenstein.

"There is an odd Italian name," he thought. Grinstein soon learned Hauenstein had been the architect of Continental's successful international expansion in recent years, so he called Gordon Bethune, the legendary, now-retired Continental Chairman and CEO.

"Oh yeah," Grinstein recalled Bethune saying of Hauenstein. "Terrific, absolutely first class."

Bethune, recalling the same conversation, remembered Grinstein had one reservation: "He's too expensive." Bethune's answer to that? Grinstein couldn't afford to *not* hire him. "He's going to save you $30 million the first year," Bethune said. "If you don't hire him, you're crazy."

Next Grinstein called Bethune's old deputy at Continental, Greg Brenneman, who was now an independent consultant. "Terrific," he said of Hauenstein, who, as it happens, was at Alitalia on behalf of Brenneman, whom the Italian carrier had hired for turnaround advice. So Grinstein placed a call to Hauenstein in Rome, only to be told he was traveling in Canada. "Oh shit," Grinstein thought. "He's leaving." Air Canada, Grinstein reasoned, had likely beaten him to the punch in pursuit of the rising star.

But Grinstein managed to reach Hauenstein in Canada and suggested they meet. "Well, I'm on my way to Houston," Hauenstein told him. Houston! This, of course, was where Continental was based; perhaps he was going back to work there, in a more senior role this time? Fortunately, Hauenstein agreed to stop in Atlanta, where he ultimately agreed to become Delta's new point man for route planning.

This was hardly the only executive change at Delta. With bankruptcy looming, a substantial number of top people were leaving, in some cases concerned those controversial pensions awarded in 2002, no longer protected in the event of a bankruptcy filing, were looking more vulnerable than ever. A few weeks before Hauenstein joined Delta, CFO Michael Palumbo announced his resignation. He was replaced by an internal candidate named Ed Bastian, who had been a key figure in formulating and executing the company's recent turnaround initiatives. Meanwhile Jim Whitehurst, a Grinstein favorite (originally hired, like Bastian, by Leo Mullin), became chief operating officer.

The great question before this new assembly of actors was bankruptcy—and whether Delta could avoid it. Knowing it would need to arrange financing to sustain its operations in the event it did file, executives got to work on soliciting potential debtor-in-possession, or DIP, loans. These are special loans available to bankrupt companies that allow DIP lenders to jump to the front of the payback line, superseding all other creditors, many of whom won't ever get fully paid back. As unfair as that might seem for those other creditors, the idea is to help bankrupt companies stay in business while they restructure, thereby preserving jobs and giving the firm a second chance. In other words, without DIP financing, everyone could lose everything. Separately, a recent change to U.S. bankruptcy law limited a management team's exclusive right to stay in power and offer its own turnaround plan—but only for cases filed *after* Oct. 17, 2005. That meant if Delta were to file before then, its management team would be less exposed to eventually losing control of the process to an outside group offering an alternative plan of reorganization, likely one involving new executives. Other new provisions would force management teams to make quick decisions about renewing leases with vendors and partners while also prohibiting executives from being paid retention bonuses unless they could prove they've been offered jobs elsewhere. In other words, were bankruptcy to become unavoidable, better to file before Oct. 17 than after.

But Delta wasn't ready to file just yet. On July 26, in a message to employees, Grinstein lamented the company's weak second-quarter financial results, blaming them on heavy exposure to low-cost competition, overcapacity along the east coast, soaring interest costs, another $95 million in pension contributions and a remarkably high $1.1 billion in fuel expenses. This was almost $400 million more than Delta had spent in the same quarter one year earlier, he wrote, and "every penny increase in the average annual cost per gallon of jet fuel drives approximately $25 million in additional mainline fuel expense." On the bright side, Delta was on its way to having the lowest non-fuel unit costs among the Big Six and managed to improve unit revenues somewhat too. "In light of what we have accomplished together so far, there can be no doubt that Delta's transformation plan is delivering results. What is also clear is that it is not enough."

Then came mention of the "b" word. "As many of you are aware, given our financial situation, there is renewed speculation about bankruptcy. We have been candid about the risk that a number of factors, some of which are beyond our control, will affect our ability to avoid a Chapter 11 filing. However, we are still working to pursue an out-of-court solution, even as we face increasing financial pressures."

That work involved the resumption of Delta's fuel hedging program, although by this time hedging wasn't cheap—the "counterparty" taking the airline's bet that fuel prices would continue rising would want to be well compensated for the strong possibility that Delta was right. Delta managed to renegotiate its GE loan covenants, buying itself more time but—less helpfully—agreeing to keep more cash on hand. It deferred additional aircraft deliveries, slowed capacity growth by removing some planes from its active fleet while adding some new Caribbean routes, tweaked operations to further reduce aircraft ground time, revamped its website and, on Aug. 15, sold its wholly owned Atlantic Southeast regional airline unit to an independent regional airline, giant SkyWest, for $425 million. It was still trying with Song, at one point announcing flights between Hartford and Los Angeles, an impossibly "thin" market, as airlines call routes with limited demand, even had it not launched in the dead of the off-peak autumn.

Against these efforts were headwinds of even greater force, including credit card processing agreements set to expire Aug. 29. So Delta stood to lose its ability to immediately collect cash when its customers used credit cards to pay for future flights, which nearly all of them did. In fact, the processing companies were demanding Delta set aside hundreds of millions of dollars in cash as a sort of insurance fund in case it suspended operations, which would trigger a rush for refunds among customers with future reservations—refunds for which the credit card companies could otherwise be left holding the bag. On July 7, terrorist attacks targeting London's Underground and killing 52 civilians—7/7, the day became known—momentarily dampened the international travel boom. On Aug. 19, the U.S. Justice Department expressed opposition to a bid by Delta, Northwest, Air France/KLM, Korean Air and Czech Airlines to coordinate prices and schedules on international routes. By this time, Delta's stock was trading at a 43-year low, and debt rating agencies were further downgrading its credit, accelerating the vicious cycle: Worse credit ratings mean higher interest costs, which in turn drain even more cash. "The airline's already slim chances of avoiding bankruptcy are dwindling rapidly," Philip Baggaley, an analyst at the credit rating agency Standard & Poor's, wrote. Pilots, meanwhile, were still rushing for the exits as they became eligible for early retirement, taking their lump-sum payments and further draining Delta's cash. Some pilots were themselves suggesting more pay concessions, highlighting their nervousness about what would happen to their careers, let alone their pensions, if Delta entered bankruptcy.

Any hope of avoiding that fate, alas, washed away with the floodwaters of a natural disaster. On Aug. 29, 2005, Hurricane Katrina hit Louisiana's coast, creating a surge of water that, along with the storm's winds, caused more than $80 billion in damage. The greatest devastation occurred in the city of New Orleans, whose flood barriers failed to hold, leaving about 80 percent of the city under water. Nearly 2,000 people lost their lives, and many more lost their livelihoods. In the months that followed, tens of thousands of New Orleans residents left the city, eventually causing its population to decline by more than 100,000 people, many of whom migrated to Houston and elsewhere in Texas.

Delta, New Orleans' second busiest airline after Southwest and the top airline in many other communities along the Gulf of Mexico that the storm also devastated, naturally saw its operations disrupted, causing further financial losses. But Hurricane Katrina's deepest blow to the airline industry came from the fuel price spike it caused. The storm knocked offline refineries that accounted for 13 percent of America's jet fuel production. Crude oil prices were now touching $70 per barrel, although their post-Katrina rise was a seemingly modest 4 percent. The real problem, because the refineries were disabled, was the cost of refining the crude into jet fuel, which is what airlines actually buy. Overnight, already high jet fuel prices jumped 33 percent to $2.30 per gallon.

In a final move before what was now an inevitable Chapter 11 filing, Delta on Sept. 7 announced a drastic 26 percent capacity cut at Cincinnati, where its armada of regional jets and heavy dependence on connecting traffic meant mounting losses. Some of these planes moved to Atlanta and Salt Lake City, resulting in new routes like Atlanta-Bloomington, Ill., and Salt Lake City-Columbus. It announced a new Atlanta-Maui route too and—most importantly—affirmed its international expansion, offering new or expanded service to 41 airports abroad. This included more Caribbean flying as well as a push into Central America and a new Atlanta-Düsseldorf flight. Since the start of 2005, in fact, Delta had now added or announced 21 new international destinations. Finally, the airline sold its remaining Boeing 767-200s, "the least efficient widebody" in its fleet.

But on Sept. 15, four days after the fourth anniversary of the 9/11 attacks, Delta filed for Chapter 11 bankruptcy protection in the U.S. Bankruptcy Court for the Southern District of New York. Northwest Airlines, with better revenue prospects than Delta but deeper labor cost problems, filed that same day. Years later, that coincidence could be seen as having foreshadowed that the two airlines would someday be inextricably linked for happier reasons. But for now, the fact that two giant airline corporations could fall into a court-protected restructuring simultaneously was hardly shocking. Since 2000, Tower Air, Kitty Hawk, Pro Air, Fine Air, Legend Airlines, National Airlines, TWA, Midway Airlines, Sun Country, Vanguard, US Airways, United, Hawaiian, Midway again, Great Plains, Atlas Air, US Airways again, ATA, Southeast Airlines and Aloha had all filed for bankruptcy. Delta's statement: "The action we have taken is a necessary and responsible step to preserve Delta's value for our creditors, customers, employees, business partners and other stakeholders as we address our financial challenges and work to secure our future. Delta is open for business as usual and will continue normal operations throughout the reorganization process. Our customers can be confident that they remain our No. 1 priority and that their travel plans and SkyMiles are secure."

The Delta and Northwest filings meant both airlines considered themselves to be in a "zone of insolvency"—they would run out of money sooner or later if they didn't file for bankruptcy, so better to get on with things and restructure. But Northwest, however unsustainable it might have been over the long term, still had $1.5 billion in cash and thus didn't need to round up DIP financing. Delta had no such luxury. It, by contrast, took more than $2 billion in such loans, mostly from Morgan Stanley and Delta's old friends GE and American Express. Of this total, $1 billion would go to pay off prior loans, with the rest available for operations and investments. The covenants attached to the new financing demanded Delta maintain certain levels of operating profits and liquidity and placed limits on how much capital spending it could undertake—fancy new airplanes, in other words, were unlikely.

The filing put Delta's transformation plan in high gear. For starters, it permitted the company to stop its large cash contributions to underfunded pension plans, although Delta didn't move to terminate any plans—at least not yet. Court protection, most importantly, would permit Delta to streamline its messy fleet and hub structure by rejecting aircraft and real estate leases—in other words, rather easily get rid of planes and gates it didn't like. The airline could also more easily cut employee compensation again, especially with respect to pilots, whose contract and pensions were now potentially subject to termination.

Amex was concerned Delta might terminate its credit card deal, a step Grinstein personally assured his counterpart Ken Chenault, on the eve of filing, he would not do. "We had an agreement," Grinstein recalled, "and lo and behold, I come in one morning and my telephone is ringing off the hook, and everyone is screaming at me: 'The credit cards have been canceled!'" One of Chenault's underlings, unaware of the agreement between Grinstein and Chenault, had taken the step to protect Amex.

"So I had to call [Chenault]," Grinstein said, "and say 'Look, you and I had an understanding.'" The credit cards were quickly working again.

Delta did, on the other hand, use bankruptcy to back out of other obligations. Still, even that wouldn't be enough.

"Bankruptcy doesn't save your company," Continental's former CEO Bethune observed of airlines in situations like Delta's. "It will fix your balance sheet, but it won't fix your company if you run a shitty company. You're just going to run through that money too. That new capital is going to be pissed away." (In Bethune's estimation, that's exactly what had happened at Continental shortly before he took over: "They were all high-fiving when they emerged from bankruptcy in '93, and by the time they got to '94 they had run through half the money.")

On Oct. 19, Delta CFO Ed Bastian, in a presentation to pilots, detailed Delta's turnaround progress thus far, including $5 billion in profit improvement measures since 2002, which would be completely realized by the following year, 2006. But the company, he said, needed more—$3 billion a year more to ensure it was 1) competitive against low-cost rivals, 2) capable of generating sustainable cash flows and operating profits, 3) in compliance with its lender covenants, 4) strong enough to attract new equity investors and 5) able to emerge from court protection with a healthy balance sheet. Bastian furthermore stressed that all stakeholders should sacrifice equally and that strong employee morale and customer service were "key ingredients to the ultimate success of the airline."

So how would Delta achieve that extra $3 billion annually? More than $1 billion would come from revenue synergies linked (for example) to further network internationalization. Another $970 million would come from non-labor cost savings now possible thanks to flexibility in rejecting and renegotiating leases and contracts. But $930 million would need to come from labor via pay cuts, benefit cuts, increased productivity and more outsourcing. And of this $930 million, $325 million, or a little more than a third, would have to come from the pilots.

Hoping to win support for this difficult message, Bastian went on to describe how Delta's domestic yields had fallen 23 percent since 2000, while its average fuel price had nearly tripled. Its unit costs were now 26 percent higher than the average of its three main low-cost rivals Southwest, JetBlue and AirTran. Delta needed to narrow that gap to 10 percent. This would require a 21 percent reduction in unit labor costs, achieved through the $930 million in cuts. Even after the late 2004 cuts, Delta's pilots still earned the highest wages in the industry. The most senior Delta captains flying a latest-generation 737, for example, earned $173 per hour compared to $163 for an equivalent pilot flying the equivalent plane at Continental, $158 at American, $139 at JetBlue and $129 at the now-restructured United. Delta was now proposing to bring its figure to $139, matching JetBlue. A senior captain flying widebody Boeing 777s would, under Delta's proposal, see his hourly wage drop from $216 to $174, below that offered by American, Continental and United.

As Bastian made the pitch for savings, Hauenstein was amplifying Delta's push abroad with two key masterstrokes that would greatly enhance revenue generation.

First, he knew widebody 767s could be far more productively deployed overseas, where yields were rising and competition limited, rather than fighting winless battles of attrition against low-cost carriers in places like yield-sensitive Florida. Smallish cities like West Palm Beach and even Fort Myers still had multiple 767 flights each day to Atlanta. Jacksonville, rather small too and just 270 miles from Atlanta, had six 767 daily flights there each way. This meant not only very low fares (because this was way too much seat supply for the market, so Delta had to sell cheap seats to fill the flights) but also more time spent on the ground loading and unloading the large planes than in the air flying the short distance. For a sense of how out of balance this was compared to the rest of the U.S. industry, compare those six daily widebody flights in each direction between Atlanta and Jacksonville, and so many others in so many other shorthaul markets, to *a total of just four domestic widebody flights each day in the entire country* at Hauenstein's old airline Continental—and those were exclusively between the airline's two biggest hubs, Houston and Newark. Longhaul-capable aircraft, Hauenstein reasoned, should be flying longhaul.

Secondly, he began to redeploy narrowbody 757s from domestic to international service, a strategy he had also pioneered at Continental. This was a plane traditionally considered inappropriate for international service, given 1) a preference among longhaul travelers for roomier widebody planes and 2) the fact that most narrowbody aircraft couldn't fly all that far anyway. But 757s were unique among narrowbodies in an important way: They certainly didn't have the greatest shorthaul economics—their engines were just far more powerful than what was necessary to fly, say, between New York and Miami, so they burned a lot of fuel. But that same power meant they had a range of roughly 4,000 miles, far more than other narrowbodies and enough to fly from the northeastern U.S. to parts of western Europe. Because they had fewer seats than widebodies, they were easier to fill in markets that might not otherwise support any service at all, and Hauenstein had found at Continental that passengers turned out to care more about convenient flights to where they were going than whether the airplane had one aisle or two. So the 757s were bound to produce far better returns flying abroad in mainline colors than at home dressed in lime green Song colors.

To be sure, Hauenstein's impatient approach to change triggered some initial resistance and even resentment. "We didn't know who the hell this guy was," remembered Joe Kolshak, the head of operations. "Glen would make these statements about the Delta people, which I thought were kind of patronizing, and I'd call him out on it. He'd say, 'They're very nice people, but...'"

Eventually, though, "Glen won me over and we became very good friends. Because what I liked about Glen was, he would tell you the way he saw it." And more often than not, the way he saw it, Kolshak realized, made sense.

"I remember standing up in the boardroom," Kolshak recalled, "and saying 'You know what? My job as the chief operations officer is to do everything I can to make Glen successful.'"

That might have sounded obvious. But it's not how things had been at Delta—or, in fairness, at many airlines. Historically, operational people told commercial people what was possible, and they worked within those constraints.

"Why," Kolshak recalled Hauenstein asking him, "can't we fly the 777s to Mumbai? The marketing guys tell me we can't because the range is 'x.'"

Why? Well, because that was farther than Boeing, the manufacturer, had said the plane could fly.

"Glen," Kolshak replied, "nobody's ever asked me that."

Kolshak talked to Boeing, which confirmed that yes: The specifications had been very conservative, and the plane could fly safely from Atlanta to Mumbai. He worked with Boeing, the engine manufacturer GE and safety regulators to change those specifications. Delta began flying the 8,510 miles from Atlanta to Mumbai, a victory for Delta's network planners and operations team alike.

"It was them showing up with a problem and we'd solve it," Kolshak said. "We really prided ourselves on being able to make marketing's dreams come true."

Hauenstein, incidentally, would eventually become Delta's fourth highest paid executive, earning more than $5 million in total compensation during 2013. Gordon Bethune had said Jerry Grinstein couldn't afford not to hire Hauenstein. Grinstein had listened.

Among other network moves, Delta was gearing up to serve Copenhagen from Atlanta. It was re-entering the New York JFK-Tel Aviv market, where it would challenge Continental's Israel service from Newark. It was penetrating secondary markets like Budapest and Managua and even Kiev in the Ukraine.

Just two weeks after entering bankruptcy, Grinstein abandoned SimpliFares once and for all. And just one month after that—with Grinstein's own doubts having been confirmed by those of his new network guru Hauenstein, who, from day one, had in management meetings outspokenly mocked the low-cost airline-within-an-airline— Song stopped singing, permanently. Years later, JetBlue's David Neeleman would recall with a smile: "We killed Song."

Delta tried to save face by noting that Song's JetBlue-like inflight amenities had become so popular with customers that Delta would incorporate them on its main-line flights even after Song's demise. It wasn't, in other words, a total loss: Delta had learned valuable lessons from Song. But they were expensive lessons.

"To tell you the truth, I could have learned that from JetBlue," Grinstein recalled. "I didn't need Song."

Even Leo Mullin, the man who had overseen the creation of Song, acknowledged—reflecting years later—it had been time to put the cow to pasture. Song, he said, had come about because of "the presumption that we would have a high cost structure continuing on the legacy side. And as soon as the bankruptcies occurred, all of a sudden the cost structures became competitive and Song was no longer necessary. I probably would have stopped it too."

Delta then began the process of rejecting leases on 40 aircraft that it had already parked by the time it filed for bankruptcy but of which it couldn't, until now, rid itself. By the end of 2006, it would dispose of 80 more planes and, in doing so, reduce its fleet complexity by leaving itself four fewer types of aircraft to manage.

Executives and board members accepted another round of pay cuts. Grinstein himself saw his pay fall by 25 percent. Delta sold its oldest 767s. Comair saw more job cuts, and Delta got rid of some unwanted airport gates, including several in Orlando, where Delta had long been the top airline. This year, 2005, would be the last year that Delta would carry more passengers than Southwest to see Mickey Mouse. Delta did, on the other hand, open its first sales office in China, anticipating it might win new flying rights coming available in 2007.

No longer, however, could it do these things unilaterally. Now a judge, tasked with looking out for the best interest of Delta's creditors, had to sign off on everything. So the airline's executives, led by Ed Bastian, set out explaining the airline's plan to turn the business around, not at its General Offices ("the G.O." or "the Gen," as employees call it) in Atlanta but in a courtroom in New York City. Almost immediately, Delta set about addressing the issue of pilot costs, hoping to convince the judge to permit the abrogation of its ALPA contract, as it requested to do with a "Section 1113" motion to the court on Nov. 1. If disallowed, Bastian argued, the company would breach its lender covenants before long. "There are two significant cost items," Bastian argued, "that are beyond Delta's control: jet fuel and pilot labor costs.

"With regard to jet fuel," he continued, "Delta is, of course, at the mercy of the market. Delta's pilot labor costs are governed by the ALPA agreement and can only be changed through negotiations with the pilots or with the judicial relief sought by this motion... A negotiated agreement with ALPA remains Delta's preferred solution. In the absence of such an agreement, however, there is simply no doubt in my mind that rejection of the ALPA agreement, and implementation of Delta's Section 1113 proposal, is necessary for the reorganization of Delta." Mainline pilot costs, Bastian went on to explain, accounted for 35 percent of total mainline labor costs.

Delta's broader turnaround called for between 7,000 and 9,000 more job cuts by the end of 2007 based on an assumption of $65-per-barrel oil. In December, after tense court hearings, Delta and its pilots—who were not only employees but were also, because of how much the company had taken from them and how much it owed them, among its key creditors—reached a temporary deal that saved $140 million. The deal cut hourly pilot wages by 14 percent and instituted other pilot pay and cost changes equivalent to another 1 percent hourly wage reduction beginning Dec. 15, 2005. Those provisions would remain in effect until Delta reached a more comprehensive agreement with ALPA or a neutral panel "issues its final order as to whether Delta is authorized to reject the pilot collective bargaining agreement under the legal standards of Section 1113." The pilot rank and file approved it—58 percent voted in favor. At the very least, Delta had a deal to survive the off-peak winter, during which it feared burning $500 million in cash. But pilots were far from happy, threatening what Grinstein called a "murder-suicide" strike if their contract was nullified.

The final months of 2005 were no less tense, both inside and outside the courtroom. Another two hurricanes—Rita and Wilma—disrupted U.S. air traffic. Oil prices did ease slightly, ending the last two months of 2005 just below the $60 mark. But that was small consolation. *The Economist* noted that if fuel prices hadn't increased during the year, the world's airline industry would have recouped all the $43 billion in losses it had recorded since 2001. On Delta's competitive radar, United finally had most of its labor rebellions under control and secured new financing to exit bankruptcy, while Delta was just beginning its own dirty work. The Star Alliance boosted its strength in Europe with the merger of Lufthansa and Swiss. Continental, while seeking flight attendant concessions, made a killing by selling its shares in Panama's Copa Airlines, which had emerged—thanks largely to its part-owner's tutelage—as one of the industry's most profitable airlines. Northwest, in bankruptcy like Delta, retreated to its three main hubs (Detroit, Minneapolis and Memphis) and secured new labor cuts after breaking its mechanics union. American was asking for labor concessions out of court. Southwest was enjoying its invaluable hedge protection. AirTran added Charlotte, Detroit, Indianapolis and Richmond to its menu of Atlanta destinations. And William Franke, the former America West CEO whom Doug Parker replaced, never really did retire. Instead he dedicated his time to investing in a new breed of "ultra-low-cost carriers" like Spirit Airlines, which was re-building the old US Airways Caribbean hub from Fort Lauderdale under the leadership of Ben Baldanza, the very person who had built the hub for US Airways.

On the other hand, some positive yield tailwinds emerged as 2006 approached. The economy remained strong, with big gains in the stock and real estate markets and the debut of new companies like a video sharing site called YouTube. Independence Air, although not yet quite gone, was in bankruptcy and seemingly heading toward liquidation. JetBlue was suddenly running into trouble, experiencing operational difficulties in New York and unable to make its new 100-seat Embraer 190s work economically with $60 oil: The airline's unit costs—its cost to carry one passenger one mile—were far higher with these smaller planes. AirTran, for its part, saw its operating margin in 2005 fall to less than 1 percent, from 3 percent a year earlier and 9 percent the year before that. Delta was also happy to enter 2006 knowing international demand remained robust and the U.S. was moving closer to reaching an "open skies" pact with the European Union that might, among other things, grant Delta the access it coveted at London Heathrow—access only American and United, among U.S. carriers, had until now. In Asia, meanwhile, China was blossoming as a global economic power.

At Atlanta, Delta's greatest hub—perhaps the greatest airline hub of them all—the fact remained that "AirTran was a giant pain in the ass competitively," as Grinstein would later describe. But AirTran didn't have Delta's historic ties to Atlanta. And AirTran couldn't take anyone to China. "And so one of the things that we did," Grinstein recalled, "was a really conscious effort to re-establish those community ties with Atlanta. And we assigned executives to various cultural organizations and spoke with every damn Rotary and business club and chamber and law firms and God knows what. You know, to establish that link with Delta. And as Delta also expanded internationally, it also gave Atlanta, which is a very internationally conscious city—an internationally connected city—a realization of how absolutely essential Delta is to its future in a way that AirTran never can fill."

And the new post-merger US Airways? In October, it formally emerged from bankruptcy, stronger and more confident than ever.

2006

"A lot of gas-sucking pigs"

For the people who pilot airplanes for a living, the horrors of 9/11 were particularly wrenching. Eight of their co-professionals—Captains John Ogonowski, Victor Saracini, Charles F. Burlingame and Jason Dahl, and First Officers Thomas McGuinness, Michael Horrocks, David Charlebois and Leroy Homer—were, on Sept. 11, 2001, murdered in violent, face-to-face, on-the-job confrontations with their terrorist killers.

Captain Lee Moak, for his part, was not on duty that day. At the moment when American Airlines flight 11 hit the North Tower of the World Trade Center, he was enjoying a serene morning with his wife—the two were eating breakfast at the Coffee Break in Clinton, Conn., a two-hour drive northeast of New York City. As he was eating, Moak looked up at a television screen—"a small, you know, old-school TV," he recalled—and saw news reports about the first plane hitting the north tower. It wasn't long before he realized his help might be needed at the airport. So he raced home to put on his uniform and began the drive to JFK. He made it through Connecticut and through Westchester County and through the Bronx, all the while grappling with unanswered questions and haunting concerns for his fellow pilot professionals. But he never made it to JFK. Traffic was stopped at the Bronx-Whitestone Bridge into Queens, which, like all bridges into the city, was closed because of concerns about potential additional terrorist attacks. There was nothing Moak could do but turn back and head home.

A few days after 9/11, Moak, a Delta 767 captain, stepped up his activity with the Air Line Pilots Association, becoming the executive administrator for the carrier's pilots—their union leader. Moak, after nine years as a Marine Corps fighter pilot, started his Delta career in 1988, a time when the company was sailing through the turbulent aftermath of deregulation, making money year after year and sharing much of the bounty with its workers. And the pilots? "They would do anything to help the company and make sure the company was successful," Moak recalled. But then came the shock of the early to mid-1990s, when a brief oil spike and recession, along with new competitive threats, compelled the company to ask for pilot concessions, abruptly depleting many years of built-up trust. This "internal, out-of-court restructuring," as Moak called it, proved a defining moment for management-pilot relations at Delta, and the sourness and bitterness it engendered were still fresh when ALPA planned to strike the airline in 2000. It was yet another event that made the old days of cooperation feel like ancient history. Moak had lived through the difficult pay cuts and the stressful strike preparations, just as he had lived through the euphoria of winning back the concessions, and then some, in what became the richest pilot contract in the airline business.

Now, just months after this contract was signed, Delta was hemorrhaging money, and Moak was one of the key employee representatives responsible for doing what ALPA could do to ensure the hard-won gains weren't lost. It was a comparatively rich contract, sure, but for the pilot who was buying a house, or paying a child's tuition or deciding how much money to allocate for summer vacation, what mattered was the paycheck he or she now expected each month. If that paycheck suddenly got smaller, lives would inevitably be disrupted in painful ways—people forced to abandon their homes, abruptly change their lifestyles and even file for personal bankruptcy. Hardship would beckon. A smaller paycheck would strain relationships, spoil dreams and stunt careers.

ALPA's job was to avoid such disruptions at nearly all costs, a job that got a lot harder on Sept. 11, 2001. Nobody was asking for concessions yet, and hope remained that the adverse impact of 9/11 might quickly fade, replaced by a quick revenue and profit rebound. But 9/11 wasn't, Moak and his colleagues were being told, the only threat to Delta and its ability to afford the new pilot contract. The industry was changing: new LCC competition, new ways of shopping for fares, new business traveler habits and so on. This was the lens through which Delta's management team viewed the post-9/11 world.

Moak and the ALPA leadership saw things through a different lens. Eight fellow pilots had just died in an attack on the United States, implying greater stresses and challenges for an already stressful and challenging profession. Delta pilots had swallowed painful givebacks, fought for their restoration and deserved their new contract. They were flying, furthermore, for the airline with the best balance sheet in the business.

These drastically different visions of a post-9/11 world were destined to clash, as they did almost immediately after the attacks. ALPA seethed when executives responded to the traffic slowdown by furloughing about 100 pilots a month for 13 months, part of a "disconcerting" strategy of downsizing and cost cutting. "They were making decisions that almost appeared spur-of-the-moment," Moak said years later. "We didn't have a collaborative relationship. We weren't working well together at that time." Moak was upset even about some of management's decisions that didn't impact pilots directly. "They didn't do their best work, and it really hurt the airline." A prime example in Moak's mind? The creation of Song. Officially, the pilots were agnostic about Song, as long as its pilots were mainline Delta pilots receiving mainline Delta compensation and working under mainline Delta work rules—as they indeed were. Agnostic—but not without an opinion. "It was another failed business strategy of many that were occurring under that management team at that time," Moak said.

Maybe. But did Moak and his colleagues governing ALPA have any better ideas for a company clearly facing competitive challenges and mounting losses?

Well, running the airline wasn't their job. But ALPA did rally its Delta membership's support behind one specific criticism of management: that executives were negligent in not effectively petitioning the U.S. government for more help. "Delta was trying to compete, perhaps with low-cost carriers," Moak explained years later. "But they [management] weren't addressing the core problem."

What was that core problem? "Government policy that was supporting low-cost carriers [and] forcing legacy carriers to compete on an un-level playing field," Moak said. An example: government willingness to give JetBlue valuable takeoff and landing slots at New York JFK. "They were given special treatment and special access that the U.S. flag carriers were not afforded, and ultimately it was quite a disaster," he said. In ALPA's mind, the government was "picking winners," a term normally used pejoratively by the champions of *capital*, not, as in this case, the champions of *labor*.

In 2004, Leo Mullin left, clearing the air for a honeymoon of sorts. "I felt it was positive that Jerry Grinstein replaced Mullin," Moak later said. But this didn't change the political realities of labor unions. Elected union leaders, like any politicians seeking votes, sometimes blame bogeymen for unpleasant realities. By 2004, it was difficult to imagine how Delta could avoid bankruptcy without asking for pilot concessions. But this reality didn't make rank-and-file pilots any less hostile to the executives doing the asking—especially after those executives had agreed to reward themselves with bonuses and bankruptcy-proof pension guarantees. Ultimately, it's the rank and file who must vote to approve any concessions their leaders negotiate. And those leaders had tentatively agreed to pay and benefit cuts worth a billion dollars. For some pilots, take-home pay would plummet 40 percent. ALPA negotiators also agreed to allow Delta to freeze defined-benefit pension plans. From now on, in other words, the company would make no promises about how much anyone would get after retirement. It would instead merely promise fixed *contributions* along the way to their accounts, which might or might not ensure a comfortable income after retirement—who knows what stock and bond markets will do over many years? The 2004 deal included givebacks in the areas of medical benefits and job protections against outsourcing too.

Harsh as these measures were, rank-and-file pilots, seeing few alternatives, ratified the deal. But in the next leadership election, in the summer of 2005, John Malone, the leader who negotiated the concessionary deal, lost. The winner? Lee Moak.

Moak assumed his new responsibilities in the autumn of 2005, just after Delta filed for bankruptcy despite the massive 2004 pilot givebacks. This cruel twist of fate was understandable enough, given the impact of impossibly high fuel prices that nobody foresaw. But that made it no less painful for pilots, who stood to lose more than any other workers.

The honeymoon for Moak and Grinstein didn't last long, not with the company asking for another $325 million in annual concessions—and not with Moak's 6,000 constituents still licking their wounds from a year earlier. Moak, as union leaders do, used incendiary language to build support for what he knew would inevitably be another raw deal—inevitable, so much more than even the prior raw deal, because now the company had the unique rules of bankruptcy to get what it wanted. All throughout United's recent bankruptcy, for example, union leaders had verbally bombarded management, hoping to build credibility among members by riding a wave of anger. "In Medieval times," one United union leader had said, in a rather memorable quote, and certainly not the only one, "people guilty of this kind of greed would have been boiled in oil."

Moak was less colorful, but he did step up the rhetoric. "We will make Herculean efforts to impress upon Delta management that the Delta pilots will not be their ATM," he wrote in late 2005, in a letter to pilots. "If management's action is to destroy the airline, I can't control them," he told the Associated Press several months later. In bankruptcy, as Moak had been reminded most recently by what befell pilots at United and US Airways, the normal process of labor relations—one governed by the Railway Labor Act of 1926 and monitored by the National Mediation Board—gave way to more company-friendly and union-unfriendly means to scrap collective bargaining agreements, nullify pension plans and get quick concessions. "They almost have superpowers," he lamented, referring to what the company could do while in bankruptcy.

Still, management couldn't truly do absolutely whatever it wanted—not after Frank Lorenzo had abused the bankruptcy laws to win labor concessions in the 1980s, prompting new laws that required a bankruptcy judge to consider the arguments of both management and unions. At Delta, the job of making management's case fell to Ed Bastian, who said without new labor cuts, the company could not meet the terms of its loan covenants and—ultimately—could not survive.

In normal circumstances, airline workers can only strike after the National Mediation Board—consisting of three members appointed by the U.S. president (of whom only two can be from the president's party)—declares a negotiating impasse. Even then, the union must first wait through a 30-day cooling off period. And even *then*, if there's still no settlement, the president can appoint an emergency board to deter a strike, a step often taken with great political calculation. President Bill Clinton, for example, used an emergency board to stop American's pilots from striking in 1997, although he did not do so when Northwest pilots walked off their jobs the following year. A likely reason: Northwest's pilot union was ALPA, a national organization affiliated with the powerful AFL-CIO umbrella union, which, in turn, is a major supporter of America's Democratic Party. American's pilots, by contrast, belonged to less politically influential Allied Pilots Association, an independent union representing only American's pilots.

For Delta's new executive team—now led by Jerry Grinstein, Ed Bastian and Jim Whitehurst, with Glen Hauenstein manning the network—yet another round of pilot concessions was essential, just as it had been in 2004. The airline had, after all, lost another $2.2 billion in 2005, excluding special items, exceeding even the 2001, 2002 and 2003 losses—only 2004 had been worse. The 2005 bloodbath, moreover, was all the more frustrating given all the work everyone in the company had done, and all the personal financial pain they had endured, to lower costs, only for those efforts to be obliterated by an uncontrollable surge in fuel prices. On top of that, 2005 had started out with a good measure of revenue optimism. But that too washed away in a flood of excess seats in the marketplace—too much supply relative to demand always means lower fares.

From 2001 through 2005, a half decade of hell for America's Big Six legacy carriers, Delta managed to grow its revenues 16.6 percent, from less than $14 billion to more than $16 billion. But its operating costs grew 17.5 percent, leaving the company worse off than it was the year of 9/11. The annual interest payments on Delta's debt, meanwhile, ballooned by 137 percent. By 2005, it was spending nearly a billion dollars annually not on its people or its planes or on pleasing its passengers—but just paying interest on its debt because of its past borrowings. Cumulative net losses, everything included, had now reached $12.4 billion in those five miserable years, one of the worst strings of financial losses for any airline ever—and by far the worst ever in Delta's long history.

For the rest of the industry, meanwhile, 2005 was a bit more encouraging. Collectively, the U.S. airline industry eked out a tiny operating profit—its first since 2000—as revenues grew a bullish 12 percent, driven in large part by a 15 percent increase in international revenues. U.S. airlines were also carrying more passengers than ever, flying more seats more miles than ever before and, even more importantly, filling a greater percentage of those seats than ever before. They were doing all this, moreover, with 119,000 fewer workers than they had five years earlier, meaning far greater labor productivity—internet bookings meant ever fewer call center agents, for example, and although some innovations like mobile phone boarding passes were still years away, others like airport kiosks had, during those five years, become commonplace. Nevertheless, the industry's net result for 2005—a figure that, unlike the operating result, includes taxes and interest payments—was still stained red, highlighting a severe debt burden.

The question: Would the second half of the thus-far dismal decade, the half beginning in 2006, mark the start of a turnaround? As harsh as the prior five years had been, after all—and they were unprecedentedly harsh—the airline industry had always been cyclical. Perhaps the cycle would turn up in 2006?

Discouragingly, Delta didn't start the second half well. In the month of January alone, it lost $213 million excluding special items. It lost another $138 million in February before nearly breaking even in March, a peak month for Delta's Florida routes, when healthy airlines flying those routes typically earn outsized profits. Delta also faced a growing problem of managers at all levels, frustrated by one too many pay cuts, leaving the company. This was especially vexing in the area of information technology, where workers once again enjoyed an attractive job market following the dot-com dip a few years earlier. Employees of all sorts, for that matter, enjoyed the opportunities presented by a now-booming economy—why put up with pay cuts at a failing airline when you could work for a fast-expanding company in the go-go housing, finance, retail or energy sectors? In time, with all the distractions inherent to full-scale restructuring, bureaucratic processes were becoming wasteful and out of control. One management-level employee hired in 2006 recalled settling in at a desk in Delta's headquarters building and receiving a packet of forms for new hires. The packet came from the airline's human resources office two floors down in the same building—but had been sent via FedEx, surely connecting at the admired cargo airline's hub in Memphis. That same headquarters building—the General Offices— had gone from drab to dilapidated; employees still recall plumbing issues, including one that left parts of the building smelling like sewage. Forget beautification: Delta didn't even have money for standard upkeep. At about the same time, Delta was more publicly earning all kinds of bad headlines, including one for losing a dog who was on her way home from the Westminster Kennel Club Dog Show, where she had won a best-in-breed award. She had escaped from a dog carrier while she was in transit at Delta's JFK terminal, another woebegone facility.

All this, however, was—in retrospect—a distraction from an emerging truth: that underneath the outward signs of gloom and distress was an industry turnaround in the making, one that, even if Delta was at the moment recovering more slowly than its peers, would eventually put Delta at the forefront of that turnaround. The year was not even a week old when, on Jan. 5, 2006, Independence Air, the airline with the impossibly low fares and the impossibly high costs, the "suicide bomber" reaping so much havoc on industry pricing, went to airline heaven. The new post-merger US Airways was slashing capacity along the east coast as GE redeployed many of its leased planes to other airlines outside the U.S. JetBlue was, for the first time ever, losing money, just like other airlines. Just like other airlines, after all, it was a victim of high fuel prices. But it felt that fuel shock even more acutely. For one thing, its new Brazilian jets now arriving—the Embraer 190s that would hold just 100 pas-sengers, with the hope of bringing low-cost service to midsized cities without the populations to fill larger jets—didn't have the economics for low-fare flying when fuel was expensive, as it now was. Plus, the average distance of a JetBlue flight—air-lines call this "stage length"—was rather long, and long flights, of course, burn the most fuel. They also tend to generate somewhat higher fares than shorter flights, but the helpful increase in fares is usually less than the unhelpful increase in fuel costs. Furthermore, as a rather young airline, JetBlue's biggest cost advantage over its competitors was the labor cost advantage of its junior workforce—and now labor costs were an ever-shrinking portion of its total cost base. They just didn't matter as much, in a sense. JetBlue lost money for all of 2005, as it did again in the first quarter of 2006. It was actually putting more money into its fuel tanks than into the pockets of its workers. Yes, it had come to that: Some airlines were starting to pay more for fuel than for salaries, wages and benefits, something that had never before been the case.

JetBlue's problems were perhaps best described by none other than Doug Parker, the US Airways CEO, in an April letter to his employees

To: US Employees (especially to our Charlotte-based team):

In announcing JetBlue's intention to add a handful of regional jet flights from JFK to Charlotte and Raleigh-Durham yesterday, JetBlue CEO David Neeleman made the following comment:

"Charlotte and Raleigh-Durham have natural ties to New York, but until now, the people of North Carolina have overpaid for sub-standard service." As US Airways is the largest provider of service from Charlotte to New York, we can assume that at least some of Mr. Neeleman's remarks were targeted at us. A number of you were upset by these remarks, so I thought I should share my views with you.

First, I know David pretty well, and I can assure you he is a genuinely good person. That he chose to make such a remark is probably indicative of the stress that JetBlue is under, and we should not take his remarks personally. JetBlue is experiencing a relative profitability decline that is unprecedented in our industry. It is probably very hard for them to hear that US Airways (who they'd counted on being gone by now) is expecting to be profitable in 2006 (excluding transition-related expenses), while they have disclosed that they expect to be unprofitable.

Their problems are serious and structural: 1) they have a low cost structure that is driven primarily by a low average age (low seniority employees, low maintenance on new airplanes for three years, etc.); 2) to maintain a low average age, they must grow; and 3) there are no more growth markets in our industry (which is where our survival really hurt them). And their problems are well appreciated by the financial markets. Since our merger, US Airways stock has appreciated over 100%, while JetBlue is down about 20%. It doesn't appear that our customers are overpaying; rather it appears that passengers aren't willing to pay JetBlue enough for them to be profitable.

Some of this is likely due to their own service. While US Airways has been the leading on-time major airline since our merger, JetBlue has

been among the worst! To characterize arriving late in JFK with a TV in front of you as better service than being on time in LGA with a first class cabin, an award-winning frequent flyer program, business clubs and a global alliance, suggests that JetBlue may be looking at the wrong service standards.

The fact of the matter is JetBlue is struggling mightily, and the hard-working employees of US Airways are a big reason why. Rather than get upset by their comments, we should keep them in context.

US Airways is going to be here long after JetBlue—that was not their plan, and they are trying to figure out what to do about it.

We, on the other hand, know what to do—we will compete aggressively, we will focus on running our own race and we will win. Thanks so much for taking care of our customers, and please keep it up.

Sincerely,
Doug

AirTran too, although it had eked out its seventh straight year of operating profits in 2005, was feeling the squeeze as fuel rose to one third of its operating costs in the first quarter of 2006, a quarter in which it lost $5 million. The longtime Delta tormentor, although certainly glad to see Independence Air disappear, naturally saw its business under pressure in Atlanta now that Delta was operating more than 1,000 flights a day there, an unprecedented buildup that forced AirTran to look for business elsewhere, notably Midwestern markets like Chicago and Milwaukee and Akron-Canton. BWI, the airport south of Baltimore that also serves parts of Washington's metropolitan area, was another growth market. By late 2005, in the wake of Delta's Operation Clockwork, about a third of AirTran's seats were no longer flying to or from Atlanta. AirTran was also, incidentally, retreating from its buildup at Dallas-Fort Worth, where American defended its turf with vigor. Back in Atlanta, Delta even terminated an agreement to accept AirTran customers during operational distress, such as if AirTran canceled a flight and needed to reaccommodate stranded passengers—these agreements are normally commonplace between even the fiercest competitors. And AirTran's pilots, who now enjoyed higher wage scales than Delta pilots (although the average Delta pilot still earned more thanks to far higher average seniority), were clamoring for a new contract. AirTran's pilots, unlike JetBlue's at the time, were represented by a union.

Even Southwest, although (thanks to its hedges) paying less for fuel than its competitors, was nonetheless paying an increasing amount as that hedge protection gradually weakened. It had essentially pre-purchased 70 percent of its 2006 fuel at a price equivalent to $36 per barrel of oil, for example. That was still a huge advantage—but a dwindling advantage compared to the $26 it had paid for 85 percent of its fuel needs in 2005. Sure enough, even Southwest began to raise prices, with its average one-way fare surpassing $100 by the end of the year. Low-cost carriers were disproportionately disadvantaged by extreme fuel prices—a counterintuitive economic irony is that low-cost airlines, which are designed to win with cost advantages rather than revenue advantages, are less able than other airlines to manage a fuel cost crisis. Southwest had its hedges and modern 737s, sure. And AirTran and JetBlue had their state-of-the art, fuel-efficient planes too, no small matter when dealing with expensive fuel. But underneath all their attractiveness... their new planes, their junior workforces, their streamlined business models, their lack of legacy pensions, their economies of scale achieved through constant growth... underneath all of all this was a core principle that superseded everything: They needed to keep fares low to stimulate demand among discretionary travelers. After all, being a low-*cost* carrier was merely a means to an end, and that end was being able to keep *fares* low. Now, keeping fares low was becoming increasingly difficult. With fuel costs (which impact all airlines more or less equally) having become such a big percentage of overall costs, low-cost competitors, whose costs are relatively low thanks to things other than fuel, now had *less of an overall cost advantage* over their legacy competitors—and *just as much of a revenue disadvantage* as always.

Fares, naturally, were rising everywhere as domestic capacity shrank, as higher fuel costs pressured airlines to increase revenues and as international markets boomed—international markets the low-cost carriers, with their short-range airplanes, were ill-equipped to exploit. Delta was among many carriers to implement fuel surcharges on international routes; these rose in tandem with fuel prices. Back at home, meanwhile, Delta and Northwest were now slashing capacity in bankruptcy. American was grounding many of its older MD-80s, further tilting the supply-and-demand balance toward the industry's favor. And the U.S. economy, fueled by a spasm of home buying—and certainly not hurt by the stimulative effect of airfares that were still cheap, in historical terms, for consumers and businesses—just kept growing.

Domestic capacity was also falling as big carriers outsourced a larger portion of their domestic flying to regional partners, a move primarily to reduce labor costs but one that also meant replacing larger planes with smaller ones. Captain Duane Worth of Northwest Airlines, who was then head of the national Air Line Pilots Association, noted that since 9/11, legacy airlines had cut 6,000 pilot jobs, while regional airlines had added 7,000. By early 2006, regional carriers such as Comair, Atlantic Southeast, SkyWest, Chautauqua, Freedom Airlines and Shuttle America were operating more than 20 percent of Delta's domestic capacity, measured by available seat miles (the number of seats available for sale times the number of miles they fly). That 20 percent figure was a higher percentage than at most airlines, because Delta had negotiated greater scope to outsource—a more flexible "scope clause"—in its 2004 pilot concession deal. But others were similarly as enthusiastic, none more so than Northwest, which purchased the carcass of Independence Air just to get its operating certificate (because it's easier to buy an existing certificate than to establish a new one) in order to launch a new regional unit called Compass

Airlines, the creation of which became possible only in the confines of bankruptcy. Northwest would own Compass, but Compass wouldn't offer its employees the kind of pay and benefits that employees working directly for Northwest could expect.

All this regional flying activity, importantly, coincided with even greater yield gains in these markets—yield, remember, is how many cents, on average, a passenger pays to fly one mile. These smaller markets were a refuge of sorts, uncontested, as they were, by low-cost carriers and their full-sized jets, which were too large to penetrate smaller markets, either because their runways weren't long enough or—even more commonly—because their local economies weren't big enough. Also at about this time, many of America's small- and medium-sized communities were furiously plugging into the booming global economy. In the Golden Triangle region of Mississippi, for example, surrounding the tiny airport in a town called Columbus were a steel factory owned by Russian investors and a helicopter factory owned by the parent company of Airbus. Executives at both companies had exactly one connection to the world: three daily 50-seat jet flights to Atlanta on planes painted in Delta's colors but actually flown on its behalf by regional airlines. Foreign automakers were dotting the American south with factories, taking advantage of non-unionized labor and the weaker U.S. dollar, for sure. But of no small importance was being just a quick Delta flight away from Atlanta, because if you could make it there, you could make it anywhere—the world was just a nonstop flight away. Cincinnati, meanwhile, was building engines for the world's airplanes, Salt Lake City was sending Utah's minerals to industrializing economies around the globe and New York City was what it had always been: a center of all things international.

The airline labor market was changing too, and not only because of the availability of young pilots willing to work for less at regional airlines. Mechanics were actually an even greater victim of outsourcing, as carriers closed some of their own maintenance facilities, particularly those responsible for labor-intensive "heavy checks" required once every few years. Well-trained mechanics were working in China and El Salvador and Singapore for far less money and with few of the restrictions imposed by in-house unions. Northwest, in fact, as it was navigating through bankruptcy, had just broken its mechanics union by operating right through a strike, with remarkably few disruptions, by using outsourced replacements. Technologies like internet check-in and self-service airport kiosks, all the while, continued to make flying less labor intensive on the ground. And in the air, all but a few planes flying in 2006 required just two pilots, not three.

Distribution costs were falling too, and not only because of the internet. In 2004, the Bush administration removed many of the rules governing competition between global distribution systems, the electronic supermarkets that travel agencies use to book tickets for their clients. These GDSs had been heavily regulated since the days when American would use its Sabre system to manipulate markets by hiding competitors' flights. But American no longer owned Sabre, and the internet made fare shopping far more transparent, making these regulations somewhat obsolete. So now, airlines had the freedom to list their flights in one system but not another—or to list some of their fares in a system but not, perhaps, their cheapest fares, which might only be available on their own websites. This naturally gave carriers new negotiating leverage, because the main advantage of a GDS was supposed to be that it presented a wide range of convenient and affordable options. And airlines used that new leverage to hammer down their booking fees. Ultimately, what emerged was a model whereby airlines promised to list all their fares in the major systems (which made GDSs happy) in exchange for lower fees (which made airlines happy)—"full-content agreements," these were called.

Airlines in 2006, more generally, were reaping gains from earlier investments in self-service technologies (such as the kiosks), new planes, electronic ticketing, advanced revenue management, flight management software and curved "winglets" added to the ends of wings, which increased fuel efficiency. To be sure, these advances were no cure-alls to the many woes which still cursed the industry: expensive fuel, high taxation, a fragmented competitive landscape and ultra-sensitivity to demand and cost shocks. But momentum was shifting in favor of the U.S. "Big Six"—American, United, Northwest, Continental and US Airways and, of course, Delta.

Even the first-quarter loss for Delta, the laggard, had a silver lining: It was a significantly smaller loss than the one for the same period one year earlier. What's more, big cost cuts were coming, from pilots and elsewhere, and these would further improve results. And Delta was still winding down Song—its last flight would be May 1. But it didn't even have to wait that long to turn the corner. In April, Delta earned a $22 million net profit excluding special items. Then $8 million in May. And then a hearty $145 million in June. The turnaround was underway.

And the bankruptcy process? From a financial standpoint, "progress" would understate what Delta was achieving. More accurately, it was conducting a catharsis. Already by mid-February, it had court approval for $200 million worth of savings from renegotiated or terminated aircraft contracts with lessors and bankers. It had reworked or rejected real estate and vendor contracts too and could quickly impose pay and benefit cuts on non-pilot employees, nearly all of whom were not unionized. With its funds from Amex and GE, Delta was able to pay for day-to-day operations as well as for the hefty fees charged by its lawyers and consultants—no surprise given that United had just spent more than $300 million on professional fees during its own bankruptcy.

Delta also managed to secure concessions from its Comair pilots and mechanics—remember, Delta owned Comair—although the regional unit's flight attendants threatened to strike. And the court approved a package of financial incentives for senior executives to discourage them from leaving. Naturally, Moak criticized the incentives, which were worth about $14 million. His most vociferous criticism, though, was directed toward the bankruptcy judge herself, who had also faced criticism from other stakeholders; she gave up the case in January, ostensibly for health reasons, not because ALPA had asked her to remove herself after she called pilot pay "hideously high" and said—as *USA Today* reported—"the only 'good thing' about pilots is they must retire at 60." The very fact that a general interest national newspaper was focusing not only on a bankruptcy case involving a giant airline (that was to be expected), but on the case's judge, was unusual. Prudence Beatty's courtroom "demeanor causes turbulence," blared the headline. Beatty, the accompanying story said, "does not always stay on point" and "regularly interrupts witness testimony with her personal stories about flying." (The story also quoted her defenders, such as a law clerk who had worked for her, saying she could be "offensive" but was "brilliant.")

Also in January, the airline secured a $300 million letter of credit from Merrill Lynch, which offset the cash that Delta's nervous processor of Visa and MasterCard payments forced it to hold in reserve—credit card issuers promise protection to their cardholders, meaning those issuers could be on the hook for huge sums of money if an airline goes out of business and can't provide refunds for trips that have been purchased but not yet flown. The following month, February, Delta won court approval to hedge about 26 percent of its fuel needs.

As Delta was conducting its catharsis, moreover, some of its rivals were encountering heightened pressures. American, for one, which barely escaped bankruptcy after last-minute bankruptcy-like concessions in 2003, now had $20 billion in debt, not to mention souring labor relations made worse by another spat over executive bonuses. Helped though it was by Delta's retreat from Dallas-Fort Worth, American was beginning to feel nervous about all the restructuring its rivals were undertaking—in the commoditized airline industry, the airline with the highest operating costs was often the least profitable, because consumers aren't willing to pay more to fly a particular airline just because it pays its pilots more than other airlines pay their own pilots. After more than three years under court protection, United finally managed to exit bankruptcy in February. But it did so with a business plan premised on $50 oil, a Song-like LCC called Ted that wasn't proving any more successful than Song and revenue projections that were already undermined by Southwest's targeted attacks, including a decision to enter United's Washington Dulles hub. Even a dismissive rival like Continental, the airline that once said Delta needed "adult supervision," was clearly wary as its rival slashed costs. AirTran, on the other hand, said it actually wanted Delta to start profiting so it would act more rationally; its executives often complained a desperate Delta hurt both airlines.

***

Delta was indeed becoming a different Delta, a different Delta from the one that priced erratically, dumped capacity into markets and fought desperately for market share in Florida, bloodying everyone, itself included, while doing so. Song and SimpliFares were gone. So was a lot of capacity, thanks largely to Delta's ability to use bankruptcy to shed planes. Indeed, Delta slashed capacity 9 percent in the first quarter of 2006. But nothing better exemplified Delta's dramatic transformation than the globalization of its network.

Bankruptcy is a powerful cost-cutting tool. But it's less helpful for growing revenues. And Delta had just as much of a revenue problem as it had a cost problem. Growing revenues wasn't as easy as tearing up a contract or handing back a plane to a lessor. "We've been tremendously successful on the costs," Ed Bastian told the Bloomberg news service at the time, "but if we don't dent the revenue deficit, I'll be honest: We're not going to make it." Cutting capacity certainly helped unit revenues, because the reduction in supply squeezed up average fares, but cutting capacity wasn't going to solve Delta's problem. What might actually solve Delta's problem: recognition that its largest planes were more profitably deployed abroad than at home.

Or even more bluntly: longhaul-capable aircraft actually flying longhaul routes.

Thus began an unprecedented international expansion involving far-flung points around the globe, masterminded by Glen Hauenstein and his deputy Bob Cortelyou, the same duo that had internationalized Continental. Already in 2005 Delta was operating new flights from Atlanta to Moscow, New York JFK to Barcelona and New York JFK to Berlin, while returning to the Atlanta-Buenos Aires and Atlanta-Rio de Janeiro markets. It also added a slew of new markets in Mexico, the Caribbean and Canada, some from Cincinnati and Salt Lake City as well as from Atlanta and New York. It even began flying from Paris to Chennai in India, relying on passengers connecting from its own flights to Paris but also from those of its partner Air France.

That was just the beginning. Recognizing Atlanta's ability to suction passengers from just about anywhere in the country, Delta sent planes from its largest hub to Athens, Venice, Nice, Copenhagen, Düsseldorf and Edinburgh—and those were just the new destinations in Europe. It added Atlanta flights to Tel Aviv in Israel, to Quito in Ecuador, to Managua, San Pedro de Sula, Roatán and San Salvador in Central America and to a dozen more points in Mexico, the Caribbean and Canada.

Delta was no less aggressive from New York JFK, where it had fewer connecting passengers to feed longhaul flights. But it didn't need as many connecting passengers there, because it could draw from a giant and wealthy local population base. So it added new JFK flights to Budapest, Dublin, Manchester, São Paulo, Mumbai and even Kiev in the Ukraine, a market no other U.S. airline had touched—and one that offered financial incentives for airlines that agreed to launch flights, a common economic development strategy. Delta was doing all of this, moreover, without buying any new planes—it simply took 767s (and later 757s) that had been languishing on domestic routes and sent them as far away as they could fly.

This international offensive was the centerpiece of Delta's strategy to reinvigorate its revenues. But Hauenstein and his team were making domestic moves too. First, they were following through on plans to greatly reduce the airline's dependence on Florida, a market with big volumes but low fares. In 2005, Delta had flown nearly 18 million seats to Florida; in 2006, that number would drop to 14 million, a 21 percent drop. It accomplished that by "downgauging," or flying smaller aircraft—no more big twin-aisle 767s flying from Atlanta to cities as small as Fort Myers, now that these 767s were instead flying to places like Kiev—and by reducing the number of daily flights on most routes, like Atlanta-Tampa, which it would now fly just eight times each day, each direction, rather than 13.

Hauenstein also cut heavily in Cincinnati, which no longer had the regional jet first-mover advantage of a half decade earlier—competing hubs, like Continental's in Cleveland, had upgraded from turboprops to RJs too. At the same time, if customers were no longer so wowed by regional jet comfort, airlines were even less wowed by their economics: They were dogs in an era of high fuel prices, burning a lot of expensive fuel while producing, at most, 50 passengers worth of revenue to cover the costs. So Delta slashed Cincinnati capacity, in most cases keeping routes but reducing the number of daily flights on those routes.

With cuts like these, Delta's domestic capacity in the first half of 2006 plummeted 14 percent compared to the same period a year earlier while international capacity was *increasing* 16 percent, driven by a 26 percent jump in Latin American capacity and a 13 percent rise in capacity to Europe. And the story didn't end there.

To make all the new international flights work, Hauenstein knew he needed to feed them as many passengers from around the country as possible, a task that required the fine art of scheduling airplanes at just the right times so that passengers from many cities all arrive at the hub airport with enough time to make their international connections—but not so much time that they choose an airline offering a shorter total journey time. To that end, Delta began piping new feeder routes into its Atlanta hub. There was Kalamazoo, Mich.; Atlantic City, N.J.; Binghamton, N.Y.; Bloomington, Ind.; Champaign, Ill.; Madison, Wis., and more, many of them college towns with growing numbers of students spending semesters or summers abroad. The idea was that if just a few people per day from these places connected to an international flight, the aggregation of all those people could fill widebody airplanes. An airline's revenue-generating power, after all, doesn't depend on the number of flights it offers but rather the number of possible itineraries, nonstop and connecting alike.

Delta was also determined to become more relevant in Los Angeles, the second largest airline market in the U.S. after New York—and like New York, a highly fragmented market that no single carrier dominated. At the main airport LAX, Hauenstein added nearly 20 new routes, including many to Mexico. Delta's Salt Lake City hub got new routes too, in some cases with new 70-seat regional jets that were far more economical than the 50-seaters (because they burned just a bit more fuel but had up to 20 more paying passengers) and more of which Delta was now allowed to fly thanks to earlier ALPA concessions on outsourcing. And outsourcing was precisely Delta's strategy: It took planes away from Comair, which it owned, and redistributed them to even lower-cost regional airlines like SkyWest and Chautauqua.

Getting New York right was, perhaps, the greatest challenge, and the one with the highest stakes. Los Angeles would always have its limits for Delta, and Salt Lake

City was simply too small to be a major profit center. So much of the company's future rested on the success of two hubs: Atlanta, perhaps the strongest hub in America, and New York JFK, a hub contested by countless airlines domestic and foreign alike, with a limited number of domestic pipes to funnel in passengers for international flights—most of New York's domestic flights, JetBlue's JFK off-peak offerings notwithstanding, were at LaGuardia Airport, at the opposite end of the New York City borough of Queens and much closer to Manhattan.

In a brilliantly devilish move that killed two birds, Delta hired a cheap regional operator called Freedom Air to begin adding 50-seat jets, one by one, at JFK. They fed Delta's bevy of international flights, yes. But the sheer number of new planes also gummed up operations at the airport, wreaking havoc on JetBlue's schedule reliability. By the summer of 2007, in fact, JFK was so badly congested that regulators felt compelled to reinstitute regulations on adding new flights from the airport. Delta's flights certainly suffered too, but if a seven-hour journey to say, Paris, was delayed by an hour, that's a delay most travelers could tolerate—and anyway, how else were they going to get to Paris? But an hour delay that nearly doubled the journey time of a JetBlue flight to Washington or Boston? This had more adverse consequences. Besides, more than two thirds of JetBlue's flights flew into and out of JFK. Befuddle its operations there and, well, checkmate. Why would Delta have done such a thing? "Hauenstein said we can't beat 'em head to head, so we'll just mess with their operation," JetBlue CEO David Neeleman speculated years later. "It really affected the airport."

Was it a dirty trick? "I look at it as 'bravo,'" Neeleman's lieutenant at the time (and future successor) Dave Barger recalled years later of the move—which, to be clear, Delta never explicitly acknowledged. "I can't prove it, but that's certainly the conclusion we've made regarding Delta congesting, intentionally, Kennedy Airport. Brilliant. And they ended up with a large slot portfolio on the backside of it"—slots Delta could later use for more productive purposes.

Partly, of course, Delta simply had to find something to do with all its toxic 50-seaters, and the JFK deployment was the least bad among bad options. It couldn't shed many 50-seaters overall, because it was locked into its deal with SkyWest. So it used them as weapons of retaliation, not only against JetBlue but also against AirTran and others. When AirTran announced new Atlanta flights to Seattle, for example, Delta responded with a CRJ-200 blitzkrieg on its rival's top Orlando markets—Orlando markets AirTran had launched, remember, partly to diversify away from Atlanta and away from markets where it competed directly against Delta. Delta knew these flights—new high-unit-cost flying in low-fare markets—would certainly lose money. But they wouldn't lose *too* much money in the context of a giant global airline, and they would send an important message to AirTran that further incursions into Delta markets would not go unpunished. Delta was also, however, starting to receive more and more 70-seat and even 90-seat jets, including 70-seat Embraers that were less cramped than typical regional jets. These new jets felt more like full-sized narrowbody airframes—not so different from a 737, for example, although without the middle seats that passengers don't like anyway. These were the E-Jets that JetBlue was regrettably introducing to its fleet (in its case a larger version and with 100 all-economy seats). Delta's 70-seaters were flying more productively in higher-yield markets. It also used these Embraer 170s in markets where it knew it would lose money but where it needed to have a presence if it was going to be the preferred airline in a given city. In New York, for example, it didn't want to fly full-sized narrowbodies against American on the LaGuardia-Dallas route—the more seats it offered in that market, the more money it would lose. So it flew the 170s and kept an important line, connecting two important dots, on its route map without losing too much money in the process. Ditto for the hotly competitive LaGuardia-Chicago O'Hare route.

The network team brought other innovations to flight schedules, including one that, even if not as sexy as announcements of exotic longhaul destinations, was just as important: seasonal and day-of-week scheduling. Operating the same schedules day in and day out, as airlines had generally done, certainly had its advantages. It was simple. It was consistent. And Southwest had become the most successful airline in the history of the world largely thanks to intense utilization of assets—especially keeping its airplanes in the air as many revenue-generating hours per day as possible. Sure, sometimes flights weren't all that full and fares weren't all that high, but as long as fuel wasn't exorbitantly expensive, whatever revenue did come in might be enough to cover the costs, especially considering the costs were lower precisely because the planes were flying so much—the cost of owning an aircraft, for example, could be spread among many more productive flight hours. These were economic realities of what was largely a fixed-cost industry—in other words, costs that were, remember, roughly the same regardless of how much an airline flew, and so the unit costs, or the costs of flying a given number of seats a given distance, declined when the airline flew more and could spread those fixed costs among more seats flying more miles.

But now fuel, a *variable* cost, was exorbitantly expensive—the more an airline flew, the more it spent on this ever-growing expense. So while it remained true that an airplane didn't make money on the ground, these days, sometimes the airplane at least lost less money on the ground than in the air, if a flight wasn't very full or fares weren't very high. Demand—this part had not changed—is not the same in January as it is in July. It's not even the same on a Monday as it is on a Tuesday. So airlines had always taken for granted that meant one thing: lower fares on Tuesday than on Monday, because of fewer people chasing roughly the same number of seats. But Hauenstein figured he could turn that upside down. Instead of the same number of seats but lower fares when demand was lower, Delta could get the same fares as on high-demand days if it simply flew less when demand was lower. So fly less it did, during off-peak seasons and on off-peak days, by parking its oldest and least efficient aircraft at those times (a tactic, incidentally, that Northwest had also been using, seemingly with success).

Delta also wasn't shy about operating flights infrequently in markets with limited demand, including some overseas markets where demand merited perhaps just four flights per week rather than daily service. Business travelers, of course, like daily service. But leisure markets like Atlanta-Venice or Atlanta-Nice were more appropriately served less regularly to keep supply in check, relative to demand, and thus keep fares rather high. A market like Atlanta-Paris, to be sure, with its heavy corporate travel demand and passengers connecting on both ends thanks to the Air France partnership, was served no less than three times daily. This was dynamic airline scheduling at its finest.

Rivals were taken aback by Delta's hyperactive network reconstruction. Continental, with its long history of condescension toward Delta dating back to Gordon Bethune's "box of rocks" comment in the late 1990s—never mind that Delta's network team had in some ways borrowed from the same playbook they had authored at Continental—publicly questioned the sanity of sending so many planes abroad, at once, to places many American had never heard of. This was the airline, after all, that had started Song and introduced SimpliFares. In a conference call with Wall Street analysts in early 2006, Jeff Smisek, Continental's president, managed to insult not just the idea but also Delta's people: "Frankly, they're taking more business risks than I would if I had their execution capabilities, but that's their decision."

The airline's more understated CEO Larry Kellner explained why, in his view, Continental's international growth made more sense than Delta's. "I think the difference is," Kellner said, "if you look at Delta at JFK versus us at Newark, we've got a true hub operation in Newark with a broad base of connecting traffic and the gates to maintain that…. So I think competitively, we're in a little different position at Newark than Delta is at JFK."

Smisek jumped back in: "How they'll do in Kiev in the winter is a question that's best addressed to them." Translation: Everyone knew how Delta would do in Kiev in the winter. Not well.

What Smisek and other critics perhaps didn't fully realize about Hauenstein's selection of markets like Kiev—Kiev, seen as the most marginal of all Delta's new markets, had become the industry metaphor for Delta losing its mind—was that Hauenstein himself didn't believe *all* the markets would be profitable. He was even downright doubtful about one or two—he reluctantly let his staff convince him to try Düsseldorf, a market he himself had exited back in his Continental days; flying there from Newark, he remembered, hadn't worked well. But he understood something important. For all the airline industry's unique and daunting challenges, one advantage this industry has over others is that its most important physical assets— aircraft—are actually very flexible. Building an expensive factory in the wrong place can sink a manufacturing company. But an airplane deployed to the wrong destination can rather easily be redeployed somewhere better. Given that even the best airline network forecasters had imperfect records, it was better to try everything that made any sense at all, Hauenstein reasoned, than to try nothing. As long as he was right more often that he was wrong, Delta would be better off for having taken the risk. If Delta didn't shoot, it would never score.

Over at American's headquarters (CentrePort, it's called) near Dallas-Fort Worth International Airport, the airline's CEO Gerard Arpey joined the Delta-bashing on his own earnings call, if somewhat less caustically than Smisek. He criticized not just the selection of markets but also the whole idea of seasonal scheduling. "We'll see how they do," he said. "But what we've been focused on the past couple of years is looking at all of our international markets and asking ourselves which of these markets are going to be successful operated for a full year. So you're going to find over time that our schedule, if you look at it, has become and will increasingly become flatter and flatter, so the summer doesn't look a whole lot different than the winter." He was, of course, differentiating his airline from what Delta was doing.

Five years later, most other airlines were, like Delta, varying their schedules by season and even by day of week. American, the holdout, was what Delta had been: bankrupt.

For now, with all the bold new 2006 routes, Delta had indeed been right more often than it had been wrong. Not every new market worked: Atlanta-Edinburgh was one flop. But others like New York-São Paulo proved highly lucrative. Still others like New York-Kiev, while not big money-makers, hardly did as badly as Smisek and others predicted. Even in the winter.

And Düsseldorf? Flown from Atlanta rather than Newark, it proved a winner thanks to companies like ThyssenKrupp, a Düsseldorf-based manufacturer with a plant in Mobile, Ala., which German executives could reach conveniently via Delta's Atlanta hub. International markets like these were growing rapidly in the mid-2000s, and Delta had the right hubs to serve them.

Even with the network-driven revenue improvements, work remained on the cost side of the equation. A lot of work. Delta still needed a pilot agreement, which, at the end of 2006's first quarter, remained elusive. Pilot savings were now doubly essential, not only to keep ahead of extreme fuel prices but also to ensure Delta had sufficiently competitive labor costs to make its international strategy successful. If routes to marginal destinations like Budapest were going to work, they would work only with a labor cost advantage. Atlanta's international routes, for their part, depended on connecting passengers, who are by nature more price sensitive than nonstop passengers, because they can usually choose to connect at other hubs if the price isn't right. And international routes at New York JFK, although less dependent on connecting traffic, were dependent on local New York travelers who—unlike their counterparts in most other metro areas—did indeed have an array of other nonstop options on many routes. On the New York-Frankfurt route, for example, Delta was competing head to head against Lufthansa and Singapore Airlines, both well regarded by travelers for their products in the air and on the ground (and by investors for their sterling balance sheets). Continental too, with a better service reputation than Delta, was flying to Frankfurt from Newark. So Delta needed a cost advantage—most obviously achieved through labor savings—to offset its inherent revenue disadvantage.

Delta's latest request for pilot concessions was a tough sell, to be sure. But this time it had more leverage. It was in bankruptcy now, and on Nov. 1, 2005, the company's lawyers filed a court motion to terminate the contract signed with ALPA back in June 2001, the one that had already been amended with harsh concessions in November 2004. But Delta didn't actually terminate the contract, because both sides agreed, on Dec. 12, 2005, to amend it again. That was just an interim agreement with interim pay and benefit cuts, an agreement crafted to buy more time for negotiations on a long-term deal. So negotiate they did, for three more months, with escalating intensity—but still no deal.

To improve its negotiating leverage, ALPA requested and got approval from its members to strike if Delta terminated their contract. This alone hurt the airline, which lost business as a result—many travelers and their agents booked on other airlines to avoid the threatened disruption, costing the company "millions of dollars per week in lost sales."

Jerry Grinstein saw the strike threat as a bluff, albeit a costly one to the airline. "I don't think Lee Moak is a guy who would lead them into that disaster," Grinstein said years later. "And I think he knew that we weren't trying to take advantage of the pilots, or take advantage of ALPA. But there were things that had to be put together if we were going to save that company."

Management made sure the pilots knew that according to the terms of Delta's bankruptcy DIP financing, a suspension of flights for more than two days—due to a strike or just about any reason other than a 9/11-like event—would trigger a default and ground Delta forever.

"I don't think he [Moak] ever was going to strike," Grinstein concluded.

Ironically, while it wrangled with pilots, Delta was holding ceremonies around the country to celebrate the retirement of the "Spirit of Delta," the 767 that employees helped the company buy the last time things were this dire, back in 1982.

On March 13, representatives from both sides met at a Washington, D.C., hotel to argue their case before a panel of three neutral and independent arbitrators who had experience settling labor disputes. This in itself was unusual: During bankruptcy, the bankruptcy court usually handled such matters. But both sides had agreed to the arbitration panel—that was part of the December 2005 interim deal. The hearings ran from March 13 through March 23, with both sides delivering their arguments.

After appearing before the panel, both sides continued negotiating for several more weeks, pressured by panel members to reach a deal on their own. Finally, on April 14, just before the panel would have announced its decision, Delta and ALPA struck a grand bargain.

The so-called Letter of Agreement No. 51 gave Delta $280 million in annual savings, or $45 million less than the $325 million it originally demanded. But the airline did get more flexibility to outsource small plane flying—flexibility the company said "directly and materially enhances Delta's revenue-generating capacity." The deal, of course, also prevented a devastating strike.

LOA 51, as Delta pilots who worked for the company then still call it, also extended the interim agreement's 14 percent pay cut, this time until Jan. 1, 2007. This, of course, was on top of the 33 percent cut pilots swallowed in 2004—LOA 46, as they bitterly recalled that one. On Jan. 1, 2007, pilots would get a 1.5 percent raise and then another 1.5 percent in both 2008 and 2009; the agreement ran through Dec. 31, 2009. These raises, moreover, would possibly be larger depending on Delta's operating profit margins, the sort of risk-sharing arrangement that was becoming more common in the airline industry. And the company agreed to a separate profit-sharing plan worth 15 percent of the company's pretax income, with the percentage rising to 20 percent for any amount exceeding $1.5 billion—a sum that at the time, for a company struggling to keep flying, seemed unimaginable. The idea: If the company does well, employees do too.

The scope clauses covering regional jet flying permitted Delta to outsource another 15 76-seat jets in 2007 and then another 30 in 2008, plus an additional three for each new mainline jet added to Delta's fleet. These 76-seaters were the most economical of the sub-100 seat planes that were then flying. In total, Delta could now outsource a total of 200 larger regional jets—that is, those with more than 50 seats.

LOA 51 also addressed the matter of pilot pensions, which Delta was convinced needed to be terminated given the lump-sum retirement option that would constantly threaten both liquidity and operations. In fact, somewhat controversially, Delta had followed the lead of United and US Airways and stopped making its normally required catch-up payments into the pension fund after it filed for bankruptcy. Thanks to additional lobbying by Grinstein and a new law that President Bush would sign in August, non-pilot plans were frozen but not terminated, meaning current employees would get the defined benefits they had already accumulated but no new ones, and newly hired employees would not get any; going forward, everyone would get defined contributions through a 401(k) plan. But the pilot plan, including its lump-sum option, simply had to go, and ALPA agreed to let it go in exchange for an unsecured bankruptcy claim of $2.1 billion and $650 million worth of bonds. ALPA could use the money to compensate its members for their lost pensions.

The decision to terminate the pilot pension plan alarmed the PBGC, the government's pension insurer, which would pay pilots part of what they had lost. The agency didn't like the idea of Delta dumping liabilities on the taxpayer while still compensating pilots with claims and bonds—an abuse of the insurance system, in its opinion. Retired pilots were unhappy too—imagine buying a house based on a steady stream of pension checks promised by a company from which you had long ago retired, only to see the amount of those checks suddenly slashed. But Delta managed to resolve the disputes with both the PBGC and retirees. The retirees, in fact, got $800 million worth of unsecured claims, to be paid out when such claims were settled after Delta emerged from bankruptcy.

On April 21, ALPA's leadership approved LOA 51. Rank-and-file members ratified it May 31. And there it was: On June 1, 2006, just in time for the peak summer travel season, Delta had the pilot cost cuts it wanted.

With dramatic cost savings now in hand, with its network dramatically revitalized and internationalized and with the economy booming thanks to spending binges by government and home-buyers alike, both fueled by debt, the skies were finally brightening for Delta, even if fuel prices remained stubbornly high, jumping back above $70 a barrel in the spring.

But there was one more critical piece to the turnaround puzzle. If Delta was to become a truly global airline, one respected by business travelers at home and abroad, it would have to sell itself better. Despite previous efforts to modernize its image, many people still saw Delta as the country bumpkin of the airline industry—friendly, perhaps, but hardly stylish or sexy.

The makeover job fell to Jim Whitehurst and his various marketing teams, which were tasked with showing the traveling public that this was a different Delta. That was easy enough in Atlanta, where Delta's brand was ubiquitous alongside brands like Coca-Cola and CNN—and where, as a result, even routine Delta news was often on the front page of the *Atlanta Journal-Constitution*. But New York City? The world's media capital was a harder sell, made harder still by Continental's success marketing itself as the airline for New Yorkers, never mind that its Newark hub, however convenient it might have been to lower Manhattan, wasn't even in the state of New York, let alone the city. Throughout Manhattan, Continental was blanketing the city's subways, taxis, buses and even phone booths (although in decline, these were still around in the mid-2000s) with striking blue signs featuring the tagline "Work Hard, Fly Right" following terse but penetrating messages only a brusque New Yorker could love. They didn't have to use the word "Delta" for travelers to recognize the target:

- Like New Planes? Good, So Do We.
- There's a Term to Describe Old Planes: Theirs.
- Eating the Competition's Lunch... If They Served It.
- See the Real Chinatown. New Daily Nonstop Service to Beijing.
- The Most International Nonstops. No Fine Print.

It was Delta, of course, flying mostly older planes on international routes. It was Delta (although not only Delta) that didn't serve free meals anymore on shorthaul routes. It was Delta that didn't fly to China. And it was Delta that was bragging—unjustifiably, in Continental's mind—that because Newark was really in New Jersey, Delta was New York's No. 1 international airline. To be sure, Continental's ads took aim at other airlines too: "This subway can't take you to Berlin. Neither can United." But Delta was enemy No. 1, never mind that both carriers were still SkyTeam partners. At a Bear Stearns investor conference that spring, Continental's Jeff Smisek just couldn't resist the opportunity to zing his part-partner, part-rival: "We have a modern and fuel efficient fleet, unlike some of our competitors, who've got a lot of gas-sucking pigs." An equal-opportunity insulter, he also launched a verbal missile at bankrupt carriers in general: "Our network competitors have screwed their employees."

This time, Delta was prepared to respond. It launched its own New York City advertising offensive, bragging about its status as the only airline flying to all 50 states—part of why it started flying to Wilmington, Del., was just so it could say that—and the only airline flying to five continents. By year end, it was boasting service to 300 destinations worldwide, more than any other airline in the world.

But winning in New York would take more than just selling its network. So in a new campaign that debuted in 2007, Delta—with the help of New York City ad firm called SS+K—bombarded the city with a tagline, "Change Is," with those two words followed by an example of the carrier's newly upgraded services and offerings:

- Change Is: Adding to the New York Skyline
- Change Is: Clean Planes and Dirty Martinis
- Change Is: Legroom Isn't Just for Exit Rows Anymore
- Change Is: Never Being Bored Onboard

Delta, as it happens, is the triangle-shaped Greek letter that, in mathematics, represents "change." That triangle-shaped letter, in turn, inspired Delta's age-old "widget" logo. But that logo, last tweaked in 2004, was now refreshed with a three-dimensional look and was, for the first time, all red, although it was almost always surrounded by the familiar navy blue that previously formed the top part of the widget itself. Delta was stylizing itself, complete with a modern sans-serif font that might have appeared more at home at a European carrier. Was this forward-looking or ridiculous? People might have perceived Delta as many things, good and bad, but stylish wasn't generally one of those things.

To further revamp its image, Delta spent big to associate itself with popular celebrities and events. In no realm was this more evident than in sports, where Delta sponsored various teams including baseball's New York Mets, who in 2006 managed to oust the Atlanta Braves from their position as division champions, a position they had held more than a decade. Delta, of course, was the official airline of the Braves too—and of the New York Yankees and the Cincinnati Reds and other teams playing in cities where it had a big presence. In 2006, it also signed two young baseball stars as "brand ambassadors." One was David Wright, the all-star third baseman for the Mets. The other was Jeff Francoeur, not just an Atlanta Brave but also an Atlanta native. In one memorable television advertisement, Francoeur appeared to hit a baseball all the way to Copenhagen, one of Delta's many new destinations. To gain wider viewership, Delta also put commercials like these on YouTube, the still-rather-new video sharing service, which—also in 2006—Google purchased.

Associating with sports figures is one thing. But if you really wanted to be cool in the 2000s, you had to hang out with Apple. All the hippest people in America—and certainly in New York City—seemed to have its iPod music players just as they would soon, in 2007, have its iPhones. So in late 2006, Delta teamed with Apple and Panasonic to outfit more than 100 Delta planes with iPod chargers at every seat. Delta worked marketing deals with Nintendo and Netflix. And if all this weren't cool enough, Delta sponsored the Latin Grammy Awards, held in New York City that year, and the Sundance Film Festival in Utah, not far from Delta's Salt Lake City hub. Not stopping there, Delta further advanced its 21st-century image by sponsoring LGBT (lesbian, gay, bisexual and transgender) events, something that had the added benefit of making its LGBT employees feel proud of their employer.

Delta stepped up its charitable activities too, donating miles and money to a number of causes, including two closely associated with Atlanta: civil rights and Habitat for Humanity, the latter tied to former president Jimmy Carter, the Georgia native who had deregulated the airline industry. Delta painted an entire plane pink to raise awareness for breast cancer. It got an award for supporting military personnel, including the nearly 1,000 whom Delta employed, about 350 of them on military leaves of absence in 2006. To promote its commitment to good works, it painted a 767 with the words "Delta's Force for Global Good" and unveiled it at a ceremony featuring the rock legend Jon Bon Jovi, never mind that Jerry Grinstein "had no idea who the hell Jon Bon Jovi was—I mean, he could have been a bartender in Marietta, Georgia, for all I knew," Grinstein recalled.

Delta was no longer livin' on a prayer. But it was still living on money lent by GE and Amex. In 2006, though, it was turning itself around, both financially and operationally. It was making good progress, for example, with its punctuality, driven by internal initiatives and a new Atlanta runway, which opened in May. Soon Delta was issuing press releases boasting of an on-time performance record better than AirTran's. It began to invest heavily in onboard amenities too. Song was dead, yes, but many of its product features would live on elsewhere at Delta—Delta's claim when it closed Song that Delta would actually "tap the best features of its highly acclaimed Song product" turned out to be more than just face-saving spin (although it was that too). All 48 Song planes, indeed, retained their satellite televisions but were reconfigured with first-class cabins, an important sales tool for cross-country flights. Eventually 100 757s, assigned to flights exceeding 1,750 miles, would feature the modern Song-like economy cabin.

To operate profitably on international flights, a competitive business class cabin was essential, for several reasons. One was that premium passengers accounted for a disproportionate share of a flight's revenue. Just as importantly, corporations signed travel contracts with airlines based partly on the appeal of their premium products. Winning the Coca-Cola account in Atlanta was easy enough, but Delta was competing against Continental and American for huge New York City accounts like JP Morgan Chase, Verizon, Pfizer and so on. To help it with that endeavor, Delta introduced a new "Business Elite" product with the latest thing in premium flying: lie-flat seats, on ultra-long 777 journeys, anyway. It hired a celebrity Miami restaurateur, Michelle Bernstein, to revamp inflight menus. It introduced new inflight cocktails with names like the "Mile-High Mojito." Its flight attendants, now outfitted in Richard Tyler-designed uniforms, handed passengers redesigned amenity kits. It replaced cloth seats with leather ones. It changed inflight lighting to brighten cabins. It installed power outlets for passengers to recharge their laptops. And it cleaned its planes more often and more thoroughly. At one point, employees—Gerald Grinstein was one of them—volunteered to tidy up plane cabins during overnight shifts in what became known as "Delta After Dark." Delta did get into a bit of hot water with cleaning workers, though, who thought Delta might be trying to eliminate the overnight cleaning shift. "This is not a cost-cutting measure," the company reassured them.

Some other rank-and-file workers rolled their eyes too. "It is ironic," one pilot wrote on a message board, "that a senior management [team] that has spent millions on $1000/hour consultants to lower employee costs now attempts to reach out by asking employees to work for free." But many were won over by Grinstein's insistence on volunteering on the overnight shift himself.

Why was deep-cleaning the planes so important? "Have you ever seen a 767 that flew nonstop from Honolulu to Atlanta?" Grinstein asked. "I mean, it's full of crushed macadamia nuts and these Polynesian sugared drinks or some damned thing. It's the dirtiest aircraft you can imagine." Delta After Dark was part of a broader campaign called "SCOT:" safe, clean and on time.

Safe, clean and on time. Was Delta setting its sights high enough?

"When they first brought up 'safe, clean and on time,'" Grinstein recalled, "I said, 'How about bags?'" He knew the airline had a warehouse full of mishandled bags.

Not letting "great be the enemy of good?" The "art of the possible?" Pick your cliché—the impatient, high-achieving CEO was about to be reminded of it.

"Wait a second," he recalled staff members replying. "Let's do the achievable."

Losing fewer bags? That would have to wait until next year.

On the ground, Delta installed passport readers on its check-in kiosks, installed power charging stations in boarding areas, opened a seventh Crown Room lounge in Atlanta's airport and re-designed Atlanta's check-in and security areas—all part of a $14 million appropriation for airport improvements. In addition, it revamped its website to include better flight search functions, the ability to check in for flights online and print boarding passes at home—and a Spanish language version for 43 million Hispanics living in the U.S., not to mention the millions of Spanish-speaking Delta customers flying from Latin America and Spain. At least as importantly, Delta signed updated distribution deals with Worldspan, Sabre, Galileo and other global distribution systems, or GDSs, the electronic flight supermarkets that travel agents use to book travel for their clients. Although many leisure travelers now bypassed agents and their GDSs, booking directly on airline websites, big-money corporate travelers continued to use these intermediaries for the added value they offered: the ability to handle complex itineraries, support back-office accounting and so on. Many leisure travelers, meanwhile, continued to use online travel agencies like Expedia, Travelocity, Orbitz and Priceline, which were, in turn, powered by GDSs. But although airlines like Delta still needed the electronic supermarkets, the electronic supermarkets needed the airlines just as much, because without a major airline's inventory, few agents would use the system. Combined with GDS deregulation, this reality enabled Delta to negotiate significantly lower GDS fees.

SkyTeam, Delta's alliance, suffered a setback early in 2006 when six of its members—Delta, Northwest, Air France, KLM, Alitalia and CSA Czech—had little choice but to withdraw their request to coordinate fares and schedules on transatlantic routes after the Department of Transportation opposed the plan. But SkyTeam grew more powerful in other ways, such as new codesharing between Delta and KLM and with newly invited members like China Southern and Russia's Aeroflot. These airlines, after all, represented two of the four giant "BRIC" countries that, along with Brazil and India, were capturing the world's attention with their stunningly fast economic growth.

Separately, Delta promoted the 25th anniversary of its SkyTeam frequent flier plan, with its 40 million members, including 700,000 elite-level "Medallion" members. Jeff Robertson, who oversaw SkyMiles, later said program members spent 28 percent more with Delta, on average, than non-SkyMiles members, and members had rather high average annual household incomes of $96,500. They also, in 2006, used their miles to redeem 2.8 million "free" seats on Delta, many of which would have otherwise gone empty. They redeemed another 100,000 seats on partner airlines, also using SkyMiles awarded by Delta for miles flown—or sold, for big bucks, to American Express and other partners. Many first class seats on shorthaul flights are occupied by upgraded elite-level travelers, a perk that makes the miles worth chasing.

By mid-2006, Delta really was a changing airline. Its costs were much lower than before, its image improving, its network internationalized, its fleet restructured and its products and services upgraded. But what about the real test? Was it making money again?

The answer, made clear that summer, was a resounding yes. From April through June, Delta earned a quarterly net profit (not just a more easily attained *operating* profit), excluding special accounting items, for the first time since 2000, a major milestone for the company. In the six months from April through September, meanwhile, which coincided with the peak spring and summer travel seasons, Delta earned an operating profit of more than a half billion dollars, good for a 6 percent operating margin, thanks to a 9 percent increase in revenues and a 2 percent drop in operating costs compared to the same period a year earlier. Labor costs, with pilot concessions now in place, dropped a dramatic 20 percent. Delta was able to achieve this, moreover, with an average oil price during those six months of $72, a level no one had imagined a few years earlier. Just a year earlier, remember, Delta's own then-CFO had said, "No commercial airline's business works at $50 to $60 a barrel for oil," and no one inside or outside Delta seemed to think he was wrong. Now, not just any airline—but the very airline whose finances he had overseen—had a business that indeed seemed to be working not at just $50- to $60-per-barrel oil, but above $70 too. Delta's fuel costs, in fact, increased just 4 percent despite the per-barrel crude price spike, moderated by the disposal of the company's least fuel-efficient planes, the helpful hedges and fuel conservation efforts like taking weight off planes. It was also able to achieve its sharp profit turnaround despite an unprecedented route reshuffling, which led international revenues to spike 28 percent—they now accounted for 27 percent of total passenger revenues. Domestic revenues increased too despite big capacity cuts and 60 fewer airplanes overall.

But the journey wasn't finished. Delta's 6 percent margin for April through September was on par with most of its rivals, including American, United, Continental and US Airways. But Northwest, which had entered bankruptcy the same day as Delta, was pulling well ahead with a 10 percent figure, as close to industry leader and hedge-master Southwest's figure above it as it was to Delta's below it. Delta, furthermore, still faced lingering labor unrest at its Comair unit, and it remained worried about fuel: "If crude oil moves into the $80 range," a nervous Jerry Grinstein said, "I think we're going to have to go back and re-tool, and we're going to have to get more costs out." He did, however, add: "I'm not going back to the employees.... That is a promise."

***

Nevertheless, the mood at Delta was as good as it had been in years. It was generating not just strong accounting profits again, but also strong "free cash flow"—in other words, it was quite simply cashing a lot more checks than it was writing, the ultimate key to digging out of a debt hole. It was even hiring back furloughed pilots and flight attendants to support international expansion. Much of the hardest restructuring work was behind it, and management now felt confident of a bankruptcy exit by early 2007. The economy was still going strong, not just in the U.S. but globally. Everyone was in an international mood as they watched Italy beat France—two major SkyTeam markets—in July's World Cup final. Delta's buddy in philanthropy, Bon Jovi, had a new hit single, "Who Says You Can't Go Home?" a perfect motto for the many immigrants throughout the U.S. now endowed with nonstop Delta flights to their far-flung homelands. Few people noticed the 2006 launch of a new company called Twitter, which would soon create a social media messaging phenomenon—in 140 words or less. And Americans enjoyed their American Idol, their Black Eyed Peas, their Da Vinci Code and their Nintendo Wiis.

In early August, though, the airline industry mood soured when British police uncovered an extremist plot to detonate liquid explosives aboard at least 10 planes flying across the Atlantic. Thankfully, the perpetrators were arrested and jailed before anyone died. But the episode rekindled fears of flying and resulted in another round of new airport security procedures that proved costly and time-consuming.

The color-coded U.S. terror alert was raised a notch, and travelers could no longer bring bottles or tubes of liquid through security—a restriction that, only slightly modified, would endure for many years.

The mood darkened further on the morning of Aug. 27, when Delta flight 5191, a 50-seat CRJ-100 en route from Lexington, Ky., to Atlanta, operated by Delta's wholly owned regional unit Comair, crashed as it was taking off, killing 49 people. The lone survivor was the one of the pilots—the first officer—who suffered brain damage and other severe injuries. The cause, according to investigators: pilot error. Pilots had chosen the wrong runway, one too short for a regional jet.

The fatal accident and the new security fears broke the feeling of momentum, casting a blanket of gloom on Delta as summer turned to autumn. The security threat had financial consequences, erasing an estimated $40 million from Delta's profits. And by late summer and early fall, there were new concerns about the engine of the current economic expansion. Housing prices were starting to plateau and even fall in some markets, although the impact on household spending was alleviated somewhat by the easing of oil prices back to about $60 per barrel by winter.

None of these setbacks, however, stopped Delta from stepping even more forcefully on the international growth accelerator. The summer of 2006 saw not just the launch of many new overseas routes but also the announcement of many more to come. In perhaps its most important move, Delta finally obtained the right to serve the New York-London market, the world's busiest intercontinental market. United, as it happened, wanted to expand in booming Asia but hadn't invested in new longhaul airplanes while in bankruptcy. So it grabbed planes from Atlantic markets and sold Delta its New York JFK-London Gatwick authority for $21 million. London Gatwick, unhappily for Delta, was not London Heathrow, the preferred airport among business travelers. But at least Delta could tell potential corporate accounts that, yes, it did fly to the U.K. capital—the world's biggest airline market, one that was almost a third larger than even giant New York, counting all passengers using all the airports serving each city.

Hauenstein and his team announced new service to Prague too. And to Pisa and Vienna and Bucharest and Shannon. It was hard to think of a European city that *wasn't* on Delta's list. But Europe was just the start. Delta said it would go back to Dubai, a market it briefly served before 9/11 but which had since blossomed into one of the world's great aviation hubs, spearheaded by the local airline Emirates. With oil prices soaring, riches were flowing into the Arabian Peninsula at an astounding pace, with much of the money reinvested in the city-state's real estate and tourism sectors. United, in fact—also chasing oil money and in its case U.S. military contracts too—launched service to Kuwait at about the same time.

Another new market was Seoul, Delta's first foray into East Asia since opening Tokyo service in 1987. Atlanta, for all its advantages, was not a particularly well-positioned hub for East Asia, because travelers from the northern half of the U.S. tended to fly over the North Pole, and travelers in the western half tended to fly over the Pacific—no reason, in other words, for anyone in New York, Chicago, California or Texas, the big population and wealth centers of the country, to backtrack to Atlanta en route to the Far East. But Seoul made sense to Hauenstein for several reasons. One was Atlanta's large population of ethnic Koreans. Second, Korean Air was a close Delta SkyTeam partner (meaning more connecting passengers to fill planes). And third, there was the large flow of U.S. military traffic traveling to and from Korea. Atlanta is, after all, well positioned to handle traffic from large U.S. bases like Fort Bragg and Camp Lejeune in North Carolina.

In India, Delta began flying nonstop to Mumbai from New York, eliminating the need for passengers to make a connection, usually through Europe. India, of course, was another of the booming BRIC economies, one with a large number of nationals living in the U.S. It wasn't an oil exporter like Russia or Brazil. It didn't have the manufacturing base that China had. But India did have a vibrant software sector, handling back-office and call-center work for many U.S. companies.

And the cosmopolitanism didn't end there. Delta was also going to Africa, the least economically developed continent but one flush with funds from mineral and energy exports. At the same time, Delta recognized a large neglected market of African immigrants living in the U.S., who yearned for a convenient and affordable way to visit home. So Delta flew to Accra in Ghana. And it flew to Johannesburg in South Africa with a stop in Dakar, Senegal. Many of its targeted passengers for these routes, incidentally, previously flew to Paris first, where they connected to one of Air France's many flights to Africa. Needless to say, Air France wasn't thrilled about its partner taking that traffic away.

Back in the Far East, Delta badly wanted to jump on the China bandwagon, with the country's economy growing by double digits every year, with U.S. companies enthusiastically investing in the country and with American tourists eager to visit the once-closed Middle Kingdom. The problem: The air service bilateral agreement with mainland China restricted U.S. airlines to just six daily flights, four operated by United (Chicago and San Francisco to Beijing and Shanghai), one by American (Chicago-Shanghai) and one by Continental (Newark-Beijing). But a recently negotiated update to the bilateral would provide one of the incumbents with an additional flight in 2007—United wound up winning that with an application for Washington-Beijing. And then in 2008, a new round of awards would be granted, this time to any U.S. carrier that wished to apply. Naturally, as the largest U.S. carrier not yet serving China, Delta was all but assured of being selected. Not content to wait until 2008, however, Delta began drumming up business in 2006, opening a sales office in Shanghai. In October, Jim Whitehurst welcomed a delegation of Chinese officials to Atlanta, visiting the city to study its experience hosting the summer Olympics in 1996. Beijing was to host the games in 2008.

To serve all these far-flung destinations, 767s, with their limited range, weren't going to do the job. And 777s, the largest and longest-range aircraft in its fleet? Delta had a mere eight of them, compared to about 50 each at United and American.

Fortunately, another five 777s, their delivery dates pushed back during the crisis years, were due in 2008 and 2009. Delta decided to change its order, though, to the ultra-long-range version of Boeing's 777, known as the 777-200LR ("LR" meant "long range.") These could fly nonstop from either Atlanta or New York to Tokyo, Tel Aviv, Mumbai, Dubai, Seoul and just about anywhere else—all with just two engines, no less, rather than the gas-guzzling four required for the longest-range planes in the fleet at United and Northwest, the 747. And although Delta refrained from buying the next-generation Boeing 787s or Airbus 350s that Northwest, Continental, US Airways and others around the world were eagerly buying, Delta did place an order in late 2006 for 10 737-700s, a narrowbody plane with a rather long range, capable of handling U.S. routes to the northern half of Latin America. Delta had also ordered 50 larger 737-800s.

In the meantime, Delta continued to fund its international buildup by transitioning seven Boeing 767-400 aircraft from domestic duty, bringing to 20 the number of aircraft moved from domestic to international flying just since the spring. In addition, it purchased 10 over-water-equipped 757s, capable of flying to either Hawaii or Europe, from American. American had inherited these 757s from its ill-advised acquisition of TWA and saw little use for them. Delta, on the other hand, had big plans for them. But in general, U.S. airlines were not growing their fleets much, even with the recent resurgence in industry yields. One Wall Street airline analyst, David Strine of Bear Stearns, forecast seat supply growth of just 0.6 percent in 2006 and 3.3 percent in 2007.

Even JetBlue and AirTran were dialing back growth plans by deferring aircraft deliveries. Nor was Southwest growing much overall, despite new flying opportunities thanks to the repeal of a federal amendment restricting operations from its home airport, Dallas Love Field. Fred Reid's Virgin America was still stuck at the gate, bogged down by rivals protesting the influence of its foreign shareholder Richard Branson—was he merely a minority investor, which would have been legal, or did he control the airline? Another new startup called Skybus, although it had ordered no fewer than 65 Airbus 319s, had a business model that few people took seriously.

September was a month of anniversaries, one marking a year since Delta's bankruptcy filing and another marking five years since the 9/11 attacks upended the airline business. After just 12 months, Delta had radically rehabilitated its prospects. And after just five years, U.S. airlines had a radically different set of challenges to confront. Before bankruptcy, Delta was among America's highest-cost airlines. Now it was one of the lowest. Before, it was a predominantly domestic airline. Now it was more of an international one. Before, it was losing money. Now it was making money.

Before 9/11, meanwhile, fuel was cheap. Now it was exorbitantly expensive. Before 9/11, labor was expensive. Now it was much less expensive, the consequence of pay cuts, benefit cuts, job cuts, outsourcing and new labor-saving technologies. Before, distributing airline tickets was expensive. Now the cost of that was falling too. Before, 50-seat regional jets were a powerful weapon. Now they were increasingly a liability. Before, America was at peace. Now it was fighting two overseas wars and a broader one against international terrorism, with air travel on the front lines. Before, airport security was almost an afterthought. Now it was a choke point for travelers, depressing shorthaul travel in particular and costing airlines countless millions in lost time and higher taxes. Before, America's finances were as good as they had been in many decades. Now government spending was growing faster than at any time since Lyndon B. Johnson was president—but this time with plummeting revenues due to two large tax cuts. Before, the world seemed smaller but dominated by a strong and healthy American economy. Now, the U.S. economy was still growing but not as quickly as emerging economies like China, India, Brazil and Russia. China in particular was now America's most important trading partner, stocking its Walmarts and filling its houses with inexpensively built goods and then sending the money it earned from this activity back to America too, by lending it to the U.S. government. All the money Americans were paying to fill their cars and SUVs with gasoline was also getting recycled (in this case from oil-producing nations) back into American financial markets, further swelling the supply of money to which U.S. banks had access, and which they, by the nature of their business, needed to lend out, even if that meant lending to homebuyers with poor prospects of paying it back. Self-destructive as that might seem later, it didn't seem that way in a cloud of hyper-complex lending contracts, the triple-A assessments by firms paid to judge the creditworthiness of borrowers, the practice of packaging bad loans with the good ones and the ease of selling these packages to someone else, who would then sell them to someone else.

Financial markets weren't alone in living a lie. A world of false assumptions extended to American cultural life too. Just as those home loans weren't really as good as they seemed, neither were some of America's most iconic sports figures of the post-9/11 years. In 2002, the cyclist Lance Armstrong won his fourth straight Tour de France, followed by his fifth straight in 2003, and then his sixth and his seventh. In baseball, a bulked-up Barry Bonds of the San Francisco Giants won the National League most valuable player award in 2001, 2002, 2003 and 2004. His American League rival Alex Rodriguez, playing first in Gerald Grinstein's hometown Seattle before moving to Texas and then to the bright lights of New York City, became perhaps the biggest baseball star of them all. In 2001 and 2004, Roger Clemens won baseball's annual Cy Young award given to its best pitcher, first with the New York Yankees and then with the Houston Astros. These players and others, it would later emerge, had allegedly been cheating. Tiger Woods, meanwhile—the winner of the 2001, 2002 and 2005 Masters golf tournaments and nine other "majors," as golf's most important tournaments are known, during the decade—was engaged, it would also later emerge, in a different kind of cheating.

There was no apparent cheating in the airline business, although investors feeling cheated by the sector's massive post-9/11 losses might have disputed that. But even this was changing. For all of 2006, in fact, U.S. airlines earned a collective net profit (excluding special accounting charges), their first after five consecutive years of red ink. The growing economy certainly helped, but the true hero was capacity discipline. ASM capacity (remember, that's available seat miles, or the number of seats on offer times the number of miles they flew) barely grew at all—just 0.3 percent. And even that meager overall growth was only because of 6 percent international growth, which was more than justified by strong demand growth. Domestically, capacity shrank nearly 2 percent, lifting pricing power, measured by yields—the number of cents an average passenger paid to fly one mile—almost 6 percent. Overall demand, in fact, grew nearly eight times as quickly as capacity, leaving planes fuller than they had ever been.

As the skies brightened, airlines and their stakeholders began to take a closer look at the wisdom of consolidation. The America West-US Airways deal, despite messy labor and IT integration headaches, was working better financially than any-one—perhaps even Doug Parker and Scott Kirby themselves—expected. Revenues were up, costs were down and the whole industry was benefiting from the merged airline's big capacity cuts. In Europe, meanwhile, the Air France-KLM merger was proving at least as successful, generating big revenue premiums by combining two global networks at a moment when globalization was intensifying. Emboldened Air France was now on the verge of buying Alitalia, a dysfunctional airline if there ever was one, but an airline with a rich base of Italian corporate travelers nonethe-less. Lufthansa's takeover of Swiss International Airlines was going well too, while elsewhere in Europe, Air Berlin and TAP Portugal each acquired local rivals and Richard Branson merged his Belgian airline with a local rival. Ryanair too tried to buy an airline, Aer Lingus, but regulators said no. In greater China, Hong Kong's Cathay Pacific purchased a rival called Dragonair. In India, the top private airline Jet Airways was negotiating to buy its rival Air Sahara. And back in the U.S., United CEO Glenn Tilton, who had hired Goldman Sachs to analyze prospective mergers, was publicly extoling the virtues of consolidation every chance he got.

Northwest too, just to be prepared, hired the investment banking advisory firm Evercore Partners to examine potential merger scenarios. AirTran, although happy to see Delta cutting capacity and pricing seats more rationally, was nonetheless feeling pressure from its giant rival, especially in Atlanta, prompting AirTran to make a hostile takeover bid for a smaller Milwaukee-based airline called Midwest Airlines. Passengers liked Midwest, notably for the chocolate chip cookies it baked aboard its flights—flight attendants delivered them while they were still warm. AirTran liked Midwest for its strong position in Milwaukee, within driving distance of Chicago's wealthy northern suburbs, and for its fleet of Boeing 717s, an aircraft type that both AirTran and Midwest, but few other airlines in the world, happened to have. Separately, AirTran also formed a loose marketing partnership with Denver's Frontier Airlines—the two would essentially refer passengers to each other via their respective websites—to bolster its weak coverage west of the Mississippi River.

Everyone in the industry knew enough money was sloshing around America's financial markets to finance potential mergers. Wall Street wanted deals, which minted handsome advisory fees along with welcome lending opportunities. And airlines did too, especially after US Airways-America West and Air France-KLM increasingly pushed aside memories of past debacles, most recently American-TWA. Airlines instead focused on the promise of greater pricing power, greater global coverage and greater clout with suppliers.

Delta had little interest in merging with anyone, at least not before emerging from bankruptcy as a newly healthy and independent airline. But that time now appeared near, with an exit envisioned for the first half of 2007. Grinstein, his job nearly done, announced in October he'd retire in 2007, urging the board of directors to appoint one of his top two executives—CFO Ed Bastian or COO Jim Whitehurst—as his successor.

But Grinstein's vision for a gentle stroll into the sunset was not to be. Just past sunrise on Nov. 15, 2006, Delta's CEO was shaving. The radio was on in the background. National Public Radio was reviewing the morning's news.

"All of a sudden," he would recall years later—with no warning—"I hear USAir is making a hostile bid to take over Delta! Lucky I didn't cut my freaking throat!"

It was true. Doug Parker, emboldened by the success of his last takeover, was offering $8 billion to buy control of Delta. US Airways would pay Delta's unsecured creditors, the true controllers of Delta's destiny, $4 billion in cash and another $4 billion in US Airways stock. These creditors were the suppliers, bondholders, labor unions, government agencies and anyone else to whom Delta owed money—everyone from the airports handling Delta's flights to the firm that cleaned its carpets, all making nearly 8,000 claims for some $84 billion. Most importantly, though, were nine of the largest creditors appointed to what's called an "unsecured creditors committee," a group that would ultimately vote on which exit plan offered them the best chance to recover as much as they had lost. Creditors wouldn't get all the money Delta owed them. But they would get some. And the better the business plan, the more they'd get.

The nine unsecured creditors in Delta's case were: 1) the pilot union ALPA, 2) the plane-maker Boeing, 3) the engine-maker Pratt & Whitney, 4) The Coca-Cola Company, which supplied Delta with most of its onboard non-alcoholic beverages 5) the federal government's pension insurance agency (the PBGC) and four companies representing bondholders: 6) US Bank, 7) MacKay Shields, 8) Fidelity and 9) Bank of New York. The nine would each have one vote, and the exit plan chosen by the majority would then be voted on by the wider pool of creditors, which typically go along with the committee's recommendation. The committee also had two non-voting members: the airports in Atlanta and Cincinnati.

US Airways certainly got the creditors' attention. Although the total of all creditor claims was $84 billion, the market valued them at just a fraction of that: about 25 percent less, in fact, than the $8 billion US Airways was offering. "The market" in this case referred to the active buying and selling of claims, especially among hedge funds and other asset management companies. Delta might have borrowed

$50 million from a bank, for example, making that bank a creditor with a $50 million claim. But the bank, knowing it would never get its full $50 million, might sell that claim to another investor for $10 million, with that investor hoping the claim would be worth $15 million when it was ultimately converted into stock in the new Delta. So the great question now for anyone holding Delta claims, however they acquired them, was which Delta would be worth more: Grinstein's independent Delta? Or Parker's vision of a Delta fused with US Airways?

2007

"Now heaven is Rio and hell is Lagos"

By the fall of 2005, Gordon Bethune was comfortably if a bit restlessly retired. For 10 years, the tall, tough-talking Texan had been chairman and CEO of Continental Airlines, a basket case when he took the helm in late 1994 and one of the nation's strongest, healthiest and well-liked carriers when he left at the end of 2004. Early in his tenure, Bethune came within a whisker of merging Continental with Delta. In 1997, after learning Ron Allen had been fired, Bethune flew to Seattle to speak directly with Delta board member Jerry Grinstein, offering to buy the company—"I saw the shot and I took it," Bethune said. Grinstein knew Bethune well, as it happened, from Grinstein's days running Western Airlines, where Bethune was his top maintenance executive.

But Delta's board, after an emergency weekend meeting, rejected the offer. Members told Bethune they were prepared to fight it "tooth and nail." Not confident of winning a hostile takeover attempt, Bethune backed off.

That same weekend, meanwhile, Delta hired Ron Allen's replacement Leo Mullin, a task the board had suddenly considered more urgent because the lack of a CEO—the power vacuum—was leaving Delta vulnerable to another takeover bid. A new CEO from outside the industry, who wouldn't have left a good job and moved his family for a temporary role, would be a clear signal that Delta intended to proceed independently.

Later, Continental's controlling shareholder, the private equity firm TPG, actually considered turning the tables and selling Continental to Delta. But Bethune persuaded Continental's board (including TPG's representatives on the board) that there was a better offer: a transaction with Northwest that would give Northwest part ownership of Continental but keep Continental independent. This also, of course, meant Bethune could keep his job. Key to winning the boardroom battle was

Bethune's insistence that a Delta takeover would destroy employee morale, because Mullin wanted to place Continental's workers at the bottom of an integrated seniority list. And for employees like pilots, seniority lists are crucial, determining everything from pay to promotions to who's forced to work on Christmas.

Three years later, pressured by the U.S. Justice Department, Northwest sold its Continental shares back to Continental, although Northwest retained a so-called "golden share" that effectively gave it veto rights over any future merger that Continental might contemplate. But all talk of industry mergers would cease a year later, when the 9/11 attacks threw the industry into turmoil. On the day of the tragedy, Bethune was in his office when his operations chief called with news that a plane had struck the World Trade Center. He rushed down to the airline's board room, where the board was scheduled to meet that morning anyway and where someone had wheeled in a TV in time to see United flight 175 crash into the south tower. He asked his board coordinator to quickly rent 10 Avis cars—with all flights grounded, these would soon prove vital—as the team turned its attention to monitoring the whereabouts of all 150 or so Continental planes currently in the air, anxiously ticking off each one as they safely landed. The main topic on the agenda for that morning's board meeting: Continental's 2002 financial plan, which Bethune "ceremoniously threw in the trash can."

Just four days later, with its revenues obliterated, Continental laid off 20 percent of its staff, although it avoided the need to ask for a government loan guarantee, relying on its good reputation with lenders to secure capital from the private sector. Unlike most of its competitors, Continental didn't use a *force majeure* provision to get out of providing contractually required medical and other benefits for laid-off employees because, Bethune said, "the people that we didn't lay off were looking to see how the other people were being treated." Years later, he would still take pride in being voted (in an annual *Fortune* magazine survey) among America's 100 best employers that year. "Even after laying off 12,000 people," he said. "And they got to vote."

Continental also, critically, would avoid bankruptcy, not because it wasn't pressured by the aftershock of 9/11, and not because it wasn't pressured by Southwest's ability to reduce fares and expand service thanks to lucrative fuel hedges. "What saved our ass," Bethune recalled, was that half of Continental's revenue came from international flights, which were immune to Southwest's sting, and which by mid-decade were booming. Delta, only belatedly, had followed Continental's example and internationalized, hiring Continental's ex-network planner Glen Hauenstein to do it.

In retirement, just as when he had been running Continental, Bethune wasn't one to keep his opinions to himself. A favorite with the media for his colorful quotes, Bethune gained attention for publicly lambasting executives he thought inferior, politicians he thought ignorant and consultants he thought clueless, such as one who told him Continental should be more like Southwest. "And I look at this guy and say, 'What am I supposed to do with these 20 DC-10s we own?'" Bethune recounted. The aging widebody DC-10s—planes that would never exist at all-domestic

Southwest—were Continental's only available tool to serve some key international markets. "'I mean, you stupid shit, we don't have a blank piece of paper here.' It's like a man who marries a woman who has three children and he says, 'Let's go do a family planning session.' What for? We've already got it. There isn't anything to plan."

Bethune's approach to improving Continental? "I had a great idea: Why don't we fly to places people want to go? Shit, write that down!"

One of his favorite stories was the day of the 2003 New York City blackout, when the region's airports were without power. American, United and Delta understandably canceled most flights at JFK and LaGuardia. But business travelers heard Continental was still operating from Newark—even though the power was out there too. They headed there instead. It was true. Airport staff equipped with flashlights were checking tickets, while TSA security workers equipped with handheld metal detector wands screened passengers. Anyone holding a full-fare ticket on another airline was welcomed, processed and escorted to the boarding area. Continental made $2 million that day. "Shit," Bethune said, reflecting a decade later. "Turn the lights off every night!" Continental was becoming known as the reliable, upmarket airline for corporate travelers.

But no subject was more the target of Bethune's wrath than Delta. While still CEO, he constantly railed against Delta's pricing strategy, referring to its management team as "dumber than a box of rocks." He blamed Delta for hiring the management consultancy McKinsey and listening to its advice to launch Song, and with aircraft he judged inappropriate, no less—"moronic thinking," he called it. Leo Mullin, he declared, "didn't know the front end of the airplane from the back" (an insult Bethune didn't reserve only for Mullin but also for other competitors and predecessors). He wondered aloud how Delta could launch Song after so many other airlines had launched similar projects that failed. "It always amazed me that we [Continental, which launched an LCC called Continental Lite before Bethune was hired] burned our finger by putting it in the candle. And then you see Ted, for United. You see Song. You see the same morons doing the same thing over and over again, expecting a different result. Of course they're all failures. They all lost their ass. Why wouldn't you learn from others? I mean, read a book. Look out the window."

In Bethune's view, Delta's predicament was avoidable. "Here's a company that is based in Atlanta, who has one of the strongest balance sheets in the history of aviation, had loyal employees that even bought them a 767," he recalled. "And they took that thing and threw it into the crapper. Management did it."

How important is good management? "Well, if you took a look at the history of the Kentucky Derby, there was a four-year period where one jockey, riding three different horses, won three of four races. So it's not just the horse. It's the jockey. And when you have a 300-pound jockey on your ass, you can't win."

Bethune's influence on America's airline industry did not end with his retirement, and it did not end with mere colorful media commentary. Although uninterested in returning to the business as a chief executive, he gladly, five days before Christmas in 2006, at age 65, accepted a handsomely paid job as an advisor to Delta's creditor committee, the committee that was now weighing a decision of great consequence for itself and for the entire U.S. airline industry. Should the creditors support Delta's standalone restructuring plan? It was, after all, already starting to produce results: Costs were down, revenues were up and Delta was making money again. Or should the creditors support the US Airways takeover plan, which would create a giant airline with nearly $2 billion in promised synergies?

Bethune studied the dueling proposals. Doug Parker, for one, was convinced Bethune understood the logic of the US Airways options. "He got it," Parker recalled years later. "He just instantly seemed to get it."

By the first day of 2007, both plans were on the table: the US Airways plan revealed to the public back on Nov. 15, 2006, and the Delta standalone plan filed with the court Dec. 19.

The audacious idea to chase an airline the size of Delta actually wasn't Parker's. It came to him from his trusted lieutenant Scott Kirby, who was by then enjoying a reputation within the industry as a master of the fine art of managing revenues through deft pricing and capacity maneuvers. But it was, when Kirby first raised the subject to Parker, still early 2006, just months after the last merger, the one in 2005 between America West and US Airways. "Gosh, you must be kidding," Parker, speaking years later, recalled reacting initially. "But you couldn't argue with the enormous benefits," he remembered, "and there was this small window that was closing. It would be the only shot." The timing wasn't perfect, but Parker and Kirby couldn't choose the timing.

The idea was compelling enough that US Airways hired restructuring advisors to evaluate the potential benefits of a US Airways-Delta merger—and to assess in greater detail what Delta had already done in bankruptcy and whether additional improvements were possible. Even more convinced after those discussions, Parker phoned Grinstein during the summer of 2006 to assess Grinstein's interest in what the US Airways people internally were calling "Project Green."

"And he was polite, as Jerry always is," Parker recalled. Polite but unambiguous: He had no interest.

"It was what we called the 'polite stiff arm,'" Parker continued. "And so then we sent a letter saying that we really wanted to talk."

That was on Sept. 29.

Dear Jerry:

It has been a few months since I called to let you know that US Airways would be interested in talking with Delta about a potential merger. At the time you indicated you had some internal issues you needed to address before you would be in a position to talk with anyone about alternatives to your standalone plan. Given the substantial progress you have made with your restructuring, I am hopeful your internal issues have been addressed and we can begin a meaningful dialog about entering into a transaction.

Let me begin by saying we are very impressed by the restructuring progress you and your team have engineered and are implementing. Delta seems well on its way to being able to emerge from bankruptcy as a standalone airline and I am sure you are extremely proud of your team. We also believe, however, that a merger with US Airways would, for Delta's stakeholders, be a superior alternative to any standalone plan, because of the considerable synergies a merger could produce. Our experience suggests a transaction completed before Delta emerges from bankruptcy would create significantly more value than any transaction that closes post-emergence...

The letter went on to detail the merits of a merger. But on Oct. 17, Grinstein responded:

Dear Doug:

I have shared your letter of September 29, 2006 with the Delta Board of Directors and reviewed with them this response to you.

As a preliminary matter, let me thank you for your kind words about the Delta team and the restructuring progress we have made to date. Important milestones have been reached in our reorganization plan, and we are confident of Delta's ability to emerge from bankruptcy as a strong, viable airline. Given the work that remains, we believe it would not be productive to engage in the type of exploratory discussions that you propose at this time.

The Board and management of Delta have been, and will remain, focused on enhancing value for our stakeholders. It is in this context that we will continue our work on our reorganization plan, and we will determine if and when it would be in the interests of our stakeholders to initiate discussions regarding possible extraordinary transactions with third parties.

We have also discussed your letter with our official creditors committee and its advisers, who have expressed support for this response.

Respectfully,
Gerald Grinstein

But Parker was determined to do a deal. Sure, he preferred a consensual one. Yet he was willing to take his offer straight to Delta's creditors, who—remember—were essentially the airline's board of directors while it was in bankruptcy. Technically, only Grinstein and his team had the legal right to offer a Delta turnaround plan, merger or no merger—that was one benefit management got by filing when it did on that day in 2005 when Northwest did the same, before the bankruptcy laws were due to change. But by taking his offer public, Parker might woo enough creditor support to pressure Grinstein into working with him. So on Nov. 15, US Airways publicly announced its $8 billion offer. Parker sent another "Dear Jerry" letter—this time an open letter for everyone to see—explaining his move:

Dear Jerry:

Last spring we had a conversation about a potential merger of US Airways and Delta. As you know, following that conversation, I sent you a letter on Sept. 29, 2006, outlining our thoughts about a transaction, describing the significant benefits that could be achieved for both of our respective stakeholder groups from this type of transaction and proposing to meet with you and your team to work together to further consider and develop our proposal. I was disappointed that you declined to meet or even enter into discussions in your letter of Oct. 17, 2006. Because the benefits of a merger of US Airways and Delta are so compelling to both of our companies' stakeholders, we believe it is important to inform them about our proposal. Therefore, we are simultaneously releasing this letter to the public....

He continued:

This proposal presents an opportunity for Delta creditors to receive significantly higher recoveries than they can receive under any standalone plan for Delta. It is also an opportunity for US Airways shareholders to benefit from the significant upside potential of the combination. Consumers will benefit from expanded choice as well as the reach and services of a large-scale provider within the cost structure of a low-fare carrier. Our employees will benefit from a more competitive employer and our willingness to adopt highest-common-denominator employee costs.

As I expressed to you previously, I understand that you and your team have worked extremely hard on your own restructuring and greatly respect all that you have accomplished to make Delta a healthy, viable airline. We simply believe that a combination with US Airways will produce even more value for your creditors and our shareholders, and that this is a unique opportunity to create an airline that is even better positioned to thrive long into the future, whatever that future might bring to the industry, greatly benefiting our employees and customers.

We and our advisors, Citigroup Corporate and Investment Banking and Skadden, Arps, Slate, Meagher & Flom LLP, are ready to commence due diligence and to negotiate definitive documentation immediately, and request that you agree to work with us so that this alternative to your standalone plan can be quickly and fully developed. We are prepared to meet with you, Delta's Board, Delta's Official Committee of Unsecured Creditors and any major Delta creditor or other stakeholder to achieve this outcome. I believe we owe it to our respective stakeholders to pursue this opportunity vigorously.

I look forward to hearing from you soon.

Respectfully,
Doug Parker

With that out of the way, Parker and his team worked furiously to sell the benefits of the merger proposal, which was now hostile. Always with the ears of creditors in mind, he spoke tirelessly about the $4 billion in cash that they'd receive plus nearly 80 million shares of US Airways stock worth another $4 billion. This amount was, he continued, 25 percent higher than the current market value of all the unsecured claims creditors held against Delta. What's more, Delta's creditors would own 45 percent of a combined airline, which would produce synergies worth another $1.65 billion, of which $935 million would come from combining the two route networks, cutting capacity 10 percent, capturing more corporate contracts and creating a giant frequent flier program with enormous appeal to travelers and—by extension—to various vendors wishing to buy miles for the purpose of rewarding and incentivizing their own customers when they used credit cards, stayed in hotels, rented cars, sent flowers to loved ones and so forth. And the other $700 million? That would come from cost savings. Not cost savings by rank-and-file layoffs—that would be a nonstarter with employees, whose support was important—but cost savings from eliminating overhead and renegotiating contracts with airports, distributors, vendors and aircraft suppliers.

Such enticing value creation, Parker insisted, could only be achieved now, with Delta still in bankruptcy and thus still afforded certain leverage and legal rights to cut costs. As it happened, aircraft markets were booming again, so lessors would be willing—even happy—to let Delta out of its lease obligations and instead send airplanes overseas, where foreign airlines were clamoring for more capacity. That had certainly been the case during the US Airways-America West merger as well. More than half of the expected cost synergies, Parker said, were only possible in the confines of bankruptcy protection. Do it now or lose the opportunity forever, was the underlying message.

If there were any doubts about the ability to hit these lofty synergy targets, Parker emphatically pointed to the America West-US Airways merger, which had already hit all its synergy targets and then some. The new Delta, more generally—"Delta" would indeed remain the name—was a powerhouse in the making, poised to be No. 1 across the Atlantic, No. 1 at 155 airports and No. 1 up and down the busy eastern seaboard. Particularly enticing was the prospective pricing power it would command in the southeast, which was dominated by Delta's Atlanta hub and US Airways' Charlotte hub: Some small southeastern cities had nothing but flights to Atlanta and Charlotte. Internationally, the airline would have its choice of joining either the Star Alliance, of which US Airways was a member, or SkyTeam, Delta's alliance. And it would be run by a new management team without the scars of bad ideas like SimpliFares and Song.

What's more, most big US Airways shareholders—including PAR Capital, the carrier's largest shareholder—supported the deal. And this support, ultimately, was for owning a piece of the new Delta, an airline Delta's creditors, too, had the chance to own. Besides, Parker argued, look at United's creditors, whose claims turned to ownership stakes in the restructured United when it exited bankruptcy in February 2006. That stock was performing far worse than post-bankruptcy US Airways stock—proof, went the argument, that mergers create more value than standalone turnaround plans.

The hostile takeover would be financed with cash borrowed from Citigroup—$7.2 billion in cash, to be precise, of which $4 billion would fund the cash offer to Delta's creditors. The rest would pay off Delta's high-interest debtor-in-possession loan from GE Capital. Importantly, US Airways assured creditors that they wouldn't have to wait long to see their money. America West took just four months to close its US Airways takeover once the merger was announced, and Parker estimated a Delta deal could be signed, sealed and delivered by the end of the first half of 2007. But to achieve this ambitious schedule, Delta's management would need to cooperate by agreeing to 1) open its financial books with the purpose of conducting due diligence and 2) postpone a Feb. 7 hearing to evaluate its standalone exit proposal.

The persuasion campaign didn't stop there. For US Airways to emerge victorious, it would need to cultivate at least some support among Delta's employees, if for no other reason than to alleviate creditor concerns that employee hostility would make a merger unworkable. To this end, Parker not only promised no layoffs for non-management personnel but also the "highest-common-denominator" pay he had referenced in his letter to Grinstein. Pay and other contractual terms for each work group, in other words, would be harmonized to the level of the more generous airline. So if Delta mechanics earned more than US Airways mechanics, all mechanics at the merged airline would work under the Delta terms. And Parker repeatedly argued that consolidation benefits all workers: An airline with a much stronger balance sheet and much stronger clout with suppliers—an airline that was "too big to fail," he could have said, two years before that term would be widely used to describe giant troubled banks—implied job security and opportunities for career advancement. US Airways was planning to cut capacity by 10 percent, yes, but without any impact on front-line jobs. It was also hinting quietly to union leaders and pro-labor politicians that a merger would mean Delta's many non-union workers might become unionized.

US Airways also set out to ease the concerns of small communities, especially those in the southeast, whose local economies depended on Delta's air service and which in some cases would have been monopolized but for the competition between Delta and US Airways. Consumer groups and corporate travel advocates had similar concerns about rising airfares more generally, and to this US Airways again retorted with evidence from the America West merger. The combined airline, enabled by merger synergies, had actually lowered fares, it claimed, since the deal. Besides, it was America West whose 2002 fare restructuring—a less clumsy and more appropriately pursued forerunner to Delta's SimpliFares—helped put downward pressure on airfares nationwide. US Airways, Parker was suggesting, was pro-consumer, not anti-consumer.

Did consumers, communities and coalitions of business travelers believe him? Actually, that wasn't the key question. The key question was whether the U.S. Department of Justice would believe him. It was DOJ, recall, whose hostility to the proposed United-US Airways merger in 2000 had scuttled that deal. Delta's creditors might think the world of a Delta-US Airways merger, but if Justice said no, such a deal would be consigned to irrelevance. So the day after it went public with its offer, US Airways delivered a presentation entirely dedicated to addressing these concerns—"Proposed US Airways-Delta merger will not reduce competition," was the title of the first PowerPoint slide. It went on to explain how the airline business had changed dramatically since 2000, with low-cost carriers now carrying more than a third of all air traffic along the east coast, ensuring intense fare competition. AirTran was keeping Delta honest in Atlanta, for example, and that wouldn't change. Nor would low-fare pressure from Southwest and JetBlue. Just as importantly, a combined US Airways-Delta would control just 18 percent of all domestic seat miles, hardly what you'd call a monopoly. On the contrary, the industry would remain highly fragmented, contested by a large number of airlines: American, United, Continental, Northwest, Southwest, JetBlue, Alaska Airlines, AirTran, Frontier, Spirit, ATA, Midwest, Sun Country, Allegiant, USA3000 and so on. Not in the past 30 years, US Airways said, had the DOJ challenged a merger in which the industry's leading firm would have less than a 30 percent market share.

Only two nonstop routes—Cincinnati-Charlotte and Cincinnati-Philadelphia—would go from two competitors to just one. Another 11 nonstop routes were flown by both airlines but by others too. And 81 percent of all US Airways and Delta passengers had access to low-cost carrier flights, either at the same airport or at airports nearby. US Airways promised it would remain in all markets and sell one of the two northeast corridor shuttles that competed against each other—the Delta

Shuttle or US Airways Shuttle—and expressed its willingness to do more based on DOJ feedback, which the department commonly gave before issuing a ruling. But would that even be necessary? Yes, in name, this was the same DOJ that had signaled it would block the United-US Airways merger in 2000. But in reality, it was quite a different DOJ, one whose leadership was appointed not by President Clinton but by a more *laissez-faire* President Bush. It was a DOJ that had approved giant combinations like AT&T Broadband and Comcast; JP Morgan Chase and Bank One; and Procter & Gamble and Gillette. The legislative branch was potentially more hostile to a big airline merger, especially after late 2006, when Democrats took control of Congress, putting the anti-merger James Oberstar of Minnesota back in charge of the House of Representatives Committee on Transportation and Infrastructure. But the executive branch, not the legislative branch, had more direct sway over whether mergers were approved or rejected.

Parker's arguments were winning converts, especially among hedge fund investors that purchased Delta bankruptcy claims hoping these claims would rise in value, as many thought they would thanks to the US Airways merger proposal. But as 2006 turned to 2007, time was running out. Many of the things Delta intended to do in bankruptcy—restructure its labor and lease costs, for example—were now done. And the hearing for Delta management to present its standalone exit plan was still scheduled for Feb. 7.

US Airways needed to get that date postponed, and it had an idea for how to get creditors to agree. On Jan. 10, it raised its offer. Now it was proposing not $8 billion but $10.2 billion, including not $4 billion in cash but $5 billion, with the rest paid in stock. Creditors, moreover, would now own not 45 percent of a combined airline but 49 percent. In the background, meanwhile, was a helpful development in oil markets: Crude prices had fallen from $74 per barrel six months earlier to just $55 by January, a 26 percent drop. And Delta's creditors surely understood by now that as oil prices go, so go the fortunes of the airline business. Alone or merged, Delta would be better off than it would have been months earlier. Everyone was feeling more bullish about the industry.

But Gerald Grinstein was feeling no more bullish about a merger with US Airways. Throughout the entire saga, Delta's CEO remained not just opposed to the hostile offer but enraged by its brazenness. And he didn't want to keep his rage to himself. "I mean, I wanted everyone to hate USAir—to absolutely despise those bastards for doing that," he recalled. So he went out and bought doormats and put the US Airways logo on them, and he placed them at the door to each executive's office with a sign: "Wipe feet before entering." And he ordered Hauenstein in the route planning department to launch new spite flights into US Airways strongholds: New York JFK-Phoenix, for example, and Salt Lake City-Charlotte and Salt Lake City-Pittsburgh.

More substantively, Grinstein and his two top deputies, Ed Bastian and Jim Whitehurst, pressed their case for rejecting US Airways. On Dec. 11, the triumvirate, along with legal and financial advisors, met Delta's board of directors and did their best to spook it with tales of past mergers gone awry. Grinstein warned of antitrust concerns, criticized Parker's "flawed economic assumptions" and described "overwhelming labor and cultural issues." The US Airways plan, he added, would soak the company with $23 billion in debt—compared to $11 billion for the Delta standalone plan—while unwinding all the restructuring progress already achieved. And strategically, US Airways would be a poor fit for Delta, resulting in an airline still devoid of a major presence in Asia or on the U.S. west coast and without a strong hub in the middle of the country. If mergers in general made little sense right now, *this* one made even less sense than most. Delta would surely have to end its domestic alliance with Northwest and Continental too, reducing the merger's benefits. Grinstein emphasized the antitrust issue, for the DOJ's potential rejection was emerging as a major source of doubt for many creditors. The merger, Grinstein affirmed, would create more than 2,000 city pairs—in other words, origins and destinations, regardless of the connecting points passengers used to travel between them—where the airline would control more than 90 percent of the traffic. How would even a relatively *laissez-faire* DOJ approve that kind of stranglehold? And even if the DOJ *did* approve the deal, it would likely require precious slot divestitures at key airports like Washington Reagan and New York LaGuardia, opening the door to more punishing low-fare competition in these markets and—yet again—reducing the merger's benefits. Southwest's Herb Kelleher, in fact, had recently called both Parker and Grinstein, eagerly asking if they'd like to sell any such assets. Southwest, heaven forbid, might even show up in Atlanta.

US Airways, Grinstein continued, essentially got lucky with its recent America West merger, which coincided with the demise of Independence Air, industry capacity cutting and strong economic growth. Its synergy estimates for a Delta merger, meanwhile, underestimated considerations like the negative drag from transition costs. In addition, a merger would reverse Delta's promising internationalization efforts (because US Airways was an overwhelmingly domestic airline), increase fleet complexity and threaten to undermine gains in operational reliability and service quality.

At the same time, Delta's executives trumpeted their own record of success in turning around the airline, which now had a rightsized domestic network, a vastly expanded international network, the lowest unit costs among its peers, a 50 percent reduction in debt, improved liquidity, major customer service enhancements, a simpler fleet and income statements—for the first time in years—with black bottom lines.

On Dec. 15, Delta's board of directors—a collection of leaders from various walks of life—accepted these arguments and voted to reject the US Airways offer, citing "unacceptably high risk that it could not be consummated in the manner suggested by US Airways" and an assessment that it "was not in our best interests or in the best interests of our creditors, as well as our other stakeholders." But this was largely symbolic. The true test was convincing the creditor committee to do the same. Two days after presenting to the board, Delta's management delivered the same presentation to the committee and anxiously awaited a verdict.

On Dec. 19, Grinstein sent Parker a letter, informing him of the board's decision. This time, he didn't even address him familiarly as "Doug."

Dear Mr. Parker:

The Board of Directors of Delta Air Lines has unanimously rejected US Airways' merger proposal. The Board concluded that our creditors, as well as the company's other stakeholders, are best served by moving forward with our standalone Plan of Reorganization.

Our Board of Directors considered many compelling factors during its thorough review of the US Airways proposal and determined that our standalone Plan of Reorganization filed today will provide superior value as well as faster recovery and greater certainty of execution. Further, we concluded that your proposal is structurally flawed. It represents an unacceptably high risk of not achieving antitrust clearance because it would harm consumers and communities due to its substantial anticompetitive effects. It has overwhelming labor issues precluding attainment of claimed synergies and depends on achieving "synergies" that are premised on faulty economic assumptions. In addition, the proposal would saddle the company with a precariously high total debt load and reverse Delta's progress, eroding the value of the Delta brand. Finally, US Airways continues to experience significant integration problems and has not successfully completed its prior, smaller merger with America West; it is not equipped to simultaneously integrate a substantially larger company.

The Board of Directors believes that the antitrust issues inherent in your proposal are grave, based on Department of Justice ("DOJ") standards. Moreover, a DOJ review process would be prolonged, thus unacceptably extending the period Delta would be forced to remain in bankruptcy. In addition, the Delta unit of the Air Line Pilots Association has said—and Delta agrees—that our pilot contract would prohibit the combined company from implementing the capacity reductions that are the economic foundation of the proposed transaction.

We believe that the proposal would have a demonstrably negative impact on the actual value delivered to our creditors. Your proposal radically overestimates synergies and erroneously states there is an urgent need to complete a transaction while Delta is still in bankruptcy. At the same time, it downplays the impact on employees and the traveling public, all of whom would suffer from less service and resulting higher prices to many destinations.

Our vision for a fundamentally different airline that provides superior value and quality is working, as our significant progress during the year makes clear. These accomplishments—along with the strength of our brand and the resolve of our people—are the strong foundation we're using to build further success and position Delta for intense domestic and international competition.

As part of its review, the Board concluded that Delta is better served by continuing to focus on its plan to pursue new international market and revenue opportunities from the solid base of our right-sized domestic network, a best-in-class network cost structure, and high levels of customer service. Your proposal, on the other hand, would drain or dilute both the value and quality our company has worked hard to create, including superior service levels.

For all these reasons, Delta's Board and management have rejected the US Airways proposal.

Sincerely,
Jerry Grinstein

In the meantime, Grinstein enlisted the support of various communities and airports by frightening them with suggestions that, for example, "the downsizing of the Charlotte hub is inevitable," given its overlap with Atlanta. Same for Pittsburgh, given its overlap with Cincinnati, and same for Salt Lake City, Phoenix or Las Vegas— at least one of them would have to shrink, because all three largely handled many of the same traffic flows. Internationally, he argued, Philadelphia's service would inevitably shrink because nearby New York could handle the same markets. Remember, he said, how St. Louis lost much of its air service after American bought TWA. Small communities would perhaps suffer most, for a merged Delta would be the largest carrier in 127 of these communities, of which only 14 had low-cost carrier competition. Further frightening consumer groups and companies that spend small fortunes on air travel, Grinstein's team said a Delta-US Airways merger would create 31 overlapping nonstop routes impacting 12 million passengers. Of course, this argument was made for the ears of DOJ antitrust lawyers too.

Just as importantly, Grinstein worked to rally Delta's employees to his side, highlighting the labor troubles that followed the US Airways-America West merger— the merged company had, by that time, completed a joint labor contract, covering employees at both airlines, with just one work group. Pilots were fighting bitterly about how to integrate their seniority lists. In a Delta-US Airways merger, there would be nine potential disputes over union representation, 10 potential disputes over seniority integration and nine potential negotiations for joint agreements. Grinstein loudly highlighted Parker's plan to slash capacity by 10 percent, which would actually violate a clause in the new Delta pilot contract mandating that in the event of consolidation, total hours flown could not fall below pre-merger levels. This would, Grinstein conjectured, result in the elimination of 10,000 jobs, including 900 mainline pilot jobs as approximately 180 planes were removed from the fleet.

Delta organized what it called the Velvet Rope Tour, a series of sessions where employees would gather to learn about Delta's new business plan and provide opinions and feedback to management. It was in these sessions that managers spoke of the "substandard service" offered by US Airways, which contrasted with Delta's rapidly improving service. Leading the charge was a new human resource chief, Mike Campbell. Like Glen Hauenstein, he came from Continental—another former protégé, in other words, of Gordon Bethune. One of Campbell's early contributions: motivating Delta employees with a rewards program that gave everyone $100 for every month in which the airline exceeded goals for on-time performance and customer service. By now, $25 million worth of awards had been given. And perhaps most persuasively, Delta in November started recalling pilots and mechanics, bringing them back to work and demonstrating all the while that the Delta standalone plan was good for job growth. To emphasize the point, it confirmed orders for new aircraft too.

In a video message to employees, Grinstein again tried to rally the troops: "We are saying no to US Airways," he stated firmly. "The US Airways proposal just doesn't make sense for Delta.... The people of Delta have said no, loudly and clearly. And now, after careful consideration, Delta's board of directors has joined them to reject US Airways' proposal.... Delta believes the US Airways proposal would be bad for everyone: bad for creditors who want to preserve and grow Delta's value and strong brand, bad for consumers who want to keep low fares and great service, bad for small communities and businesses who want to keep competition and growing worldwide access and convenience and bad for Delta's people, who want to keep their jobs and hard-earned benefits.... Delta's plan has shown that it is working, and our progress has been tremendous. When the history book is written on the restructuring of this industry, Delta will be the greatest turnaround story in it."

Lee Moak, the elected leader of Delta's unionized pilots, had been 35,000 feet above Greenland, piloting a flight from Europe back on Nov. 15, when he got a message, via the cockpit ACARS system used by airlines use to communicate with pilots, that US Airways was trying to buy Delta, confirming rumblings he had heard. "I knew I was going to be busy when I landed," Moak recalled. And he would remain busy for months, shuttling between meetings with Delta management, Delta pilots, politicians and other stakeholders. But there was one person he couldn't recall hearing from: Doug Parker.

Parker didn't question that account. "I don't think I ever spoke to Lee Moak," he confirmed.

Parker, so focused on convincing creditors of the financial value of the deal, and regulators that this financial value would not cause too much financial pain for consumers, had perhaps underestimated the influence of Delta's employees, particularly its pilots.

And from the beginning, Delta employees vehemently opposed the US Airways takeover, best exemplified by a spirited campaign to "Keep Delta My Delta," the brainchild, according to Lee Moak, of Delta pilots (although Ketchum, a public relations firm, won an award for its role in developing the campaign). The slogan appeared on buttons employees wore on their uniforms lapels—Delta made an exception to a rule against wearing buttons—and shouted at employee rallies. At one of these rallies, on Dec. 17, workers shouted that US Airways should go back to the desert, referring to the company's headquarters in Tempe, Ariz., near Phoenix. ALPA was particularly active, with Lee Moak at one point holding an anti-merger press conference in front of the abandoned US Airways headquarters in Crystal City, Va.—a not-so-subtle hint that Atlanta too could lose its airline. ALPA would spend $15 million of its own money to fight the US Airways bid.

Local politicians from throughout America's South joined Delta's workers and held their own press conferences to denounce the merger plan, barking about the devastating effect it would have on their economies. At one such event on Dec. 19 in Columbia, S.C., the message was clear. "Consumers should be very concerned about this," Neil Stronach, a Delta vice president of operations, told a crowd at the airport. "Fares would and will go up." As he spoke, other Delta leaders delivered similar messages at no fewer than eight other "Keep Delta My Delta" rallies that day alone in places from other southern state capitals like Tallahassee, Fla., and Charleston, W.V., to hub airports like Cincinnati, Salt Lake City and—of course—Atlanta.

By the time US Airways increased its offer on Jan. 10, the issue had reached Washington, where the Senate—or more precisely, the Senate Committee on Commerce, Science and Transportation—was watching closely. So on Jan. 24, the committee held a hearing on airline consolidation, inviting Parker and Grinstein to testify, along with a leader from the International Association of Machinists and Aerospace Workers (the IAM union), a representative of the Consumer Federation of America and the assistant secretary for aviation and international affairs at the Department of Transportation. In addition, Johnny Isakson, one of Georgia's two U.S. senators (and not a committee member), testified in support of Delta's standalone plan.

After an opening statement by the powerful committee chair, Sen. Daniel Inouye of Hawaii, Sen. Jay Rockefeller of West Virginia defined the interests of small communities, such as those in his largely rural state. Then came Isakson:

> *"I asked to do this today because I wanted to introduce the President and CEO of Delta Air Lines. I wanted to introduce him for a couple of reasons. He's a very humble man, and I was afraid he wasn't going to tell you all of the great things about what he and Delta Air Lines employees have done during difficult times. But second, I think it's important to have a perspective into why the Commerce Committee is looking into the state of aviation in this country and what has gotten us to the point that we are. My background in this is not just by being*

from Atlanta and knowing Delta. My background is, in the six years preceding my election to the U.S. Senate, I served on the Aviation Committee in the House. I was there and saw the after-effects of 9/11 on the aviation industry, watched with horror what happened in that affair. Watched further as gas prices spiraled, and the cost of running of an airline spiraled out of sight, with little or no control. And I watched a great airline, Delta, go through very difficult times, as did every airline in the aviation business. I watched them go to the depths, and I've watched them now come back to the heights of what everybody would hope would happen."

The DOT representative spoke next. Then came one of the two stars of the show: Doug Parker. His opening statement discussed the industry's post-9/11 challenges and how America West, by buying US Airways, benefited many stakeholders and could now do the same by merging with Delta.

"We believe we have an opportunity to make US Airways a better and more efficient competitor through our proposed merger with Delta. We believe the proposed merger would be good for all employees. There would be no furloughs of front-line employees of US Airways or Delta, and we will raise every employee to the highest common labor cost. We believe the proposed merger would be good for the communities we serve. No domestic city with US Airways or Delta service today will be without service after the merger, and no hub will be eliminated. In addition, we believe the merger will be good for consumers. We will implement our customer-friendly pricing in more markets to more destinations. Even after this merger, our industry will still be highly fragmented and highly competitive. Low-cost carriers are committed to continued, aggressive expansion. This is an important time for our industry. The market is bringing about positive change, and it should be allowed to continue. I would encourage Congress to let the market work, so long as any transaction is compliant with the antitrust laws. My fear is that, if we do not do that, future hearings will not be on the opportunities facing our industry but about the overwhelming challenges—and ultimately, the need for additional industry bailouts."

Next came Gerald Grinstein:

"I appreciate the opportunity to discuss my views about the impact of consolidation on the airline industry, generally, and US Airways hostile takeover attempt of Delta, specifically. In case there's any question of the hostile nature of it, take a look behind me at all of the people from

Delta who have come here today to let you know by their presence how strongly they feel about this. Congress is right to carefully examine this important public policy issue, because the decisions made now will affect the competitive landscape for years to come. Your decisions on consolidation, including any decisions made about the proposed US Airways/Delta merger, will impact consumers and communities across the country. If this deal is allowed to go forward, it most certainly will trigger broad industry consolidation, and the likely outcome will leave US Airways/Delta the weakest of the carriers, with little West Coast and Asia presence and a staggering debt load of $24 billion.

"In many ways, the market has already helped restructure the airline industry, so it is not clear to me that consolidation is inevitable. But if consolidation does happen, it should happen in a way that does not unfairly penalize employees, does not harm consumers and communities and provides long-term value for all stakeholders. To ensure this, each transaction should be evaluated on its own merits. A US Airways/Delta merger, a merger that is even more anti-competitive than the proposed United/US Air merger rejected in 2001 by the Department of Justice after 18 months of hearings, is the poster child of the worst kind of merger, and on its merits, should be rejected."

He emphasized the support of his employees:

"With me today is Captain Lee Moak, Chairman of the Delta chapter of ALPA, the union representing 6,500 pilots. And, by the way, Delta has called all of the pilots off of its furlough list.... Everyone has been offered a position. We also have members of Delta's Board Council, the group representing nearly 40,000 Delta employees, and Cathy Cone, chairman of Delta's Retiree Committee, representing more than 36,000 retired Delta people and their families. They are steadfastly united in their opposition to the US Airways deal, and let me note that ALPA and the retirees are two of the largest creditors of Delta."

And he emphasized the potential impact on fares:

"With less competition, fares will increase. Again, US Airways denies this, but one only has to look at the track record. Since its merger with America West, for every market where US Airways has lowered fares, the average fares increased in four times as many markets. Maybe that's why tens of thousands of people from all 50 states and 105 countries have joined together in the rallying cry, 'Keep Delta my Delta.' This deal is bad for Delta people, bad for the traveling public and bad for

*small communities. And this hostile takeover is nothing more than a
company's ill-conceived plan to eliminate its principal competitor, and
it should be rejected."*

The Senate hearing, perhaps unsurprisingly for a body in which Wyoming's
500,000 residents have just as much representation as California's 35 million, degen-
erated into a discussion about rural air service. But on that score, Parker was the one
under pressure. Even Senator Trent Lott of Mississippi, a free-market Republican
ostensibly committed to letting businesses act as they see fit, made clear that all
politics is local when he expressed opposition to the merger. He was, after all, from
a region Delta and US Airways dominated. "There's something worse than prices
that are too high," he said, "and that's no service. We've dealt with both of those."

"And you pay an outrageous price to fly," he continued, "just to Atlanta. And
then you can fly, you know, all over the dang country, to the big cities, for one third
the price." Again, a senator from rural America defending his state.

Parker was also under pressure when the topic turned to employees. Sen. Frank
Lautenberg of New Jersey, for example, closed his questioning with this: "I want to
ask one last thing here of you. And that is the pension benefit. The pension obligations were reduced by $5 billion as a result of your reorganization. If you can come
up with $5 billion in cash for the merger, shouldn't US Airways pay those pensions
back before buying other airlines?" The room, filled with Delta employees, broke
out in spontaneous applause.

Parker's response was a good one: "Senator, as you well know, given your business background, the $5 billion is not our money. And indeed, it's more than $5
billion—we actually have committed financing for this merger of around $8 billion
at this point. That money is not ours. That money is Citigroup's money and Morgan
Stanley's money, which they are willing to loan to us if we do this transaction." For
what it was worth, this was true of the banks' money. Parker didn't have a choice
between the merger and the pensions. It was the merger or nothing at all.

But the hearing's momentum was clearly in Grinstein's favor.

Drawing on his past experience working as a senate aide, Grinstein, who knew
Congress well, pulled out all the ammunition, at one point even noting that US
Airways was a customer of the European manufacturer Airbus, while Delta—by
implication, patriotic Delta—was a Boeing airline. And he relished telling Senators
that "there are no bonuses in place now for any executive at all."

Back when Parker first went public with his takeover attempt and got all the
headlines, Grinstein told his staff of Parker: "He gets the first day. But that's the last
good day he has." More than two months later, on this day in Washington, Grinstein
had the better day. "What I wanted to do by going to Congress," he recalled years
later, "was demonstrate to the creditors committee you're never going to get this
damn thing through, so don't even dwell on it.... Parker didn't have a very good day,
and the message got through just as it should have."

The Senate theatrics only added to Delta's momentum, building steadily as management hammered home the message about labor and regulatory uncertainty. But what would Gordon Bethune say? What would he tell the creditors who had hired him to assess both options?

"There was bigger reward with USAir, but there was bigger risk," he recalled. "There were fewer rewards with the Delta organization internally—and less risk. 'I can't tell you which one is the right one for you,'" he continued, characterizing what he had told them, "'but you can believe only 80 percent of what's being told to you by Delta. And maybe you can only believe 70 percent of what's being told to you by USAir. And they're almost the same, but neither one of them is going to do what they say they're going to do, because they're just overstating the results. Both have risks."

But US Airways had more risks.

That didn't, however, quite settle the matter. Some bondholders who had purchased Delta bankruptcy claims on the open market, and who liked the idea of turning around and selling them to US Airways at a profit, felt unrepresented on the official creditors committee and formed their own unofficial committee to advance the takeover proposal, urging Parker not to withdraw his offer by his self-imposed Feb. 1 deadline. This was the deadline, more specifically, for Delta's official creditors committee to postpone the scheduled Feb. 7 bankruptcy court hearing regarding the standalone plan and instead allow for due diligence—in other words, allow US Airways to examine Delta's financial accounts and apply for regulatory approval. The unofficial committee was basically telling Parker: keep the offer alive even if the official committee does nothing by Feb. 1, because the bondholders will continue to press the case.

But on Jan. 30, US Airways presented its financial results for the fourth quarter of 2006—good results, as it happened—and dismissed the idea of extending the deadline. Feb. 1 would be the take-it-or-leave-it date. Speaking to Wall Street airline analysts that day, Parker told one of them: "We've had a number of suggestions from a lot of creditors, who don't feel like they're being represented by the official committee, telling us, you know, 'Stick with us, we'll go block this, et cetera.' We have told them we have no interest in that plan. We have given a deadline of Feb. 1 to the official committee. They know exactly what they have to do, and they know if they don't do it, our proposal is gone. And although I believe we could form a blocking position and go through those sort of gyrations, we're not interested. If this committee is not willing to do what it should do for the people it represents, people that have been defaulted upon by Delta management, that we're trying to get back at least as much of their money as we can to them—if they aren't willing to do that for those investors, we're not willing to pursue this transaction anymore, and that's their decision to make.... I can't imagine that they don't make the right decision, but they still haven't made it. So we will see. But if they don't do it, we're gone."

On that same day, Delta advanced its cause by lining up $2.5 billion in financing to fund its plan to exit bankruptcy. The money, much of which would go to repay its higher-interest loans from American Express and GE Capital, would come from six giant financial institutions that were enjoying a golden age of Wall Street lending: JP Morgan, Goldman Sachs, Merrill Lynch, Lehman Brothers, UBS and Barclays Capital. Creditors were also swayed by promises to appoint additional members of Delta's new board that would form upon exiting from court protection. In addition, Delta's top executives would receive a significantly smaller stake in the combined company than United's executives received when their airline exited bankruptcy.

So on Jan. 31, the nine voting members of the official unsecured creditors' committee—Boeing, Pratt &Whitney, Coca-Cola, ALPA, the PBGC, US Bank, MacKay Shields, Fidelity and Bank of New York—"determined that [we] will support the standalone plan of reorganization... that will be filed later this week [and] reached this determination after engaging in extensive discussions with representatives of Delta and US Airways over the last two months and upon consideration of the advice of the Creditors' Committee's legal, financial and industry advisors." Why did they reject US Airways? "Timing" and the "risks associated with... successful consummation" of the deal.

Later that day, US Airways formally withdrew its offer, accompanied by bitter words of frustration and disappointment: "We are disappointed that the committee," Doug Parker said in an official statement, "which has been chosen to act on behalf of all Delta creditors, is ignoring its fiduciary obligation to those creditors. Our proposal would have provided substantially more value to Delta's unsecured creditors than the Delta standalone plan. We would have created a better and more financially stable airline that offered more choice to consumers and increased job security to its employees. Our merger would have been able to be consummated in a reasonable timeframe, and we would have been able to obtain all requisite regulatory approvals.

"The publicly traded bonds of Delta have fallen precipitously since rumors of this committee decision were leaked last week, reducing the implied market valuation of what Delta's unsecured creditors can expect to recover in these cases by over $1.5 billion. We empathize with the investors who purchased Delta bonds at increasingly higher prices since our offer was announced last November and thank them for their support of our proposal and their confidence in our team. It is now clear that there will not be an opportunity with the committee to move forward in a timely or productive manner, and as a result, we have withdrawn our offer."

Grinstein had won the battle.

On Feb. 7, as planned, Delta—back in bankruptcy court—formally disclosed its detailed exit plan. And after crossing some t's and dotting some i's, it emerged from bankruptcy April 30, reincarnated as a new airline with a fresh cost structure, a reinvigorated workforce and a network that was no longer notable only for its domestic and leisure orientations. Now it was gaining traction in the minds of global business travelers.

Parker, reflecting years later, pointed to two key reasons why his plan failed.

One was that he hadn't done enough to cultivate support from Delta's workers, a lesson US Airways would take so closely to heart that, in a future bid, it would appear to prioritize engendering the support of employees even above engendering the support of management—and that time, its efforts would succeed. But not with Delta.

"So we put all of our focus on the creditors and driving value to them," Parker recalled, "and the view was if the creditors vote for it, this is going to get done and that's where you should go. And what we missed in that is the employees of Delta, who obviously didn't think it was a good idea, and we didn't focus on [them]. I think naively our view was, 'Okay, well this isn't where the game's being played.'"

In retrospect, perhaps this should have been clear after the rough congressional hearing in which Jerry Grinstein was flanked by his employee supporters. But that's not how Parker saw it at the time. "When it was over, we didn't say, 'Okay, well now the deal's over,'" Parker said. "To the contrary, we said, 'Okay, we got that over with. But that's not the real game. The real game is with the creditors' committee. That's where we've got to focus, with the bondholders.'"

But "that hearing was more important than we gave it credit," Parker reflected, "because even the bondholders then looked and said, 'Well, wait a second. It's one thing for the numbers to say we're going to get all this value, but those guys have got to go try and run an airline. Well, the people don't want to do it with them. And what kind of airline is that going to be? How are they going to manage that?'"

If that was easy for Parker to see in retrospect, it was even easier for Lee Moak, the Delta pilot leader. "I think that USAir learned from that that the employees do mean something and that they can affect the process," he said.

The second reason for the deal's failure, in Parker's estimation, was one less romantic than the idea that Delta's employees helped kill the deal (although they certainly did) but just as important. This second reason was an idea that seemed present in the mind of Delta's bondholders. Although they were impressed by the money US Airways was offering, many of these bondholders also owned bonds of Northwest Airlines, which, of course, was preparing its own emergence from bankruptcy. And just wouldn't it be great, these bondholders seemed to think, if Delta were to exit bankruptcy alone and then merge with Northwest? "So as they were talking to us," Parker recalled, referring to the Delta bondholders, "it was like, 'Yeah, yeah, we want consolidation. But what we really want is Delta and Northwest to get together, because that will help both of our bonds.... There's a better deal for us.'"

Just before midnight Jan. 31, the day Delta's creditors had made their fateful decision, Doug Parker was arrested in Scottsdale, Ariz., for driving under the influence of alcohol. He would later plead guilty to the charge and serve one day in jail.

Media accounts at the time connected the obvious dots: the failed bid and the drunken driving. But Parker, speaking years later, said the two were actually unrelated. He had been at an event related to the annual Phoenix Open golf tournament.

He was going from that event to another with a friend, who asked Parker to drive because the friend had been drinking wine during dinner.

"I said, 'Sure, I'm fine,'" Parker said. "And I drove. And it turns out I wasn't fine. So it was a big mistake on my part, but it had nothing to do with the transaction."

Parker, despite what was widely speculated at the time, hadn't been drowning his sorrows that night because of Delta. But that didn't mean he was happy about what had happened—or more precisely, what hadn't happened.

Anger, in fact, was still festering on March 2, when US Airways applied for traffic rights to Beijing. The airline was clearly motivated by a desire to complicate Delta's long-held dream of flying to China. That's not to say US Airways was nothing if not married to Delta. On the contrary, it was posting solid profits and reporting strong revenue gains, gains that would persist strong throughout 2007. In January it announced new flights to Zurich, the wealthy Swiss banking center; to Brussels, the capital of a European Union feeling triumphant from the long strides it had taken since being torn apart during World War II; and to Athens, the Greek capital still basking in the afterglow of the 2004 Olympics. Still, US Airways was a predominantly domestic carrier in an internationalizing world, one vulnerable to low-cost carriers, minimally attractive to global travelers and still—in the minds of men like Doug Parker and Scott Kirby—eager for industry consolidation.

And the idea of further U.S. airline consolidation did not die with the collapse of Parker's Delta plan. In fact, it had more life than ever. Thanks to the U.S. Federal Reserve and other central banks responsible for supplying economies with money, and thanks to banks with the power to create new money through lending, money was everywhere, not just for Americans buying new homes but also for airlines, be they airlines wishing to chart their own courses or airlines wishing to buy other airlines. The money so readily accessible to Delta and US Airways for their business plans was Exhibit A. But easy money also fueled AirTran's proposed takeover of Midwest Airlines and United's courtship of Continental. Even Southwest's CEO, at an investor conference in April, went out of his way to remind everyone that his airline was no stranger to mergers, having bought Muse Air in the 1980s, Morris Air in the 1990s and a piece of ATA in the current decade. In Australia, a group of investors secured huge debt financing for a proposed takeover of Qantas. In Europe, Germany's No. 2 airline Air Berlin bought a smaller rival called LTU. In Latin America, a dynamic young low-cost carrier called Gol bought the rotting carcass of Varig, once a symbol of national might and now a symbol of bloat and inefficiency. India's government merged its two state-owned airlines Air India and Indian Airlines. And back in the U.S., so long as there was industry fragmentation, a robust global economy and oceans of capital looking for returns, airline consolidation would remain a hot topic.

Delta, for its part, was not necessarily opposed to merging. It was just opposed to merging with US Airways. Northwest Airlines, which was also coming out of bankruptcy with a fresh start, seemed a most likely partner for Delta.

Merging would have to wait, however, for Delta had a more immediate task at hand. It needed a CEO to replace Gerald Grinstein, who would retire—really, this time—now that his chief task of restructuring the airline was finished. Grinstein wanted one of his two top lieutenants—Ed Bastian and Jim Whitehurst—to succeed him. And he urged the newly constituted board of directors to choose either of them. But Gordon Bethune, as advisor to the creditors' committee, had others in mind. Bethune thought Bastian was not ready for the job, and he thought Whitehurst never would be. A better move, Bethune thought, was to lure Larry Kellner, Bethune's replacement at Continental. And if not Kellner, then Kellner's No. 2, Jeff Smisek. But neither had much interest in leaving Continental.

So Bethune thought of someone else—someone who *was* willing to leave his job. And Delta's board was listening, for it was Bethune who had recommended Glen Hauenstein, the network planner who was masterminding Delta's stunningly successful internationalization while rightsizing dying domestic hubs. "They had Cincinnati running on steroids and losing their ass," Bethune recalled of the situation a few years earlier. "It was all screwed up, and Glen new exactly what to do." Then Delta hired Bethune's former human resource chief, Mike Campbell. "They finally hired people who knew what the fuck they were doing!"

To Bethune, Richard Anderson was someone else who knew what the fuck he was doing. Early in his tenure at Continental, Bethune watched as his fellow Texan transformed a troubled Northwest Airlines maintenance department, bonding with mechanics as if he were himself a mechanic, not a former Texas prosecutor. Anderson had left his job as a prosecutor because corporate lawyers earned more money, according to a profile in *USA Today*. Before joining Northwest, he was at Continental, where he first caught the eyes of executives for his deft handling of legal matters after a fatal DC-9 crash near Denver. After joining Northwest, Anderson familiarized himself with all aspects of airline management, electing to transfer from the legal department to the maintenance department, of all places. One reason for that unusual move: It would, he calculated, open a clearer path to the top of the food chain, for in the legal department, that path was clogged by someone above him, another ascending lawyer named Doug Steenland.

Bethune worked closely with Anderson after Continental and Northwest became alliance partners, by which time Anderson—just as he had calculated could happen if he took a detour from the legal department to maintenance—had leapfrogged Steenland to become Northwest's CEO. He had become CEO, more precisely, in that fateful year of 2001, seven months before 9/11. His full tenure at Northwest would span 14 years, ending when he left the company—and the airline business altogether—in late 2004, becoming a senior executive for United Healthcare, one of the nation's top medical insurance companies. Like the time he moved from being a government prosecutor to a corporate lawyer, Anderson was again moving to a job with much higher pay.

At United—the insurance company, not the airline—he would earn $4.3 million annually. But he never lost his enthusiasm for the airline business. He would call Bethune from time to time, saying "Don't you forget I'm down here if you need help..."

Bethune told Delta's board: "He's stupid, because he's making a gazillion dollars, and has his own G4 [a Gulfstream corporate jet] and would quit that job and come work for you." Bethune also sold Anderson's experience running a maintenance division, where treating employees with respect was critical. Bethune, after all, had gotten his own start in maintenance too. There he had learned the supreme importance of motivated employees. "You know how much faster I can fix an airplane when I *want* to fix it?" he asked rhetorically.

Delta's board of directors listened. On Aug. 21, 2007, it named Richard Anderson— who in April had already been appointed a non-executive board member—as chief executive officer to succeed Gerald Grinstein. He would be just the eighth man in Delta's 78-year-old history to run the airline, following Woolman, Dolson, Beebe, Garrett, Allen, Mullin and Grinstein.

In the months leading up to Anderson's appointment, Delta largely upheld the promises made by the champions of a standalone emergence from bankruptcy. After managing a solid 4 percent operating margin in the off-peak first quarter, Delta reached nearly 10 percent in the second quarter, driven by double-digit unit revenue gains on international routes. During the first half of the year, it increased international capacity 19 percent and managed to grow international revenue a stunning 32 percent; most of Delta's new international markets were succeeding.

At the same time, Delta cut domestic capacity 5 percent but still managed to grow domestic revenue 3 percent. Delta had cut its most unproductive flying. And this was an excellent demand environment, further buttressed on the cost side by Delta's 12 percent drop in labor costs. As for fuel, virtually tied with labor now as the airline's No. 1 cost item, prices were still extremely high. But at least they were off a bit from highs reached a year earlier. Overall, since seeking court protection from creditors in the fall of 2005, Delta had slashed $2 billion from its cost structure, eliminated its pilot pensions, dumped 188 airplanes, outsourced a chunk of its regional jet flying and reduced its debt from $17 billion to $8 billion. It also remained less unionized than its legacy peers and wouldn't have to pay income taxes for years thanks to $8 billion of past losses it could use to offset its newfound profits.

Importantly, Delta's management-employee relations had improved dramatically. Despite fresh memories of pay cuts and job cuts, workers had been galvanized by the US Airways takeover attempt and had rallied alongside management to stop it. In a final measure generating enormous goodwill, Grinstein refused to accept any special payouts when he retired—no stock, no bonuses, no severance. In fact, he asked the company to use the money to which he was entitled to instead fund two new charities for scholarships and hardship assistance for Delta employees, retirees and their families. Employees had a newfound pride in their company and pride in their SCOT campaign: safe, clean and on-time.

Immediately after the US Airways takeover bid failed, the company, in a symbolic gesture of renewal, re-illuminated the lights of a large Delta sign at Atlanta's airport, a sign whose lights had been turned off to save money during bankruptcy. More substantively, Delta again began raising wages, in addition to the profit sharing it was distributing and the shares of stock it was awarding.

More specifically, Delta's post-bankruptcy compensation program gave its roughly 39,000 non-union, non-executive employees 3.5 percent of the company's stock, worth about $350 million. Employees could hold their shares or sell them with no restrictions. They also received lump-sum payments collectively worth $130 million, with each worker receiving a check amounting to about 8 percent of his or her annual pay. In addition, they'd receive at least 15 percent of Delta's annual pre-tax profits, a generous profit sharing plan by industry standards. The company would also put at least 2 percent and up to 7 percent of employee pay into a new 401(k) defined-contribution pension plan, adding additional retirement security to benefits already earned under Delta's previous and more traditional defined-benefit pension plans, which—remember—were frozen, not terminated for all employees except pilots. Not stopping there, non-union employees would have an opportunity to further boost their pay through monthly incentive bonuses linked to Delta's punctuality, flight completion rate and baggage handling performance. And perhaps best of all, Delta, moving "toward an industry-standard pay structure over time," gave all non-union workers a 4 percent wage hike.

Unionized pilots, working under their collective bargaining contract, were similarly poised to reap greater financial rewards as Delta exited bankruptcy. Their renegotiated contract called for future pay hikes, and pilots too would be eligible for both profit sharing and the Shared Rewards program, as it was known, based on the company's operating performance. Critically, ALPA's deal with management to allow for not just a freeze but a complete termination of their pension plan meant pilots would receive bankruptcy claims that they eventually sold for $1.2 billion. ALPA got the claims in exchange for its concessions, and although it could have used them to acquire a major equity position in the new Delta, it instead cashed in and distributed payouts, with each pilot getting about $185,000 on average—senior pilots more, junior pilots less.

Although Grinstein refused any stock in the new Delta, the rest of the management team—about 1,200 people—did receive about 2 percent of the new Delta's stock, worth about $240 million. But they did not receive any additional lump-sum payouts and would not receive across-the-board pay increases until frontline employees reached industry standard pay. Senior executives did have the opportunity to reap greater bonuses linked to the company's performance, but their total compensation was nonetheless modest relative to their peers at other airlines and in other industries. United's management team, for example, had received not 2 percent of company equity when it emerged from bankruptcy, but 8 percent. Needless to say, Delta's move impressed the non-union rank and file in particular. They would repeatedly reject future unionization drives, including one in October to lure flight attendants.

Also in the months leading up to Anderson's arrival, Delta retired aging planes like Boeing 737-200s, 737-300s and 767-200s. It introduced HBO programming on its newly installed inflight television, enabling travelers in all cabins to view some of the era's most popular programs: "The Sopranos," "Sex and the City" and "Entourage." It hired a nightclub owner to design inflight cocktails with names like the Summer Sizzle. It temporarily rented storefront space on Manhattan's West 57th St, where it opened a Sky360 shop showing off its latest inflight services.

Delta used a Boeing 757 to honor Hank Aaron, the legendary Atlanta Braves baseball slugger. The television talk show host Ellen DeGeneres taped one of her episodes aboard a Delta flight from Los Angeles to New York. It launched a voluntary carbon offset program for environmentally conscious passengers. It celebrated the 25th anniversary of its SkyMiles frequent flier program by announcing improved member benefits. And it began replacing 50-seat regional jets—once viewed by passengers as an upgrade from turboprops but now scorned for their cramped cabins relative to newer models—with larger regional jets outfitted with first-class cabins. One of Delta's first moves early in the year, in fact, was buying 30 additional CRJ-900s from Canada's Bombardier. These were planes with much better operating economics than their 50-seat predecessors, all the more so now that Comair had slashed its labor costs. Delta outsourced some CRJ-900 flying to third-party carriers too.

Jim Whitehurst, who would soon leave Delta shortly after Richard Anderson, rather than he, became Delta's CEO, liked to cite the example of Starbucks. At an old-style coffee shop, patrons seated in padded booths get personalized service from a waiter who takes your order, serves it to you in a ceramic mug, brings you a refill on demand and buses your table after you leave. In Starbucks, by contrast, you wait in line, you order from a clerk, you leave a tip, you wait again while your order is being prepared, receive the coffee in a paper cup and then wind up sitting on an uncomfortable bar stool if the handful of comfortable chairs are already taken. If you want a refill, you have to do it all again and pay a second time. But Starbucks, while keeping its costs rather low, offers a "21st-century experience" and most importantly a good core product—i.e., good coffee. "Let's be honest," Whitehurst said, during an investor presentation, of the customer experience at Starbucks. "You feel a little younger than you really are. You're a little hipper than you really are. You feel kind of urban. And those are all the emotional kinds of buttons that Starbucks is pushing." Delta was trying to push those same buttons by offering Summer Sizzles and episodes of "Sex and the City." And it aimed, like Starbucks, to push those buttons while keeping its costs low.

But most importantly, Delta threw all of its management might at becoming the most operationally reliable airline in the industry. Ultimately, reliability was to an airline what coffee was to Starbucks: a core product. Run your flights on time and deliver your bags on time, and before long, your revenues will rise (as travelers come to prefer your airline) and your costs will fall (because operational inefficiencies are expensive).

Sure enough, by 2007, Delta was becoming the most punctual airline among its peers. And while Atlanta's new runway explained some of that improvement, so did Delta's own initiatives. Sometimes it had merely been a victim of its own southern hospitality, such as when well-intentioned employees would delay flights so that a late-arriving connecting passenger wouldn't be left behind. The problem was that one late departure, particularly if it was early in the day, would become not only a late arrival but several more late arrivals throughout the day, and thus cause perhaps dozens if not hundreds of other passengers to miss their own connections, all in the name of trying to do the right thing for one passenger.

So departing on time—"D-zero," i.e., a departure not even one minute late, in airline parlance—would take precedence over everything except safety. "And if there were seven nuns going from New Orleans to Montréal" and in danger of missing their connection in Atlanta, Grinstein said, emphasizing the importance of inflexibility in this one regard, "they're going to have to take the next flight."

But several problems still needed attention. One was baggage handling, which still lagged the rest of the industry in reliability. The problem was Atlanta's old bag handling system, built long before the airport was handling 90 million passengers a year, as it was now. In 2006, remember, Grinstein had been told bags would have to wait until next year. This was next year. So Delta invested $100 million to upgrade the system to one with wider conveyer belts and optical scanners—ramp workers no longer needed to drive the bags between terminals for connecting passengers. Another bottleneck was the on-time performance of its regional airlines, notably Atlantic Southeast, which had been a Delta subsidiary, but which Delta had recently sold to SkyWest in a fire sale. In March 2007, Delta decided to use its own ground staff to work regional flights leaving Atlanta, giving it more control over the operation—the greater reliability, it reasoned, would be worth the higher wages it might have to pay.

But far more serious were the operational challenges in New York, where JFK Airport simply didn't have enough space to operate efficiently at peak times, a problem exacerbated by the FAA's badly outdated air traffic control system. Delta, remember, had contributed to the problem through its bare-knuckled strategy of scheduling large numbers of new flights with small jets and turboprops, ostensibly to feed traffic to its new international flights—but also, although it never publicly acknowledged this to be its intent, having the effect of sabotaging JetBlue's operation. During the summer of 2007, however, delays became so bad that the flying public began pressuring Washington for a solution. Delta decided to act unilaterally. It reduced, for example, its average hourly daily departures at JFK by 6 percent during congested periods. It moved some of its flights to western Europe from the afternoon rush hour to after 7 p.m. It tweaked schedules to leave more time for connecting customers, not to mention the employees handling their connecting bags. It added staff. It removed all turboprop aircraft. And it replaced smaller regional jets with larger ones, thereby carrying more passengers with the same number of aircraft. Overall, Delta was still planning to grow its total capacity, measured by seat miles (seats times the distance they fly) by 20 percent the following summer. But it would do so with only 11 percent more departures. Before long, the FAA decided to re-impose slot caps at JFK, which were previously phased out, starting in 2000, following an act of Congress.

As Delta's operational team worked on making Delta safe, clean and punctual, Glen Hauenstein and his network planning team were hardly letting up on their global transformation push. On the contrary, they were stepping on the accelerator, emboldened by one success after another. Starbucks, however consistent and trendy the experience and however good its coffee, was nothing if not located along the paths of bleary-eyed commuters heading to work. And an airline, however safe, clean and on time, was nothing if not located in cities with lots of people, large economies or along the paths of major travel corridors. For at the end of the day, the airline business is a real estate business, and the airlines with the best hubs win.

Well Atlanta, as Hauenstein said repeatedly, is "Boardwalk," the best real estate on the board, the best place to connect travelers into and out of Florida, the unofficial capital of the fast-growing southeast, a big business center in its own right and—increasingly—an extremely well-positioned international hub. "And the old saying used to be," Hauenstein recalled during an investor presentation, "to get to heaven or hell you had to go through Atlanta.... But the world has changed. And maybe that answer is still the same, to get to heaven or hell you have to go through Atlanta. [But] instead of heaven being Fort Lauderdale and hell being Tallahassee, now heaven is Rio and hell is Lagos."

He wasn't kidding about Lagos. Nigeria's largest city was a gold mine for airlines, catering to oil workers from cities like the energy center Houston, for which Atlanta was a perfectly situated gateway. With 160 million people, Nigeria is Africa's most populous country and the world's seventh most populous. But establishing operations there wasn't easy. Operations chief Joe Kolshak remembered two pictures he received via email from Delta employees stationed in Lagos: "One had this big burly guy walking down the street. And he had this chain that looked like something you would tow a car with, and at the other end of it was a hyena with a muzzle on. And the other one had this guy and another individual with a chain and two baboons on the end of it."

When Hauenstein first broached the subject of flying to Senegal's capital Dakar, nobody on the operations team had ever been there. "I remember," Kolshak said, "we got our Google Earth, we zoomed in, we're looking at it and we see the little shanty town on one side of the runway. We knew that British Airways and others had problems with stowaways in the wheel well. They probably jump over the fence, they jump in the wheel well and they'd be a block of ice when you landed somewhere. So, we knew we need additional security." Delta crews flying there, meanwhile, needed guards on the buses they took from the airport to their hotel, which itself had to be secure. Issues like these were old hat for an airline like Delta's partner Air France, which had long penetrated deep into Africa. But they were new for Delta, which was focusing much of its growth on a region it hadn't touched until recently.

"Now again this year, we're I think up about 20 percent in [transatlantic capacity] year over year," Hauenstein said in late March. "But really when you break that down, core European markets are essentially flat, and all of the development is to places like India, places like Africa—places that it's not so easy to get to but where the market sizes are huge. And again, I think everybody says, 'Well if you can do it, why can't the other carriers?' [But] you have to have the right gateways. You can't do it if you live in Charlotte. Charlotte-Accra is not going to work. I can tell you that.

"Again, Atlanta is the Boardwalk of airline hubs," he said. "And for an airline that was so focused on getting that last guy who wanted to go from Buffalo to Tampa, you can see that we've incredibly changed who Delta is in just a year and a half. And we see Atlanta as a gateway, particularly from not only Europe into the U.S., as really the front door to the U.S. and certainly the southeast, but also into Central America and Mexico.

"And so our goal," Hauenstein continued, "is a lot of global diversity and a lot of domestic diversity so that we can continue to move our assets around. One of my favorite lines that I use in my department all the time is: 'It's a really bad business, but at least our [assets] are mobile.'"

Disney, in other words, can't move Disney World in response to changing demand patterns. But Delta could decide whether or not to fly an airplane to Orlando.

"Last but not least," Hauenstein said of the questions he often heard from skeptics, "'What do you have that the other carriers don't have?' You know, we have industry-leading costs, we have great people, we have a global brand, we have the right gateways and we have the airplanes."

Delta, of course, was also expanding from New York JFK, an airport serving the world's second largest airline market (after London), although it was a far more competitive market than Atlanta. There was certainly no shortage of international traffic in the world's quintessential international city, but Delta still had the age-old dilemma of lacking domestic feed traffic for its global flights from JFK because domestic travelers preferred to use LaGuardia Airport. Continental's Newark hub, by contrast, was a strong domestic *and* international hub rolled into one, with its own giant market, on the New Jersey side of the Hudson River, of customers who strongly preferred it over either of the other airports. But Hauenstein, as he recreated Continental's international strategy at JFK—one that, remember, he himself had masterminded while working for Gordon Bethune—replicated its domestic strategy too. He added numerous new JFK domestic flights despite the LaGuardia dilemma. The reasoning: With so many new international flights, there would be enough connecting passengers flowing into JFK after all, filling planes even without the folks heading to LaGuardia. He added a lot of new transcontinental routes in particular, routes where many LCCs didn't compete and where the only one that often did, JetBlue, didn't have premium class cabins. And speaking of JetBlue, Delta was still hammering its operations by overscheduling regional jets.

To a lesser but still significant extent, Delta made moves in Los Angeles, the country's second largest market. This was an equally tough task given Delta's relative lack of brand recognition and frequent fliers in California, where Southwest had long dominated shorthaul travel, with United and Alaska Airlines also big players. But Delta had valuable, underutilized terminal facilities at LAX. In addition, Hauenstein saw long-term international expansion potential from LAX, expansion that could someday address Delta's lack of Asian exposure. United, as it happened, was strong in Los Angeles but flowed most of its Asian traffic through its better-positioned San Francisco hub. This meant foreign carriers dominated the Los Angeles longhaul market. For now, Delta focused its LAX expansion on shorthaul routes to Mexico and West Coast business markets like Seattle, while also hiring a rather desperate regional carrier called ExpressJet to inexpensively operate some domestic flights using the Delta brand.

In the meantime, Delta's Salt Lake City hub, benefiting from the market's fast population growth, was finally profiting. So was Cincinnati, thanks to massive downsizing. In the fall, Salt Lake City earned its first Delta flights to Paris. In March, Delta, determined to compete in Boston—which, like Los Angeles, no single carrier dominated—signed a new airport lease agreement there. In booming South America, it applied for the right to fly new routes to Colombia and signed new marketing partnerships with Aerolineas Argentinas and with Gol, a Brazilian low-cost carrier, foreshadowing what would years later become a far deeper relationship. Back in New York, Delta was adding service from LaGuardia too, doubling flights, for example, to Chicago, a stronghold for both United and American.

By July 2007, Delta was flying an incredible 114 new routes it hadn't flown the year before. This included everything from the 145-mile hop between Boston and Albany to intercontinental forays like New York to Mumbai, Accra, Bucharest and Pisa. Delta's menu of Atlanta flights, once so overwhelmingly domestic, now included Seoul, Dubai, Vienna, Prague and Johannesburg via Dakar.

And that was hardly the end of it. In the fall, Delta finally won its long-sought rights to serve China, enabling it to start selling Atlanta flights to Shanghai; it also applied for Atlanta-Beijing. And it announced Atlanta-Stockholm, and New York-Tel Aviv, and New York to Edinburgh and New York to Dakar, Amman, Cairo, Nairobi, Malaga, Lagos, Cape Town, Panama City, Guatemala City, Trinidad and Tobago and to not one but two Costa Rican cities, San José and Liberia.

To do all this, Delta—aside from redeploying more 767s from domestic routes—bought 15 over-water equipped 757s from American, which had inherited them from TWA. Delta used these planes to fly shorter routes to Europe—another idea Hauenstein had pioneered at Continental and was now stealing from himself—thereby freeing up 767-300ERs for longer routes like JFK-Cairo. Delta freed up a few more planes by abandoning a few routes, such as Atlanta-Nice, that had turned out to be a little *too* creative. It also stopped flying from Paris to Mumbai and Chennai and freed up more 767s by suspending Atlanta-Maui and Cincinnati-Honolulu flights. More provincially, meanwhile, Delta angered a U.S. senator from New York named Hillary Clinton when it abandoned the Binghamton, N.Y., market. The former first lady and then-current presidential hopeful, *USA Today* reported, penned a letter to Richard Anderson saying the company's decision "will undoubtedly prove detrimental to the economy" in Binghamton.

Distractions like that aside, Delta was thrilled to learn of a breakthrough in aviation trade talks between the U.S. and Europe. For years, U.S. diplomats had attempted to coax European nations, one by one, into signing aviation free trade agreements, otherwise known as open skies pacts. To do so, they promised antitrust immunity for alliances between each nation's major airline and its U.S. partner. The Netherlands, for example, motivated by KLM's desire to coordinate transatlantic fares and schedules with its U.S. partner Northwest, was the first country, in 1992, to sign an open skies treaty with the U.S.

The Northwest-KLM joint venture proved so profitable that Lufthansa convinced the German government, in 1996, to sign an open skies deal with the U.S. And in 2001, Air France convinced its traditionally protectionist government to follow suit. But there were holdouts, including the most important market of all for transatlantic travel, one accounting—all by itself—for roughly 40 percent of all trips. Virgin Atlantic pushed for open skies between the United Kingdom and the U.S. But mighty British Airways did not—unless, that is, it could get antitrust immunity with American, an idea regulators from both countries worried could be too unfavorable for consumers. Twice—once in 1996 and again in 2001—they had refused to approve antitrust immunity for British Airways and American unless the carriers surrendered so many slots at London's congested Heathrow Airport that the airlines, in their judgment, would be left worse off than with no immunity at all. So after all these years, the U.K. remained a largely closed market, with Heathrow open to only two U.S. airlines: United and American. And it was Heathrow that sat at the center of the aviation universe, a hub of hubs for global business travelers. Sure, New York's roughly 100 million annual passengers dwarfed almost any other global city. But New York itself was dwarfed by London and its roughly 150 million.

European diplomacy was changing by the mid-2000s, though, with European Union negotiators claiming jurisdiction for aviation policy. They wanted to scrap the patchwork of agreements between individual member states and the U.S. in favor of an E.U.-wide "horizontal" agreement covering the whole union. And that's what they got with a landmark E.U.-U.S. open skies agreement signed in April 2007, which would take effect less than a year later despite the U.K.'s reluctance. As it happened, British Airways wasn't the only critic of the deal. Virgin Atlantic and others didn't like the final language either because it didn't go far enough on the issue of foreign ownership rights: Some European airlines hoped to take advantage of a weak dollar to buy control of their struggling U.S. peers, but this would still be forbidden. And

U.S. airlines would gain the theoretical right to fly within Europe—say, between London and Paris—whereas European airlines would not be able to similarly fly between Boston and Chicago, never mind that commercial logic worked against such routes anyway.

Delta, for its part, was anything but critical. On the contrary, the new open skies pact would have two greatly beneficial implications for Delta. First, it would mean access—finally!—to London Heathrow. Second, it would present the opportunity to jointly plan transatlantic fares and schedules with its key SkyTeam partners. Immediately, Air France transferred some Heathrow slots to Delta, which announced new Heathrow flights from New York JFK and Atlanta, scheduled to launch as soon as open skies took effect in 2008. In June, Delta re-submitted its application for antitrust immunity with Air France/KLM, Northwest, Alitalia and Czech Airlines, this time confident the DOT wouldn't oppose it, for now there was an open skies pact.

Air France, for its part, was just as eager to tighten its alliance with Delta because it had quickly learned, after buying KLM in 2004, just how profitable joint ventures, or JVs, could be. In October, the two carriers—Air France and Delta, although not yet KLM or anyone else—signed a revolutionary JV that covered $1.5 billion of annual revenue generated on 19 daily flights between the U.S. and the E.U. Beginning in April 2008, the two would place their two-letter IATA codes, DL and AF, on each other's hub-to-hub flights, jointly sell each other's flights though their respective sales and distribution networks and—most remarkably—share profits on these routes, splitting not only all revenues but also all costs based on a formula tied to each carrier's capacity contribution. They would, in other words, form a virtual merged airline across the Atlantic.

Air France would even take advantage of new regulatory realities and launch nonstop flights between London Heathrow and Los Angeles, a risky maneuver away from its Paris stronghold, the first time one of Europe's giants would launch longhaul service from a rival's hub. Delta, meanwhile, announced its Salt Lake City-Paris flights, as well as flights to Lyon from New York JFK and to Orly Airport in Paris, also from JFK, complementing its existing flights to the main airport Charles de Gaulle. The clear message to regulators: Granting antitrust immunity for JVs is good for consumers because it makes many new routes like these economically viable. Therefore, they should say yes to the addition of KLM, Northwest and Alitalia to the Delta-Air France JV.

And that wasn't all. The venture was designed to expand (by the summer of 2010) to include all transatlantic flights involving Europe and the U.S., plus North Africa, Russia and parts of the Middle East, covering about $8 billion in annual revenue. To manage it, the carriers established a steering committee to oversee nine working groups responsible for coordinating day-to-day actions in the areas of route planning, revenue management, sales and distribution, products and services, frequent flyer program, operations, IT, finance and cargo. Air France employees would spend lots of time in Atlanta, and Delta employees would spend lots of time in Paris.

To be sure, so tight an alliance had its difficulties, and not just those related to the gaping cultural canyon between France and the American South. How, for example, would the two airlines split revenue for a passenger flying from San Diego to Marseilles, connecting in Atlanta and Paris? This journey, of course, involved not only one transatlantic flight but two domestic flights too. Splitting costs was even more difficult, for it was difficult to say how much of an airline's fixed costs for, say, management salaries or aircraft lease payments should be allocated to jointly marketed transatlantic routes rather than to other non-JV routes. Unions had to be assured one airline wouldn't grow while the other shrank—theoretically, a jointly-run entity could assign all transatlantic flying to the lower-cost airline, in this case Delta, and both airlines would benefit. What if each airline intentionally assigned its oldest and least fuel-efficient planes to the JV routes, thereby dumping half of those costs on the other partner? How would Air France, already angry about Delta's big African buildup—Air France had long handled a lot of U.S.-Africa traffic via Paris—prevent further sabotage of its markets? How would the two treat Continental, which was also still in SkyTeam but not part of the venture? At one point, Air France—to Delta's great dismay—had sold well-timed Heathrow slots to Continental. Needless to say, executives from both carriers spent many long hours negotiating the venture's fine print, which they never disclosed publicly.

JV or no JV, by the summer of 2007, no doubt remained that Delta's radical network revamp was a giant success. International markets, now 40 percent of Delta's capacity, were where the money was and where low-cost competitors weren't. They were markets where rising fuel costs were more easily recovered through surcharges because demand was less elastic—and through rising fares from foreign points of sale, because foreign currencies were rising somewhat in tandem with rising U.S. dollar-priced fuel costs. They were markets where Delta could escape its dysfunctional dependence on low-yield domestic traffic. They were markets Continental couldn't tap nearly as aggressively, for by 2007, it no longer had any longhaul planes to spare. United was expanding internationally, but it was more focused on the Pacific. American's high costs were preventing it from expanding aggressively. Delta, by contrast, was winning by taking advantage of its post-bankruptcy costs, which were also lower than those of most of its European competitors. It was taking advantage of deft "follow-the-sun" scheduling, removing planes from Europe in the winter, for example, and redeploying them to Africa and India. (American, remember—as its CEO had made clear in late 2006—didn't believe in this sort of seasonal scheduling.) Delta was winning by attracting international travelers with improved punctuality, new inflight products and new services like helicopter transfers between JFK and Manhattan for certain elite customers. And it was taking advantage of its improved service and its improved *esprit de corps* among front-line workers—a different kind of *esprit* from the one that had characterized Delta's family-like atmosphere for much of its history. Family? "Do you want your dumb goddamn cousin flying the airplane, or would you find the best pilot?" former Continental CEO Bethune said of the distinction. "I don't want a family. I want a team."

Indeed, Delta was thrilled to be playing offense abroad rather than defense at home. And even at home, markets were improving thanks to industry capacity cuts and—ironically—thanks to high fuel prices, which largely neutralized the low-cost carrier business model. That's because most airlines of all business models paid roughly the same amount for a gallon of jet fuel. So now that fuel made up such a large percentage of all costs, the non-fuel cost items that gave low-cost carriers their big advantages just didn't matter as much. And as early as the first quarter of 2007, Delta had shockingly earned a higher operating profit margin (excluding special accounting items) than even the one low-cost carrier that *did* have a massive fuel cost advantage: mighty Southwest. Southwest, although still well hedged, was raising fares to make up for the increasing percentage of fuel costs its hedges didn't cover, meaning airlines like Delta were no longer forced to match very low fares—and anyway, Southwest, which didn't have so much as a single flight at key Delta hubs like Atlanta and Minneapolis, was attacking United and US Airways far more aggressively than it was attacking Delta. At young Virgin America, meanwhile, the airline's CEO (and Delta's former president) Fred Reid was forced to leave the company by the DOT, which was concerned about Richard Branson's influence at what was required to be a U.S.-controlled carrier. And more importantly, Virgin's new flights were competing more directly against American, United and Alaska Airlines than against Delta. AirTran was still making money, but having paid 8.28 cents to fly one seat one mile in 2003, it was now paying 9.57 cents, the consequence of much higher fuel prices, which—remember—disproportionately hurt low-cost carriers. JetBlue, after an operational meltdown, fired its founder David Neeleman, replacing him with the former head of Continental's Newark hub. And the new LCC startup Skybus, never mind a million other problems with its business model (such as that large volumes of people weren't interested in flying nonstop between cities like Columbus, Ohio, and Greensboro, N.C., no matter how cheap the fare), certainly had no chance with oil prices surging past $50 per barrel. Domestic pricing power, meanwhile, was returning to a degree, highlighted by the return of Saturday night-stay restrictions on discounted tickets, just like in what were, from the perspective of an airline like Delta, the good old days.

Delta was the fastest growing of the seven major airlines (the big six legacy airlines—Delta, American, United, Continental, Northwest and US Airways—plus Southwest). Its financial health had improved so much that its credit card processor started withholding less cash from Delta between the time passengers booked their tickets and when they actually flew (because it no longer worried it could be on the hook for the money if the airline no longer existed by the time a customer's travel date rolled around). At Wall Street airline conferences, Ed Bastian was typically the most bullish presenter in a room that, by summer, was feeling increasingly bearish as sirens began to sound in the housing and credit markets.

Even by year end, with the word "subprime" firmly in the vernacular, Delta's traffic and revenue trends were looking strong. It was running record load factors, and its summertime unit revenues had jumped 20 percent from two years earlier. It was now the best among peers in punctuality, up from fourth two years earlier. Its mainline unit costs had dropped 10 percent. And its debt had plummeted from $17 billion to less than $8 billion.

Healthier finances meant it could invest in new technologies like "winglets"—upturned wingtips to cut fuel burn—and thinner seats that weighed less and enabled greater seating density without sacrificing passenger legroom. With lower labor costs thanks to bankruptcy, Delta's maintenance operation was insourcing a lot of third-party work and generating $300 million in annual revenue. And regional jet flying, even though still burdened by uneconomical 50-seat jets, was healthier thanks to more outsourcing and lower costs at Comair.

The whole global airline industry, it seemed, was experiencing an age of prosperity. Non-U.S. carriers were enjoying a significant discount on the things like jet fuel that they purchased in U.S. dollars, because the U.S. dollar was weak. In Europe, where LCCs got a late start, airlines like Air France/KLM, Lufthansa and British Airways were enjoying unprecedented profits thanks to not only strong European currencies and economies but also to booming longhaul traffic, highly protective fuel hedges, weaker U.S. rivals and the fruits of consolidation.

Three airlines in the Arabian Gulf region of the Middle East—Qatar Airways, Etihad and most of all Dubai-based Emirates—were growing at a hyperactive pace, benefiting from gargantuan flows of oil money into their region. In Turkey, a once-stodgy Turkish Airlines was discovering the geographic power of its Istanbul hub, enabling it to become one of the fastest growing airlines on earth. In Brazil, an airline landscape once characterized by three dysfunctional airlines—Varig, Transbrazil and VASP—was now characterized by two success stories: TAM and Delta's new partner, the low-cost carrier Gol. India was a surprisingly early convert to the idea of airline deregulation, which led to new airlines and surging traffic growth. China moved more slowly on deregulation but nonetheless saw its airlines grow dramatically thanks to its booming economy. Southeast Asia, led by the indomitable Singapore Airlines and an ultra-low cost carrier called AirAsia, was similarly witnessing an airline industry awakening. No wonder, with all this activity, that Boeing, which had sold about 500 airplanes in 2003 and 2004 combined, sold more than 1,000 in 2005 alone, another 1,000-plus in 2006 and a record 1,423 in 2007. Airbus was no different, selling more than 3,000 planes from 2005 through 2007 while also debuting its ultra-jumbo 500-seat Airbus 380, first flown by Singapore Airlines in October 2007. Across the globe, the phenomenon of commercial air travel was reaching the masses.

Back in the U.S., for the first time since United declared bankruptcy in 2002, none of the Big Six U.S. airlines was operating under court protection—in June, Northwest Airlines was the last to exit Chapter 11. In the meantime, the economy was still growing, the Sun Belt was still booming demographically and America's genius for innovation was once again on display when Apple's Steve Jobs unveiled the iPhone.

(How significant would the iPhone be? Research in Motion, the Canadian manufacturer of the BlackBerry smartphones that had become ubiquitous in corporate America at companies like Delta, didn't seem worried. "How much presence does Apple have in business?" its co-founder Mike Lazaridis asked *The Guardian*, not stopping before answering his own question: "It's vanishingly small." Many Wall Street analysts were similarly unconcerned. "I'm sure the iPhone will do well, and I'm sure there are consumers who need to have the latest and the greatest devices," one of them told CNN Money. "But it's not a corporate type of device.")

By 2007 more than 80 percent of Americans, by Southwest's count, had flown on an airplane at least once, up from just 15 percent in 1971. Naturally, this democratization of air travel contributed to America's enormous prosperity and economic revitalization since the troubled 1970s. And now airlines themselves, more than just serving as a vehicle to that prosperity, were sharing in it.

But for U.S. airlines, still nursing their post-9/11 wounds, it was an uncomfortable and insecure prosperity. Not only were oil prices still high. Worse yet, their downward momentum early in the year dramatically reversed in the second half of the year. In July 2007, the price of a barrel of crude oil jumped back above $70. In September it touched $80. The next month: $86. And then $93 for the last two months of the year. On the day of the 9/11 attacks in 2001, when a barrel of oil cost $28, even $50 was unthinkable. By late 2004, $50 was reality, and $100 was the new unthinkable. Now that psychological frontier was on the verge of being crossed too, and no airline, not even one so dramatically restructured as Delta, could be sure of its future.

High oil prices, to be sure, were having an impact on American families too. The more they paid to fill their cars with gasoline, the less they had to spend on other goods and the less they had to repay credit card and home mortgage debts. Half the cars on American highways, moreover, were not really cars at all but sport-utility vehicles and light trucks that burned large amounts of fuel, making a bad situation worse. *Fortune* pointed out nine of the world's 10 largest publicly traded companies were either firms that sold oil or firms that sold the cars that burned oil—No. 1 Walmart was the only exception. And even Walmart, which employed more Americans than the U.S. Army, would note how sales volumes dropped when gasoline prices rose. At the same time, many home buyers had taken mortgages whose payments weren't due to kick in until a year or two after they moved in. Now they were kicking in.

Just how serious would all this be? Nobody at the time knew for sure. But as early as January 2007, *The Wall Street Journal* was running headlines like "Subprime Lenders May Face Funding Crisis." In February: "Faulty Assumptions: In Home-Lending Push, Banks Misjudged Risk." On March 15: "Market's Fall May Augur a Waning Appetite for Risk—Change in Attitude Could Raise Cost of Capital Globally." April 2:

"Subprime Pullback May Crimp Consumer Spending." May 30: "Debt Bomb: Inside the 'Subprime' Mortgage Debacle."

As *The Economist* wrote, "The American mortgage industry was rotten from top to bottom, from buyers lying about their incomes to qualify for loans, through brokers accepting buyers with poor credit histories, to investors who bought bonds in the secondary market without conducting enough research."

Riskier lending practices among mortgage lenders—encouraged by a glut of cheap money triggered by the Federal Reserve's monetary stimulus after the dot-com bubble—were coming home to roost. And these original lenders weren't the only ones affected. So were many investors and Wall Street investment banks holding securities whose values were linked to these loans.

Soon, one out of every eight subprime borrowers was behind on mortgage payments. Roughly 30 subprime mortgage lenders collapsed in the early months of 2007. *The Economist* cited the example of a 24-year-old stuck with millions of dollars in debt after buying seven houses in five months, believing their prices would rise, as home prices seemingly always had. But now they were falling, threatening to detonate a $10 trillion U.S. residential mortgage market. In June, a prominent investment bank called Bear Stearns discovered two of its funds holding mortgage debt had become virtually worthless. In August, a rival bank called Lehman Brothers had to close its subprime lending unit. Even in Europe, France's BNP Paribas saw three of its mortgage funds collapse. "No one knows," *The Economist* wrote in September, "how bad things will get."

In July, the U.S. stock market dropped precipitously, and in August, the U.S. economy lost jobs for the first time since 2003. Delta was more or less seeing solid demand for its flights throughout the year, but it couldn't help being nervous. At one point in 2007, Alaska Airlines CFO Brad Tilden noted fuel prices had moved more in seven months than they had moved in the seven *years* before that. This wasn't just expensive. It was frustratingly unpredictable to a degree that made planning future schedules nearly impossible: High fuel prices generally favored flying less (because less supply of anything, including airline seats, tends to push prices up, and higher fares were the only thing that might help airlines pay the fuel bill), but airlines had no idea what fuel prices would be tomorrow, let alone many months from now, when it was time to actually operate the flights they were planning today. The fuel spike also forced Delta, late in the year, to increase fees for standby travel, reservation changes and other requests. It also implemented a hiring freeze after again cutting capacity. And it missed its fourth-quarter profit guidance.

Competitive pressures, all the while, remained intense. American opened a new JFK terminal that appeared especially inviting compared to Delta's dilapidated New York facilities. AirTran had slowed its growth, sure, but it was still growing, with new Atlanta routes to San Diego and St. Louis, for example. A revitalized Spirit Airlines, with an ultra-low-cost Ryanair-like business model, had entered Atlanta and was building a Caribbean hub from Fort Lauderdale. New startups with names like Silverjet, Zoom, MAXjet, Eos and L'Avion were stepping into the transatlantic market from New York and elsewhere. JetBlue teamed up with Ireland's Aer Lingus and sold a large stake in itself to United's close partner Lufthansa. The regional carrier ExpressJet was launching independently branded domestic service.

In October, former Vice President Al Gore won the Nobel Peace Prize for his campaign to stop climate change, reflecting a growing worldwide concern about carbon emissions from sources that included airlines. Minds were beginning to conjure a scary thought: that airlines might one day be blamed by the public for climate change in the way tobacco companies were blamed for cancer. The International Air Transport Association, or IATA, was tasked by its member airlines—most airlines around the world with the exception of a few key LCCs—with debunking what airlines considered myths about the industry's environmental record. Only with intense lobbying could airlines forestall expensive regulations and taxes. IATA was similarly charged with addressing concerns about infrastructure and security and passenger rights legislation and airport curfews and many other policy matters that threatened the industry's economic viability. Airlines understood their critical role in the global economy. But many governments seemingly did not.

So there was Delta, in many ways feeling better than ever, in many ways feeling just as vulnerable as ever. The expensive oil, the darkening economic clouds, the unrelenting competitive pressures and the future policy threats all made for a rude greeting to Richard Anderson and his ambition to make Delta an unwavering post-bankruptcy success. If all this weren't troubling enough, the U.S. airline industry remained highly fragmented, with 16 sizeable airlines all chasing a fragile market rattled by extreme fuel prices and economic uncertainty. Delta itself, meanwhile, was increasingly competing on a global playing field, and it was doing so with fewer planes than United and American and with a negligible presence in the hottest aviation market around: Asia. Perhaps, Richard Anderson thought as 2007 turned to 2008, Delta and its industry were ready for some more consolidation after all.

2008

"You didn't want to be where
American ended up being"

Doug Steenland, then the No. 2 executive at Northwest Airlines, was driving to work Tuesday morning, Sept. 11, 2001, shortly before 8 a.m. Central Time, when his wife called to tell him that—according to the morning news program she was watching at home—an airplane had hit one of the two World Trade Center towers in New York City.

By the time Steenland reached his office in Eagan, Minn., what had happened was all too clear. What wasn't yet clear was how the country's airlines would manage the situation. For Steenland and his boss Richard Anderson, job No. 1 was working with the operations control staff to ground the airline, as directed by the FAA, while accounting for all employees spread throughout the world. The drama was thick. On one flight from Amsterdam, the board of directors of Northwest's close partner KLM was en route to Detroit to inspect a new airport terminal that would open in a few months. Their plane turned back to Amsterdam, in accordance with what had quickly emerged as the general rule for longhaul pilots that day: If you were less than halfway to your destination and had enough fuel to return to your departure airport, you would turn back; if not, you would proceed to North America, usually a Canadian airport.

In one case, a Northwest flight coming from Tokyo did not have enough fuel to turn back and hoped to land in Vancouver. But Vancouver's airport was already beyond packed. It had no space for the Northwest plane. "Basically," Steenland recalled years later, "we had to beg the FAA to let it come into Seattle. And they finally let that happen. But just to show you the fear of the day, it came in under fighter escort. It was clear to everyone that if the plane deviated at all in any material way from its glide slope"—an airplane's normal descent toward a runway—"the fighter planes were not going to let it get very far."

Then there was the matter of keeping the business afloat. One of Steenland's first discussions after the tragedy dealt with the need to immediately draw down every penny from the revolving credit line the company had with its banks—in other words, to actually borrow the money to which it was entitled but (until now) didn't need. Northwest's CFO Mickey Foret knew as well as anyone else that lots of cash would be flowing out in the days and weeks to come, while little would flow in. The bankers resisted during the next 48 hours, arguing the terrorist attacks represented a "material adverse change" that invalidated the credit line agreement. But Steenland (himself a shrewd lawyer) and his team successfully defended their right to the cash.

Tensions were still high later that week when Northwest received the green light to restart its operations. About two hours before the launch, Steenland and Anderson received a disturbing report: Police had arrested four people at New York JFK for impersonating pilots—they were wearing Delta pilot uniforms. Should Northwest call off the launch? That's indeed what it did, postponing things until the next morning.

As it happened, just five months before the fateful 9/11 attacks, Northwest Airlines, then the nation's sixth largest carrier by revenues, had appointed a new CEO and a new president. Both appointees were longtime Northwest executives, having joined the company in 1990 and 1991, respectively. Both were lawyers. And both had climbed the Northwest ranks while working alongside some of the airline industry's other future luminaries, including AirTran's top executives Joe Leonard and Bob Fornaro and American's future CEO Doug Parker.

These two men, Richard Anderson and Douglas Steenland, were entrusted to preserve Northwest's recent string of impressive profitability. After a tumultuous early few years of the 1990s, Northwest produced double-digit operating margins in 1994, 1995, 1996 and again in 1997. And 1998 might have been a great year too, had a bitter two-week pilot strike in the heart of the peak summer season not cost the company a billion dollars. But with pilot peace eventually restored, Northwest earned solid profits once again in 1999 and then again in 2000. Anderson and Steenland, of course, were key decision makers during this era of prosperity, so they got credit for helping to create it. Entering the new decade, hopes were high.

But then came 9/11. Like all other U.S. airlines, Northwest was suddenly fighting for its life. Planes were grounded, cash was evaporating and many travelers refused to get on an airplane. When it came time to tally the results for 2001, Northwest's passenger revenues had plummeted 14 percent, its unit revenues were down 9 percent and 24 of its planes were out of service, only half of which were back by year end. International revenues were down even more drastically, and in the fourth quarter of 2001, capacity—measured by available seat miles, or ASMs—was 16 percent below what it was a year earlier. Net losses amounted to more than $400 million.

That Northwest Airlines was even still in business by 2001, nearly a quarter century after airline deregulation, was testament to one critical feature of its network.

Since 1978, so many other airlines had come and gone, but Northwest survived and often thrived thanks to its privileged position on routes to the Far East. Only United had anything close to what Northwest could offer in Asia, and even it was a latecomer. Northwest's Asian network started coming together in the aftermath of World War II, when Washington awarded it flying rights based on its experience flying to the Pacific via Alaska. It began flying to Tokyo in 1947, but its biggest break came in 1952, when the U.S. signed a bilateral aviation treaty with Japan. Normally, these bilaterals designate certain airlines from each country to operate between the two countries. But in this case, Japan was only several years removed from its defeat in World War II, and the U.S. had more than enough negotiating leverage to ensure that Northwest and Pan Am were able to fly not only between Japan and the U.S. but also between Japan and other countries in Asia, using what airlines call "fifth-freedom rights." Northwest and Pan Am, in other words, could operate Tokyo hubs, becoming rare examples of airlines with hubs outside their home nations.

That same year, 1952, Japan became an independent country again, and Northwest helped it launch a new airline called, appropriately enough, Japan Airlines. This was in conjunction with America's broader effort to resurrect the war-ravaged nation, once a bitter enemy but now a country envisioned as a bulwark against communist Russia and communist China. Northwest, in fact, briefly flew to Shanghai before a young communist revolutionary named Mao Zedong defeated Chiang Kai-Shek's nationalist army and turned China red. Manila, Seoul and Taipei were other early Asian destinations served by Northwest, which was now calling itself Northwest Orient.

Northwest wasn't a new airline. Its origins dated to the early years of civil aviation—1926, to be exact, when it carried mail between Minneapolis and Chicago. The next year brought passenger flights, and by 1941 it was a publicly traded company. The 1950s saw the introduction of Northwest flights from Minneapolis to Florida, catering to an increasingly affluent post-war population seeking vacations in the sun. Still, it was the Pacific network that buttered Northwest's bread, and new Boeing 707 jets were, for the first time, enabling it to fly across the vast Pacific Ocean without a stop in Alaska. In the 1970s, it began replacing these with giant Boeing 747s, the largest planes in the business.

Best of all, Northwest was making money year in, year out, acquiring a reputation for ruthless cost management along the way. The company even removed doors from restroom stalls to keep workers from idling away from their desks. Most offices were windowless, lest workers waste precious time staring at the scenery. Managers worked not five days per week but six. One of them was Joe Leonard, the future CEO of AirTran, which, as the lowest-cost U.S. airline, had become such a thorn in Delta's side. "That was where I got my basic training in cost control," Leonard recalled. "You either got it done, or you left."

Something was working, because Northwest, after decades of profits in the post-war regulated era, managed to make money after deregulation too. Even during the early years of the 1980s, when fuel prices spiked and new entrants stormed the scene—and when perennially profitable Delta stumbled to a loss—Northwest made money. Remarkably, Northwest made money during every single year of the 1980s, unperturbed on its still-lucrative Pacific routes by low-cost carriers. The 1980s were a golden era for Japan, in particular, whose real estate market soared and whose export-based conglomerates had Americans thinking their country's best days were behind it. These routes were benefiting, furthermore, from heavy losses and severe management dysfunction at Pan Am, Northwest's only competitor in the region. Throughout the 1980s, it was still calling itself Northwest Orient and promoted its service using the former Minnesota Vikings star quarterback Fran Tarkenton. Even domestically, Northwest's stronghold in the part of the country stretching from roughly Minneapolis to Seattle attracted less low-cost carrier competition than, say, California or Florida.

Still, the 1980s weren't all fun and games. In 1985, Northwest awoke to the unwelcome news that United, America's largest airline by almost all measures, was buying Pan Am's Pacific route network in what amounted to a fire sale. Now Northwest would have to compete against a much stronger rival. Worse yet, United had a much larger domestic market with which to feed its Asian flights, and it was based in Chicago, one of the four cities Northwest connected nonstop to Tokyo (Seattle, Anchorage and Honolulu were the others). Whereas United could feed its Chicago-Tokyo flights with passengers connecting from countless other U.S. cities, large and small, Northwest would have to fill its flights with travelers originating or ending their journeys in Chicago. It was also in the early 1980s that United became the second airline after American to start a frequent flier program (Delta was third), further cementing the loyalty of Chicago travelers.

This posed a serious dilemma, one Northwest decided to address by merging with another airline. The 1980s, of course, were merger mania in the airline business, prompting all sorts of speculation and chatter about who would combine with whom. On August 11, 1985, the *Chicago Tribune* ran an article under the headline: "Northwest En Route to Change." It spoke of rumors putting Northwest together with Eastern, American or a certain company in Atlanta. "Wall Street speculation," the report said, "is that the most likely partner for Northwest, if there were a marriage, would be Delta—a similarly conservative company."

But that was not to be. Not that decade or the next, anyway. Instead Northwest, in 1986, merged with its local Minneapolis rival Republic Airways. Republic itself had merged with another airline—Hughes Airwest in California—six years earlier, also in hopes of building scale as the impact of deregulation unfolded. And it had established hubs not just in Minneapolis but in Detroit and Memphis too (or "Snow-town, Motown and No-town," as some people called the group of hub cities). Republic suffered losses in 1980, 1981, 1982 and 1983, returning to profitability—and only barely—in 1984. One of its problems: an overreliance on domestic routes, in not so different a way from how Northwest suffered an overreliance on international routes. The two seemed a perfect fit.

Or were they? The new Northwest, now minus the Orient in its name, had indeed become a more balanced airline with its strong Pacific network, plus a few Atlantic routes, supplemented by a strong domestic network. But airline mergers are easier to devise on paper than they are to execute on the ground, and execution in this case proved—to put it mildly—messy. The $884 million fusion was, at the time, the largest airline merger in history, creating vast complications for combining fleets, IT systems, procedures and policies. And the most complicated task of all was merging two heavily unionized workforces. All these difficulties, in fact, would leave a big scar on the collective minds of future airline executives and airline investors, instilling them with fear and uncertainty about the unpredictable risks of merging two carriers.

If Northwest was famous for its frugality, it was also known for its less-than-lovable labor relations, perhaps best exemplified by the bitter 1998 pilot strike. Longtime CEO Donald Nyrop had on several occasions confronted unions, and his successor Steven Rothmeier was no less accommodating. Upon becoming CEO in 1985, the stern Vietnam veteran immediately issued a memo to all office employees demanding they be at their desks by 8 a.m. But running the airline like a drill sergeant didn't prevent it from suffering severe post-merger integration problems, including awful on-time performance, countless customer complaints and fighting between members of different unions. The merger transaction also left Northwest, once so allergic to debt, heavily leveraged.

The mood darkened further when, on Aug. 16, 1987, a Northwest MD-82—one that had come from Republic—crashed after taking off from Detroit, leaving 156 people dead; only a four-year-old girl somehow survived. Investigators blamed the pilots for forgetting to extend the wing flaps and slats. In 1990, three Northwest pilots were convicted for flying while intoxicated, further damaging the carrier's already soiled reputation. Many passengers were now calling Northwest "Northworst."

Nevertheless, the 1980s were the age of the leveraged buyout—the LBO. Investors bought companies with borrowed money—borrowed money that the company would be obliged to repay. And for all its post-merger challenges, Northwest proved a popular target for would-be LBO investors, including the California oil magnate Marvin Davis. It was his bid in early 1989 that set off a wave of other offers, including one by Pan Am, which was on life support—but nonetheless convinced its bankers a loan to buy Northwest would save it. In the end, Northwest's board of directors, in June 1989, accepted a $3.6 billion bid, most of it borrowed, led by Alfred Checchi, a former hotel executive turned investor and his business partner Gary Wilson, a former Disney executive. The group of buyers also included a visionary Dutch airline called KLM, which was willing to invest some $400 million in hopes of tapping the rich U.S. market, not so much for passenger business at the time but for cargo. The Netherlands was a small market compared to European countries like Germany, France and the U.K., which all had bigger airlines competing against KLM. Besides, British Airways was looking to buy part of United and later USAir, while SAS was eying Continental, Lufthansa was eying American and Swiss was eying Delta.

One reason the Checchi/KLM bid proved victorious: It was generally (although not enthusiastically) supported by unions, which viewed it as the least bad of multiple evils. In fact, the labor tensions and service problems did ease quite a bit after the change in ownership, although not without a few antagonistic moments, such as one described on Sept. 9, 1990, in the *Minneapolis Star-Tribune*: "At the Northwest station in London, for example, Wilson introduced himself to agents and staff as their 'new owner,' to which one replied, 'Dogs have owners. We're employees.'"

In the early 1990s, by which time Anderson and Steenland had joined the company, everyone was disappointed, for Northwest would get hammered by a run-up in fuel prices, an economic recession tied to that run-up in fuel prices and a slowdown in international travel caused by a U.S.-led war to oust Saddam Hussein from Kuwait and preempt him from making a move on Saudi Arabia, the world's most important oil producer. Northwest's long string of annual profits broke in 1990.

Under its new CEO John Dasburg, who had worked with Checchi at the hotel chain Marriott, Northwest expanded its network by buying struggling Eastern's presence at Washington's National Airport and some additional Asian routes from Hawaiian Airlines. It nearly established a hub in Atlanta when Eastern collapsed, studied a bid to buy Australia's airline Qantas, held merger talks with Continental, moved to acquire the bankrupt Midway Airlines, almost bought the Trump Shuttle serving the Boston-New York-Washington corridor and bid for some of Pan Am's international routes that ultimately went to Delta. Although those deals never came to pass, an important marketing pact with Northwest's new part-owner KLM enabled Northwest to earn some money in Europe and even enabled the Dutch airline to start the first-ever scheduled longhaul flights from Northwest's home in Minneapolis-St. Paul. Northwest also arranged a less consequential marketing deal with America West. And Northwest also had some political clout under its new owners: One of its board members was Walter Mondale, a Minnesota native who had served as Jimmy Carter's vice president before running unsuccessfully, in 1984, for the presidency.

But never mind all that. After the Iraq war, Northwest's losses went from bad to worse, topping $300 million in 1991 and topping $1 billion in 1992. High fuel prices and intense competition remained a problem, as they were for Delta too in the early 1990s—and for most every other airline, for that matter, save Southwest. And Northwest joined Continental in suing American for what they alleged was predatory pricing in 1992 to try to put them out of business. But Northwest had other problems, including higher-than-average labor costs and heavy debt obligations dating from the 1989 leveraged buyout. Also troubling: developments in Japan, a crucial Northwest market. At the start of the 1990s, an extraordinary buildup in real estate and stock prices came crashing down, turning the miracle Japanese economy—which had awed so many nervous Americans—into a chronic case of economic stagnation and deflation that would linger for two decades. Sure enough, Northwest's Pacific network started losing money in 1989, having morphed from an engine of profits to a loss-making drag.

As the *Minneapolis Star-Tribune* wrote, Northwest in the early 1990s was burning cash even faster than it was burning fuel. Happy though Minnesotans were when baseball's Twins claimed victory in a thrilling 1991 World Series, their hometown airline was heading toward bankruptcy. Only by the skin of its teeth did Northwest avoid insolvency, getting last-minute labor concessions from reluctant unions. It was these labor concessions, in fact, that helped Northwest quickly restore profitability, coinciding, as they did, with the beginning of the mid- to late-1990s economic boom.

But Northwest's sharp turnaround was about more than just lower labor costs—and more too than just a healthier balance sheet following an out-of-court debt restructuring. At least as important was a landmark development involving its major shareholder KLM. As it happened, the early 1990s brought a change in U.S. government policy, motivated by the desire to pry open international airline markets. The strategy was to promise foreign governments open access for their airlines to the U.S. plus immunity from antitrust laws for their national carriers if they wanted to collaborate with their U.S. partners. KLM loved this idea, and if KLM loved it, the Dutch government loved it too. Soon came the first-ever U.S. open skies deal, removing all route restrictions between the U.S. and the Netherlands and allowing KLM to jointly manage its transatlantic routes with Northwest. On the other hand, the Bush administration stopped short of allowing European airlines to exercise management control of their U.S. partners, as British Airways unhappily discovered when it tried to buy USAir.

These changes were not without controversy. During the 1992 presidential campaign, the populist, anti-globalization candidate Ross Perot even mentioned the Northwest-KLM deal by name. In the third and final debate with George H.W. Bush and Bill Clinton, the Texan billionaire said:

> *"We're getting ready to dismantle the airline industry in our country, and none of you know it. And I doubt in all candor if the president knows it. But this deal that we're doing with [British Airways] and USAir and KLM and Northwest—guess who's on the president's campaign big time? A guy from Northwest. This deal is terribly destructive to the US airline industry. One of the largest industries in the world is the travel and tourist business. We won't be making airplanes in this country 10 years from now if we let deals like this go through.... We hammer-lock the American companies—American Airlines, Delta— the last few great we have, because we're trying to do this deal with these two European companies. And never forget, they've got Airbus over there, and it's a government-owned, privately owned, consortium across Europe. They're dying to get the commercial airline business. Japan is trying to get the commercial airline business... I don't think there are any villains inside government on this issue, but there's sure a lot of people who don't*

understand business. And maybe you need somebody up there who
understands when you're getting your pocket picked."

The Northwest-KLM deal went through, and the U.S. was still making airplanes
10 years later. And Bill Clinton won that 1992 presidential election, which coincided
with the end of the Cold War, a major drop in oil prices and the beginning of an
economic boom driven by stunning new information technologies, including the
internet. The glorious second part of the 1990s had begun, a part that at Northwest
would be marred only by the crippling pilot strike of 1998. Fuel prices were low,
demand was strong and Northwest's management team, which included Anderson
and Steenland, earned a reputation for ruthless competition. Frontier Airlines, for
one, learned this the hard way. In the summer of 2004, it launched two daily Los
Angeles-Minneapolis nonstops, encroaching on one of Northwest's most lucrative
domestic routes. Instantaneously, Northwest increased its daily frequencies from six
to eight, slashed fares and launched two daily flights in one of Frontier's most lucrative
markets: Denver-Los Angeles. Frontier was gone from the market within months.
But it was lucky compared to Sun Country, a small startup airline that in 1999 tried
operating scheduled low-fare service from Minneapolis. Three years later, unable
to withstand Northwest's aggressive capacity and pricing tactics, it was bankrupt.

Thanks to what would become a powerful transatlantic joint venture—the first
of its kind—Northwest's pockets were starting to fill again. Cooperation with KLM
involved reciprocal frequent flier benefits, standardized product features and, most
importantly, having hubs on both sides of the Atlantic. Airlines have outsized selling
power at their hubs because of frequent flier loyalty and a captive corporate travel
market. And they can generate lots of connecting traffic at their hubs too because
of the large menu of flights they offer. So now Northwest and KLM, before any of
their competitors, could operate hub-to-hub flights across the Atlantic, able to
offer connections not on one end of the routes but on both. It was like United flying
between Chicago and San Francisco or American between Dallas and Miami—in
each case, the airline had hubs on both ends—with all the pricing power this implied.

Almost by accident, Northwest and KLM had some excess aircraft to deploy
one summer, and in a "let's-just-try-it-out" moment, the airlines scheduled them
between Amsterdam and Northwest's Minneapolis and Detroit hubs. Just try it
out? The flights made a lot of money, generating a few passengers flying nonstop
between these cities (who were willing to pay premiums for the privilege) and many
more connecting passengers. By the summer of 2000, Northwest-branded planes
were flying from Amsterdam to Detroit four times a day. KLM-branded planes
were doing so once a day. And it didn't really matter which airline was operating
a flight, because both airlines shared all revenues and costs equally. Such frequent
flights between two medium-sized cities separated by an ocean would never have
been possible without all the traffic generated by passengers connecting to points
beyond Detroit and Amsterdam.

KLM wanted to go even further, talking to British Airways about a merger and to three similarly undersized rivals—SAS, Swissair and Austrian Airlines—about a four-way alliance that would have been called Alcazar. But BA was wary of KLM's big equity stake in Northwest, and Alcazar talks fell apart when Swissair insisted Delta, not Northwest, be the alliance's exclusive U.S. partner.

But it would be wrong to say Northwest and KLM cooperated together like two close friends who never argued. On the contrary, they were more like spouses who loved each other but fought often, such as in 1995, when Northwest schemed to prevent KLM from exercising stock options KLM had obtained in 1993 for helping its ally avoid bankruptcy. KLM even sued, arguing it should have the right to lift its ownership stake from 19 percent to 25 percent, the maximum U.S. law would have allowed. The two couldn't agree on jointly ordering planes from Airbus, even when both were greatly interested in buying the same twin-aisle 330s Airbus was selling. They couldn't reach a consensus on common specifications, even disputing which way the cockpit switches would turn. As one Northwest executive remembered it, "We were never close to getting it done. [It was] one step too far."

But even if the marriage wasn't always blissful, the revenue surpluses that joint transatlantic routes were generating proved a powerful incentive against divorce. In 1997, in fact, the two decided to deepen their integration. As part of that arrangement, KLM agreed to sell its 20 percent stake back to Northwest, creating a more balanced partnership. The following year, 1998, Northwest would snatch Continental from the arms of Delta just as the two were ready to merge, only to face a Justice Department that blocked Northwest from merging with Continental. The two nonetheless formed a close alliance, and Northwest gained a so-called "golden share" in Continental, with veto rights over future mergers involving Continental. KLM was no longer Northwest's master; now Northwest was Continental's.

The start of the new decade, the 2000s, was thus filled with hope. Northwest was making money, the joint venture with KLM was a big success, and even if labor costs were still high relative to the industry average, at least fuel costs were low. Low-cost carriers, while making life miserable for Delta, US Airways, United and others, were less interested in Northwest's upper Midwest markets—"it's cold, it's dark and it's all ours," remember, went the devilish internal mantra. "A hammerlock on the hinterlands," wrote *The Wall Street Journal*. In some cases, in fact, not only were LCCs not making life miserable for Northwest: *It* was making life miserable for *them*, still assaulting their markets by dumping capacity and low fares into their markets, lest they get any unwise ideas. In 2000, Spirit Airlines sued Northwest, alleging it violated the Sherman Antitrust Act when it bombarded the Detroit-Philadelphia and Detroit-Boston markets with low fares right after Spirit entered. Spirit, not playing by Northwest's rules, had based itself in Detroit.

At the start of the 2000s, Northwest was profitable enough to invest in new technology too. In 2000, it became the first network airline to permit domestic systemwide online check-in via its web site. And in January 2001, it ordered 52 new aircraft: 24 widebody Airbus 330s, 20 narrowbody Boeing 757s and a handful of 747s and 319s. One month later, CEO John Dasburg left Northwest to run Burger King, a Miami-based fast-food chain, leaving the top job at Northwest Airlines to his deputy Richard Anderson.

Seven months later, of course, came calamity. Anderson found himself facing an entirely new set of circumstances. Northwest was once again losing money and burning through cash faster than it was burning through jet fuel—jet fuel, keep in mind, that was now skyrocketing in price.

Net losses in 2002 were even worse than in 2001, prompting Anderson to once again highlight Northwest's labor cost dilemma: "In light of the cost adjustments made at many of our competitors, it is imperative that we reduce our labor expenses so that we can restore Northwest to profitability," he said in a press release dated April 16, 2002. At the time, wages and salaries alone accounted for 40 percent of Northwest's total operating costs. In October, the airline announced it would close its aircraft maintenance base in Atlanta; its call center in Long Beach, Calif.; and several city ticket offices throughout the country.

Just as it did in 1993, however, Northwest coupled its assault on labor costs with a more uplifting revenue initiative. Back then it was the alliance with KLM. This time Northwest was adding Delta to its existing alliance with Continental. But this alliance, although it involved helpful codesharing and frequent flier reciprocity, was far less integrated than the KLM alliance—Northwest and Delta, for example, couldn't jointly plan routes or price seats in the way Northwest and KLM could. And the deal did little to alleviate the pain from the start of what would be an ongoing elevation in oil prices, the Iraq war and SARS, a health epidemic that hurt Northwest, because of its outsized Asian exposure, more than most U.S. airlines. Northwest's debt went from $3 billion in 2000 to $5 billion in 2001 to more than $8 billion by 2004 (or more like $15 billion, counting off-balance-sheet lease obligations). By October of that year, Richard Anderson had seen enough. He left for a more lucrative gig running United Healthcare. His replacement: Doug Steenland, the man who had helped form the joint venture, the man who had negotiated an end to the 1998 pilot strike and the man whose chief task now was to save the airline from bankruptcy.

These were awful times for the U.S. airline industry, particularly on the domestic front, where Northwest—long insulated from domestic scourges like LCCs that plagued other legacy airlines—was this time feeling a greater impact than most from a new problem: Delta's SimpliFares initiative. Northwest needed big revenue premiums—i.e., high fares—to compensate for its labor cost disadvantage, and these premiums were disappearing as Delta brought down fares. "We believe that fare simplifications of this nature are revenue negative and that this initiative will adversely affect industry revenues," Northwest said in an annual report. In this sense, Northwest was the opposite of Delta: Northwest had more of a cost problem than a revenue problem, although both carriers had their share of both problems.

Things were more hopeful abroad. KLM, still looking for a merger partner, found one in Air France. And when the two completed their groundbreaking merger in the spring of 2004, Northwest followed them into the SkyTeam alliance.

Also in 2004, Northwest pilots agreed to $285 million in concessions including pay and benefit cuts, as well as the right for the airline to use larger outsourced regional jets. In the meantime, Northwest made headway in restructuring its debt and credit lines. And it stopped serving free meals for economy class passengers on domestic flights. In May 2005, even as financial uncertainty was becoming greater than ever—even as the specter of bankruptcy was nearing—Steenland felt confident enough to order Boeing's new 787 Dreamliner, a plane with the right economics to restore Northwest's Pacific profits. Months earlier, it had ordered more twin-engined Airbus 330s too, eager to replace tri-engined DC-10s whose descent into obsolescence was accelerating as fuel prices spiked.

Back on the domestic front, Northwest was fortifying its firepower in the so-called "heartland" region, the U.S. Midwest. It built mini-hubs in Indianapolis and Milwaukee, supplementing its three key strongholds of Detroit, Minneapolis and Memphis. None of these three hubs, by the way, suffered the sort of costly congestion that rivals suffered at airports like Newark, New York JFK and Chicago O'Hare. Detroit had opened its gleaming new airport terminal in 2002, and internationally, the KLM venture was as strong as ever, covering $3 billion in revenue—"the industry's most integrated alliance," Northwest proudly claimed, and nobody rose to dispute that. Its alliance with Continental was "highly profitable for both airlines." The carrier had become a technology leader too, with 35 percent of ticket revenue generated from its website and greater systemwide use of airport check-in kiosks than its competitors. And since 2001, Northwest had achieved $1.7 billion in improvements from cost cutting and revenue enhancements.

But it wasn't enough. Northwest had lost $3.6 billion since 2001, including $716 million in just the first half of 2005. Its aging planes were ill designed to profit with oil prices exceeding $70 per barrel. Yes, low-cost carriers were less of a threat at Northwest's hubs than they were at other airlines' hubs, but they were a threat nonetheless: Average fares between Detroit and Washington Dulles fell 77 percent after Independence Air entered the market. The company's pension obligations were a giant burden. Unit labor costs remained the industry's highest, and even the recent pilot concessions were temporary: Absent another deal, everything would "snap back" in just two years. Northwest was making little headway with its three other major unions representing flight attendants, airport workers and mechanics. It hastened to emphasize the industry's impossibly high tax burden—in just the second quarter of 2005, it paid more than $296 million in fees and non-income-related taxes. Asian routes, meanwhile, flown with high-cost labor using high-cost aircraft, continued to lose money, demonstrated by the airline's decision to suspend New York-Tokyo service. Total company losses amounted to some $4 million per day, losses unsustainably funded through borrowing and asset sales.

In Hurricane Katrina's wake, Northwest Airlines filed for bankruptcy on Sept. 14, 2005—the same day Delta filed. But Unlike Delta, which was already almost penniless, Northwest—although clearly on an unsustainable trajectory—filed with $1.5 billion still left in its coffers, making it less dependent on external financing. In any case, it was operating under court protection from creditors all the same. And it was determined to use this protection, and to use all the other tools bankruptcy affords, to make its business profitable again.

It had actually achieved one key goal just before the bankruptcy filing. Way back in 1999, Northwest's mechanics, impatient for a pay hike following the new contract pilots had achieved by striking a year earlier, threw out their union in favor of a small, tough-talking, startup outfit calling itself AMFA—the Aircraft Mechanics Fraternal Association. AMFA, in fact, had defeated the mighty International Association of Machinists, or IAM, even after the IAM had won praise for compelling management to hire back six workers dismissed for alleged violations of company policy (although the union was unable to do much for another worker fired for showing up to work in a clown suit). More substantively, its popularity began to wane when it negotiated a tentative contract many members judged inadequate. They were highly skilled workers, they felt, and as such should be paid more like pilots than like their unskilled brethren. "Guess what, guys?" Doug Steenland said, recalling management's view of what the mechanics wanted. "That doesn't work."

But AMFA emerged victorious and quickly acquired a reputation for championing unreasonable demands, even after the company's financial distress in the early 2000s. Management called it a "rogue" union. "Irresponsible to the core," Steenland said. "Leadership, particularly at Northwest, that you just simply couldn't deal with." Not that the rank-and-file mechanics themselves were all unreasonable people, in Steenland's view. But "all of a sudden they're now run by the Taliban."

Management, however, had one ace up its sleeve. AMFA, unlike the IAM, was not part of the national AFL-CIO, a coalition of unions with political muscle in Washington. This meant paradoxically, although AMFA was more militant than the IAM, Northwest actually had a better chance of breaking this union by letting it declare a strike, as it was threatening to do, and then using the occasion to hire replacement workers. Pilots, flight attendants and customer service workers, represented by unions that were affiliated with AFL-CIO, quietly made clear to management they would not support AMFA's actions with sympathy work slowdowns or other actions—the mechanics, after all, had voted out one of their fellow unions. "If we were trying to do this with another AFL-CIO union?" Steenland recalled years later. "Not a chance."

So without further delay, Northwest spent $125 million to train some 1,200 contract mechanics and more than 300 management mechanics, working closely with the FAA to ensure its approval of the process. At midnight on Saturday, Aug. 20, 2005, AMFA struck, triggering the contingency plan. Hundreds of replacements were standing by in hotel rooms, ready to report to work at the midnight shift change.

The company arranged buses and police escorts to bring them—new toolboxes in hand—past the AMFA picket lines.

The plan worked with remarkably minimal disruption—Northwest had proactively pared its schedule a bit that first weekend but operated the more conservative schedule rather smoothly. Going forward, the airline unilaterally implemented new terms and conditions of employment, saving $200 million annually. Northwest would from now on outsource most of what airlines call "heavy maintenance"—periodic overhauls of an aircraft that can last days. The in-house mechanics that remained to do "line maintenance," such as routine tasks in between flights, would be non-unionized.

Even while never questioning the decision to break the union, Steenland felt bad for the individual mechanics who lost their jobs. "It was tragic," he said. "These were in general decent human beings who were highly skilled. These are licensed mechanics and talented people who just made a bad choice when they voted in this other group.... The core rank and file just wanted to go to work and do their jobs and didn't want to be bothered by any of this stuff, and be paid fairly."

"Half of them were crying" as they left work that night, Steenland recalled, "because they knew they weren't coming back. They knew that their union had led them down the path of no return."

His email inbox, meanwhile, was filled with comments, good and bad alike. One Minneapolis-area resident wrote: "You've got a big set of balls." (That was a compliment.)

Years later, when observers would marvel at management and unions at various airlines who not only got along cordially but even sometimes found themselves sitting on the same side of the table—fighting together for mergers, for example—those observers would sometimes forget that a key turning point in airline management-union relations had occurred in the summer of 2005. "A lot of that mindset started when people looked at what happened with AMFA, and they basically said, 'Oh my God,'" Steenland said. "I think it really did sort of reshape the business."

The airline would stay in bankruptcy from September 2005 through May 2007, a 20-month period that coincided with another strong uplift in industry demand, albeit a sharp increase in fuel prices too. But combined with a $2.4 billion reduction in operating costs (including $1.4 billion in labor savings), pension relief legislation from Congress and more than $4 billion in total debt reduction, Northwest quickly became profitable again. Following scope clause concessions from pilots, management also ordered modern 76-seat jets to replace geriatric DC-9s for smaller domestic markets and started an all-new regional subsidiary called Compass Airlines to operate them. Not stopping there, Northwest bought its regional partner Mesaba while renegotiating terms with another regional partner called Pinnacle.

By the time it emerged from bankruptcy, Northwest had dramatically restructured itself, just as Delta had. Delta, to be sure, had fallen farther and faster—and had its feet planted more squarely on death's doorstep when it filed for bankruptcy, making its turnaround more unlikely. But Northwest's efforts were herculean in their own right: non-fuel unit costs slashed 14 percent, unit labor costs slashed 37 percent, unit revenues up 12 percent and—most importantly—the restoration of profits. In fact, restoration understates the case: Northwest became one of the most profitable airlines in the industry. In 2006, it managed a $330 million net profit excluding one-off accounting items, along with a 6 percent operating margin, topping everyone but Southwest. The next year proved even better: a $542 million profit and a 9 percent operating margin, this time slightly better than even Southwest.

Delta had exited bankruptcy with management and employees practically on the same side of the table, unified in their opposition to the hostile US Airways bid. If such an alliance would have seemed merely strange at most of Delta's competitors, it would have been patently unimaginable at Northwest, where managers internally—complementing the "it's cold, it's dark and it's all ours" line to describe the domestic geography it dominated—had another mantra to describe the take-no-prisoners approach to restructuring, starting with breaking AMFA just before the bankruptcy filing: "We'll do it once, we'll do it right and we won't have to do it again."

This was truly a new Northwest, with new labor contracts, a simplified and renewed aircraft fleet and a refurbished balance sheet. Its regional network was finally rightsized with the right planes. Its Pacific network was rapidly replacing DC-10s and 747s with 330s. Its Atlantic network, amplified by the still-highly-profitable KLM joint venture, was further fortified by re-diverting 757s to Europe, just as Delta had done, although Northwest, never with a network as unwieldy to begin with, didn't have to conduct a network revamp as radical as the one Delta had undertaken. Northwest had the strongest cargo business of any U.S. airline thanks to its routes in Asia, where so many of America's imports were produced. It was eager to exploit the fast-growing Chinese market and awaited regulatory approval to enlarge its transatlantic JV to include Delta and Air France. The new U.S.-E.U. open skies agreement meant it could soon fly to London Heathrow. To protect its heartland markets, Northwest joined with the investment group TPG to take control of Milwaukee-based Midwest Airlines, outmaneuvering Atlanta-dependent AirTran, which had also wanted to take over Midwest and its Milwaukee hub. Unlike Delta, Northwest—even if ruthless in some regards—left bankruptcy without having to terminate anybody's pension plan.

"To this day," Steenland recalled years later, "I'm walking through the airports in Minneapolis and Detroit, when I'm there on occasion, and it's rare if I don't have somebody coming up to me saying, 'Hey, I really appreciate you saving my pension, because it really makes a difference.'" Although not terminating them, Northwest did freeze its plans, meaning no future benefits would accrue.

Thanks to a combination of its own renewed prospects, its Pacific route rights used as collateral and the global capital glut, Northwest had no problem refinancing older loans at better interest rates. Its equity was back on the New York stock exchange. Its closest rival, Chicago-based United, which competed for many of the same connecting passengers, never did quite restructure so dramatically, emerging from its bankruptcy with uninspiring financial results—the "do it once/do it right" line was an allusion to this.

So Northwest, like Delta, entered 2008 feeling—in so many ways—better than ever. But also like Delta, Northwest had reasons to feel insecure, reasons to feel its progress, however monumental, would be no match for the violent forces of the airline business. The real estate bubble had popped, and the international financial system was in flames, with nobody certain just how fast and far that fire would spread nor how much damage it would do. Unemployment in the U.S. rising. America's auto industry, so critical to Northwest because of its Detroit hub, was in deeper trouble than even the airlines. But troubled the airlines were too, with the industry still excessively fragmented. Northwest, for its part, for all its strength in Asia, the U.S. heartland and Canada, was virtually absent in Latin America and the southeastern U.S. Its hubs were small, requiring lots of lower-yielding connecting traffic to support international service. Memphis was America's bankruptcy capital. Tokyo's airports were building more airport capacity, implying future opportunities for competitors. Detroit was losing population. And Minneapolis-St. Paul, although growing, was still only the 16th largest metro area in the U.S., just ahead of San Diego, St. Louis and Tampa—not exactly the best platform to exploit a boom in international traffic.

And something else made Steenland nervous too. Northwest had "an awful lot of eggs" in one basket, namely the KLM relationship. And now KLM was controlled by Air France, which was clearly hitching itself to Delta's wagon. So what would happen if Delta chose to merge with, say, United, taking Air France and KLM with it? This would leave Northwest with not only an uncompetitively small domestic market but also a giant hole in Europe. Losing KLM would be like Sonny losing Cher.

Then there was the matter of Northwest's labor relations, which were still—to understate the case—less than serene. In one highly publicized incident, management handed booklets to some ground handling employees suggesting ways in which they could save money in their daily lives to adapt to post-bankruptcy wages. One of the suggestions: Don't be shy about fishing things out of the trash. More meaningfully, Northwest suffered a major operational disruption in the summer of 2007.

Even though Northwest pilots (unlike those at Delta) hadn't lost the pension benefits they had accumulated so far, the Northwest pilots had swallowed even deeper pay cuts and work rule concessions than the Delta pilots. One of the changes proved exceptionally unpopular: Pilots would now commute to work more often, no small matter in an industry where commuting often means not a short car or subway trip to work, but standing by for an empty seat on a flight to a hub airport. Sick calls began to rise. At the same time, management was eager to use every last ounce of its newly won authority to schedule the airline more efficiently. But there turned out to be such a thing as too much efficiency. The FAA restricts how many hours pilots can work each month, and Northwest's crew schedulers were coming so close to those limits that normal flight delays, plus the higher-than-average number of sick calls, led to inevitable pilot shortages by the end of the month. Timing magnified the problem: This was the busy summer season, meaning large numbers of outraged travelers and few empty seats on other flights to accommodate the passengers from canceled flights.

"To be completely honest, we probably got one work rule concession too many out of the pilot group," Steenland allowed. "People who had built their entire life schedule around having three trips a month that they then had to commute to, now they were looking at a fourth." So management agreed to relax the onerous new commuting requirements in exchange for other productivity improvements that the pilots didn't mind as much. After all, Steenland was asked years later, pilots are hard-working people—right? "You could make a judgment, on an absolute basis, whether they were working hard or not compared to the rest of the world," he said. "For them, they were working hard."

Then there was the matter of oil prices. Happy New Year? On Wednesday, Jan. 2, 2008, the price of a barrel of benchmark West Texas Intermediate crude touched $100 for the first time in history. Even adjusted for inflation, this was similar to levels last seen after the Iranian revolution and the start of the Iran-Iraq war some 30 years earlier. Like Delta and other U.S. carriers, Northwest had asked for so many painful concessions from its employees, its business partners and its investors to counteract the cancerous effects of constantly escalating fuel prices. If oil prices had gone from $20 to $50 to $75 and now $100 in a matter of a few years, who was to say to what levels they would reach next? Delta and Northwest had done so much to become profitable businesses again. But because of fuel prices, it might not be enough.

Perhaps, many people were concluding, the answer was consolidation. Fewer, more powerful U.S. airlines might be better able to adjust capacity and pricing to fuel price changes. The bigger the airline, the more markets it would dominate, meaning the more wherewithal it would have to cut capacity and raise fares without losing traffic and revenue to competitors.

Already in the closing weeks of 2007, Wall Street and the airline industry were abuzz with airline merger talk. But this was only partly motivated by fear of fuel prices *per se*. Consolidation was also looking more attractive due to a related sharp fall in airline share prices, which made potential takeovers cheaper. Consolidation, in other words, was becoming both more desirable and more feasible.

Delta, for its part, was now worth less than half what US Airways had been willing to pay for it. The US Airways-America West transaction, although bedeviled by labor tensions and operational hiccups that caused some non-financial observers to consider it a failure, had actually been a big financial success for both carriers, neither of which had been likely to survive without the other. The message: bigger was better. The Air France-KLM merger too had proved a resounding success, and Delta, for one—such a close partner of the Franco-Dutch giant—knew all about that. At the same time, Delta did not want to relive the US Airways scenario, in which a hostile suitor forced it to defend itself—next time, the ending might not be so happy.

If these weren't reasons enough to think merger, the U.S.-E.U. open skies agreement reinforced the notion airlines would increasingly compete on a global battlefield rather than a national one—and size, scope and scale would be advantages when competing against intercontinental rivals. There was an altogether different reason too. In 2006, the Democrats, riding a wave of frustration with President Bush's handling of Iraq, Katrina and social security reform, captured control of both houses of Congress. And among other things, this meant the coronation of Rep. James Oberstar of Minnesota as chairman of the House Committee on Transportation and Infrastructure, giving his anti-consolidation fervor a powerful platform. And as he preached from this platform, carriers were constantly reminded 2008 would bring another election, this time determining Bush's successor in the White House. That successor looked likely to be Senator Hillary Clinton, the wife of Bill Clinton, the same Bill Clinton whose justice department had taken an active stance against airline mergers—recall the opposition to Northwest's proposed acquisition of Continental in 1998 and to the United-US Airways deal in 2000. Getting a deal done while Bush was still in office, in other words, was preferable.

But that still didn't fully explain the industry's urge to merge. Ultimately, control of a publicly traded company rests with its shareholders, and one shareholder in particular was buying large ownership stakes in both Delta and United. Pardus Capital Management, an investment firm based on Madison Avenue in New York City, made a living buying up lots of shares in companies, which gave it clout to force strategic changes. The idea was that these strategic changes would then boost the company's stock price, yielding a profit for Pardus. It was hardly alone in this strategy, as American Airlines discovered when an Icelandic investment firm began buying shares with the intention of compelling it to sell AAdvantage, its lucrative frequent flier program. But for Pardus in late 2007, the target was Delta, of which it became the single largest shareholder.

Pardus wanted Delta to merge, either with United or Northwest. And to press its case, it hired none other than Gordon Bethune, the former Continental chief who had played a role in the Delta-US Airways drama earlier in the year (and who had advised Pardus against advocating for a Delta-Continental merger, ostensibly because of Continental's relatively high cost structure). Pardus called on other large stakeholders in Delta to pressure it to merge. And Pardus also became the largest shareholder in United, whose CEO Glenn Tilton was every bit as much a proponent of consolidation as Doug Parker at US Airways.

Tilton, a former oil man, had guided United through its long bankruptcy but remained convinced—especially following United's rather lackluster post-bankruptcy financial results—that the industry's only path to salvation was consolidation. He was willing, in fact, to step aside and let Anderson run a combined Delta-United, as Pardus was suggesting. By November, Pardus had amassed 7 million shares of Delta stock and 5.6 million shares of United stock and was arguing the two companies could do an all-stock merger.

In late October 2007, Delta's new CEO Richard Anderson, now back in the airline business, softened his initial statements on consolidation, in which he had sounded reluctant. In Delta's presentation to Wall Street of its 2007 third-quarter earnings, speaking from Paris, where he was working on consolidation of a different sort—consolidating transatlantic operations with Air France/KLM—he said:

> *"Before I close, I would like to address a topic that has been on the minds of many of the people on this call and observers of the industry. And this is true both within the broad investment community and the airline industry in general. And that's the issue of consolidation. This industry, including Delta, and candidly all of the major network carriers, are products of consolidation, and we fully expect that this evolution toward a more consolidated industry will continue. I would even say that it makes sense and could make sense for Delta if it's done thoughtfully—from a position of strength—and is in the long-term best interests of Delta's shareholders and its employees. As a result we are evaluating the best path forward for Delta. There are obvious benefits that could accrue from consolidation for our shareholders and employees. Remember that our employees are our greatest asset. The magnitude of change that they have accomplished over the last year, two years, is a testament to the importance that they play in the future of Delta. They're crucial—their support is crucial to our continued success. As such, we will take a balanced view toward consolidation and its impact on Delta, while keeping focused on any execution risk, while being certain that we do our very best to create shareholder value."*

In November, Anderson, under heavy pressure to do a deal, crafted a statement that directly addressed Pardus, which itself had sent a letter to Delta's management proposing a United deal:

> *"We appreciate receiving Pardus' views on the best course for Delta's future. We have been consistent in our public statements that Delta believes that the right consolidation transaction could generate significant value for our shareholders and employees and that strategic options should be evaluated. With oil at over $90 a barrel, this analysis takes on a heightened importance as we factor those prices into our long-term planning process.*
>
> *"Prior to receiving this letter, Delta's Board of Directors had established a special committee of the Board to work with management to review and analyze strategic options to ensure Delta maintains its leadership position in the airline industry, including potential consolidation transactions."*

During bankruptcy, Jerry Grinstein had spoken with other airline executives, including Doug Steenland, about whether merging made sense. But they concluded a deal while both companies were in bankruptcy would prove too complex. When Delta's new board of directors assembled after the airline emerged from bankruptcy, hedge funds that had purchased its claims pushed for, and won, the right to appoint members with a pro-consolidation bent. This included, generally speaking, Anderson, although he had reasons for reluctance too. For one thing, he had just stepped back into the industry. He also knew the difficulties of merging two giant airlines: integrating complex IT systems, managing a mixed fleet and navigating the interests of labor groups, for example.

One thing Anderson was determined to preserve was Delta's labor relations, which were once again excellent in the aftermath of the US Airways attempted raid. Indeed, he insisted that if a merger were to happen, the new airline would absolutely keep the Delta name, absolutely stay in Atlanta and absolutely protect the seniority of Delta's employees. Still, would Delta's pilot union, historically wary of mergers, entertain one now?

Lee Moak was watching all this with intense interest. One lesson the pilot union leader learned while Delta was in bankruptcy, he recalled years later, was to "develop relationships with the legal teams, the investment bankers and the restructuring specialists in Manhattan." By staying close to Wall Street, in other words, he would stay informed of any merger momentum and not be caught by surprise. He knew full well, therefore, what Pardus was trying to do, and he immediately took a hard line against it. In a November letter to his rank and file, Moak defiantly asserted his opposition: "Pardus' demand for a merger between Delta and United is a poisonous vision built upon an artificial timeline and focused primarily on a financial transaction. In essence, the demand is nothing more than another version of a hostile takeover of Delta Air Lines." In his meetings with Pardus managers, he found them "very aggressive." He called the company a "renegade" hedge fund and proclaimed: "We demonstrated in the case of the US Airways assault on our company, we can stop a consolidating event that is not in our best interests, and we will treat the demands by Pardus no less seriously than those presented by US Airways last year."

But importantly, Moak's position on consolidation had some nuance. In fact, he wasn't reflexively opposed to any and all mergers. During the US Airways drama, ALPA had established a strategic planning group charged with analyzing industry trends and assessing their impact on Delta and its workers. So Moak saw what everybody else was seeing: skyrocketing oil prices, and even the biggest industry players like Delta had limited power to raise fares in response. He saw credit markets drying and the economy weakening. He saw how Southwest, still armed with heavy fuel hedges, could undercut any airline that dared to raise fares. He saw JetBlue and AirTran, although challenged in their own right by rising fuel prices, still growing. He saw Virgin America enter the scene and carriers like Air France and KLM merging abroad. He saw how U.S. carriers were falling behind on product and service standards in an internationalizing marketplace. He saw how US Airways and America West, however messy their integration, had saved themselves from oblivion by merging. He saw how industry business partners like American Express, General Electric and Citigroup seemed willing to do anything to keep giant airlines from disappearing, and how merging Delta with any other carrier would indeed create the most giant airline of all. Sure, pilots prefer organic growth. But given current industry conditions, growth via consolidation was a far more realistic possibility. "Although I'm a firm believer in organic growth," Moak said years later of his thinking at the time, "as we get later into that summer, oil skyrockets to $147. By now, I'm a few years into this job and I really understand—I have a better understanding of the economics. I realized we're not going to survive through this. I'm watching other airlines liquidate."

Moak also knew all too well that in bankruptcy, union bargaining leverage dramatically weakens. So the last thing he wanted, for this reason and a million others, was for Delta to wind up back in bankruptcy. And looking ahead, he felt comfortable with the idea of working for a merged airline led by Richard Anderson, the man whose CEO candidacy ALPA itself, as a creditor in Delta's bankruptcy, had supported the summer of 2007. Moak was impressed by Anderson's intimate familiarity with airline operations. But most enticingly for Moak, a merger transaction represented a rare opportunity to renegotiate a brutal bankruptcy-era contract that would otherwise be locked in for several years. ALPA would have renewed leverage to negotiate pay hikes, scope protection against regional jet outsourcing, an equity stake in the merged airline and greater pension contributions to help allay the losses pilots suffered when Delta terminated their old plan.

So Moak warmed to the idea of "rational" consolidation and told Anderson he was ready to support a deal if the terms were right, if pilots were protected and if pilots received an equity stake in the new airline. Moak told his union members: "At some point [a merger] may become inevitable or even desirable."

But a merger with whom? A Delta-United combination would surely create a powerful giant, underpinned by United's Asian network and its hubs in the nation's top business markets. But even though the two networks (unlike Delta and US Airways together) didn't have much overlap, the sheer size of the combination might kindle some government opposition, even from the Bush administration. More importantly, United was a founding member of the Star Alliance and had a close relationship with Germany's Lufthansa, another founding member. Delta was one of four founding members of the rival SkyTeam alliance, of which its close partner Air France was another. Further complicating matters, Air France was now merged with KLM, whose joint venture with Northwest was still producing big profits. Not all those relationships could survive a Delta-United merger, implying lost value from the start. In addition, United's costs were higher than Northwest's, United was more exposed than Northwest to Southwest and other LCCs and in late 2007 and early 2008, United wasn't running a smooth operation.

In the meantime, Lee Moak, in talking to his pilot union counterparts at United, found little common ground on a subject of monumental importance: the integration of pilot seniority lists. In the career of a pilot, seniority is everything. Unlike a management employee, it's hard to base pilot pay and promotion on merit—all pilots are highly skilled, and they're all tasked with the same critical assignment: flying planes safely. Anything less is unacceptable. So pilot pay and promotion are instead based on seniority. The pilot with the most tenure at the company will fly the biggest planes at the highest pay rates, won't have to work on Christmas and is first in line for any new opportunities that arise—if the airline buys even larger planes commanding even higher wages, for example. Junior pilots, all the same, will work their way from first officers to captains, from smaller planes to larger ones and from shorthaul to longhaul flying—a more efficient way to fly a lot of hours in a short period of time—based on their own seniority rankings.

Merging two pilot groups naturally complicates matters, as demonstrated by the ongoing seniority dispute between US Airways and America West pilots. By 2008 the groups still weren't integrated, three years after their companies merged, with one side livid about an arbitration ruling that left some pilots better off than others. (No one imagined then they *still* wouldn't integrate for another half decade.) America West pilots had argued they should be atop the list, because US Airways was on the verge of liquidation when the merger happened, so its pilots should be happy to have jobs at all. US Airways pilots, who were generally more senior, argued they should be on top because of this greater seniority. Further complicating matters, pay scales were higher at America West than at US Airways, which had twice been through bankruptcy. But only US Airways had widebody intercontinental flights. Would a US Airways widebody pilot, for example, be forced down to lower-paying narrowbody flying because an America West pilot, who previously flew narrowbodies, could bump the US Airways pilot down the seniority list? US Airways, moreover, still had pilots on furlough because of all its bankruptcy-era capacity cuts; America West did not. What would happen to these pilots? US Airways pilots argued for seniority list integration (SLI) based on date of hire, which would put even young America West's most senior pilot—who was hired in 1983, 17 years after the most senior US Airways pilot—far down the list. America West pilots argued for a formula that gave little weight to time and tenure. Among the endless number of difficult questions at stake: Which one of those two pilots should rank No. 1?

After a year of unsuccessful negotiations between the two pilot groups, an arbitrator issued his ruling, which devised an integration formula that left US Airways pilots livid, leading them to form their own breakaway union. The pilots never integrated, and the arbitrated ruling was never implemented. And none of this drama was unique to the US Airways-America West merger. On the contrary, just about every past airline merger, including American's takeover of TWA just prior to 9/11, faced similar tensions.

Richard Anderson's skepticism was perhaps understandable, therefore, when Lee Moak pledged something unprecedented in airline history: a seniority integration list agreement *in advance of the merger's closing.* If he could deliver that, it would remove a large element of uncertainty, greatly smoothing the push toward a merger, and with it a new pilot contract that included wage hikes and an ownership stake in the newly created company. "At first, it was pretty strange to hear labor saying something like that," remembered Moak, regarding management's reaction to its proposal. "It was just like 'that's pretty much impossible to do. Nobody has ever delivered a [pre-merger integrated] seniority list.' But after a while they warmed up to it."

Shortly after Northwest emerged from bankruptcy, its long-term strategic vulnerabilities—never mind its current standout financial performance—compelled Doug Steenland to think about merging. He spoke with Richard Anderson, who, although not opposed to the idea of merging, had just (in September 2007) taken Delta's reins, was just getting his bearings and wasn't yet ready to negotiate a merger. Steenland spoke with Larry Kellner, the CEO of Northwest's longtime partner Continental. He spoke with American's CEO Gerard Arpey. He met several times with United's Glenn Tilton. These people, in the meantime, were all speaking with each other.

As Steenland explained years later, "You didn't want to be where American ended up being"—that is, without a chair when the merger music stopped, suddenly the smallest rather than the largest of America's "Big Three" global airlines, and, because American hadn't gone through bankruptcy, the one with the highest costs.

It didn't take Anderson long to reacquaint himself with the airline industry, learn his way around Delta—and, in November 2007, reach back out to Doug Steenland.

The fact that the two knew each other well, having risen through the ranks at Northwest to each, in succession, eventually run the airline—and now, concurrently, run two of the largest airlines—was not a reason to merge. But it didn't hurt.

"I think it mattered," Steenland said. "One, I think we both knew each other pretty well and had sort of collectively been through a lot—you know, 9/11, the pilot strikes, the various financial challenges post-9/11 that the airline faced and the like. I think there was a level of experience of having dealt with each other for a long period of time that facilitated things."

The two, in other words, already had a level of trust that might otherwise take time to develop—and they spoke the same Northwest language.

"There was sort of a shorthand that could be used," Steenland said. "I think it helped that because of his Northwest experience, Richard knew the airline pretty well and so found credible various presentations that we were making." And "he knew we were going to be straightforward and candid."

By January 2008, Delta had tilted away from United, and discussions with Northwest were underway in earnest. One important fact: the better-than-even odds that a combined Delta-Northwest would stay largely non-union. Delta, after all, was considerably larger than Northwest. So if most of Northwest's people wanted to remain unionized and most of Delta's people wanted to remain non-unionized, when adding up their votes in any future representation elections, the unions would likely be out at Delta, "whereas if it did something with a bigger airline"—an airline like United, which was roughly Delta's size—"it ran the risk of losing that," Steenland said.

As Anderson met with his former colleague and now counterpart Steenland, Moak met with his ALPA counterpart at Northwest, Captain Dave Stevens. And by March, the two former military pilots reached what Moak had proposed and few other people in the labor or management ranks thought possible: a handshake agreement on seniority list integration.

The airline consultant Michael Boyd had once said of airline mergers and their labor integration risks: "You can end up with Hatfields and McCoys in the cockpit.... Full-blown mergers are a mess. If you're going to invest in an airline these days, do it with your ex-wife's money so you can get even." And few people rose to dispute that. But here were Delta and Northwest on the verge of a merger agreement that included not only support from their respective pilot groups—that was rare enough—but even an agreement on a process to integrate seniority lists.

But sure enough, progress suddenly stopped. Stevens, sensing dissension from his pilots, got cold feet. There would be no pre-merger seniority list integration agreement. The deal was on the verge of collapse. Some investors, incidentally, were happy. They too were getting cold feet, in their case nervous about the deal as fuel prices continued to rise and the health of the U.S. economy continued to fall.

But having come this far, Anderson and Steenland were determined to do the merger, with the pilots or without the pilots. This created a massive dilemma for Lee Moak: Should he withdraw his support for the merger? Or should he sign a separate peace with management—in other words, a contract agreement that covered only the Delta pilots? This would imply a post-merger situation in which Delta pilots would be making a lot more money than their Northwest counterparts, with seniority lists kept separate, just as they still were at US Airways and America West. Indeed, post-merger US Airways was still two separate airlines—and would long remain so—when it came to crew scheduling and pilot pay. And however messy the situation was operationally, the airline was doing reasonably well financially.

Moak didn't have to look far to be reminded of just how grave the economic situation was getting nor to understand the importance of locking in a deal now. Oil prices were soaring, airlines were filing for bankruptcy, financial institutions were collapsing and Delta itself was dialing back its growth plans.

This was all the justification he needed to support a merger—Northwest pilots be damned—and so he proceeded to negotiate a slew of new contract benefits for Delta pilots only. Sure enough, upon securing these contract changes in a document called Letter of Agreement No. 19—LOA 19, as Delta pilots still remember it—the merger was ready to be announced.

And so it was. On April 14, 2008, Delta Air Lines and Northwest Airlines, two companies that had led their industry for decades but had fallen into bankruptcy on the same day four years after 9/11, announced they would become one company. By this time, Pardus had long since sold its Delta shares at a loss. Northwest shareholders would receive 1.25 Delta shares for each Northwest share they owned. Delta shareholders would own 55 percent of the combined company and Northwest shareholders 45 percent, in an all-stock transaction worth $17.7 billion. The airline would be based in Atlanta and run by Richard Anderson, with a 13-member board of directors: seven from Delta, five from Northwest and one selected by ALPA. "Today we're announcing a transaction that is about addition, not subtraction," Anderson said.

In proclaiming the news to the world, Anderson and Steenland stressed benefits for employees, small communities, consumers and the U.S. economy as a whole. "In an industry where the U.S. network carriers have shed more than 150,000 jobs and lost more than $29 billion since 2001," a press release read, "the combination of Delta and Northwest creates a company with a more resilient business model that is better able to withstand volatile fuel prices than either can on a standalone basis. Merging Delta and Northwest is the most effective way to offset higher fuel prices and improve efficiencies, increase international presence and fund long-term investment in the business."

Non-pilot employees stood to benefit too. Frontline staff at both airlines were promised a "fair and equitable" process for seniority integration, a 4 percent equity stake in the new airline, no involuntary furloughs, protection of existing pension plans and reciprocal travel privileges on both airlines, beginning even before the transaction closed.

Ten days later, on April 24, Anderson and Steenland appeared on Capitol Hill to cultivate support from Congress. At a House Judiciary Committee hearing, the two executives, accompanied in the chamber by Delta employees, enumerated their long list of arguments about why the merger would benefit a whole host of stakeholders. "We aren't coming here to ask you for financial support," said Anderson, "We just want the ability to do what is in the best interest of our companies, our employees, our shareholders and the communities we serve." One thing they specifically addressed: their intention to keep all their hubs, soothing concerns by the committee's top Republican, Steve Chabot, who hailed from Cincinnati, Delta's weakest hub. "We are fortunate," Anderson reassured him, "that in Cincinnati we have strong companies there.... We have General Electric engines. We have Procter & Gamble, which is Delta's largest customer in the world. And they tend to fly more on more premium fares, so it pushes up the business mix." Steenland said similar things about Memphis, Northwest's weakest hub, to Steve Cohen, a Democratic Congressman from there. Steenland said, for example, that Memphis-based FedEx was one of its five largest customers—yes, one of the airline's most important customers was another airline, albeit one of a different ilk. When FedEx's executives and salespeople flew around the world, they did so on Northwest.

The merger, as it happened, would meet no resistance from Congress and no resistance from the Bush administration, whose justice and transportation departments issued their approvals later in the year. Shareholders in both companies would likewise approve the merger deal without much resistance.

But there was still the open question regarding the pilots. For the Delta group, the situation was best captured by a letter from Lee Moak to his rank and file on the day the merger was announced. In it he called for members to ratify LOA 19, describing in detail exactly what Delta pilots would be getting:

Dear Fellow Pilot,

Today, the boards of Delta Air Lines and Northwest Airlines jointly announced their intent to merge the two carriers under the Delta brand.

Unlike traditional airline merger scenarios, the proposed merger is unique in that, for the first time in the history of airline mergers, the Delta pilots, through their union representatives, have participated from the formative stages of the proposed merger. This past Saturday evening, your MEC [Master Executive Council] voted unanimously to conditionally approve proposed contractual modifications to the Pilot Working Agreement, codified in Letter of Agreement 19. Soon, you too will play a crucial role through the membership ratification process as you decide whether to ratify these changes. If you approve Letter 19, then we will know the terms on which we will participate in the transaction, and Letter 19 will take effect on the date the corporate transaction closes.

In my letter of March 17, I described [our] efforts to achieve an overall comprehensive agreement consisting of a transition agreement, a joint pilot contract and an integrated seniority list in the event of a corporate merger. Letter 19 is not that agreement. The contractual modifications and associated returns of Letter 19 will apply only to pre-merger Delta pilots. Pre-merger Northwest pilots will continue to work under their current agreement until together we negotiate a joint pilot contract for the merged airline covering both groups. What Letter 19 does do, however, is provide us with the certainty of returns instead of our having to negotiate later in the face of rising fuel costs and a declining economy.

But let's be clear about one thing in particular: the Delta MEC welcomes the Northwest pilots as partners in the building of the new merged airline, and we look forward to working with the Northwest MEC to bring about the rapid completion of a new joint contract and a fair and equitable integrated seniority list to take effect on the effective date of the new joint agreement.

With that said, I want to provide you an update of the events that led up to today's announcement and the reasons behind your elected representatives' decision to unanimously ratify Letter 19 and support the merger, as proposed, between Delta and Northwest.

Nearly one year ago, both Delta and Northwest emerged from Chapter 11 as restructured carriers, thanks in very large part to the sacrifices of each airline's pilots. Those sacrifices were investments in the future of our respective carriers, and we have the right to protect and defend those investments.

Over the months following Delta's exit from Chapter 11, we carried millions of our passengers safely to their destinations as we had done before and throughout the bankruptcy process. But there was a difference. For the first time since the 9-11 attacks, our companies began to report profits.

Discouragingly, the price of oil continued its meteoric rise and with it, speculation increased that long-anticipated industry consolidation was just around the corner.

In November, the rhetoric increased when The Wall Street Journal *reported that hedge fund Pardus Capital Management, LP, was attempting to force a merger between Delta and United. The story was met with an immediate response from the Delta MEC establishing its position on any proposed industry consolidation. In essence, we made clear that while we do not oppose industry consolidation and that the "right" consolidation opportunity could draw our support, we would not support a transaction for transaction's sake. Further, the Delta pilots would be critical participants from the beginning in any consolidation discussion and potential resultant event, not an afterthought to be considered at a later date.*

Over the next several months, we continued to repeat this message. We soon established our relevance in a process where labor has historically been excluded. Having read the last several Chairman's Letters, you are no doubt familiar with what has taken place since Pardus' ill-conceived attempt to shape our future.

Since my last letter, the financial difficulties that Delta and the rest of our industry face have not gone away. In fact, they have intensified. Oil remains above $100 per barrel, having increased at a historically steep rate since Delta exited bankruptcy. The economy is suffering, and many economists assert that we are entering a recession; others argue we are already in one. The credit markets have become increasingly difficult if not impossible to access. Just this month, Aloha, ATA and Skybus ceased operations and Champion Air will shut its doors on May 31. Last week Frontier filed for Chapter 11 protection. Legitimate concerns exist about the long-term financial viability of several other carriers.

Delta is not immune to these pressures, and they must be realistically addressed in the context of our broad goal which has not changed–that the Delta pilots will work for a company that has long-term viability with pay, benefits, working conditions and retirement commensurate with the responsibility and experience required of our profession. With that goal in mind, we remained actively and aggressively engaged with Delta's senior executives as they continued to consider consolidation options. The purpose of that engagement was to determine what courses of action, to include opposing or supporting any proposed merger, would best support our overall goal.

While we were unable to reach an overall agreement with the Northwest MEC, the Delta MEC remained determined to find an alternative to the traditional merger process, an alternative that would provide for a superior outcome not only for the pre-merger Delta pilots, but eventually all pilots of the merged corporation.

After careful analysis and deliberation of the facts, the Delta MEC concurred with Delta's senior executives and our financial professionals that a merger between Delta and Northwest was financially superior to a standalone Delta. That determination led to the negotiation of Letter 19, a tentative agreement between Delta management and the Delta MEC which, if ratified, will provide certain modifications to the current Pilot Working Agreement designed to facilitate the proposed merger with Northwest and provide returns for the value our participation brings to the merger.

Elements of Letter 19 include:

– A three and one-half percent equity stake in the merged Company in fully tradeable stock at the close of the merger

– Annual pay raises beginning with a five percent raise on January 1, 2009 and followed by four percent raises every January 1 through January 1, 2012. On January 1, 2011, Delta pilot pay rates will exceed the Letter 46 rates, without even considering the equity each pilot will receive.

– A one percent increase to the [pension plan] contribution rate beginning in January 2010.

– Furlough protection–with certain exceptions, no pilot may be furloughed as a result of the merger for a period from merger announcement until 24 months after the close of the merger.

– An increase in the full-pay sick leave bank from 240 hours to 300 hours.

– The ability for a pilot returning from disability to refill his full pay sick leave bank once every four years instead of once in a career.

– An increase in 737-700 pay rates to match the 737-800 pay rates.

– In return for these improvements, we would provide various modifications to our scope clause to enable Delta to proceed with the merger. For example, we would allow the Company to place the Delta code and brand on Northwest flights on an unlimited basis after the close of the *merger, provide greater flexibility on minimum block hour protections during the merger process, and permit the Company to retain Northwest's large stake in Midwest Airlines (previously purchased by Northwest Airlines) while maintaining their separate operational status.*

Your MEC unanimously adopted and enthusiastically endorses Letter 19. Soon you too will be asked to vote on Letter 19. Our role in the proposed merger will then rest with you.

If you choose to ratify Letter 19, its terms will become effective at the close of the corporate transaction. We will actively support the merger through legislative and other efforts. We will join management to seek Department of Justice antitrust approval in a timely manner.

If you decide not to ratify Letter 19, it will become null and void. In that event, what happens next is unclear but we will retain our rights to seek to reshape or even oppose the proposed merger...

Anger and hope will never be effective strategies to counter the challenges we face, and change is never easy, but as we have become intimately familiar with over the years, it is one of the few constants in our industry. A key difference this time, however, is that the Delta pilots can choose to be an agent of that change rather than a bystander to it.

Your union leadership chose to craft a new and, I believe, far superior solution—one with a substantially brighter outcome for the pilots of the merged corporation than the traditional merger scenario. As your MEC recognized, we have a historic opportunity before us. I encourage you to read and understand all the information you receive. Talk to your elected representatives. Seek out answers to your questions. Make every effort to attend a pilot road show.

Then, when the ratification window opens, I join the Delta MEC in strongly encouraging you to vote in favor of ratifying Letter of Agreement 19.

Fraternally,
Lee Moak, Chairman

Some Delta pilots weren't swayed. One argument against LOA 19 was that they'd do better by waiting until their current contract, filled with concessions extracted during bankruptcy, became amendable on the last day of 2009, just a year and a half from then. Management and the union, in fact, were required to exchange opening offers less than a year from now. "Our pilot group has paid dearly for the mismanagement of this airline," one anti-LOA 19 campaigner wrote in an ALPA newsletter, "and our amendable date represents what is so far our best opportunity to significantly correct the abuses of bankruptcy."

Moak and others countered with a reminder: that airline labor contracts never really expire. They just become amendable at their end date, so the Dec. 31, 2009, date had little practical significance. Airline labor negotiations, governed by the Railway-Labor Act of the 1920s, commonly drag on for years before a new contract agreement. And with industry conditions becoming graver by the day, there'd be little chance management would agree to something more lucrative. The only way Delta could offer a better contract, the argument went, was if merger synergies paid for it.

As the debate churned within the Delta pilot ranks, Northwest pilots had their own decision to make. When the merger was announced, the position of Dave Stevens was clear: no to any merger that awarded gains to the Delta pilots but not the Northwest pilots. He too went to Capitol Hill for a merger hearing, this one held on May 14 by the House subcommittee on aviation, chaired by Congressman Oberstar, the anti-merger crusader from Northwest's home state of Minnesota. After Anderson and Steenland, also testifying, reiterated their arguments about why the merger was good for everyone—and after Lee Moak also spoke in favor of the merger—Stevens issued his declaration of opposition:

> "We recognize that the combined company has the potential of becoming a stronger and more viable airline. However, the Northwest ALPA Master Executive Council and our pilots strongly oppose the merger as it now stands.
>
> The total economic potential of the combined corporation will not be achieved without a joint pilot contract which is the only way for all of the predicted revenue enhancements and cost savings to be realized. A joint contract would also resolve potential labor discord which is counterproductive to achieving economic success. Given the current high cost of fuel, the broad economic downturn and substantial costs related to an airline merger, the future viability of the combined company will be in question if it is unable to take advantage of every revenue opportunity. A critical evaluation of the economics of the proposed merger is in the best interest of all groups affected by the merger. Management of the two airlines has stated that the merger will produce greater profitability as a result of a series of synergies that allow increased revenue and reduced costs. They will predict a financially stronger airline, one better to serve all its stakeholders including its customers. According to management, these synergies will result from an end to end merger rather than a traditional overlap production merger.
>
> However, many of the synergies and therefore much of the economic benefit management is counting on will be unavailable without a common contract that includes the Northwest pilots. Indeed, for the new combined Delta-Northwest to have any chance of fully realizing its potential, all employee groups must be treated fairly regardless of their

pre-merger carrier. Why is this true? Without a joint pilot contract, the two airlines' flight operations must remain separate. Without a single airline operation, much of the needed revenue growth and cost savings will not be achieved. Layer in the bad will created by contractually treating Northwest employees as B Scale, and the matters will be even worse.

We appreciate Delta management's statement of optimism that we can obtain a common contract and an integrated seniority list prior to the date of corporate closing. However, we believe actions speak louder than words. To date, we have no negotiating session scheduled. Furthermore, Delta management has found the time to reach a tentative agreement with Delta pilots effective on the date of closure that excludes Northwest pilots. The more we review this document, the more questions we have as to Delta management's intent. We feel there is no reason to have several of the provisions in the new Delta pilot contract if the intent is truly to have a joint contract before closing. We are concerned that the reason for this agreement may be to put economic pressure on the Northwest pilots to agree to an unfair seniority list. We will not do that. Contract terms can be changed. Seniority lives forever. We agree with the statement from Delta that in their analysis a merged Delta-Northwest airline is stronger than a Delta standalone airline. However, our review shows that as currently structured, the same is not true for Northwest. Given the current structure of this merger, we believe a standalone Northwest is stronger than a merged Delta and Northwest.

Our review also shows that Northwest Airlines is the best place of any legacy carrier to weather the current high cost of fuel and economic downturn. Northwest has an enviable route system that includes the Pacific hub, a flexible fleet a fuel efficient order book of Boeing 787 aircraft and the most relative cash on hand of the legacy carriers.

We understand that integrating the operations of these two large carriers will require a delicate balancing act to minimize the employee discontent and maximize the employee harmony required to access the proposed synergies necessary for the merged carrier to be successful going forward. However, the steps to date will largely have the effect of maximizing employee discord.

Rather than a joint statement by Mr. Anderson and Mr. Steenland that the new carrier was committed to a fair and equitable integration of the workforces, we have only the statement of Mr. Anderson that he will protect the seniority of Delta employees with the implication being that current Northwest employees will have to fend for themselves. Rather than negotiating a joint contract, Delta chose to negotiate contract improvements only for Delta pilots.

Notwithstanding the events leading to this point, the officers and representatives of the Northwest MEC are willing to negotiate with Delta management and Delta ALPA. However, time is critical. There is a small window of opportunity remaining in which to conclude a joint contract and a joint seniority list outside the traditional merger process. I have tried in this statement to explain to you, Northwest ALPA's concern about the current situation. I ask that you evaluate this merger in the current context. I urge you to critically examine management's promises and statements of their present intentions. Will the company meet its financial obligations and manage to abide by its promises to maintain current service and hubs or will it shrink and shed thousands of jobs? What will the loss of those jobs mean to the broader economies of the States and regions affected? Will this merger work if management cannot achieve the expected synergies? In short, what happens if the merger does not succeed? We believe the marketplace shares our concern as evidenced by tremendous loss of value of the share price of both companies since the merger announcement. In our view, the proposed merger is risky for Northwest and Delta passengers, communities and employees. With the price of oil, the weak economy, the closed credit markets and the huge costs of combining the two companies, there will be no margin for error. As it now stands, the combined company will not have access to the predicted synergies due to lack of a joint pilot contract."

Moak's view, of course, was that the separate peace between Delta and its pilots would—as he said at the hearing—"provide a solid framework for a new joint collective bargaining agreement to include the Northwest pilots." And he said he remained committed to not only a joint contract but also an integrated seniority list before the two companies became one.

Later, in a back-and-forth question and answer period, Oberstar began attacking Moak:

> **Oberstar:** *Now let me ask Captain Moak first. How many aircraft do you think or might you speculate that are likely to be retired in the new Delta?*
> **Moak:** *Chairman Oberstar, I believe, like I said earlier, that although there are announced domestic capacity drawdowns related to the price of fuel, in the press announcement of the new global Delta, there are 20 additional wide body planes that will be coming and there are many markets that will be added. I believe that.*
> **Oberstar:** *Captain, if you believe that, then I have a bridge I would like you to buy, if you believe a press release issued by your company. They can't tell you on their sacred oath and word and trust, and you have to read it in press release?*

Moak: What I am saying is this: I am not going to jump on the man-agement bandwagon or apologize for things that other managements have done. But if you are going to vilify every single management team, eventually you are going to have a management team that arrives that is trying to work through the problems. This is a difficult time, difficult problems. Now through the collective bargaining process, okay, the Delta pilots modified their contract. However, we worked together with the Northwest pilots over the last three months in what was a first-ever attempt to negotiate a contract before a merger was announced. We weren't successful, but we are not giving up. We are years ahead of everybody else. We will get it done. I am confident of it. We raised the bar for the Delta pilots over the next few years. It is approximately a 20 percent pay raise. It increases the retirement for the Delta pilots, for the Northwest pilots, and I am confident we will get it done. I will say it time and time again. I am working with Captain Stevens. We welcome them, and we are going to get it done. But for some of his equipment, some of his pilots, it will be a 35 percent pay raise over the life of the agreement. That is the right thing to do. As far as equity, there is equity for all the employees. I know we haven't completed the negotiation with Captain Stevens and the Delta management. But I am going to stand here, I am sitting here, telling you that I believe there is equity for the Northwest pilots also. There has to be to make this work. So I think the collective bargaining process—you are seeing it work. We are working together. We are going to get it done.

And indeed, they got it done.

Stevens understood the merger was going to happen with or without his support. So the real question was whether to continue working under the old Northwest bankruptcy contract or agree to a new contract and a process for an integrated seniority list, in doing so bringing his members under the new Delta contract, with all the big benefits that entailed. Stevens resumed talks with Moak, and sure enough, the two came to an agreement. On June 24, 2008, they announced a groundbreaking deal on seniority list integration *before* the merger—in an industry, recall, where that often didn't happen even years *after* a merger.

The task wasn't an easy one. Northwest pilots were on average more senior, because 3,200 Delta pilots had retired early from 9/11 through the run-up to bankruptcy, collecting some $2.5 billion worth of lump-sum pension payouts. Northwest pilots were quick to point out Delta pilots stood to benefit from the new Boeing 787 Dreamliners Northwest had ordered. They also argued their airline's Asian network afforded the combined pilot group unique job security (never mind that Northwest's Asian routes were losing money; the Atlantic routes flown together with KLM were what had kept the company alive). Delta pilots said theirs was the bigger company and the one essentially taking control of Northwest. Northwest pilots highlighted the fact that more of them would retire in the near future, creating greater promotion opportunities for Delta pilots. There were questions about how to rank pilots who flew 757s domestically versus those who flew 757s internationally. Should all international flying be treated the same, or should there be a "super premium" for the largest widebody jets? Northwest had giant 747s, after all. Delta pilots said their proposal for seniority integration should carry more sway because Northwest pilots would be getting a larger percentage increase in pay with the new joint contract. And so on.

Ultimately, the two sides agreed to submit the matter to a three-member arbitration panel, which issued its ruling in December. It rejected a date-of-hire-based system advocated by the Northwest side, because this would have given Northwest pilots all the highest-paid international flying, considering their higher average seniority. But it also rejected the Delta group's proposal based on status and aircraft categories, which would have left a large number of Northwest pilots at the bottom of the list, making them more vulnerable to furloughs at a time when airlines were indeed furloughing workers because of fuel costs and the economic situation. Instead, the panel created a modified status and category system that included a temporary "fence" keeping each pilot with the aircraft his or her airline had brought to the merger.

Predictably, not everyone was happy. But ultimately, if the merger proved a success—creating more wealth and growth opportunities for everyone—grievances and grudges would be forgiven. But would the merger really create more wealth and growth opportunities?

There were plenty of skeptics, and not just those pointing to the difficulties of integrating two labor groups. Some felt Northwest was selling itself short, and to a rival that was not long ago considered an industry basket case. This was, after all, Delta, the company that had exasperated the rest of the industry by launching SimpliFares and Song. Northwest, meanwhile, had emerged from bankruptcy with outsized profit margins and a large war chest of cash, making it best positioned, or so the argument went, to go it alone. In 2007, it earned a princely $542 million net profit excluding special items, more than any other airline in the U.S. Its 9 percent operating margin for the year was also best among U.S. mainline carriers, beating even Southwest.

Northwest would have the option, these skeptics argued, of merging with another carrier, perhaps US Airways, but on better terms and as the senior partner. Or perhaps Northwest would best be served by buying small airlines in the region of the country it dominated, from the Midwest (hence the acquisition of Midwest Airlines) to the Pacific Northwest—it actively considered buying Alaska Airlines, which, despite its name, was actually based in Seattle. Northwest still, remember, held its golden share in Continental, which dated from 1998, when Northwest had invested in Continental after Washington refused to allow the two carriers to merge outright. This golden share effectively made Northwest a consolidation kingpin: It could veto any deal involving Continental. Because United and Delta didn't plan to get together, and because US Airways and Delta would likely never get together given the bad blood there and the same antitrust concerns that had helped kill the deal, industry consolidation was largely stalemated. Northwest held all the cards.

If Northwest had good reason to not accept Delta's overtures, meanwhile, the arguments against merging from Delta's own perspective were perhaps even more compelling. Was it about to pollute the rare management-labor goodwill that it had achieved during the US Airways takeover attempt? It was, after all, planning to merge with an airline characterized by a history of toxic relations, an airline that had advised its workers to fish through the trash. Most of Delta's non-pilot workforce was non-unionized, moreover, and this advantage would be jeopardized as heavily unionized Northwest workers were added to the mix.

Delta would indeed have the Asian network it long coveted. But it was an Asian network that had lost money all decade. It was inheriting a hub in Memphis, a city that ranked a lowly No. 46 in terms of population among U.S. metropolitan areas. Detroit was a notorious symbol of economic decay, saddled, as it was, with an automotive industry on the verge of collapse. Minneapolis, at least, was one of the nation's more profitable hubs thanks to its relatively healthy economy and demographics and its status as gateway to the U.S. northwest. But if Delta learned one thing during its dramatic turnaround, it was that international flying represented the key to sustained profitability, and Minneapolis did not have the geography or population base to become a major global hub. Milwaukee, a Northwest stronghold after its partial takeover of Midwest Airlines, was another smallish market, one still besieged by an angry AirTran—in late January, the LCC announced three daily Milwaukee flights to New York's LaGuardia Airport. The combined Delta-Northwest network, furthermore, would lack clout in the critical states of California and Texas, and in the western U.S. more broadly.

The fleet would be messy too. Delta was inheriting Northwest's ancient DC-9s and its almost-as-ancient 747s, planes whose obsolescence grew with each uptick in fuel prices. The core of Northwest's fleet, meanwhile, consisted of Airbus 320s and 330s, which were completely incompatible with Delta's Boeing fleet. More generally, merger skeptics pointed to the management distractions such a giant integration would entail during such a volatile time for the industry. Sure enough, Delta's stock price and Northwest's stock price tumbled in the days after the merger was announced, reflecting investor skittishness.

But Anderson and Steenland had powerful arguments of their own—arguments they enumerated in multiple discussions with investors in the weeks and months following the merger announcement. The transaction, they assured those investors, would by 2012 produce $1 billion in synergies, exactly the sort of gains that were needed to confront an out-of-control fuel market, declining economic fundamentals and an airline industry that was becoming more global. The new airline would have $7 billion in liquidity, with great potential to raise additional funds from credit card companies and others enticed by access to what would be, with more than 60 million members, the world's largest frequent flier plan. Clout would also grow with aircraft manufacturers and other suppliers. Unlike the US Airways proposed takeover deal, with all the leverage it would have entailed, this deal involved no additional debt at all. And because both carriers had just been through bankruptcy, a merged Delta-Northwest's cost structure—even after giving all its workers a raise—would still be below those of its principle global competitors, United, American and Continental, if not quite below that of US Airways, which needed a lower cost structure because its network, and thus its revenue potential, was far weaker.

This was a truly global network. The new Delta would be No. 1 to Europe, No. 1 to Japan and No. 1 to Africa. The airline's sales representatives could now walk into a multinational firm and say, "We can take you just about anywhere." This was true in a giant market like New York, yes, but it was equally true in a large collection of smaller markets, from Kansas City to Baltimore to New Orleans, where signing a corporate contract with Delta was now a whole lot more attractive. About 40 percent of the combined carrier's revenues would come from international routes, a figure that would hopefully rise to 50 percent.

And it wasn't just the amount of international flying that made the deal attractive, but the balance across all regions. A full 55 percent of Northwest's international capacity touched Asia, for example, making it highly vulnerable to a demand shock in the region, as it had learned during the SARS epidemic in 2003. Only 7 percent of Delta's capacity touched Asia, but a full 30 percent touched Latin America and the Caribbean, compared to 10 percent for Northwest. The combined network, helpfully, wouldn't be overly exposed to any one region—the next time Asia endured a rough patch, some aircraft could be shifted to Europe or Latin America, or vice versa. Northwest also happened to be a leader in Canada, which was economically integrated with the U.S. Midwest.

Then there was the SkyTeam factor. Northwest's phenomenally successful joint venture with KLM could be expanded to include Delta and Air France. There would be no need for either part of the merged carrier to change global alliances, and the longstanding domestic alliance between Delta and Northwest meant cooperation wouldn't start from scratch. United and Lufthansa, for their part, had a less mature relationship, US Airways had no close transatlantic partners and American and British Airways never were able to receive the antitrust immunity (ATI) necessary for close cooperation. On the contrary, Northwest, Delta, Air France and KLM, just weeks before, had received preliminary DOT approval for ATI among all of them, an important step toward creating an entity commanding 27 percent of all transatlantic traffic.

Speaking of which, one relative benefit of a Delta-Northwest merger—compared to, say, the failed US Airways bid for Delta—was that U.S. regulators should be less skeptical of this merger, even if that fact would seem more apparent years hence than it did at the time. "It wasn't obvious to us at all that there was going to be this sort of smooth antitrust sailing," then-Northwest CFO Dave Davis would later recall. "As a matter of fact, we were very concerned about whether we were going to get antitrust approval because airlines in the past like United-USAir and others had been turned down. So I think now... after multiple mergers have taken place, you can look back in hindsight and say these things get approval. But at the time, the history was that they didn't get approval. I mean there was concern, at least on our side, with whether it was Delta or Continental or American, anybody—whether the government was going to allow these mergers. We didn't presuppose anything."

And never mind fleet complexity. There would indeed, after all, be some fleet synergies too. In business schools throughout the U.S., Southwest's simplified all-Boeing 737 fleet, 500 planes strong by 2008, had become a ubiquitous case study in efficiency. But simplicity also limits flexibility. Southwest could not fly overseas. It could not fly to markets with too few people to fill 737s with (in Southwest's case) at least 122 seats. It could not upguage and downguage when demand fluctuated. The new Delta, by contrast, would have 800 mainline planes plus another 600 regional jets, divided into many sub-fleets, most with their own economies of scale. That's something the simplicity hawks didn't fully understand. It's one thing for an airline with just 50 airplanes to have multiple fleet types—that would indeed be inefficient. But the new Delta would have about 125 Airbus 320-family planes and 75 Boeing 737-family planes, for example. Yes, their missions would overlap to some extent. But there were enough of each to create staffing and maintenance efficiencies. In fact, one quirk actually made the different fleet types not only tolerable but even desirable: Because the fleets were *so* different—only the 757 was in both fleets— there would be no need to merge maintenance programs for most aircraft types, making it quicker and easier to obtain a single FAA operating certificate to operate as one airline. Having to decide which of two 737 or 767 maintenance procedures to adopt, in other words—the Delta or the Northwest one, if both airlines had the same planes—would have actually delayed integration. (And the 757s that the two airlines did have in common? Those would indeed later reveal themselves to be a big integration headache not only because of the pre-merger airlines' different mainte-nance procedures but also because the merged airline would have more than a dozen different variations of the plane: not only differently sized 757-200s and 757-300s but—even among the more numerous 757-200s—different seating configurations, lavatory configurations, kitchen configurations and so forth.)

In addition, Delta still had a large (and non-unionized) maintenance and repair unit that was so skilled and efficient that it profitably insourced work from other airlines. Well, now its mechanics and engineers would gain competencies in Airbus aircraft.

And the diverse fleet, for whatever complexities it might present, would also present the opportunity to much more precisely match the right airplane to the right route—and even more precisely than that, at the right time. Northwest's giant 747s had long been too big for a lot of the routes they were flying from midsized hubs like

Detroit. And when an airplane is too big relative to the number of people who are willing to pay rather high fares to fly a route, an airline needs to discount fares to fill seats—and this, in turn, can wipe out profits. But those same 403-seat jumbo jets that weren't optimal for a lot of Northwest routes could be perfect for a busy Delta route like Atlanta-Rome in the summer or Atlanta-São Paulo in the winter—Delta's largest plane had just 275 seats, meaning it couldn't even meet all the demand that existed in some markets. Smaller Delta 767s, meanwhile, could handle these same routes during off-peak times. New York JFK-Amsterdam could benefit from replacing Delta's 767s with Northwest's larger Airbus 330-200s, while Portland-Amsterdam could gain by doing the opposite. Delta's domestic route network, meanwhile, had a lot of short routes throughout the south, in particular, that were tailor made for Northwest's DC-9s—they were geriatric and burned a lot of fuel, no doubt, but they were perfectly sized, and the differential in fuel economy doesn't add up as much on shorter routes. Before the merger, Delta flew many of these routes with undersized regional jets. In Cincinnati, 757s were proving too large; Northwest's Airbus 319s were just what the doctor ordered. Back on the international front, new growth opportunities—funneling Northwest's Midwestern passengers to Latin America via Atlanta, for example, or Delta's Southeastern passengers to Asia via Detroit—justified exercising purchase options on another 20 additional widebody aircraft. Pilots, to be sure, welcomed that. Northwest's 330s, meanwhile, were much younger than Delta's similarly sized 767s, removing the need to place another expensive widebody order.

Anderson and Steenland were confident wage hikes and ownership stakes for all employees would preserve Delta's constructive relationship with workers. And there was a fair chance mechanics, flight attendants and airport workers would remain non-union, because—Anderson and Steenland, remember, had long ago realized this was a unique advantage of *this* merger over a merger involving Delta and a larger airline—non-unionized Delta workers would outnumber the unionized Northwest workers in a representation vote. As for pilots, the support both ALPA groups would eventually provide greatly de-risked the integration process and ensured quick synergies from scheduling crews together.

There would, of course, be some costs to merging. The new Delta pilot contract sure wouldn't be free. Nor would painting planes, combining IT systems, changing airport signage and standardizing products, services and procedures. But this would be more than offset, Anderson and Steenland stressed, by the billions of dollars in synergies, 70 to 80 percent of these from revenue gains achieved through fleet redeployment, network optimization and grabbing market share from other less worldly airlines. Mergers carry costs, yes, but they also promise cost savings in the areas of IT, sales, facilities and overhead—an operation previously supported by two management teams would now need just one.

Back at Delta and Northwest, Anderson and Steenland continued their focus on planning for integration—they couldn't actually do anything until receiving regulatory clearance but were free to establish 26 planning teams with representatives from each carrier. The two executives also took a public role in defending the merger from critics, including one *Wall Street Journal* columnist who called on the government to block the deal. That prompted the airline chiefs to pen a rebuttal, which the newspaper published June 25:

Not All Airline Mergers Make Sense, But This One Does

In "The Second Death of the U.S. Airlines" (Business World, June 18), Holman W. Jenkins, Jr., is correct that fuel prices approaching $140 a barrel present remarkable challenges for the entire industry, but he is wrong in questioning the Delta-Northwest merger just because other U.S. airlines were unsuccessful in their merger discussions. The truth is, this merger makes even more sense with oil prices at these record levels.

Last October, as oil prices reached $80 a barrel, both airlines independently reviewed strategic alternatives using a range of fuel assumptions. We came to the same conclusion: The right merger would create a company with the financial and marketing strength to overcome the many challenges facing the industry and also better position the company over the long term.

But the right merger would demand certain characteristics: a global, end-to-end network with little overlap, a proven international alliance partner, a strong balance sheet and competitive cost structure, significant revenue and cost synergies, manageable integration costs and the potential to harmoniously integrate employee groups.

After extensive analysis, both airlines concluded that this merger met all those criteria. It will produce over $1 billion in annual cost and revenue improvements, while one-time transition costs will be less than $750 million, spread over four years. These synergies will strengthen the merged airline in any economic environment. However, if oil prices remain high, the synergies enable us to offset increased fuel costs, a benefit not available to either carrier on a stand-alone basis.

Our route systems have little overlap, and the merged carrier will provide service, with our SkyTeam alliance partners, to virtually every point in the world, a significant competitive advantage at any oil price.

Further, if extraordinary oil prices force further capacity reductions, the revenue-generating capability of our world-wide network will better allow us to rationalize capacity by trimming frequencies rather than eliminating destinations, an option not readily available to airlines with smaller networks.

Unlike previous airline mergers, Delta-Northwest is a merger of choice. Delta and Northwest are the two strongest network airlines, with the strongest balance sheets and best-in-class cost structures. This means at closing the merged airline will be financially viable, have access to the capital markets and be immediately competitive.

There is no assurance oil prices will retreat from current levels. In fact, some observers predict prices will continue to rise. Delta and Northwest, having planned for this environment, stand ready to face the challenge. Integration planning is on track and when the regulatory review of our transaction is completed later this year, we will be well-positioned to integrate our airlines efficiently and deliver industry-leading returns, whatever the economic environment may be.

Richard Anderson
CEO, Delta Air Lines
Atlanta

Doug Steenland
CEO, Northwest Airlines
Eagan, Minn.

But there were more immediate worries. Conditions on the battlefield weren't getting any easier. Alarmingly, Delta incurred $137 million in net losses (excluding special accounting items) during the first half of 2008, and it would have lost a lot more than that without $354 million in gains from settled fuel hedge contracts. Northwest, for its part, suffered $271 million in first-half losses. So here were two airlines, which had just cleansed their cost structures in bankruptcy, that where now again losing money—this after such a promising finish to 2007.

Why the sudden relapse? Once again, oil was the culprit. Now prices were above $100 per barrel, reaching an average of $105 in March. In April, oil hit $112. Then $125 in May and $134 in June, reaching a high of $147 in mid-July. Delta and Northwest, being what they believed to be rather conservative, had built their companies to survive at $100 oil. But now prices were close to $150. How much higher would they climb?

This was more than a crisis for just America's airlines. It was a crisis for America. Throughout the country, drivers were allocating more and more of their disposable income to gasoline—and less and less to everything else. On July 2, *USA Today* ran an article describing how high gas prices were devastating rural towns that depended on long-distance car trips for supplies and diesel generators for electricity. Towns had to cancel county fairs, a ritual of summertime. Schools had to cancel field trips. Another *USA Today* piece noted 60 U.S. communities had lost scheduled airline access altogether. Detroit's Big Three auto manufacturers and their dealers weren't just selling fewer cars; they were also selling far fewer fuel-thirsty light trucks and sport-utility vehicles, their most profitable products. General Motors SUV and truck sales were running nearly 30 percent below prior-year levels, while Japan's Toyota saw sales of its partly battery-powered hybrid car—the Prius—spike 54 percent. The cost of food rose as supermarkets paid more to transport items from farm to shelf. Walmart, the nation's largest retailer and largest private employer, would explain how "gas prices are probably the No. 1 predictor of discretionary spending in our stores." Most consequentially, American homeowners became increasingly unable to make their mortgage payments, a particularly troubling trend because ownership of those mortgage loans had become dispersed throughout the world.

At least one group of stakeholders—the oil companies—enjoyed the oil shock. Texas-based ExxonMobil, in just the first six months of 2008, recorded net profits of nearly $23 billion. For perspective, Delta's total *revenues* for those six months, never mind its profits, were less than $14 billion. The incumbent governor of Texas, Rick Perry, his state awash in oil money, would become one of the longest-serving governors in U.S. history. Of course, America's geopolitical rivals were thrilled too. Russia's autocratic Vladimir Putin would—even more brashly than Perry—use endless oceans of oil money to essentially buy himself more than a decade of power. More alarmingly, America was now transferring a significant portion of its wealth to hostile nations like Iran, with large sums finding their way to anti-American militant groups. As *New York Times* columnist Thomas Freidman liked to say, America was funding both sides in the war on terror.

Each day, newspapers and television news programs discussed and debated how this oil crisis came to be. Some cited fast-growing demand from emerging markets like China and India. Population growth drove demand too, as did fuel subsidies in poor nations and the craze for fuel-inefficient SUVs in the U.S. At the same time, political instability in the Middle East, exacerbated by the U.S. invasion of Iraq, created uncertainties about supply. So did limited spare capacity in Saudi Arabia, the most important global supplier of oil. In Nigeria, militants were attacking oil pipelines. In Venezuela, an OPEC member, the anti-American firebrand Hugo Chavez had seized control of the state-owned oil company, leading to labor strikes, severe declines in productivity and a near 25 percent fall in exports to the U.S. in the seven years leading up to 2009. Countries like Russia and Mexico had a lot more oil to produce, but they didn't have the appropriate technical expertise and shunned foreign investors who did. Nobody in oil-producing countries, moreover, was eager to see another re-run of the 1980s and 1990s, when oil prices had crashed because production outpaced demand growth. And everywhere, production costs were rising amid a shortage of skilled oil workers.

U.S. airlines, for their part, pinned part of the blame for the oil spike on financial "speculators" who were buying and selling the oil futures contracts that determine prices. The airlines urged Congress to pass laws restricting such activity. Were the "speculators" really to blame, and anyway, could the government have done anything that would have helped rather than causing even worse unintended consequences? Likely not. But oil had certainly become much more than a cost input for businesses like airlines. It was now an asset class where all sorts of investors—from hedge funds to pension funds to day traders—placed their money. After all, by mid-2008, investing in oil certainly looked more attractive than buying securities backed by residential mortgages, which had been the hot investment a few years earlier but had become toxic. Refinery costs were also surging. The cost of turning crude oil into jet fuel was at times running higher than the oil itself had cost a few years earlier—in other words, the impact of per-barrel crude oil prices surging from $50 to $100 to nearly $150 was even worse than those numbers themselves suggested. The weak U.S. dollar meant producers abroad would lose value unless they raised prices. And some people blamed the Federal Reserve for loose monetary policies that never quite caused much-feared inflation in goods and services—China's low labor costs and efficiencies at retailers like Walmart saw to that—but had indeed fueled dangerous inflation in financial assets like mortgage-backed securities and commodities like oil.

Not all global airlines saw the oil spike as an unmitigated disaster. Although none liked paying exorbitant jet fuel prices, carriers in places like the Middle East and Russia at least saw their revenues surge, offsetting some of the cost pain. Emirates, for its part, its customers flush with oil money, kept adding planes, adding destinations, adding workers and adding to its profits. It also debuted its giant new Airbus 380 aircraft, choosing New York as its first market.

If only U.S. carriers were so lucky. Sure, Texas, with all its oil—and Houston more specifically—remained a strong market for airlines. Continental's Jeff Smisek, then the Houston-based company's No. 2 executive, told investors July 19, "Here in Houston... [oil companies] are living large and flying all around the world up front and spending money like drunken sailors." ("Up front" is industry slang for premium cabins.) But Continental's Houston situation was the exception. Far more common were airlines trying to raise fares to recoup at least some of what they were paying for fuel. This was dangerous, of course, because the economy kept deteriorating: An average of about 140,000 jobs evaporated each month from January through August, including 49,000 manufacturing jobs, 40,000 construction jobs, 29,000 retail jobs, 13,000 finance jobs and 6,000 transportation jobs.

Boyd Group International, an airline consultancy, analyzed fare data and found U.S. carriers charging an average one-way fare of $191, or $166 excluding taxes and fees. But the cost of fuel per passenger, the study explained, was about $139, leaving just $27 to pay for everything else, including wages and benefits. By contrast, in 2000, average fares were $188, or $168 without taxes, and the fuel cost per passenger was just $32, leaving $136 for other costs and—this is a business, after all—profits.

To the public, and to even many front-line airline employees, it was all very confusing: Flights were clearly packed full. Fuller than ever before. Fuller, even, than in the go-go days of the late 1990s, that rare period of nearly universal prosperity for airlines. But what employees and consumers couldn't see was that these flights were not making any money. The Boyd Group also found that "most of the nearly full flights for July and August will be carrying passengers that paid fares well below the new fuel-driven break-even point." Not only was fuel expensive. Just as importantly, airlines—as they sold tickets to passengers, who would travel at some future date—had no idea what they would actually pay for the fuel that would help them carry those passengers. Travelers often buy their tickets well in advance of their journeys—sometimes months in advance—creating a significant lag time between when the product is priced and when the costs are incurred. Raising fares in reaction to a fuel spike, in other words, isn't a terribly effective tool to recoup costs in the short term. If fuel prices were high and stayed high, well at least supply could be cut, driving fares higher to compensate for those higher costs. But with costs wildly spiraling upward, it was anyone's guess what the proper fare should be six weeks from now. And schedules are planned many months in advance.

So the U.S. airline industry was breaking again. More than a few insiders saw the latest fuel cost shock as more challenging than even the post-9/11 demand shock. In just the April-to-June quarter, generally a peak period for demand, U.S. carriers collectively lost $934 million. Fares had to go higher. And there was only one way to make that happen. Capacity—large amounts of capacity—had to be removed from the system. Some people were asking whether there could even be an airline industry at all if fuel prices kept surging. "There's always going to be an airline industry in this country, and the only question is: What's the size of it going to be?" Doug Steenland told CNBC, the popular business news network. "The price of oil went from $26 in 2002 to over $70 in 2007, but 2007 was a great year for the airline business…. Over time, the industry will adjust…. It will eventually reach equilibrium." Airlines, in other words, could profit with fuel at any cost if they could properly match supply with demand and get passengers to pay the fares necessary to compensate for those high fuel costs.

On June 4, United, its hubs under relentless attack by Southwest and now Virgin America, announced plans to reduce domestic mainline (i.e., non-regional-jet) capacity an extraordinary 17 percent to 18 percent. One of the markets it exited: San Francisco-Atlanta, conceding the traffic to Delta. A hundred planes would leave the fleet. Between 1,400 and 1,600 people would lose their jobs. And Ted, United's low-fare unit, which never really had any better chance than Delta's Song, would close its doors. United also, incidentally, hired Delta's Joe Kolshak to run its operations.

On that same day, Continental, its oil industry traffic surging in Houston but its banker traffic plummeting in Newark, cut 6 percent of its schedule and 3,000 jobs. One month later, American, with its increasingly uncompetitive labor costs, followed a May announcement about capacity cuts with another 11-to-12 percent cut in available seat miles, axing 7,000 jobs in the process. US Airways cut capacity 6 to 8 percent, along with 1,700 jobs. As a result, business travelers, as described in a Bloomberg article at the time, were not only forced to pay higher fares. They were forced to spend more time on the road too because of so many flight cutbacks. They spent more time in their cars driving to distant airports because nearby airports no longer had service—indeed, small and rural airports experienced some of the steepest cutbacks. They spent more time at airports when they missed a flight and had to wait longer for the next one. They spent more nights in hotels because flying out and back on the same day became harder to do with fewer frequencies—the first flight of the morning and the last one at night were often the least profitable and thus the first on the chopping block. Some who booked in advance found their flights had been canceled, forcing them to scramble for alternatives. The airline industry's problems were becoming corporate America's problems.

Other capacity was leaving the scene involuntarily. Throughout the world, the fuel plague was killing smallish airlines one by one. Airlines with names like Adam Air, Alpi Eagles, Oasis Hong Kong, Nationwide, EuroManx, Aerocondor and Magnicharters perished. A crop of young transatlantic startups catering to premium passengers—Eos, MaxJet and SilverJet—died too, as did Zoom, a transatlantic startup for budget travelers. Within the U.S., the upstart Skybus, with its nonstop $10 flights between cities like Columbus, Ohio, and Greensboro, N.C., failed. So did Aloha Airlines and ATA. In April, Frontier, an LCC getting hammered at its Denver base by Southwest, filed for bankruptcy. Deep capacity and cost cuts would help it cling to life.

To be sure, the Big Three LCCs—Southwest, JetBlue and AirTran—were also feeling the pain. For them, and particularly for the latter two, the 2008 fuel shock was unequivocally worse than the 9/11 demand shock. Back then, the shock represented a tremendous opportunity to steal price-sensitive passengers from bloated legacy giants like Delta. Now, those legacy rivals were leaner and meaner. And more importantly, fuel was an equal-opportunity assassin, hurting LCC cost structures just as much as everyone else's. Or actually, even more so. Because an LCC's labor, distribution and overhead costs were lower, fuel made up a greater percentage of overall costs. At AirTran, for example, fuel accounted for a remarkable 46 percent of total operating costs in 2008. At Delta, the figure was less than a third. Or put another way, the areas where LCCs did have a cost advantage, including labor, were becoming less important relative to the one big area where they did not: fuel. All the things LCCs had done so well throughout the decade, and especially *this* decade, just didn't matter as much anymore. Predictably, the LCCs slowed their capacity growth dramatically.

Nor did LCCs have much international traffic, and it was international traffic that was still holding up relatively well in 2008. Years later, the idea that the rest of the world could have emerged unscathed from the U.S. mortgage market meltdown would seem daft—the global financial crisis would be so deep and so widespread that it would come to be known, for short, by its acronym, GFC. But in mid-2008, the question of whether "contagion" would ensue was still considered legitimate. Delta and others had a much easier time raising prices on international routes, sometimes by introducing fuel surcharges. Within the U.S., pricing power was limited by both the sagging U.S. economy and the simple fact that so many different airlines were competing.

A third factor was Southwest's hedge protection, which enabled it to charge lower fares than it otherwise could have charged—fares other airlines felt compelled to match, even if they couldn't break even with those fares. But by no means was Southwest immune to the industry crisis. In 2008 it was still paying just $51 for 70 percent of its fuel, a huge bargain. But inflation on the other 30 percent was hardly negligible—the company expected its total fuel costs to rise by $500 million that year. Higher fuel costs also meant many off-peak flights, especially in the early morning and late in the day, were no longer economically viable for Southwest, just as they had become unviable for other airlines. And cutting those flights meant a reduction in aircraft utilization, which for four decades had been one of the secrets to Southwest's success. In addition, Southwest's labor costs were rising, especially as its heavily unionized workforce demanded higher wages to compensate for smaller profit-sharing checks than the ones to which workers had long been accustomed. As a result of these cost pressures, Southwest too gradually raised fares, lifting its self-imposed fare cap, for example, from $299 to $399. Nor did it help that Southwest had a large presence in sunny markets like California, Florida, Phoenix and Las Vegas, where the collapse in housing prices was most acute.

If Southwest's best days were perhaps behind it, could Delta's best days—even in these dark days for the industry—be yet to come?

Delta was now in a better position to cope than its LCC rivals, quite a contrast from the post-9/11 period, when its balance sheet started out strong but so much else—its network, its labor costs and so on—made it highly vulnerable. Now it had a cost advantage over United, American and Continental too, and it had a revamped network that was producing revenue premiums. If the Northwest merger produced the synergies it was promising, that would be yet another advantage.

Nevertheless, Delta and Northwest—still operating independently unless and until they got final approval for their merger, hopefully that autumn—had to take protective measures, including more capacity cuts. On June 18, Ed Bastian, Delta's No. 2 executive after Richard Anderson, presented the company's action plan to a gathering of airline investors attending a Merrill Lynch conference in New York. His PowerPoint presentation, "Challenging Times Require Aggressive Action," highlighted a 13 percent reduction in domestic capacity for the second half of the year, with Orlando—and Florida more generally—losing a lot of service. By year end, up to 20 mainline aircraft and up to 70 regional aircraft would leave the fleet. As it happened, Delta's domestic capacity in the summer of 2008 was already 23 percent below its level three years earlier, when it was on the verge of filing for bankruptcy. Its international capacity, by contrast, was up an astounding 77 percent since then and would continue to grow another 14 percent in the second half of 2008 compared to the same period in 2007.

Counterintuitively, Delta's relatively weak position in the largest longhaul international market—London—was now a blessing. The new open skies deal that took effect in March meant lots of new capacity at London Heathrow, including Delta's own new flights there. For American and United, with large portions of their transatlantic capacity concentrated at Heathrow, this new competition hurt. But Delta was earning its money abroad in more off-the-beaten-path places like Moscow and Istanbul. Middle East routes like Dubai and Africa routes like Lagos, Accra and Dakar were "incredibly strong," Glen Hauenstein said. Latin America and India were doing well too. By serving many overseas cities from Atlanta, meanwhile, Delta was able to suction connecting traffic from much of the U.S., including California, Texas, Florida and—especially for routes to Latin America—even the northeast. What's more, even as U.S. companies and households found their travel budgets pressured by fuel and recession, foreigners, lured by the cheap dollar, were visiting the U.S. in record numbers. In 2007, 57 million of them visited, breaking the previous high set in 2000, the year before 9/11. Visits from the United Kingdom, the largest overseas market, grew 7 percent from a year earlier. Arrivals from Germany grew 10 percent. And France, where Delta was strongest thanks to its cooperation with Air France? From there, visits soared 26 percent. China: up 18 percent. India: up 39 percent. Brazil: 22 percent. And so on. All told, foreign visitors would spend $123 billion in the U.S. that year, outspending U.S. travelers abroad by $18 billion and lowering America's current account deficit.

So even as it ended service to places like Islip and Bellingham and Atlantic City at home, Delta was adding routes to Cape Town, Sydney, Tel Aviv, Monrovia, Luanda, Malabo, Edinburgh, Málaga, Lyon, Stockholm, Amman, Tegucigalpa and Georgetown abroad. Delta, now brashly calling itself "America's flag carrier to the world," also used newly won rights to finally serve booming China, launching Atlanta flights to Shanghai. It began connecting Paris to its Salt Lake City hub. It later announced new flights to oil-rich Kuwait and won rights to serve Bogotá and Buenos Aires from New York. It applied for rights to serve Manaus and Fortaleza in Brazil. Hauenstein, meanwhile, wasn't shy about quickly axing new routes that didn't profit. It scrapped plans—before the first flight even departed—to serve Orly Airport south of Paris. It pulled out of Bucharest and Vienna and stopped flying to London Gatwick from New York. Like Orly, Nairobi was announced but never launched. Airlines often spend months deliberating the viability of potential new international routes, analyzing sophisticated mathematically derived forecasts based on economic, demographic and industry traffic data. Hauenstein's approach: Things are changing so quickly that—although he and his staff certainly did their share of analysis—better to rely partly on trial and error, if a route seemed to make some sense, than to leave expensive longhaul-capable planes wallowing in Orlando. Better to take full advantage of the fact that planes, unlike factories, are mobile assets that are easily moved around. If you're right more often than you're wrong, erring on the side of being more aggressive, rather than less, will work out better than never shooting and never scoring, even despite the inevitable dud routes.

Rivals were jumping on the international bandwagon too. That summer, Continental added Cleveland-Paris and Newark-Mumbai. American added Moscow, Milan, Barcelona and London Stansted. United added a few new Asian routes and US Airways a few new European ones. But none had the planes, the cost structures nor perhaps the courage to expand abroad as rapidly as Delta. Besides, rivals seemed to be doing more international subtraction than addition: United, for one, exited Denver-London, San Francisco-Taipei, San Francisco-Nagoya and Los Angeles-Frankfurt.

Delta, like its rivals, was also taking action on the labor front. But it was doing so without involuntary layoffs or salary cuts. Instead, it used voluntary buyouts to reduce its headcount by 4,000, saving $200 million a year. In fact, shortly after the merger announcement, it offered all non-union workers a 3 percent wage *increase*. And in June, management was thrilled to learn flight attendants had voted against unionization. To further save on non-fuel costs, the airline closed nine airport lounges and further reduced Comair flying. New long-range 777s were coming. So were versions of narrowbody Boeing 737s with the range to fly rather deeply into Latin America. On the pricing front, Delta joined its peers in bringing back so called revenue management "fences"—in other words, rules like Saturday night-stay requirements for certain fares—which had faded away in the first half-decade following 9/11. SimpliFares, in other words, were as distant a memory as ever. As Delta cut domestic capacity, meanwhile, it focused its cuts mostly on non-hub flying—Boston-Los Angeles was one route that got the ax. It did not, by contrast, cut capacity on Atlanta routes that overlapped with AirTran, whose fortunes, by mid-2008, had taken an alarming turn for the worse. AirTran would later consider itself lucky to have been blocked—by Northwest, remember—from acquiring Midwest; in retrospect, the acquisition might have doomed the company. In July, AirTran cut nearly 500 jobs and shrank its flying 5 percent after posting a negative 6 percent operating margin in the second quarter. Its days of profitably picking at Delta, like a vulture at a carcass, were long gone.

Delta happened to have a good fuel hedge book too. No, not nearly what Southwest had—that was true. But with oil prices shooting past the $100 mark, Delta's fuel hedge portfolio would at one point be valued at some $1.5 billion. It had nearly half its expected fuel needs hedged for the second half of 2008 at $2.76 per gallon, well below the "spot price," or the unhedged price. Delta was also saving on its fuel bill by installing a new line of ultra-light airplane seats.

The marketing team, meanwhile, was busy solidifying Delta's image, most notably in New York City. The airline, already the official sponsor of the Mets, became the official sponsor of the more mighty Yankees too, although neither New York team advanced to the postseason in 2008. The airline held an inflight concert with Grammy winner John Legend. It sponsored the Sundance Film Festival in Utah, the U.S. ski and snowboarding teams and street festivals hosted by the Food Network, including one with stars from the popular television shows Curb Your Enthusiasm and The Daily Show. It burnished its charitable credentials too, working with the American Red Cross and continuing its longtime support for Habitat for Humanity. The marketing team also scored a viral YouTube hit with a new inflight safety video featuring a tall red-haired flight attendant who came to be called "Deltalina" for her resemblance to the actress Angelina Jolie.

Northwest was certainly doing its share of adjusting to the fuel shock. It moved to cut its post-summer domestic capacity another 5 percent, retiring as many as 20 additional airplanes. Domestic mainline capacity would contract sharply as geriatric DC-9s were replaced by new 75-seat regional jets with better operating economics. There was some international expansion, including a new Detroit-Shanghai route. But gone were Minneapolis-Paris (for the winter) and the just-launched Detroit-Düsseldorf and Hartford-Amsterdam routes (forever). Northwest cut travel agency commissions in the Japanese market, where travel agencies still had great sway over even leisure travelers. And together with Delta, it established those 26 integration teams to plan for actions to take once the merger was finalized. In July, the carriers also announced their joint executive team, gleaning talent from both sides. Delta people would remain in charge of network planning (Glen Hauenstein) and human resources (Mike Campbell), for example, while Northwest people would assume control of fleet planning (Nathaniel Pieper) and information technology (Theresa Wise). Delta's Ed Bastian would temporarily be chief of Northwest until the two airlines became one.

So Delta's battle plan was in place. It featured five key principles that Richard Anderson described to Wall Street:

1) "We will be aggressive with respect to managing capacity, domestically and internationally but particularly in the domestic market. We've evidenced that with the steps that we took last October and this past March and we will continue that vigilance."

2) "Second, we came out very quickly in response to fuel with a very aggressive cost management plan that was really based on a lot of innovative productivity enhancements across our businesses. And we will continue to be very aggressive in being certain that we're pushing productivity in the industry."

3) "Third, we're pushing fare increases and fee increases. You'll see in our results, we had 12 percent [revenue] growth in this quarter."

4) "Fourth, we will maintain high levels of liquidity between our cash and our revolver [i.e., the company's credit line]. Our liquidity is over $3.6 billion, and will be building through the quarter."

5) "And fifth, we're merging with Northwest Airlines."

The reference, in the third point, to fees was perhaps somewhat buried. But it touched on a strategy that would, in fact, prove enormously important to the industry as a whole. Of the many dynamic airline industry responses to fuel costs, one of the most dynamic—and most controversial—was charging passengers extra for a range of products and services that were previously included. This was not entirely unfamiliar. As early as 2003, Delta itself was selling snacks aboard its planes. But the proceeds from selling food—even full meals—were marginal. In February 2008, United sparked a media frenzy by telling passengers—those buying nonrefundable domestic economy tickets who aren't elite frequent fliers, anyway—they would now need to pay $25 to check a second bag; one checked bag would still be included. United's media team spun the move as justice for passengers that didn't have bags: They'd now have access to lower fares and wouldn't have to subsidize their heavy-packing flightmates. In other words, people could pay for the extra services they wanted and not pay for the extra services they didn't want.

Other airlines—including AirTran, which increasingly needed any money it could find—quickly matched. Delta and Northwest followed. Eventually, so would all U.S. airlines with just one exception: Southwest.

But that was only the beginning. American, which had waited until late April to follow United's charge for second bags, came forth just a month later with something even more stunning: It would charge for even a *first* checked bag. Passengers—again, at least non-premium shorthaul ones—would pay for any bag they couldn't carry aboard. Most airlines, including Northwest, matched the move. But Delta did not, at least not for many months—it hoped to generate nearly as much revenue, but more goodwill among passengers, by instead increasing fees for the second checked bag above what others were charging for that. But Delta was forgoing too much badly needed revenue. By November, it relented and aligned its bag fees with nearly everyone else's. Southwest and JetBlue would long remain the only holdouts in offering a free checked bag (and in Southwest's case two—it loudly made its "bags fly free" policy a part of its brand).

Bags would prove the biggest money-maker in a larger push toward what came to be called ancillary revenues. Airlines levied and raised fees for booking offline, changing an itinerary, standing by for an earlier flight, sitting in seats with more legroom, pillows, blankets, priority boarding, curbside check-in, inflight entertainment and so on. One European low-cost airline, Ireland's Ryanair, had become famous for pioneering the idea of charging for just about everything, and in doing so, it became one of the world's most profitable airlines. Its fast-talking, foul-mouthed CEO Michael O'Leary even dangled the notion that one day, all tickets would be free, with all the airline's revenues coming from ancillaries. Indeed, at one point about a fifth of Ryanair's passengers were flying on "free" tickets, although high fuel prices eventually meant an end to these giveaways.

Most U.S. carriers never went quite as far as Ryanair. But they were now charging for bags and seats and food, and by doing this, they were raking in tens and soon hundreds of millions of dollars per year. There was some resistance, for sure, like when United tried charging for meals on flights to Europe, or when US Airways tried charging for even water, soft drinks, juice and coffee—both of those initiatives failed when customers pushed back and competitors didn't match. The strategy was bad for the industry's image too, generating headlines like one in the *New York Post*: "SKYWAY ROBBERY - $15 BAG FEE TO HIT FLIERS." Still another in the *New York Daily News* read: "PILLOW FIGHT AT 30,000 FEET: FLIERS PEEVED AT JETBLUE'S $7 FEE FOR SLEEP KIT." And yet another: "AIRLINES BATTLE

SOARING FUEL PRICES BY STICKING YOU WITH NEW FEES TO CHECK LUGGAGE." Comedians had a field day: Jay Leno joked American was now charging $15 for even *emotional* baggage.

But for airlines, ancillary revenues were no joke. They were an extremely important tool to offset fuel inflation. They also coincided with the advent of new technologies like inflight Wi-Fi, which American pioneered in August, followed by Virgin America and Delta shortly thereafter; Delta would later leapfrog and offer Wi-Fi on more aircraft—eventually its entire shorthaul fleet, other than the smallest regional aircraft—than any other airline, although its smaller nemesis AirTran would be the first to offer fleet-wide Wi-Fi, no exceptions (in its case on 136 aircraft), by the following summer of 2009. One nice thing about Wi-Fi was that unlike fees for services that had previously been included, which passengers saw as punitive, nobody complained about paying for Wi-Fi—it was an entirely new amenity for passengers to take or leave. Delta also, meanwhile, joined its peers in accepting new forms of payment like eBay's PayPal and equipping its flight attendants with handheld credit card readers, all the better to push inflight sales.

As it happened, oil prices did begin to ease a bit in the month of August, to an average of $117 per barrel from an average of $133 (and, remember, a peak of $147) in July. But the mood in America wasn't improving. Somewhat paranoid Americans—who had feared the Russians would beat them militarily and scientifically in the 1960s, the Arabs would destroy their economy in the 1970s, the Japanese would buy all their golf courses in the 1980s and the Mexicans would suck away all their jobs in the 1990s—now saw China as the bogeyman, the rising power that lent America its money and took all its manufacturing jobs. And now China was hosting the summer Olympics, earning more gold medals than the Americans and displaying a discomforting talent for grandiose ceremonies using legions of people performing in unison. All the while, the U.S. economy was sinking.

On Sept. 15, 2008, the investment bank Lehman Brothers, with heavy exposure to subprime mortgages, ran out of money, and nobody was willing to lend it any more. Nobody would buy the company either, even in a last-minute fire sale. Which left the U.S. government with an awful choice: "spray the investment bank with public money or let it burn," *The Economist* wrote.

Six months earlier, Uncle Sam—fearful of the impact a failure would have on the entire financial system, and, by extension, the entire U.S. economy—had elected to spray Lehman's rival Bear Stearns with public money. Lehman, as it happened, was even bigger than Bear, and it owed more money to more people. If it failed, the ripple effect would be enormous. But the Bush administration and the Federal Reserve knew repeated bailouts would only encourage more risky behavior in the future—moral hazard, as it were, a term that wasn't new but was becoming more familiar to more people. And the U.S. public, with a predisposition toward mistrusting both Wall Street and Washington, was already reaching for pitchforks. In the end, Lehman Brothers was left to burn.

And all hell broke loose. Just one day earlier, the esteemed Merrill Lynch, which had also amassed extraordinarily reckless exposure to subprime mortgages, had no choice but to hastily sell itself to Bank of America, which months earlier had bought Countrywide Financial, at one time the nation's largest home lender but one that was disproportionately infected with subprime toxins. Several days before that, two oddly constructed New Deal-era companies called Fannie Mae and Freddie Mac, created to boost home ownership in America, had also succumbed to the subprime virus. Washington had little choice but to nationalize them.

One day after the Lehman debacle, AIG, the country's largest insurance company, created an even greater dilemma when the world was shocked to learn it had written billions of dollars in insurance policies, known as credit default swaps, on bundles of mortgages that were now all but worthless. Counterparties to those transactions—the people and companies who had won the bets, so to speak—were all demanding cash at once, and AIG, which couldn't pay them all, had just one place left to turn: Uncle Sam. And for all the worries about moral hazard and public opinion, Uncle Sam knew that if AIG failed, so would a large number of those counterparties, including all major banks, which made up America's financial system. The millions of Americans insured by AIG would lose their policies. And airlines would be affected too—not only did AIG insure aircraft, and not only did it offer travel insurance to passengers, but it also owned the world's largest aircraft leasing company, ILFC.

So the U.S. stepped in with an $85 billion loan in exchange for an 80 percent ownership stake. AIG was simply too big to fail. The cost of failure would have been far greater than the cost of rescue.

But if only that were the end of it. From bank to bank, Wall Street was burning. Lending between banks froze, because nobody trusted anybody else to repay. It was all happening a few blocks from where the World Trade Center had fallen seven Septembers ago.

On Sept. 25, a giant but insolvent Seattle-based mortgage lender called Washington Mutual sold itself to JP Morgan. An even bigger lender, Charlotte-based Wachovia, agreed to a takeover by Wells Fargo, which had outmaneuvered Citigroup. A few weeks later, Citigroup—itself now on the verge of collapse—was partly nationalized. Morgan Stanley turned to a Japanese bank for equity. Goldman Sachs turned to Warren Buffet.

To stop the panic, the Bush administration devised a plan called the Troubled Asset Relief Program, or TARP, which would use up to $700 billion of taxpayer money to buy so-called "toxic assets" like subprime mortgages from financial institutions, thereby removing the germs from the system. But this required approval by Congress, which on Sept. 29 voted no. Stock markets plummeted, and Treasury Secretary Hank Paulson pleaded for a re-vote. He finally convinced recalcitrant Republicans, and on Oct. 3, the measure passed the House of Representatives. As Federal Reserve chairman Ben Bernanke explained: "A lot of this goes against American values of self-reliance and responsibility, and I'm very, very aware of that,

[but] I would give the following example: If your neighbor smokes in bed and sets his house on fire and you live in a neighborhood of closely packed wooden houses, you could punish him very severely by refusing to send the fire department, and then he would probably learn his lesson. But unfortunately, in the process, you'd have the entire neighborhood burning down."

And this wasn't just the neighborhood burning. It was the whole American economy and beyond. The subprime virus was taking down some of Europe's financial institutions and municipal governments, which had bought Wall Street products stuffed with mortgages from home buyers who couldn't repay their loans, some of whom had been tricked by lenders who were incentivized to do more and more deals. The book "All the Devils Are Here: The Hidden History of the Financial Crisis" describes first-time homebuyers who never even moved into their new properties because they couldn't afford the very first payment. With home values plummeting, Americans could no longer use their properties as collateral for new loans. Worse, many now found themselves "under water," meaning their houses were worth less than what they owed. The fire that began on Wall Street was spreading to Main Street.

It was spreading to America's businesses too, businesses big and small alike, causing unemployment to spike and industrial production to plunge. Before long, with auto sales at their lowest levels since 1993, Detroit's Big Three auto manufacturers, directly and indirectly responsible for hundreds of thousands of jobs, were forced to beg Washington for TARP money. The venerable General Electric, a big builder of aircraft engines and the owner of a giant aircraft leasing company, found its GE Capital arm caught up in the financial whirlwind, forcing it, like Goldman Sachs, to turn to Warren Buffet for emergency capital. GE also staved off disaster by tapping financial markets that were only alive thanks to timely government support. Airlines themselves watched warily to gauge the impact. Delta had some beneficial hedge contracts with Lehman that were now worthless, but its overall exposure there was minimal. With the clouds already darkening in late August, it had borrowed the entire billion dollars of its revolving credit line—everybody was grabbing as much cash as they could—and negotiated better terms for its credit card processing agreement. Appearing on Fox News, Virgin Atlantic founder Richard Branson said his company got the scare of its life when its British bank HBOS nearly collapsed before being rescued by a rival bank. Virgin had about $2 billion deposited at HBOS and was told it couldn't withdraw the money during the height of its crisis, when the bank looked likely to dissolve. Had it had done so, Branson said, Virgin Atlantic might have "disappeared."

One great fear was deflation: the potential prices would fall because of a lack of economic activity. Every bit as scary as hyper-*inflation*, *deflation* encourages people to stop spending today in expectation of getting a better price tomorrow. So that fear—never mind that actual deflation never broadly materialized—led to a further drop in economic activity, fueling a vicious downward spiral. Talk of another Great Depression was everywhere. As the government felt compelled to spend, tax receipts were falling because of the drop in business activity, worsening the nation's already severe fiscal shortfalls. Since the start of the decade, tax rates had dropped significantly at the same time entitlement spending was rising significantly, never mind two overseas wars that were still raging, with no end in sight.

There was plenty of blame to go around: Wall Street's irresponsibility, loose money policy at the Fed, global financial imbalances, unethical mortgage originators, ill-informed home buyers, lax government oversight, financial deregulation, insanely complex derivative contracts and ratings agencies that seemed to stamp anything that came across their desks, no matter how toxic, with triple-A ratings. By the end of the party, Wall Street was creating investments linked to investments linked to investments with exposure to subprime junk—in other words, betting on the same bad mortgages multiple times. Spreading risk, which can be extraordinarily useful when done properly, doesn't work when everything is bad. The amount of debt grew to astounding levels. Niall Fergusson, a Harvard historian, would look back and identify six causes for the debacle: 1) excessive bank leverage, 2) a failure by ratings agencies to accurately assess the risk of securities tied to subprime mortgage loans, 3) an asset price bubble that the Federal Reserve failed to address, 4) the sale of derivatives with no regard to their systemic risk potential, 5) the political push to have everyone own a home and 6) China's voracious appetite for U.S. bonds to keep the Chinese currency depressed, in order to help its exporters.

And oh, if this drama weren't enough, there was the small matter of an election scheduled for November, pitting the one-time head of the Senate's aviation subcommittee, John McCain, not against Hilary Clinton, as had been widely expected, but against a young U.S. senator from Illinois named Barack Obama. On Nov. 4, Obama won, becoming the first African American president in a country where African Americans, a century and a half earlier, had been slaves. This inspired an America yearning for good news, tired of hearing about one depressing news story after another, including the revelation that a respected Wall Street investor named Bernie Madoff wasn't so respectable after all. He turned out to have swindled more than $60 billion from his clients.

Airlines, meanwhile, were still flying, but they were flying with fewer passengers. "The situation remains bleak," IATA, the airline industry's global trade association, wrote. "The deterioration in traffic is alarmingly fast-paced and widespread. We have not seen such a decline in passenger traffic since SARS in 2003."

And Delta? It was less pessimistic, as was evident Oct. 15 in Richard Anderson's remarks during the company's third-quarter earnings presentation. "I want to focus on a topic that has dominated the headlines in recent weeks: the credit crisis and how it is impacting Delta," he said. "The turbulence in the markets coupled with a soft economy and high fuel prices have created a pretty significant financial storm, the effects of which have rippled through the economy in every market around the world and touched almost every consumer and business. I just want you to know we're well positioned to weather the turmoil in the market." He talked about Delta's proactive capacity cutting, about its staff reductions, about its pre-arranged financing for upcoming aircraft deliveries and about its strong cash balance. And, he said, "as the industry deals with the turbulent times in the credit and equity markets and the potential for a global recession, there is a key difference that sets us apart in our ability to manage through challenging times, and that's our merger with Northwest."

But Delta did lose money in the third quarter, which is usually the best quarter of the year. Then, in the off-peak fourth quarter, it suffered a massive $340 million net loss (excluding special accounting items). In a reversal of fortune, its fuel hedges were now becoming a liability: Hedges were really, in effect, an agreement to purchase future fuel at today's prices. Sure, for most of the decade, that was a fancy way of saying "discount." But no longer. And these wrong-way hedge contracts, moreover, required large amounts of precious cash to be set aside as collateral: Delta, like its competitors, was paying dearly for a privilege that was no longer even helping. In December, Ed Bastian told investors to expect a decline of revenues, during 2009, of between 8 and 12 percent. It was, he said, "the worst industry revenue environment in history, ex 9/11."

The clouds, however, held not one but two silver linings for U.S. carriers. Demand was falling, yes. But so was supply, following aggressive cutting all year—and supply cuts, remember, prop up airfares. Also falling: oil prices. In September, they had dipped below the $100 mark to an average of $77 in October, then $57 in November and just $42 in December. Oil hadn't been this cheap since the summer of 2004.

The race to the bottom was on. Demand, supply and oil were all in freefall. The question for airlines: Which would fall fastest?

2009

"Half the time we were unified, and half the time we were trying to kill each other"

One evening during Delta's darker days, Larry Kellner met Jerry Grinstein for dinner in Atlanta. The men were running rival airlines, Kellner in charge of Continental since succeeding Gordon Bethune in late 2004, Grinstein in charge of Delta since succeeding Leo Mullin earlier that year. Rivals though they were, Delta and Continental were domestic marketing partners too, hence the routine meeting. Grinstein, born in 1932, was 27 years older than Kellner—old enough to be his father. Grinstein was 73, and at about 9 p.m., as he was dropping off his fellow CEO at Atlanta's airport, Grinstein remarked to Kellner that his evening wasn't finished. Leading by example, he would head straight from the airport to Delta's aircraft hangars to clean planes on the late shift. Kellner was awed.

"You know, most 70-year-olds wouldn't even want to be there, much less be willing to go through that," Kellner said. "And it made a huge difference."

Continental's other U.S. partner, of course, was Northwest. Kellner, Bethune's finance chief since the beginning of Continental's own remarkable turnaround in the mid-1990s, was there when Delta nearly merged with Continental in 1998, and when Northwest agreed to buy Continental instead. He was there when the U.S. Justice Department said no to that deal. And he was there when, in 2002, Leo Mullin invited Northwest and Continental to join SkyTeam and to form a three-way domestic marketing alliance with Delta.

But the world had changed a lot since then. By 2007, Delta was a born-again airline with dramatically lower costs thanks to bankruptcy plus a team of Kellner's ex-colleagues including Glen Hauenstein (who revamped Delta's network) and Mike Campbell (who revitalized its employee relations). Another ex-Continental employee, albeit one from before the Bethune era, was Richard Anderson, with whom Kellner had worked while Anderson was CEO of Northwest and with whom Kellner would work now that Anderson was CEO of Delta—Delta, Northwest and Continental, remember, remained partners.

But Anderson's first message to Kellner, after Anderson became CEO of Delta in late 2007, was hardly a routine re-acquaintance now that Anderson had rejoined the airline industry. The new Delta board of directors was assembled with consolidation in mind, and Anderson wanted to speak with all his major partners and rivals. "Richard was very transparent and said, 'Look, we need to do something. Can we come over and talk to you guys?'" Kellner recalled years later.

"We knew he was making the rounds."

Anderson sketched out his objectives. He valued the three-way alliance with Northwest and Continental, but he also wanted a true merger, and a three-way merger was a non-starter, given regulatory realities. Delta could merge with one of the two but not both. By then, a Delta-United deal was looking unlikely. Would a Delta-Continental deal be possible?

Kellner was skeptical, most of all because he knew what Delta really needed: a global network that included heft in Asia. Northwest could give them that; Continental could not. "If you left the meeting and sat back with a white board," Kellner said, recalling his meeting with Anderson, "you would come to the conclusion: Well, they ought to merge with Northwest, based on what they want, which is a global platform. Because, I mean, we can't give them Asia. But Northwest can." Continental had strength to Latin America and especially Europe, but so—already—did Delta.

Kellner was also skeptical about Delta's choice of chairman: Daniel Carp, the former chief of Kodak, who had no airline experience. "You always worry when you have split leadership at an airline," meaning a CEO who is not also chairman of the airline's board of directors. "From a good corporate governance standpoint, it may be great to split the roles," he said, alluding to an increasingly popular belief among investors that a board could not properly oversee a company if the top manager, whom the board should be overseeing, is not only on the board but at its helm. But "from a labor negotiations standpoint," he said, the split was bad. At Continental, pilots would speak directly with chairman David Bonderman, a high-profile airline investor—he was also chairman of Europe's Ryanair.

Gordon Bethune himself, while an advisor to Pardus Capital, urged against pushing for a Delta-Continental merger, in part because of Continental's pension obligations. But that aside, Continental was a healthy airline—as healthy as one could be during the fuel spike of 2007 and early 2008, anyway. It didn't necessarily need to merge.

But of one thing Kellner was sure: Continental couldn't stay in SkyTeam if Delta and Northwest merged. A combined Delta-Northwest would relegate Continental to a second-tier status with a muted voice. "We're not going to do anything if they do nothing," Kellner said later of his thinking at the time. "But if they did something, we would need to do something." Something meant three options: 1) somehow reposition Continental within SkyTeam, upholding its influence, 2) merge with another airline or 3) change alliances. "We could not be a junior partner in SkyTeam and succeed."

Despite amicable talks with Anderson and Steenland, the first option simply wasn't tenable. For one thing, Continental had built up international service at its Newark hub dramatically in the years since joining SkyTeam, while Delta had done the same at New York JFK, creating lots of overlapping and competing service—a passenger on New York City's subways at the time, looking at competing Delta and Continental advertisements making their respective cases for why each airline was truly New York's most global, could be forgiven for not realizing the two airlines were partners. So Kellner began speaking with American and British Airways, members of the oneworld alliance. He happened to be friends with American's CEO Gerard Arpey and was friendly with his deputy Tom Horton too; Kellner and Horton had, in particular, worked together on the creation of Orbitz, an online travel agency originally backed by the airlines. On paper, the numbers looked good—better, in fact, than they did for the SkyTeam scenario. But there was one big problem: "That deal had antitrust hair all over it," Kellner recalled. Indeed, the justice and transportation departments would not look kindly on the dominance that a combined American-Continental would have in the greater New York City area, the nation's largest air travel market.

That left United, a Star Alliance leader, which enthusiastically entertained the idea of merging. But it would be a merger or nothing at all: United had no interest in inviting Continental into Star without a merger, United CEO Glenn Tilton, the former oil man who had taken United through bankruptcy and who was now the industry's most outspoken proponent of consolidation, told Kellner. Or as the message sounded to Kellner: "You can't sleep with us without getting married."

Kellner and his team, instinctively a more merger-wary group, nonetheless continued the conversations. Despite the risks, they were intrigued by the idea of a combined United-Continental network. It would have hubs in the five largest economic centers of the country—New York, Los Angeles, Chicago, Washington and Houston—plus San Francisco, Denver and Cleveland. United's Asian strength, furthermore, would mix well with Continental's European and Latin American strength. A merged United-Continental network, Gordon Bethune said at the time, was "checkmate." And one important roadblock was gone. Northwest's "golden share" in Continental, which prevented the latter from doing a deal without the former's consent, would automatically go away if Northwest itself was involved in a merger, whether with or without Continental. And by early 2008, Northwest was clearly on a path toward merging with Delta. Continental would be free to merge with whomever it wanted.

So Kellner and Tilton, together with their staffs and their legal and finance teams, worked to hammer out a deal. One of the meetings between the two CEOs took place at the Hay-Adams hotel in Washington, D.C., across from the White House. There, they thought they could avoid the media. "It's a place where, you know, it would not be unusual for me to be in there, maybe with somebody," Kellner recalled. "It would not be unusual for Glenn to be in there meeting somebody." They even exited the hotel 20 minutes apart.

But the ruse didn't work. Sure enough, someone had recognized them. The word was out. By the spring of 2008, everyone was speculating on when the Delta-Northwest and United-Continental deals would happen.

Kellner, however, was getting nervous as the talks progressed. Since their start, oil prices had done nothing but spike, crossing the $100 mark. The economy had done nothing but sink. In March, Bear Stearns collapsed. "It's hard to overstate how bleak things looked in '08," Kellner said.

United's own finances, meanwhile, were going from bad to worse, as Continental could see up close after the two airlines agreed to examine each other's accounts. United had earned below-average profits in 2007. And it suffered a mammoth $537 million net loss in the first quarter of 2008, which it revealed April 22, seven days after Delta and Northwest announced their merger. United had $11 billion in debt and swirling questions from Wall Street about its ability to comply with bank loan covenants. "This was obviously a very difficult and challenging quarter for us and for the industry," Glenn Tilton told analysts in a conference call. United hadn't hammered down its costs during bankruptcy to the degree that Delta and Northwest had done. It was slow to cut capacity immediately after 9/11. It had wasted money creating and sustaining Ted. Its hubs were in Southwest's crosshairs. Its labor relations were still tense. Its revenues now ranked just third among U.S. legacy carriers, having been surpassed by Delta even before it merged with Northwest. While Delta was hyper-aggressively exploiting international markets, United, despite ostensibly better global gateway hubs, largely seemed to sit and watch.

Day by day, Kellner became increasingly convinced that a merged United-Continental would have little margin for error. On top of the concerns about the deteriorating financial markets, stabilizing United's earnings would require an immediate and massive capacity cut. By Continental's analysis, this would mean having to ground United's entire fleet of narrowbody 737s, as Kellner knew Tilton himself itself would surely conclude—both used the same analytic software from a company called Sabre, so both were coming to the same kinds of dire conclusions. Jobs were going to be lost. And before a merger could be approved by regulators, Tilton and Kellner would surely be dragged before Congress and asked for assurances that jobs would not be lost.

Kellner knew Continental's lawyers could have come up with a reassuring but careful statement about avoiding job losses, which would have remained technically correct, even if jobs were eventually lost. But how could Larry Kellner go before Congress and tell lawmakers—no matter how crafty the language, no matter how delicately he parsed words—that big downsizing would not follow?

He could not.

"There was no way I was going to sit in front of Congress and be deceptive in testimony about what we planned to do," he recalled years later. "I said if we're going to do this, we've got to be through the front door about what we need to do." If nothing else, Kellner would otherwise lose trust among Continental's workers, a trust Gordon Bethune had built against all odds. A decade and a half earlier, just before Bethune took over, Continental had been a bankrupt airline controlled by union hate figure Frank Lorenzo. Now it regularly ranked among the best employers in America.

Kellner had to be careful though. If Continental didn't merge with United, would United instead merge with US Airways, leaving Continental alone against a bulked-up United, a bulked-up Delta and an American closely tied to British Airways? Indeed, Glenn Tilton and Doug Parker were speaking.

Decision time was coming. To merge or not to merge? That was the question on Saturday, April 26, 2008, when Continental's board of directors assembled in Houston, debating the company's fate late into the night. In the end, it was Kellner's call.

Maybe other executives thought soaring oil prices and a sagging economy were the reasons to merge. Kellner thought they, combined with United's increasingly shaky finances, were the reasons *not* to merge. He believed the risks were too great. And just as importantly, "we made a calculated bet, which turned out to be right: If they can't figure out how to make this work with us, they will not go merge with Airways"—US Airways, that is, due to labor obstacles. If he was right about that, he didn't have to merge defensively.

There was still the important alliance matter: If United really wouldn't have sex without marriage, Continental might soon find itself abused, in its current relationship, by a merged Delta-Northwest. But however important that was, it wasn't important enough to bet the company. Kellner was walking away from the deal.

Early Sunday morning, Kellner attended a March of Dimes charity event, where he and his fellow executives had to act as if nothing was happening. Nobody—not even Glenn Tilton, for whom Kellner had high personal regard—knew what Kellner and Continental's board had decided. By noon, the team was back at Continental's downtown Houston headquarters, preparing a message to employees and a press release for the media—and getting ready to set up meetings with key investors in Boston and New York to explain the decision, once it became public knowledge.

"And so then I called Glenn," Kellner recalled, "and said Glenn, 'Let me show you a draft of what we're going to put out. I don't want you to be blindsided here. You've been a great partner and I'm really sorry and you know, we love you, but we just don't think a merger makes sense for us.'"

Tilton was unsurprisingly disappointed. But he told Kellner he empathized with Kellner's predicament. It was Kellner, after all, who would have been in charge of the combined airline.

But if Tilton himself could empathize with why Continental rejected United, the bankers involved in the proposed deal—who stood to earn hefty sums if it went forward—could not. They were irate. One of their arguments: Kellner was crazy to not merge now while Bush was still in office; who knew what kind of administration would come next? But Kellner's right-hand man Jeff Smisek, himself a Harvard-trained mergers-and-acquisitions lawyer, saw this as nonsense: United and Continental had so little network overlap that any justice department would approve it, especially if the Delta-Northwest deal was approved.

Of course, Kellner knew Continental's decision not to do a deal with United was not necessarily "not ever." It was, because of everything happening in the world and at United, "not now." He knew the two airlines' paths might someday cross again.

He just didn't know how soon.

That Monday morning, a few hours before boarding a flight to Boston for a Tuesday morning breakfast with investors, Kellner looked down at his BlackBerry, at a time—2008—when nearly every executive still had such a device. Looking back up at him was a message from none other than Glenn Tilton.

"Interested in Star? Call me."

"Holy shit!" Kellner thought to himself. Perhaps the biggest downside to not merging, the alliance conundrum, could be resolved more easily than Kellner ever imagined.

United had been bluffing. It was more promiscuous than it had professed. It *was* willing to let Continental become its alliance partner without merging, which is exactly what Kellner originally wanted. Sure, Tilton preferred a full merger. But despite his rather strong hand, he knew he didn't hold all the alliance cards. If he continued to prevent Continental from joining Star, Continental might indeed resign itself to a future as a second-class SkyTeam member. Or, Tilton worried, it might turn to American, British Airways and their oneworld alliance. And he was right to worry. That Wednesday, British Airways admitted it had been speaking with Continental.

But by the time that news emerged, Kellner had already, during the previous 24 hours, all but dropped oneworld as an option. Because on Tuesday, just one day after Tilton's email, the two airlines, showing no bitterness about the last-minute breakup at the altar, were talking again. This time they were talking about how Continental would transition away from Delta and SkyTeam to Star, and how Continental, United, Air Canada and Lufthansa would collaborate on a transatlantic joint venture.

Everyone involved in the talks knew a deal would emerge—there was just too much to gain and too little to lose. But the details took nearly two months to negotiate. On June 19, the two airlines went public with their announcement: "Continental Airlines and United Airlines today announced a framework agreement to cooperate extensively, linking their networks and services worldwide to the benefit of customers and creating revenue opportunities and cost savings and other efficiencies. In addition, Continental plans to join United in the Star Alliance, the most comprehensive airline alliance in the world."

Switching alliances—unwinding relationships, technological ones especially but also legal and personal ones, with a dozen airlines, and forging new ones with two dozen others—took more than a year. Until the final cutover on Oct. 27, 2009,

Continental continued to work with Delta and other SkyTeam members with little sign of bitterness. Larry Kellner remembered Richard Anderson acting "incredibly personable and gracious" during the transition. "And I think the key that makes the industry work," Kellner said, "is that, you know, while we're all fierce competitors, we also all sat on the ATA board together lobbying the government on terrible issues after 9/11. And so half the time we were unified, and half the time we were trying to kill each other."

So at the start of 2009, a new alignment of America's airline sector was taking shape. Delta and Northwest were now one airline. United and Continental were moving toward an overseas joint venture, not to mention membership in the same alliance. And American, for its part, had reapplied for antitrust immunity to coordinate transatlantic fares and schedules with British Airways. US Airways, the other remaining Big Six legacy carrier, remained eager to merge but simply couldn't find a willing partner after its talks with United—with whom it remained a Star Alliance partner, albeit the sort of second-class citizen Continental didn't want to become in SkyTeam—fell apart. Then there were the mostly shorthaul players, including three big LCCs—Southwest, JetBlue and AirTran—and some smaller players like Frontier, Virgin America, Spirit, Allegiant and Hawaiian. And then there was Alaska Airlines.

Despite its name, Alaska Airlines was not based in Alaska. Its headquarter city and chief hub was Seattle, although it certainly did have a large and profitable business flying people to, from and within the state of Alaska. It also had a big presence up and down the west coast, including the giant California market and even into Mexico. It was not exactly a low-cost carrier: It offered a business class cabin and touted good service, not just low fares. And importantly, it readily partnered with other airlines. All that talk about relationships outside marriage? This airline was downright polygamous. Alaska shared flight codes to boost sales of two-carrier itineraries, and it allowed its own passengers to accumulate and redeem—"earn and burn," as airlines call it—Alaska Airlines frequent flier miles on numerous other airlines. And it allowed those airlines' passengers to earn and burn their own miles on Alaska. This was not a cheap strategy: Alaska had to buy more miles from other airlines to award to their passengers than it sold to those airlines (because more of their passengers flew Alaska, but wanted to accrue miles within other airlines' loyalty plans, than vice-versa). And it had to buy more airline tickets for its customers on other airlines than it sold to those airlines, because its own customers wanted to redeem their miles to fly other airlines to distant places around the world, where Alaska didn't fly, more often than those other airlines' customers wanted to redeem their miles to fly Alaska. No, not a cheap strategy. But a winning strategy, demonstrated by the carrier's excellent reputation with travelers and a long history of financial success, never mind that it competed head to head against Southwest on many routes.

As it happened, two of Alaska's partners were Delta and Northwest. And almost immediately after the merger, Alaska and Delta updated and expanded their partnership to include more benefits for their mutual customers. A Delta SkyMiles "Medallion" (elite) passenger traveling from Minneapolis to Sacramento via Seattle, for example, using one flight operated by Delta and the other by Alaska, could now get her benefits—including upgrades, when seats were available—on both airlines.

This was no small matter for Delta, which, for all its new post-merger network heft, didn't have a west coast hub. And not having a west coast hub presented problems for its Asian franchise—Pacific Rim cities like Los Angeles, San Francisco and Seattle, after all, had deep economic and cultural links to Asia. Delta would soon realize it had other Asia shortcomings too. But for now, its beefed-up partnership with Alaska enabled the launch of new west coast international flights, including Seattle-Beijing and even Los Angeles-São Paulo. The tightened relationship also represented another instance of U.S. airlines working with each other rather than only against each other.

And U.S. airlines could use any help they could get. For at the start of 2009, their home economy was disintegrating. Rapid if controversial actions by Congress, the Federal Reserve, President Bush and the new president—President Obama—helped avert utter catastrophe by mobilizing the federal government to act as a lender and spender of last resort. But the situation was nonetheless bleak. Badly undercapitalized banks weren't lending. Families across the country suddenly owed more money for their homes than those homes were worth. Everywhere, small businesses were closing. State and local governments saw their tax bases collapse. And unemployment reached levels not seen in many years.

It was yet another frightening start to yet another year. The decade that had already brought 9/11, the Iraq War, SARS and a massive fuel spike now brought a monumental economic collapse.

When the industry reported final figures for 2008, the picture was as grim as it was clear. America's airlines had lost another $9.5 billion, excluding special accounting items. After small operating profits in 2006 and 2007, red ink was back, and in a big way. Carriers cut capacity 2 percent in 2008, but even while they were flying less, their expenses spiked 15 percent, driven by the big surge in fuel prices during the first half of the year—oil averaged an even $100 for the full year. Revenues, by contrast, grew just 7 percent. Airlines, in other words, managed to pass along only some of the fuel bill to their customers. U.S. airline employment shrank again too, by another 1 percent. As what's now called Airlines for America, the industry's trade association, put it at the time: "The U.S. airline industry continues to be confronted by a systemic inability to cover its cost of investor capital or, for that matter, to exceed break-even profitability on a sustainable basis."

Would 2009 be another year of misery? The year's opening months weren't encouraging. Revenues were falling even more dramatically than most airlines had predicted. At the same time, because of capacity cuts, non-fuel cost pressures grew, because airlines were becoming less efficient: Just as Southwest had long ago invented the low-cost model by flying the same planes more, and by getting the same number of employees to take care of more customers, now planes and people were more often sitting idle, serving fewer customers. "Fixed costs" like aircraft leases were the same each month, even if the planes were flying less. Planning became more difficult too: Travelers began booking tickets later than usual, creating more uncertainty when forecasting future revenues. It was classic deflation: Airfares were now falling, encouraging cash-strapped travelers to wait before buying. Airlines like Delta that still had pension obligations saw the assets in their pension funds plummet as stock markets tumbled. Fuel hedges, once a blessing, were now a curse in more ways than one. Not only did they obligate airlines to pay more for fuel than they would have paid had they never signed the hedge contracts. They also required airlines to set aside enormous cash reserves as collateral to guarantee they could settle these wrong-way bets.

Nor could airlines take much advantage of falling fuel prices to at least lock in the newly low prices for future needs. That's because the "futures curve," which the market uses to price derivative contracts, showed oil rising again in coming months. So the market was betting oil would reverse course and rise again, meaning banks had little desire to let airlines lock in low prices for future needs.

How cursed could one industry be? Airlines' greatest dream (falling fuel prices) had finally come true, and yet this dream-come-true was causing almost as much misery as it was eliminating.

So even as revenues were plunging, costs weren't dropping in tandem to nearly the degree that might have been expected. There was no rainbow in sight. At the same time, airlines were immensely frustrated that a giant $787 billion federal stimulus, signed into law by President Obama in February, featured virtually nothing for airlines, never mind their role in facilitating commerce and trade. Of the $787 billion, fully 27 percent took the form of tax cuts—of which not a penny went to airlines, which had already considered themselves more overtaxed than the rest of America. Worse yet, Obama—responding to public outcry over corporate and public money spent on lavish events while so many ordinary people were suffering—was even urging companies and governments to cancel meetings and conventions. But the cancellations themselves, of course, were causing more ordinary people to suffer, because the people who would have been taking care of the alleged "fat cats" were none other than people like pilots, flight attendants and airport staff, not to mention countless hotel, rental car and other travel industry workers, who were being furloughed. Congress, meanwhile, was attacking airline alliances and the outsourcing of maintenance tasks to workers overseas.

So the last thing airlines needed was an accident. But on Jan. 15, US Airways flight 1549, an Airbus 320, had just taken off from New York LaGuardia when it lost power in not one but both of its engines. The crew, led by Captain Chesley Sullenberger, a former air force pilot, and First Officer Jeffrey Skiles, had no way of getting back to the airport—or any airport. "We're going to be in the Hudson," Sullenberger told air traffic controllers. Successful emergency water landings for commercial airliners are almost unheard of. But there, in the heart of the world's media capital, for all to see, the plan worked. Flight attendants Donna Dent, Doreen Welsh and Sheila Dail orchestrated the evacuation. Rescue crews quickly arrived. "Sully," as the soon-to-be celebrity would come to be known to all of America, didn't leave the slowly sinking aircraft until all passengers and all other members of his crew were safely aboard lifeboats. Everyone survived. The media called it a "miracle on the Hudson."

Colgan Air flight 3407, a Bombardier Q400 turboprop flying on Feb. 12 as a "Continental Connection" flight from Newark to Buffalo, ended more tragically. All 49 people on board plus one on the ground died. The captain, Marvin Renslow, seemed to have made a basic error: pulling back on the "stick" rather than pushing it forward when the plane, flying in bad winter weather, began to stall. The idea that pilots of a stalling plane should attempt to dive, rather than climb, to regain airspeed is counterintuitive to non-pilots but fundamental in the cockpit. Both he and his first officer, meanwhile, might have been fatigued; she, Rebecca Shaw, had commuted to work all the way from her parents' home in Seattle, where she and her husband lived, seemingly partly because they couldn't afford more on a sub-$20,000 regional airline co-pilot salary. In addition to the human toll, the disaster would have a costly legacy for U.S. airlines, which would face strict new rules regarding pilot rest and the amount of experience required of pilots before they could carry passengers.

Then on June 1, 228 people aboard an Airbus 330 en route from Rio de Janeiro to Paris died when the plane crashed off the coast of Brazil. The incident might have seemed to have nothing in common with the Colgan crash—in this case, an intercontinental widebody jet, not a small turboprop, had crashed in a different hemisphere—except that in the most important way of all, it had everything in common: Investigators blamed the accident partly on the fact that the pilots didn't recognize that the plane, flying in bad weather, had begun to stall. So they didn't push forward on the stick to dive, in an attempt to regain airspeed. The operator of the plane: Delta's joint venture partner Air France.

That marked the start of a horrible month. June was rock bottom for airlines. Not because Michael Jackson died, nor even because General Motors filed for bankruptcy, although those two things happened that month. And not, even more relevantly than the GM bankruptcy, because oil prices—was there no justice in the world?—were rising again: A barrel that had cost just $42 in January now cost $70. No, the real cause of airline dismay in June 2009 was demand. Not only was the economy still a mess. But starting in April, an influenza epidemic—the H1N1 virus, as all the world would come to know it—appeared, devastating air travel at first to Mexico and then to northeast Asia. In May, Mexican carriers had seen their traffic fall almost 40 percent. Now in June, Asian carriers lost 15 percent of their traffic. And U.S. carriers with lots of Mexican and Asian routes shared in the suffering.

Delta was no stranger to the despondency of early 2009. For all of 2008, it endured more than $500 million in losses, excluding one-time accounting items but including figures for Northwest. Passenger revenues fell 1 percent. Cargo revenues fell fully

24 percent: Northwest's 14 cargo-only 747s, fuel guzzlers assigned to carry freight in a world that was no longer shipping as much freight, were now a liability, not an asset. At the start of 2009, a massive $1.1 billion of Delta's cash—18 percent of its total liquidity, i.e., cash and cash equivalents—was set aside as fuel hedge collateral. As it happened, Delta had more of its fuel hedged than most airlines—Southwest, with even more, was the only notable exception—and now, remember, being heavily hedged was a bad thing. As bad as a half-billion-dollar annual loss had seemed, that was downright tame compared to $693 million *during one quarter,* which is exactly how much Delta lost in just the first quarter of 2009. Passenger revenues sank another 18 percent. Management grounded all those dedicated 747 freighters, raised bag fees, offered more early retirement incentives to reduce headcount and—in a big strategic reversal—cut even international capacity as well as domestic.

London, with its ravaged financial sector, was suddenly a weak market. So Delta abandoned the Seattle-London route. Travel demand to India had dropped after November 2008, when a major terrorist attack killed 166 people in Mumbai, including several at the Taj Mahal hotel, where Delta's crews would sometimes stay. Days later, Israel invaded the Gaza Strip, causing bookings for Delta's Tel Aviv flights to plummet. Chasing oil money in markets like Dubai and Moscow had worked well when oil money was pouring into these places. But the inflows had stopped. At home, demand in Northwest's Detroit stronghold dropped in tandem with the city's terrible economic predicament, symbolized by the travails of the Big Three auto companies. And Delta's New York flights, especially the "shuttle" markets to Washington and Boston, felt the impact of the finance sector's problems. The long-marginal Cincinnati hub, which relied on corporate traffic, was particularly weak. Business class demand was bad everywhere. The CEO of Walmart, whose employees rarely flew business class to begin with, told the interviewer Charlie Rose company travelers could no longer even automatically use the airport closest to the company's headquarters in Bentonville, Ark. If the fare was much cheaper at Tulsa, a two-hour drive away, they had to fly from there. Said Ed Bastian during Delta's first-quarter earnings call: "We're in the worst global recession of this generation, and the revenue environment remains weak and uncertain."

And with the recession spreading globally and businesses slashing their travel budgets, suddenly it was better to have more exposure to the domestic routes and leisure routes that had long been so toxic for legacy airlines—this after Delta had just spent three years internationalizing and courting business travelers. US Airways, with its limited international exposure—one of the reasons it tried to buy Delta was to address this weakness—was now the best positioned among what, after the Delta-Northwest merger, had become the Big Five legacy carriers. And LCCs, in a flashback to the first few years of the decade, were cruising again as cash-strapped travelers looked for value, even if that meant foregoing frills. And with jet fuel cheaper in 2009 than it had been in 2008, LCCs' non-fuel cost advantages—their more productive workforces and so forth—once again "mattered" more and gave them huge overall cost advantages. These cost advantages, remember, had somewhat evaporated when fuel costs, a cost item where LCCs have no inherent advantage over legacy airlines, had become such a big percentage of overall costs for all airlines, low-cost and legacy alike. Indeed, America's LCCs would go on to have an excellent 2009, outperforming the Big Five by a wide margin. Southwest, which endured its first quarterly loss in more than two decades in the January-to-March period, then recovered and earned a full-year operating margin of 5 percent. AirTran, which barely survived 2008, earned 8 percent. JetBlue? Nine percent.

But for Delta, the second quarter, which included the awful month of June, once again brought red ink—a $199 million net loss, excluding special items. Sensibly enough, Delta—recognizing the awful demand environment—had cut supply 7 percent. But total revenue declined an unfathomable 23 percent. At the beginning of the year, Ed Bastian based his cautious optimism on the fact that, with fuel prices and seat supply both falling, revenues would have to fall by an unprecedentedly steep amount for Delta to lose money. Well, guess what? Revenues were now falling like never before. Bastian's team estimated the H1N1 epidemic alone had cost Delta between $125 million and $150 million during the second quarter, most of that lost in Asia, a region where—remember—it wouldn't have had much exposure if not for its recent merger. Delta's wrong-way fuel hedges, for their part, contributed $390 million in losses.

On June 11, Richard Anderson and Ed Bastian addressed employees with a memo titled, "Global Recession and Rising Oil Prices Forcing Additional Changes to Our Business." It read:

> *We are all seeing negative impacts from the global recession and rising oil prices not only in the news, but also in our communities and personal finances. Clearly, the airline industry is not immune. Industry passenger revenues have declined nearly 20 percent in the first four months of the year compared to the same period in 2008. That trend is expected to continue in the near term. On top of this, cost pressures from rising jet fuel prices—up more than 20 percent since the start of the year—coupled with softer travel demand due to the spread of the H1N1 virus, have created a difficult business environment.*
>
> *These forces that are affecting the industry are creating significant headwinds for Delta. Declining revenues will overtake the more than $6 billion in total benefits we expected this year from lower year-over-year fuel prices, merger synergies and capacity reductions.*
>
> *This morning, at an investor conference in New York, we will announce additional steps to align our capacity with market demand, preserve liquidity and ensure Delta's long-term success. This plan includes reducing our system capacity by 10 percent compared to 2008. Capacity reductions will begin in September. In this environment, our merger*

makes more sense than ever and we will continue to accelerate our integration, as it gives us a competitive advantage and strengthens our financial foundation. We also will maintain tight controls on our costs and capital spending.

Customer demand for international travel has fallen significantly. Accordingly, we plan to reduce our international capacity by an additional 5 percent from what we announced in March, for a 15 percent total reduction in international capacity. This fall's capacity reductions will target routes that have experienced losses in the current economic climate and with higher fuel prices, including:

- *Suspending nonstop service from Atlanta to Seoul and Shanghai and instead routing customers for these flights over Detroit or Tokyo, or on nonstop SkyTeam partner flights.*
- *Suspending nonstop flights from Cincinnati to Frankfurt and London-Gatwick. Cincinnati customers will still be able to reach these and many other international destinations via our other European gateways.*
- *Suspending nonstop service between New York JFK and Edinburgh.*
- *Reducing weekly frequencies connecting Atlanta and Detroit to Mexico City and postponing some previously planned seasonal service between non-hub cities and Mexican beach destinations due to the impact of the H1N1 virus on customers' travel plans.*

In keeping with our long-term business plan, we continue to grow the global footprint that is a cornerstone of our successful strategy. While we must reduce capacity this year, our international capacity this fall will still be more than 20 percent larger than it was before our global expansion began in 2005, and we are adding more than 20 new markets to our international network in 2009, including:

- *Los Angeles-Sydney*
- *Salt Lake City-Tokyo*
- *Detroit-Shanghai*
- *Atlanta-Johannesburg*

By leveraging the unique strengths of our network, hub structure and alliances, we continue to provide the most travel options for our customers.

The additional capacity reductions mean we again must reassess staffing needs. While the challenges of the current environment preclude us from making guarantees, our goal remains to avoid any involuntary furloughs of frontline employees.

We will not allow the economy to negatively affect our merger integration—in fact, the current environment gives additional urgency to accelerate our efforts. You will see us move more quickly to rebrand and consolidate facilities, repaint aircraft and ramp up our frontline training activities.

These are tough times and people often ask what they can do to contribute. Your most important contribution is to stay focused on doing your job well. We must all continue to deliver excellent customer service, run a strong operation and execute our Flight Plan. The entire industry is dealing with a difficult economy and rising fuel prices, but no one else has the opportunities and the people to match Delta in successfully navigating this crisis. Do what you do well, and we have no doubt that we will win.

Thank you for the incredible work you do for our customers every day. Together, we are building a stronger Delta.

Was this yet another example of the airline business being an exercise in futility, a money-losing endeavor from the get-go, a hopeless cause?

Actually, no.

Someone watching very closely could recognize that buried beneath the red ink of early 2009 were foundations of strength that hadn't been present during earlier crises. This time really *was* different for U.S. airlines, including the Big Five. And as 2009 moved from summer to autumn, and from autumn to winter, the encouraging changes became ever more clear for all to see.

For starters, the oil super-spike from 2002 through mid-2008 really had been broken, even if the force that broke it was an economy so bad that demand for oil had plummeted. True, per-barrel oil prices did begin an uncomfortable ascent in the early months of 2009. But after reaching $70 in May, they stayed between $70 and $80 for the rest of the year. And $70 to $80 was child's play for airlines that now had business models premised on $100-plus oil. And that wasn't all. Remember how airlines had refined their thinking to recognize that high oil prices *per se* weren't as much of a problem as oil price volatility, because of how volatility made planning so difficult? Well now the marked *lack* of price volatility during these six months made planning easier. And oil refining spreads, which determine actual jet fuel prices, had dropped too.

Legacy hedges had prevented carriers from enjoying the big drop in fuel prices that accompanied the economic crisis. But these hedges were wearing off. So were the large cash collateral postings required when current prices were far below hedged prices. Delta's hedges, in fact, were in the money again by the third quarter of 2009.

Hedge headaches were at least as bad for overseas rivals, and this time, the U.S. dollar was strengthening, forcing many foreign carriers to pay more than they otherwise would for their fuel—the currency movements that had long cushioned them from the worst of the oil spike were now working against them. Many began retreating from U.S. routes. Emirates even pulled its jumbo Airbus 380s out of New

York. These capacity cuts—reduced competition, in other words—helped U.S. airlines that flew abroad. European airlines like Air France/KLM, Lufthansa and British Airways, with much greater exposure to longhaul, cargo and premium demand, benefited from that exposure when longhaul, cargo and premium markets boomed in 2006 and 2007. Now these were the most toxic markets.

For all the additional losses that U.S. airlines incurred during the first half of 2009, most managed to avoid a cash crunch. Carriers did, to be sure, scramble for capital like squirrels collecting nuts for the winter. And they were getting it. The cost of this capital, to be sure, wasn't cheap. In one transaction, Delta paid investors a yield that exceeded 9 percent, a giant spread relative to what investors could get lending money to the U.S. government—or relative, for that matter, to the interest rates at which banks had, just a few years earlier, had been lending money to home-buying consumers with the shakiest of financial credentials. But that 9 percent yield transaction was in September 2009, one year after Lehman's collapse, and it enabled Delta to stay highly liquid during an uncertain time. Delta also asked for—and got—more financing from American Express. And it was able to refinance expensive Northwest debt by using Asian route rights and airport slots as collateral. Why were investors so willing to buy airline debt during what seemed like another of the industry's darkest hours? Maybe they recognized the foundations of strength below the surface. Maybe they thought things had gotten so bad that they could only get better. Maybe it was simply the airline capital paradox invoking itself again: For airlines, it's easy to lose money but also easy to raise money.

All the while, distribution costs continued their long trajectory downward. Airline websites were getting better by the year, and American's CEO Gerard Arpey boldly suggested someday, third-party distributors should pay airlines to access their content, not the other way around. Richard Anderson agreed.

Already in March, there were some economic rays of sunlight peaking through the clouds. That's when the stock market started rising again—what would later be remembered as the beginning of one of the greatest multi-year bull markets in history—taking airline stocks along for the ride. Cheaper gasoline relieved the strain on U.S. households. Interest rates were low, for those who could get a loan, anyway—not everyone was as fortunate as airlines. And the federal stimulus, while adding more debt to an already heavily indebted national balance sheet, and while not helping the airline industry much directly, succeeded in cushioning the fall in aggregate demand and total output.

And the LCC threat? Would this be another replay of the early 2000s, when Southwest, AirTran and JetBlue ran roughshod over legacy carriers, including Delta? No. It would not.

Most importantly, the LCCs, although their earnings indeed surged during 2009, were just like the legacy carriers in their capacity restraint. During the year, Southwest actually shrank its capacity 5 percent. AirTran shrank 2 percent. JetBlue grew, but just barely: 0.4 percent. Their renewed success was based on two main factors: the fall in oil prices and the fact that many consumers and businesses were "trading down," that is, accepting fewer frills and foregoing benefits like frequent flier miles, all to save money. But without growth to create labor and fleet efficiencies—growth was the LCC equivalent of what McDonald's called its "secret sauce"—their non-fuel unit costs were rising sharply: up 7 percent for Southwest, up 5 percent for AirTran and up 9 percent for JetBlue. What's more, LCCs were increasingly beating up not only on legacy airlines but on each other, best exemplified by bloody battles between Southwest and AirTran in Baltimore, Milwaukee and Orlando. Meanwhile, they were also going rather easy on Delta, notwithstanding Southwest's entry to Minneapolis and New York LaGuardia. Even more indicative of the trend and more helpful for Delta: AirTran's steady push away from Atlanta. In 2000, 91 percent of its capacity touched Atlanta. Now the figure was less than 50 percent, the consequence of focusing growth on those cities where it was battling Southwest: Baltimore, Milwaukee and Orlando. With Glen Hauenstein's network and pricing departments breathing down its neck, AirTran remarkably felt more comfortable picking fights against the great Southwest than against Delta.

And that was logical. Sure, AirTran still claimed to have a 47 percent cost advantage versus Delta. But it also had a huge revenue disadvantage, a disadvantage that was only growing as Delta increasingly re-established respect among Atlanta business travelers. AirTran CEO Bob Fornaro, Joe Leonard's successor, saw the US Airways takeover attempt as the turning point, when Atlanta's businesses and residents rallied around Delta and did their best to support it and fly it. The ensuing years weren't kind to AirTran, which, after nearly running out of money in 2008, had to sell or defer the deliveries of no fewer than 50 planes from its original fleet plan, even after fortuitously losing the battle to buy Midwest just before the financial crisis, a transaction which, in retrospect, might have bankrupted it. But for all its recent troubles, AirTran still claimed a 4 percent cost advantage over even Southwest. Even among the low-cost carriers, AirTran was as low-cost as they came.

Not being the lowest-cost producer anymore was reason enough for Southwest to worry. But it wasn't the only reason, even as Southwest touted its 37th consecutive year of profits, an unmatched achievement in the airline business. One giant problem: Its hedge shield, so instrumental in keeping its traditional business model alive during the half decade that followed 9/11, was now gone. It was now paying roughly the same price for fuel as everyone else. In fact, when oil made its way back up to the $70 range in the second half of 2009, this was a bigger adjustment for Southwest than it was for others, because it hadn't fundamentally adjusted its business—by, for example, furloughing employees and cutting the wages and benefits of those who remained—in the way others had. Southwest had, though, cut capacity. It had stopped hiring. It searched for new revenues too—low costs were no longer enough—and that meant signing corporate contracts, paying for third-party distribution to travel agencies and even levying fees, if not for most bags then at least for other extras. It tried partnering with other airlines such as Canada's WestJet, but Southwest's simple IT systems proved woefully inadequate. And it had outsized exposure to Sun Belt states like California, Arizona, Nevada, Florida and others that had been hit especially hard by the housing meltdown.

Round after round of labor cuts throughout the industry, all while Southwest watched from under its hedge umbrella, meant its pilots now earned higher wages than any of their industry peers. They still tended to work more productive schedules, and they were still, on average, less senior than their legacy counterparts. But the cost gap was shrinking. So Southwest, eager to shrink headcount now that its capacity was contracting, felt compelled to offer early-retirement incentives. In August, it tried to consolidate its position against United in Denver by buying bankrupt Frontier Airlines, which happened to fly to Atlanta too, albeit with just a few daily flights from Denver. But the prize slipped away, because Southwest made its bid contingent on pilot unions from both carriers reaching an agreement on seniority integration, which—unlike the Delta and Northwest pilots—they weren't able to do. Southwest's pilots wanted to send the Frontier pilots to the back of the seniority line, while Frontier pilots wanted their tenure to count for something. In the end, Frontier's creditors chose a buyout offer from Republic, a small-jet regional operator.

So for January through March, Southwest had a losing quarter—its first in two decades. And although it still had enough strengths, efficiencies and market power to recover solidly later in the year, its vulnerabilities were clear enough. It was also, happily for Delta, limiting major offensives to United's Denver hub—that was about the only place it grew substantially in 2009. And it would later attack American's St. Louis hub and pick a fight with JetBlue in Boston.

JetBlue itself was a very different carrier in 2009 than it was in, say, 2003. David Neeleman was now off in Brazil starting another airline called Azul—"blue" in Portuguese. JetBlue was busy attacking American in the Caribbean and pursuing higher-cost, revenue-chasing strategies like partnerships with Ireland's Aer Lingus and others. In late 2007, in need of new capital, it had sold a 19 percent stake in itself to Lufthansa, which wanted a New York shorthaul presence because its U.S. Star Alliance partners United and US Airways didn't have much of one. But the Star Alliance was now welcoming Continental, complete with its robust Newark hub. So the commercial relationship between Lufthansa and JetBlue became less necessary from Lufthansa's standpoint, and it never really evolved. In any case, JetBlue's growth focus, to Delta's delight, was no longer New York. Instead, JetBlue was growing in Boston, where Delta had already dramatically cut its seat count by more than 30 percent since just before it filed for bankruptcy in 2005. In particular, it had quit some of the price-sensitive Florida routes that interested JetBlue.

Delta and the LCCs, meanwhile, weren't the only ones doing the downsizing. During the final quarter of 2009, even as revenue pressures started to ease, United's capacity was down 11 percent compared to the same quarter a year earlier. American and Continental had each cut 8 percent, US Airways 5 percent and Alaska 10 percent. Delta, for its part, was 4 percent smaller, with a huge 20 percent reduction in transatlantic flying offset somewhat by growth to Latin America and more modest downsizing at home. Together, this willingness to contract supply despite the negative unit-cost implications—the inefficiencies as planes and people sat idle at airports more minutes during the day—created one of the three critical pillars to the industry's underlying health.

A second pillar was consolidation, led by the giant Delta-Northwest merger but also the cooperation between United and Continental, which was deeper than the cooperation Continental had with Delta and Northwest before those two merged.

The third pillar? Charging extra for just about everything other than safe transportation. Ancillary revenues, led by bag fees, were bringing the industry hundreds of millions of dollars in new revenue. Sure, airlines often had to lower base fares a bit when they implemented new fees. And there were some associated costs, including the burden bag fees placed on operational performance once everyone started bringing all their worldly possessions aboard flights to avoid fees. Still, overall, operational performance actually improved—all the capacity cuts had already meant fewer planes flying around and less congestion at airports. And even if the bag fees caused some headaches "above wing"—i.e., during boarding—down below, now there were fewer bags to load into aircraft bellies. That meant fewer bag handlers and fewer on-the-job injuries, further reducing costs. The public wasn't thrilled. But airlines tried to redirect anger away from themselves and toward heavy-packing fellow passengers: Why, they said, should you have to subsidize someone else's bags? That, they explained, is what happens to light packers when checked bags are included in everyone's fares. In the end, fees for bags and preferred seats and booking over the phone and buying food and pillows and blankets on board were home runs for airlines. They were, moreover, a more stable revenue source than fares, because the fees were mostly immune from price wars. So now if base fares dropped by a certain percentage, the total amount collected from a given passenger didn't decline by nearly as much.

So all airlines, to one degree or another, were building important defenses against the inevitable future shocks that would surely come. But no airline was building stronger defenses than Delta. And none was performing as well.

Yes, Delta lost money—a lot of money—during the dismal first half of 2009. But its operating losses were less than those of its Big Five rivals. The relative outperformance was even more pronounced in the second quarter, when Delta actually eked out a small operating profit, excluding special items, never mind the H1N1 epidemic. Nor does this tell the whole story. Masking formidable strengths were those wrong-way fuel hedges, to which Delta had greater exposure than most of its competitors. In the second quarter alone, these cost Delta a massive $390 million, without which Delta would have earned a $191 million net profit. And again, that was during one of the worst quarters for demand in airline history. Bad news was good news, because day by day, those underwater hedges were wearing off, meaning Delta's underlying strength would eventually enable it to prosper.

No wonder Delta was smiling in a rainstorm. Its memories of 2002 through 2005 were still vivid: the labor cost problems, the network problems, the LCC problems.... This time there was none of that—just some ill-timed derivative contracts that would work themselves out and a macroeconomic demand problem that would surely ease as the economy recovered. And this time, Delta had a powerful merger from which to mine many synergies, a merger that was—as was becoming increasingly clear—working better than almost anyone had expected.

Delta's newly enlarged network was winning it a greater share of corporate contracts, just as it had envisioned. Revenue and cost synergies were exceeding targets. IT systems integration, a perennial time bomb for airline mergers, was proceeding with exceptional smoothness. Managers at all levels were executing the unsung details of unifying two different sets of service standards into one, a task that included everything from deciding which soft drinks to serve (this was actually an easy one—Atlanta-based Coca-Cola, of course!—although Delta also asked for and received a bid from Northwest's supplier, PepsiCo) to which bags to use for collecting inflight trash.

Perhaps most remarkably, the new Delta was starting to feel like the good old Delta, the pre-1990s Delta that longtime employees remembered for its amicable management-labor relations. The company was now paying bonuses to front-line workers when the company met operational performance goals—in 2008 alone, it distributed more than $65 million this way. Put another way, incentives were aligned: When the company did well, so did its workers. One of Delta's first moves after closing the merger was to change the numbers on everyone's employer identification badges so that nobody would know if you had come from Delta or Northwest. The idea: Nobody should care. This was all one team. The company built a new employee dining hall at its Atlanta headquarters. It opened a medical clinic for employees, no small matter in a country where health care costs were skyrocketing. At a time when overseas outsourcing angered many Americans, Delta brought call center jobs back to the U.S. from India. In April, Delta gave nearly 70,000 of its employees two free airline tickets—confirmed, not standby—to anywhere the airline flew. "The free tickets," Delta said, "are in recognition of how hard employees have worked during the past six months to consolidate Delta and Northwest into the world's largest airline."

During those six months, frontline employees also received wage increases and 15 percent of the company's stock. Lee Moak and the pilots, for their part, delivered on their promise to integrate seniority lists within a mere 90 days after the two companies became one, an unprecedented feat. The first mixed Delta-Northwest crew flew together, in March 2009, less than five months after the merger. Other work groups rejected unionization—the company's meteorologists, unionized at Northwest but not Delta, were an early example. Mechanics, also non-union, quickly agreed to a seniority integration list of their own. Flight attendants, outfitted in stylish new uniforms, did the same. There were still some unresolved questions about whether those flight attendants and some other groups would elect to join unions when it came time to hold their own elections. But throughout 2009, the rising morale at Delta was palpable. And it was in stark contrast to the bickering at some other airlines, most notably American, which was stunned to learn its pilot union, the Allied Pilots Association, was actually lobbying against its proposed joint venture with British Airways.

The old Delta was showing its smiling face again, in employee break rooms and cockpits and hangars and aircraft cabins everywhere. But when it came to dealing with certain other stakeholders, its Northwest-style toughness dominated. Ruthless capacity moves and pricing against LCC invaders continued. Anderson and his team engaged in public spats with the American Society of Travel Agents, the International Association of Machinists and three regional airlines whose 50-seat jets had fallen out of favor. Management negotiated its way out of a 1992 deal that obligated Northwest to keep its headquarters in the Minneapolis area. Critically, Delta reached an extended lease deal with Atlanta's airport, where it was paying just $5 per passenger—some other large airports charged double or triple that.

All the while, ancillary charges continued expanding—checked bags on some international flights, for example, now carried fees. With a flexible, non-union workforce, Delta Tech Ops, the airline's maintenance unit, was thriving, winning new contracts from carriers like Hawaiian Airlines, South America's LAN and EVA Air of Taiwan. Like Delta Global Services, a ground handling business, Tech Ops earned big profits.

Back at the core passenger airline, 346 planes were outfitted with inflight Wi-Fi by the end of 2009. Passengers traveling from some airports could now use their mobile phones to check in for their flights and retrieve their boarding passes. And Delta actively engaged with new social media platforms like Facebook and Twitter to communicate with customers, particularly young ones.

America's talented young millennials, as the generation had come to be known, weren't only impressed with Delta's adoption of new technology. They were also impressed with Delta's corporate social responsibility. The airline partnered with the American Red Cross to provide relief after a devastating earthquake in Haiti (in early 2010). It remained actively involved with Habitat for Humanity and Earth Day environmental causes. It proudly boasted of a perfect 100 percent rating in the 2010 Corporate Equality Index, distinguishing the company as one of the country's best places to work for lesbian, gay, bisexual and transgender (LGBT) employees. Initiatives to promote breast cancer awareness included an inflight Melissa Etheridge concert, serving pink lemonade aboard flights and lighting up the New York JFK air traffic control tower pink.

But nothing captures the attention of many New Yorkers quite like baseball's Yankees and Mets. Delta not only continued sponsoring both but also opened hospitality suites at the newly opened Yankee Stadium and Citi Field. And it held a contest: Whichever of two players—Derek Jeter of the Yankees or David Wright of the Mets—had the highest batting average at the end of the season,

Delta would donate money to the charity of his choice. (Jeter won.) Delta's brand exposure certainly didn't suffer when the Yankees wound up winning the 2009 World Series.

AirTran, as it happened, struck a deal to sponsor the Atlanta Falcons that year—the NFL team in Delta's own hometown! But no matter: Delta was comfortably dominant in Atlanta. What it wanted was to win in New York, where it had to stand out among many airlines vying for supremacy. So it sponsored the Tribeca Film Festival too. And the New York City Wine & Food Festival. And so on.

But when it came to marketing, no weapon was more powerful than the SkyMiles frequent flier program, which now had 74 million members. It was, of course, the reason why American Express had on several occasions thrown Delta a financial life saver, perhaps even rescuing it from oblivion—Amex was as dependent on Delta's miles as Delta was on Amex's money. But Amex did exercise considerable influence over the program's rules and benefits—anything that devalued the miles would devalue its all-important mileage-granting credit cards. (Frequent fliers on internet chat sites had years earlier taken to deriding the program as "SkyPesos" for what they considered to be constant devaluations.) It was with Amex's consent, in 2009, that Delta introduced a new "diamond" Medallion status tier for the company's very best customers—those who flew more than 125,000 miles annually.

Delta also made it easier for all Medallion members—silver, gold, platinum and now diamond alike—to requalify the following year by allowing excess miles beyond the tier attained to "roll over" and count toward the next year's qualification requirements. So if someone flew 50,000 miles and qualified for gold, and then flew another 5,000 before Dec. 31, those last 5,000 miles would count as the first 5,000 the following year, rather than the year starting at zero, as had always been the case. (This wasn't pure altruism. Delta realized frequent fliers often had a perverse incentive to stop flying their favorite airline late in the year, after they had qualified for one tier but clearly wouldn't hit another—perhaps those 5,000 miles, "wasted" from a qualification standpoint with Delta, could have helped a very frequent flier attain status on another airline. Now there was a reason to keep flying Delta, because the excess miles would make qualification next year that much easier.)

Just after the merger, Delta's SkyMiles chief Jeff Robertson sat down with both Richard Anderson and Doug Steenland to scrutinize, line by line, the Delta and Northwest frequent flier plans—the best aspects of each would be kept in the merged program. Indeed, the involvement of the two CEOs themselves was testament to the importance of SkyMiles. Actually, there was even better testament to its importance. In November 2007, Robertson, speaking at an IATA conference in Athens—and revealing figures Delta would never again reveal publicly—said SkyMiles generated about $2 billion in annual revenue for Delta with just roughly $1.5 billion in costs. So SkyMiles was producing an astounding $500 million profit for a company that in 2007 earned a total net profit, excluding special accounting items, of $418 million. SkyMiles was the unsung hero of Delta.

Delta even awarded flight attendants bonuses for signing up new SkyMiles members in flight. Some members were in it just for the free tickets, once they collected enough miles. But frequent business travelers? They wanted Medallion status. Because Medallions got special treatment: first class upgrades, shorter security lines, priority handling in the boarding area, special call center numbers for faster service and so on. It's these elites that the Big Five were most eager to please, for a mere 5 percent of Delta's frequent fliers produced a quarter of its total passenger revenue. Delta once considered shrinking its domestic first class cabins, because many people sitting in those seats hadn't bought first class tickets; they were SkyMiles Medallions who had been upgraded. Removing some first class seats could enable Delta to add many more economy seats and sell more tickets. But after analyzing the possibility closely, Robertson determined doing so would have actually cost Delta $1 billion in annual revenue. Why? Because the possibility of getting upgraded was driving loyalty in the first place. It's why an Atlanta-based road warrior whose company booked him on Delta during the week took his family on Delta for weekend trips too, even if AirTran was a bit cheaper.

SkyMiles members as a whole, even averaging in those who weren't Medallions, were an incredible demograhic. The average member was a 37-year-old married home-owner with—remember—a household income of $96,500. When they booked tickets on Delta, SkyMiles members spent 28 percent more, on average, than non-members. And because they were so eager to earn free travel, Delta was able to sell about $1 billion worth of miles every year to everyone from American Express to hotel chains and rental car companies (which all had to buy the airline miles they awarded to their own customers) to even flower delivery companies, which—like so many other merchants, large and small alike—used miles to lure customers, who were addicted to those miles.

Together with Northwest, Delta's frequent flier plan now had greater scale and scope. Delta also had more negotiating leverage with its partners over how much they would have to pay for miles: If the idea of not being able to award Delta or Northwest miles, when both airlines were separate and smaller, had previously scared a hotel chain into paying the old price for miles, imagine how much scarier the idea was of not being able to offer miles on this merged global giant—and how much higher the new price was. Medallion status too became all the more attractive: Delta even used it to woo other airlines' customers in hotly contested markets.

Atlanta, of course, was not hotly contested, at least when it came to big-time corporate travelers. Delta owned the market. New York, however, was a different story. The world's second largest airline market in the world—only London is bigger—was nobody's fiefdom. It was a three-way combat zone involving Delta, American and Continental, and Delta was more determined than ever to win. And not, primarily, to win the New York area family traveling to Disney World—those were the old days. What Delta wanted now was the big-money corporate traveler flying around the globe.

Beginning in 2006, with Hauenstein's global transformation plan, Delta had become more relevant to New York's business travelers. Companies that signed contracts with Delta now had access to many new international destinations from JFK plus better schedules to the U.S. west coast. The merger helped too. While Northwest happened to have the weakest New York presence of the then-Big Six airlines, it did give Delta that ostensibly more rewarding frequent flier program to pitch, plus additional Asia connections via Detroit. Since 2006, Delta had also upgraded its premium services. It spent heavily to advertise itself throughout Manhattan while attaching its name to New York's cultural institutions and sports teams. It even created a new senior vice president position just to oversee New York—everything related to New York. In the meantime, operations were improving after 2008, when the FAA—responding to near-gridlock at JFK during the prior summer—re-imposed slot restrictions at the airport.

Nevertheless, Delta's New York business had two critical shortcomings. One was its old JFK terminal, inherited from Pan Am—"Worldport," a 1960s vision of the future. Although preservationists would later fight to save it because of its historical importance to global aviation, most people seemed to consider it ugly and inconvenient, more reminiscent of a dilapidated bus station than a global gateway. The second shortcoming was Delta's limited access to London Heathrow, the busiest overseas airport for U.S. business travelers. With the new U.S.-E.U. open skies agreement, Delta was at least able to squeeze itself in. But just barely: It got enough slots from its partner Air France/KLM to operate a mere two daily JFK-Heathrow round trips. American, for its part, operated five, and would together with British Airways operate 11 once their joint venture received regulatory approval. Virgin Atlantic, nearly half owned by Singapore Airlines, was the other big player in the market, with four round trips of its own, not to mention—like British Airways—another two daily Newark-Heathrow round trips. In 2009, with financial companies reeling, limited Heathrow exposure was a blessing. But everyone knew that situation wouldn't last. Once the economy recovered, Heathrow access would be instrumental to winning business in New York.

As Hauenstein and his team bent their minds around these two dilemmas, with no obvious solutions, an unrelated opportunity emerged, one that would make Delta a stronger player in New York not at global JFK but at shorthaul LaGuardia Airport. Corporate travelers welcomed Delta's international and transcontinental buildup at JFK. But when these same travelers flew domestically, they wanted to fly from LaGuardia, which was much closer than JFK to Manhattan. (Continental's Newark hub was reasonably convenient too—less so from most parts of the city than LaGuardia but more so than JFK.)

In the summer of 2009, Delta had a sizeable presence at LaGuardia. After the merger, in fact, it became the airport's No. 1 carrier, measured by the number of seats it offered. But it was far from a dominant No. 1. American was nearly as large.

US Airways had actually been No. 1 before the Delta-Northwest merger and was still a close No. 2. US Airways had a newer and nicer terminal too.

But US Airways was losing money at LaGuardia, partly because of its gleaming terminal, a hefty real estate obligation it had assumed during better times. Business travelers liked its shuttle service to Washington and Boston as well as its frequent flights to Charlotte, home to what was now America's largest bank: Bank of America. It also offered better service than Delta to small communities in upstate New York and New England. But US Airways was virtually absent at JFK and Newark. And its international presence overall was weak. As Doug Parker quickly learned after buying it, US Airways made much of its money in just two places: Charlotte, with many of the geographical and cost advantages of Atlanta although on a smaller scale, and Washington, D.C. At Reagan National Airport, just across the Potomac River from the epicenter of American political power, US Airways offered nearly 200 daily departures, accounting for nearly half the airport's total service. The yields were high, and so were barriers to entry—this airport, like LaGuardia, was slot controlled. Delta, meanwhile, had the same kinds of disadvantages at Reagan National that US Airways faced at LaGuardia.

So each airline had unwanted assets that could make the other stronger—US Airways' scraps at LaGuardia and Delta's at Reagan could help Delta conquer New York and US Airways further dominate Washington. But could they set aside their mutual hatred for each other, just a year and a half after Delta had bitterly and successfully fought off US Airways' hostile takeover bid? For inspiration, they might have looked to baseball's New York Mets, who play their games at a ballpark so close to LaGuardia that airplanes on final approach sometimes distract opposing teams, and their National League eastern division rivals, the Washington Nationals. Teams within the same division rarely trade players; better to share the mutual benefit with a team that's not in direct competition. But the prior baseball season, the two had nonetheless completed a trade—two players from the Nationals in exchange for one from the Mets—whom the teams believed would make both teams better.

Could a different sort of trade between New York and Washington make two *airlines* better? In August, Delta—never mind whatever lingering feelings it had about US Airways—agreed to send 42 of its Reagan National slot pairs, each good for one daily round trip, plus international flight rights to fly to Tokyo and São Paulo, to US Airways. And US Airways? It would send no fewer than 125 LaGuardia slot pairs to Delta. The two would also swap gates, meaning Delta would move into the more modern US Airways facilities at LaGuardia. And it was ready to invest $40 million to make those facilities even better.

The deal meant Delta could double its presence at LaGuardia, linking small communities to the north with small communities to the south—in other words, a LaGuardia connecting hub. It could also replace the 50-seat regional jets and even smaller turboprop planes US Airways was using with larger jets, thereby growing total seats the only way possible at an airport that was otherwise growth restricted due to slot controls. Now it could offer the world from JFK and the only nonstop flights to smaller shorthaul destinations from the airport corporate travelers preferred, LaGuardia, something no other airline—when competing for big-money corporate contracts—could promise. But one high hurdle remained: Even if the airlines considered the transaction just a slot swap—not so different from the baseball trade between the Mets and Nationals—it was more technically considered a purchase of slots, which wasn't permitted under current law. So the two airlines needed special regulatory permission, which wouldn't come easily.

New York, of course, wasn't the only market where Delta was making changes. At its struggling Cincinnati hub, it revamped its fare structure once again and cut more capacity—Cincinnati had become conspicuously less vital to Delta's network now that it controlled Northwest's Detroit hub, which, never mind the city's economic malaise, was a more profitable hub than Cincinnati. Conversely, Delta added markets from Salt Lake City, whose economy was faring relatively well during the recession thanks to a booming mining sector and residents moving in from high-priced California. Salt Lake City also happens to be roughly equidistant to Denver, Phoenix, Los Angeles, San Francisco, Portland and Seattle, making it a geographically well-placed transportation hub. In the old Northwest heartland, Republic Airways—yes, the same Republic that had snatched Frontier from under the nose of Southwest—came along and mercifully purchased Delta's share of Midwest Airlines. Delta didn't get nearly as much money as Northwest originally paid, but so be it: This was a welcome exit strategy, with Southwest and AirTran beating each other's brains out in Milwaukee and Midwest, with nowhere to go, caught in the middle as collateral damage. Fares from Minneapolis-St. Paul were under some pressure after Southwest showed up there on the Chicago and Denver routes. Still, the hub was a strong one, boosted by a relatively stable local economy led by companies like United Healthcare, Richard Anderson's former employer, and retailers like Target and Best Buy. It was also a well-placed gateway to the Great Plains, where booming agriculture prices lifted incomes throughout the 2000s. Nor was there much LCC competition on routes to places like Montana and the Dakotas. Now those places were cold, dark—and all Delta's.

International flying was certainly tough during the economic doldrums of 2009. But Delta, for all its early success at changing this fact, at least remained—for better or worse, and mostly for better at the moment—less exposed than some of its rivals to premium traffic. In Tokyo, its sizeable operation from Narita Airport to beach markets like Honolulu and Guam was doing well thanks to a strong yen—this made vacations particularly affordable for Japanese tourists. Latin American economies held up rather well during the crisis too. And just as importantly, Delta was following the advice of Johnny Mercer's classic 1944 song—accentuate the positive, eliminate the negative—by aggressively moving airplanes around in line with the shifting winds of supply and demand. If a route worked in summer but not in winter, it became a summer-only route. If it worked Friday but not Tuesday, it flew Friday but not Tuesday. That might sound logical enough. But few giant global airlines had ever achieved anything nearly as dynamic. Varying schedules by season and day of week, after all—even if it had some benefits—was costly and complex; American's CEO Gerard Arpey, remember, had (in 2006) scoffed at the idea that it was even advisable. In the meantime, Atlanta, the jewel of the crown and the top source of profits, continued to get new routes. In 2009, traffic at almost every major airport shrank, and Atlanta was not immune. But in 2008 Atlanta had still grown while the nation's second third, third and fourth busiest airports—Chicago O'Hare, Los Angeles and Dallas-Fort Worth—all shrank dramatically, by at least 5 percent. By reducing its presence in Washington, meanwhile, Delta was acting in line with a strategy to concentrate its ammunition at its major hubs, rather than fight losing battles as an underdog in former focus cities like Boston, Indianapolis and Orlando. These sizeable non-hub stations, along with the Cincinnati hub, took the brunt of Delta's capacity cutting.

A good network is a network with strong hubs, for sure. But just as importantly, a good network is a network supported by the right planes in the right places. And Salt Lake City, for one, became a stronger hub when Delta moved Northwest's Airbus 320s there. These were single-aisle planes capable of reaching all the way to the east coast, unlike Delta's MD-90s, which held roughly the same number of passengers. In Minneapolis, conversely, those same 320s offered more range than was necessary— from the center of the country, an MD-90 could reach almost anywhere. Aircraft cross-fleeting like that was one early way that the whole—as companies always say but don't often deliver when they merge—really was adding up to more than the sum of its parts.

But then there were parts Delta just didn't need. So it sold some 757s and ancient DC-9s. It put fuel-saving "winglets"—extensions at the ends of wings—on some of its planes. And its most toxic fleet type of all? "This combined carrier had way too many 50-seat regional airplanes," Glen Hauenstein said in a November investor call. So Delta looked for every opportunity to eliminate those.

Delta was most conspicuous, though, for what it was *not* doing with its fleet. On Dec. 8, 2009, United announced firm orders for 25 Boeing 787 "Dreamliners" and 25 Airbus 350s. These were next-generation midsized widebody aircraft that could transport a couple hundred passengers to just about anywhere in the world. Perhaps most impressively, they promised significant fuel savings, thanks to new engine technology and lightweight "composite" material, rather than aluminum, for the airframe. A year earlier, American had ordered up to 100 787s, contingent on reaching a contract deal with its pilots. Continental had 25 787s on order. Even US Airways, never mind its limited international network, held orders for 350s.

But new airplanes aren't cheap. And Delta, with a religious-like devotion to shrinking its debt obligations, recognized a key reality about the airline business: Airplanes were an airline's single biggest capital expense. So if it kept its aircraft spending to a minimum and continued to generate the positive cash flow that was now streaming in during even the toughest of quarters, it would have lots of cash left to pay its creditors and, for that matter, its employees. True, older airplanes burn more fuel. But by Delta's calculations, other airlines overestimated how much of a problem that was. A new plane's efficiency, in other words, was often outweighed by its capital costs. And older airplanes were particularly perfect for the variable schedule that Delta was increasingly adopting: Parking an airplane on Tuesday is far easier to stomach when the plane's mortgage was long ago paid off, making it a variable-cost aircraft—it only costs money when it's in the air burning fuel. New airplanes, for all their fuel efficiency, carry big ownership costs and thus cost money when they're on the ground. The tradeoff is not so different from what a consumer faces when deciding whether to purchase a newer, more efficient car: Replacing an old car with a Toyota Prius hybrid might pay off, but only if it's driven almost constantly.

Granted, passengers tend to prefer newer planes—this, along with increased fuel burn, was another drawback to old aircraft. What passengers really hate, though, aren't old aircraft, but aircraft that feel old. If Delta could save millions by keeping its old planes, it would have plenty of cash to spend on better seats and more of the frequent and intense cabin cleaning it had already implemented—so passengers wouldn't even notice the age of the planes—not to mention better airport facilities, better training and so on. And who knew? Maybe someday, Delta would even have enough cash to pay dividends to its shareholders.

Needless to say, planes eventually must be replaced. But on the narrowbody front, Delta scoured the market for unwanted MD-90s, picking them up here and there when the price was right. Their overall economics, even counting their lousy fuel burn, were surprisingly good, taking into account their virtually nonexistent ownership costs. And as for widebodies, Delta was in no rush to buy 787s or 350s, not with its 767s and 330s still far from retirement. So without much fanfare, Delta renegotiated Northwest's 787 contract with Boeing, deferring deliveries far into the future—more than a half decade later, it was still unclear when or even if Delta would ever take the aircraft. When Northwest placed the order, 787s seemed a perfect tool for connecting Detroit and Minneapolis with Asia. They might enable some new Latin America service too. But now they'd be less critical, with Delta's 767s able to handle some of Northwest's west coast routes to Tokyo, and with Delta's 777s providing more longhaul flexibility in general. Midwestern flows to Latin America could be channeled through Atlanta; from there, 767s had more than enough range. Remarkably, giant Delta had just four new airplanes scheduled for delivery in all of 2010: two ultra-long-range 777s and two 737s. Anderson's and Bastian's contrarian approach to aircraft buying was becoming clear for the world to see.

But if Delta was sheepish about new plane shopping, it was just the opposite regarding alliance formation. Nobody knew better than Anderson how lucrative Northwest's joint venture with KLM had become. And Air France quickly learned this truth when it assumed control over KLM. In the spring of 2008, Delta and Air France had implemented their own JV. Now it was time to fuse the two JVs into a four-way arrangement. On May 20, 2009, the two companies, both consolidation pioneers, announced a beefed-up venture whereby both would share all revenues and costs for routes between North America and Europe (as well as between Amsterdam and India, and between North America and Tahiti). The two companies would also cooperate on some routes between North America and Africa, the Middle East and India, as well as on flights between Europe and several countries in Latin America.

The two would act like one across the North Atlantic, where they controlled an imposing 25 percent of all capacity, generating annual revenues of some $12 billion. The combined schedule, about half flown by Delta and half by Air France/KLM, included more than 200 flights and roughly 50,000 seats each day, with nonstop links connecting hubs on both sides of the Atlantic with each other and with secondary cities on the other side. The agreement covered not just the nonstop transatlantic routes but also even the revenues and costs tied to connecting passengers "behind" and "beyond" these hubs, as network planners refer to the traffic that feeds hubs.

How would it be managed? With an executive committee consisting of the three CEOs plus a management committee of representatives from marketing, network, sales, alliances, finance and operations. In addition, 10 separate working groups would assume responsibility for implementing and managing decisions pertaining to network, revenue management, sales, product, frequent flyer programs, advertising and brand, cargo, operations, IT and finance. Helpfully, the broader SkyTeam alliance was now taking a more activist approach to develop new alliance-wide products (such as multi-airline around-the-world passes) and share best practices, to the extent antitrust laws permitted. SkyTeam opened its first centralized office in Amsterdam—Star and oneworld, the other two global alliances, had long ago established such offices—and led an effort to have all members paint at least one of their planes in a special alliance-themed design. The first plane to sport the SkyTeam paint scheme? A Delta 767.

Delta formed another JV too, albeit a much smaller one. In July, it announced a tie-up with Australia's Virgin Blue, which was partly owned by Sir Richard Branson's Virgin Group but was otherwise unaffiliated with London's Virgin Atlantic or San Francisco-based Virgin America. The motivation for the Delta-Virgin Blue JV was simple: Both carriers had just launched flights between California and Australia—in Delta's case, Los Angeles-Sydney flights—and the market went overnight from being a comfortable United and Qantas duopoly to a four-carrier brawl. Virgin and Delta, the two marginal carriers, faced the longest odds. The JV meant they would no longer compete—three Australia-U.S. ventures rather than four—and could provide traffic feed on both ends, which for Delta meant the ability to sell tickets to more places within Australia and the South Pacific.

The North Pacific, on the other hand, posed much greater strategic uncertainties. For years, East Asia was a black hole for Delta, save for a lone Atlanta-Tokyo route. That, of course, changed with the merger and the addition of Northwest's Tokyo hub. At the time of the merger announcement, Northwest served the Japanese capital nonstop from no fewer than six cities on the U.S. mainland: Detroit, Minneapolis, Los Angeles, San Francisco, Seattle and Portland. It also flew nonstop from Detroit to Osaka and Nagoya, and from several Japanese cities to U.S. beach destinations like Honolulu, Guam and Saipan. Also from Tokyo, it offered intra-Asia markets like Singapore, Manila, Guangzhou, Bangkok, Hong Kong, Shanghai, Beijing, Seoul and Busan—the "interport" markets, as these were known internally. Even giant United, with a Tokyo hub of its own, didn't offer as much as Northwest.

So what was the problem?

The problem was that the Japanese market was poised for big changes. In December 2009, Japan and the U.S. signed an open skies agreement. As is usually the case with free trade agreements, this one was great news for consumers and for would-be new entrants into the market—in this case, aspiring airlines. But as is also often the case, the news wasn't as good for incumbents like Delta. In addition, Tokyo's two major airports planned to expand their runway and terminal capacity—again, great news for everyone except incumbent airlines, who profited by hoarding the limited supply in a high-demand market. Delta's hub was at Toyko's longhaul airport, Narita. But soon, the more convenient Haneda Airport, preferred by business travelers because of its proximity to central Tokyo, would be able to handle some international flights too. So could Delta ever move its entire Tokyo hub to Haneda? No: U.S. carriers would receive just a small helping of Haneda departure and arrival slots. Nobody yet knew exactly how many and which carriers would get them, but there was no way Delta would get enough to move its hub.

Worse yet, the Japanese government signed that open skies agreement for one main reason: Japan's two major airlines—Japan Airlines and All Nippon—had reversed their long-held aversion to such an agreement. They too had begun sensing the power of alliances—everyone recognized how successfully Delta and Air France/KLM were working together—and an open skies agreement would likely mean antitrust immunity to form similarly tight JVs with their U.S. partners. Alas, Delta was not one of those partners: Japan Airlines was now in oneworld, aligned with American, while All Nippon was a longtime Star Alliance member, linked to United. When the music stopped, Delta would be the airline without a chair.

The backdrop to this conundrum was a Japanese market that remained rich but stagnant, its economy barely growing and its population actually shrinking. Japan was an expensive place to do business, especially with respect to labor costs. Scheduling flights to Tokyo was always tricky: Should flights be timed to please travelers going only to Tokyo, or should they be optimized to connect well with flights to onward destinations? And although Asian economies had boomed in the 2000s, the growth occurred not in Japan but in China, which now had more of its own nonstop service from the U.S.—"overflying" Toyko, as airlines call such hub bypassing—while other travelers increasingly traveled between the U.S. and China through other Asian gateways, most notably Seoul. During the last few months of 2009, Delta's executives would spend a great deal of time grappling with this Asia problem.

There were other problems to manage in the closing months of 2009, including a public relations black eye when a Northwest flight from San Diego to Minneapolis overshot its destination by 150 miles, losing contact with ground controllers for more than an hour. The pilots told investigators they had become distracted while using their laptop computers, which weren't allowed in the cockpit.

Then on Christmas Day, a passenger from Nigeria aboard Northwest Flight 253 from Amsterdam to Detroit attempted to set off a bomb sewn to his underwear. Fortunately for the 290 people aboard the Airbus 330, the bomb didn't fully detonate, in part thanks to efforts by passengers and crewmembers, who overpowered the would-be bomber. The plane landed safely. Several months later, the al-Qaeda leader suspected of plotting the attack died in a CIA drone strike.

One week earlier, a United Nations climate change summit in Copenhagen reminded airlines of their exposure to potential initiatives to curb greenhouse gas emissions. A year before that, the European Union had voted to include commercial aviation in its carbon trading system. Officials in some countries blamed airlines for a disproportionate share of climate change because the global airline industry was growing rapidly and because some scientists believe high-altitude emissions cause more harm than emissions on the ground. IATA, the airline trade body, reminded critics aviation was responsible for just 2 percent of total carbon emissions worldwide. Still, airlines feared they could come to be seen by the public like tobacco companies, blamed for being bad corporate citizens, attacked by lawyers and subject to even more taxation.

Back in the U.S., with American politics consumed by health care legislation—"Obamacare," as critics were deriding it—Senator Ted Kennedy, one of the fathers of airline deregulation, died. He was 77. A plan was now in place to end the war in Iraq, but the war in Afghanistan was degenerating, requiring an additional troop "surge." The national debt hit $12 trillion.

For Delta, though, the closing moments of 2009 were filled with hope. For the year, it lost another $1 billion net, excluding special items. But set aside hedge losses, which were wearing off day by day, and Delta would have had a net *profit* of $291 million. This was on $28 billion in total revenues, $8 billion more than American, the second largest U.S. airline by this measure. Worldwide, only Lufthansa and Air France/KLM had greater annual revenues, and only because these companies had larger cargo, maintenance and catering units. In terms of passenger revenues alone, no carrier was larger than Delta. No carrier, for that matter, had more twin-aisle widebody airplanes, symbols of intercontinental heft.

And as for the merger naysayers? During the year, Delta estimated it had achieved $700 million in merger-related synergies, with another $600 million to come in 2010, as pilots from both airlines began flying together, as reservation systems were merged, as more cross-fleeting took place and as the Delta-Air France/KLM JV published its first joint transatlantic schedule. In December, the FAA granted Delta and Northwest a single operating certificate—or "SOC," by the acronym workers at merging airlines know well. A year after Delta had become one company financially, now safety regulators recognized it as one airline too.

Even during quarters when Delta lost money from an accounting perspective, it managed to generate positive cash flow—that is, it collected more money than it spent. It ended 2009 with $5.4 billion in "unrestricted liquidity" (cash plus investments that could quickly be turned into cash), a $400 million increase from the start of the year. It had repaid debt and cut capacity 6 percent. Fuel prices weren't cheap, but they were stable—and they remained far off their 2008 highs. Late in the year, industry fares slowly began to rise with signs of economic recovery and with Southwest no longer positioned to play spoiler—its hedge armor was now stripped away, and it had to slow its growth in an effort to raise fares, just like everyone else.

Globally, the industry was following in the footsteps of Delta and Air France. It was consolidating. In Latin America, Colombia's Avianca announced a merger with Central America's TACA. China Eastern would merge with Shanghai Airlines. And Lufthansa purchased British Midland, a carrier with valuable Heathrow slots coveted by both British Airways and Virgin Atlantic. Back in the U.S., meanwhile, airlines retreated to their major hubs. American folded up the tent at its long-withering St. Louis hub; US Airways did the same at Las Vegas. Continental, meanwhile, readily admitted it was watching Delta closely. If Delta continued to produce such excellent results, then Continental might reconsider a full merger with United. For now, in any case, it was busy hitching itself to United through their new JV.

On Dec. 15, Delta's management team held its annual investor day event to discuss the latest developments in the business, along with expectations for 2010. Optimism, even if only cautious optimism, filled the air. Executives talked about the $1 billion they planned to invest to install flat-bed business class seats, expand inflight entertainment, add first class service on larger regional jets and open new Sky Club lounges. They detailed past and future merger synergies, the recent demand improvements and fare increases, the stabile oil prices, the falling debt levels, the alliance initiatives, the ancillary revenue initiatives, the grand plans for New York— including the planned slot swap with US Airways—and Delta's willingness to cut capacity and refrain from binging on airplanes. Leaders proudly boasted of how management and labor were working as a team—lest there be any doubt, Air Line Pilots Association representatives were at the event to prove it. Union leaders, after all, didn't attend investor conferences at most airlines, other than sometimes to picket them, and they certainly didn't stand side by side with management. Delta, for the first time, was even talking about return on invested capital, or ROIC, targets—in other words, how much money it would earn relative to each dollar invested—a welcome change from the time when pleasing investors meant assurances of its mere survival.

"Well," Ed Bastian told investors that day, "for 2009, as everyone in this room well knows, 2009 was a very, very challenging year for us. It wasn't just challenging for the airlines, wasn't just challenging for Delta. It was challenging for our global economy. And despite the unprecedented economic weakness that we experienced, as we look back on 2009, we believe that at Delta Air Lines, we weathered the storm in solid fashion and are well poised and positioned for a successful 2010."

One thing Delta didn't speak about that day: its Asia problem. But that evening, Glen Hauenstein was on a flight to Japan.

2010

"We're a powerhouse in New York, and they'd like to be"

In 2009, Japan Airlines was two years shy of turning 60. And like most 60-year-olds, it was feeling nostalgic for the days when it was 30. Three decades prior, the airline was young, healthy, vigorous and on top of the world. For much of the 1980s, it was the free world's largest international airline (Aeroflot was the largest overall) and its largest cargo airline too. These were the days of Japan's economic ascendancy, when its population was still growing, its exporters still dominating global industries, its real estate market still booming, its average incomes still rising and its tourists still fanning out across the globe in ever greater numbers, the finest Japanese-built cameras hanging from their necks. This was the age when American children played Nintendo video games, watched Japanese cartoons, listened to Sony Walkmans (or was it "Walkmen?"; the Oxford English Dictionary accepted both) and grew up to drive Toyotas and Nissans.

In many ways, the 1980s were to Japan Airlines what the 1960s had been to Pan Am: a golden age—maybe not so golden financially, but golden by the standards of growth, status, resplendence and glamor. Japan Airlines had come a long way from its birth in the 1950s, when Northwest Orient, as it was then known, helped it launch. Already by the 1960s, Japan's miracle economy had turned Japan Airlines, or JAL, into a major cargo airline, leading to a cargo alliance with Air France. In the 1970s, JAL followed Pan Am's lead and flew ultra-jumbo 747s, just as Japan's economy was becoming the world's second largest. More than just an airline, it was a symbol of national pride and an instrument of national government, transporting the imperial family for their trips abroad and Prime Minister Kakuei Tanaka, in 1972, for his historic olive-branch visit to China. By 1979, more than 4 million Japanese citizens were traveling overseas annually.

JAL's go-go 1980s began with the collapse in oil prices and shifted into fifth gear during the second half of the decade. In 1985, the U.S. government, under pressure from manufacturers, farmers and other export-based companies, worked with Japan, the U.K., France and West Germany to significantly depreciate the dollar. And although export-oriented Japan wasn't thrilled to see its own currency appreciate, this was better than the U.S. Congress passing laws to—in an even more painful way—make Toyotas and Hondas more expensive for American consumers.

A stronger Japanese yen, in any case, led to a surge in buying power for Japanese companies, which naturally began buying assets overseas, and for Japanese households, which naturally took more trips overseas on Japan Airlines. They also bought more real estate, sending the price of property soaring. Japan Airlines itself brashly bought hotels in Hawaii. All the while, Japanese outbound travelers increased from about 5 million in 1985 to more than 10 million in 1990. Oil was cheap too, all the more so for JAL, which was buying it in strengthening yen. Cold war détente meant JAL could now fly over the Soviet Union's airspace en route to Europe, saving time and money. New aircraft, meanwhile, meant nonstop flying from Tokyo to the U.S. mainland—no more stops in Alaska. So JAL made money every year from 1986 through 1991, enjoying the same favorable conditions as its one-time mentor and now rival Northwest Airlines.

Japanese tourists didn't only want to visit Hawaii. Nor, after getting their own Tokyo Disneyland theme park in 1983, were they content to see Mickey at home. Nor were they content, even, to see him in California. Their pockets filled with amplified buying power abroad, Japanese tourists wanted to see Mickey in Florida, and JAL happily obliged. It didn't quite fly to Orlando. But in 1986, it began flying to Atlanta, where it negotiated a cooperative agreement with Delta, which was then Orlando's top carrier.

The next year saw JAL's privatization, undertaken with expectations that the good times would last forever. But they didn't. Already by the mid-1980s, new and stronger competition was creeping into JAL's most important routes linking Tokyo with the U.S. Delta flew to Tokyo for the first time after winning new flying rights from Portland. American entered at the same time. And United, America's largest airline, had replaced the dying Pan Am in Tokyo after buying its Pacific routes. JAL's domestic rival All Nippon, meanwhile, received more rights to compete against JAL internationally.

More traumatically, a giant real estate and stock market bubble was quietly building during the latter half of the 1980s. In 1990, it popped. Then came the first Gulf War, which depressed international air traffic. With that came a fuel spike and then, for Japan, two full decades of economic stagnation, increasingly accompanied by a shrinking and aging population.

During the 1990s, Japan Airlines faced many of the same pressures its U.S. counterparts were facing: new competition, battles with unions and inevitable cost cutting. But unlike its U.S. counterparts, JAL didn't even enjoy the extremely low oil prices of the late 1990s. Instead, the benefits were spoiled by a weak yen and an Asian financial crisis. And 1998 marked the start of domestic airline deregulation in Japan, which led to bloody fare wars following the launch of LCCs, including one called Skymark. JAL had to sell some of its real estate holdings, launch low-cost units of its own and—in 2002—merge with Japan's third largest carrier, the domestic-oriented Japan Air System (JAS).

This led to a virtual duopoly within Japan among non-LCCs—Japan Airlines and All Nippon were now the only major players in that realm. But for JAL, not even *this* environment of limited domestic competition was enough to bring happiness. On the contrary, the first decade of the 2000s was filled with dismay. Along with much higher fuel prices and a still-stagnant home economy, JAL faced a storm of new competitive challenges, led by the emergence of Seoul as an alternative longhaul gateway.

Two Korean carriers—Korean Air and Asiana—became the airlines of choice for many international business travelers flying into and out of booming China, which by the late 2000s had surpassed Japan to become the world's second largest economy. Korean Air and Asiana eventually built networks of more than 30 Chinese destinations. What's more, unlike in Tokyo, where Haneda Airport handled mostly domestic flights and Narita mostly international flights, and these flights didn't connect with each other, nearly all of Seoul's traffic was concentrated at one airport. So someone in, say, Osaka or Sapporo could more easily reach the rest of the world via Seoul than via Tokyo. As it happened, Koreans themselves were growing richer by the year, the country's powerful exporters like Samsung and Hyundai reminiscent of their Japanese counterparts' earlier days. In 2010, Korean Air surpassed $10 billion in revenues—still smaller than JAL and All Nippon but on par with other Asian giants like Cathay Pacific and Singapore Airlines.

Speaking of Singapore Airlines, it was now flying jumbo, amenity-laden Airbus 380s into Tokyo. Emirates was in Tokyo too, and like many of JAL's international rivals, its service was at least as good, while its costs were far lower. The 2000s also saw the LCC revolution, pioneered 30 years earlier in the U.S. by Herb Kelleher, arrive throughout much of Asia. Dynamic newcomers like Malaysia's AirAsia and Australia's Jetstar began showing up in Japan, in some cases directly competing against JAL. Korean LCCs, including low-cost units owned by Korean Air and Asiana, were entering Japan too. Within Japan, meanwhile, Skymark, long just a marginal threat with limited ambitions, suddenly began expanding rapidly after replacing widebody planes with more appropriate narrowbodies. But that wasn't to say it had forgotten about widebodies. Soon, it would even place an order for giant Airbus 380s! Had it lost its mind? Perhaps. Still, JAL would feel the pain of competing against all this capacity. More immediately threatening, meanwhile, was Japan's expansion of high-speed bullet trains, which competed against airlines in major domestic markets.

Making matters worse, JAL experienced several worrying safety incidents in the mid-2000s. They weren't lethal, but instances of exploding engines and tires falling off planes worried regulators and travelers alike. At one point, Japan's ministry of transport, concerned JAL's constant cost cutting and job cutting might be affecting safety, ordered the company to prepare a plan to address the issue.

From 2000 through 2009, JAL's international capacity plummeted by nearly 50 percent. And during the same period, the number of Japanese visitors to the U.S. dropped 43 percent, from 5.1 million annually to 2.9 million. Trends like these forced JAL to rethink its fleet, an armada of jumbo jets that were now too big for its needs. Of course, rightsizing a fleet of hundreds of jets took years, and by the end of the decade JAL still had too many 747s, four-engined planes that were all the more problematic in an era of extreme fuel prices. Many of JAL's smaller planes were becoming obsolete too, and many of its domestic planes were flying with a far greater percentage of empty seats than was normal for the industry. The only thing worse than spending a lot on fuel is spending a lot on fuel to carry seats that aren't even occupied by paying passengers.

JAL tried hard to cope with this endless storm of challenges, repeatedly cutting costs and even offshoring jobs to lower-cost countries like Thailand. But with nine unions resisting change and many of its costs like fuel and airport charges largely outside its control, losses accumulated, pension deficits swelled and debt reached gargantuan levels. JAL actually managed modest operating profits in 2007 and even in 2008, when hedges and a strong yen buffered the impact of fuel's super-spike.

But then came 2009. For Japan Airlines, it was the year from hell. The economic meltdown emanating from the U.S. was spreading to Asia. As Martin Wolf of the *Financial Times* noted, the value of consumer spending in the U.S. alone during the mid-2000s boom was larger than the economies of China and India combined, underscoring the grave implications for Japanese exporters of consumer goods. In the fourth quarter of 2008, Japan's industrial production shrank by a shocking 21 percent compared to the same period a year earlier. To a much greater extent than Delta and other U.S. carriers, JAL had outsized exposure to the crisis' three hardest-hit markets: longhaul, premium and cargo. Unlike in the U.S., there had been no recent consolidation in Japan—there were, after all, just two major airlines. There was no ancillary revenue revolution. Sure, JAL—like its U.S. counterparts in this regard—did aggressively cut capacity, but only in line with a contraction in demand that was at least as steep. Besides, from 2005 through 2008, while JAL was downsizing international flying 15 percent, its rival All Nippon—feeling emboldened by the fact that its international flights had, in 2006, started making money for the first time ever—actually *increased* its international capacity 12 percent.

So while Delta headed into the macroeconomic tempest of 2009 bulked up through a merger, armed with new ancillary revenues and relieved of competitive capacity pressures, JAL headed into the darkness without any such tailwinds. Things went from bad to worse when, in the spring of 2009, the H1N1 virus devastated traffic in northeast Asia. In its April-through-September fiscal half year, JAL's international yields (the amount of money each passenger paid to fly one mile) plummeted 36 percent from the year prior, while total international revenues—because flights were emptier—fell an even steeper 43 percent. The company would end the year with $2.5 billion in net losses, an operating loss margin of negative 10 percent and (just like Delta on the eve of its bankruptcy) more than $20 billion in debt. Only with government support and concessions from creditors did it manage to stay in the air.

Something had to change, for on top of all that had gone wrong in the years leading up to 2009, 2010 would bring a new set of uncertainties. Both Tokyo airports were expanding, and although this would bring new growth opportunities, it would also bring new competition. Two new smaller airports on Tokyo's outskirts, one in Ibaraki and one near Mount Fuji, were also opening and trying to lure LCCs. And Japan's government, looking for ways to stimulate the sleepy economy, began liberalizing aviation treaties with other Asian nations, in doing so opening the market to more foreign competitors. There was also, of course, a foreign competitor—one with a Tokyo Narita hub, no less—that had just become larger and more powerful. Delta was now by any measure, and by a wide margin, Japan's largest foreign airline.

How would Japan Airlines and All Nippon compete in this brave new world? As they looked for answers, both carriers recognized an inescapable trend. After the U.S. and Europe implemented an open skies agreement in 2008, carriers on both sides were more or less free to collude with each other. It was the trigger that enabled Delta's joint venture with Air France/KLM and an impending JV between United, Continental and Lufthansa. American and British Airways, although the focus of greater antitrust scrutiny, appeared likely to jointly operate flights as well. Might similar JVs work wonders for Japan's airlines?

As it happened, Japan Airlines and All Nippon were scheduled to be the first airlines in the world to fly Boeing's new 787 Dreamliner—JAL alone had ordered 35 of them. So they needed new places to fly them. Sure enough, these machines were perfectly suited for U.S. routes. They had the right economics, range and size to serve a host of new markets that previous generations of aircraft simply couldn't serve profitably. San Diego and Boston were two examples—JAL's 767s were the right size but without enough range, while its 777s had adequate range but too many seats.

With this desire for U.S. partnerships and more U.S. market access, plus the imminent addition of new airport capacity in Tokyo, the stars were aligned for a U.S.-Japan open skies agreement, which the two countries indeed reached on Dec. 12, 2009. All Nippon would form an antitrust-immune transpacific JV with its Star Alliance partners United and Continental. Japan Airlines would do the same with American Airlines, its oneworld alliance partner since 2006 and codeshare partner since way back in 1998.

Or would it?

Seven thousand miles away in Atlanta, network general Glen Hauenstein and his lieutenant Bob Cortelyou had several key priorities for Delta's network as 2010 approached. One was cultivating merger synergies by moving planes around. Another was deciding where to most appropriately cut capacity in response to the economic bust. Still another was ensuring smooth execution of the newly enlarged JV with Air

France/KLM. A fourth: finding solutions to two key choke points in Delta's quest for global supremacy. One of these was New York City, which Delta finally managed to link with Europe's most important airport, London Heathrow, and where its position at LaGuardia Airport stood to expand significantly if the government approved its slot swap with US Airways. The other hole to patch? Asia.

When Delta merged with Northwest, one of its reasons for doing so was access to Asia. And that's indeed what Delta got. But Northwest's Asian franchise, with its hub at Tokyo's Narita Airport, hadn't earned consistent profits in years, afflicted, as it was, with many of the same problems plaguing Japan Airlines: a weak Japanese economy, the challenge posed by Korean carriers, an aging fleet of oversized 747s and so on. So post-merger Delta was now the largest U.S. airline in Japan, even larger than United. But that didn't translate into profits. Naturally, the export collapse and H1N1 scare of 2009 made matters worse.

And those facts barely began to explain Delta's Asian dilemma. In 2010, two developments stood to further weaken its Asian position. First was the expansion and internationalization of Haneda Airport—however much of a problem this was for JAL, it was that much more of a problem for Delta, all of whose service was concentrated at now-unloved Narita. Second was the newly planned transpacific JVs involving Delta's four key competitors for passengers flying between the U.S. and northeast Asia. Sure, Delta might itself win some new slots at Haneda, but nowhere near the number it would need to completely move its hub from Narita, the less convenient airport situated further from the city. At best it would have a few Haneda flights to the U.S. and the rest of its flights at Narita, implying a split operation similar to what JAL had—or, for that matter, similar to the debilitating split operation Delta itself had in New York.

This wouldn't be such a big problem if Delta at least had an alliance partner in Japan, one with which it could share traffic and coordinate schedules and fares. But it didn't. Japan had just two airlines of consequence, and both were taken: All Nippon was committed to United, while Japan Airlines was committed to American.

But just how committed? In All Nippon's case, there was never any question of its desire to work with United and Continental, with their mega-hubs in cities like San Francisco, Los Angeles, Washington and Chicago, precisely the cities where Japanese carriers flew. Besides, United had a Toyko Narita mini-hub of its own, one that was smaller than Delta's, to be sure, but large enough nonetheless to support flights to Singapore, Taipei, Seoul and Bangkok. United also flew the Tokyo-Honolulu and Tokyo-Guam routes, both huge draws for Japanese tourists. And Continental operated a Micronesian unit that depended on Japanese tourists. United and Continental were perfect partners.

American, on the other hand, had a far weaker presence in Asia, which gave Hauenstein an idea: Might Delta persuade Japan Airlines to drop American and form a JV with it instead? *The Wall Street Journal* reported that Richard Anderson, in October 2008—right after the Northwest merger was finalized—instructed his vice president of strategic alliances to approach JAL. In December 2008, that executive, Vinay Dube—a former American employee—met with his JAL counterparts to introduce the idea. American, the *Journal* said, learned about Delta's interest in January 2009, but JAL told American it had no interest in changing partners. Later, in August, two JAL executives even flew to American's Fort Worth headquarters to reassure its CEO Gerard Arpey in person.

But by this time, JAL's financial situation had become grave: It lost about $1 billion in the April-to-June quarter. And Delta had a trump card it was now ready to play. In September 2009, Delta President Ed Bastian called JAL CEO Haruka Nishimatsu and offered $500 million if JAL would switch alliances. Some would be in the form of an equity investment, which would make Delta a key shareholder in JAL.

Nishimatsu, who had spent his entire career at JAL, assumed the chief executive position in 2006 after the airline's bout with safety issues claimed his predecessor in a boardroom coup. Nishimatsu quickly established a reputation for personal frugality, taking the bus to work, wearing modest suits and eating at the employee cafeteria, as profiled by international media including CNN and CBS News. He further endeared himself to staff by walking the front lines and soliciting suggestions from the rank and file. But he was also a seasoned finance executive who understood all too well how dire JAL's problems were. And he had spent part of his career working from JAL's office in Frankfurt, giving him insight into the world of business outside corporate Japan. He was now working frantically to keep the company from falling into bankruptcy.

So Nishimatsu listened attentively when a team of Delta executives pitched the idea of switching alliances. Delta, they explained, not only carried more passengers between the U.S. and Japan than American but also more passengers between the two countries than any airline, period. Delta's Asian presence was far larger than American's, and the SkyTeam alliance was stronger in Asia than oneworld, which didn't have any Korean or mainland Chinese members. Air France/KLM was also promising to deepen its existing ties to JAL. And Delta was stronger financially and strategically than American, which by late 2009 was looking more and more like the sick man of the U.S. airline sector, burdened, as it was, by a cost structure never cleansed by bankruptcy. Many of its problems, in fact—high labor costs, stagnant network planning, heavy debt, aging planes—weren't so dissimilar from JAL's.

Nishimatsu, however, was not the only person whose opinion counted. Japan's powerful government bureaucrats were now deeply involved in the predicament too, following $1 billion in taxpayer-funded survival loans to JAL granted during June, the worst month of the H1N1 crisis. The bureaucracy, it seemed, had warmed to Delta's offer. Perhaps that wasn't such a surprise: In addition to the merits of Delta's arguments themselves, Delta, after all, had inherited Northwest's long-established team of government relations and sales executives based in Tokyo, some of whom had close ties to the corridors of Japanese political power.

American was shocked to learn about Delta's equity offer. Immediately it responded with a counteroffensive. Its weak balance sheet couldn't support a big equity infusion to match Delta's offer, so American partnered with the airline investment group TPG to make an offer. Its contacts and connections in Japan weren't nearly as extensive as Delta's, so it hired the former U.S. transportation secretary Norman Mineta, a Japanese-American, to lobby Japanese officials. CEO Gerard Arpey appealed personally to his counterpart Haruka Nishimatsu.

American reminded JAL why they had been partners in the first place: JAL was originally attracted to American because of its gateways in New York, Los Angeles and Chicago, America's three largest cities. If the two developed their relationship into a JV, JAL would also have the opportunity to send its U.S. passengers to a large array of destinations through American's Dallas-Fort Worth hub, the country's fourth busiest airport after Atlanta, Chicago O'Hare and Los Angeles. Do Japanese passengers, the message implied, really want to go to Detroit, Minneapolis, Atlanta and Salt Lake City? American furthermore reminded JAL, whose fortunes depended on business passengers, of Delta's greater historical reliance on leisure travelers. American, in fact, still outfitted many longhaul planes with not just a business class cabin—Delta had that—but a separate first class cabin too. American's inflight product was better.

American emphasized to JAL that in SkyTeam, it would have to share the stage with Korean Air, which itself had antitrust immunity with Delta, even if the two weren't really taking advantage of it. China Southern was a SkyTeam member too. JAL, in other words, would remain a far bigger fish in oneworld. Because of oneworld's loose restrictions on members cooperating with airlines outside the alliance, JAL could maintain partnerships with Air France/KLM and others. JAL actually codeshared with Korean Air too, and it could continue doing so. If JAL stayed in oneworld, American would share its knowledge in areas like corporate forecasting and aircraft maintenance while offering wisdom gained from its own out-of-court restructuring in 2003—exactly what JAL was trying to accomplish. The message to bureaucrats, meanwhile, was less carrot and more stick: If JAL turned to Delta, American would slash capacity to Japan.

Other oneworld members supported American's campaign. Australia's Qantas promised to cooperate with JAL on a new low-cost carrier for Japanese routes. British Airways promised deeper cooperation on Europe-Northeast Asia routes. Finnair and South America's LAN likewise pledged tighter cooperation. As persuasive as these promises were, however, American knew Delta was the more powerful player in Japan. But American's trump card? Precisely the fact that Delta was the more powerful player in Japan.

JAL would be taking a huge risk by aligning itself with Delta, American asserted, because U.S. antitrust regulators wouldn't grant antitrust immunity. Delta and JAL together would control more than half of all seats flying between the U.S. and Japan and an even higher percentage of the total number of passengers flying between the two countries. American and JAL had fewer than a third of the total seats combined, and without JAL, American would lose significance to transpacific passengers, leaving U.S. consumers at the mercy of just two giant JVs linking the world's first and third largest economies. Delta countered that its share of true transpacific seats, if combined with JAL's, would reach just 40 percent. But that didn't include beach markets between Japan and Hawaii, Guam and Saipan. American didn't even fly any of these routes. Delta and JAL together controlled nearly 70 percent of those markets. Might the U.S. government, American asked, force a combined Delta-JAL JV to shed some Hawaii routes, if it would even approve such an alliance in the first place?

American, unfortunately, was in the delicate position of making these alarmist antitrust arguments at a time when it was nervously awaiting approval for its JV with British Airways, a venture its rivals were arguing was itself anticompetitive. But that didn't stop American from reminding JAL that antitrust concerns were what had killed past combinations like United-US Airways (in 2000), Delta-US Airways (in 2007) and American itself and British Airways, with earlier JV attempts not once but twice (in 1997 and 2001). Delta, of course, was no stranger to using the antitrust card to get what it wanted—it had propagated the fears that killed the US Airways takeover attempt long before regulators ever actually got a chance to review the matter.

A decision would not come quickly, however. JAL's financial situation grew worse, and in October, a government-backed panel of restructuring experts reviewed the company's predicament and assessed its chances of avoiding bankruptcy. Just weeks earlier, a revolution of sorts had occurred in Japanese politics, with the country's long-dominant political party, the LDP, voted out of power. The new ruling party, the DPJ, promptly installed new cabinet ministers, including a new transportation minister, who needed time to assess the precarious situation. In the meantime, JAL announced another restructuring, this one involving nearly 7,000 job cuts and the axing of some 50 routes. The days when JAL was the free world's biggest airline seemed as distant in the rear-view mirror as... well... the term "free world."

All the while, American and Delta, their executives working from nearby hotels in downtown Tokyo, intensified their lobbying campaigns. American touted up to $100 million in revenue and cost synergies if JAL stayed put. Delta said it would pay for the cost of switching alliances. American said JAL would suffer $500 million in lost revenue in the first two years after switching. Delta increased its offer to more than $1 billion in aid, including $500 million in equity, plus asset-backed financing and revenue guarantees for any short-term losses from switching. American, together with TPG, essentially matched the offer.

In early December, the CEOs of both carriers got a chance to make their pitches directly to Japan's transport minister Seiji Maehara. Richard Anderson went first, followed by Gerard Arpey a few days later.

"We give the opportunity to make certain that JAL holds its rightful place as the leading airline in Asia," Anderson told the press after his meeting.

"[We offer] far more commercial and financial benefits, far less risk and the best chance for JAL to achieve long-term success," Arpey countered.

Delta appeared to have won. Maehara publicly criticized American's pitch, accusing Arpey of spending too much time criticizing Delta rather than stressing the benefits of his own offer. "American promoted itself to a certain extent, but it spent most of the time explaining why JAL cannot partner with Delta," Maehara told the *Kyodo News*. "To be honest, I wish they had given us a slightly more forward-looking explanation."

Vocal factions within JAL supported the Delta option. Many in the government bureaucracy were clearly impressed by Delta's status as not only the world's largest airline but also one of its financially strongest. Some Japanese newspapers pointed to Delta as the near-certain winner. Also helping Delta: the fact that it perhaps better understood key cultural nuances. One Japanese minister invited Arpey to Tokyo for a half-hour meeting. Arpey told his staff that no, he wasn't making a 14-hour trip for a 30-minute conversation. American's Japanese staff finally convinced Arpey that yes, you do indeed go all the way there for the 30 minutes.

But as December turned to January, no decision had yet emerged regarding whom JAL would choose as its partner. Again getting in the way was the urgency of JAL's survival—and to what degree the government was willing to contribute. There was even some talk of keeping JAL alive as a domestic-only airline, handing its international routes to All Nippon. Cooler heads prevailed on that score, but ultimately, on Jan. 19, 2010, JAL filed for bankruptcy in the Tokyo District Court, wiping out shareholders. Taking charge was the country's Enterprise Turnaround Initiative Corporation (ETIC), financed by both taxpayers and Japan's big financial institutions. It had been created to resuscitate chronically sick firms.

Five days before the bankruptcy filing, Japan's most widely read newspaper, the *Yomiuri Shimbun*, reported "Japan Airlines and Delta Air Lines on Friday [Jan. 15] reached a basic agreement on a comprehensive tie-up that mainly features codesharing flight services." Delta was the winner, although with the government now committed to ensuring JAL's rescue, it decided against accepting any new foreign capital. Delta would get its alliance but not an ownership stake, which was fine with Delta. Dangling equity, after all, was merely a means to an end. That end: a partnership.

But there was no final decision yet. On Jan. 20, American held a conference call to discuss its financial results for the fourth quarter of 2009, which happened to be by far the worst of any U.S. airline. In any event, CEO Gerard Arpey summarized American's offer to JAL: "American, oneworld and TPG had previously made a substantial offer to assist JAL and the government of Japan in their efforts to secure JAL's long-term future. We recently presented an enhanced proposal that will deliver approximately $2 billion in commercial value over three years to JAL from relationships with oneworld members. In addition, the proposal includes an improved capital investment of $1.4 billion, which would include $1.1 billion from TPG and up to $300 million from oneworld, should it be welcomed and deemed appropriate by JAL and the government of Japan. JAL's restructuring will occur through a process similar to our Chapter 11 process, and it appears at this point that the prospect for an external capital investment is being downplayed by the parties involved in JAL's restructuring. In any case, we believe that our proposal offers all stakeholders the best solution at the lowest risk to ensure JAL's long-term financial success."

But Arpey's deputy Tom Horton, responding to a question from JP Morgan analyst Jamie Baker, acknowledged the possibility of losing the battle. "We think it should be an easy decision," Horton said. "But that said, if JAL were to choose otherwise, we would huddle with our oneworld partners and consider our alternatives there. And there are other carriers around the world who have expressed an interest in joining oneworld, and we would go consider that. We would evaluate other carriers in the region, both those that are not represented by alliances and those that are. We would take a clean sheet of paper to this."

Added Arpey: "And Jamie, it probably goes without saying, but we would of course also move aggressively to block any form of cooperation between the dominant carrier in the region and certain anticompetitive outcomes from 65 percent of the traffic between the United States and Japan being controlled by one partnership. I would be astonished if such a partnership could come together and pass any form of antitrust scrutiny, let alone ATI [antitrust immunity]. I think ATI is a nonstarter. It would make a mockery of the whole notion of open skies. It would make a farce of the whole process. The thought that the carriers that have had the duopoly in that market where other airlines, including American, have been prevented from competing in Japan for 50 years—that open skies would lead to *them* having an immunized partnership—would be a joke."

Horton again: "And despite press reports otherwise, we continue to have an active dialogue with JAL, with the government, with the banks, with everybody who is relevant in this process"

On Jan. 26, Delta held *its* fourth quarter conference call. Unlike American, it didn't mention the JAL matter in its prepared remarks. But responding to a question from Dan McKenzie, an equity analyst at Rodman & Renshaw, Ed Bastian used the opportunity to again remind JAL of the benefits of switching to SkyTeam: "We have had, as you mentioned, a fairly visible discussion of what the benefits to JAL would be with Delta versus the current alliance to which they belong, and we believe the benefit to JAL was in the hundreds and millions of dollars per year, about $400 million from moving to SkyTeam, but we obviously expect significant benefits back to Delta and the other SkyTeam members as well."

Later in the call, Richard Anderson expressed confidence U.S. regulators would approve a Delta-JAL JV, noting it would have less control of the U.S.-Japan market than antitrust-immune partners American and LAN have in the U.S.-Chile market. Besides, he said, the Star Alliance, not SkyTeam, would remain the largest alliance in Asia. Ed Bastian, meanwhile, hinted that even if approval for antitrust immunity never came, just yanking JAL from oneworld to SkyTeam would be a big plus—for Delta, anyway.

JAL, for its part, now in bankruptcy, would receive massive tax breaks and debt relief, but only in exchange for yet another draconian turnaround plan, this one involving 16,000 job cuts over three years, more pay cuts, more route cuts and vast reductions in pension obligations. The company would update "obsolete and overly complicated" IT systems, reform management, sell non-core units, merge airline subsidiaries, stop flying cargo-only planes and reform pension and procurement policies. Oh, and one more thing: Haruka Nishimatsu would be out as chief executive.

To replace him, the ETIC turned to a national icon. Dr. Kazuo Inamori, then 77 years old, had spent a lifetime creating two of Japan's most influential companies from scratch. He founded the ceramics and electronics giant Kyocera at age 27, just as Japan began its recovery from the devastation of World War II. His next act was the creation of KDDI, which became his country's second largest telecommunications firm. He was a celebrated entrepreneur like Steve Jobs, a celebrated management guru like Michael Porter, a celebrated business titan like Jack Welch—and even a Buddhist monk, all in one. One thing he didn't have was aviation experience. But he was called upon to use his unique talents to rescue an iconic airline that was gasping for dear life.

His first day on the job was Feb. 1, 2010. And one of his first big decisions on the job was whom to choose as a partner: Delta or American. According to local news reports at the time, some government officials actually expected him to waste no time and announce a commitment to Delta at the press conference introducing him and his new management team. Instead, Inamori's deputy, JAL's newly appointed president Masaru Onishi, told questioning reporters: "Instead of being tied to previous discussions, we are currently examining the issue from scratch under the new management."

Indeed they were. Inamori and Onishi met with the Delta and American executives. At one meeting in a Tokyo hotel, Arpey appeared with—at Inamori's request—Willie Walsh, the CEO of British Airways, who would years later recall how the American CEO was articulate and "incredibly passionate" in making the case that JAL should remain their partner. So passionate, in fact, that Arpey's words began racing out of his mouth so quickly that the translator in the room could no longer keep up.

Walsh jumped in. "Dr. Inamori," he said. "I don't know if you've understood anything Gerard has said. But I hope you've felt the passion that this guy has for the relationship." Inamori and the translator both broke into laughter.

That lighthearted moment aside, Inamori quickly saw the attractiveness of joining with Delta. But he also saw the risks. The U.S. Department of Transportation, hearing lots of noise about the likelihood of JAL choosing Delta, went out of its way to inform Japanese officials that the tie-up, should it happen, would be subject to a robust antitrust review. So Inamori called the DOT himself and heard the same thing: Approval for antitrust immunity would be no slam dunk, and a review of JAL-Delta would surely take longer than a review of JAL-American. And one thing JAL didn't have was time.

Further uncertainties entered Inamori's calculating mind. Switching alliance partners would cost money, and although Delta had agreed to pay for these costs, the changes would take time—again, time JAL didn't have. Inamori also realized American stood ready to retaliate with pricing, capacity and other weapons at its disposal, and here too Delta's promises to compensate for any losses were ill defined. If American slashed prices on the Tokyo-Los Angeles route, for example, how much would JAL lose, and for how long? A switch, moreover, would confuse customers who were already wary of flying a bankrupt airline with a recent history of safety troubles. A switch would introduce new management and operational complexities, potentially distracting from JAL's immediate goal of getting out of bankruptcy.

As hefty as the expected Delta synergies were, they would take an estimated three years to realize. Would JAL even be around in three years? JAL would need to move its Chicago flights to Delta's Detroit hub, flow passengers through Atlanta rather than Dallas, and so on—a lot of work for a frantically restructuring airline. JAL, of course, would also be a bigger fish in the oneworld sea, rather than having to share northeast Asian traffic with Korean Air. Delta itself liked to say one of its advantages on transatlantic routes was that it was Air France/KLM's only U.S. partner—no need to share traffic in the way United shared Lufthansa's traffic with Continental and even Air Canada.

If there was one factor that tipped the scales, it was the simple fact that loyalty counted for Dr. Inamori, who stressed the role of ethics in corporate management. Remaining with JAL's longtime partner American felt like the more loyal and ethical thing to do.

So that's what he did. On Feb. 9, 2010, Inamori put an end to the four-month courtship battle, announcing JAL's intention to remain with American Airlines. JAL wouldn't take any of American's or TPG's money now that it had sufficient government support to stay in business while restructuring. But the two airlines would, just three days later, submit their DOT application for immunity from U.S. antitrust laws, enabling them to coordinate prices and schedules on transpacific flights. Approval came that autumn.

Delta's valiant attempt to solve its Asia problem had failed. It would remain partner-less in the important Japanese market, where United and American, Delta's two most important international rivals, both got the JVs they wanted. And Delta's Narita hub stood threatened by the coming internationalization of Haneda. It was an awful day.

And the day was young.

***

Also on Feb. 9, Delta got more bad news. The Federal Aviation Administration (FAA), part of the U.S. Department of Transportation, technically accepted Delta's slot swap with US Airways but with a giant caveat: They would need to divest a substantial number of LaGuardia and Reagan National slots to airlines that held less than 5 percent of the slots at each airport—in other words, their low-cost rivals Southwest, JetBlue and AirTran. That defeated the purpose of the swap, negating much of any benefit Delta would get by consolidating its grip on LaGuardia and much of anything US Airways would achieve by doing the same at Reagan. Sometimes regulators kill a deal not by rejecting it outright but by imposing conditions so tough that the companies no longer find the deal worth it. This was one of those times.

The FAA ruling specifically called for 20 of the 125 LaGuardia slot pairs involved in the transaction, and 14 of the 42 at Reagan, to be divested. A slot pair, remember, permits one departing flight and one arriving flight. The main pilot union at US Airways, angry its airline was axing jobs in New York, applauded the FAA. But Lee Moak and the Delta pilots—the Delta pilots, who had broken with convention and supported the Northwest merger—condemned the FAA's decision. "For both the consumer and labor," Moak said, "the reality is that the long-term interests of both are best served by a vigorously healthy, profitable, flourishing airline industry. And when the government interferes in the free-market process through overly intrusive regulation, that simply cannot happen."

All on one day, regulatory threats had torpedoed Delta's grand strategy for Asia, and regulatory demands had torpedoed its grand strategy for New York.

The difference in New York, though, was that perhaps this wasn't the end of the story. Rather than walk away, Delta and US Airways proposed a compromise: They would divest not 20 slot pairs at LaGuardia but 15, and not 14 slots at Reagan but four and a half. These slots would go to four airlines: JetBlue at Reagan and AirTran, Spirit and Canada's WestJet at LaGuardia. Conspicuously absent from that list: Southwest, which US Airways in particular was eager to keep out of Reagan.

But regulators again said no. Perhaps they were swayed by Southwest's timely reminder that Delta, just three years earlier, had argued a US Airways takeover of Delta would have created unacceptable dominance at Reagan and LaGuardia. The FAA and DOT insisted the airlines surrender 20 and 14 slot pairs at LaGuardia and Reagan, respectively, and that they do so by auctioning them off to the highest bidder—no backroom deals with individual airlines to isolate Southwest. Delta released a statement: "We are disappointed the DOT and FAA rejected a proposal that would provide clear consumer benefits in both the Washington, D.C., and New York markets. There are no winners in this decision—consumers lost, communities lost and our employees lost. Even our competitors lost."

And regulators *still* weren't done spoiling Delta's February. Four days after the JAL and slot swap disappointments, the DOT said yes to American's proposed JV with British Airways and Iberia, two airlines that would (in April) announce their own merger. Suddenly transatlantic competition was getting tougher. American and British Airways had failed twice before to obtain antitrust immunity, but this time, the airline market between Europe and the U.S. was an open skies zone, with more transatlantic competitors at Heathrow. The DOT did, however, force the airlines to sell or lease four Heathrow slot pairs to rivals, two for Boston flights and two for flights to any U.S. city. Still, this was far less burdensome than the 16 slot pairs mandated in 2002, when the DOT last ruled on an American-British Airways alliance proposal, another example—like the slot swap—where regulators didn't say "no" but might as well have.

The JV airlines also had to amend their agreement slightly to provide a promise to grow from their multiple hubs. Justifying its decision, the DOT cited consumer benefits such as lower fares, better schedules, of new routes, reduced travel times, reciprocal product benefits and greater competition against the already immunized SkyTeam and Star Alliance ventures. American, British Airways and Iberia would control just 22 percent of all U.S.-E.U. passengers, less than SkyTeam and Star, although they would control fully 47 percent of the U.S.-U.K. market, which alone accounted for about 30 percent of the entire transatlantic market.

Delta wasn't the airline most upset about the ruling. That distinction went to Virgin Atlantic, whose founder Richard Branson called it "a kick in the teeth." But Delta, even though it actually managed to acquire the four slot pairs slated for divestment, understood all too well that its franchise in New York would be further challenged by American and British Airways working so closely together. Delta would never, for example, be able to match their offering on the big-money New York JFK-London Heathrow route, the busiest overseas route in the world.

Indeed, a frustrating start to 2010. Delta had lost three big battles, losses that impacted two of its most important markets: Tokyo and New York. Battles lost, yes, but Delta was still winning the larger war. It was still outperforming its peers (most notably American) financially as the new decade began. It was still stunning rivals with the efficiency and smoothness of its merger integration. It was still trending upward on nearly all service metrics, from on-time performance to lost-bag rates to inflight product ratings. In a U.S. airline industry that was uncharacteristically managing the economic downturn better than many of its counterparts abroad, Delta was re-emerging with the reputation it had held during its long era of glory, a reputation that evoked financial strength, cordial employee relations and tactical acumen. The new Delta was gaining a reputation for broader *strategic* acumen too—and for style and grace and intercontinental flair. And if Delta was increasingly making its customers and employees and shareholders happy, it was doing just the opposite to its competitors, having inherited Northwest's take-no-prisoners approach to competition. If the new Delta was starting to resemble the old Delta, it was doing so minus the old Delta's shortcomings. That Delta was sometimes seen as a country bumpkin Disney World airline with a good balance sheet, yes, but lacking cosmopolitan cool. This Delta was getting it done on Wall Street *and* Madison Avenue.

The new decade didn't wait long before providing America's airlines with good news. The first quarter brought nearly universal reports of rising demand and yields in all categories of traffic, including premium traffic, corporate traffic, leisure traffic, domestic traffic and international traffic. Although U.S. economic growth was recovering more slowly, oil prices had more or less comfortably stabilized at less than $80 per barrel. Industry capacity was far more restrained than before the bust, and fewer flights meant reductions in costly delays and bag mishandling. In 2009, U.S. carriers handled 618 million passengers, down from 652 million the year prior and 679 million the year before that. Airlines, Delta included, were shrinking their way to redemption. In the meantime, carriers were leaner after a decade of job cutting. They had improved their ratios of flights per worker. New technologies like mobile boarding passes were further enhancing productivity. Airlines slashed capital expenditures, retreated to their fortress hubs, charged extra for all kinds of products and services that were once included and deepened partnerships with airlines abroad. The first decade of the new millennium, which arrived with great hope after the boom of the late 1990s, had instead yielded terrorism, war, disease, accidents, bankruptcies, liquidations, new government burdens and punishingly high fuel prices. But for airlines that made it through the storm, a new decade promised better times ahead.

Delta, for its part, now had "SOC," a single operating certificate, meaning Delta and Northwest could operate as one airline. Most Northwest planes were now painted in Delta colors. A single revenue management IT system now managed all flights. Merger synergies crossed the $1 billion mark in early 2010. Delta and Northwest pilots were flying together. Stunningly, the IT team managed by Theresa Wise from Northwest, together with the reservation system supplier Travelport, executed the near-impossible: an uneventful cutover to a single reservation system. So many other reservation system migrations, including the one undertaken after the US Airways-America West merger, had resulted in significant operational disruptions. Better yet, Delta was targeting another $600 million in merger synergies in 2010.

Even in East Asia, Delta's strategic predicament notwithstanding, 2010 brought signs of a robust economic recovery, one that would radically improve traffic and profits for nearly all airlines in the region, even—no, *especially*—Japan Airlines, which went on to become extraordinarily profitable. Exports bounced back. Memories of the H1N1 crisis quickly faded. Back at home, Delta continued to dump 50-seat regional jets and eventually managed to reduce its overall fleet by more than 70 planes but still fly the same seat-mile capacity, an incredible increase in productivity. In 2010, just 15 new planes were scheduled to arrive. Delta's commitment to invest $1 billion in product and service improvement was on track, boosted by steady inflows of cash from operations. These inflows, moreover, adequately relieved pressures from higher wages granted to workers, while enabling large cash contributions to employee pension plans. Maintenance costs were also increasing, but only because of Delta's conscious decision to let planes age instead of spending billions to replace them prematurely. Preparations were underway to replace the airline's large fleet of 757s, long and narrow planes with about 200 seats each. But there was no urgency to do much more than that in the near term. In fact, Delta extended leases on aging 747s—it spruced up their interiors, of course, so that only an airplane enthusiast would realize how old they were—and picked up more geriatric MD-90s in the equivalent of airplane flea markets. It bought nine, for example, from China Eastern.

The pricing team, meanwhile, was cognizant of the fact that ancillary fees were far more inelastic than base fares, which is another way of saying raising them was easier. Raise a base fare by a penny, and your flight could get buried on the computer screens travel agents and consumers use to shop, where flights can be sorted from cheapest to most expensive. But when Delta raised first- and second-bag fees again in January 2010, people just paid. Soon Delta was granting exemptions to anyone with Delta-branded American Express cards, thereby enhancing the value of the cards. By 2010, of course, base fares across the U.S. airline industry happened to be rising anyway, partly because the economy was recovering but perhaps more importantly because Southwest, its hedge protection gone and its labor costs rising, was hiking fares repeatedly. Its decision to break from the herd and *not* charge bag fees and ticket change fees, in fact, added another layer of pressure to raise base fares to make up for what it wasn't earning from ancillaries. Southwest was losing its reputation as the industry's low-fare airline, and the rest of the industry, including Delta, loved that fact.

In January, Delta's hardball negotiating tactics were on display when its regional partner Mesa Air filed for bankruptcy after Delta canceled a 22-plane contract. Delta cited poor operational quality, which allowed it to get out of the contract, which it otherwise couldn't terminate yet. Mesa said nonsense: If Delta was truly concerned about reliability, rather than the lousy economics of 50-seaters, why did it only cancel the contract for 50-seaters and not for larger regional jets, which Mesa also operated on Delta's behalf? And anyway, as for Mesa's many cancellations—it acknowledged it did have a lot of these since 2008—many were at JFK, where Delta itself was seemingly overscheduling flights to gum up JetBlue's operation. In any case, Delta got what it wanted.

In February, Delta's president Ed Bastian, the company's second in command, secured a seat on Delta's board of directors, which was still chaired by the industry outsider Daniel Carp. It was Carp, remember, whom Delta's creditors selected after the airline emerged from bankruptcy in 2007. And it was Carp's independent board, acting on behalf of the creditors, which hired Richard Anderson and pushed him to merge.

The merger with Northwest had succeeded beyond anyone's expectations. And now Delta was the largest airline in America and by some measures the most profitable. During the second quarter of 2010, Delta reported a net profit (excluding special accounting items) of $549 million, more than any other airline on the planet. Its operating margin was 11 percent, the company's highest springtime figure in a decade. Revenues skyrocketed 17 percent from the same period a year earlier, and cash poured in—$1 billion of it in just three months. This enabled Delta to pay off $345 million in debt and put aside another $90 million to share with employees, not even counting the nearly $700 million Delta had injected into its employee pension plans during the first quarter.

The second quarter performance was all the more remarkable in light of several significant market disruptions beyond Delta's control. On April 14, a volcano in Iceland began spewing ash, creating a giant cloud over much of Europe. Europe's safety authorities—unnecessarily, most airlines believed—closed the continent's airspace for nearly a week, causing more than 100,000 flights to cancel. After 9/11, by contrast, U.S airspace closed for just three days. The worst impact came Sunday, April 18, and Monday, April 19, when approximately 30 percent of all worldwide air service was grounded, according to IATA. HRG, a large U.K.-based travel management company, said 40,000 of its clients were stranded. IATA pinned the total revenue industry revenue impact at $1.7 billion through April 20, although the profitability impact was offset somewhat by about $110 million in daily fuel savings while aircraft were grounded. But airlines had to pay for employee overtime, and they had to provide hotels and food for their stranded passengers and then figure out how to get them to their destinations.

Naturally, European airlines were most affected—the ash cloud cost Delta's partner Air France/KLM about $200 million. But Delta itself was not immune. From April 14 through April 19, Delta canceled roughly 400 transatlantic flights. And of course, it shared Air France/KLM's losses—a profit-sharing JV with nothing but losses that week. The ash cloud dented Delta's quarterly profit by about $20 million.

On April 20, disaster hit closer to home, with less direct impact on airlines but meaningful implications for key Delta markets along the U.S. Gulf Coast. Shortly before 10 p.m., an explosion rocked the offshore Deepwater Horizon oil rig—licensed by the British oil giant BP—killing 11 workers and causing some 4 million barrels of oil to spill into the Gulf of Mexico, off the coast of Louisiana. It was an environmental disaster and an economic one too for countless tourism- and fishing-dependent Gulf communities like Gulfport, Miss., Mobile, Ala., and Pensacola, Fla.—Delta was the top airline at all of these. Richard Anderson, appearing on *Charlie Rose* years later, said "if [Delta] had run the oil platforms in the Gulf of Mexico, with our safety systems, the result would have been different."

The year would also feature major earthquakes in Haiti, Chile, New Zealand and China. Ethiopian Airlines, Libya's Afriqiyah Airways, Air India Express, Pakistan's Airblue and Cuba's Aero Caribbean all suffered fatal accidents, as did a Polish military plane that killed many of the country's top political leaders, including the president. There was political unrest in Bangkok, an escalating drug war in Mexico, tensions on the Korean peninsula, more violence in the Middle East and the ongoing war in Afghanistan. But the turmoil was accompanied by a strong economic recovery in most of the world, accented by stable oil prices, making 2010—to the surprise of many observers—one of the best years ever for the global airline industry. It followed, of course, one of the worst years ever, one that nonetheless killed only a surprisingly few, smallish airlines—no major airlines perished, thanks in many cases to government rescues. Japan Airlines had been just one example.

Atop this newly healthy global industry stood none other than Delta Air Lines, with its $30 billion-plus in annual revenues. And with size came enormous economies of scale and scope, without the diseconomies of labor unrest and operational chaos that typically spoil airline mergers. How global was Delta? Well, it was the only North American airline present in South Africa when the country hosted the FIFA World Cup that summer. It was the only North American airline serving Lagos and Istanbul, Málaga and Moscow, Budapest and Brasilia, Nice and Nagoya, Pisa and Prague, plus Amman and Düsseldorf and Cairo and others. Where *didn't* Delta fly?

Delta's rivals were now asking a different question: Should they consider merging too? If Delta and Northwest could do it, and do it so successfully, why couldn't they?

Doug Parker needed no example to follow. His airline, America West, had initiated the consolidation wave by buying US Airways, which in turn nearly bought Delta, ultimately driving Delta into the arms of Northwest. Parker remained uncomfortable in a globalizing world where US Airways lacked the international heft to compete against its four larger rivals—Delta, United, American and Continental—and lacked the low cost structure to compete against Southwest and other low-cost carriers, at least in the long run. It was managing well enough for now, driving ancillary revenues more aggressively than most of its rivals—too aggressively sometimes, as when it had started charging for coffee, juice and even water but quickly backtracked after customers revolted. It also adopted a contrarian approach to hedging fuel: It simply didn't do it, accepting some risk but saving untold millions in premium payments.

Parker was thrilled to hear Continental, in the spring of 2008, had lost its nerve at the altar after nearly marrying United. United and Continental agreed to become allies, yes, further marginalizing US Airways within the Star Alliance. But United was still single and available, with its CEO Glenn Tilton still eager to consolidate. So Parker and Tilton talked in mid-2008, making some headway before the financial crisis put everything but survival tactics on hold. Now, in 2010, conditions were looking healthy again, so talks re-started. United was very much interested, and the two carriers managed to overcome a key obstacle to merging: a clause in the US Airways pilot contract that would have triggered automatic big wage hikes in the event of a merger. United and US Airways, of course, had also almost merged in 2000 before a combination of DOJ opposition, the bursting of the tech bubble and United labor unrest torpedoed the deal. This time the hurdles looked less problematic. The two airlines, with a deal in principle worked out, got as far as discussing who would run the combined company—Tilton and Parker were both interested. United proposed Tilton be the CEO, with Parker, from the smaller airline, serving under him as president. Parker said no: He liked Tilton, but he wasn't going to take a demotion. If Tilton became CEO—a result Parker could accept—Parker would leave.

But it was all moot.

When Continental heard what was happening, alarm bells rang. At the beginning of 2010, Larry Kellner retired. Replacing him was his longtime deputy Jeffrey Smisek, a tall, thin, wise-cracking corporate lawyer with gray hair, a penchant for criticizing Washington and degrees from Princeton and Harvard. Smisek was instrumental in Continental's decision to walk away from United in 2008—he was concerned then about United's financial state and the state of the credit markets. But his unease about Continental's strategic positioning as a standalone carrier never disappeared. Continental's old ally Delta was now a significantly larger competitor, and a combined United-US Airways would be bigger still, with the independent American also exceeding Continental in size, scale and network scope. Even Kellner later conceded Continental perhaps had gotten luckier than he realized at the time when United and US Airways didn't merge in 2008. "If they did it, fine," was how he, years later, characterized his team's thinking at the time. "We don't think it's bad for us. We'll pick up the pieces. We'll do something." But maybe Continental had dodged a bullet, having perhaps been, "in hindsight, a little too confident in 2008 about how bad things were and where we were positioned versus the other guys. But you know, I think if I knew everything I know today, we could've played some other strategies in 2008.

"But it's like anything with 20/20 hindsight," Kellner said. "You know, give me next week's *Wall Street Journal*, and I'll be rich."

At a March 9, 2010, investor conference hosted by JP Morgan, Smisek spelled out his thoughts about Continental's new alliance with United. "We're now partners with people who want us to succeed," he said. "In our prior alliance"—the one with Delta, of course—"we were partners with someone who wanted to kill us, and it was a lot like being married to a woman who wants to poison your food. It's just generally not a good idea, and we thought it best if we leave that alliance. We were given the opportunity to do so. We did, and the Star Alliance is working very well for us."

But at the same conference, he did little to conceal an unmistakable preoccupation with Delta's new market might, both acknowledging and downplaying the threat. "I think they've done a very good job with their merger, candidly," he said. "I think they're very professional about it, and I think it's gone relatively smoothly, as these are quite complex—certainly, merging airlines is quite complex. [But] I think it's premature to know how well that merger will do"

"I think we'll continue to watch Delta," he continued. "It's important for us to watch them. They are, as they continue to remind everyone every day, the world's largest airline. [But] we are a big threat to Delta. We're a powerhouse in New York, and they'd like to be. We are a growing threat to them in the Pacific. You watch the fight over JAL. They were taking out their checkbook and spending money like drunken sailors. And they see us, they see the Pacific joint venture. They see Star Alliance. They see our partnership with All Nippon Airways. [And] we are very strong in Latin America, where they have great ambitions as well."

Smisek defended Continental's 2008 decision to walk away from United—with an emphasis on 2008. "I've been very clear with all of my co-workers"—Continental's longstanding term for its employees, dating back to when Bethune's team saved the company—"with [Wall] Street, with anyone who asks me, that when we chose to [walk away from] United, it was a point-in-time decision. And I think, candidly, it was the right decision at the time. I voted against it, myself, as a member of management and a member of Continental's Board.

"That said," he emphasized again, "that was a point-in-time decision, and we'll continue to watch the competitive dynamics. And if we think it's in our best interest to bulk up defensively, we'll do so."

When *The New York Times*, on April 7, 2010, broke the news that United was talking seriously with US Airways, the need for Continental to act became obvious. Two days later, on April 9, Glenn Tilton was celebrating his birthday in Santa Fe, N.M., when his cell phone rang. It was Jeff Smisek.

Times really had changed since the spring of 2008. In the spring of 2010, United started showing extremely strong profit margins, with its costs still on the high side, yes, but its revenue surging from the recovery in premium, longhaul, Asia and cargo demand. At the same time, it was doing much better operationally after hiring Delta's pre-merger operations chief Joe Kolshak. Southwest, which had mercilessly attacked United in the California, Chicago, Washington and Denver markets, eased its assaults once its hedge shield dissipated. And United's chief rival American was struggling with even higher costs, unions threatening to strike, Virgin America crashing yields on transcontinental routes and an ultra-LCC called Spirit that was stealing its Miami traffic to the Caribbean with a hub at nearby, low-cost Fort Lauderdale. Soon, Spirit would even charge not only for all checked bags but even for *carry-on* bags while—never mind the public outcry—earning extraordinary profits. Continental's profits, for their part, were improving too, in part thanks to a newfound acceptance of ancillary revenues—the airline, long a holdout in offering a more bundled product than its peers, had finally started charging for inflight meals, for example. More importantly, it expected a princely $350 million in bag fees for the year. And even *more* importantly, fuel costs were much lower and much more stable in the spring of 2010 than they had been in the spring of 2008.

United preferred Continental over US Airways not just because of what seemed like a more attractive merged network. In addition, United's pilot union was strongly opposed to a US Airways deal, as its leader Wendy Morse made clear April 8 in a public statement: "Media reports of United Airlines and US Airways being 'deep in merger discussions' have caused a great deal of consternation among the pilots I represent. United pilots share the view of many industry analysts and experts that a United merger with US Airways is unlikely to achieve significant synergies. In addition, the considerable legal hurdles to such a combination will only serve to distract United's management team from solving its own pressing issues. The pilots of US Airways and America West have yet to achieve operational integration more than four and a half years after the airlines merged. US Airways pilots face years of litigation as they attempt to work through their operational integration difficulties with America West pilots. United pilots certainly would not benefit by being drawn into that situation."

In 2008, Continental—although it hoped United would merge with no one at all—had been willing to watch it merge with US Airways rather than being drawn defensively into a merger. Then, Kellner had called Tilton's bluff and won; United, it turned out, would merge with Continental or no one at all, and because Continental had said no, United merged with no one. But Smisek in 2010? He was unwilling to make the same bet. And anyway, the market environment was vastly different now. So just three weeks after reviving their talks, on May 3, 2010, United and Continental announced they would merge.

"I didn't want him to marry the ugly girl," said Smisek, characterizing his arguments to Tilton about why United should choose Continental rather than US Airways. "I wanted him to marry the pretty one. And I'm much prettier."

United shareholders would own 55 percent of the new company, Continental shareholders the other 45 percent. The new airline would be called "United" but feature Continental's logo. Continental's Jeff Smisek would run it from United's Chicago headquarters, with a mixed management team gleaned from each airline. For the first two years, United's Glenn Tilton would be its non-executive chairman. And this time, unlike two years ago, United and Continental would not have to cut capacity, would not have to scramble for financing and would not have to integrate while navigating severely depressed demand conditions.

The route network Gordon Bethune had once described as "checkmate" was now reality: strength in all geographies and powerhouse positions in the country's most important business, political and cultural centers. With about $34 billion in combined revenues, the new United would soar past Delta to become America's largest airline by that measure (although shorter-haul Delta would still carry more passengers). The new United would also have the largest frequent flier plan in the world, one with 91 million members, surpassing Delta's 74 million and American's 64 million. Executives targeted at least $1 billion in annual merger synergies after three years, and with little hub overlap, regulators would have few reasons to oppose the deal. Pilots, too, seemed broadly supportive—not long before the merger announcement, Continental had offered its own pilots the Delta pilot contract, including all its terms and conditions, plus $1 an hour more in wages.

What did Delta think of all this? Naturally, it had some concerns. The new United would be a formidable competitor, perhaps one that could win back some corporate business it had lost to Delta when Delta's network grew stronger. Quickly, the marketing team set about reassuring passengers that Delta was still the best even if no longer still the biggest. As one of its new advertisements proclaimed: "No one who flies is waiting for a bigger airline. They're waiting for one that's committed to making flying better."

And whatever concern Delta had was tempered by the merger's positive implications for the rest of the industry. The rising consolidation tide was lifting all boats—or all fares, as it were. A less competitive industry is an industry with fewer fare wars and turf battles. It's an industry with more capacity discipline. In addition, no one could be sure the new United could integrate its information technology, its workforces and its planes as efficiently as Delta had done. Its pilots, for starters, did not—unlike Delta's—have a pre-merger agreement on pay and seniority integration. And there was no way United would ever have unit costs below Delta's, especially if it offered its pilots the Delta contract. Anderson, Bastian, Hauenstein and the Delta team also recognized that sometimes it's better to dominate smaller hub cities than to share the pie at larger ones. True, the new United was stronger in Chicago, for example, a much bigger business and population center than Atlanta. But United shared Chicago O'Hare with American. And to a lesser but important degree, it shared the city with Southwest, which by now offered a massive 225 daily departures at the city's other airport, Midway. Southwest had no presence in Atlanta.

The United-Continental merger would be the biggest deal of the year. But it wasn't the only one. Several months earlier, yet another two airlines had come together, if on a far more limited scale. American, seeking answers to its growing problems, was watching with frustration as Delta snatched New York City corporate travel accounts. Long-awaited regulatory clearance in February for American's JV with British Airways and Iberia would certainly help. But some more heft at New York JFK would help too. So American called JetBlue.

For Dave Barger, who had succeeded JetBlue's founder David Neeleman in 2007, opportunities in New York were becoming less interesting than those in cities else-where. Long gone were the days when JetBlue could simply steal Delta's lunch money on New York runs to Florida, charging low fares and profiting handsomely thanks to cheap fuel. A bet on new 100-seat Brazilian jets small enough to theoretically bring low fares to smallish markets proved unworkable, as fuel prices kept rising. In the world of 2010 rather than 2000, Delta was a fierce competitor in New York, and JetBlue, like everyone else, had to cultivate revenue growth wherever possible. Smartly, it had built a profitable network of flights to the Caribbean, where Southwest couldn't fly because its aging IT systems couldn't accommodate international flying. Just as shrewdly, JetBlue had positioned itself as the airline for Boston business travelers, exploiting opportunities in a market where American, Delta and US Airways were all downsizing. What JetBlue also wanted, though, perhaps more than anything else, were slots at Reagan National Airport in Washington. It came close to getting some in the compromise slot swap deal engineered by Delta and US Airways. But regulators had again said no.

American, as it happened, was willing to trade eight slot pairs at Reagan National, plus one pair at Westchester County Airport north of New York City, to JetBlue in exchange for 12 slot pairs at New York JFK. Not stopping there, the two carriers agreed to an interline partnership so passengers could book joint itineraries on a single ticket. Frequent flier reciprocity would follow. The agreement covered only a handful of non-overlapping routes, though, and stopped short of codesharing.

Any more intense relationship might have upset pilots at JetBlue, who were not unionized and urged by management to stay that way. American's unionized pilots would have been even more wary: They had strict restrictions on management's ability to codeshare, fearing outsourcing of flights to lower-cost airlines such as... well... JetBlue. Separately, American belatedly stepped up its activity in New York by appointing a new vice president for the market, expanding its marketing activity in the city, launching new service to Madrid, Manchester, Rio de Janeiro and Costa Rica and winning new JFK flight rights to Tokyo's Haneda Airport. It launched a slew of new domestic markets too, including several aimed squarely at Delta—five daily Atlanta flights from LaGuardia, for example. American also reacted fiercely to Delta's decision to enter the LaGuardia-Chicago market, at one point offering triple bonus miles. The oneworld alliance, meanwhile, now run by a former Delta executive (Bruce Ashby) who had in 1996 helped launch Delta Express, moved its headquarters from Vancouver to Park Avenue in New York.

Limited though it was, the new American-JetBlue friendship marked yet another instance of U.S. airlines cooperating rather than competing, consolidating rather than fragmenting. With fuel prices still high enough to discourage new startup carriers, meanwhile, the industry appeared to be on structurally healthier ground than at any time in its past. And investors recognized this, as reflected in rising airline share prices. Delta shares, trading for about $4 in early 2009, were selling for more than $14 barely one year later.

The true impact of these mergers would unfold over months and years. But Delta, with its head start, was in the meantime lighting up the profitability scoreboard. In 2010's third quarter, thanks to a great peak summer season, Delta blew away its peers with a 14 percent operating margin. Its net margin exceeded 10 percent—this was even more impressive, because it spoke to the increasing strength of Delta's balance sheet—outperforming everyone except its increasingly close ally Alaska Airlines, which did slightly better. The Atlanta hub, still the jewel in Delta's crown, was of course making money, with Atlanta-LaGuardia and Atlanta-Los Angeles still the two highest-revenue routes in the company. But domestic routes overall were doing well—the Minneapolis hub was particularly strong. Detroit was resurgent too after the auto industry bailout. Even in Asia, Delta's day of reckoning was forestalled thanks to a strong yen (which gave the Japanese newfound purchasing power when traveling abroad), JAL's deep capacity cuts and a recovery in demand following the H1N1 scare—Delta would actually add some new beach destinations from Tokyo. And as Richard Anderson proclaimed July 19: "The merger integration is for all practical purposes successfully complete."

Delta, having learned the lesson from its ill-advised purchase of Comair a decade earlier, now moved to sell two of the regional carriers it had inherited from Northwest—Mesaba and Compass—for a combined $83 million. And speaking of Comair, whose usefulness was now exhausted, Delta moved to dramatically shrink its fleet from 97 planes to just 44 by 2012. At the same time, Delta's regional partner

SkyWest, which had bought Atlantic Southeast from Delta in 2005, acquired SkyWest's rival ExpressJet—yet another example of consolidation. Delta also added first class cabins to its larger regional jets; even planes with 65 seats would have first class. This enabled elite frequent fliers with upgrade credentials to claim their bounty on an ever-greater array of flights in Delta's network.

Recognizing its disadvantage in Tokyo, the U.S. DOT awarded Delta two of the four Haneda routes that became available with the new U.S.-Japan open skies agreement—only four because of lingering space constraints at Haneda. This meant Delta could launch service from both Detroit and Los Angeles to Tokyo's preferred airport, although restrictions on what times Haneda-U.S. flights could actually operate made the Detroit flights particularly tricky to schedule at convenient times. Delta also launched or announced new Detroit flights to Shanghai, Seoul, Hong Kong, São Paulo and Rome, positioning the airport as a convenient and less congested alternative to Chicago. Delta also added domestic flights from Los Angeles, and New York JFK flights to Iceland—it would become the only U.S. airline to fly there. It even scheduled Atlanta flights to Luanda, the capital of oil-rich Angola in southern Africa. And no wonder: Paris-Luanda was, for a time, the highest yielding route in Air France's entire route network. Not stopping there, Delta also applied—successfully—for the London Heathrow slots that American and British Airways were forced to surrender, enabling it to start Heathrow service from Boston and Miami.

When Apple in 2010 released its latest product sensation—the iPad—Delta quickly put it to good use, setting up iPad kiosks in its New York airport terminals, enabling passengers to order food without leaving the gate area. And speaking of digital era sensations, Facebook became a booking channel, its page outfitted with a flight search engine. This accompanied a revamped website, updated mobile applications for iPhones and Android phones and newly installed re-charging stations throughout airport gate areas.

This boosted Delta's New York appeal somewhat, but what it still really needed was a replacement for its dilapidated JFK terminal. On April 26, at an aircraft finance conference in the Grand Hyatt near Grand Central Station in Manhattan, Delta's Senior Vice President and Treasurer Paul Jacobsen used the term "third world" to describe its JFK facilities, saying international visitors arrive at the terminal and say: "This is not the New York I've seen on 'Friends' and 'Seinfeld.'" Jacobsen also, incidentally, reminded conference attendees that a decade earlier, Delta had been an investment-grade airline. Implied: It was determined to recover that distinction.

For now, though, Delta was willing to pressure its balance sheet by committing to a $1.2 billion upgrade of its JFK facilities. In August, Delta and the Port Authority of New York and New Jersey announced a plan to expand and renovate JFK's Terminal 4 while demolishing Terminal 3. The airline itself took responsibility for the contracting, design, management and construction, bearing the risk of any cost overruns. But the Port Authority would issue $800 million in bonds to fund the majority of the project, with money for repayment of these bonds coming largely from higher rents Delta would pay to occupy the facility. One regrettable aspect: Delta's partners Air France and KLM would remain in a separate JFK terminal, meaning flight connections weren't as convenient as the airlines and passengers might have hoped. But that aside, Delta was thrilled to finally be getting a state-of-the art home at New York's international gateway. And although expensive, by only partly demolishing its existing facility—Pan Am's Worldport—Delta actually paid less than American had paid years earlier to construct an all-new JFK terminal.

"International" was still the key word. Devastating though the global economic slowdown was to global commerce, the world economy was bouncing back strongly in 2010, with emerging markets like China, India, Brazil, Russia, Turkey and Africa leading the way. And for all the economic trauma of late 2008 and 2009, airlines still saw international markets as the source of future profits. Developed markets were rebounding more slowly, with the U.S. experiencing a jobless recovery that was clearly visible in the airline sector. Employment at U.S. carriers inched up slightly in 2010 but was still 6 percent below 2006 levels, according to the DOT's Bureau of Transportation Statistics.

There was one major region of the world, however, where economic conditions were getting worse. Already by late 2009, it was becoming clear that Greece, a member of the eurozone currency block, was hopelessly overleveraged, with government debts equal to more than 100 percent of the country's gross economic production. It was on the verge of default. So the European Union and the International Monetary Fund had little choice but to provide €110 billion in rescue funds. Before long, Ireland would need a bailout too. Then Portugal. Then Greece again. Italy and Spain, two much larger economies, scrambled to avoid the same fate, imposing emergency budget austerity. Even in more advanced economies like Germany and the U.K., banks were hit hard by the U.S. subprime crisis, followed by this eurozone sovereign debt crisis—German and French banks, in fact, were among Greece's largest creditors. All of this further reduced demand for goods and services, including air travel, spreading recession throughout the European Union.

Suddenly Europe's major airlines were in trouble. Having outperformed their U.S. peers throughout most of the 2000s, the tide was reversing. Just as U.S. carriers were solidifying their future with their "three Cs" reforms—consolidation, capacity cutting and charging for everything—European carriers were hit with economic sclerosis at home, exacerbated by a depreciating euro, which increased the cost of fuel. The volcanic ash debacle made this bad situation worse, as did a rash of new taxation imposed on airlines by European governments desperate to patch holes in their budgets. In 2007, Greek airports handled 16.5 million passengers. In 2010, the number would fall to 15.4 million, on its way to less than 13 million two years after that. Europe's carriers also suffered a rash of labor unrest as not just airline workers, but air traffic controllers and airport staff too, staged strikes. Street protests in cities like Athens and Lisbon depressed critical tourism revenues.

Among Europe's major airlines, few were hit harder than Delta's partner Air France/KLM. As at Southwest in the U.S., the powerful hedge shield it had against high fuel prices had worn off and was now a liability. To the west, U.S. routes were doing fine thanks to its cooperation with Delta. But to many markets east, Gulf carriers like Dubai's Emirates, Abu Dhabi's Etihad and Qatar Airways, plus Turkish Airlines too, were aggressively adding capacity. All had significantly lower labor costs and faster-growing local economies. Rivals like Lufthansa were chipping away at its lucrative African business too, while LCCs like easyJet were hammering Air France and KLM in their home markets, causing massive losses at Air France's shorthaul operation, in particular. In 2009, Air France/KLM as a whole tumbled to a gruesome $1.6 billion net loss excluding special items. It was hurt disproportionately by its heavy exposure to cargo, premium and longhaul revenues. Losses eased somewhat it 2010, but the company still lost more money, excluding special accounting items, than any other airline in the world.

Air France/KLM, to be sure, still had many strengths, and it was far from the basket case it had been in the early 1990s. It still had a powerful global network with lots of routes to fast-growing emerging markets. Its service levels were well respected by global business travelers. It was dangerously indebted, yes. But it was also innovative. In 2009, Air France had created a new premium economy product with a comfort level and price between economy and business class. Much smaller Virgin Atlantic had done this years earlier, but among giant global airlines, Air France/KLM was an early adopter of what would become a powerful worldwide trend, perfect for companies forced to cut their travel budgets that didn't want to stick their employees with barebones economy. The Atlantic, meanwhile, remained a sea of calm for Air France and KLM, relatively speaking, testifying again to the power of international joint ventures.

To make their international JV more powerful still, Air France/KLM and Delta—on July 5, 2010—announced Italy's Alitalia would join the group. Nobody would mistake Alitalia for a successful airline. If Air France/KLM thought it had problems of its own, they were nothing compared to Alitalia's endless cycle of massive losses followed by government bailouts. The carrier seemed to be on strike more often than it was flying. But it did have a route network capable of pumping valuable Italian corporate travelers directly across the Atlantic or through the Paris and Amsterdam hubs. The traffic feed from wealthy regions in northern Italy, most notably, provided enormous value to Air France/KLM's hubs, which is why Air France/KLM had agreed to a full takeover of Alitalia in late 2007, when the global economy still appeared strong.

Thankfully for Air France/KLM's own sake—much as AirTran had thankfully been blocked by Northwest from purchasing Midwest Airlines—an Italian politician named Silvio Berlusconi, eager to stoke nationalism while trying to win back the Italian prime ministership, sabotaged the deal. Alitalia instead merged with a local rival called Air One. Several months prior to that, however, the victorious

Berlusconi was forced to deal with reality. On Aug. 29, 2008, Alitalia was placed into bankruptcy protection, with much of its debt and bad assets dumped onto taxpayers. The reincarnated Alitalia still needed more capital though, and selling the carrier's art collection—yes, it really had one—wasn't going to suffice. So on Jan. 12, 2009, it sold 25 percent of itself to Air France/KLM, which outbid Lufthansa, which similarly coveted Alitalia's traffic base in northern Italy. Air France/KLM paid about $450 million.

With the addition of Alitalia, the Delta-Air France/KLM JV represented approximately 26 percent of total transatlantic capacity, with annual revenues exceeding $10 billion. The JV would now feature seven key hubs: Amsterdam, Atlanta, Detroit, Minneapolis, New York JFK, Paris and Rome. It didn't do much for the giant London market. But in large swaths of Europe, and into Africa and the Middle East too, SkyTeam—including the JV, an alliance within an alliance—was a powerhouse. This JV was also the most developed and most mature of the three big transatlantic JVs. United, Air Canada and Lufthansa were just getting started on true revenue sharing, and unlike Delta, Air France/KLM and Alitalia, the Star carriers refrained from cost sharing. The just-approved American-British Airways JV was similarly focused on revenue sharing only. Only Delta's JV was a true profit-sharing JV, a virtual merged airline across the Atlantic.

Before long, the SkyTeam airlines really were scheduling transatlantic flights without regard to what logo adorned the aircraft—"metal neutrality," in industry jargon. They did have to work within pre-defined capacity allocations for each carrier, which were in place mainly to reassure unions that Air France, for example, couldn't outsource all its flying to Delta, whose labor costs were lower. But what they could do—and did do—was have Air France handle all New York-Paris flying, recognizing Air France's more premium product, including the true longhaul first class cabin that Delta lacked, worked well in such a premium-heavy market. Delta, on the other hand, would handle Philadelphia-Paris, a route Air France had previously flown.

Why didn't Delta, Air France/KLM and Alitalia just merge into one company? Because even had they wanted to do so, foreign ownership restrictions on both sides of the Atlantic, advocated most forcefully by U.S. unions but also even by the U.S. Defense Department (which considered foreign control of U.S. carriers a security issue), prevented full cross-border mergers. Europe's negotiators pushed for liberalization of these laws in open skies talks with the U.S. but failed to achieve more than token concessions. So JVs, alliances, codeshares and other forms of cooperation became all the rage, serving as a next best option to merging. SkyTeam alone, as it celebrated its 10th anniversary, would in 2010 welcome seven new members scattered around the globe, namely China Airlines of Taiwan, Romania's TAROM, Indonesia's Garuda, Aerolineas Argentinas, Vietnam Airlines, China Eastern and Shanghai Airlines, that last one plucked away from the Star Alliance when China Eastern bought it. The Chinese members, in particular—China Southern was also already in the club—gave Delta hope it could stay strong in East Asia following its setback in

Japan. Delta, remember, couldn't cooperate with these alliance members as closely as it could with Air France/KLM and Alitalia, with which it had the antitrust-immune JV. But it could at least promise its passengers recognition of their SkyMiles status and so forth when they traveled to ever more vast regions of the world.

Delta recruited partners on a bilateral basis too—those that didn't join SkyTeam, in other words—including the Brazilian LCC Gol, with which it signed a codeshare pact. Gol, because of its status as one of the two largest airlines in the giant Brazilian market, was able to get away with Alaska Airlines-style polygamy: It signed a codeshare pact with American too. Less important airlines wouldn't have had such flexibility. The Canadian LCC WestJet, which was fed up with Southwest's inability to execute a planned marketing pact due to IT shortcomings, was not a less important airline. So it signed marketing pacts with Delta and American too. Delta, although it canceled codesharing with its former part subsidiary, Milwaukee's embattled Midwest Airlines, signed new codeshare deals with Hawaiian Airlines and Air Nigeria while reinstating codesharing with Aeroméxico. (Aeroméxico's biggest boost of all in 2010 would come not from this but from the fact that its archrival Mexicana, a oneworld member, would in September collapse.) It was all part of Glen Hauenstein's pursuit of what he called "360-degree schedule strength."

To be sure, full mergers were happening too, and not just United-Continental. In 2010, British Airways fully merged with Iberia—one company, even though the two separate national brands would endure. LAN and TAM, the two most powerful airlines in South America, agreed to become one while also (for the moment, at least) retaining separate brands. Caribbean Airlines bought Air Jamaica. Aegean Airlines agreed to fuse with Olympic Air. And back in the U.S., the United and Continental mega-merger plan was just the beginning.

Back in April, when United and Continental announced their blockbuster deal, AirTran's CEO Bob Fornaro, with his gravelly Long Island-accented voice, uttered a sentiment that might have surprised some stakeholders. Fornaro was open, he suggested, to a merger. But hadn't AirTran just tried a merger, bidding for Midwest before Northwest and its financial partner TPG stepped in and snatched it? And hadn't that pursuit proved unwise in retrospect, occurring, as it did, just before the financial meltdown? Indeed, had AirTran succeeded in buying Midwest, which by 2010 was barely surviving, the resulting impact on AirTran's own balance sheet might very well have killed it. Even having dodged that bullet, after all, AirTran suffered a serious liquidity scare in 2008, a year in which it lost more than $100 million.

For AirTran, maybe a deal would be risky. But in 2010, was *not* doing a deal even riskier?

A sharp turnaround in 2009, a great year for LCCs around the world—Delta, for all its progress, still had a small net loss that year, whereas AirTran earned big profits—didn't make Fornaro feel secure. Hauenstein was hammering AirTran hard in Atlanta by throwing lots of capacity at it, driving fares down to levels where even low-cost AirTran couldn't profit, forcing more of its growth into more marginal territory. The Atlanta business community, moreover, as Fornaro himself said, had rallied around Delta during the US Airways takeover drama and more or less remained loyal thereafter as the new and improved Delta offered increasingly good service. More generally, AirTran, however low its costs and nimble its operations, simply didn't have the financial muscle and market power possessed by its larger rivals, some of which were growing even larger.

Deep in the heart of Texas, meanwhile, the happy world of yesteryear was quickly fading for the legendary Southwest Airlines. Throughout the 1980s and 1990, fuel was cheap, aviation taxes were low, economic growth was steady, airport security was hassle-free, skies were uncongested, competitors were bloated, Southwest's key markets like California and Texas were lands of opportunity and Herb Kelleher had found a way to do the impossible: consistently make money flying airplanes.

But Herb's more buttoned-down successor Gary Kelly faced tougher operating conditions. The 2000s saw skyrocketing fuel prices, rising taxes and airport costs, airport security hassles (to which Southwest was the most vulnerable of all airlines, because it specialized in short routes where people could choose to drive instead), wage inflation, an eventual erosion of massively lucrative fuel hedges, a giant economic recession, restructuring legacy rivals and a new breed of dynamic LCCs with even lower wages, even more flexible work rules, more advanced IT systems, international exposure and superior inflight products. One of these LCCs, AirTran, even managed to achieve the unthinkable: lower overall unit costs than the mighty Southwest itself.

Kelly understood the need for change. So he raised fares, added flights to business centers like Boston and New York, turned Denver into the major growth focus Chicago and California had once represented, upgraded Southwest's pricing and revenue management practices, distributed tickets through corporate travel agencies, chased corporate contracts, added ancillary charges for perks like priority boarding and lobbied hard to change a law that restricted Southwest's flying from Dallas Love Field. After losing its partnership with WestJet to the north, Southwest signed one with an LCC to the south, a Mexican airline called Volaris. It won 18 slot pairs at Newark when regulators forced Continental to surrender them as a condition for approving its United merger. Southwest revamped its frequent flier plan and began outfitting its planes with Wi-Fi. It even tried buying Frontier Airlines before pilot seniority issues got in the way.

For all of these changes, though, a key ingredient to Herb Kelleher's business model was missing: Southwest was not growing anymore. In fact, it had *cut* capacity 5 percent in 2009 and another 3 percent in the first six months of 2010. For the entire first decade of the 2000s, average annual growth was a modest 6 percent, this after growing at a 14 percent annual clip in the go-go 1990s. Growth was what had long enabled Southwest to keep its unit costs so low even though it paid its people (especially its senior employees) rather well, because it was always hiring new people at entry-level wages, holding down its average pay rates. And as it flew more, it achieved more scale and became more efficient in nearly every way imaginable.

But the growth had stopped. It had to stop, because the world had changed. Growth always—at every airline, everywhere in the world—helps hold down unit costs. But it also always—at every airline, everywhere in the world—does something less benign: It depresses unit revenues too, because more supply of anything relative to the same amount of demand means lower prices. And because of high fuel prices—which Southwest was now as powerless to control as every other airline—for the first time in Southwest's history, growth had begun holding down unit revenues more than unit costs. So it had to stop growing.

Organically, anyway.

Another way to grow is to buy the growth. And actually, Southwest wasn't a stranger to takeovers. In 1985 it bought a fellow Texas airline called Muse Air. Seven years later, it bought an impressive Salt Lake City-based LCC called Morris Air, pitting it more directly than ever against Delta—Delta had a Salt Lake City hub that it too had acquired, in its case when it bought Western Airlines back in 1987. Morris Air had been run by a young and restless David Neeleman, whom Herb Kelleher planned to groom as his successor. As it happened, the entrepreneurial Neeleman didn't last long at Southwest, leaving to help found WestJet in Canada and then JetBlue in New York. More recently, Southwest, in addition to trying but failing to buy Frontier, had succeeded in buying what was left of ATA—mainly airport assets that, among other things, enabled its Chicago Midway hub. But now it was after a bigger fish.

AirTran couldn't escape Gary Kelly's attention. It was, after all, Southwest's only significant lower-cost competitor. The two competed closely up and down the east coast to Florida, overlapping most prominently in Baltimore and Orlando. AirTran had Boeing 717s, smaller jets capable of serving markets that were too small for most of Southwest's 737s—additional growth potential, in other words. It flew internationally too, mostly to the Caribbean. It had a sizeable presence in Boston and slots at New York LaGuardia and Reagan National in Washington. And enticingly, AirTran had Atlanta, which after all these years remained conspicuously absent from Southwest's giant nationwide route network—an airline from as far away as Korea served Atlanta, but America's second largest domestic airline (behind Delta) did not. Georgia was on Gary Kelly's mind.

Kelly called Bob Fornaro in the spring of 2009, the *Atlanta Journal-Constitution* reported, suggesting the two discuss a merger. "When Gary called," Fornaro told the *AJC*, "first of all, I wasn't sure what the subject would be.... I was really unsure." The attractiveness of fusing with Southwest didn't take long to register.

The vulnerabilities of AirTran's thin balance sheet would disappear. AirTran's shareholders would win. So would its employees. Soon, executives and lawyers began working on a deal, cloaked in secrecy by avoiding any mention of the two airlines—Southwest was "Cowboy" and AirTran was "Falcon," references to their hometown NFL teams.

More than a year later, on Sept. 27, 2010, Southwest and AirTran announced a $1.4 billion merger, creating a behemoth with 685 airplanes and 43,000 workers, serving more than 100 airports and 100 million passengers annually. The new Southwest promised $400 million in annual synergies by 2013.

"Southwest is looking for growth opportunities," Kelly beamed. "And I'm happy to say that we have found a way to grow." He added: "We kind of liken it to the '90s when we had big pools of growth opportunities. We had California. Then this decade we had Chicago, and of course recently, we've had Denver. In terms of us filling our network gap, the major market that we don't touch domestically that our business customers in particular want is Atlanta. So this is very clearly a strategic move for us to fill that gap."

Delta's Atlanta hub was finally in Southwest's crosshairs. But for now, in the waning days of 2010, Delta had other things to think about. Or more precisely, other things to celebrate. At its annual investor day event Dec. 15, executives waxed glowingly about the company's breathtaking turnaround, one of the most spectacular in the annals of American corporate history. Sure enough, Delta had another strong quarter from October through December, again beating United, American and US Airways. Among the revelations that investor day: Just 5 percent of Delta's customers accounted for 26 percent of its revenue. This elite group of fliers consisted of road warriors who practically lived in the air, best personified by George Clooney's character in a movie of the era, "Up in the Air." That character flew American. But more and more real-life corporate travelers were choosing Delta.

Delta was taking airline management to a new level, going so far as to conduct research that involved monitoring passengers' heart rates throughout their journeys. (Heart rates, Delta found, jump when going through security, when preparing to board the plane and when arriving at the baggage carousel to claim checked luggage.) Delta was also investing heavily in information technology, particularly in the areas of network management, revenue management, flight operations, ticket and ancillary service distribution and—perhaps most importantly—customer service, equipping airport agents with handheld computers and reviving the old practice of deploying red-coated agents (the "red coats," as longtime Delta fliers knew them) to assist travelers in the terminal.

Anderson and Bastian, at that investor day, said investors should count on a company driven by maximizing returns on their investment. To emphasize the point, Anderson discussed Delta's unconventional aircraft procurement strategy.

"You know, this industry has been a bit focused on shiny new airplanes," Anderson said. "And often times, shiny new airplanes may not produce returns. And it should be less about the marvel of the machine and more about the marvel of a return on invested capital, and that orientation is an important part of what we are about."

What was perhaps the greatest marvel of all, and perhaps the most compelling element of the Delta turnaround miracle, was how much the airline's employees had benefited since the dark days of bankruptcy and the years leading up to it. In 2010, employees earned another $313 million in profit sharing money on top of their wage increases, improved benefits, performance bonuses and greater job security. Delta, in other words, would have been even more profitable if only it didn't have to share so much of the bounty with its employees. That was a problem it was happy to have.

But would Delta remain a largely non-union company? At the start of 2010, the answer wasn't clear. Pilots were represented by ALPA and always had been. And it was clear early on that mechanics would remain non-union because of what had happened at Northwest—Doug Steenland chased the AMFA union off the property by flying through its strike. AMFA, with little support among the mechanics still employed by Northwest after the strike, voluntarily decertified itself in February 2009. Delta quickly and unilaterally—without asking for anything in return—raised the pay of all Northwest mechanics to more generous Delta levels and made them eligible for profit-sharing and operating-performance bonuses. The airline was quick to remind them too that they no longer had to pay any union dues. "This is fantastic news for Delta and the new TechOps team," the division's president Tony Charaf said. "As I've said many times in the past, our flexible workforce has always been an advantage as we grow our global customer base." While most other airlines felt compelled to outsource many of their heavy maintenance jobs overseas, Delta was able to keep much of this work in house and even *insource* some work from its competitors.

What was so different at Delta that enabled it to take what was a *cost* center at airlines like United and American—and turn it into a *profit* center? Especially considering Delta did, to be clear, pay its mechanics rather well? The key was the "flexibility" Charaf had mentioned.

Or as Ray Valeika, a retired Delta senior vice president who had overseen TechOps during his time at the airline, explained: "I could take a guy working on one model type of an engine and if I needed more employees in another area, I could move him over. In some cases with unions, you can't do that."

And that wasn't all.

"Another example, which is really a big example," Valeika continued, "was the ability for us to select our 'leads' based on ability and capability as opposed to seniority. So we could have young leads.... We allowed the employees to select their leads and have them vote, picking a lead based on who they thought were the best employees, whereas most union leaders are strictly a function of seniority—once you got senior, you could bid for the job and you got it. It didn't mean that you were qualified, competent or anything else. It meant that you'd been there a long time."

Fortunately for Delta, that wouldn't change. But what about the airline's other front-line employees, including its large groups of flight attendants and airport agents, who were non-union at Delta but unionized at Northwest?

Several national unions sensed a moment of opportunity after Delta's merger with union-heavy Northwest. Campaigns to organize the combined airport and flight attendant workforces might not be that difficult, union leaders reasoned, especially amid the uncertainty the 2008 merger had brought to employees. And then the unions got a major break.

By supporting President Obama in his 2008 election bid, unions now had a friend in the White House. They had contributed large amounts of money to his campaign. Sure enough, among voters hailing from a union family, Obama won 59 percent of the vote to John McCain's 39 percent, according to a survey for the National Election Pool by Edison Media Research/Mitofsky International. To return the favor, the Obama administration, through the National Mediation Board that governs labor relations in the airline sector, instituted a new rule—over objections from Georgia's congressional delegation—that made it significantly easier for unions to organize workers. Members who didn't vote at all would no longer be considered to have voted "no," as had long been the case. Only a majority of "yes" votes among people actually voting, rather than among all eligible voters (whether they voted or not), would be required in order to unionize.

The new rule, incidentally, came as airlines were already smarting from a new Obama administration rule levying high fines—millions of dollars for just one flight—for keeping passengers stranded aboard aircraft on the ground for more than three hours. This so-called "tarmac delay rule" would have unintended consequences, however: When bad weather threatened, carriers felt compelled to cancel countless flights to avoid even one lengthy "tarmac delay" rather than do their best to operate all flights. Regulators also nixed a planned joint venture between Delta and Virgin Blue, the Australian airline backed by Richard Branson's Virgin Group.

United's Jeff Smisek was the most outspoken about Washington's aviation policy. At a JP Morgan investor conference, he ranted:

> "The day that I rely on government to help this industry, you should make sure that I get fired... because every time they try to make things better, they just make things worse. An example of that is long tarmac delays. That's solving a problem that doesn't exist. I mean, long tarmac delays are extremely rare. They do occasionally occur. There's no question about it. But, having a rule that requires us to cancel flights at three hours or suffer a fine of $27,500 per passenger is inane. And so, what we do in the face of a fine like that is, we're going to cancel a lot of flights.
>
> "The reason they're on the ground is because we use the very finest 1950s ground-based radar technology in our air traffic control system. So, the government sticks us on the ground because they refuse to invest in the highways in the sky, right, because no congressman ever looks up as far as I can tell. And then they fine us when, as a result of their incompetence, we're held on the ground, right? And so, we'll cancel flights.
>
> "Well, many passengers, at 2 hours and 45 minutes, they really want to go to L.A. or Mumbai or wherever. But, the government, by God, says we're going to fine you $27,500. Guess what we're going to do? We're going to cancel the flight. And with the loads we've got today, you're not getting

there for maybe days. And so the government's inconveniencing more passengers by passing what is, candidly, a very stupid rule."

It was a rant that would have sat well with the ascendant "Tea Party" movement that helped wrest control of the House of Representatives from Democrats in the fall of 2010. But anti-government rants aside—and keep in mind, some airline executives were highly supportive of President Obama's economic stimulus efforts—the new union voting rule is what specifically threatened Delta's "direct" (i.e., non-collective-bargaining) relationship with its workers. And it came at a time when other airlines throughout the world were fighting bruising battles with unions. British Airways endured multiple flight attendant strikes, for example, and Virgin Atlantic came close to a pilot strike. Much closer to home, Spirit Airlines, a rising star in the U.S. airline sector, grounded its operation from June 12 through June 17 when pilots walked off their jobs, in what had in recent years become a rare occurrence in the U.S. Some suggested the ALPA union had pushed for the Spirit strike as a message to management at much larger United: Give us a fair contract, or this will happen to you. United and Continental pilots were already publicly blasting management for slow-moving contract negotiations.

But what about Delta?

Early in 2010, results from the airline's first union representation election of the year came back: Flight simulator technicians had voted against joining the International Association of Machinists. Just 40 out of 91 eligible workers had voted in favor of organizing. It was a small group, yes, but a good early start for Delta and its efforts to keep its non-pilot workforce union free. But that was before the new rule took effect: For now, as long as the union had only 40 "yes" votes out of 91 eligible voters, it didn't matter how many of the rest actively voted no. That would change starting in May.

The first big test—flight attendants, some 19,000 crew members voting under the new union-friendly rules—came in the fall. Organizers from the AFA-CWA union campaigned vigorously for a yes vote, with management working just as strenuously for the opposite result. At one point, Richard Anderson himself accused union leaders of bully tactics against workers and their families. Well, the same week in November when Republicans won big in Washington, Delta won big on the labor front. The attendants defeated unionization, with 53 percent of those actually voting—that's what mattered now—opposing the union. It was the third time in 10 years Delta's flight attendants had rejected union representation. This vote had been more in doubt than the others because of the new rule and especially because Northwest's more pro-union flight attendants had a say. Delta didn't hurt its chances by cleverly announcing a recall of furloughed attendants just as the voting was taking place.

As with the mechanics, the continued non-union status of its flight attendants enabled Delta to—although paying them rather well—maintain a level of flexibility its competitors could only envy. "You have some flexibility on the number of flight attendants you can put on widebodies," Gerald Grinstein, recalling his days as CEO, explained. "Sometimes you use six, sometimes you use seven, sometimes you use more…. It's geared really to what kind of passenger service you want to have." In fact, when Delta began installing inflight screens with live television and movies and music and games, it yielded the pleasantly unexpected surprise of reducing the work demand for flight attendants, because passengers were more preoccupied with the entertainment. So Delta could fly with less staff, and because there was no union, "we didn't have to go back into a negotiation just to adjust the number of flight attendants," Grinstein said.

Two weeks after flight attendants rejected unionization, on Nov. 18, 2010, "below-wing" airport workers delivered the same result. Of 10,593 people voting, 53 percent voted no. Work groups accounting for more than 40,000 people had now rejected unionization.

"Once again, Delta people have clearly stated their preference for working directly with their leaders to make Delta a great place to work for all employees and the global airline of choice for our customers," Delta's human resources chief Mike Campbell said. "In multiple elections across many work groups, tens of thousands of Delta employees continue to reaffirm the importance of maintaining the generations-old set of values set forth by our founder C.E. Woolman."

Less than three weeks after that, another big victory: Delta's "above-wing" airport workers—those working not on the airfield but in the terminals assisting passengers—rejected unionization too. Nearly 13,000 of them had voted. Nine different work groups, small and large alike, had now sided with management and declined third-party representation.

"These results are stunning," a thrilled Richard Anderson exclaimed. "There is no better testament to how well the direct relationship works at Delta than the voices of the majority clearly stating time and again they want to preserve our special relationship and values. Through numerous campaigns by several unions, even with the voting rules changed in the middle of the process, Delta people have said 'no.' It is time to move forward and bring everyone together."

It was also time to show the world that 2010, one of Delta's greatest years ever, was—to borrow a term then fashionable to describe the broader economy—the "new normal."

2011

"We are no longer interested in giving it back in the winter"

Ten years after 9/11, America was a changed nation. And its airlines were operating in a changed environment. The country had entered an age of terrorism, prompting heavy military and security measures that included two expensive overseas wars and a revamp of airport screening. Economically, the U.S. had suffered its worst crisis since the Great Depression. Still, by 2010, inflation-adjusted GDP had grown 18 percent since 2000 to nearly $15 trillion, even after shrinking 3 percent in 2009. The population had grown just 10 percent during the same period, implying substantially greater wealth per person, although this good news was tainted by expanding gaps in wealth distribution: By 2010, 15 percent of the population was living below the poverty line, the highest figure since the early 1990s. In the meantime, war spending, social spending, stimulus measures and a series of tax cuts during the terms of Presidents Bush and Obama left the U.S. treasury with enormous deficits and debts.

The population was older in 2010 than in 2000. While the overall number of people in the U.S. grew by just 10 percent during the decade, the number of people 65 and older grew 21 percent, with people aged 45 to 64 increasing in number by an eye-popping 32 percent. This shifting demographic reality provided the backdrop for arguably the greatest economic challenge of America's future: how to provide health care to a population aging so quickly. Those 45-to-64 year olds, in their peak earning and tax-paying years, would soon retire, leaving a much smaller generation behind them to pay for all their needs. In the meantime, people continued to move south and west from northeastern and Midwestern population centers, fueling 20 percent population growth in Nevada, Arizona, Utah, Idaho and Texas, with North Carolina, Florida and Delta's home state of Georgia not far behind. On the opposite end of the scale was Michigan, whose population declined in tandem with the fall of America's Big Three auto makers. Rhode Island, Ohio, New York and hurricane-ravaged Louisiana grew, but only barely.

The New York, Los Angeles and Chicago metropolitan areas remained the country's three largest population centers, but all saw population increases of just 3 to 4 percent in the first decade of the 2000s. By contrast, Dallas-Fort Worth grew 23 percent, surpassing Philadelphia to become the No. 4 metro area. Also closing in on Philadelphia was Houston, with 26 percent growth. Atlanta, now ranked No. 9, enjoyed similarly explosive population growth of 24 percent, fueled partly by economic opportunities generated by Delta's global links. Delta's hub cities Minneapolis and Salt Lake City grew by double digits too, although Detroit certainly did not—its population *shrank* 4 percent.

The rise of energy-rich Texas as the country's most dynamic economic and demographic center highlights another characteristic of the post-9/11 decade. Oil prices, so closely correlated with the health of America's economy since World War II, went from unusually cheap to unusually expensive, sucking trillions of dollars of wealth out of the country. Sure, U.S. GDP grew 18 percent in the 2000s. But it had grown 35 percent in the 1990s and 36 percent in the 1980s, two decades when oil was mostly cheap.

The stunning run-up in fuel prices, of course, contributed heavily to the bankruptcies of United, US Airways (twice), Delta and Northwest, four of America's Big Six airlines. In a mad scramble to survive as fuel prices spiraled higher, U.S. scheduled passenger airlines slashed the equivalent of about 140,000 full-time jobs. The industry still employed a lot of people: 388,641 people in September 2011. But 10 years earlier, before 9/11, the figure was more like 520,000. Despite the staff reductions, however, U.S. carriers were actually producing more seats—and generating more traffic and more revenue—than before 9/11, thanks to new labor-saving technologies like web check-in and contract concessions compelling workers to do more for less. Some jobs, especially those involving maintenance work, were simply outsourced—people were still doing the work, but those people weren't directly employed by the airlines. The sciences of pricing and revenue management had evolved too. In 2000, airlines filled 72 percent of their seats. In 2010? Fully 82 percent, a massive differential.

Another big reason U.S. airlines were producing more with less: internationalization. Although total capacity measured by seat miles increased 2 percent from 2000 through 2010, domestic capacity shrank 4 percent. The actual number of domestic flights grew 10 percent, but many former "mainline" routes—i.e., those previously not farmed out to smaller airlines—now did indeed feature smaller regional jets with fewer seats. Domestic passenger counts, meanwhile, rose a mere 5 percent in 10 years. Southwest, with its many ultra-shorthaul markets of less than a few hundred miles, saw some of the greatest contraction in demand. Where driving was an option, travelers stayed away from time-consuming airport security hassles. Southwest's CEO Gary Kelly, making the point, noted that measured by pure number of seats—in other words, not taking into account distance—industry capacity on domestic routes had plummeted 17 percent from April 2000 through April 2011. So yes, airlines were logging more miles and operating more flights and filling more seats and expanding abroad. But the decline in actual seats within the U.S. was unmistakable. "That, by any stretch of the imagination, is a huge reduction in industry capacity," remarked Kelly, who would call the first 10 years of the 2000s a "lost decade."

From 2002 through 2005, fuel was still priced low enough, and legacy carriers were still burdened with costs high enough, that low-cost carriers like Southwest, JetBlue and AirTran could play offense. But the tide began to turn in 2006, and five years later, no major airline—legacy or LCC—was expanding beyond a few percentage points per year. The LCCs had run into some harsh new realities that, although never causing them quite the turmoil that their legacy brethren had earlier experienced, did force them into uncomfortable strategic adjustments. They now had no choice, for example, but to aggressively chase corporate flying contracts, a game they were far less eager to play than the old game of winning by having massive non-fuel cost advantages over their legacy competitors—back then, the LCCs' revenue disadvantage mattered little because their cost advantage was so massive. Fuel, in that sense, especially after Southwest's hedges wore off, was the great equalizer between legacy carriers and LCCs.

The great changes of the post-9/11 decade were visible through countless windows. Consider Google, whose revenues in 2000, when it was just a year old, amounted to $19 million, about half of what Continental Airlines generated in a *day*. By 2010, Google was hosting the world's most visited website and generating $22 billion in annual revenues—more than American Airlines. Its net profit of $4.2 billion in the recession year of 2008 was roughly equal to the net profits of Lufthansa, Air France/KLM and British Airways combined—in the boom year of 2007!

Ten years earlier, Southwest was the world's one and only major low-cost airline. There was no JetBlue, Virgin Blue, AirAsia, Gol, Air Arabia or Vueling (which would all become major LCCs). Canada's WestJet had a mere 16 planes, Ryanair had just introduced its first new-generation 737 and easyJet was still a few months from going public with its shares. Air Berlin was a charter airline, Norwegian a regional feeder. ValuJet briefly thrived as an LCC in the early 1990s, but by 2000 it was a loss-making, 47-airplane carrier renamed AirTran.

But by now, in 2011, it was hard to believe that barely more than a decade earlier, giants like American, United, Delta, Northwest, Continental and US Airways, in markets where Southwest hadn't yet shown up, allegedly had an unfair competitive grip on the nation's most important routes, triggering political backlash and antitrust investigations. How quickly that situation had disappeared in the post-9/11 years. In 2000, LCCs—which, at the time, really meant just Southwest and a few other small players—accounted for 12 percent of all seat-mile capacity within the continental U.S., according to a calculation by AirTran. By late 2009, they were on their way to surpassing 30 percent.

Globally, one of the great developments of the 2000s was the rise of the Arabian Gulf carriers, headlined by the stunning expansion of Dubai's national airline Emirates. Brazil's TAM, Panama's Copa and Chile's LAN gave the concept of creative destruction a good name by transforming Latin America from an airline intensive care unit to one other regions looked to for inspiration. Korean Air and Asiana, although hardly profit machines, did manage to capitalize more than anyone else on China's enormous economic growth. Ethiopian Airlines and Kenya Airways showed the way in an Africa that remained over-regulated and under-stimulated. Jet Airways gave Indians a quality alternative to Air India, and Aegean Airlines gave Greeks an alternative to Olympic. Old warhorses Singapore Airlines, Cathay Pacific and Qantas—however challenged by LCCs and Arabian Gulf upstarts—completed a decade of unqualified, if not uninterrupted, financial success, fueled by deregulation, economic growth and technology.

Speaking of technology, 10 years earlier, new-generation narrowbodies like Boeing 737-700s and -800s had only recently entered service with a handful of airlines. Same for the latest Airbus 320-family planes, which similarly offered LCCs and non-LCCs alike the range and economics to profitably fly routes that previously had no service or were served with less-than-ideal aircraft. The success of the Gulf carriers rested in part on new long-range widebodies like the Boeing 777-200LR—"LR" for "long range"—which enabled them to stretch their networks across continents, and with a fuel-sipping twin-engine (rather than gas-guzzling quad-engine) airplane, no less. At the turn of the millennium—difficult as this might have been to believe by 2011—American, United, Delta, Northwest and US Airways were all still flying 727s, three-engine narrowbody aircraft that required three-person cockpit crews.

Technology also played a giant role in reducing the industry's non-aircraft cost base, most importantly in the area of ticket distribution. In 2000, 25 percent of Southwest's ticket sales came from its website. In 2010, the figure was 78 percent. In 1999, American spent almost $1.2 billion on travel agent commissions alone, helping it secure $18 billion in revenue. By 2011, it spent $100 million *less* to secure $24 billion. New and better ways to process passengers on the ground and entertain them in the air had arrived. E-tickets, online check-in, self-service airport kiosks and on-demand inflight multimedia were just some of the new technologies that were mostly science fiction on 9/11 but commonplace by 2011. In short, technology had enabled the airline industry to both lower its costs and—in some cases, anyway—provide better service.

The second great change enabler was deregulation. On Jan. 1, 2000, the U.S. had 37 open skies agreements with other countries. The one it signed with Japan in 2010 was its 95th. One of them, signed in 2007, was with the European Union, effectively opening the busy U.S.-London Heathrow market to more competition. Airline liberalization brought even more radical change throughout the developing world. Widespread removal of barriers to air service yielded the birth of LCCs, more competition, improved service, lower fares and vastly better route networks. And deregulation of global distribution systems—those fare and schedule supermarkets used by travel agencies—helped airlines lower their costs.

Economic growth was a third enabler of industry change. Even with the heavy downturn in 2009, global economic production expanded from roughly $40 trillion in 2000 to more than $60 trillion by the decade's end. That's a far greater increase than the growth in the world's population, which was only about 10 percent for the decade. That means the average person became wealthier and more apt to fly. At the same time, business and tourism became more globalized than ever, creating new demand for cross-border air service. According to data published by the International Civil Aviation Organization (ICAO), the world's airlines transported 2.3 billion passengers and 4.3 trillion RPKs in the peak year 2008, up 54 percent and 63 percent, respectively, from 10 years earlier. They did it more efficiently too, with capacity up just 47 percent. That's because load factors—essentially, the percentage of seats that were occupied—had risen seven points.

Still, it was far from a triumphant decade. Giovanni Bisignani, the IATA chief Leo Mullin hired just after 9/11, called the opening decade of the 2000s the 10 worst financial years in aviation history. Supporting his claim was a brutal statistic: Global industry losses from 2000 through 2009 had amounted to $49 billion, or nearly $5 billion per year. The four-letter F-word—fuel—was the culprit. On Jan. 1, 2000, the per-barrel price of oil was $26. Even this figure was up significantly from late-1990s lows, when an Asian financial crisis depressed demand. By 2004, the price averaged $42. Then $57, then $66, then $72—and by 2008, having touched $147, the average full-year price was an even $100, plummeting briefly in 2009 but trending back to the $100 mark by early 2011.

Sure enough, new-generation airplanes and enhanced operational procedures made the industry 20 percent more fuel efficient compared to a decade earlier, according to IATA. But fuel outlays, which were responsible for little more than 10 percent of total operating expenses at the beginning of the decade, had ballooned to more than 32 percent by 2008. Airlines were on a treadmill, running harder just to stay in place.

An era of extreme fuel prices did contribute to economic growth in some regions like the Middle East, Russia and Africa—in that sense, it was good for the airlines based there, at least on the revenue side of their ledgers. And pricey oil opened new opportunities for others who launched new "chase-the-oil-money" routes—Delta played this game to the extent it could by flying to places like Nigeria and Angola. But overall, expensive fuel was the chief reason for the industry's decade of heavy losses.

The chief reason. But not the only reason.

The decade also saw hugely destabilizing incidents of terrorism, war, natural disasters, health epidemics, disruptive foreign exchange volatility and multiple economic shocks, including the bursting of an internet stock bubble and the worst global recession since the 1930s. The airline industry's role in global warming became controversial, putting the industry on the defensive. For all the deregulation championed by some visionary politicians, governments simultaneously imposed burdensome new airport security procedures and ever-higher taxation, did little to lift foreign ownership restrictions, failed to sufficiently modernize the industry's public infrastructure, subsidized and protected loss-making airlines and—on anti-trust grounds—threatened to block various forms of cooperation.

Not surprisingly, airlines unprotected by their governments collapsed by the dozen. Swissair, Sabena, Ansett Australia, Skybus, Independence Air, Transbrazil, VASP, Sterling, Aerocalifornia, Air Afrique, Silverjet, Aloha, Mexicana, ATA, Oasis Hong Kong and Adam Air—some with long histories, others gone soon after they launched—were just a few of the dearly departed. Others like TWA, Varig, Virgin Express and Northwest lost or largely lost their identities following mergers. But the more important trend was not how many airlines disappeared. It was how few major ones went away. Japan Airlines, Alitalia, Olympic, Air India, Aerolineas Argentinas and even Air Canada were among those that were on the brink but ultimately got help from their governments.

No single market, however, had a more disheartening decade than the U.S. The period began with a weakening American economy, which only got worse after the 9/11 terrorist attacks, the most debilitating such event in industry history. Washington had to step in with bailout money and emergency loans. A weak dollar made fuel even more expensive than it was for overseas rivals. One by one, the nation's big airlines—United, US Airways twice, Delta and Northwest—declared bankruptcy. American barely avoided it. Pay and pensions were slashed, labor and regional flying were outsourced, planes were parked and route networks were downsized—all this *before* the economic collapse that began in late 2008. By then, the whole sector, LCCs included, was slashing capacity. Fortunately, access to capital was never really an issue, with suppliers, business partners, Wall Street and takeover-minded rivals ready to step in. But the pain was intense.

Just how lost was the "lost decade?" Well, from 1990 through 1998, U.S. carriers grew their passenger counts by 32 percent, according to data published by what would later be renamed Airlines for America, the industry trade association. From 2000 through 2008, by contrast, the growth was merely 11 percent. Focus exclusively on domestic flights, and the numbers are even worse: 34 percent growth in the 1990s and a paltry 8 percent in the 2000s. Overseas travel by Americans increased just 15 percent from 2000 through 2008, held in check by the weak dollar and fuel surcharges that inflated fares, according to the U.S. Office of Travel and Tourism Industries. Inbound visitors to the U.S. in those eight years, meanwhile—depressed, as these visits were, by new visa restrictions imposed after 9/11—increased just 13 percent.

It was in the context of this turbulent decade that Delta had stumbled from financial strength on Sept. 10, 2001, to bankruptcy on Sept. 15, 2005. The post-9/11 demand shock, the war in Iraq, the run-up in fuel prices, LCC attacks and an unaffordable pilot contract were all responsible, along with some self-inflicted wounds like Song. But then came one of the most remarkable turnarounds in the history of corporate America. Six years later, by September 2011, Delta was the king of its jungle.

The new decade began with the Atlanta-based giant outperforming its peers at home and abroad, with strong profits and cash flows. In 2010, Delta's best year since the late 1990s, net debt fell by $2 billion, unit revenues rose by 13 percent and unit costs excluding fuel were more or less flat. No longer just managing to survive, Delta generated a 10 percent return on its invested capital, a figure high enough to attract whole new categories of investors. Delta wasn't merely just outperforming other airlines. It was a real company! Once a slave to lenders, it was now paying far less in interest to its bankers and bondholders. Remarkably, the airline managed to generate the same amount of revenue in 2010 as it had generated in 2008, but with 165 fewer aircraft—one reason for this was that the international fleet actually increased by 10 planes. Delta was also adding some used MD-80s from the bargain bin and some larger regional jets, but aircraft investment was otherwise minimal, freeing money for investments in product, service and facility upgrades. This was clearly showing, with Delta's customer satisfaction scores, corporate market share and reliability metrics all trending toward the top of the industry rankings. Delta was also using its hefty cash surplus to market its brand, especially in New York City, by spending heavily on sports and entertainment sponsorships. A more targeted focus for marketing dollars were the 5 percent of customers who accounted for a quarter of Delta's revenues—the "road warriors." Newsletters for corporate travel buyers, with names like *The Transnational,* which had long been blanketed by Continental advertising during that airline's remarkable surge in popularity among big-spending business travelers, now often featured Delta advertising most prominently.

Delta's strength was also evident in its strikingly benign labor relations. Even after merging with heavily unionized Northwest, Delta remained a largely non-union company. Pilots were still unionized, of course, but flight attendants, mechanics and ground workers were not, giving management unusual flexibility in adjusting to change. As Ed Bastian would tell a room full of investors in May 2011, "Our non-union status has a lot to do with the productivity opportunities that we have, in terms of being able to be more efficient."

And the company's one major labor contract wasn't even yet "open," or subject to renegotiation. The ALPA pilot agreement, covering about 11,000 pilots and signed in conjunction with the 2008 Northwest merger, didn't become amendable until the last day of 2012. Only four other work groups were represented at all. One covered a few hundred Delta dispatchers. Another covered roughly 2,000 workers at Comair, a Delta-owned regional airline, but Comair was in the process of significant downsizing anyway, on its way to eventual closure. American and United, by contrast, had countless outstanding issues to address with their heavily unionized workforces. American's flight attendants, as they picketed airports throughout the country, charged executives with "managerial incompetence" and "moral contempt." They were also threatening strikes, as were unions at many other airlines around the world—Air Canada, British Airways, Virgin Atlantic and Qantas were among the biggest but were certainly not the only ones.

"When other major airlines were announcing involuntary furloughs, outsourcing and hiring freezes," Richard Anderson said in February 2011 in a memo to Delta's workforce, "Delta kept its commitment to no frontline involuntary furloughs as a result of the merger. We were bringing reservations jobs back to the U.S.; we were insourcing in TechOps, cargo and airport customer service; and, in the last year alone, we added more than 4,000 new frontline jobs."

As 2011 began, the groundbreaking merger was all but complete, removing a major demand on the company's capital and finished just as United-Continental and Southwest-AirTran were getting to the tough parts of their own mergers—the parts Delta, but few other merged airlines in history, had managed smoothly. There was hardly any assurance they would handle their integrations as smoothly as Delta had done. The Delta-Air France/KLM-Alitalia joint venture similarly had a leg up on its younger rivals, and it was more deeply integrated too.

Offering so much more to its customers than ever before—so much more in terms of network, services and reliability—Delta was earning revenue premiums relative to its rivals in many markets. In other words, people were willing to pay more to fly Delta than to fly other airlines. And it was achieving this even as it maintained a roughly 10 percent non-fuel unit cost advantage against United and the ailing American, even despite all the post-merger Delta wage hikes. Lower costs and higher revenues meant outsized profits.

And all this was happening in one of the most benign operating environments U.S. airlines had ever known. Access to funding was inexpensive and plentiful, and all large airlines were shrinking or barely growing capacity even as demand was steadily recovering. The practice of charging for bags and other ancillaries yielded billions in incremental revenue—Delta, for its part, saw its maintenance, ground handling, tour package and private jet businesses contribute some $700 million in supplemental revenue during 2010. Consolidation was monumentally important too. Gordon Bethune had once said an airline is only as good as its dumbest competitor. And after three major mergers, there simply weren't as many competitors to make dumb pricing and capacity decisions. In fact, the five largest U.S. airlines now controlled 85 percent of domestic capacity: United 21 percent, Delta 20 percent, Southwest 20 percent, American 14 percent and US Airways 9 percent. In western Europe, by contrast, the top five airlines had a mere 45 percent of their equivalent to the "domestic" market, in their case referring to intra-western European traffic: Ryanair 14 percent, the Lufthansa Group 10 percent, easyJet 8 percent, Air France/KLM 6 percent and British Airways/Iberia 6 percent.

These were good times for airlines everywhere. In terms of traffic volume, 2010 had been the best year in aviation history. Across the globe, airlines transported close to 2.5 billion passengers, according to ICAO. That was 6 percent higher than the downturn-era levels of both 2008 and 2009—topping those years was easy enough—but also about 5 percent higher than record-setting 2007. Measured by revenue passenger kilometers (RPKs)—in other words, considering not just the number of passengers but also how far they flew—global air traffic had last peaked in 2008 but reached a new-all time high in 2010. Capacity too—measured by the number of available seats multiplied by distance—set a record, but barely. Available seat kilometers (ASKs) were up less than 2 percent from the previous high in 2008 and less than 4 percent from 2009. So with traffic up significantly more than capacity, passenger load factors (the measure of how full flights are) rose more than three points, from 76 percent to 79 percent—here again, an all-time record.

But 2011 wouldn't be quite so rosy. And once again, the airline's version of kryptonite was responsible. Fuel prices, which had behaved so manageably in 2010, began yet another upward spike in early 2011. After averaging about $2.15 per gallon during 2010, prices averaged $2.86 in the first quarter of 2011 before reaching $3.27 in April. Per-barrel oil prices (using the benchmark West Texas Intermediate crude, or WTI, index) surpassed $100 again in March and neared $110 in April.

A key driver of this latest spike was a series of political revolutions in North Africa and the Middle East—the "Arab Spring," collectively they would become known—starting in Tunisia and spreading to Egypt, Libya, Syria, Bahrain and Yemen. Iran, meanwhile, which violently suppressed an uprising of its own in 2009, was in 2011 getting closer to becoming a nuclear power, a fact that spooked the U.S., Europe and rival Middle Eastern powers like Israel and Saudi Arabia. The resulting geopolitical uncertainty from all this led to worries about oil supply disruptions. A recovering world economy and corresponding growth in demand for oil also contributed to oil's rising value. So too, probably, did a global savings glut that looked to hard assets like gold and oil as investments because interest rates were extremely low—investors needed to put their money somewhere, and oil looked like a safe bet.

Then came another shock. On March 11, 2011, a giant undersea earthquake off the coast of Japan triggered a massive tsunami with waves exceeding 130 feet high. As the waves crashed down in the northeastern Tohuku region, more than 15,000 people lost their lives. Homes, buildings, railroads, airports and dams all suffered damage. And most frighteningly, so did the Fukushima nuclear plant. Delta was there to help, donating heavily to the recovery effort, including $1 million in cash to relief efforts, among other contributions.

This humanitarian disaster, coupled with the latest fuel spike, reconfirmed the reality—lest anyone had forgotten—that the airline industry was still a nasty, brutish and shock-prone business. But had Delta built impenetrable defense mechanisms to deal with such disruptions? Would industry shocks in 2011 prove less traumatic than in the past? Would this time really be different?

The first quarter of 2011 was indeed a losing one for Delta, with margins down from the same period in glorious 2010. A 30 percent increase in fuel prices drove up total costs by a mammoth $610 million, while the Japan earthquake erased about $35 million in revenues, with additional losses expected for the second quarter—Delta, remember, was still the largest U.S. airline in Japan, which accounted for about 8 percent of its total systemwide revenues. In addition, unusually harsh winter storms caused flight cancellations that depressed revenues by another $90 million. And the heartache didn't stop there. Even more significantly, Delta's heavy exposure to transatlantic markets wasn't helpful at a time when Europe's economies were deteriorating. Now Portugal was on the brink, becoming the third country after Greece and Ireland to run out of money and turn to the European Central Bank and the International Monetary Fund for a bailout. Fingers were crossed that the much larger economies of Spain and Italy wouldn't be next. As bad as the consequences were from fuel prices and Japan and weather, Delta's management hinted losses on transatlantic routes—shared, of course, with Air France, KLM and Alitalia—were the biggest reason for the first quarter earnings decline. To be sure, Delta wasn't exactly an innocent bystander to whatever excess capacity plagued the transatlantic market, having upped its own first-quarter capacity there by 16 percent.

So the bad times were back—yet another example of false hope. Maybe the airline industry's defensive walls weren't as thick as presumed. Maybe the "three Cs" of consolidation, capacity cutting and charging for everything weren't quite the powerful shock absorber they were supposed to be. Maybe Delta's phenomenal performance was a flash in the pan, an anomaly, a brief interlude of calm before another set of storms.

But it wasn't.

Delta's 2010 revival was no fluke. The anomaly was what it experienced in the first quarter of 2011, a rare abundance—even for an airline—of simultaneous disruptions. And looking closer at Delta's performance, even in that rather cursed quarter, there were clear signs of impressive resilience. First, keeping in mind U.S. airlines routinely lost money in the off-peak first quarter, the $320 million net loss was mild by historical standards. Delta's operating margin was just negative 1 percent. Delta also paid an average of $2.89 per gallon for fuel compared to United's $2.78 and American's $2.75, saving just $78 million from its fuel hedges—again, an anomaly, considering there was no reason to believe Delta would perpetually pay more than its competitors for fuel. And although total operating costs rose 16 percent, revenues almost kept pace despite all the disruptions, rising an impressive 13 percent despite just 5 percent more capacity. Fuel was getting more expensive, yes, but so were airfares.

By its own estimates, Delta recaptured about 70 percent of its higher fuel costs with revenue gains, with an even greater rate on domestic routes, Latin American routes and non-Japan Pacific routes. Then there were non-ticket revenues, which also grew sharply, not just from ancillary services sold to passengers but also surging cargo performance and the SkyMiles frequent flier program, which was now more than ever a quiet but giant cash cow. Bookings for the upcoming spring and summer, meanwhile, continued to look strong other than to Europe and Japan, resulting in free cash flow generation of nearly half a billion dollars. Money was flowing in despite the accounting loss.

Just as importantly, Delta didn't sit still in the face of these new pressures. On the contrary, it reacted with great speed and forcefulness, slashing Japan capacity by more than 15 percent, suspending its just-launched Detroit and Los Angeles flights to Tokyo's Haneda Airport, initiating seven of the industry's 17 fare hikes through late April, eliminating roughly a quarter of all flights from its underperforming Memphis hub, refinancing its bankruptcy-era loans at much lower interest rates, increasing fees for second checked bags on European routes, reducing planned capital expenditures by $300 million, restructuring its fuel hedge portfolio, parking another 20 mainline planes—including some international widebodies—and phasing out countless 50-seat regional jets and propeller planes. The shedding of aging Saab 340 propeller planes, in particular, forced the suspension of flights to many small communities, whose chief access to the outside world was air service to big hubs like Minneapolis and Atlanta. Thief River Falls in Montana was one such community: Delta's flights, subsidized by taxpayers, flew with 88 percent of their seats empty. Among others losing service were Muscles Shoals, Ala., and—in Mississippi—Greenville, Hattiesburg and Tupelo. All four of those "Old South" cities had been on the front lines of the 1960s civil rights movement, a movement that greatly benefited from Delta's transport links to otherwise isolated areas. One figure who cited this contribution was Andrew Young, the civil rights leader who served as "New South" Atlanta's mayor throughout much of the 1980s before eventually serving on Delta's board of directors and helping it win flight rights in Africa at a time when Delta's rival Continental was denied access.

The goal for non-fuel unit costs, always a key performance indicator, was to reduce them to 2010 levels by the end of 2011. Phasing out older and less efficient planes more prone to costly maintenance was one way to achieve this. Another: the old trick of coaxing more senior employees to retire early through voluntary exit programs, the latest of which attracted more than 2,000 willing Delta workers. Management also made more efficient use of facilities and real estate in Atlanta, Minneapolis, Cincinnati and Memphis, selling some buildings it no longer needed.

One striking example of innovation was Delta's decision to change the way it compensated passengers for overbooked flights. Airlines, on any given flight, sell more tickets than they have seats because they know a certain percentage of passengers, especially those with refundable or changeable tickets, won't show up. Predicting this no-show rate is a rather precise science, but sometimes an oversold flight has more passengers than seats. When that happens, gate agents announce a compensation offer for volunteers willing to surrender their seats and take a later flight. If no volunteers are willing to take the airline's first offer, the agent at the gate can raise the ante and then raise it again and again until someone bites. But this can get expensive for the airline. So Delta revamped the process in its favor. It began asking for volunteers not at the gate, during the final frenetic moments before departure, but when passengers checked in at kiosks or online before passing through security. There the airline's systems (without distracting busy gate agents) could ask:

If we need your seat, would you volunteer, and if so, what compensation would you accept? At the gate, agents would already have a list of volunteers and could choose the ones who had bid the lowest.

In February, following the lead of some of its partners and competitors, Delta announced a new section of extra-legroom seats on all longhaul international flights. "Economy Comfort" provided up to four additional inches of legroom and 50 percent more recline than standard economy class seats. Passengers sitting in these seats could also board early and enjoy complimentary liquor—Delta had a few years earlier restored complimentary beer and wine, but not liquor, in economy. This was a way of achieving two objectives: raising ancillary revenue from economy ticket holders willing to pay $80 to $160 for more comfort and rewarding buyers of full-fare unrestricted economy class tickets plus high-tier SkyMiles members with better seats, in some cases for no additional charge. United had actually pioneered its similar "Economy Plus" concept more than a decade earlier. But now various forms of extra-comfort economy seating—from the basic extra-legroom seats United and now Delta were offering to the true premium economy section (complete with extra width and better meals) Delta's partner Air France offered—were catching on across the industry. Delta's early returns were so good that it quickly expanded the concept to its domestic fleet. In the same vein of rewarding loyal customers, Delta and its SkyTeam partners also developed an alliance-wide "SkyPriority" service, which ensured priority handling at the airport for anyone with at least mid-tier elite status on any SkyTeam airline. Most members had long offered some of these services anyway. But instead of an unpredictable patchwork across the alliance, now a Delta Medallion member could be assured of expedited check-in, security screening, boarding and bag handling when flying, say, Vietnam Airlines, Kenya Airways, Aeroflot or China Southern.

And that's not all Delta did for its SkyMiles members. Also in February, it became the first major U.S. airline to reverse a decade-long trend of tightening mileage expiration policies. In fact, SkyMiles would never expire. This meant more liability on Delta's balance sheet and no more reinstatement fees from people paying to get their expired miles back. But it also made the program more attractive to fliers and partners, most importantly American Express. Delta realized there was no sense in doing anything to discourage loyal customers—even those who didn't really fly much but felt a deep loyalty to Delta—from accumulating SkyMiles. (This did little to please truly frequent fliers, who already moaned about what they considered frequent mileage devaluations—in other words, more miles required for the same award travel. Now, even more miles would chase the same scarce award seats.)

Generally speaking, Delta was among the more generous U.S. carriers in terms of providing amenities to economy travelers, from free snacks on domestic flights and the free wine and beer on longhaul flights, to personal television even on many shorthaul flights and—now—the chance to earn miles that would never expire.

But more importantly, Delta was also out to impress the big-money frequent fliers, matching competitors by lowering the status threshold required for achieving top-tier SkyTeam benefits, most notably lounge access when flying longhaul economy on partner airlines—this would now be available for members flying 50,000 miles annually rather than only at the 75,000-mile level. Another move: special Medallion parking spaces at Atlanta Braves baseball games. This mild escalation in generosity was, in fact, a broad industry trend. Across the U.S. airline sector, big carriers were—to varying degrees—making modest customer-friendly policy changes, following years of taking away privileges, tightening restrictions and levying new fees.

At the same time, management knew it had no choice but to sustain its cost-control efforts. "We're counting on [expensive fuel] being the new norm for the industry," Ed Bastian told investors at a conference in May. "And one of the challenging aspects that we've all experienced over the last few years is despite all the hard work we have conducted through the merger, the integration, the restructuring [and] the rebuilding of the franchise, we continue to chase high oil prices. And every time we think we get there, it seems like prices move another notch further, eroding the profitability of the business." But, he said, "sitting and hoping that high fuel prices are going to go away or that fuel prices are going to fall is not a strategy."

Attacking distribution costs, however, *was* most definitely a strategy. By 2011, the practice of selling airline tickets had changed dramatically from the old days, when travel agents sold about 80 percent of all tickets—all those except the ones sold by airline agents at call centers, airport ticket counters and airline city ticket offices. ("CTO" was, in the industry, a once-ubiquitous but now-vanishing acronym.) Travel agencies, to be clear, were still a critical link in the distribution chain, especially measured by value, not volume. According to PhoCusWright, a market research company, agencies accounted for a full 61 percent of the $110 billion in revenue U.S. airlines generated in 2010. The biggest of these agencies were corporate travel management firms like American Express, which big firms hire to manage all aspects of their employee travel, from booking tickets to controlling costs and ensuring traveler safety. Then there were the online travel agencies like Expedia, originally launched by Microsoft, and Priceline, which went on to thrive again in the years after Delta sold its investment.

But that still left 39 percent of all ticket sales booked directly on airline websites and through airline call centers. This proved a big threat to another critical link in the distribution chain: the global distribution systems (GDSs), which provide fares and schedules to travel agencies. These companies, which airlines themselves originally created, charged airlines hefty fees for every flight segment an agent booked. To drive the most price-sensitive leisure passengers directly to airline websites, airlines cleverly withheld their cheapest fares from GDSs, making them available only through airline sales channels—why pay big commissions and fees to sell tickets to the least profitable passengers? Sure enough, the bargain hunters indeed migrated away from agencies, hurting them and their GDS partners. This led to a compromise: The GDS companies agreed to lower their booking fees if airlines agreed to provide them with all their flights and fares, including the cheapest ones—no exceptions.

In 2006, for example, Delta had signed a new seven-year "full-content agreement" with Sabre, the largest GDS in the U.S.

But that wasn't the end of the story. By 2011, airlines were earning billions from their new lines of ancillary products and services, most of which the GDSs, and thus travel agencies, weren't capable of selling. Airline websites, by contrast, had blossomed into sophisticated retail outlets, offering a wide array of travel products, inflight services and airport perks, merchandized with graphics and consumer-friendly interfaces. Just as importantly, airlines were on their way toward personalizing offers just like Amazon.com, so that an elite frequent flier might someday be offered a fare package including inflight Wi-Fi and two free checked bags, while a first-time flier might just be offered a cheap no-frills fare.

Frustrated at not being able to sell in such a dynamic fashion via travel agencies, which high-paying corporate travelers tended to use, American, for one, decided to get bold. It launched a high-profile effort to get agencies to connect directly to its internal systems rather than rely on the old ways of obtaining static fares and scheduled content—not customized for travelers, because airlines didn't even know who the flier would be until after he or she bought a ticket—through GDSs. The GDSs were welcome to connect to American's internal systems too, but American's point was that the old model of doing things was no longer acceptable.

But Sabre and another GDS company called Travelport, which together controlled 92 percent of all GDS bookings in the U.S., weren't ready to abandon their old ways—not if it meant they'd be cut out of many transactions or not sufficiently compensated for investing in new technologies needed to enable new selling techniques. Fortunately for them, they still retained great influence with travel agencies, which were often compensated for using the GDSs and which worried about their ability to compare fares across many competing airlines, something that was easy on an old GDS screen. What followed were volleys of accusations, angry press releases and—the airline alleged—a major boycott of American's flights. Next came a federal lawsuit, in which American accused Sabre of "seriously [injuring] American's business," organizing "secret collusive boycott agreements," being a "ring leader in a classic hub-and-spoke conspiracy" and "planning [these] attacks for five years." It also accused Sabre of doubling its booking fees twice during negotiations and said domestic GDS booking costs, even after falling 34 percent in recent years, were still triple what a direct booking costs, not to mention that the airline still couldn't personalize an offer for an individual traveler.

American had taken all the risk. Delta, on the other hand, couldn't lose. It took some market share from American in cities like New York, where the two competed closely. And Delta enjoyed its status as a free rider while American advanced the cause—and bore all the expense—of being able to sell more dynamically, which is something Delta wanted too.

And to be clear, even though American waged the riskiest war—against the giant GDSs themselves—it's not as if Delta did nothing on the distribution front.

On the contrary, it got aggressive, for example, with "meta-search" sites that scour the web for low fares, sending shoppers to the site that has the best deal—Kayak was the most notable of these companies. Delta forced Kayak and others to send anyone who wanted to buy a Delta ticket to delta.com, not an independent online travel agency. Delta might still have to pay a small referral fee to Kayak, but this was a reasonably efficient distribution channel, as long as customers did indeed end up purchasing their tickets directly from the airline—remember, not only did this mean lower costs than had that customer purchased the ticket on Expedia or elsewhere, but now Delta could interact directly with that customer and offer him or her lots of ancillary services. Sure enough, the airline saw its website traffic jump. Delta also ended its partnerships entirely with a dozen or so smallish OTAs, and it reworked fare rules to limit how agencies and tour package providers could sell its inventory. They could no longer, among other things, offer Delta's lowest fares if they bundled its flights on an itinerary with other carriers, which the intermediaries commonly did if, say, Delta was cheapest for the outbound flights and US Airways was cheapest for the return. Now it would have to be all Delta to get Delta's lowest fares. Eventually, Delta would sign more limited GDS deals that enabled sales of some, although not all, ancillary products, including Economy Comfort seats. The airline was now targeting non-ticket merchandising revenue of $1 billion by 2013.

As 2011 turned to spring, the demand weakness and yield deterioration on transatlantic routes became increasingly worrisome. Delta had already cut capacity there 9 percent in 2009 and another 3 percent in 2010. But then it grew the market 16 percent in the first quarter of 2011, only to see its load factors fall six points. Air France/KLM and Alitalia had cut capacity in tandem with Delta after the financial crisis. Still, results were getting worse. Both of Delta's European partners were struggling mightily, beset by the weak economy, a fluctuating euro, labor strikes by air traffic controllers, fuel prices spiking anew, expensive new security directives, the volcanic ash cloud, higher taxes and an onslaught of new capacity from Arabian Gulf carriers on longhaul routes and low-cost carriers like Ryanair and easyJet on shorthaul routes. (Qatar Airways, in a symbolic blow, even won sponsorship rights to the Tour de France.) For Air France, shorthaul routes, in particular, were bleeding money, and although these routes weren't part of the joint venture and thus not Delta's losses to share, the overall distress was disconcerting. Air France/KLM also happened to have more exposure than most of its peers to Japan and to unrest in places like Syria and the Ivory Coast. In 2009, it had lost an Airbus 330 en route from Rio de Janeiro to Paris; its pilots seemed partly to blame. It was now flying enormous Airbus 380s ordered long before the financial crisis. Europe planned to soon force airlines to join an expensive emissions trading scheme. In 2011, Air France dismissed its CEO and brought back Jean-Cyril Spinetta, the hero of its turnaround and merger with KLM. And its close but troubled partner Alitalia? It was just as troubled as ever.

It was in this context that on May 19, the three partners agreed to a joint 7-to-9 percent cut in post-summer transatlantic passenger capacity. Negotiating the cuts wasn't easy, with each side dealing with different fleet and labor issues, but the agreement testified to the JV's ability to react when events required action.

Delta itself cut overseas routes—some permanently and some only during off-peak periods—to Berlin, Athens, Manchester, Stockholm, Copenhagen, Abuja, Kiev, Fortaleza, Amman and Cairo. Tellingly, none of these cities was a SkyTeam hub. Glen Hauenstein and his team were doing more than just cutting. They were fine-tuning flight schedules to an unprecedented degree, flexing capacity up and down depending on the season and the day of the weak.

"The transatlantic has always been a seasonal game," Hauenstein explained in an earnings presentation, "and I remember Freddie Laker with his famous speech about how any idiot can make money on the transatlantic during the summer. It is the winter months that count. And that goes back to 30 or 35 years ago. And what was true then still remains the same today: that the transatlantic is quite a seasonal market, and the game is to not give back the profits you make in the summer in the winter."

For those 30 or 35 years, everyone had known it, but nobody had really done much about it.

Airlines had always accepted, to one degree or another, that of course off-peak winter fares would be lower than peak summer fares. The truth, as Delta realized, was that winter fares could be nearly as high as summer fares. Airlines just had to fly a lot less to achieve that. They had to take huge amounts of supply out of the market to better match supply with reduced off-peak demand, so that they would no longer have to fill flights with bargain seekers, who brought down average fares.

So Delta was now planning to fly 20 percent fewer transatlantic seats in the winter of 2011 and 2012 than it would fly in the summer, and it could do this in large part because of its non-union workforce, which didn't have contractual restrictions against seasonal and part time work, and because of its older planes, which didn't carry big mortgage or lease payments—unlike newer aircraft, they could be parked on days when they weren't needed, because they didn't really cost much money while they were inactive.

"We continue to increasingly 'variabilize' our flying levels to the strength of the demand season," Ed Bastian said during that same earnings call. "Historically, you have never seen that level of flexibility. It is what you need to do. For us to make the money we are making this summer and give it back in the winter? We are done doing that. We need to make money year round. We will make more money in the summer, but we are no longer interested in giving it back in the winter."

Delta cut in other regions too, including the Memphis-led cuts at home. In fact, the only region that continued to see more capacity was Latin America, where markets like Brazil, Perú and Colombia were still seeing big increases in air traffic demand. Delta was simply done offering flights that didn't make money, whether that meant cutting entire routes or just certain seasons or days of the week. Or as Ed Bastian said: "We are going to be getting out of markets that don't make sense for us, that we can't 'price for fuel.'" Markets, in other words, that might have been profitable at a different point in history.

Delta wasn't alone in this regard—its nemesis US Airways, for one, was also actively fine-tuning its schedules according to seasonal and day-of-week demand patterns. But Delta was a leader in the area, and it was eons ahead of a rival like American, which—remember—had even expressed public skepticism for the idea of seasonal scheduling. Management foresight deserved most of the credit. But Delta's advanced accounting IT systems, in which Leo Mullin had invested heavily during his modernization of the airline in the late 1990s, were unsung heroes too. These systems enabled management to better understand the true profitability of individual routes and flights, something that was notoriously difficult for airlines because of questions about how to properly allocate costs like management overhead to a certain flight, or how much revenue that flight truly contributes to the success of other flights because of the connecting traffic it provides.

Delta was bucking conventional airline wisdom. It was raising wages and bonus payments for workers. Its aversion to buying new planes meant more costly maintenance. Its heavy investment in inflight amenities and operational reliability didn't come cheap. And its capacity cutting meant less intensive use of its people and planes, something that went squarely against what for decades had been the most successful airline business model: the high-utilization model invented by Herb Kelleher at Southwest (i.e., keep the planes and people busy in order to drive down unit costs).

But it was working. Cost pressures were effectively neutralized by balance sheet improvements, smarter distribution policies, managing down unit labor costs through early retirement schemes and managing down unit aircraft costs by retiring inefficient regional planes. "Delta has a long history of having the lowest unit cost of all legacy carriers, and we intend to maintain that advantage," Hank Halter, Delta's chief financial officer, said.

At the same time, Delta's tactics were driving up revenues. Customers willingly paid more for an airline with content and motivated staff, not to mention on-time flights with better seats and food. Capacity cutting squeezed up fares. And even flying old planes—as long as they were clean and reliable and had interiors that had been updated to the point that passengers didn't even notice they were old—had a silver revenue lining: The same mechanics who expertly worked on Delta's fleet also produced insourced income by working on other airlines' airplanes. So Delta, going completely against the industry grain, proceeded to buy even more used MD-90s, an aircraft no longer even in production, from its old flame Japan Airlines.

Speaking of Japan Airlines, something strangely miraculous was occurring there. The immense human tragedy left behind by the tsunami/earthquake/nuclear disaster had indisputably crushed air travel demand, especially inbound travel from other nations. Still, Japan Airlines was reporting phenomenal profits, rising to the top of the industry league tables. Its turnaround efforts were proving a huge success. Its cost cuts, network cuts, jobs cuts and debt cuts during bankruptcy were so massive that not even an earthquake could shake them. In the summer of 2011, with the Fukushima nuclear reactor still a hazard, JAL earned an unheard-of 26 percent quarterly operating profit margin.

And the story got stranger still. It wasn't just JAL. All Japanese airlines— including United's partner All Nippon Airways and the previously sleepy low-cost carrier Skymark—were thriving in the wake of the crisis. How was this so?

The answer to the riddle: the value of Japan's currency. To the consternation of exporters like Toyota and Honda, the yen had risen to an extremely strong value relative to the U.S. dollar. And while this was a curse for those exporters, because their cars had become more expensive for Americans and others, it was a godsend for Japanese airlines, which earned most of their revenues in now-strong yen but were buying fuel and airplanes priced in cheap dollars. So when fuel prices spiked for everyone else after the Arab Spring, Japan's airlines were protected.

And so, in a way, was Delta—at its Tokyo hub, anyway. To be sure, its strategic vulnerabilities there remained as vexing as ever. But for the time being, its routes from Japan to Hawaii, in particular, were thriving. For Japanese tourists with strong yen in their pockets, Hawaii had become a relatively cheap destination. And for Delta, like its Japanese rivals, fueling planes in Tokyo was now cheap relative to the strong revenue environment. More generally, the sharp capacity cuts Delta and others enacted after the earthquake matched weaker demand with less supply, on top of the massive capacity cuts JAL had made during its bankruptcy.

So Japan was a bright spot for Delta in 2011, never mind its longer-term vulnerabilities there. Still, Japan was a shrinking market, not a growth market. And Delta—without a local partner—didn't stand much of a chance of becoming the market's airline of choice.

But there were two markets back in the U.S. where Delta felt it did have a fighting chance of becoming the carrier of choice. And these were not just any two markets, but the two largest U.S. markets of all.

Los Angeles, the No. 2 market, was as tough a battleground as ever. But Delta's determination to win there was evident from its sponsorship of the wildly popular Lakers basketball team, which had been the NBA's champions in both 2009 and 2010. Delta also sponsored the city's hockey team, the Kings. (Baseball's Dodgers had signed a sponsorship deal with JetBlue, another airline vying for a share of the highly fragmented market). For the more musically inclined, Delta paid to become the official airline of the Grammy museum. On the network front, it added more frequencies to San Francisco and Las Vegas, two hyper-competitive markets but ones highly important to Los Angeles travelers—no big company there would likely give a corporate flying contract to an airline that didn't offer these. There were the new Tokyo Haneda flights too from Los Angeles and new flights to Miami, Cancún and elsewhere. Finally, the DOT reversed its initial refusal and granted consent to Delta's pending joint venture with Virgin Blue, which was renaming itself "Virgin Australia," providing a huge boost for Delta's new Los Angeles-Sydney flights. This

JV was, of course, far more limited than the giant JV Delta had with Air France/
KLM and Alitalia. But it was a JV nonetheless, highlighting growing industrywide
enthusiasm for JVs, sparked in large part by the success of Northwest-KLM and then
the expanded Delta-Air France/KLM arrangement itself. These JVs, to an even deeper
degree than alliances, were a next-best solution in a world where, even after years of
progressive fare and schedule deregulation, all-out cross-border mergers remained
prohibited by foreign ownership laws. Between Los Angeles and Sydney, Delta would
cooperate with, not compete against, Virgin. Because of their virtual merger, there
would essentially be three airlines—Delta/Virgin and the more established Qantas
and United—not four.

While new routes, new sponsorships and a new JV with Virgin Australia made
Delta a stronger player in the No. 2 market Los Angeles, No. 1 New York remained
the far more important strategic market for Delta. New York was where Delta had a
much larger presence, and a much stronger one too, most notably across the Atlantic.
Its London Heathrow problem was indeed still a problem: It didn't have a partner
there, unlike American, which now had antitrust immunity with British Airways.
Even so, Delta was winning corporate accounts and generating strong revenues in
New York. And in 2011, it sensed another big New York opportunity.

Actually, it was an old opportunity, revived under new industry conditions.
A year earlier, Washington had refused to allow Delta and US Airways to execute
a swap of Washington Reagan and New York LaGuardia takeoff and landing slots
unless they agreed to surrender so many slots to LCC rivals that the deal would
no longer make sense. But the world had now changed, and Delta and US Airways
knew it. Southwest was now present at Newark after Continental agreed to lease it
slots as part of Continental's own effort to win Justice Department consent for its
merger with United. And Southwest had itself merged with AirTran, which provided
it additional access to New York LaGuardia and first-time access to Washington
Reagan—AirTran served both. So Southwest could no longer moan as credibly that
it was being excluded from the big-revenue airports in New York and Washington.
And JetBlue, after swapping slots with American, was now present at Reagan too.

So in May 2011, Delta and US Airways revived their proposal. This time
Delta would get 132 LaGuardia slots pairs, not 125. US Airways would still get 42
Reagan pairs. Now that Japan and the U.S. had signed an open skies treaty, Tokyo
rights didn't matter (US Airways could have flown there with or without a deal
with Delta), but it would still get the rights for two daily flights to São Paulo by
2015 plus $67 million in cash. The carriers offered to give up 16 LaGuardia slot
pairs and eight Reagan slot pairs for newcomers, fewer than the original numbers
demanded by regulators—those regulators, Delta and US Airways hoped, would
recognize and appreciate the changed circumstances. Not only did LCCs now
have more of a presence at these capacity-constrained airports, the two airlines
argued, but the United and Southwest mergers had sharpened competition in the
northeast more generally.

The idea worked. In July, the DOT tentatively accepted the proposal; final approval would come in October. Carriers with fewer than 5 percent of the slots at each airport—i.e., all major LCCs—would be eligible to bid for the surrendered slots, with the two slot-swapping carriers even being able to keep the proceeds of the auction. JetBlue would later outbid Southwest and others, getting more access to both Reagan and LaGuardia, with Canada's WestJet also obtaining some LaGuardia slots.

Delta now had greatly amplified access to an airport domestic New York business travelers prized. It also had a new growth market—or put another way, a much better place to put planes than Memphis and Cincinnati. Delta's plan was to approximately double the number of nonstop destinations it served from LaGuardia, including the addition of some destinations not previously served by US Airways. It would replace turboprop aircraft currently operated by US Airways with larger regional jets, in doing so adding as many as 4 million additional roundtrip seats annually at LaGuardia without increasing congestion, because what caused congestion was the number of flights, not the number of seats. Delta would furthermore take control of US Airways' Terminal C and build a 600-foot connector between it and Delta's existing terminal as part of a $117 million overall investment in modernizing the facilities. Delta would keep its popular hourly Boston and Washington shuttle at its six gates at the separate Marine Air Terminal. And by doing all this, it would create an estimated 6,000 new jobs in New York, winning it friends among politicians eager to tout job growth at a time when unemployment remained stubbornly high in almost every part of the nation except places like Texas, Oklahoma and North Dakota, which had oil.

So Delta was downsizing across the Atlantic in response to the euro crisis, across the Pacific in response to the Japan crisis and domestically in markets like Memphis, Cincinnati and Washington. It was upsizing in Los Angeles and New York, with some growth to Brazil, where the Obama administration was easing visa laws to promote tourism, and even to London, where Delta began flying nonstop from Miami and Boston after winning the slots American and British Airways had to give up to get their JV. Detroit got a new route to Shanghai. Atlanta again got its previously suspended flights to Shanghai. And even Pittsburgh, an old US Airways hub, got nonstop service to Paris. Things were steady, meanwhile, in Salt Lake City, Detroit, Minneapolis and the hub of all hubs, Atlanta. Delta's profit-sharing partner KLM began flying to Miami from Amsterdam, while Air France began flying to Orlando from Paris.

Delta was adding new partners too. The SkyTeam alliance redoubled its efforts to better cover East Asia and the Middle East by inviting China Eastern and Xiamen Airlines in mainland China, China Airlines of Taiwan (not to be confused with mainland China's Air China, a Star Alliance member), Indonesia's Garuda, Middle East Airlines of Lebanon and Saudi Arabian Airlines. Outside SkyTeam, Delta had its new marketing partnerships with WestJet and Air Nigeria, the reincarnation of Virgin Atlantic's ill-fated Nigerian airline.

More significantly, Delta deepened a partnership with Aeroméxico, its country's top airline and the only Mexican airline catering to longhaul business travelers. This wasn't just a simple codeshare and frequent flier partnership. In August 2011, Delta paid $65 million to buy 4 percent of its fellow SkyTeam member. The two weren't allowed to form an antitrust-immune JV because the U.S. and Mexico, oddly enough, did not have an open skies agreement. But Delta and Aeroméxico did just about everything short of that, working as closely as legally possible in the areas of joint selling, maintenance, airport co-location, systemwide codesharing and mutual recognition of each other's elite customers. A constantly troubled headache for its government owners of most of its history, Aeroméxico had begun experiencing a sharp earnings renaissance after its chief rival and fellow state-owned carrier Mexicana collapsed in 2010, an event that punctuated an epidemic of collapsing Mexican carriers—Aerocalifornia, Aladia, Alma, Aviacsa, Avolar and Azteca were just the ones that started with the letter "A." The triumphantly surviving Aeroméxico went on to secure union concessions, sell shares on Mexico City's stock exchange, renew its fleet and thoroughly modernize its management. The Delta-Aeroméxico deal, moreover—unlike the Delta-WestJet deal—was an exclusive deal for Delta: Aeroméxico was forbidden from forming a partnership with any other U.S. airline.

And Delta didn't even stop there. Flush with cash thanks to its excellent streak of profits and success in paying down debt, the formerly bankrupt and domestic-heavy airline from Atlanta decided to buy its way into Brazil too. Years earlier, Gordon Bethune's Continental had made one of the great airline investments of all time by buying a large stake in Copa, a Panamanian airline that—blessed by good geography and other natural advantages but also thanks to the tutelage of what was then perhaps the best managed U.S. carrier—went on to become one of the global airline industry's perennially most profitable airlines. Now Delta—was *it* now the best managed U.S. carrier?—was hoping to replicate the trick with not just Aeroméxico but also with Gol, an LCC that had started life in the early 2000s, eventually growing into Brazil's largest domestic airline by some measures. It was Gol that had bought the carcass of the old legacy carrier Varig, providing Gol crucial slots in São Paulo and Rio de Janeiro, by far Brazil's two largest airline markets. But Gol's profitability record was notoriously volatile: After a strong 2010, it ran into trouble during 2011 after being stung by higher fuel prices, tougher competition from the merged LAN-TAM and a domestic fare war thanks partly to the emergence of Azul, the new airline launched by JetBlue's founder David Neeleman. In July, taking a cue from its consolidating U.S. counterparts, Gol purchased its smaller rival Webjet. Then in December, it sold part of itself to Delta for $100 million.

It was a timely moment to buy, for Gol's share price had dropped more than 50 percent in the preceding year. As with Aeroméxico, the investment gave Delta a seat on the company's board of directors and deeper commercial ties including expanded codesharing, maintenance cooperation, coordinated sales efforts, airport co-location, reciprocal lounge access and status recognition for each other's best customers. And it struck another blow at American, which had to drop its own codeshare partnership with Gol. By year end, Delta itself—the airline that had begun as a crop duster in Monroe, La.—was operating 5,500 daily flights to 343 destinations in 63 countries. And including its partners? The equivalent statistics were 18,000 daily flights to 1,164 destinations in 187 countries.

By the time Delta announced the Gol deal in December 2011, a number of other big developments had transpired that year at Delta, in the airline business and in the world at large. First Americans were heartened by the killing, in May, of the 9/11 mastermind Osama bin Laden. But in July, a massacre in Norway, of all places, left the impression that nowhere was safe from extremism.

Also in July, more prosaically, Atlanta's former mayor Shirley Franklin joined Delta's board of directors. So did David G. DeWalt, chief of the computer security firm McAfee. In August, a bitter federal budget struggle involving the White House and a sharply divided Congress brought the country within a whisker of defaulting on its national debt; it escaped the abyss only with a messy last-minute compromise that called for deep military and social spending cuts if a "super-committee" of lawmakers couldn't come up with anything better. In a side show to that, however, carriers benefited from a summertime fight over funding the FAA, which resulted in airline ticket taxes going uncollected for several weeks. Airlines could essentially pocket the money instead.

August also brought Hurricane Irene, which badly disrupted air service on the U.S. east coast and raised some questions about the recently implemented "tarmac delay rule," designed by its backers to prevent airlines from leaving people stranded aboard airplanes waiting to take off or park at a gate or face fines that could add up to millions of dollars for even one flight. Well, by the summer of 2011, major U.S. airlines had canceled more than 100,000 flights since the start of the year—or more than 2 percent of all flights—according to a FlightStats analysis for Bloomberg News. The figure was on pace to be the highest since 2001, the year 9/11 grounded the entire industry for several days. Part of this was unusually bad weather in busy markets, including Hurricane Irene in the northeast and wintertime ice storms in Atlanta and Dallas. But the new rule had actually created a perverse incentive for airlines to cancel flights: Rather than doing everything possible to operate every flight, even if that risked a long tarmac delay, they were doing everything possible to avoid the multi-million-dollar fines. So they had begun proactively canceling countless flights before storms to avoid the possibility that even one of those flights might fall afoul of the tarmac rule. And because flights were fuller than ever before, cancellations meant affected passengers would sometimes have to wait days before they could get seats on other flights.

The new tarmac rule was among a string of new DOT mandates imposed on airlines, including restrictions regarding how they advertised their fares and fees (no more advertising cheap base fares that didn't include taxes, for example), additional compensation for passengers involuntarily denied boarding, bag fee refunds when bags were lost, a four-hour international tarmac delay rule to go along with the three-hour domestic one and a requirement to allow penalty-free cancellations up to 24 hours after passengers booked their flights. Carriers did dodge a bullet, though, when the DOT deferred a decision on whether to force carriers to sell their ancillary services through global distribution systems.

In October, cancer killed the iconic Apple CEO Steve Jobs, eliciting worldwide elegies to his creative genius. Two months later, a far less praiseworthy figure—the North Korean dictator Kim Jung Il—lost his life. The last American combat troops left Iraq. And America's economy slowly improved as Europe's trended in the other direction. U.S. unemployment was easing, even if only modestly; the auto industry was healthy again; so was the country's financial system; and a technological revolution was leading to a collapse in domestic power grid prices although not, sadly for airlines, oil prices. Even in the oil markets, though, there was good news: In 2009, domestic supplies had actually begun increasing for the first time since 1991. That marked a step toward energy independence at a time when the U.S. still imported 4.3 billion barrels of oil annually at an average price of about $62 per barrel. Americans were sending $267 billion of their money out of the country for this purpose, of which 41 percent went to OPEC countries.

The year 2011 also marked an important transformation in the market for airplanes. The run-up in fuel prices had counterintuitively proved a great blessing for the two great airplane builders of their time, Airbus and Boeing. Expensive fuel rendered older planes ever more economically obsolete, with some models like the Boeing 727 and Airbus 300—still mainstays of some airline fleets a decade earlier— now all but relics, almost nowhere to be found among passenger airlines. Adding to the pressure for newer planes were growing demands among environmentalists and politicians to reduce carbon emissions, demands that the industry needed to take seriously lest it wind up like the tobacco companies years earlier, whose reputations were in ashes and whose legal exposure was seemingly infinite.

With narrowbodies—the single-aisle planes that form the backbone of U.S. domestic flying—Boeing did best with its latest 737s, especially the -800 version, with about 160 seats in Delta's configuration, and the -900, with about 20 more seats. Southwest and AirTran were big users of the smaller -700, but these were falling out of fashion as higher fuel prices and higher load factors encouraged airlines to operate fewer frequencies with larger planes. The Airbus 320 family similarly offered several versions, with larger 320s and 321s—which competed closely against 737-800s and 737-900s—having become more popular than smaller 319s.

And these larger narrowbodies were flying off the shelves. By 2011, the order backlogs at Airbus and Boeing were downright enormous, with some airlines forced to wait years before getting the planes they wanted. Yet technology—especially engine technology—was evolving. Airlines wanted new narrowbodies with new engines, but Airbus and Boeing were reluctant to oblige—why spend billions of dollars designing something new when the current models were still selling so well? Well, Canada's

Bombardier, known for its regional jets and turboprops, was attempting to crash the narrowbody party by giving airlines what Airbus and Boeing didn't seem to want to provide: an all-new model with next-generation engines. Bombardier's new aircraft program would be called the CSeries. Airbus had seen enough. Better, it concluded, to cannibalize its own current-generation A320 program than to let Bombardier take the orders. So as the calendar turned to 2011, Airbus had begun offering a "new engine option"—or "neo"—for its 320 airframe. One of the two available engine types was the same one that would hang on the CSeries' wings. The Airbus 320neo, which would generate thousands of orders before the first one ever flew, was an instant success—to Bombardier's chagrin, an exponentially greater success than the CSeries, which had started the new-engine party.

Boeing had to do something. Its most important customers, including Southwest, were pushing it to go bold and develop not just a newly engined 737 but an-all new narrowbody airframe too, making use of the composite materials Boeing was using in its revolutionary 787 "Dreamliner" widebodies. Boeing, however, had learned its lesson from nightmarish 787 production problems and didn't feel an all-new 737 could be ready until the mid-2020s, leaving Airbus to enjoy a new-engine narrowbody monopoly for years—the 320neo would debut in 2016.

The pressure on Boeing grew when American, having neglected fleet renewal for most of the 2000s due to its financial distress, opened negotiations for a massive narrowbody order. Unwilling to lose American as a customer, and to lose years of sales to Airbus, Boeing decided to develop its own re-engined 737: the 737 MAX. On July 20, 2011, American placed one of the largest aircraft orders in aviation history, actually splitting the order by taking hundreds of airplanes each—a mix of current and new-engine models—from both Airbus and Boeing.

Southwest, United, JetBlue, Alaska Airlines, Spirit, Frontier, Virgin America and Hawaiian Airlines all joined American in buying re-engined 737s or 320s. Only two major U.S. airlines did not. One was US Airways, which was still hoping to merge with another carrier and assume that carrier's existing plane orders. The other? Delta.

Delta was again marching to its own beat, accepting some aircraft inefficiency in exchange for preserving capital for paying down debt, increasing employee compensation to preserve harmonious labor relations and investing in customer service.

That's not to say Delta was doing nothing on the aircraft front. In fact, not only was Delta not doing nothing. It was benefiting as much as any other airline from the availability of new models even though it didn't order even a single one. How? Because as soon as the new models were announced, the current models—no less efficient than they were a day earlier—suddenly became less desirable in the eyes of many airlines. Less desirable meant cheaper. And cheaper was the way Delta liked its airplanes.

In 2011, Delta's narrowbody fleet featured roughly 125 Airbus 319s and 320s inherited from Northwest, 80 Boeing 737s (mostly -800s), 170 DC-9 and slightly newer MD-80/90 series planes and 170 Boeing 757s. The 737s were relatively new, but most of the other fleet types were about 20 years old, on average, with the DC-9s averaging a stunning 34 years in service.

But rather than replacing all of them in one giant order, Delta decided to focus on the 757s. Not only were they old and increasingly inefficient, but they were a messy collection of units from both Delta and Northwest—more than a dozen different versions, in fact, all differently configured, each with its own three-character designator (like "75H") in Delta's systems. The complexity caused scheduling and maintenance headaches. Some, like those that had flown for Song, had a nice seat-back entertainment system. Those that had flown for Northwest, which—always the more Spartan airline—offered no shorthaul inflight entertainment, did not. One unloved variant from Northwest was designated the "75N." ("Do you know what the 'N' stands for?" a flight attendant working a 75N flight asked a customer whom she realized had industry knowledge. "Nasty!")

Contrary to some speculation, Delta had no pre-conceived affinity for Boeing, with which it once had an exclusive supplier contract. Delta, after all, was really part Northwest, run by Northwest's former CEO, and Northwest was an Airbus airline. Delta just wanted the best deal. It pitted Boeing's 737-900 against the Airbus 321, both roughly the same size as the 757s they would replace. The negotiations lasted months, covering everything from the timing of deliveries to various aircraft specifications and of course price. When decision time neared, Airbus seemed to have the better offer. By August, sales teams from both manufacturers gathered at Delta's Atlanta headquarters. They were seated in separate conference rooms, preparing their final sales pitches. With Delta leaning toward Airbus but its negotiators shuttling back and forth between rooms, Boeing suddenly came forth with a surprise. It involved, of all things, toilets.

In Florida, a company called B/E Aerospace, which provided seats and other aspects of an airplane's interior, was working on a new concept for its lavatories, redesigning them in such a way that they would be smaller—so much smaller, in fact, that airlines could add extra seats to their 737s. In Delta's case, this would mean four extra seats to sell aboard the 737-900 at no extra cost to the airline—revenue that would flow straight to the bottom line in an industry where even one passenger could make the difference between profit and loss. Boeing and B/E Aerospace weren't really quite ready to start marketing the new lavatories, but Boeing—realizing a multi-billion-dollar aircraft order could depend on this innovation—put its ace on the table. Airbus had no such card. For Delta, that was the clincher.

On Aug. 25, Delta and Boeing announced an order for 100 current-generation 737-900s for delivery between 2013 and 2018. Delta was not adding new capacity. It was merely replacing 757s plus some 320s and even widebody 767s (some of which still flew shorthaul routes) as they retired. The new 737-900s would be extended-range "ER" versions that could fly any domestic route Delta offered, and they could do it 15 to 20 percent more efficiently than the planes currently flying the same routes. Along with the new space-saving lavatories, the planes would also feature Boeing's new "Sky

GLORY LOST AND FOUND

Interior" with amenities like adjustable mood lighting. They would have expanded carry-on baggage space and an energy-efficient LED lighting system. Importantly, "the size and timing of the order will allow Delta to maintain its annual capital expenditure run rate between $1.2 billion and $1.4 billion over the next three years and will not impact the company's $1.2 billion of capital expenditures projected for 2011. Capital discipline is key to the company achieving its $10 billion adjusted net debt target by 2013," the airline said in a statement.

In a subsequent discussion with investors, Delta dispelled any notion that the order was just the start of a buying binge. Ed Bastian affirmed there would not be a "second step of aircraft [purchases], whether it be with Bombardier or Embraer or Boeing or Airbus…. We are done talking about aircraft for the near to medium term."

Richard Anderson was quick to add: "We are not buying shiny objects here. Our goal here is to improve the P&L [profit-and-loss statement] with a modest order of airplanes, Because… 30- to 35-year-old airplanes have higher maintenance costs. If you can take down the maintenance costs and have more efficient operations, you improve CASM [the standard industry measure of how many cents it costs to fly one seat one mile.] And if you stay within our march to get to $10 billion in net debt, you will actually improve the P&L of the airline…. And it really is conditioned upon owning the airplane and not leasing the airplane." That last point was an important one: Delta, bucking yet another industry trend—one toward leasing rather than buying aircraft—saw great value in buying planes and using them for many years.

Delta continued to produce excellent results in the second half of 2011, earning a $765 million net profit excluding special items during the peak third quarter. That was more than any other airline on the planet aside from (of all airlines!) Japan Airlines, which was in the midst of a turnaround as epic as Delta's, and post-merger United. But in the fourth quarter, United—after an excellent 2010 and first three quarters of 2011—began hitting a wall. Delta, by contrast, had another strong quarter covering the last three months of the year, earning a $379 million net profit (in the entire world, only JAL earned more) and blowing away all rivals with an 8 percent operating profit margin, almost unheard of for a longhaul legacy carrier in the off-peak winter. The off-peak capacity cutting was working. Almost everything Delta was doing was working.

Capping off the year was a new agreement with American Express, which agreed to pre-pay $675 million for frequent flier miles it could later award to its credit card customers, who also got priority boarding, waived bag fees and discounted lounge access. Delta got even Amex to pattern its cash payments to counteract the seasonal cash patterns of ticket sales. For U.S. airlines, cash flows tend to be light during the summer, for example, when many travelers have already booked their summer travel and don't plan to go anywhere in the fall. That's when the bulk of the Amex cash would pour in.

Measured by stock market capitalization—in other words, the total value of a company—Delta was now the most valuable airline in the U.S., surpassing even

366

Southwest to become the eighth most valuable airline in the world, trailing mostly East Asian carriers as well as No. 5 Ryanair. But its market cap in late 2011 was still just $7 billion, trifling compared to corporate leaders of other industries. ExxonMobil, amassing wealth that would have made John Rockefeller blush, was alone worth more than twice as much as the top 75 airlines combined!

The airline industry would never match the oil industry's profits. But that fact took nothing away from Delta's triumphs, which were again on view at what had become an annual December investor day conference. This time it was on a chilly but dry day, 11 days before Christmas, at an old church in New York City.

Delta, the old leisure carrier that had focused on taking people to Disney World all those decades, ended 2011 with more domestic first-class seats than any of its rivals. Delta.com was getting a million daily visitors and generating $8 billion in annual revenue. The airline would soon have new state-of-the-art airport terminals in Atlanta and New York. A new ad campaign told fliers it would "Keep Climbing." Of its 2012 capital expenditures, only 14 percent of the money would be for new airplanes, with 60 percent designated for upgrades to its existing planes.

"Just think," Ed Bastian said that day. "A few years ago, if I had told you that we would be paying $130 a barrel all-in for oil, that we have a war going on in the Middle East, that unemployment in this country is stubbornly sticking at a 9 percent level, that our two most important economies, both the U.S. and Europe, are wobbly at best, and maybe in the initial throes of a post-recession dip, and we also have a slow recovery building in Japan, but going slower than any of us would like, you would have thought we would be on our knees. You would have thought that we would be burning the furniture, we would be out trying to raise cash at any cost, that we would be struggling, we would be talking about survival."

Survival? Delta was, of course, in reality doing far more than merely surviving.

The brain trust of a now-prospering Delta was free to bend its minds around the airline's remaining strategic challenges rather than figuring out how to get through the day. One of these strategic challenges was London. Another was Asia. Yet another was finding some way to mitigate the notoriously violent swings in fuel prices—high fuel prices *per se*, Delta had learned, could be managed if those high prices were rather stable, but volatility was still highly unwelcome. The finance team was now looking for new ways to reward investors. The fleet team needed to manage its small-jet phase-out while abiding by pilot scope restrictions on larger regional jets. The labor team pondered the future as the 2008 pilot agreement approached its Dec. 31, 2012, amendable date—12 months could pass quickly in labor negotiation terms.

Delta was just as busy assessing the broader industry landscape, no easy task following sweeping changes brought on by a succession of mergers and joint ventures. Who, for example, was the real United: the United that had kept pace with Delta for

2010 and most of 2011, or the United that had begun faltering in recent months? United was, to be sure, benefiting enormously—even more so than Delta—from American's deep problems, because United and American had dueling giant hubs, side by side, in Chicago. But the jury was still out as to whether United could do all the things it needed to do to integrate two airlines: combine reservations systems, frequent flier programs, websites, product offerings, ticket policies and—oh, yes—labor groups.

US Airways, having been spurned by United, was doing rather well but feeling just as vulnerable as ever because of its heavy reliance on the domestic market. It was now, incidentally, a smaller airline overall, measured by revenue, than domestic-only Southwest. Questions surrounded Southwest itself: Could it integrate AirTran smoothly? Could it compete head to head against Delta in Atlanta? Could it, along with other LCCs like JetBlue, prosper in a world of high fuel prices (which, remember, actually meant less of an overall cost advantage for LCCs) and limited domestic growth opportunities? Could it prevent its labor costs from spiraling upward? Were Spirit and Allegiant, both generating enormous profit margins, taking Southwest's place as the standard bearers for youth, innovation, dynamism and disruption?

As for American, its losses simply couldn't continue without drastic action. Its labor costs were excessively high relative to its rivals. Its pilot scope clause made its regional network uncompetitive. It was weak in Asia, even after retaining JAL as a partner. It was late in getting antitrust immunity with British Airways and Iberia. It was fighting costly wars against its distribution partners. It appeared asleep as Delta and others moved into frontier markets like Africa and varied their flight schedules by season and even day of week. Since 2005, in an ever-globalizing world, American had downsized its international capacity 4 percent while the U.S. industry as a whole had *grown* it 13 percent. Spirit and JetBlue were ruthlessly attacking American's Latin American and Caribbean markets. Southwest had won the battle to deregulate the Dallas market. Having stood idle as others merged, American didn't have the scale to compete against Delta and United. At one point, Richard Anderson suggested American was playing the old and discredited game of chasing market share instead of profits, especially in New York and Los Angeles, even as it was bleeding red ink. "This is not a hobby," Anderson said scornfully.

On top of it all, American had an unbearable debt load, huge pension liabilities, a giant new aircraft order to finance and a rash of retiring pilots, who were, rationally enough, responding to incentives in their contracts to retire early whenever American's share price was declining. And American's share price was declining.

American had long prided itself on being the only global U.S. airline that had never filed for bankruptcy.

That changed on Nov. 29, 2011.

2012

"If you saw the prices, you could never pass on that deal"

In an industry filled with uncertainty, one thing had long been certain: Southwest Airlines, in any given year, would produce better profit margins than Delta. Forget even about the post-9/11 era, when the comparison was downright silly—Southwest made money every year, and Delta lost money every year. Reach back even to those three memorable years that closed the 1990s, when Delta scored an 11 percent operating margin in 1997, and then a 12 percent operating margin in 1998, and then a 13 percent operating margin in 1999. Even then—even in those glorious years—Southwest was better every year, with margins of 14 percent, 16 percent and 17 percent.

This was Southwest, the airline with 39 straight years of profits, the airline that had never laid off a single worker, the airline that had used low fares to democratize air travel, the airline that had profited from 1991 through 1994 while the rest of the industry was losing $13 billion, the airline that had managed not only profitability but a *double-digit operating margin* in 2001, of all years—the year of 9/11—and then further profits in all four quarters of dreadful 2002. It was the airline with the best balance sheet in the business, the airline familiar to any business school student ever assigned a case study on good management and the airline founded by a business icon—Herb Kelleher—whom *USA Today*, in 2007, had ranked No. 5 on its list of America's 25 most influential business leaders of the past quarter century, behind Bill Gates and Steve Jobs but ahead of Jack Welch and even Warren Buffett. This was Southwest. And sure enough, it again beat Delta again in 2010—10 percent to 8 percent—in a year that was triumphant in every other way for Delta.

But then came 2011.

For the first time since the Southwest miracle took shape decades earlier, Delta's operating margin, in 2011, beat Southwest's, 6 percent to 5 percent.

What was perhaps most surprising wasn't that this happened. No, what was most surprising of all was that for anyone paying close attention, this changing of the profitability guard wasn't... well... really all that surprising.

Ever since the watershed moment of the financial crisis, the undercurrents of the industry had changed, propelling Delta forward and Southwest back, at least relative to its own high standards. The problem wasn't that Southwest was any less good at the things that had enabled it to dominate the industry for nearly four decades. The problem was that the world had changed, and those same things—at which Southwest was every bit as good as it had always been—simply didn't matter as much anymore.

Delta was the airline now grabbing attention for its ability to capture new revenue, not via Southwest's old model of stimulating traffic with low fares, but by improving its products, services, flight schedules and alliance offerings. Southwest's old weapons of war—used so effectively against Delta in the Ron Allen, Leo Mullin and Gerald Grinstein years—had been defanged by high oil prices, legacy carrier restructurings, a structural decline in Southwest's bread-and-butter ultra-shorthaul markets (where travelers could opt to drive) because of airport security hassles, IT shortcomings, an inflight product some people considered stale, rising labor costs and a heavy reliance on areas of the country like California, Arizona, Nevada and Florida that had been battered even more than most by the residential real estate collapse.

Managing costs—something Southwest had always mastered—was now an exercise with limited scope for self-improvement. Fuel accounted for nearly 40 percent of Southwest's total operating costs in 2011, and Kelleher's successor Gary Kelly couldn't do much about that. Labor was another 30 percent, and Kelly couldn't do much about that either, not without breaking from tradition and laying off workers or slashing wages and benefits—or, absent that, rapidly growing capacity to justify rapidly hiring new workers, whose entry-level wages would bring down average overall labor costs.

Southwest, to be sure, still had lower unit costs—the cost of carrying one seat one mile—than legacy airlines like Delta. But the gap was narrowing as high fuel prices proved a great equalizer and as legacy carriers exorcised many of their cost demons in bankruptcy. So Southwest, no longer sheltered from these harsh realities by its old hedge umbrella, was forced to play a revenue game—and this, unlike the cost game, was a game legacy carriers, with their global networks and giant frequent flier plans and multifaceted fleets, were better equipped to play. But Southwest had no choice. With cost differentials muted, it had to play this revenue game, so it entered high-revenue airports like New York LaGuardia and Boston Logan, revamped its Rapid Rewards loyalty plan, increased the percentage of its passengers who connect (rather than fly nonstop) from a quarter to a third, tried (but failed) to buy Frontier Airlines, lobbied successfully to overturn federal restrictions limiting its flying from Dallas

Love Field, squeezed more seats aboard its aircraft, added some modest ancillary fees for various services, improved its flight scheduling and hired a large airline IT company called Amadeus to implement a new reservation system, one that would enable international flying, codesharing and other complexities.

Most boldly of all, Southwest orchestrated a 2010 takeover of its lower-cost rival AirTran, which was itself on a similarly troubling trajectory: robust growth and profits in the immediate post-9/11 years giving way to fuel headaches and a born-again Delta getting nasty in Atlanta.

To Southwest's credit, many of its revenue efforts were succeeding. From 2007 through 2012, Southwest—including AirTran's figures both before and after the merger—managed to increase operating revenues by $5 billion despite offering fewer flights. Costs were up too, to be sure, but solid (although not spectacular) profits continued.

Delta was no stranger to competing against Southwest, which had a big presence in Salt Lake City and carried lots of passengers—to and from Florida, for example— whom Delta might have otherwise carried through Atlanta. But Southwest itself had never actually been in Atlanta. Until now.

By buying AirTran, Southwest had become an instant Atlanta powerhouse, with nonstop service to no fewer than 60 cities, including New York, Los Angeles, Chicago, Dallas-Fort Worth, Houston and San Francisco, all key Delta markets. It even served some nearby international markets, mostly in the Caribbean. True, Glen Hauenstein's aggressive pricing and scheduling tactics put AirTran on the defensive, causing it to begin diversifying away from Atlanta. But Atlanta was still by far AirTran's most important market, and now mighty Southwest was assuming its footprint.

So was Delta alarmed by Southwest's arrival at Atlanta, Delta's largest and most profitable hub?

Publicly, at least, Delta downplayed the threat. Far from a nightmare, Richard Anderson and other Delta executives said the Southwest-AirTran merger might even be a good thing for Delta, because the merged airline would have higher costs than the independent AirTran had. They mocked Southwest's unusual boarding procedures and welcomed Southwest's plans to scrap AirTran's business class product, its extensive online travel agency distribution and its assigned seating. Most importantly, Delta knew Southwest could never achieve the merger's planned synergy targets without fare increases. Michael Boyd, a consultant, said at the time that Southwest's history of lowering fares when entering new markets couldn't be repeated this time—AirTran, with its lower costs, had already depressed fares in Atlanta as low as they could go given current fuel prices, and higher-cost Southwest would have to charge more, not less.

Boyd also pointed out a more nuanced but perhaps even more important problem with Southwest's Atlanta plans: Although a fair number of passengers on AirTran flights to and from Atlanta actually began or ended their journeys in Atlanta, the majority were merely connecting in Atlanta—just as countless Delta passengers did—between two other cities. AirTran purposely scheduled tightly packed "banks" of flights to facilitate these connections. Southwest, on the other hand—although it gladly welcomed connecting passengers—still optimized flight schedules across its network for point-to-point passengers. That's because these passengers tend to pay a premium for convenient, nonstop service. And point-to-point flights are more efficient to support from a labor perspective—this mattered for an airline like Southwest that paid rather high wages—because if they are spread evenly throughout the day rather than packed together in banks arriving and departing all at once, a smaller number of gate agents, for example, can work more flights. One agent, in other words, can staff the boarding gate for two flights departing 45 minutes apart from each other, but obviously not for two flights departing at the same time. But flights optimized for point-to-point travelers, rather than for connecting passengers, would not—just as obviously—attract as many connecting passengers, because the average length of their layovers, and thus their total travel times, would be longer. And Southwest made clear that as it integrated AirTran, Atlanta would indeed resemble other Southwest markets, with schedules geared more toward point-to-point passengers. Meanwhile, the number of people who actually wanted to travel to or from Atlanta—the point-to-point market—was limited. At the same time, Southwest was saying it would continue growing its total presence in Atlanta. But if the number of point-to-point travelers wasn't going to grow (because only a finite number of people actually want to fly to or from Atlanta) and if the number of connecting passengers was likely to shrink (because Southwest's schedules wouldn't be as useful for them), that meant total demand for Southwest's flights would shrink, not grow. So how could Southwest grow in Atlanta? The numbers didn't add up. Boyd calculated that of AirTran's roughly 180 daily departures, connecting passengers alone filled the equivalent of 100 of them. "Cut the connecting hub, and the majority of these consumers are gone from the future Southwest system," he wrote at the time.

Southwest's Gary Kelly didn't take the verbal punches, whether from Delta itself or others, lying down. In a presentation to Wall Street about the merger, he reminded Atlanta's travelers that Southwest was the only airline that "doesn't charge those ridiculous fees." And he said Southwest would indeed lower fares significantly in Atlanta, stimulating new demand in at least two dozen Southwest stronghold markets that AirTran never served or underserved—Atlanta-Chicago Midway was one example.

Who would be correct? The answer hadn't yet been clear in 2011, partly because Southwest took a slow approach to integrating AirTran. In fact, Southwest-branded planes didn't even show up in Atlanta until February 2012. Market dynamics, in other words, were changing slowly. But Southwest was clearly mobilizing for war, spending lavishly on an advertising campaign that blanketed the city with ads proclaiming it "Atlanta's hometown airline." Delta hit back with "70 years as Atlanta's hometown airline." Southwest called attention to its "bags fly free" policy. Delta reminded people who held Delta-branded Amex credit cards that their bags flew free too. "Atlanta at Last; Good-bye High Fares," Southwest boasted. "Improving First Class," Delta retorted, "Begins by Offering One."

Journalists loved the story. "Move Over Delta, Southwest to Fly Out of Atlanta," read one headline. "The Battle for Atlanta is Heating Up," proclaimed another. "Game On: Delta and Southwest Duke it Out." "Southwest Eager for a Seat in Atlanta." And so forth.

This was no minor skirmish over some trivial outpost. In 2011, for the 14th year in a row, Atlanta's airport was the world's busiest, handling more than 92 million people. For Delta, Atlanta was bigger, in terms of weekly flights, than its second and third biggest hubs, Detroit and Minneapolis, *combined.* In the summer of 2012, Delta would operate more than 1,000 flights each day, each way, from Atlanta, compared to fewer than 400 at New York JFK and LaGuardia airports combined. No single hub was as important to, say, American or United. American, at its largest hub Dallas-Fort Worth, scheduled just 750 daily departures. United flew about 650 from Houston and a bit less from Chicago. Put another way, Atlanta was still Delta's nerve center, still its most important market by far—in absolute terms, anyway, the most important market for any airline anywhere in the world. Penetrate its defenses there, and Delta's tower of success would come crashing down. Beat Delta in Atlanta, as AirTran had learned years earlier, and you beat Delta, period.

Atlanta wasn't nearly as important to Southwest's overall health. But it was important nonetheless. By 2012, Atlanta had become Southwest's fourth busiest airport after Chicago Midway, Baltimore-Washington and Las Vegas. Winning there would be no small matter.

Alas, Southwest could not win in Atlanta, for all the reasons Delta and Michael Boyd had pointed out. And it was only a matter of time before Southwest itself would reach the same conclusion. It ended flights to Washington Dulles, Seattle, Dallas-Fort Worth, Sarasota, Fla., Bloomington, Ill., Atlantic City, N.J., White Plains, N.Y., and Newport News, Va., meaning fewer people flowing through the hub to fill other flights. Southwest and AirTran combined would soon operate 12 percent fewer departures from Atlanta than AirTran alone did in 2011, while the number of nonstop destinations the two brands offered fell by fully 20 percent. Southwest would remove 15 AirTran destinations from its Atlanta flight menu, unable to make them work with its higher-cost, more point-to-point-focused business model. In the summer of 2010, AirTran had operated 210 daily flights from Atlanta. By five years later, Southwest would whittle that down to just 125. In doing so, it eliminated hundreds of Atlanta-based jobs.

AirTran's Atlanta hub, as it happened, was already struggling when Southwest acquired it. In fact, those 210 daily departures in 2010—impressive as that figure might sound—were well short of AirTran's peak of 265 in the summer of 2008. It still profited in some key markets like Atlanta-New York and Atlanta to the Caribbean. But many of its shorter-haul corporate travel markets like Atlanta-Charlotte and Atlanta-Jacksonville were problematic. And when Southwest stepped into the picture and began bringing all of AirTran's workers up to Southwest's much higher wage scales, cost inflation was immediate—however well something worked for AirTran, that same thing often worked less well for Southwest. And Southwest's union contracts prohibited the heavy airport staff outsourcing AirTran had used.

Southwest's downsizing in Atlanta was a gift to Delta. And it wasn't Southwest's only gift. Delta, as it had correctly predicted would be the case, enjoyed competing against an airline with no business class cabin, no assigned seating and no inflight entertainment. And Southwest's famously low fares? Indeed, they weren't so low anymore. The Rapid Rewards revamp and other revenue initiatives helped, but the bulk of that $5 billion revenue expansion from 2007 through 2012 came from good old fashioned fare hikes. Southwest still served its popular peanuts. But the days of cheap "peanuts fares," as it had branded them during its 1990s expansion across the U.S., were long gone.

In fact, because of its insistence on not charging for bags, seat assignments or itinerary changes—despite the billions of dollars these practices was reaping for its competitors—Southwest was facing even *more* pressure than other airlines to raise its base fares. Southwest also refused to sell its tickets through third-party online travel agencies like Expedia, Travelocity, Orbitz or Priceline—it was wary of being easily comparison shopped and wary of paying fees to the agencies and the global distribution systems they used. This strategy might have worked well enough in, say, Austin, a longtime Southwest stronghold where, as at Cheers, everybody knows your name. But it worked less well in a more competitive market like... well... Boston, the town that's home to the Bull & Finch Pub featured in Cheers. There, not so many people knew Southwest's name, let alone the fact that southwest.com was the only place to buy Southwest tickets online. Numerous consumers—nobody knew how many—would never even think to check with Southwest. And Atlanta was more like Boston than Austin.

Wall Street analysts and other stakeholders increasingly pressed Southwest to change its ancillary and distribution strategies. They often pointed to the rising airline superstar Spirit Airlines, which was earning huge profit margins while charging the lowest base fares in the industry. Its secret: extremely aggressive ancillary fees and, less importantly, an agnostic approach to distribution. Even ultra-low-cost Spirit happily sold through online travel agencies. It simply passed the added costs along to consumers. Why couldn't Southwest do this?

Southwest's technological challenges created yet another advantage for Delta. Because Southwest's systems were so outdated, the Southwest and AirTran networks—even though under one financial roof—weren't connected via codeshare for more than two years, something Delta and Northwest were already doing on the day they merged. So Southwest got virtually no network synergies in the interim. For a while, travelers couldn't even take the more basic step of booking AirTran tickets on Southwest's site and vice versa. There was brand confusion too: AirTran passengers still had to pay for checked bags; Southwest passengers, of course, did not.

(If Southwest was so sure bag fees were a bad thing, some analysts wondered, why wasn't it getting rid of them at AirTran?) In the meantime, Southwest's acquisition of AirTran eliminated Delta's lowest-cost competitor at its most important airport.

Was Southwest's purchase of AirTran a mistake? Well, it did get some benefits: the elimination of its own lowest-cost competitor, less head-to-head competition in markets like Baltimore and Orlando, its first-ever international service, some slots at Reagan National and LaGuardia and so forth. And Southwest could now, at least, link Atlanta to its most important business markets like Chicago and Houston, giving its customers in those places access to an important commercial center that was previously absent from the Southwest network. Plus, it got all of AirTran for—probably—less than Southwest would have had to pay for AirTran's 137 airplanes alone, not to mention the rest of the airline's commercial value.

But all airlines—including all of Southwest's competitors—benefited from the disappearance of AirTran as a competitor, while Southwest alone had to bear the cost of the merger. (One lesson of modern airline mergers had by now become clear: They are almost always good for the industry at large. They are only sometimes good for the airlines actually merging.) And Southwest probably could have gotten some modest Atlanta access—enough to put the dot on its map, so to speak—without buying an airline.

And for whatever benefits Southwest indeed might have gotten from the transaction, Southwest did not anticipate the need to downsize so heavily in Atlanta, and it did not anticipate its losses in Atlanta would prove a heavy drag on the company's financial results for years to come.

And there was one other thing Southwest did not anticipate.

By buying AirTran, Southwest inherited not just 51 Boeing 737-700s that were similar to the ones in its existing fleet but also an even greater number of Boeing 717s—88 of these, to be exact—which were an entirely distinct aircraft type requiring different pilots and mechanics. These were updated versions of the out-of-production DC-9s and MD-80/90 series planes; Boeing inherited the 717 program, which had previously been called the MD-95, after it bought McDonnell Douglas in the 1990s. The 717s never gained much traction with airlines and were now also out of production. They weren't bad planes, but with just 117 seats, U.S. carriers often preferred to fly either smaller jets with outsourced pilots earning lower pay—to comply with "scope clauses" in pilot contracts, these generally couldn't have more than about 76 seats—or larger jets with a more advantageous revenue-to-fuel burn ratio. The 717s, in other words, burned only modestly less fuel than larger jets but generated far less revenue because they carried far fewer passengers. Initially, Southwest thought it could make good use of the AirTran 717s on "thinner" (i.e., lower-demand) routes where a 737 was too much airplane. But then Southwest realized it would need to downsize Atlanta. And as fuel prices jumped significantly following the takeover agreement, the 717s—whose economics suffered disproportionately more than those of the 737s when fuel was expensive—looked increasingly like an unwanted asset.

Nearly two thirds of the fleet of the airline Southwest had just bought wasn't performing as Southwest had hoped. Aside from the competitive benefits of eliminating AirTran—which had helped other airlines too, none more so than Delta—what had Southwest really bought itself other than an Atlanta hub and a mostly 717 fleet it no longer wanted?

On the morning of Sept. 27, 2010, Nathaniel Pieper was driving to work, listening to National Public Radio. And what he heard, as he would later relay to his colleagues, nearly caused him to drive off the road. Southwest, a host said, was buying AirTran. Pieper, Delta's fleet strategy chief, immediately thought of AirTran's 717s. Never mind that these planes were broadly so unpopular that they had one of the shortest production runs of any aircraft in memory. Pieper had long coveted the 717, if only he could find a willing seller at a low enough price. Delta was different from most other carriers in that its network badly needed planes of that size, which performed most economically when flying routes of roughly 750 miles. Well, Delta had a huge number of routes like that, including many of the best corporate travel markets from Atlanta like Newark, Detroit and Chicago. That's why it had kept Northwest's geriatric DC-9s for so long and why it readily pounced on any secondhand MD-80 or -90s that became available.

Of course, when it announced it was buying AirTran, Southwest gave no indication it didn't want the 717s; on the contrary, it considered these a main selling point of the transaction. But driving to Delta's headquarters at about 7:30 a.m., Pieper dialed the cell phone of Kevin Schemm, his counterpart at Boeing, which was the actual owner of the 717s—Boeing had leased them to AirTran. Pieper was excited. But Schemm? He was sleeping. Pieper had forgotten it was still 4:30 a.m. in Seattle, home to Boeing's commercial airplane division.

When Schemm woke up, he vaguely recalled that Pieper had called, so he called him back. There wasn't much to talk about: Southwest, at this point, was happy to have the 717s. But should Southwest's feelings ever change, Boeing knew that for all the airlines in the world that had no interest in the planes, there was one that was highly interested—but only, of course, if it could pay a price reflecting the fact that no one else was interested. Delta, as it had patiently done with so many other airlines and aircraft types, was now waiting for Southwest to throw its 717s into the bargain bin.

For about the first half year after it announced it would buy AirTran, Southwest remained publicly optimistic about the 717s. Gary Kelly in March 2011: "It's a good shorthaul airplane. It's very fuel-efficient for those markets, and it's better suited for some of the smaller communities that we would like to get into."

But Kelly's underlings were beginning to whisper to him that the fleet type wasn't performing as hoped. An outsized proportion of AirTran's profits were coming from its 51 737s, not its 88 717s.

As soon as five months later—in August 2011, at an airline conference in Albuquerque hosted by, of all people, the consultant Michael Boyd, who had expressed some of the earliest skepticism about Southwest's plans—Kelly was singing a detectably more nuanced tune. He hadn't yet given up on the 717s—at least not publicly. But "I don't think it brings any unique benefits to Southwest that you can't get with the 737," he said. "Longer term, I don't see that it plays a strategic role in our fleet." By two months later, during an October 2011 earnings call, he was even more specific: "We don't see a need to have a different airplane in our fleet, like the 717, as compared to the 737. Said a different way, the 717 doesn't bring any unique capabilities for us that would justify having the ongoing complexity by having a second fleet type. So that's just a fact. Then, the question becomes, well what are we going to do about that? So I think that if we had an opportunity that was affordable for us to accelerate the retirement, if you will, of the 717s and replace them with 737s, that would be fantastic."

Once Southwest realized it had to get rid of the 717s, three-way negotiations among Boeing, Southwest and Delta began. Talks between Delta and Southwest were understandably awkward, given the competitive battle they were waging against each other in Atlanta. But interests are interests, and here was one company with an asset of which it badly wanted to rid itself and another company that badly wanted that asset.

On Dec. 13, 2011, Southwest announced a deal with Boeing to buy 150 of its future-generation 737s—the 737 MAX, Boeing's new-engine answer to the Airbus 320neo—and, for more immediate needs, 58 current-generation 737s. That was all Delta needed to hear. It knew for sure Southwest clearly wanted out of the 717s and had probably convinced Boeing to facilitate an escape from the 717 leases in exchange for the big order. So Delta tightened its negotiating stance, determined to get a sweetheart deal on the planes it wanted so badly—planes no other airline in the world likely wanted at all.

On March 13, 2012, answering an audience question at a JP Morgan investor conference, Ed Bastian acknowledged what had become an open secret: Southwest, Delta and Boeing—which actually owned the planes and had leased them to Southwest, remember—were talking. "We're looking at all arrangements," Bastian said. "And we have taken note that Southwest has indicated a desire to exit the [717] fleet. I can't tell you whether that's going to be a decision Delta can take or not."

By May 22, 2012, they had a tentative deal. Delta reached "an agreement in principle" with Southwest and Boeing to lease the 88 AirTran 717s. More precisely, Southwest would continue to lease them from Boeing Capital, and then it would sublease them to Delta. Southwest even agreed to foot the $100 million bill for painting them in Delta colors and outfitting them with Delta interiors. They would be configured with 110 seats, 12 of them in first class. Deliveries would start in the summer of 2013, arriving roughly three per month for three years.

Airlines, manufacturers and lessors never disclose the actual prices anyone pays for anything. But "if you saw the prices," Richard Anderson told investors, "you could never pass on that deal." Delta was getting a lot of useful airplanes for not a lot of money.

But the tentative deal was just that: tentative. Because in reality, this wasn't a three-way deal but a four-way deal. The fourth party, with just as much power to make or break the deal as the other three? The very Delta pilots who would fly the planes. Delta, remember, took an unconventional approach not only to fleet planning but also to labor relations. And in this case, those two realms were linked—by design.

Excluding its heavily unionized Comair regional unit and about 350 flight dispatchers, Delta's only unionized workers were its roughly 11,000 mainline pilots, who were represented by ALPA. Well now the ALPA contract was approaching its expiration date, or more precisely, its amendable date—airline labor contracts never really expire, but they become open for negotiation on a certain date. The pilot deal signed just before the Northwest merger in 2008, which covered both Delta and Northwest pilots, ran through the end of 2012. And naturally, after two extremely good years for Delta, pilots wanted their share of the prosperity.

Just as naturally, investors, recalling the rich contract Delta gave its pilots months before 9/11, feared pilot demands could torpedo the company's prosperity. But Richard Anderson, Ed Bastian and their human resources chief Mike Campbell resolved to avoid that, to somehow find a way to negotiate new contract terms that simultaneously rewarded pilots, preserved one of the industry's healthiest management-union relationships and provided the airline with economic benefits. Rapid expansion—one way to make pilots happy while reducing unit costs through greater scale—was a nonstarter, an example of the old way of airline thinking that got the whole industry into trouble in the first place: Everyone had expanded, only to see everyone's unit revenues go to pieces. Delta would not abandon its adherence to capacity discipline.

So it took a different tact: It identified a common enemy. Ten years earlier, 50-seat regional jets were all the rage among U.S. airlines, which fought to fly the planes using outsourced pilots earning a fraction of the airlines' own mainline pilots earned. But now airlines like Delta hated these 50-seaters every bit as much as their mainline pilots hated them, a change in attitude brought forth by high fuel prices—the planes would barely be economical even if the low-wage pilots instead worked for free. So Delta devised a grand bargain: It would greatly reduce the number of outsourced 50-seaters in its fleet, essentially replacing every two of these with one larger 717 flown by mainline pilots. The 717s would replace the geriatric DC-9s too, of course, but there were just 24 of those left, compared to 88 717s coming. Of course, many markets were simply too small for a 110-seat aircraft, so pilots would also agree to expand the scope of Delta's outsourcing rights for 76-seat regional jets—jets far larger, more economical and more customer friendly than the 50-seat jets. Delta already had 255 of these larger regional jets, but pilots would allow it to fly 70 more. Overall, outsourcing to regional partners would still decrease substantially, because about 200 50-seaters would leave the fleet by the end of 2015.

In summary, the deal would enable Delta to restructure its smaller-gauge domestic fleet with planes featuring lower unit costs and more comfort for customers, implying higher unit revenues. In addition, the company would separately obtain the right to vary pilot schedules by season, scheduling more intensively during peak seasons and less intensively during slow months like January and September. Management could also require crews to work more hours per month. And profit sharing would become less generous, falling from 15 percent to 10 percent of the first $2.5 billion in profit. A 20 percent rate would still apply to any annual profits exceeding $2.5 billion.

Pilots, for their part, would see more jobs back at the mainline carrier. And they'd get large wage increases, including an immediate 4 percent raise, followed by a 9 percent raise in 2013 and 3 percent in each of the two years after that. Delta would also raise its contribution to the pilots' pension plan by a percentage point each year. MD-88 pilots would now earn the same pay rates as their MD-90 colleagues. Delta would not be allowed to convert 70-seat jets to 76-seaters. Sick leave and reserve flying policies would improve. At least half of all seat-mile capacity in the Air France/KLM/Alitalia joint venture would still have to be flown by Delta crews. And pilots would now be eligible for an early retirement plan available to other workers.

All this, including the 717 deal, hinged on rank-and-file pilots ratifying the amended contract negotiated by ALPA, which at Delta was now led by a Detroit-based 767 captain named Tim O'Malley following Lee Moak's promotion to head ALPA's national organization. And not all pilots were convinced. Some of the more senior fliers wanted even greater management concessions to make up for the many rounds of pilot concessions surrendered in years past. Some didn't like the idea of having to fly more hours per month, because this meant less future hiring and therefore fewer members in the union. But O'Malley, in a letter dated May 21, 2012, cited the example of a 737 captain earning $153.42 per hour in 2008, with an 11 percent pension contribution from the company, who under the new contract would—by January 2015—earn $216.92 per hour, a 41 percent increase in base pay, not to mention an increase in the company's pension contribution to 15 percent. According to an analysis for *Airline Weekly* by FAPA.aero, a pilot employment advisory firm, a 23-year-old pilot hired by Delta under the new terms would earn $1.3 million more over the course of his or her career, through age 65, than the old agreement would have provided.

The new contract terms, O'Malley wrote, would also boost the ratio of mainline domestic to outsourced regional flying by 57 percent over the life of the agreement. If pilots rejected the agreement, new negotiations would likely drag on for years, as pilot negotiations typically did. Some younger pilots, meanwhile, were heartened by a bulge in upcoming retirements, which provided them with better flying opportunities, which would mean better pay regardless of anything else management did. It was already a remarkable feat: Delta had reached this tentative deal with ALPA seven months *before* its current deal became amendable in an industry in which negotiations often dragged on long *after* deals became amendable, with settlements often only coming as worker strikes or management lockouts loomed.

But would the rank and file vote yes?

On June 29, 2012, the results of the poll emerged. And for all the concern among management and union leaders alike that members would hold out for something even better, in the end, it wasn't all that close: 62 percent voted to approve the deal.

Many observers were stunned. The innovative deal came remarkably early in the traditional bargaining process and after only two months of negotiations. Management and union leaders alike said a deal so early in the negotiating cycle, and so good for the company and workers alike, was "unprecedented."

United's ALPA division, by contrast, was using different words to describe its own airline's management. In a letter to its members, leaders called management "intransigent" and "out of touch," noting there was no agreement on any major cost item—not wages, not work rules and not scope. ALPA picketed the airline's Chicago headquarters and petitioned the National Mediation Board to release pilots from mediation, which would start the clock ticking toward a possible strike. ALPA went on to accuse management of shrinking the airline and pushing for more labor concessions while awarding executives big bonus payments, pay hikes and stock distributions. ALPA singled out United's CEO Jeff Smisek—a protégé of Gordon Bethune, who had presided over generally good labor relations at Continental—accusing Smisek of not even showing up to negotiating sessions. Post-merger United had originally committed to negotiating a joint collective bargaining agreement, encompassing pilots from both United and Continental, by September 2010. It was now mid-2012, with no agreement in sight.

American's pilot relations were even worse. The airline was now in bankruptcy and reaching for steep concessions. Pilots at US Airways hadn't gotten a new contract since the 2005 America West merger. Workers at several major European airlines were not—as United pilots were doing—just threatening to strike. They were following through on their threats.

A few months later, Bloomberg News correspondent Mary Jane Credeur asked Delta executives how they planned to afford the new contract. Anderson: "When you look at the overall value that we're going to create as a result of unlocking the ability to re-fleet, plus the productivity that has been built into that agreement, we're confident that it will be an important part of our ability to reduce unit costs over the next couple of years, to improve our margins and our return on invested capital."

"One additional thing," Ed Bastian added. "We also reduced the profit-sharing going forward too, and that's an important part of helping to fund that cost growth."

Just shedding all those 50-seat regional jets would save $473 million in ownership costs, outsourcing fees and maintenance—many of these planes were aging and due for expensive engine overhauls. So Delta now had a fleet plan featuring larger RJs, 717s subleased at fire-sale prices, used MD-90s bought from airlines like China Southern and current-generation 737-900ERs purchased at a time when other airlines were falling over themselves for more expensive future-generation planes. And Delta was taking its time on widebodies, effectively canceling (although technically deferring deliveries on) the 787 orders Northwest had placed years earlier.

As for large widebodies, Richard Anderson had made perfectly clear that Delta had no interest whatsoever in giant Airbus 380s or Boeing's not-much-smaller 747-8s.

Linking labor relations to fleet planning wasn't entirely novel. But the traditional playbook involves dangling future fleet growth, which means future job growth, as a carrot to extract union concessions. Delta's playbook was different. It was actually shrinking fleet count overall but promising more mainline flying by outsourcing less. And although it did extract some productivity concessions, including more flexibility to vary pilot staffing by season, everyone walked away with higher pay. With the company making money again, pay—not to mention employee morale—was further enhanced by large profit-sharing checks. On Valentine's Day 2012, Delta, based on its 2011 profits, paid its employees an extra $265 million. Job applicants noticed. In one 2012 flight attendant recruitment drive, Delta received 22,000 applications for 300 job openings. Those with foreign language skills went to the front of the line.

Delta would indeed incur some wage inflation as a result of its new pilot deal, coupled with steady wage increases for non-union workers. And its defined-benefit pension obligations remained substantial too. Not for pre-merger Delta pilots—the airline had terminated their plan during bankruptcy—but for other work groups, including ex-Northwest pilots whose plans were merely frozen rather than terminated. But this was nothing Delta couldn't handle. Not with revenues trending up and most other costs trending down.

Maintenance costs, for example, declined as new planes replaced old ones and thanks to initiatives like a joint engineering venture with Aeroméxico. Distribution costs declined as more travelers—nearly 40 percent—booked on Delta's own website. Airport labor costs fell as pre-merger Northwest workers became non-union, giving management more staffing flexibility than other airlines had. Early retirement programs helped lower average wages and benefits. Reservation centers in Seattle and Sioux City, Iowa, closed. Unit costs declined as planes gained extra rows thanks to redesigned seats that were thinner and lighter and redesigned lavatories that were smaller. Interest costs declined as Delta repaid its debt. And costs fell as synergies from the merger continued to take root in areas like fleet and network planning. Combine all this with 13 percent revenue growth in 2010 and 11 percent revenue growth in 2011, achieved with barely any capacity growth, and it was no wonder Delta was thriving, no wonder it was outperforming its peers, no wonder it was emerging as one of the great turnaround stories in the history of American business.

But Richard Anderson and his team weren't satisfied. For Delta, 2011 was indeed a good year, with $1.2 billion in net profits (excluding special accounting items) and a 6 percent operating margin, best among what were now the Big Four legacy U.S. airlines (United, Delta, American and US Airways) plus Southwest. For the second straight year, Delta was earning a positive "return on invested capital," a benchmark heard more and more from the mouths of Delta executives and something airlines infrequently achieved. However, 2011 marked a step backward from 2010, when Delta had earned $1.4 billion net and an 8 percent operating margin. Was 2010—as Jack

Nicholson said in a film by the same name back in 1997, during Delta's last period of prosperity—"as good as it gets?" Delta's share price fell too in 2011. Among U.S. airlines, only Alaska Airlines and Allegiant saw their shares rise that year.

The cause of Delta's step back was as obvious as it was usual: oil prices. They had skyrocketed in response to Middle East unrest, and Delta—despite increasing capacity by a mere 1 percent—watched helplessly as its fuel bill spiked by $3 billion. It was still paying significantly more to fuel its planes than to employ its 80,000 workers. Nearly 40 percent of its entire operating cost base, in fact, was just jet fuel.

Sure, hedges helped, saving $150 million in the fourth quarter of 2011 alone. But hedges weren't a cure-all. They were at best an expensive insurance program and at worst a financial weapon of mass destruction, as Delta realized when its hedge book lost $1 billion in 2009. New planes like Boeing 737-900ERs offered fuel savings. So did the installation of aerodynamic winglets at the tips of aircraft wings, removing weight from planes and other operational adjustments. But in the end there wasn't much else an airline could do about fuel.

Or *was* there something else an airline could do?

One aspect of rising fuel costs was particularly vexing for Delta and other airlines. The price of raw crude oil itself wasn't the only thing bouncing around and spiking at inopportune times. The price to *refine* the crude oil into usable jet fuel was rising even faster. The refining margin (or "refining spread" or, even more colloquially, "crack spread") had inflated from about 13 cents per gallon a few years earlier to more like 80 cents by 2012. And airlines couldn't even easily hedge for crack spread volatility; a market for that just didn't exist. In the meantime, the U.S.—oddly enough, considering six decades of growing oil dependence on other countries—was experiencing an energy production revolution, in which new technologies were deployed to unleash large quantities of oil and gas from shale rock. So the price of natural gas, used for heating and generating electricity, was indeed plummeting in response to the new supply, because the natural gas market was largely a domestic market. But the oil market is anything but. And sure enough, oil prices had stayed stubbornly high, because what was happening in the U.S. was just one piece of the overall global picture. In addition, all the new oil being pumped from places like North Dakota (where Delta was adding flights) lacked rail and pipeline links to the nation's refineries, meaning much of the oil used for jet fuel still came from overseas imports. The same was true for automobile fuel, whose high price was hampering the U.S. economic recovery. To what degree? Well, *The Economist* estimated an 80-cent-per-gallon drop in gasoline prices would have given American households $100 billion more in annual disposable household income. And more disposable income means more money to spend on air travel.

Actually, the crack spread had become Delta's single fastest growing cost item, with an average annual growth rate of 73 percent from 2009 through 2011. Refiners had little choice but to squeeze prices upward on their relatively inelastic airline customers. The cost of crude was rising sharply, but passing this cost to gasoline stations across the country was difficult, because demand for gasoline was falling as Americans embraced smaller, more fuel-efficient cars. They were also carpooling, using more public transportation and driving fewer miles. Americans still spent $446 billion at gasoline stations in 2010, not much less than the $521 billion they spent on food at grocery stores. But the number of miles driven had peaked way back in 2004, and overall gasoline demand in the country was at a 20-year low. At the same time, cheaper natural gas meant less demand for heating oil, another one of the major products sold by refiners. Absent any pricing power with buyers of auto fuel and heating oil, in other words, refiners needed to squeeze their profits from airline fuel.

As Delta's finance executives observed this disturbing trend, they couldn't help but notice other dark clouds. Since September 2011, three refineries supplying the U.S. east coast, where Delta's operations were concentrated, had closed because their owners simply couldn't profit. This was less of a problem in America's energy belt along the Gulf Coast, which had greater access to cheaper crude oil and didn't rely as much on the European and African crude (from places like Angola and Nigeria) on which east coast refineries relied. America's largest oil refinery, measured by barrels per day produced, is located in Baytown, Texas, near Houston. The next four are all in nearby Louisiana. East coast facilities tended to be smaller, older, less technologically advanced and more subject to environmental regulations. Those facts raised further concerns about jet fuel supplies for some of the country's busiest airports, including those in New York, which (counting all area airports) had become Delta's second largest market after Atlanta.

So Delta began thinking: What if it bought itself a refinery? In the fall of 2011, according to *Platts*, the finance team began inquiring about a refinery for sale in Louisiana, which another company ultimately bought. At roughly the same time, according to the *Philadelphia Inquirer*, Delta contacted Patrick Meehan, a Republican U.S. congressman from Pennsylvania, to express interest in a refinery in a Pennsylvania town called Trainer not far from Philadelphia's airport—and, by extension, not terribly far from New York, either—which the refinery's owner, ConocoPhillips, planned to close.

After getting $30 million in financial support from the state of Pennsylvania, Delta, on April 30, 2012, announced a deal to buy the Trainer refinery complex, together with a pipeline network to supply jet fuel to airports throughout the northeast, for $150 million. To run the facility, Delta would hire oil industry veterans and establish a wholly owned subsidiary (named "Monroe," in honor of the airline's Louisiana birthplace). It would spend another $100 million to upgrade the aging refinery and to increase jet fuel production to 32 percent of the refinery's total output, up from about 14 percent. As for the production of refined products other than jet fuel, Delta would trade those to BP and Phillips 66 for additional jet fuel produced at their own facilities around the country. All told, these transactions would secure about 80 percent of Delta's domestic jet fuel needs. Whatever Trainer jet fuel it didn't use itself, it would sell to its competitors, which all faced the same situation.

As financial transactions went, the Trainer refinery acquisition didn't quite get the mainstream attention that Facebook's IPO was getting that spring. But Delta's highly unorthodox move—other airlines hedged jet fuel; Delta was buying its own oil refinery—was a media sensation nonetheless. Appearing on CNN, Ed Bastian defended the move: "We spend over $12 billion a year [on] fuel, so when you think about a $150 million bet, if that's what you want to call it, relative to the size of our spend, we don't think it's much of a bet at all."

Delta was quick to add that the price it was paying for the refinery, to address so many of the giant company's fuel needs, was less than the price it would have to pay for a single widebody airplane—a Boeing 777, for example, could cost $200 million

"One of the things that you see a lot and read a lot about," Bastian said May 17 at a Bank of America/Merrill Lynch conference, "are the aircraft manufacturers that are talking about the importance of re-gauging and re-fleeting airlines so that you can generate fuel efficiency and savings. We'd have to purchase 60 narrowbody new-generation aircraft at a cost of $2.5 billion to generate the same level of fuel efficiency that we expect to get out of the $250 million investment in Trainer.... So we thought it's a risk that's worth taking."

Specifically, Delta said the move would generate $100 million in savings for the remainder of 2012 and then $300 million annually after that. This didn't even include possible additional savings if Delta could supply its new facility with cheaper North Dakota oil, as new infrastructure (such as pipelines) emerged.

Skeptics, pointing to the unforgiving economics and operating complexities of running an oil refinery, questioned the move. "Volatile." "Capital intensive." "Uncertain." Those were just the polite adjectives people used to describe oil refining—adjectives, of course, that also described the airline business. Delta would make its own jet fuel, secure its supply in the northeast and hedge itself against soaring crack spreads. But how much would running a refinery, with a unionized workforce and aging equipment, cost? There was a good reason, some experts argued, why no new U.S. refineries had been built in decades—and why the country's major oil companies were getting out of the refining business. If oil companies couldn't make money refining oil, how could an airline? "There are three problems here," Gregory J. Millman, a *Wall Street Journal* columnist, wrote. "First, Delta won't manage the capital invested in the refinery for optimal return. Second, even if Delta were to do so, the refinery is one of the least economical in the U.S. so that its potential returns are low at best. Third, the refinery will probably require much more capital than Delta's public presentations suggest."

Was this another in a string of innovative strategic moves by an airline now considered by some observers to be the industry's best managed? Or was it a case of overconfidence and misjudgment? Only time would tell. But this much was clear: Richard Anderson was unwilling to let the vagaries of the oil markets destroy Delta's fortunes yet again. "Let's not be a victim of fuel," he proclaimed April 12 at a U.S.

Chamber of Commerce aviation summit in Washington. "If it's 40 percent of your cost structure, you can't just say it's not in your control."

Two weeks after that speech, Delta reported its 2012 first quarter results. As it had every year since 2000—and as most other airlines do too in the off-peak winter—it lost money. But it lost a lot less money than it has lost a year earlier: just $39 million rather than $320 million, never mind that the average price of fuel had jumped from $2.89 a gallon to $3.28, sending United to a $286 million loss and American to a $248 million loss.

Thus confirmed contrasting trajectories for the nation's top three airlines. Delta was strong and getting stronger, American improving some but still confined to a bankruptcy bed and United getting significantly weaker after a rather strong first three quarters of 2011—its weak fourth quarter had not been an anomaly.

United's case was particularly intriguing. The protégées of Gordon Bethune at Continental—led by CEO Jeff Smisek, Larry Kellner's successor—now dominated the management ranks. Smisek's recurrent boasts about new planes, new routes, new seats, new products, a mammoth frequent flier plan, transatlantic and transpacific joint ventures, falling debt and hub cities overflowing with Fortune 500 companies made the post-merger United indeed appear like an emperor in the making, which— sure enough—had matched Delta financially during most of 2011. At one investor conference, Smisek even celebrated Delta's success, seeing it as a prelude to what United could itself achieve after completing its still-in-progress merger integration.

How wrong he would turn out to be.

March is a busy month for most airlines. After rebuilding their savings, which are depleted during December at shopping malls, many American families stay at home during January and February before flying again in March. University students fly home or to vacation destinations for Spring Break. It's a particularly busy season for sunshine markets like Florida. So Delta had chosen January (of 2010, in its case) to undertake the most complex merger integration task of all: merging its reservation systems. As *The New York Times* noted at the time, that involved the replacement of more than 140,000 electronic devices and no fewer than 8,856 separate steps by the airline's computer engineers. As it turned out, the timing didn't really matter, because the transition went smoothly. But had things gone awry, this would have been the least bad time of the year for that to happen.

Now it was United's turn to merge reservation systems. Unlike Delta, which chose to adopt the larger merger partner Delta's (rather than Northwest's) reservation system so that it only had to retrain roughly one-third of its agents, replace one-third of its airport kiosks and so forth, United chose to adopt the system used by the smaller merger partner, Continental, which would necessitate retraining more like two-thirds of its agents, replacing two-thirds of its airport kiosks, etc. And unlike Delta, United chose to undertake this migration not in barren January—but in busy March.

Initially, problems appeared limited and manageable. But over the course of the next several months, just as the peak spring and summer travel seasons began, rather than small problems working themselves out, small problems cascaded, and all hell broke loose. Soon, United was consistently ranking dead last among its peers for on-time performance, lost bags and customer complaints. In June, it ranked 15th out of 15 U.S. airlines in punctuality, arriving on time just 70 percent of the time, a full 16 percentage points below Delta and US Airways and 10 points below American. Then in July, United's on-time rate dropped to 64 percent.

During the first six months of 2012, United was responsible for 35 percent of complaints against airlines recorded by the U.S. DOT for all of America. And things were only getting worse. The equivalent figure was 45 percent for June alone, when United received seven complaints per 100,000 passengers, compared to just 0.19 complaints per 100,000 for Southwest, the industry leader. A United customer, in other words, was 37 times more likely to complain than a Southwest customer. No other airline had more than 2.5 per 100,000. Worse, United's all-important elite ("premier," in United's lexicon) customers weren't receiving their upgrades. One got a message to contact the airline about a schedule change. After a long wait and then a long discussion with perplexed agents, she discovered only her flight number had changed. A platinum premier member living in central New Jersey, territory Continental's Newark hub had long dominated, said he instead began driving down to Philadelphia and flying US Airways, never mind its reputation for Spartan service: At least the flights were on time, and he hadn't been getting the upgrades to which he was entitled on United anyway. The IT problems affected United's revenue management and maintenance and just about every other aspect of its business, to speak nothing of the frustrations it was causing customers.

Then, far from reassuring its best customers the worst would soon be over, United taunted them. United's Chief Financial Officer John Rainey, speaking in May (at a Bank of America/Merrill Lynch conference) about changes to the airline's MileagePlus frequent flier program, said, "We had certain groups in this program that were over-entitled, if you will." Never mind that Delta was thinking similar thoughts. Or that Rainey, in further explaining that United had "re-aligned the benefits of that program with what the customers and program participants are actually providing to the program," was merely voicing what almost every other airline, including famously friendly and egalitarian Southwest, was doing too. "Over-entitled" was the last thing any customer wanted to be called, and United was the last airline in a position to call them that. The comment appeared in every major newspaper and was vilified on frequent flier websites by incredulous MileagePlus members, many of whom felt that far from over-entitled, they weren't even getting that to which every flier rightfully feels entitled: arriving "on time, with your underwear," as Gordon Bethune liked to say back when he was running Continental.

Smisek soon apologized to customers and acknowledged less success in winning corporate contracts than United had hoped. Many corporations, sure enough, were turning to Delta, whose reliability and service reputation were all the while improving. "When you're in the middle of a lot of construction," Smisek said, "people take a detour." He said service would improve, and customers would return.

But United had other problems in 2012—some of its own making, many not—even aside from the IT blow-up. The economy in China, an important market, was slowing. Cargo, important on Asia flights, where United had big exposure, was depressed. Southwest was relentlessly attacking United's hub markets and—over United's loud protestations and threats—won the right to fly internationally (such as to Mexico) from domestic-only Hobby Airport in Houston, a competitive threat for United's hub at nearby Bush Intercontinental Airport. Worse, Smisek followed through on one important threat he had made: He really did cut available seat-mile capacity by nearly 10 percent at the profitable Houston hub, a move that amounted to an own goal, because now United had to reallocate some of the service to more marginal hubs. Southwest had gotten what it wanted; United was only punishing itself.

In Washington, United's Dulles hub was suffering as federal budget cuts weakened the local economy. And as big as markets like Houston and Washington were, United didn't dominate them, or even its giant headquarter city Chicago, in the way Delta dominated markets like Atlanta and Minneapolis. Had Gordon Bethune, who had been right about so much, been wrong when he said (in 2008, prior to the first time they almost merged) a fused United-Continental would be "checkmate" because of its strong position in the nation's biggest and most prosperous cities? Could it be that the way to make outsized profits in the airline industry was not to have a plurality of service in giant markets but a dominant majority in slightly smaller ones? US Airways, after all, was—even if less spectacularly than Delta—earning good profits by dominating hubs like Charlotte and Philadelphia, not to mention high-yield, capacity constrained Washington Reagan.

When Chile's LAN merged with Brazil's TAM, United lost its Star Alliance partner in Brazil. When British Airways bought British Midland, United lost its Star Alliance partner in London. To alleviate its operational distress, United spent money adding staff and spare aircraft. In the meantime, United's pilots clamored for a new contract, one that at least matched the pay and benefits that Delta's pilots were now getting. Even the bankruptcy of United's close rival American was at least as much of a threat as an opportunity: Yes, American was cutting capacity and facing even greater pilot unrest, but it was also slashing costs and rightsizing its fleet in competitive markets like Chicago. At one point, American offered to instantly confer elite frequent flier status on anyone that held similar status on United. What was more humiliating: that a bankrupt competitor was offering to rescue United's customers from its poor service, or that the offer didn't sound so ridiculous to many of those customers?

But Delta was clearly winning business away from American too, especially when a pilot "sickout"—an unofficial work slowdown, in other words—made a mess of its operations that autumn. American faced its own strategic problems, including bombardment of its two most profitable hubs—Dallas-Fort Worth and Miami— by the surging ultra-LCC Spirit Airlines (in Miami's case via nearby Fort Lauderdale). It remained weak in Asia, moreover, and was lucky to even be relevant there after nearly losing Japan Airlines to Delta two years earlier. It certainly had better London Heathrow access from New York, but it was nonetheless losing New York corporate traffic to Delta because American lacked hourly shuttle flights to Washington and Boston. It had been slowest of all the U.S. legacy carriers to embrace the tactics like seasonal and day-of-week scheduling that had worked so well for Delta. But perhaps most problematic was American's lack of scale relative to Delta and United, in a business where scale ordained great advantages. In Buffalo, for example, American offered just five daily flights to Chicago—nothing more. United by contrast, offered 19 daily flights to four hubs. Delta? Twenty-six daily flights to five hubs. The same was true at numerous other midsized airports.

US Airways certainly understood the importance of scale. While running America West, Doug Parker and Scott Kirby bought the old US Airways to bulk up. Then they tried to buy Delta. Then they tried to merge with United. Now, six years later, American was the only big target left. So Parker and Kirby coveted American.

It's not that US Airways faced any immediate pressure to address its strategic shortcomings. It had earned decent profits in 2010 and 2011. Its Washington Reagan hub was a cash cow, all the more so since the Delta slot swap. Its Charlotte hub shared many of Atlanta's beneficial demographic, geographic and economic features, even if only on a smaller scale. Its formidable European presence was becoming an advantage as the transatlantic market consolidated into three big joint ventures, never mind that US Airways wasn't actually in one of these—it was benefiting as much as anyone else from improved pricing power. It had closed its poorly performing Las Vegas hub. It was among the most aggressive airlines in generating ancillary revenues. And more generally, all U.S. airlines enjoyed a steadily if slowly improving economy and a more benign competitive environment thanks to consolidation and capacity restraint. Indeed, even United and American, for all their troubles, would make money in 2012, albeit with profit margins well below those of US Airways, Southwest and especially Delta. In 2011, industry profits had been an astonishing $7 billion better than 2008, even though the two years had strikingly similar overall demand and fuel cost environments. Many analysts believed this time really was different, that airlines really had reformed enough to ensure financial sustainability.

But far from reassured, Parker, in April 2011, seven months before American filed for bankruptcy, presented his board of directors with an internal analysis of a potential US Airways-American merger.

In September of that year, Tom Horton, then American's No. 2 behind Gerard Arpey, approached Parker at the annual Conquistadores del Cielo meeting of airline CEOs in Wyoming and expressed interest in discussing a deal—but only after American secured new labor agreements. The next month—one month before the bankruptcy filing—Arpey tried to persuade US Airways to leave the Star Alliance in favor of oneworld, which would serve as a potential prelude to a potential future merger. About a month after the bankruptcy filing, Parker called Horton, who had replaced Arpey as CEO on the day of the bankruptcy filing, to reiterate his interest in a merger. But Horton again—thinking American's negotiating position would be stronger after, not before, it cleaned up its act—insisted he wanted to restructure his company first.

But Parker and Kirby felt bankruptcy was the reason *to merge*, not the reason not to merge. They wanted to seize control of American during its restructuring, not after it. Their experience buying US Airways, when they were running America West seven years earlier, had confirmed their belief in the flexibility of merging with a bankrupt airline. It's why they tried to buy Delta when it was still in bankruptcy. And it's why they wanted American now.

Parker and Kirby had learned something else from their experience with Delta: Just wooing the bankrupt airline's creditors wasn't enough. They needed support from the bankrupt airline's workers too. So throughout 2012, US Airways vigorously and often publicly waged a charm offensive on the investors that owned American's debt, as they had done with Delta's creditors, and—this part was new—*on the unions* that represented American's pilots, flight attendants and mechanics.

On Jan. 13, 2012, *The Wall Street Journal* reported three separate parties were "studying bids" for American: US Airways, the private equity firm TPG and—to everyone's surprise—Delta. Delta, the *WSJ* wrote, had hired the Blackstone Group, a financial advisory firm, to assess the wisdom of a bid and conducted a thorough study of the legal implications, concluding a deal, if it included concessions, would likely pass antitrust muster. Taking the possibility seriously, British Airways CEO Willie Walsh said a merged Delta-American would be a "phenomenal entity." Less enthusiastic was Air France/KLM CEO Jean-Cyril Spinetta, who publicly questioned the chances of such a combination ever winning regulatory approval.

Was Delta seriously thinking about buying American? Or was it a ploy to drive up American's price so US Airways would have to pay more? Either way, Delta was soon out of the picture, content to watch the US Airways courtship of American play out for the rest of the year. If it succeeded, Delta would face another bulked-up behemoth. But this was overshadowed by the big revenue benefits that yet another mega-merger would bring to all U.S. airlines, not to mention that a merged American would have higher costs than an independent American because (as Delta had done to facilitate its merger) American would give rank-and-file employees sizeable raises in exchange for their buy-in. Asked by an analyst, during an earnings call, about whether he considered a merged American-US Airways a threat to Delta, Richard Anderson refused to comment specifically about that potential transaction. But he said all that needed to be said with his general comment that "global consolidation is good for the business model."

These days, everything seemed to be good for Delta's business model. The second quarter of 2012 was another excellent one for Delta. Its revenues expanded

6 percent even though its capacity actually shrank 1 percent—Delta was earning more despite flying less. It was indeed taking away corporate business from United and American. "Now that we are able to offer the scale and the opportunity to New Yorkers to travel anywhere in the world, particularly our big corporates," Ed Bastian said at a Raymond James conference, "you are seeing a massive amount of share that is moving our way." Gains from financial, manufacturing, health care and IT companies were most notable.

Just as Delta was worrying less about Southwest these days, it was worrying less about JetBlue too. Gone were the days when Delta couldn't compete against the New York-based LCC's toxic mix of low fares and a superior inflight product. Now JetBlue, like everyone else, was happy to raise fares, and Delta's inflight product was increasingly competitive. And most of JetBlue's growth now was not in New York—that's the growth that had been most damaging to Delta—but in Boston and the Caribbean. And even in those markets, Delta had the financial muscle now to play hardball, at one point adding overlapping New York routes to Sarasota, Fort Myers and St. Maarten. Unlike the situation that had prevailed during most of JetBlue's history, it was now Delta, not JetBlue, that had the stamina to withstand wars of attrition.

Spirit Airlines was causing a bigger stir, evoking memories of disruptive LCCs of yesteryear by expanding rapidly and charging very low base fares. It was also attracting a lot of attention to itself with headline-grabbing policies like fees for even *carry-on bags* (not just checked bags) and outrageous email advertising campaigns that never failed to offend. Often they were sexually suggestive, such as its "Many Islands, Low Fares," or "MILF," sale—anyone under a certain age recognized that acronym, from the 1999 sex comedy "American Pie," as standing for "mom I'd like to fuck." Still others mocked subjects ranging from Tiger Woods' infidelity to an incident in which a JetBlue flight attendant lost his job after deploying an emergency slide and sliding onto the tarmac with a can of beer in each hand. The ads might have seemed to emanate from a university fraternity house, but Spirit's brainy, board-game-playing CEO Ben Baldanza had explained in 2009 to *Airline Weekly* that they were merely a pragmatic cost strategy. "People get the email and forward it to their friends," he said. "And when that happens, we don't have to buy an ad in *The Miami Herald.*" And the silly ads belied serious profits: Spirit was growing quickly and profitably, generating some of the global airline industry's highest profit margins.

Not even Spirit, though, was much of a threat to Delta, even though Detroit was one of the LCC's biggest bases and even though it had added some flights to Atlanta, Minneapolis and New York. Spirit, more to the point, was stimulating traffic that otherwise wouldn't be flying—its fares were so low, in other words, that it was in some senses competing more against movie theaters, for consumers' discretionary entertainment dollars, than against full-service airlines like Delta. And in any event, it was doing so more from American's big markets like South Florida (American at Miami, Spirit at Fort Lauderdale) and Dallas-Fort Worth. Taking nothing for granted though, the Delta pricing team devised a new line of "basic economy" fares, offered selectively in markets where Spirit competed. Unlike other discounted economy fares, these bargain-basement fares did not allow itinerary changes—not even for a hefty fee—and did not include seat assignments, not even for high-tier SkyMiles "Medallion" members. On the other hand, they did confer full frequent flier credits, another example of Delta wanting people to remain fully engaged in the SkyMiles program so that they would do other things that put money in Delta's pockets, like signing up for American Express cards or patronizing businesses that buy miles from Delta.

Internationally, Japan, although still a strategic liability for Delta, was recovering from the tsunami. In May, Delta opened a new international terminal at its most important airport: Atlanta. With the U.S. dollar still weak relative to many currencies, inbound tourism from markets like Brazil and China remained strong. A federal push to ease visa hassles, part of an Obama administration effort to boost U.S. export earnings, further contributed to more inbound airline traffic. Unit revenues were up sharply in Mexico and Brazil, owing to Delta's new equity-based partnerships with Aeroméxico and Gol, respectively. The Aeroméxico partnership was becoming so tight, in fact, that Richard Anderson even made an appearance at Aeroméxico's own annual investor day event in March. Expanded marketing deals with Canada's WestJet, China Southern and China Eastern also helped.

Delta's biggest revenue story in 2012, however, was Europe. The continent's economic crisis remained acute. And Air France/KLM was suffering from two debilitating cancers: uncompetitive labor costs and rivers of red ink from shorthaul routes, where it was helpless to compete against ruthless low-cost carriers like Ryanair and easyJet. But Delta and Air France/KLM, together with Alitalia, slashed their transatlantic capacity, especially in the off-peak winter. In late 2011, Air France/KLM had dismissed its CEO and brought back Jean-Cyril Spinetta, who promptly announced a major cost-cutting drive—this, of course, helped Delta because the two shared costs. As a result of these changes, Delta saw its total passenger revenue from its European flights jump 11 percent during the first quarter even though it had *cut* capacity by 9 percent—an unbelievable swing in fortunes resulting in a unit revenue (i.e., revenue per available seat mile) surge of 22 percent! Trends remained strong for the rest of 2012, helped along by another 5 percent reduction in capacity, which Delta announced in May.

One of the cuts: getting rid of Delta's last flights to London's Gatwick Airport. Delta, at one time or another, had flown to Gatwick from New York JFK, Boston and Cincinnati, but all that was left by the summer of 2011 was one daily Atlanta flight, which was now gone too. Heathrow, not Gatwick, was where the revenue was, and that—by the summer of 2012—was the only place Delta was, with Heathrow flights to New York JFK, Atlanta, Boston, Detroit and Minneapolis. What about Miami-London, added after American and British Airways were forced to surrender some Heathrow slots? That was now gone too. So, for that matter, were money-losing routes like Atlanta-Shanghai, Atlanta-Athens, Atlanta-Moscow,

Atlanta-Prague, Atlanta-Guayaquil, New York-Manchester, New York-Tel Aviv, New York-Berlin, New York-Budapest and Salt Lake City-Tokyo. After the summer, Delta abandoned yet other routes: Atlanta-Accra, Atlanta-Milan, Atlanta-Barcelona, New York-Istanbul, Detroit-Hong Kong and—eliciting an uproar from Tennessee's politicians—Memphis-Amsterdam.

Despite such aggressive cutting, international routes would provide 35 percent of Delta's total passenger revenues in 2012, exactly the same figure as in 2011. By dynamically moving its planes to more precisely match supply with demand, Delta was practicing addition through subtraction, raising revenues in Europe, for example, even while downsizing its network there. Strikingly, Delta was a 22 percent larger airline in the peak summer than in the off-peak winter, a far more drastic seasonal disparity than any other giant airline. This 22 percent was up from 14 percent just a year earlier, in 2011, and even that 14 percent figure had been impressive.

Domestically, Delta's fastest growing market was New York LaGuardia, thanks to the US Airways slot swap. Its fastest shrinking markets were Memphis, Cincinnati and—also thanks to the slot swap—Washington Reagan. In March, however, it did win the right to launch a new Washington Reagan flight to its Salt Lake City hub, thanks to a new round of congressional exemptions to the Reagan National Airport "perimeter rule," which didn't permit most flights to places more than 1,250 miles from Washington. That aside, the swap was working as planned, with the buildup at LaGuardia generating more connecting traffic, more corporate business and higher profit margins. "Our New York City margin is up two points despite the capacity adds in LaGuardia, so we have essentially added 45 percent to the capacity [there] without having any margin deterioration in its first year of operations," Ed Bastian said on April 25. Adding so much supply anywhere, so quickly, without any profit margin deterioration, was almost unheard of.

That same month, the airline broke ground on a $160 million expansion and renovation of LaGuardia, which included a connecting bridge between terminals, a new Sky Club lounge and additional security lanes. Renovation work was now well underway at JFK too. Delta's relentless marketing in New York, meanwhile, was gaining visibility, even more so when one of the sports teams it sponsored, the New York Knicks, briefly catapulted to center stage by the breakout performance of a Taiwanese-American point guard named Jeremy Lin. The "Linsanity" that ensued led to many eyes seeing Delta's logo and ads adorning Madison Square Garden.

Elsewhere, Detroit was benefiting from the auto sector rebound. Minneapolis was benefiting from the oil boom in nearby North Dakota. During the first half of 2012, air traffic at North Dakota's airports was up an astounding 22 percent compared to the same period a year earlier, and no other airline's hub was as well positioned as Minneapolis to capture that demand.

Delta's revenue momentum had other sources too. Service continued to get better and better, as DOT data and countless traveler surveys testified. When Delta was bleeding money and desperate to preserve cash, its ability to invest in service upgrades was minimal. Now it was making money and plowing about half the cash it was generating back into the business to make the flying experiencing better—which, in turn, helped it make even more money. It was losing far fewer bags, receiving far fewer complaints and incurring far fewer cancellations and delays. It could now afford to boost staffing during peak periods with seasonal hires, deploying more than 1,300 of its "Red Coats," for example, to assist passengers at nearly 100 airports throughout the world. Just before the busy summer, these agents completed a two-day workshop on creative ways to address the needs of passengers during travel disruptions. To reduce wait times at the airport, Delta placed kiosks on concourses—adorned by signs that said, "Need help?"—to help passengers rebook flights when things did go wrong. Automating the more routine rebooking requests freed agents to work on more complex situations.

Extra-legroom, extra-recline "Economy Comfort" seats first appeared in 2011 on Delta's longhaul flights. Well, the idea proved so successful that in May 2012, Delta expanded the concept to all two-class aircraft, even large regional jets—almost every fleet type except small turboprops and 50-seat regional jets. (A small section of extra-legroom economy seats, incidentally, was an idea United had pioneered a decade earlier with its "Economy Plus" product—a rather profitable idea, it turned out, that its competitors had ignored.) Soon, Economy Comfort became available to shoppers booking through the Travelport and Amadeus distribution systems used by many corporate travel departments—high-tier elites could select them for free, while others could pay—pleasing not only those travelers but also the airline, which was happy to have the extra revenue.

The age of the smartphone and social media gave Delta additional opportunities to enhance the travel experience for its customers. Its mobile application—or its "app," as smartphone users had by now come to call these—for iPhone and Google Android phones enabled users to purchase tickets, check flight information, select their seats, download their boarding passes, track their baggage, re-book their flights when necessary and even store a photo of their parking spaces to make finding their cars easier when they returned home. They could also receive automatic text messages with information about the status of their connecting flights. The airline also had two dozen people monitoring social media sites like Facebook, responding to comments, questions, suggestions and complaints.

Inflight Wi-Fi access was yet another area where Delta was offering more, not less. Airlines had discovered onboard Wi-Fi wasn't much of a money-maker in its own right—uptake rates were rather low. Connection speeds, moreover, could be slow when too many people used it at the same time. But online access was something many high-paying customers demanded, and so Delta—unlike any of its legacy competitors—had already made it available on every two-class shorthaul aircraft in its fleet. On other airlines, passengers could check whether Wi-Fi would be available on their particular flights; on Delta, there was nothing to check. If they were flying Delta over land (other than on its smallest jets and turboprops), on roughly 750 aircraft—no other airline came close—the answer was yes. And in June it announced its intention to expand the service to longhaul flights too, using a new satellite-based (rather than air-to-ground) system, beginning in early 2013.

The year also saw a major modernization of Delta's website, a critical sales channel that had essentially run on the same platform since 1997. Among the enhancements were smoother shopping pathways for purchasing ancillary items, whether from the airline itself or from third parties like hotel or rental car companies. Glen Hauenstein, speaking in December at Delta's annual investor day event, compared it to a car wash: "When you drive out to a car wash, they always offer the basic wash, and the basic wash, you know, is $10. And then they offer the enhanced wash, and then there is the deluxe wash, and then there is the supreme wash. And very, very few people actually just buy the basic wash." For too long, the basic wash was the only thing airlines—Delta and its competitors alike—had really offered. But that was changing.

Theresa Wise and the IT department also improved the software tools tasked with automatic re-booking of passengers during operational disruptions. Finding new flights for passengers whose original flights were canceled was no easy task, especially with flights that were, on average, 80 percent full. The introduction of Economy Comfort seating only added to the complexity, because the last thing a high-tier customer wanted, after her flight had been canceled, was a less comfortable seat on the next flight. But the right technology could solve a lot of these issues.

SkyTeam improved too. Aerolineas Argentinas, Lebanon's Middle East Airlines and China's Xiamen Airlines had accepted their invitations and joined the alliance. Corporate customers appreciated moves by Delta to provide more detailed travel expense reports, specifying not just the total cost of tickets but also the ancillary items customers bought, how many of the company's employees were rewarded with elite status, how many were upgraded and how many enjoyed bag fee waivers. The reports even detailed the average on-time and bag handling performance of the employees' flights.

By 2012, Delta was re-emerging as an industry advocate, harkening back to the post-9/11 aftermath, when Leo Mullin was the sector's unofficial spokesman. Now Richard Anderson had assumed that role. In December 2011, U.S. airlines collectively decided to revamp their trade organization, which Anderson chaired at the time. Frustrated by what they considered Washington's indifference to their outsized contribution to America's economy, airlines were ready for a more proactive approach. So the Air Transport Association was rechristened Airlines for America, or A4A. No longer could one airline veto an entire initiative or campaign. To run A4A, the industry hired Nicholas Calio, considered one of Washington's most powerful lobbyists. Calio had represented Citigroup, America's largest bank, during the crafting of the Dodd-Frank financial reform act and other high-stakes legislation and administrative rulings designed to protect against another financial meltdown. Before that, he was President George W. Bush's chief liaison to Congress, advocating for White House policies on Capitol Hill. His job now: to convince legislators airlines suffered a disproportionate tax burden and that investing in aviation infrastructure, most importantly modernized air traffic control, would be good for the American economy. More broadly, A4A wanted someone in the White House or Congress to champion their cause, much as Senator Ted Kennedy had championed the cause of airline deregulation in the mid-to-late 1970s, or as Michigan's congressional delegation has long championed the auto sector.

This was an uphill battle. Every day, news organizations—especially broadcast news—chronicled airlines that seemed to do nothing but pack passengers like sardines, leave them waiting on the tarmac for hours, lose their luggage, cancel their flights, raise fares, and—perhaps most diabolically—charge extra for everything. "And this is actually, in my book, a declaration of war on consumers!" exclaimed Peter Greenberg, CBS's travel editor, on the network's morning news show. Never mind that airlines were safer and (especially in Delta's case) more reliable than ever before, or that airfares, all the while—even if they had risen from their recession-era lows—were still at some of their lowest inflation-adjusted levels ever.

In addition to his role as A4A's chairman, Anderson was elected chair of the Metro Atlanta Chamber (MAC), which represented more than 4,000 companies based in and near Atlanta. In June 2012, he became chairman-elect of IATA, an organization representing airlines from every corner of the earth, on his way to becoming chairman a year later, succeeding the CEO of Australia's Qantas.

In his leadership roles, Anderson pushed back against efforts by the European Union to unilaterally impose carbon emissions trading on the airline industry, including non-European airlines. He told Congress the war-torn African nation of Liberia had next-generation air navigation, but the U.S. did not. He called for streamlined antitrust guidelines for evaluating airline deals, recounting how it took two years to get approval for a mere slot swap with US Airways. He called for "fair skies" as opposed to "open skies"—it's not free trade, he argued, when a carrier like Japan Airlines gets $8 billion in government money and—despite a U.S.-Japan open skies agreement—Delta can't get the Tokyo Haneda slots it wants (never mind that non-U.S. airlines regularly moaned that U.S. airlines operated at unfair advantages thanks to their country's own bankruptcy provisions). Anderson wanted visa reform too. He wanted less burdensome regulation. Delta joined a campaign called Fix the Debt, organized by U.S. firms urging Congress to address America's fiscal challenges, including its annual budget deficits, its $16 trillion in debt and its future pension and health care obligations to a swelling rank of retiring baby boomers.

And he took these concerns to Washington. In April, he spoke—with the industry's chief lobbyist Calio at his side—at an aviation summit hosted by the U.S. Chamber of Commerce. "I think," Anderson said, "we have an obligation as policy makers and thought leaders in this industry to be serious about what it is going to take to have a real national airline policy in this country. I can tell you, China does... They view aviation as a national asset." Only agriculture and the oil industry, he continued, contribute more to national GDP than the airline sector. "[But] we pay a greater sales tax on tickets than you pay for guns, alcohol or cigarettes."

One particularly thorny issue involved the Export-Import Bank of the United States, created as part of the New Deal era to help arrange financing for overseas firms buying U.S.-built products. In practice, the biggest beneficiary of Ex-Im financing, as it was known, was America's biggest exporter, Boeing. An airline from, say, Bangladesh, which wanted to buy 737s but had poor credit, could nonetheless go out and a get a loan from a bank, which in turn could rest assured of getting repaid—if the airline couldn't repay the loan, U.S. taxpayers would. In reality, the Ex-Im Bank, as it was known for short, managed its risk exceedingly well, and in all its years of existence, it earned a lot more money for taxpayers than it lost, through fees charged to airlines that applied for loan guarantees.

So what was the problem? Delta and other U.S. airlines—Delta was the most vocal—thought the arrangement was grossly unfair. Non-U.S. carriers qualified for loan guarantees that lowered their cost of borrowing, whereas U.S. carriers could not get this sort of financing, not even if they bought from Airbus. For these U.S. airlines, it was hard to say what was worse: that this subsidy was helping to lower the cost of capital for extremely profitable foreign airlines, like Ireland's Ryanair or Panama's Copa, which didn't need any help, or that it was propping up dying airlines that might have otherwise collapsed or at least not bought as many airplanes.

Shortly before the financial crisis, when Delta's credit was still weak, it had trouble finding financing for two 777 widebodies it planned to buy to fly to India. But Air India, a mess of an airline that was lucky when it was only losing hundreds of millions of dollars rather than billions, an airline alive only thanks to recurrent government subsidies, had no problem buying 777s thanks to $3.4 billion in guarantees from the Ex-Im Bank. And where did Air India fly these planes? To the U.S., competing directly against Delta but able to price its tickets, Anderson claimed, $300 to $400 lower than otherwise would have been the case due to the special financing. So together with A4A, Delta sued the Ex-Im Bank, asking the U.S. District Court of the District of Columbia "to find the Air India loan-guarantee commitments unlawful, to prevent the loan guarantees from being issued and to order injunctive relief requiring the Ex-Im Bank to comply with its statutory obligations."

On one hand, Delta and the other U.S. airlines had a point. On the other hand, the Ex-Im Bank was likely helping to create and preserve far more American jobs at Boeing and other exporters than were being lost at U.S. airlines as a consequence of the Ex-Im Bank's existence. Plus, other aircraft manufacturers like Airbus, Embraer and Bombardier benefited from similar export credit agencies, so arguably the Ex-Im bank merely leveled the playing field for Boeing more than it put U.S. airlines at any sort of disadvantage, especially considering European airlines, for example, couldn't use export credit to buy Airbus aircraft in the same way U.S. ones couldn't use it to buy Boeings.

In any event, the court didn't give Delta and its fellow airlines what they wanted. The bank had defended itself with skill, at one point enlisting the support of former President Bill Clinton. But the episode marked another example of U.S. airlines, led by Delta, asserting themselves and demanding the appreciation and recognition they felt they deserved.

Joining the lawsuit was the Air Line Pilots Association, now led at the national level by Lee Moak, the former ALPA head at Delta. Moak knew all too well that the fortunes of his members were closely aligned with the fortunes of their employers. He had seen what happened to his flock when Delta ran out of money. He had the scars to prove it. And he saw just as clearly that his support for consolidation—controversial at the time among pilots—had been, in retrospect, the right card to play. Delta and its fellow carriers became far healthier as a result, and pilots were sharing in that success even as fuel prices remained high. Now he was playing another card.

Moak concluded, exactly as airlines themselves had, that more airline-friendly government policies could help. And in some ways, ALPA possessed greater sway in Washington than its members' employers, especially among Democratic lawmakers, whose success at the polls depended on union support. Moak thus echoed Anderson's calls for a national airline policy, upgraded air navigation infrastructure, more financial support for customs facilities at U.S. airports (rather than at increasingly popular "preclearance" facilities abroad) and an end, before it really began, to Europe's emissions trading system. He applauded President Obama for relaxing visa restrictions on foreign tourists and stood alongside Delta and its co-litigators in attacking the practices of the Ex-Im Bank.

"Over the past five years," an ALPA statement read, "the Ex-Im Bank has provided financing for dozens of widebody aircraft. This financing is provided at rates that are not available to U.S. airlines, and many of these Bank-subsidized aircraft are being used to fly routes that are, have been and could be served by U.S. airlines. U.S. carriers have found that they have needed to withdraw from or not begin flying routes that might otherwise be economically viable. As a result, the Bank's financing is directly and adversely affecting U.S. airlines and their employees. Further, there is every indication that Bank financing of widebody aircraft is likely to grow rapidly and increasingly threaten U.S. airlines' ability to compete on international routes, costing ALPA members and other airline industry employees their jobs."

Anderson couldn't have said it better himself! And that was the point. A new spirit of labor-management cooperation had emerged, a spirit cultivated by Anderson and Moak alike in the interests of both of their constituencies. Sure, Moak—in a June 14, 2012, speech to the Aero Club of Washington—championed some policies airlines would oppose, including job protection provisions in open skies pacts, the retention of foreign ownership restrictions (i.e., preventing foreigners from buying U.S. airlines) and more rights for workers during bankruptcies. But he also complained of high taxation, costly consumer rights protections for passengers, TSA security hassles, the absence of regulations on oil price speculation and the presence of open skies agreements that disadvantaged U.S. airlines—all complaints that would warm the hearts of any airline management team. Anderson, for his part, when asked at the Chamber of Commerce summer about the future of unmanned aircraft, talked about a recent flight he had taken to Tokyo. The weather was rough, and the pilots had to abort not one but two landings. "I was pretty glad there were two of Delta's senior 747-400 captains on that flight," Anderson said. That was music to Moak's ears.

Back at the General Offices, or "the G.O." or "the Gen," as employees called headquarters in Atlanta, Delta's marketing team clinched new sports sponsorships in the U.S. and beyond, including one with the popular Chelsea Football Club, a Premier League soccer team, to enhance Delta's brand in the U.K. It also dedicated an airplane to Chipper Jones, the retiring Atlanta Braves star who had spent his entire Major League career in Atlanta, and offered him a free round-trip ticket to anywhere in the world. Delta's relationship with American Express was as tight as ever: Amex's CEO Ken Chenault, in fact, was the keynote speaker at a Delta leadership forum held in August in Atlanta. Richard Anderson, in his regular communications with employees—including a weekly phone message called "Right from Richard"—invoked the words of Delta's founder C.E. Woolman: "Let's put ourselves on the other side of the counter. We have a responsibility over and above the price of a ticket."

Invoking Woolman wasn't ridiculous, because the glory days seemed to have returned. Ron Allen's "Leadership 7.5" era, which Delta's now-CFO Paul Jacobsen described as a time when people and product were the first places executives went for cost cutting? That period was a fading memory. Delta's turnaround was on display again in the summer of 2012, when the airline's operating profit exceeded $1 billion in just three months. Unit revenues to Europe rose again thanks to capacity cuts, despite the London Olympics, which scared many business travelers away. Operating margin for the third quarter was 10 percent, beating US Airways by two points, JetBlue and Frontier also by two, United by three, Southwest by five, Virgin America by six and American by six. Only Alaska Airlines, Spirit Airlines and Allegiant—a smaller airline and two downright tiny ones, by comparison—had higher margins than Delta that quarter.

But Delta had several items of unfinished business. One was restructuring regional flying in line with efforts to drastically reduce 50-seat regional jet flying and incorporate Southwest's 717s. In the spring, Pinnacle Airlines, which had purchased Mesaba from Delta after the Northwest merger—and which now flew about 200 regional jets for Delta—filed for bankruptcy. Some of its creditors alleged Delta, trying to hammer down regional flying costs, had pushed Pinnacle there. Whether it bore the blame for Pinnacle's cash crisis or not, Delta was now in a position to control the airline. Its first move was to keep it alive with a $74 million debtor-in-possession loan, on the condition it renegotiate flying contracts and labor contracts. As Pinnacle's most important source of business, and with no other investors interested in rescuing it, Delta's leverage was overwhelming. Pinnacle would stop flying for United and US Airways, give Delta the right to remove 50-seaters over time and fly for Delta at highly competitive rates relative to what other airlines were paying for their regional traffic feed. After Pinnacle restructured, Delta's loans would convert to equity, and Pinnacle (which would later change its name to Endeavor Air) would become a wholly owned subsidiary of Delta. Had Delta, which had in 1999 bought now-deeply-troubled Comair, not learned a lesson about buying regional airlines? Anyone who asked that missed the point. Delta, in 1999, had paid $2 billion for Comair. It found Pinnacle, on the other hand, in the same place it looked for its aircraft: in the bargain bin.

As for Comair, by the summer of 2012, Delta had whittled its fleet to fewer than 50 planes, 16 of them 50-seaters. The 50-seaters were, moreover, some of the earliest ever built, making them even less efficient than other inefficient 50-seaters. Delta once hoped to sell Comair. But the only thing to do now was close it, which is exactly what Delta (on July 29) announced it would do. On Sept. 29, Comair's 35-year history came to an end.

Two months later, Delta furthered its regional restructuring with the purchase of 40 new two-class CRJ-900s that could hold 76 passengers, with an option to take another 30 later. Cleverly, it agreed to do the deal only on the condition that the plane's manufacturer, Bombardier, would assist with the phase-out of 60 CRJ-200 50-seaters. This implied a separate deal between Bombardier and SkyWest, which was now flying the CRJ-700s Comair had been flying. All told, these deals with Pinnacle, Bombardier and SkyWest meant Delta now had a plan to eradicate more than 200 50-seat aircraft that were otherwise contractually slated to fly for many years.

If these behind-the-scenes Delta maneuvers didn't exactly capture the imagination of most Americans that summer and fall, there was good reason why, even aside from the fact that regional flying assignments don't generally capture the imagination of most Americans. It was, after all, presidential election season again. Suspense built as August turned to September and September to October. Running for the Republicans against the incumbent Barack Obama was Mitt Romney, a wealthy businessman who had worked with Delta to turn around the troubled 2002 Winter Olympics in Salt Lake City, making the games a success by the time the athletes actually competed. The presidential race was close, but Romney was handicapped from the start. Painted as an uncaring plutocrat and often sounding like one—he wasn't concerned about what 47 percent of Americans thought, he was secretly recorded saying—his signature achievement of health care reform, while he was governor of Massachusetts, was neutralized as a campaign theme because Obama himself had used it as the basis for his own nationwide healthcare reform, while Romney now tried to explain why he was against something nationally that bore striking resemblance to what he had rather successfully implemented at the state level. Obama, meanwhile, although dogged by persistently high unemployment and a big budget deficit, won support not just for securing healthcare reform but also for ending the war in Iraq, winding down the war in Afghanistan, killing Osama bin Laden, intensifying drone attacks on terrorists, imposing crippling sanctions on Iran, rescuing the auto industry, signing a Wall Street reform bill and presiding over a steadily if slowly improving economy, underpinned by healthier real estate and financial markets. The race tightened after, in the first of three debates between Obama and Romney, Obama had one of the worst presidential debate performances in memory. But then President Bill Clinton, endorsing Obama at the Democratic National Convention in Charlotte, gave one of the great political speeches in American history. That, along with Obama's improved performances in the second and third debates, helped secure the election. On Nov. 6, Romney won easily among older, whiter and wealthier males. But victory went to Obama, who carried the northeast, the west coast and most of the Midwest. He even retained two states in the old Confederacy: Virginia and Florida, although this time (unlike in 2008) not North Carolina.

The political drama didn't stop with the election. Next was a "fiscal cliff" that a deadlocked Congress itself had created with the Budget Control Act of 2011, which set a path to steep but haphazard federal spending cuts if lawmakers couldn't work out a better deal. The idea was that the steep and haphazard cuts would be so distasteful to both sides that the sides would surely compromise. At the same time, the Bush tax cuts of 2001 and 2003 were set to expire. Abroad, meanwhile, France, Mexico, Russia and Venezuela were among other countries that held presidential elections—the former two more or less free and fair elections, the latter two more or less not. China and Japan both transitioned to new leaders too, at a time when tensions between them were escalating. The hopeful Arab Spring of 2011 turned chaotic in Egypt and even worse in Syria. Emerging market economies slowed, oil prices stayed high and the death of Whitney Houston elicited more worldwide Google searches than any other single topic. The next most searched item: a dance-filled Korean pop video called "Gangnam Style."

In the airline business that fall, US Airways kept chasing American, and United announced a new pilot contract that more or less mimicked Delta's. Delta itself fortified its network to Paris, the home of its partner Air France, with new U.S. routes and additional service on existing routes. It moved its Latin American head office from Atlanta to São Paulo. Virgin America, one of the few airlines still growing at the start of 2012, was now shrinking. But that almost didn't matter, for America's top four airlines now controlled about 80 percent of the domestic market, compared to 60 percent just a few years earlier. This alone made the U.S. airline industry more shock resistant than it had been historically.

Or was it? It didn't take long to put that question to the test. After a year of mostly mild weather, the largest Atlantic hurricane on record, Hurricane Sandy, made landfall on Oct. 24 in Jamaica. It then hit Cuba and the Bahamas before making its way north over the ocean. On Oct. 29, it came ashore again, hitting the most populous metro area of the entire country. Meteorologically speaking, it wasn't even a hurricane anymore. But no matter. New York City and New Jersey's coast suffered the brunt of $65 billion in damage, making "Superstorm Sandy," as she came to be known, the second costliest storm ever—only Hurricane Katrina in 2005 had been worse by that measure.

Sandy essentially closed the world's busiest airspace for two full days, forcing airlines to cancel 20,254 flights between Oct. 27 and Nov. 1, according to FlightStats. Delta canceled 1,293 flights, causing a massive $100 million hit to its bottom line. That included lost revenue, mitigated by money saved on fuel and crews. It also included disruptions to the startup of the Trainer, Pa., oil refinery, which produced a $63 million loss in the fourth quarter. But despite it all, Delta overall earned a $238 million fourth quarter net profit, excluding special accounting items. The most incredible accomplishment, perhaps, wasn't that Delta had earned a billion dollars in the peak summer third quarter. It's that rather than giving some of it back in the off-peak fourth quarter, it actually added to the total, ending 2012 with an outstanding $1.6 billion net profit, more than double what any other U.S. airline earned that year.

It was another great year indeed. But for all Delta had done, there was still more to do. And as 2012 came to a close, all eyes on were on two markets: London and Asia.

2013

"Very, very smart"

Already by 1984, Richard Branson, not yet 34, enjoyed wealth and fame. At age 16, the brash but always smiling self-starter from Britain disregarded his dyslexia and poor academic performance—he had dropped out of high school—and started a student magazine. At 20 he started a mail-order music business. Then a record store. And then a music label, which scored big with acts like the iconoclastic Sex Pistols and unconventional Culture Club. Branson himself was iconoclastic and unconventional, wearing a thick mane of golden hair and never a business suit. Even the name of his business empire was iconoclastic: The Virgin Group.

Obsessed with challenging the establishment, Branson next turned to an industry where, as he would later joke many times, it was easy to become a millionaire—if one started as a billionaire. Against the advice of almost everyone, Richard Branson, in 1984, launched an airline. And in doing so, he instigated the ultimate challenge to the British business establishment, targeting the government-backed, flag-carrying, empire-spanning British Airways.

Branson's timing was impeccable. The U.K. was in the thick of the Thatcher years, liberalizing its airline sector and breaking BA's protective government umbrella. So Branson, already a famed entrepreneur and music maven, bought into and soon took control of a startup airline called British Atlantic, which hoped to mimic the early success (but not the no-frills product) of People Express in the London Gatwick-U.S. market. With skillful lobbying and a little bit of luck, Branson's airline—which he had renamed Virgin Atlantic—won those coveted Gatwick-U.S. rights, beating out the more established British Caledonian. In June 1984, Virgin Atlantic operated its first flight, with a leased 747, from Gatwick to Newark near New York City.

Virgin Atlantic understood the mistakes of an earlier British entrepreneur, Freddie Laker, whom BA's aggressive pricing had pushed out of the marketplace.

Laker, in fact, had advised Branson what to expect. Sure enough, Virgin's early goings were rough, mired in fare wars against BA, People Express, TWA and Pan Am. Consumers, who were well aware of how many startup airlines had failed in the past, were at times reluctant to fly a new carrier that had just a single airplane. The press was keen to point this out. And Virgin experienced inevitable stumbles, including an engine failure on the eve of its inaugural flight and an episode in which it overbooked a flight by 200 passengers, leading to such chaos at Gatwick that police had to quell the mayhem. But soon came another stroke of good fortune: People Express began to bleed when its rival American attacked it with a new weapon called yield management, using advanced computing technology and complex algorithms to profit by segmenting passengers and matching People Express fares for budget travelers, so that they had no reason to fly the no-frills airline, while still "protecting" its high fares for business travelers, whom it had learned to identify by traits such as not wanting to remain at a destination over a Saturday night. ("Business travelers," Continental's head of revenue management explained to laughs at an IATA conference two decades later, "like to sleep in their own beds. Leisure travelers like to sleep in someone else's bed.") Years later, the idea of charging different fares to different kinds of passengers would become a basic profitability tool, but in the mid-1980s it was highly disruptive. People Express was gone by 1987; Continental purchased what was left of it, including what would become Continental's Newark hub.

A few years later, Pan Am was gone too, and TWA was a shadow of its former self, presenting Branson's greatest opportunity yet: an invitation to join Club Heathrow. When the U.S. demanded in 1991 that the U.K. amend the notorious Bermuda II air service treaty ("Bermuda Screw," some on the American side called it) to replace Pan Am and TWA with United and American, the U.K. could have asked for more rights for British Airways in return. But it instead asked to allow Virgin to join the other three, after Branson had brilliantly positioned the situation as an opportunity for London to keep British Airways from having too much market power. BA did receive some concessions, but the biggest British winner was Virgin Atlantic. It even convinced its government to give it some of BA's slots at Tokyo's Narita airport.

Even before getting into Heathrow, Virgin Atlantic was making money—in just its third full year of flying, in fact. As a new airline, its employees were all junior and earned salaries commensurate with that fact. It was much nimbler than BA, and it leveraged the dazzling marketing and self-promotion skills of its youthful and telegenic founder. Over the years, Branson would promote new routes by dressing in drag, strutting through airplanes with fashion models, appearing with celebrities and, on one occasion, bungee-jumping off a skyscraper. A daredevil adventurer, he attempted stunts like flying around the world in a hot air balloon—one adorned, of course, with a giant Virgin logo. He appeared in Apple ads and in James Bond films. A prized possession of his was a large model Concorde adorned with Virgin's livery, never mind that only British Airways and one other airline, Air France, actually flew the supersonic plane. On Virgin Atlantic, passengers could find inflight wine tastings or comedy shows, Phil Collins music pumping through the cabin during boarding, rock music videos on the inflight entertainment menu and fashionably dressed flight attendants. It all seemed to strike a chord with the affluent baby boomer generation that was then coming of travel age.

And Virgin Atlantic itself was coming of age. By the time of its Heathrow debut in July 1991, Branson had built his fleet to eight 747s flying to Newark, Miami and Boston from Gatwick and to New York JFK, Los Angeles and Tokyo Narita from Heathrow. BA, of course, was outraged at what its government had done, turning its rage on Branson with such ferocity that Branson, in response, turned to the courts, suing BA for libel. There, he was judged to have been unfairly treated; BA had to compensate him and his airline for damage BA was found to have caused. And in the court of public opinion, Branson used BA's aggressiveness to highlight Virgin's underdog status and heroic resistance to a campaign of "dirty tricks." Branson gave the BA money he won in court to Virgin Atlantic's staff.

Heathrow access enabled Virgin to move far beyond the low-fare model that had failed Branson's airline mentor Freddie Laker. Heathrow was a protected market, especially to the U.S., where BA, United and American were the only authorized competitors. While retaining a low-cost edge thanks to its junior workforce, its nimbleness, its lack of pension liabilities and its heavy use of outsourcing, Virgin went upscale, matching many of BA's premium products in its own self-styled "Upper Class," marketed as a first class product at business class prices complete with inflight massages, lavish lounges and limousine pickups.

The early 1990s, of course, weren't a good time for airlines, given the first Gulf War and the related oil price spike and recession. In the 12 months to November 1992, Virgin Atlantic lost roughly the same amount of money it had earned in the two full years prior, leaving it with a liquidity crunch. Only by reluctantly selling Virgin Records, which was by then representing stars like Paula Abdul and Janet Jackson, did Branson successfully recapitalize Virgin Atlantic and keep it flying for the long run.

Branson, in 1996, would score another major lobbying victory by playing the lead role in defeating the proposed joint venture between British Airways and American. He would repeat the feat on their second attempt in 2002. And all the while, Virgin continued to win new rights to new destinations from Heathrow every time the U.K. signed a new air service bilateral. Soon it was flying to San Francisco, Johannesburg, Delhi, Hong Kong and Sydney, to name just a few of its destinations. In 1994, it even signed its first transatlantic partnership, agreeing to codeshare with a carrier that had been locked out of Heathrow. That carrier? Delta. But the relationship didn't last long. Three years later, Virgin dropped Delta for Continental, another airline without Heathrow access. Both codeshare deals were, according to people familiar with the terms, heavily skewed in Virgin's favor, because Delta and Continental were willing to pay dearly to be able to market Heathrow as a destination—to show up as an option when corporate travel agents searched only for flights to "LHR"—even if they couldn't actually operate the service. In 2002, Virgin revived a more limited frequent flier partnership with Delta.

Virgin Atlantic produced a steady stream of strong profits from 1995 through 1999, a run that was underpinned by the global economic recovery, which in turn was underpinned by a steep fall in oil prices. But not all was well in the wider Virgin Group empire, whose railway, cola and vodka businesses were flopping. (No one realized yet that Virgin's music megastore business would soon begin hemorrhaging cash too as people dumped compact discs in favor of music file-sharing services— including illegal but popular Napster, which launched in 1999—and then Steve Jobs' latest creation, the wildly successful iPod, which debuted in 2001.) The group also ran an unsuccessful Belgian shorthaul airline called Virgin Express and would in later years back a disastrous airline venture in Nigeria and what was for years a chronically unprofitable carrier in the U.S. This messy state of affairs was actually rather typical for Branson's empire, whose strategy *The Economist* once described as "launch a company, build a brand, never mind the profits, and flog it at the right moment for a huge gain."

By "flogging," *The Economist* meant selling. And that's exactly what Branson did with Virgin Atlantic—49 percent of it, anyway—in late 1999. The carrier, at the height of its value after the recent string of profits and the escalating importance of London Heathrow as a must-have international gateway for global airlines, wasn't immune to downside risks, risks Branson and his management team understood well. Earnings were already weakening in 1999 as the Asian financial crisis compelled many carriers to reposition planes from Asia, instead sending them across the Atlantic, where the U.S. economy was booming. This, in turn, created intense competitive pressures for Virgin. Nobody knew, moreover, at what point the U.S. and the U.K. might reach a new air service bilateral that could open Heathrow to new competition; any liberalization there would hurt Virgin, which would fight against opening Heathrow to other airlines just as vigorously as it had fought *for* opening it for itself. And if the two countries did reach such an agreement, a BA-American JV could soon follow; if competing against BA and American separately was difficult enough, what would Virgin do if the two could join forces? The proper level of liberalization seemed to be that which best suited Virgin. Branson loudly called on governments to open their skies, but he did so somewhat disingenuously. He said, for example, that open skies with the U.S. must mean the right for Virgin to fly domestically within the U.S., a demand he knew was a nonstarter. By asking for the stars, which he knew he would never get, Branson was more likely to end up with the status quo, with which he was perfectly happy. The compromises that were more likely to emerge were what scared him most.

The deal to sell 49 percent of Virgin Atlantic netted Branson just short of $1 billion, an astronomical sum in retrospect, implying the entire airline was worth $2 billion, far more than it would ever be worth again. Branson, to quote *The Economist* again, was "selling his past in order to finance his future"—the future, at that time, was a rail venture. The buyer was Singapore Airlines, which was flush with cash thanks to years of profiting in a bustling home economy with good governance, low-cost labor and weak competitors. Unsure of how long the Asian financial crisis would last, Singapore Airlines wanted more transatlantic exposure and appreciated the importance of Virgin's strong brand—over-appreciated it, perhaps, in the eyes of those who question the relevance of brand equity in a business where cost structures, route networks, schedules and reliability often matter most. In any case, Singapore Airlines snatched its prize, only to soon end up wrangling with Branson over his investment in a new Australian airline, one that would compete against Ansett Australia and Air New Zealand; Singapore Airlines owned parts of both. Plans for a tightly integrated alliance withered, and Singapore and Virgin would, for the rest of their relationship, cooperate only loosely. In the meantime, Asian economies quickly rebounded and became the hot growth area of the 2000s, all while air travel in the western world stagnated amid insufferably high fuel prices. Branson's timing had again been impeccable.

Naturally, the 9/11 attacks hurt Virgin Atlantic, which was forced to slash capacity by 20 percent, including a suspension of service to Chicago and Toronto. It also pulled out of the London-Athens market, its only intra-European route. But the disruption didn't stop Virgin from following through on an earlier commitment to order six of the new super-jumbo Airbus 380s that the European manufacturer was peddling. Always the sensationalist and salesman, Branson spoke of outfitting the planes with inflight casinos and exercise rooms. As late as mid-2004, meanwhile, Virgin ordered another round of Airbus 340s, quad-engine planes other airlines had already realized were becoming obsolete in an increasingly twin-engine world of high fuel prices.

The 2000s also saw Virgin undertake a big expansion to the Caribbean, mostly from London Gatwick but also from Manchester. It was now flying to Barbados, Havana, Nassau, Antigua, Montego Bay and St. Lucia, for example. It also supplemented its business travel-oriented Heathrow flights with leisure-oriented Gatwick flights to Orlando and Las Vegas. And for most of the 2000s, Virgin continued to earn respectable profits.

Then came the global economic meltdown of 2008 and 2009, which happened to coincide with a confluence of plagues raining down on Virgin Atlantic. The U.S. and Europe had finally signed an open skies deal, and the Heathrow citadel was now open to Delta, Continental, US Airways and any other airline that could manage to get its hand on coveted takeoff and landing slots—even Air France briefly operated flights between Heathrow and Los Angeles. The open skies deal, in turn, calmed regulator unease about BA and American merging their transatlantic operations, because now they wouldn't dominate the marketplace to the same degree that they would have done without open skies. So on their third try, BA and American got their joint venture, subject to a few concessions that neither hurt them nor helped Virgin much. Making matters worse, the U.K. began imposing increase after increase in the air passenger duty, or APD, which greatly increased the cost of travel to and from U.K. airports—an increase airlines couldn't fully pass along to consumers. The APD was calculated based on distance, and as an all-longhaul airline—the longest-haul airline in the world, in terms of the average distance of its routes—Virgin was hurt most. But most maddening of all, "distance" was actually crudely calculated based not on the distance from London to the actual destination itself, but on the distance from London to the capital city of the country of a destination. So flights to Antigua, not even 4,100 miles from London, were taxed more heavily than flights to Los Angeles, nearly 5,500 miles away, because the capital of Los Angeles' country was Washington, D.C., just 3,700 miles from London. And between British Airways and Virgin Atlantic, guess which airline had more service to places like Los Angeles and which had more to places like Antigua? It was as if everything was conspiring against the Caribbean specialist, Virgin.

On top of all this, Virgin Atlantic's 49 percent stake in Virgin Nigeria, which launched in 2005, had been a nightmare from the beginning, generating heavy red ink until, in 2009, Virgin finally stripped the Nigerian operation of the Virgin brand. And no wonder: WikiLeaks had revealed not only huge losses at Virgin Nigeria but also episodes like one when government gangsters carrying baseball bats ransacked its business class lounge in Lagos. Just as punishingly, the Nigerian government, rather than let Virgin's professionals decide which routes to fly, forced the airline to fly to London from the outset, a route requiring expensive widebody planes without the time to cultivate a shorthaul feeder network. This caused an immediate cash drain. Things only turned worse when Nigeria's President Olusegun Obasanjo, who supported the Virgin Nigeria project, left office and was replaced by a less friendly successor. Virgin America, meanwhile, which finally received U.S. clearance to launch in 2007 after Branson reduced his ownership stake and former Delta president Fred Reid stepped aside as CEO (because regulators considered him too close to Branson, which could effectively give the foreigner illegal "control" of the airline), was operationally smoother but financially not much better. It chose to allocate a large portion of its capacity to the cutthroat transcontinental market—between giant cities like New York and Los Angeles—a notorious graveyard for young upstarts.

The challenges didn't end there. With fuel prices rising all decade and then spiking again after the recession, Virgin's fleet of 747s and 340s—every one of its airplanes had four engines, even though virtually all its routes could have been flown by more efficient twin-engine planes—were a giant liability. The airline recognized this in 2007, when it ordered 16 Boeing 787 Dreamliners, which Virgin said would burn 27 percent less fuel per passenger than the oldest and smallest of its 340s. But endless production delays meant Virgin wouldn't see the aircraft until 2014. As a stopgap measure, in 2009 it hastily ordered twin-engine Airbus 330 jets, but even these wouldn't arrive before 2011. Regretful it ever ordered the ultra-jumbo 380s a decade earlier, it now deferred deliveries of those many years into the future.

The right planes weren't the only thing Virgin lacked. It also lacked the right partners. As globalization spread and alliances grew in importance, Virgin was an airline without an invitation. Sure, everyone coveted its privileged Heathrow position, but it offered nothing of what alliances value most: unique destinations difficult to reach by other means. If you were Aerolineas Argentinas, say, and offered a menu of obscure domestic destinations no other airline served, then you would—no matter how bad your product, no matter how unreliable your operations—offer value to an alliance, because any airline flying to Buenos Aires could now offer its customers an array of other nearby destinations that it would never actually serve with its own "metal," as airlines say. But if you were Virgin—no matter how good your product, no matter how reliable your operations—you had nothing to offer other airlines in terms of unique destinations, because they already served all the big global destinations you served either on their own or via other partners.

Never mind marquee names like Singapore Airlines. Virgin's most important partner, as it happened, was a smaller U.K.-based airline called British Midland International, or BMI, which Virgin endlessly courted as a merger partner throughout the years, recognizing the good fit on paper between Virgin's longhaul routes and BMI's shorthaul routes. Together, these two carriers held more Heathrow slots than any other airline save BA. So together, their shorthaul and longhaul networks could rival BA. BMI, however, would fall into the hands not of Virgin but of Lufthansa, which was seduced by its Heathrow access. BMI was, however, never able to serve the U.S. from Heathrow (which is what Lufthansa really wanted) until open skies, and by that time the recession made doing so a fool's endeavor. In any case, BMI was bleeding financially, battered by the weak U.K. economy, the impossibly high taxation, high fuel prices and heavy exposure to the Middle East, where demand vaporized amid the political uprisings of early 2011—it was scheduled to launch flights to Tripoli, of all places, the day the revolution started in Libya.

BMI was still a critical ally for Virgin, however—*the* critical ally, in fact, because the two had fed passengers to each other. An estimate by OAG, a provider of airline schedules and other data, suggested a full quarter of Virgin's entire passenger traffic came from BMI, connecting onto or from various shorthaul routes. Lufthansa didn't drop Virgin as a BMI partner and was unlikely to do so. The risk: Because Virgin didn't control BMI, who knew when Lufthansa might sell it to someone else who would indeed drop Virgin?

And that's exactly what happened. In late 2011, Lufthansa sold BMI to none other than Virgin's hated archrival BA, which—never mind its soothing stated goals—rather clearly, to anyone paying attention, wanted to further dominate Heathrow and to further marginalize Virgin. Virgin had tried to raise enough money to buy BMI but simply couldn't match BA's offer. Branson was apoplectic, calling antitrust approval of the deal a "kick in the teeth."

And the bad news continued. United, which had inherited Continental's codeshare relationship with Virgin, ended that relationship—no need to continue overpaying Virgin to carry passengers now that Continental had its own Heathrow access, thanks to open skies, and would have had it anyway after merging with United. And Singapore Airlines badly wanted to dump the overpriced equity stake it never should have taken.

To appease regulators scrutinizing its purchase of BMI, BA had to surrender some Heathrow slots, enabling Virgin to start a new shorthaul service called Virgin Red, which would actually be operated by the Irish airline Aer Lingus. It would cover a few key routes like Manchester and Glasgow where the loss of BMI's traffic feed would hurt most. BA's CEO Willie Walsh began mocking Branson in public, saying at one point, "We're all looking forward to him losing more money when he starts operating those exciting services to Aberdeen." Virgin wanted to fly to Moscow too but had even lost its touch for the thing it did best: effective lobbying. New Moscow rights, available to only one new airline in the market, went to the LCC easyJet instead.

But Virgin didn't need to wait until the BA-BMI deal in 2011 and all the subsequent bad news before realizing the gravity of its challenges. In the 12 months to March 2010, the airline suffered pretax losses exceeding $200 million, by far its worst annual performance ever. Something had to give. So in the fall of 2010, Branson hired Deutsche Bank to review the carrier's strategic options and perhaps find it a new investor. Lufthansa, which now fully controlled BMI, was one rumored suitor. Another was Etihad, the hyper-growth airline owned by oil-rich Abu Dhabi.

Then Delta called. Earlier that year, its immaculately conceived masterstroke for the Japanese market—a JV with Japan Airlines—had collapsed. At that point, its plan to gain the upper hand in New York—a slot swap with US Airways—was also going nowhere. But just about everything else was going right, and Delta's financial wherewithal to think big was increasing. In New York, it didn't just want to be stronger at LaGuardia. An even more burning desire was to be stronger to London Heathrow, where by the summer of 2010, more than two years after U.S.-E.U. open skies, it had a mere two daily flights from JFK. American had five, and British Airways another six, meaning 11 for the two JV partners combined. BA also had another three frequencies from Newark. To be a player in New York City, to be relevant to its legions of corporate travelers, an airline needed to offer ample access to London, in the same way it needed to be able to offer lots of shorthaul destinations from LaGuardia. The Air France/KLM JV, for all its might in countless other European markets, did nothing to help Delta in New York-London, which was by far the most important transatlantic market of all. London, in fact—counting all its airports—is by far the world's busiest air travel market, dwarfing even New York, and Delta had only a token presence in London.

Virgin Atlantic had three JFK-Heathrow flights plus another two Newark-Heathrow flights. More generally, it had lots of Heathrow slots, a deteriorating financial position, a 49 percent shareholder (Singapore Airlines) that was eager to sell and a need for alliance partners in a world increasingly dominated by alliances. Delta, with its strong cash position and its interest in Heathrow, was interested.

So the two airlines talked that fall and then again on a separate occasion in 2011, with Air France/KLM also involved in the discussions. But it wasn't until the summer of 2012 that Glen Hauenstein and Virgin's chief commercial officer got close to a deal on cooperation that worked for both sides. Delta didn't just want to own part of Virgin. It wanted to cooperate with it, much as BA and American were now cooperating so profitably. This was a two-track negotiation, with Delta talking to Singapore Airlines, from which it would buy 49 percent of Virgin, as well as to the Virgin Group, which owned the other 51 percent and was now effectively led by Branson's No. 2 man David Baxby.

London newspapers began reporting Delta-Virgin talks in November 2010, and at Delta's investor day event one month later, Glen Hauenstein, asked about the possibility, didn't quite deny it. "At some point in time," he said, characterizing Delta's thinking, "do you need a partner? Partners are always good on the other side."

A full year later, at the airline's December 2011 investor day, Delta executives said even less—or more precisely, nothing. But by mid-2012, a deal was emerging. It was not a moment too soon for Virgin, which—after climbing its way back to small profits in the boom year 2010—had relapsed into heavy losses in the fiscal year that covered most of 2011, a year in which its pilots threatened a major strike after two years of frozen pay. The situation hadn't improved much in 2012, with business travelers staying away from London during the Olympics and with British unemployment reaching its highest rate in 17 years. The mounting distress led the Virgin Group to drop its demand for hefty annual fees to license the Virgin brand and to soften its opposition to the deeply integrated JV Delta was demanding. Delta's patience was paying off. It wanted Virgin, but it wanted it only if it could find it the same place it found its airplanes and its recently purchased regional airline Pinnacle: in the bargain bin.

On Dec. 11, 2012, the two airlines announced a far-reaching partnership. Delta would buy Singapore Airlines' 49 percent stake in Virgin Atlantic for just $360 million, a fraction of the nearly $1 billion Singapore had paid 13 years earlier. The two transatlantic partners would create a revenue- and cost-sharing JV modeled on the one Delta had in place with Air France/KLM. That JV would stay as is—no sense messing with success—covering all transatlantic markets outside the U.K., while the new Delta-Virgin JV would cover all U.K. routes to the U.S., Canada and Mexico (but not Virgin's many Caribbean routes). Delta also obtained three seats on Virgin Atlantic's board of directors and an estimated $120 million in annual net synergies, implying a quick payback for its investment. In 2008, incidentally, Continental had paid more than $200 million for a mere four Heathrow slot pairs. Delta was now buying half of an entire airline that had more than 40 slot pairs—for just $360 million.

Investors were impressed. On the day the deal was announced, Delta's market value soared by $700 million. Overnight, Delta had addressed a key shortcoming by vastly improving its appeal to the New York City business traveler.

"There were some moments when we thought it might not happen," Julie Southern, Virgin's chief commercial officer, told reporters at a New York event where the two airlines announced the deal. She delineated the promised benefits for air travelers. Then she and the "Dull Richard"—that's what Richard Anderson called himself to distinguish himself from the "Dashing Richard," Richard Branson, who wasn't present—fielded media questions.

Anderson addressed the issue of antitrust approval, expressing lawyerly confidence that if British Airways and American received immunity, so would Delta and Virgin Atlantic. He also noted Air France/KLM's "strong support for the transaction" even though it wasn't a part of it; its JV with Delta, covering everything in Europe except the U.K., would remain the larger of Delta's two European JVs. Anderson laughed when asked whether BA's Willie Walsh might be correct in suggesting the Virgin Atlantic brand would be retired within five years.

London Heathrow was the largest international destination for U.S. business travelers, and it wasn't close—Paris was large, but London was three times larger. Nearly three million people flew annually between New York and London—or close to four million counting Newark—making it America's top transatlantic route. London-Los Angeles ranked second with 1.4 million passengers, followed by New York-Paris.

So Virgin Atlantic—an airline with outsized exposure to exorbitant U.K. taxes, a suboptimal fleet of four engined-747s and 340s, a lack of shorthaul feeder traffic, no alliance affiliation and an archrival, British Airways, that had taken British Midland and teamed up with American—now had a powerful partner, one that could help it significantly in the U.S., its most important market. Virgin was still losing money, to be sure. But now it felt confident enough to forecast a return to profitability by the spring of 2015.

There was, however, some unfinished business. Should Virgin join SkyTeam? Doing so might have seemed like a no-brainer, given how close Virgin now was with Delta. But Virgin faced a Shakespearian dilemma.

When Virgin's archrival British Airways bought British Midland in 2012, Virgin didn't actually lose *all* its shorthaul feeder traffic, even though it had lost its partner. Quietly, it would actually continue to get some feed from none other than its archenemy BA. That's because in addition to BA (as a regulatory condition of its deal with American) having to give up Heathrow slots that led to everything from Little Red to Delta's London-Boston and London-Miami flights, BA also—as a lesser-noticed condition—had to give Virgin preferential prorated shorthaul fares for passengers who booked itineraries involving connections between shorthaul BA and longhaul Virgin flights. Although passengers in the modern age of alliances more often connect between partner airlines, some still book old-fashioned "interline" itineraries, as they're called, involving connections between two airlines that don't cooperate much commercially. Sure enough, a small but meaningful number of passengers did connect between BA and Virgin, just because—even though the two airlines didn't coordinate this—flights sometimes happened to connect well with one another. Airlines are generally free to negotiate what are called special prorate agreements, or SPAs, on terms that benefit both airlines. An airline wouldn't typically agree to an SPA that would help its bitter enemy, and BA, whose purpose of buying BMI was largely to tighten the noose around Virgin's neck, was in no mood to give Virgin any kind of a discount on its shorthaul seats. But as a condition of approving the BA-American JV that BA wanted so badly, regulators forced BA to do just that: sell some shorthaul seats to Virgin at below-market fares. Per the terms of the deal, this favorable arrangement would last until... well, until Virgin joined any alliance (in much the same way Northwest had held its powerful "golden share" in Continental only until Northwest was involved in a merger). Joining SkyTeam, in other words, would carry special costs beyond the usual IT upgrades and so forth that come with joining an alliance.

Even aside from that, Virgin—contradictory as the semantics of this might sound—was polygamous, depending on various bilateral relationships around the world according to what made sense in each region. Sure, SkyTeam's Delta would now be Virgin's most important partner of all. But with flights to places like Japan, South Africa and Singapore, Virgin actually had more partnerships with airlines like All Nippon, South African Airways and Singapore Airlines, which was giving up its ownership stake but not its codeshare relationship. These were all Star Alliance members, and joining SkyTeam could jeopardize these partnerships. Not only was joining SkyTeam not a foregone conclusion. It might not even be advisable at all.

With Delta's three seats on Virgin's board, meanwhile—these would be held by Ed Bastian, Glen Hauenstein and Delta's point man for the new JV, Paris-based Perry Cantarutti—the Atlanta-based giant could exercise heavy influence in London, weighing in on Virgin's most critical decisions. One of these decisions was whether to actually take delivery of the Airbus 380s it had first ordered 13 years earlier, before 9/11. Delta had made no secret of its distaste for Air France's 380s, working, it said, to keep the "ill effects of that aircraft out of the joint venture." It would now be well positioned to keep Virgin from welcoming the planes into its fleet at all.

Another big decision: how to replace the longtime Virgin CEO Steve Ridgway, who had announced he would retire in early 2013. One candidate was Julie Southern, the chief operating officer and one of aviation's highest ranking female executives.

But Delta wanted an outsider. And not just any outsider. Craig Kreeger of American Airlines wasn't anyone's first guess, if simply because of his lack of prior CEO experience and lack of name recognition. He also wasn't British, but American. But Delta knew Kreeger was the man who, perhaps more than anyone else, had built and run the American-British Airways JV for American. Who better to run an airline whose most important strategic imperative was building a JV to compete against BA and American? Kreeger, in fact, originally recruited by a search firm hired by Virgin, was interviewed by not just Virgin but even by Singapore Airlines, whose stake hadn't yet transferred to Delta when the process started, and then—later in the process—by Delta. American's CEO Tom Horton, hearing the news, probably felt as the Atlanta Braves had felt when one of the greatest pitchers in team history, Tom

Glavine, signed a contract to play for the Braves' division rival New York Mets. But he was proud his underling had been tapped for such a big role and "treated me very nicely and appropriately throughout that process," Kreeger said. "He's a class act."

In June 2013, Delta and Virgin Atlantic received American and European anti-trust immunity to jointly operate their transatlantic routes. A month later, they were codesharing. And by the end of the year, they announced a jointly planned flight schedule for the following spring. Delta also said it would move some of its London flights—including key New York and Boston flights—to Virgin's terminal at Heathrow, amplifying an advantage over BA and American, which were in separate terminals in both New York and London. That was inconvenient for connections as well as when a passenger, say, missed one New York-London flight and had to take the next one an hour later, and that next one was in a different terminal. Virgin, even before doing its deal with Delta, happened to be located in New York JFK's Terminal 4, the one Delta was now renovating.

With one swing of the ax, Delta had neutralized its last glaring New York weakness. It had the London Heathrow access it needed. But there was still the matter of Asia, its problems there not yet addressed three years after the failed attempt to court Japan Airlines.

***

One hundred sixty years earlier, as Americans moved westward to settle their vast open continent, one group trekked all the way to the country's northwest corner, establishing themselves at a settlement they called—confusingly—New York. To the relief of future geographers, they soon changed the name to honor a local Indian leader: Seattle. Like so many western cities, Seattle and nearby Tacoma boomed when the transcontinental railroad arrived, facilitating development of abundant lumber and coal resources. So more people came. Then came the Alaska gold rush, and Seattle was the jumping-off point for prospectors. According to the city's official history, Scandinavians came to work in fishing and lumbering, African Americans to work as railroad porters and waiters and Japanese to operate farms and hotels, all alongside sizeable communities of Italians, Chinese, Jews and Filipinos. In 1916, a company called Boeing began life in Seattle, and like the city's shipbuilders, it grew enormously during the World Wars, producing much of America's aerial and naval armadas. In the postwar era, the Seattle metro area gave birth to some of America's most powerful and recognizable firms. It's where Bill Gates made his Microsoft fortune, where Jeff Bezos launched the online retail behemoth Amazon and where the bricks-and-mortar retailer (as these would later come to be called) Nordstrom got its start. Starbucks, Costco and the online travel agency Expedia (originally launched by Microsoft) are all Seattle-area companies too.

So is a company called Alaska Airlines. Its name reflects the airline's beginnings in the 1930s. But after deregulation, the focus of its network in the 1980s became

Seattle, where it earned handsome profits flying to key business centers in the western U.S., all while retaining a lucrative operation to and within Alaska. The events of 9/11 certainly hurt, forcing steep cost cuts and controversial labor outsourcing in the ensuing years. Fortuitously for Alaska Airlines, the U.S. west coast avoided much of the LCC-induced fare deflation that had hit the east coast in the immediate post 9/11-era. AirTran, JetBlue, Independence Air and Delta's own Song unit all focused on the east. Southwest too was busy expanding in Chicago, Philadelphia and other cities away from the west coast, while Seattle proved less attractive for growth because costs at Seattle-Tacoma International Airport, or "Sea-Tac," were rather high. This relatively stable environment helped keep Alaska Airlines' yields relatively stable too, even during the most difficult periods.

Southwest might have disliked it for the airport costs, and hub-and-spoke airlines might have shunned it for its geography, but Seattle was in many ways a good airline market, with strong corporate demand and leisure demand alike. The summer was especially lucrative, and after Alaska Airlines added flights to Hawaii, its winters became lucrative too. The airline enjoyed a loyal following in the Pacific Northwest, not just in the Seattle-Tacoma area but also in Spokane in eastern Washington, and in Portland, Ore., where Alaska operated a secondary hub. It operated a regional airline called Horizon, which served many of the area's smaller communities. And in the state of Alaska, Alaska Airlines was a lifeline for many communities, flying not just people but also cargo in and out. It was also chief transporter of people and cargo for the state's large oil industry, which created great riches during the 2000s. In every other state, residents pay taxes to fund their state governments. But Alaska? In 2008, the year oil prices reached $147 per barrel, the state's reserve fund ran such a large surplus that every resident received a check for more than $2,000—a state government paying its residents just to live there! Needless to say, some of that money was spent on tickets with Alaska Airlines, which ran special fare sales during payout time.

Alaska also enjoyed a major presence in California, served Mexican beach markets, extended its reach transcontinentally and earned a reputation for technological prowess, becoming the very first airline to take online bookings in 1995, one of the first to roll out airport check-in kiosks in 1996 and the first to offer online check-in in 1999. Alaska Airlines also became an early adopter of what it called a "Switzerland strategy," not limiting itself to any one alliance but partnering with any airline that was interested, including airlines that competed vigorously against each other. Alaska's customers could accrue and redeem frequent flier miles on airlines all around the world. Alaska essentially had to buy miles and airline tickets from those partners—their customers could theoretically earn and burn miles on Alaska too, but in practice, Alaska bought a lot more than it sold. So it wasn't a cheap strategy. But it was an effective one. Among its partners: American, Continental, Hawaiian Airlines, KLM, LAN, Qantas and indeed Delta. Recall that in 2009, once Delta began integrating with Northwest, the combined carrier upgraded its relationship with Alaska Airlines, providing more benefits to their mutual customers.

By 2012, Alaska Airlines was posting some of the highest profit margins of any airline in the world, a remarkable achievement for an airline with neither the lowest costs nor the largest network—most of the world's other profitability standouts had one or the other. At an investor event, the airline said it had a 22 percent unit cost (the cost of carrying one seat one mile) advantage versus legacy rivals and an 11 percent unit revenue advantage over LCCs. Its unit costs, in fact, had fallen 12 percent since 2002, even as JetBlue's increased 31 percent and Southwest's 28 percent. Low costs and high revenues meant big profits. Not even the advent of California's Virgin America derailed Alaska's momentum. Ditto for challenges posed by the ultra-low-cost carrier Allegiant, which invaded an airport in tiny Bellingham north of Seattle.

For Delta, the way to address its Asian weakness seemed clear enough: assemble a network of its own Asian flights from Seattle, and feed these flights with passengers connecting from its close partner Alaska Airlines' broad menu of shorthaul flights. The pressure to do something was mounting. In Japan, Shinzo Abe was embarking on bold economic reforms to jolt the languid economy. The centerpiece of these changes involved greatly expanding the money supply, to intentionally cause inflation—unchecked inflation can be disastrous, but Japan's problem was the opposite, with *deflation* discouraging consumers and businesses from spending today, because no one wants to spend money today if they expect everything to be cheaper tomorrow. One side effect of this policy to print more yen: a sharp depreciation in the yen's value abroad. Suddenly, Japanese travelers stopped getting on Delta flights to Hawaii and elsewhere. At the same time, because jet fuel is priced in U.S. dollars, which were strengthening against the yen, the price of jet fuel purchased in Japanese yen skyrocketed, applying additional pressure on Delta's Japan flights.

The weaker yen would have large repercussions throughout the industry. No airline serving Japan was safe. But at least United and American had Japanese JV partners with whom to share the burden. Delta did not. All the while, newly available takeoff and landing slots at Tokyo's more centrally located Haneda Airport further depreciated the value and traffic-generating power of Delta's Tokyo Narita hub. The two big Japanese carriers—Japan Airlines and All Nippon—were also using their new Boeing 787 Dreamliners to fly nonstop to midsized U.S. markets like San Jose, San Diego and Boston, carrying traffic that might have connected via U.S. hubs like Detroit. Airlines call this "overflying" a hub. It's usually good for the airline doing the overflying and bad for the airline with the hub.

Seattle wasn't a perfect gateway to Asia. The metro area's population was small relative to that of San Francisco, United's Asian hub, which was also the best place to put an Asian hub based on a combination of geography, population size, economic size, business links and cultural links. But San Francisco was taken. Los Angeles, the nation's second busiest city, was a hub for everyone and no one at the same time, a place no single carrier dominated; Delta had its own obligatory flights from there to

Tokyo. Seattle also competed somewhat against nearby Vancouver, a robust Asian hub for Air Canada.

But Seattle had its upside. Geographically, it was the closest big mainland American city to northeast Asia—it was so close, in fact, that only one airplane was required to operate one round-trip per day on many routes (because it could depart Seattle, arrive in Asia and return to Seattle with another load of passengers, all within 24 hours). Most flights between the U.S. and Asia required a second aircraft, a more expensive endeavor. Importantly, no other U.S. carrier used Seattle as much of an overseas gateway—United flew to Tokyo, but that was about it. And only a handful of Asian carriers flew to Seattle. It was ripe for Delta's taking if it wanted it.

And Delta now wanted it. There had been hints of that fact as far back as the summer of 2010, when it began flying from Seattle to Beijing and Osaka, complementing the Tokyo Narita route Northwest had served for many years—giant Tokyo was almost always the first Asian city a U.S. airline served from an American gateway even if it didn't serve any others. Beijing and Osaka turned out to be just a prelude to further expansion, which revved up with the 2013 launch of service to both Shanghai and Tokyo Haneda. Delta would also "upgauge" (that's the term airlines use to describe a switch to larger aircraft) its Narita service to jumbo 747s and help fill these new seats with additional flights between Seattle and New York JFK, a market Alaska didn't serve. Delta further signaled its Seattle ambitions with investments in a new Delta Sky Club, power ports throughout Delta's facilities, expanded ticket counters and lobby renovations.

A Delta press release presented it all as a joint effort. "The international expansion and customer enhancements in Seattle," the release read, "are driven by a strategic partnership between Delta and Alaska that benefits customers of both carriers and creates more competition and travel options for consumers in the Pacific Northwest region. Under an extensive codesharing agreement, Delta customers can access more than 50 markets beyond Seattle via Alaska's domestic hub, while Alaska customers in the Pacific Northwest have access to more than 60 domestic Delta destinations, including extensive options over Delta's Atlanta and Minneapolis-St. Paul hubs. The two carriers review connecting flight schedules and make timing adjustments to shorten passenger connection times. And customers of both carriers enjoy reciprocal access to Delta's Sky Club and Alaska's Board Room airport lounges, as well as reciprocal frequent flier benefits.... More than 200,000 international passengers connected between Alaska and Delta flights during the past year."

The two carriers were perfect for each other! Or were they?

Underneath the surface of Delta's reliance on Alaska Airlines shorthaul feed was an uncomfortable reality: that relying on partner feed was riskier than relying on one's own flights. Why? Because partners like Alaska Airlines revenue-manage their own flights with an entirely different set of incentives. At a hub like Minneapolis, where Delta controlled both the shorthaul and longhaul flights, its modern origin-and-destination revenue management system might—perfectly rationally—accept a passenger who wasn't paying much for a shorthaul flight if that passenger was connecting to a longhaul flight and ultimately contributing more revenue to Delta than another passenger who would have paid more for the shorthaul flight but who would not have connected to a longhaul flight. In Seattle, Alaska had no such incentive to displace higher-paying shorthaul customers to fill Delta's longhaul flights. Connecting passengers on shorthaul flights usually pay less for those portions of their journeys than other people on the same flights who are only flying shorthaul. At best, Delta's lower-yielding passengers might have been a useful way to "backfill" seats that would have otherwise flown empty—better to get something rather than nothing for a seat.

The problem for Delta was that Alaska just didn't have very many empty seats to fill. In 2012, in fact, Alaska had filled an incredible 87 percent of its seats. With such high load factors, it was hardly desperate for incremental traffic connecting to or from Delta international flights. Sure, it would take the bookings, if the revenue was high enough. But it would have to be roughly as high as what Alaska could get from just selling a ticket on its own—and usually, it wasn't nearly that high. Alaska wouldn't want to displace a high-fare passenger traveling nonstop from Boise, Idaho, to Seattle, for example, for a Boise passenger connecting onward to Beijing if Delta, to access the Boise-Seattle seat for its Boise-Seattle-Tokyo passenger, wasn't willing to pay nearly as much as what Alaska could get on its own from the Boise-Seattle "local" passenger, as airlines call such a passenger who isn't connecting. At the onset of 2013, Alaska's business was booming. Fares were rising, and demand for seats on its shorthaul flights was surging. If Delta wanted a seat to accommodate a passenger connecting to one of its Asia flights, it would have to pay dearly.

Too dearly, from Delta's perspective.

Delta understood all too well its dependence on its ally. About a third of Delta's international passengers in Seattle were fed from Alaska Airlines, according to Mike Medeiros, Delta's vice president for Seattle, in an interview with the *Puget Sound Business Journal*. That's a large chunk. Of course, Alaska's codeshare arrangements with Delta generated $235 million in revenue for Alaska during 2013, hardly a trifling amount. But increasingly, Alaska seemed to think this was revenue it could get with or without Delta.

So the two partners failed to reach a deal to give Delta broader access to Alaska's seat inventory. That special prorate agreement, or SPA, that had been imposed on British Airways, forcing it to sell discounted seats to Virgin Atlantic? Those are the kinds of terms Alaska felt Delta was demanding. But in this case, no one was forcing Alaska to accept them.

For Delta, this was maddening. Overlay Alaska's shorthaul routes with Delta's longhaul ones on a map, and you had the perfect joint network. Delta could have the Pacific coast longhaul hub and avoid the messy matter of building a shorthaul network to feed the flights, which was particularly important in a midsized market like Seattle, where longhaul flights would always depend even more on connecting passengers than in a giant market like New York. Yet even though the airlines had all the right planes and airport gates and routes and schedules to work together, the commercial realities of 2013—ironically, that things were *too good* for Alaska—prevented it all.

Glen Hauenstein and his network planning team were not about to let this derail the Seattle project. Instead, Delta would take a more unilateral approach, adding its own shorthaul feeder flights, even if that meant competing head-to-head against its partner. Such a strategy was expensive too: Delta would now be going all in, no longer getting the milk without buying the cow. But adding its own flights could, at least, be good for labor relations, because if Seattle growth meant new capacity rather than reallocated capacity, there would be more Delta pilot jobs compared to if Delta had relied on Alaska and its pilots. In January 2013, Delta fired its first shot: nonstop Seattle service to and from Los Angeles, one of Alaska's most important routes. The new flights launched in the spring. By July, Delta's domestic capacity from Seattle was up more than 20 percent compared to the same period a year earlier.

And that was just the beginning. During the summer, Delta, advancing its original project, further expanded international service with new flights to Tokyo's Haneda Airport (the more convenient Tokyo airport, not the one where Delta had its hub) in May and then Shanghai in June. In July, it announced London Heathrow flights, which would begin in 2014. And in August it announced Seoul and Hong Kong, also due to launch in 2014.

This time, Delta's press release mentioned its partner Alaska only in passing. And lest anyone think that was an accidental oversight, Medeiros, the Delta vice president, confirmed in the *Business Journal* interview that Delta and Alaska were now "fierce competitors." Delta turned up the heat further by announcing more flights to Los Angeles and Las Vegas and another new route: Seattle-San Francisco, yet another key Alaska Airlines market. Just as provocatively, Delta offered double SkyMiles to passengers booking these routes.

The aggression continued. In November, Delta added San Diego and Portland, and it added more flights to Anchorage. It started awarding not just double SkyMiles but double Medallion status-qualifying miles, enabling customers to reach all-important elite tiers—silver, gold, platinum and diamond—twice as fast. Then came Fairbanks, Juneau and Vancouver. Then Phoenix, Palm Springs, Tucson and Jackson Hole, Wyo. Then Spokane, Maui and Calgary. And, in its first push into Alaska Airlines' successful Mexican beach markets, Cabo and Puerto Vallarta. And, penetrating deeper into regional markets Alaska long had to itself, Bozeman, Mont. By mid-2014, the Battle of Seattle was a national story, profiled in national newspapers like *The Wall Street Journal*.

Alaska Airlines certainly wasn't taking the onslaught lightly. In an industry where size matters, because "small" can mean "vulnerable," Alaska was indeed far smaller than its part-friend, part-enemy—"frenemies," analysts were calling them. But this smallness belied Alaska's ample staying power, buttressed by a rock-solid balance sheet thanks to years of outsized profits. If Delta thought all its new Seattle shorthaul service (which was almost certainly losing money, no matter how brave a face Delta put on the matter) would cause Alaska to capitulate and give Delta what it really wanted—the milk without buying the cow—it would be sorely disappointed.

Not only did Alaska not fold. In the spring of 2013, it hit back with new service from Seattle to Delta's Salt Lake City hub, a route Alaska had previously politely avoided. It expanded its codeshare relationship with Delta's rival American, taking advantage of relaxed restrictions in American's new pilot contract. It announced new service from Portland to Atlanta, the epicenter of Delta's empire.

All the while, the two airlines continued to cooperate in important ways, such as the codeshare (when Delta could manage to get seats at fares that were acceptable to both airlines) and the frequent flier reciprocity. Andrew Harrison, Alaska's vice president of planning, told investors "we'll work together where there's benefit" but "where there is... head-to-head competition, then we'll vigorously defend our core markets."

"What we're trying to do here is take the emotion out of this process," Alaska CEO Brad Tilden said, adding: "I would think that as we move forward there will be places where it is going to be in our interest to work with Delta, and we're going to support them. They're growing internationally. By itself, that should be a good thing for both of us, and so we're going to work with them to grow the connections between the two airlines. And then there are places where they are growing in north/south markets that have been long-term core markets for Alaska Air Group, and in those markets we will compete, and we'll defend what we've built over the years. But we've got a longstanding relationship with these folks. We've had a lot of competition north/south on the west coast over the years. It will be a little complicated, but that's the world we're moving into, and I think it's going to be okay."

During the remainder of 2013 and into the first half of 2014, Alaska matched many of Delta's frequent flier bonus promotions; upgraded its mileage partnerships with Delta's international rivals British Airways and Cathay Pacific and another Delta frenemy, Korean Air; and escalated its assault on Salt Lake City, launching new routes between there and Portland, San Jose, San Diego, Boise, Los Angeles, San Francisco and Las Vegas. Salt Lake City-Portland, like Salt Lake City-Seattle, was a route Alaska—although it had long stayed out of Delta's way on these—might have justified based on its own merits: Portland was an Alaska hub, and Salt Lake City was an outstation. But the rest were unambiguous shots back at Delta.

To cultivate loyalty, Delta invited Seattle-area frequent fliers to a private concert by the Canadian crooner Michael Bublé. Alaska started flying to Delta's Detroit hub. Delta won moral support from Seattle native Gerald Grinstein, who had returned triumphantly to the city after retiring from Delta. Alaska emphasized its long history in Seattle and how it still served more destinations with more flights and more planes. Delta spent money on billboards, airport signage, community involvement and a new plane it christened "the Spirit of Seattle." Alaska, on its Facebook page, reminded customers that "we unveiled the original 'Spirit of Seattle' in 2008, a nod to the beautiful city we call home." Delta became the official airline partner of the Seattle Seahawks. Alaska hired the team's star quarterback Russell Wilson as a brand ambassador. (Both teams got more bang for their bucks when the Seahawks, on Feb. 2, 2014, won the Super Bowl.)

The two airlines began removing some codeshares from each other's flights. Delta terminated ground service deals with Alaska at 13 airports, in some cases forcing Alaska to find alternative lounge facilities for its passengers. "Alliances," Alaska Airlines said, expressing frustration, "can be complicated."

To be clear, Delta wasn't only trying to punish Alaska. The whole point of the quarrel was that Delta didn't see Alaska as an economically reliable partner to feed its longhaul Seattle flights. Having its own flights could help. All the while, Delta continued to reduce the centrality of Tokyo Narita to its Asian operations so that by 2013, about half the airline's Pacific capacity didn't touch Narita. Although obligatorily telling investors that "our Narita hub is really a great asset for Delta," Glen Hauenstein conceded "it is challenged by the environment that's around it—the opening of Haneda. So I don't think we can count on that being our only way to get to Asia over the next decade or two."

Not that Delta was going to wait that long. It had one other big idea to pursue.

Sure, Japan Airlines and All Nippon were taken. But why not a closer partnership with Delta's fellow SkyTeam member Korean Air? Korea was a substantially smaller market than Japan, and Seoul was a smaller market than Tokyo. But Delta was overflying Tokyo on half of its routes to Asia now anyway, and a close partner in Korea would be especially useful for developing traffic into and out of China, whose economy was still growing rapidly, albeit less rapidly than during the mid-2000s. Korean Air also flew between more U.S. cities and Asia than any other carrier from either continent—more than even Japan Airlines or All Nippon—partly reflecting the large numbers of Korean students and immigrants throughout the U.S., in addition to revenue support from a giant cargo operation: It's easier to make a flight profitable when its belly is filled with Samsung phones. With nearly 30,000 U.S. troops stationed in Korea, it was also a busy market for American travelers. A Delta-Korean Air JV would actually be larger than either Japanese-American JV—a transpacific revenue giant. And all the regulatory concerns that dogged other JV approval processes, resulting—if not in rejection—in, at least, harsh concessions as conditions of approval? *Delta and Korean Air already had antitrust immunity!* They didn't use it much—key players from both airlines spoke perhaps once a month. But they had it, meaning a Delta-Korean JV, unlike others that had drawn so much scrutiny, would likely require only the most cursory regulatory review and nod. Unlike Tokyo, moreover, Seoul didn't suffer from split airports destroying the network effects of a hub city: Seoul has just one major airport. Seoul is a lot like Delta's Atlanta hub in that important way, and being a lot like Atlanta is usually a good thing.

There was just one problem.

Korean Air wasn't interested.

The two airlines held intense discussions in late 2012, but Korean, vigorously guarding its independence, ultimately rebuffed Delta's attempts to form a joint venture. Because of its own extensive U.S. network, Korean arguably didn't need a JV as badly as the Japanese airlines needed theirs. So it felt it had the luxury of abstaining because of the downsides inherent with JVs: sharing control, for example, of its network, scheduling and pricing decisions, while perhaps diluting the value of its inflight product, on which Korean Air had spent heavily despite its dubious financial results and heavy indebtedness. Flying Delta had become rather nice, but Korean's inflight product still enjoyed the better reputation. Korean, whether miscalculating Delta would back off or just not worrying about the consequences, wouldn't budge.

Delta knew Korean Air depended on it for traffic feed, all the more so because Korean was receiving giant Airbus 380s and sending them to Los Angeles and Atlanta. So to try to force Korean's hand, Delta said its frequent fliers would no longer earn any Medallion-qualification miles when they flew Korean Air, a major and unusual downgrade of a relationship with an alliance partner and one that would certainly discourage Delta's best customers from booking flights on Korean, because now flying Korean was no longer like flying Delta from a status-qualification standpoint. And Korean's KE code abruptly disappeared on some Delta-operated shorthaul flights on which the two had long codeshared, so that Korean could no longer market these flights to its own customers. Officially, Korean Air declined to comment, and Delta said only that "each airline determines its level of participation" in the SkyMiles program.

Pretending nothing was amiss soon became impossible. By November 2013, John Jackson, Korean Air's vice president for the Americas—speaking at the Boyd Group International Aviation Forecast Summit in Baltimore—acknowledged the tension. "It is well known we have our disagreements," he said.

Not only were Delta and Korean Air both SkyTeam members. They were both *founding* members. And not only that. They were once so close, their histories so intertwined, that Malcolm Gladwell's bestselling book "Outliers" chronicled how a safety expert from Delta literally helped turn Korean (in 2000) into a safe airline after a string of fatal crashes. But like Delta and Alaska Airlines, Delta and Korean Air were turning cold toward each other, with Delta now conveying the message that Korean couldn't have it both ways by using Delta's own loyalty program as a weapon to lure business away from Delta while refusing to form a JV. Korean, on the other hand—which had felt the relationship between the two growing gradually colder since the mid-2000s—bet customers would forego the status miles and choose what it believed (and what surveys of business travelers generally confirmed) was a better inflight product on long flights to Asia.

As with the Alaska Airlines situation, here was an arrangement Delta felt made so much sense—a maddening amount of sense—except that it didn't make any sense at all, because Delta was like a bride who had planned every element of her dream wedding but had no one to marry. The situation would remain unresolved, Korean

Air still going it alone to the U.S. and Delta still unable to secure the Asian JV it so badly desired.

So Delta turned to China, another avenue of potential answers for Delta's Asia dilemma, which—again—centered on a likelihood that Delta would lose relevance in Tokyo as U.S. flights migrated from Narita to Haneda, thereby marginalizing Delta's Narita hub. On a 2013 trip to Japan, CEO Richard Anderson pleaded with officials to provide enough slots for Delta to move all its operations to Haneda—anything short of that wouldn't help, because if Delta had to split its operations, it would lose the network effects of flights at one airport connecting to each other. The way hub math works, half as many flights at a hub can mean not half as many possible origin-and-destination itineraries—that would be bad enough—but actually more like a quarter, in the same way 10 times 10 equals 100 but five times five equals only 25. Delta could stomach having its operations split between JFK and LaGuardia because of the enormous benefits that came from giving New York corporate travelers everything they wanted. It could stomach no such thing in Tokyo, where it was a much smaller player.

But on that same trip to the Far East, hedging his bets, Anderson stopped in Beijing to pursue another line of strategic maneuvering. In Guangzhou and Shanghai, respectively, Anderson met with his SkyTeam partners China Southern and China Eastern, viewing them as future Asian JV partners.

In an interview with *China Daily*, Anderson said Delta was ready to assist its Chinese partners with management and operations knowledge sharing. And he noted Delta's help when the two carriers were seeking slots and gates at U.S. airports. "Our goal is to closely integrate our operations and systems with the two Chinese carriers," he said, also noting—anyone paying attention knew why he was saying this—that a large percentage of all China-U.S. traffic currently passes through Korea. The message: Some of those people should stop flying through Seoul and instead fly on joint Chinese-American airline itineraries. Anderson even played the nationalist card. "China should not give its aviation industry away to the rest of the world," he said.

But this was a long-term solution. The U.S. and China did not have an open skies agreement, and although they weren't legally prohibited from doing so, U.S. regulators, in practice, didn't approve JVs without open skies. That's because 1) a JV without open skies could be messy, as airlines wouldn't have the freedom to do some of the things normally covered by a JV and 2) one incentive for countries to sign open skies pacts with the U.S. was the potential for their airlines to enter into JVs with U.S. carriers. So why take away that incentive? Besides, the U.S.-China air travel market was still immature, hindered by visa restrictions and an absence of the extremely tight commercial and political ties that linked the U.S. with Japan and Korea. It was a market to watch for the future, no doubt. But Delta had an Asian dilemma in the present.

Inconclusive remedies to this dilemma notwithstanding, Delta began 2013 just where it left off in 2012, earning a first quarter net profit of $85 million, excluding special accounting items. It was, in fact, the company's first Q1 net profit since before 9/11, more than a decade earlier. Not only was Delta earning massive sums of money in the summer. Now it wasn't giving any of the profits back during the cold, dark winter. In March alone, Delta amassed a gargantuan $300 million net profit, making it the most profitable March in company history. Fuel prices were down. And unit revenues were up sharply on routes between JFK and Europe—and JFK to London Heathrow more specifically, even before the JV with Virgin Atlantic came into force. Corporate revenue—and corporate market share—continued to grow despite a decline in business from government agencies and defense firms. Business in Asia was less robust, but that didn't matter much. By 2013, even as airlines elsewhere in the world struggled with foreign exchange volatility and slumping economies, the U.S. airline sector was the healthiest it had ever been thanks to stable fuel prices, an improving domestic economy, healthier balance sheets, network enhancements, fleet upgrades, the densification of aircraft cabins with more seats and, of course, the "Three C" reforms of consolidation, capacity cutting and charging for everything. Airline workers were doing well too. Oil producers were still doing reasonably well. But consumers were indeed paying more for airfares, after three straight decades during which fare pressure was mostly downward. A Boyd Group International study found the true cost of a one-way airline ticket had spiked 29 percent, on average, since 2008, including taxes as well as ancillary fees for items once offered without charge. Adjusted for inflation, air travel was still a better deal than it had been throughout most of history. But it was more expensive than it had been a few years earlier, reversing a century-long trend of the inflation-adjusted cost of air travel almost always declining.

The first quarter was filled with activity. In January, Delta completed its take-over of the bankrupt regional airline Pinnacle, an important provider of regional feed at Delta's hubs. Pinnacle had stayed alive while it restructured only thanks to debtor-in-possession loans provided by Delta, which remembered how it felt to be on the other end of that sort of transaction, as it had indeed been just a few years earlier. The loans then converted to equity.

Pinnacle's pilots, meanwhile, ratified a seven-year agreement that reduced pay by at least 9 percent for everyone and even more than that for higher-paid senior pilots. Pinnacle, as planned, dropped its business with United and US Airways and flew just for Delta. It agreed to remove 140 50-seat CRJ-200s over the "next two to three years" while taking on another 40 larger and more efficient CRJ-900s for Delta. Sell high, buy low: None other than Delta CEO Richard Anderson himself, back in 2003 as CEO of Northwest, had spun off Pinnacle as an independent company, fetching triple the price Delta would pay to buy it back a decade later.

Delta got an important source of low-cost regional feed. Pinnacle's pilots, meanwhile, got a carrot: first crack at future Delta mainline pilot jobs. This was important because in 2007, the U.S. FAA had raised the mandatory retirement age for pilots from 60 to 65. So for the following five years, no pilot was forced to retire—they all had an extra five years to work. But now retirement time had arrived, creating a need for qualified replacements and a bumper crop of job openings. Some people feared a pilot shortage for airlines. But Hunter Keay, an airline equity analyst for the firm Wolfe Research, said in a note to investors that this was actually yet more good news for U.S. carriers, which would replace their most senior pilots with junior ones earning much lower pay.

And Delta had no problem recruiting pilots—or anyone else, for that matter. In February 2013, employees again got big profit-sharing checks, this time amounting to $372 million, or about 7 percent of each worker's annual pay. This didn't count the $91 million in bonus payments employees received for hitting certain operational goals like arriving on time and not losing bags. Later in 2013, Delta said nearly all 80,000 of its workers would get pay raises in 2014, although they would pay a little more for their health insurance. "We just finished an employee survey across the entire company," Ed Bastian bragged to investors, "in which over half of the employees in the company participated. And over 80 percent of those employees themselves consider Delta a great place to work, and they're very proud of the fact that they work at Delta and they have great trust in their leadership."

Historically, an airline was often doing better than its peers if it had happy shareholders *or* happy employees *or* happy customers. Delta? It had all three.

Delta seemed to conclude its customers were so happy with its core product, in fact, that they might tolerate a somewhat less generous frequent flier program. So Delta would require travelers to scale higher hurdles in order to attain the "Medallion" status that confers upgrades, shorter security lines, waived bag fees, priority boarding and so forth.

A decade earlier, Delta under Leo Mullin had the same idea: Why should Medallion qualification, Mullin's team reasoned, be based primarily on how far customers flew rather than how much they spent with the airline? So Delta, in 2003, had begun awarding customers traveling in its three lowest economy fare "buckets," as airlines call their numerous categories of fares, only 50 percent as many Medallion-qualification miles (MQMs) as customers who bought less restrictive, more expensive tickets. Some customers might have to fly as many as 50,000 miles in a calendar year, rather than 25,000, to attain "silver" Medallion status, the lowest tier. These three lowest fare buckets were coded "L," "U," and "T," which was convenient for outraged frequent fliers, who began ranting on message boards of the era about Delta's "sLUT fares." This outrage mattered, because in 2003, most Americans could still choose from among many airlines. So unless most of those airlines matched Delta, Delta's customers could take their business elsewhere. Well, most of those airlines did not match Delta—only Continental did, and it did so only partly (its lowest-fare customers could still get their full qualification miles if they booked directly on the airline's own website rather than by phone or via third-party agencies). And sure enough, customers defected. Delta eventually rescinded the move, reinstating more egalitarian requirements.

But now—under different management but also, more importantly, operating in a very different environment—Delta felt emboldened to try again. The new rule, announced in 2013 but not due to be implemented until 2014, required customers to meet certain spending requirements, measured in "Medallion qualification dollars," in addition to the mileage or segments-flown requirements they already had to meet. To qualify or requalify as a platinum Medallion member, for example, a customer would still have to fly 75,000 actual miles with Delta and its partners while also—this was the new part—having to spend at least $7,500 that year with Delta. Holders of Delta-branded American Express cards would be exempt if they charged at least $25,000 annually on their cards, whether they were spending this money with Delta or with any other merchant, because this was revenue for Delta: Money spent on purchases became merchant fees paid to American Express, which, in turn, purchased miles from Delta to award to the cardholders.

Many lower-spending frequent fliers expressed outrage. But elite benefits are to some degree a zero-sum game, and a minority of Delta's highest-spending customers could be happy about the prospect of not competing against as many others for, in particular, upgrades to scarce premium seats. Still, that had been just as true in 2003 as it was today, and this move wasn't so different from what Leo Mullin had tried back then.

What *was* different was that this time, Delta didn't have to wait nervously to see whether five other legacy airlines (not to mention nettlesome AirTran, with its competing Atlanta hub and its business class cabins and its rather generous elite program) would match the move, with the wait ending in disappointment when only one of the five would match. And not giant American or giant United but only smallish Continental, at that. And only partly, at that.

This time, AirTran was gone. This time, only three other legacy airlines remained. And this time, when one of those three matched Delta's move, it did so promptly and fully. And this time, it was giant United, the only airline bigger (by most measures) than Delta itself. Of the "Three Cs," consolidation was the biggest "C" of all, because it was the "C" that, by reducing competition, had made the capacity cutting and charging for everything possible—and indeed, made moves like this one possible—because any move one airline made was more likely to "stick" with fewer competitors remaining to spoil the party by not matching the move.

(Nearly a year later, in January 2014, Delta would go a step further. It announced that beginning in 2015, SkyMiles wouldn't really be miles at all. Rather, they would be points—although still called "miles"—which customers would accrue based on how much money they spent on tickets. As before, SkyMiles Medallion members would get bonus miles. As before, holders of Delta-branded Amex cards would get additional bonuses. Soon a trip from New York to Chicago could earn more "miles" than a trip from New York to London if the fare to Chicago was higher. And big spenders could earn far more miles than penny pinchers. The Medallion qualification rules, meanwhile, would remain partly based on distance but with the added spending requirements announced in 2013—silver status, for example, required 25,000 miles flown plus $2,500 spent with Delta or $25,000 spent on a Delta-branded Amex card. Simple it was not. But once again, United matched. And once again, the move—although it wouldn't truly be implemented in 2015—looked likely to stick.)

The eventful first quarter of 2013 also featured the U.S. DOT's release of its final consumer metric data for 2012. The clear No. 1 among the four legacy airlines in key categories like on-time performance, lost bags and customer complaints? Delta. And it wasn't even close. US Airways, for its part, was a clear No. 2, while American and United ranked a distant third and fourth. Big-money corporate customers were clearly noticing—Delta's revenue from these passengers was rising at a 9 percent annual clip, with increases in the double digits on transatlantic and Latin American routes. Across all regions, they were up a whopping 31 percent from companies in the banking sector, with New York's big banks clearly impressed with Delta's planned JV with Virgin Atlantic, its terminal upgrades at JFK and LaGuardia airports, the $140 million it was spending on digital technologies like mobile apps and website upgrades, its new flat-bed seats and—indeed—its excellent punctuality. This, incidentally, was another important difference from a decade earlier, when Delta had last tried to make Medallion status more difficult to attain. Back then, customers in most cities could just choose different airlines that not only had looser elite qualification requirements but were also, at least by some measures, better airlines. Now, migrating away from Delta almost always meant accepting that your flight was more likely to be delayed and that your bag was more likely to be lost. Part of the reason Delta could get away with a less generous loyalty program was that it was running one of the most reliable operations in the history of the global airline industry.

Delta's remarkable success was indeed a big airline story in the first quarter of 2013. But not *the* big airline story.

In faraway Tempe, Ariz., near Phoenix, Doug Parker, now the longest-tenured among CEOs of major U.S. airlines, was enjoying rather impressive success in his own right. In 2012, US Airways quietly earned a 6.5 percent operating margin, only fractions behind Delta's 7.2 percent. It flew exactly zero seats to Asia, where currencies and economies were frustrating airlines like Delta. Its transatlantic and Latin American networks, by contrast, were solid, and its domestic markets were booming, especially in Charlotte and Washington's slot-controlled Reagan National Airport, where it had swapped slots with Delta. But five years had passed since Parker failed to acquire Delta, which preceded failed attempts to merge with United, in an industry where size conferred great advantages and US Airways was considerably smaller than its three legacy peers.

So just as it had done with bankrupt Delta in 2006, US Airways was now chasing bankrupt American. And just as Gerald Grinstein had done in 2006, American's CEO Tom Horton was rebuffing Parker's initial advances, saying he preferred to restructure American first and only then perhaps discuss a deal. Parker again refused to accept "no" for an answer. But this time, he courted the airline's unions just as enthusiastically as he did American's creditors, something he hadn't done with Delta. "I think US Air[ways] learned from that that the employees do mean something, and that they can affect the process," Lee Moak, by now the national leader of ALPA, the pilots' union, observed of the way Parker approached American compared to the way he had approached Delta back when Moak, then the leader of Delta's pilots, had joined with Delta's management to fight the takeover.

In the spring of 2012, American's three major unions had publicly endorsed a merger with US Airways, which offered them new contracts that included substantial pay and benefit hikes, which, in turn, would be financed by expected merger synergies. These contracts were not nearly as lucrative as those that the unions had enjoyed before bankruptcy—an expensive pilot contract was one reason the airline was in bankruptcy in the first place—but they were better than the draconian terms the workers now faced. There would be no "Keep American My American" campaign like the "Keep Delta My Delta" movement that buttressed Jerry Grinstein's defenses. This time, the unions were on the side of the raider.

Horton held firm in defense of a standalone strategy. In one comment he made—in February 2012 to the *Charlotte Observer*—he seemed to underestimate his opponents. "This is not US Airways' first attempt at this," he said correctly of the airline's failures to convince Delta and United to merge with it. But then he continued: "This is a small company, very strategically limited, I would argue—not any international flying, hubs of less strategic importance." Taking the second part first, US Airways—to cite one example—actually offered more international longhaul destinations from Philadelphia (17) than American offered from New York JFK (13) despite New York's much larger and more global population. So Horton had unwittingly drawn attention to the fact that American was, in fact, remarkably un-global, relative to its huge widebody fleet and big-city hubs. And as for those hubs, US Airways actually preferred its dominance of places like Charlotte, Washington Reagan and Philadelphia over American's second- to fourth-place positions in New York, Chicago and Los Angeles. And even as for US Airways' previous plans to merge: Sure, the past two attempts had failed, but US Airways, as it existed, was nonetheless the product of multiple rounds of consolidation, as recent as the 2005 America West-US Airways merger. And even more importantly, every major U.S. airline including US Airways—except one, American—had become profitable thanks largely to the consolidated industry that resulted precisely from US Airways' more recent failed attempts. It had driven Delta to embrace Northwest and United to embrace Continental, and almost every airline—none more so than US Airways itself—was richer for it.

Horton also noted—correctly—that US Airways hadn't even unified two rival pilot groups from the America West merger seven years earlier. With so much unfinished business there, how could it pursue another merger? American's financial results were improving too thanks to sharp cost-cutting since its bankruptcy filing in late 2011. It didn't *need* to do anything. Horton pressed on with demands for 13,000 job cuts, about half of which US Airways was pledging to save if it got its way. The three big unions, meanwhile, had each claimed a seat on the nine-member creditor committee that would ultimately vote on American's future direction. They literally had a vote on the airline's future; Horton did not. Unions at US Airways, meanwhile, would also benefit from richer post-merger contracts. Doug Parker had long told employees that US Airways was at a revenue disadvantage to its larger peers, so it needed to be at a cost advantage to make up for the revenue gap, and thus it couldn't it couldn't pay its workers what larger airlines could pay theirs. Well now those same US Airways workers could be working for the largest airline of all, with all the revenue-generating power that implied. And Parker was ready to give them raises.

Merger momentum was unstoppable. On July 19, 2012, Horton and Parker, friends from their days in the late 1980s working as young analysts at American— Parker had married his wife Gwen back then at the Hilton Anatole in Dallas—met for an early morning breakfast at the Jefferson Hotel in Washington, D.C. Horton was less defiant, essentially saying he was open to a merger but not necessarily with US Airways—other possibilities included JetBlue, Virgin America, Alaska Airlines and Frontier. A day earlier, Parker—flanked by *union leaders from American*, with all the symbolism that implied—had appeared at the National Press Club blocks from the White House, publicly advocating his plan. Horton, for his part, on July 23 told a gathering of corporate travel executives in Boston that American's turnaround plan was on track, that its network and alliances were strong, that lots of new airplanes with new inflight amenities were coming and that American would soon unveil a new logo and aircraft livery. He also said American believed in consolidation, although he didn't elaborate. On Bloomberg Television, he wooed creditors with the company's second-quarter financial results, pointing to solid profits for the first time in years, industry-leading unit revenue gains and lots more profit improvement to come once labor costs were reduced, something that was certain thanks to bankruptcy protection. "We're making a lot of progress winning corporate accounts," he added. He said again he had long believed in industry consolidation, but only on the right terms for American and only after American fixed its other problems and emerged from bankruptcy. He also said it was he who—one year earlier—had first approached Parker, not the other way around. Horton's message: We don't need a merger but would consider one.

But Horton's resistance looked more and more futile. In August the two companies signed a non-disclosure agreement to evaluate each other's finances, a standard precursor to a merger. In the meantime, American suffered a severe spike in cancellations and delays because of a sharp increase in pilot sick calls and maintenance write-ups—pilots were allegedly refusing to fly because of nonessential maintenance issues that usually waited until the next scheduled maintenance check.

By the end of 2012, merger talks were in full swing, covering critical questions like how much ownership each airline's shareholders would get and who would run the combined carrier. The new year opened with American's board set to discuss a proposed deal, which American's main unions and creditors supported. In the meantime, US Airways shares appreciated more in 2012—166 percent!—than any of the other 499 companies in the Fortune 500. Investors liked what Parker was doing. In a last-ditch attempt to torpedo a deal, Horton—although now claiming to be agnostic—pushed for an integrated pilot seniority list as a prerequisite for merging.

But the train had left the station. On Valentine's Day 2013, Parker and Horton stood side by side to announce an all-stock merger transaction. American and US Airways would combine forces to create the world's largest airline, retaining the American name, American's Dallas-Fort Worth headquarters and American's one-world alliance affiliation. But Parker would run the new airline (although Horton would stick around as chairman for a year). American's stakeholders, including creditors, would get 72 percent of the new company. US Airways shareholders would get 28 percent. Suddenly, Delta had a strong new competitor.

Or did it? On Aug. 13, 2013, the U.S. Justice Department, together with six state attorneys general and the District of Columbia, stunned the airline world with a lawsuit to block the $11 billion merger on antitrust grounds. "Business people aren't supposed to be surprised," Parker told *The Wall Street Journal*, "but we were absolutely surprised.... We had five senior lawyers working on this thing, and they never thought we'd be sued." The suit alleged "hundreds of millions of dollars" harm to consumers in the form of higher airfares and reduced service. Parker, having neglected to lure union support for his torpedoed Delta deal, had this time neglected to appease Washington. A trial was set for Nov. 25, 2013.

But this time was different in other important ways—ways that worked to Parker's benefit. This time, tens of thousands of unionized workers stood to lose higher pay and benefits if Justice stopped the merger, and they made sure to let the Obama administration know. Many states and cities stood to gain greater air access to more overseas markets, so they too mobilized on behalf of the merger. The attorneys general who had sued to block the merger began cutting deals—no severe air service cuts in their states, for example, in exchange for their support. Ultimately, on Nov. 12, 2013, Justice agreed to settle the case out of court in exchange for gate and slot divestitures at key airports. Most importantly, American agreed to surrender 52 slot pairs at Washington Reagan plus 17 slot pairs at New York LaGuardia and two gates each in Boston, Chicago O'Hare, Dallas Love Field, Los Angeles and Miami. American also promised to preserve its hubs (no significant reductions in Phoenix, for example, for at least three years) and to preserve small-city service from Reagan. Only domestic LCCs like Southwest, JetBlue and Virgin America would be permitted to obtain the new Reagan and LaGuardia slots, although Delta urged regulators to let *it* buy the slots at Reagan, where it had not long before traded away dozens of slots to none other than US Airways, because—it said—only *it*, not the LCCs, had the planes and the business model to link the airport to small communities. (The regulators laughed.)

In any event, the American-US Airways merger was a done deal. The two companies became one on Dec. 9, 2013. Delta would indeed have to compete against a bulked-up American, one with 1,511 airplanes, 560 new planes on order, 101 million frequent fliers and more than $1 billion in expected synergies by 2015. Would this jeopardize Delta's miracle turnaround?

Quite the opposite, Delta's executives said. At a JP Morgan investor event in early 2013, Ed Bastian, mindful of the additional pricing power all airlines would enjoy, had said he welcomed the prospect of an American-US Airways merger. One fact was inescapable: Just four U.S. airlines—all products of recent mega-mergers—now controlled a full 85 percent of all domestic airline seats. Add JetBlue and Alaska, and the figure topped 92 percent. And as Delta could see, United was stumbling badly following its merger with Continental, and Southwest's acquisition of AirTran, far from shaking up Atlanta, had further cemented Delta's dominance there. Bastian also pointed out that mergers take time. "The reality is there is only one deal that really has been concluded and completed," he said, "and that's the Delta-Northwest merger. That's fully integrated. So from my perspective, I think we're still in the relatively early innings of the benefits of consolidation, because these deals still have a couple of years before they're fully integrated, fleets are rationalized, new labor rates are set. And the benefits of those across the entire industry landscape are yet to be seen."

But this much was known: The Big Six of the terrible post-9/11 era were now the Big Three. That alone put the U.S. airline industry on surer footing than ever, even with oil prices still high, averaging $98 in 2013, up from $94 in 2012. "We've all known consolidation was the answer to a lot of the industry's problems," Gordon Bethune told *Fortune* magazine back in 2007, adding: "It's just that Doug's the only one with the balls to go and do it." That was after Doug Parker's attempt to buy Delta, which followed his America West takeover of US Airways and preceded his US Airways merger with American, with the Delta-Northwest and United-Continental mergers—both caused by Parker's other overtures—sandwiched in between.

Parker and his team had helped shape the U.S. airline industry. But he wasn't the man on top—at least not yet. That distinction belonged to Richard Anderson. It was Anderson who presided over the country's most profitable airline, and it was Anderson who, in June 2013, assumed his role as ambassador for the global airline industry, becoming chairman of the International Air Transport Association, or IATA. A month earlier, on one night, the interviewer Charlie Rose, on his influential television talk show, had welcomed just two guests: the legendary basketball coach Phil Jackson, mastermind of 11 NBA championships, and Richard Anderson. In a 25-minute interview, Anderson answered a question about consolidation and airfares by arguing there's still "plenty of contestability in the marketplace." He defended bag charges by noting Delta's $150 million investment in Atlanta's bag handling system, which made the system more reliable—customers were paying more but getting more. And when asked which airline's service he admired most, he predictably answered Virgin Atlantic. He also boasted of having bought the oil refinery, of a fourth straight year of "really strong profitability," and—he seemed most proud of this—of Delta's unusually strong rapport with its workers. "We have the best labor relations in the world," he said.

Anderson continued winning praise from some of his fiercest competitors, such as British Airways chief Willie Walsh, who lauded Anderson both generally and specifically—Delta's investment in Gol, for example, was "very, very smart." Lufthansa's CEO Christoph Franz told *Airline Weekly* Anderson was "one of the great leaders of our industry, even on a worldwide basis."

Delta had a reputation for being smart but also tough. Its approach to both Alaska and Korean Air—an approach that channeled the old ruthlessness for which Northwest had been famous—impacted other relationships too. SkyTeam member Aeroflot, according to Russian news sources, contemplated a defection to the Star Alliance because—the reports said—of a frayed relationship with Delta. Aeroflot was said to be frustrated with the bilateral agreements it had with Delta, which covered formulas for calculating how revenue would be split for joint itineraries and terms for frequent flier cooperation. Aeroflot remained in SkyTeam. But by mid-2013, Delta's SkyMiles chart of Medallion-qualification mileage accruals on partner airlines had basically become a ranking of the importance of other airlines in Delta's eyes. Delta customers got the most MQMs when they flew Air France/KLM, Alaska, Alitalia, Aeroméxico, Gol, Virgin Atlantic or Virgin Australia. Never mind that four of the seven weren't even in SkyTeam. Six of the seven were either equity partners or JV partners, or both, with Delta. The seventh, Delta's frenemy Alaska, paid Delta a king's ransom for its miles. Delta customers got no qualification miles at all if they flew Korean. Most other SkyTeam airlines fell somewhere in between.

Delta's toughness was also on display in Dallas, where it expressed its intention to bid for Love Field gates American was forced to divest. If Delta got its way, it would offer two-class service (Southwest couldn't offer that) to key business destinations and one-stop service to the world (Southwest couldn't offer that either) from the downtown Dallas airport via Delta's hubs. In Boston, where JetBlue was now top dog, Delta announced three new overlapping destinations: Las Vegas, Jacksonville and Richmond, plus a second daily frequency to Los Angeles and some Saturday-only Caribbean flights. Why? Because that was the price it exacted on JetBlue for launching Boston flights to Delta's Detroit hub. Delta was defending Detroit the same way Northwest had done throughout the years.

Delta wasn't afraid of taking on its rivals in California, even adopting a high-frequency shuttle-like schedule in the extremely competitive Los Angeles-San Francisco market. Just like its New York-Boston-Washington Shuttle in the northeast corridor, Delta's new California shuttle featured hourly weekday flights, free newspapers, dedicated check-in counters and complimentary snacks. In Memphis, on the other hand, ignoring pleas from local politicians and business leaders, Delta was now flying just 90 weekday departures. On Saturdays, it operated—how's this for variable scheduling?—just 18.

The spring and summer of 2013 brought another round of spectacular profits, helped by declining fuel prices. Delta's oil refinery was still losing money in its own right, but Ed Bastian repeatedly insisted refining spreads (the markup after crude became jet fuel), which were falling, would have been substantially higher without the fuel Delta's Trainer, Pa., facility was pumping into the market. In May, Delta opened its upgraded terminal at New York JFK, celebrating the occasion with a media event featuring New York mayor Michael Bloomberg and Virgin's Richard Branson.

Also in May, Delta thrilled investors with a capital deployment plan that included quarterly dividend payments, share buybacks, further debt repayment and contributions to its frozen pension plans to reduce its future liabilities. All this was possible thanks to booming cash generation from Delta's day-to-day operations, which amounted to $1.3 billion in the second quarter of 2013 alone, followed by $1.2 billion in the third quarter. Even after subtracting the cash Delta spent on airplanes and other investments, free cash flow for the two quarters amounted to a weighty $1.4 billion. No other airline came close.

That's partly because subtracting what Delta spent on airplanes—normally by far the largest capital expenditures for airlines—didn't imply subtracting all that much at all, because Delta was paying rather little for its fleet. In early 2014, Delta would operate its last scheduled DC-9 flight, finally saying goodbye to an aircraft type for which Delta had been the launch customer in 1965, less than two years into Lyndon Baines Johnson's presidency. Since 2008, the airline had retired more than 350 planes, including DC-9s, yes, but also 50-seat CRJ-200s and 34-seat Saab-340 turboprops. The last DC-9 flown was an old Northwest bird originally bought by Republic Airlines, the airline Northwest (then called Northwest Orient) bought in 1986. But all these years later, Delta was still buying the DC-9's descendant MD-90s, at pennies on the dollar compared to a new 737-800. The prices were so attractive that Delta was happy to grab one whenever it could even just for spare parts, because the sum of the prices of an airplane's parts is usually far higher than the cost of a whole airplane. A big in-house parts inventory for old aircraft might not have done most airlines a lot of good. But Delta's large non-unionized maintenance operation continued offsetting a big disadvantage of old aircraft: their propensity to need fixing. In April, moreover, Delta announced its intention to upgrade its 182 MD-88 and MD-90 planes with new avionics suites, reducing their fuel burn by enabling them to pursue more efficient flight paths (and confirming these planes would be around for many years to come, because otherwise Delta wouldn't bother making an investment like that).

In the fall of 2013, Delta started taking its first 717s from Southwest. Simultaneously, it began receiving the first of 100 brand new Boeing 737-900ERs designated to replace Delta's oldest 757s. Newer 757s, for their part, were standardized and densified with additional seats. The 737 purchase showed Delta wasn't averse to buying new planes. In fact, it opportunistically added 10 Airbus 330s and 30 321s to its order book in September. But these were current-generation airplanes, not the future-generation 737 MAXs and 787s or 320neos and 350s that Boeing and Airbus were now selling, and that other airlines were voraciously buying. Other than the 787s Richard Anderson had ordered when he was CEO of Northwest, an order Delta had effectively canceled (although technically deferred many years into the future), Delta in 2013 had no orders for any next-generation planes—not the MAX, not the neo, not the widebody 350, not the new Bombardier CSeries. (Delta did hold options to convert the last 40 of its 737-900ER deliveries to the future-generation MAX version of those.) Anderson did express (to both Reuters and the Associated Press) an affinity for the stretched 787-10 Boeing was selling. But in general, he was wary of buying any new aircraft technology, mindful of the how the 787-8s now flying were dramatically different from what he had signed up for at Northwest years earlier. Let other airlines overpay and then find out the true performance of what they had ordered. Delta could buy planes later, once they were cheaper and that performance was known.

Not even a squabbling U.S. government could derail Delta's momentum. A 16-day federal government shutdown in October, orchestrated by dissident Republicans loosely organized under the "Tea Party" banner, cost the U.S. economy about $24 billion, according to various estimates, with airlines among the affected. Delta, for its part, said revenues declined an estimated $20 million to $25 million as a result of lost bookings. But never mind. In the October-to-December quarter, Delta produced another $558 million in profits.

The end of 2013 brought the death of Nelson Mandela, the fallout from the Edward Snowden affair and a Red Sox World Series victory. It also brought another symbolic reflection of Delta's rise. The airline's shares once again joined the Standard & Poor's 500 index, a collection of some of the largest U.S. companies by market value. S&P had dropped Delta just before it filed for bankruptcy in 2005, leaving Southwest as the only airline member. But now Southwest's market value was roughly half that of Delta, which was now the world's most valuable airline.

And no wonder. On Jan. 21, 2014, Delta reported its annual results for 2013. The highlight: a massive $2.7 billion net profit, more than double what it had earned in its previous best year ever, and more than any other airline had earned—anywhere in the world—in the 100-year history of commercial aviation.

Epilogue

June 17, 2014, was a special day for Delta Air Lines. It was the company's 85th anniversary, a perfect occasion to celebrate the opening of a 68,000-square-foot museum celebrating its illustrious history. It was there, on the grounds of Atlanta's giant airport, that Georgia's governor Nathan Deal officially proclaimed June 17 Delta Air Lines Day, a day to honor a company employing more than 30,000 people in Georgia alone. More than just a job provider, though, Delta had played a vital role in building Atlanta into one of the country's top business centers. It helped America's Sun Belt transform into a magnet for migration and investment in the post-World War II era. It played a supporting role in advancing the Civil Rights movement. It made the vast American continent a smaller place. It linked America to the rest of the world.

June 17, 2014, was also a perfect occasion to marvel at what Delta had achieved since its traumatic bankruptcy filing in 2005. There were so many reasons why it might not have recovered its past glory, a glory prevalent through most of its first seven decades of flying. While still in bankruptcy, Delta had almost lost its independence to US Airways. In 2008 it had taken a risky chance on merging with Northwest, just months before the onset of a giant economic meltdown. The new decade brought gradual economic recovery but also a return to extremely high oil prices—on June 17, 2014, the price per barrel was $107. A bold attempt to snatch Japan Airlines from the clutches of American had ended in failure.

Nevertheless, by 2014, Delta was well on its way to five straight years of profits that were large and getting larger. During 2013, Delta had earned more money than any airline in the history of the world. And during the first half of 2014, it was on pace to earn even more—a lot more. It was now carrying 165 million passengers annually, more than the entire population of Russia. During 2014's peak summer season, Delta's already industry-leading operational performance got better: more than 2,000 fewer cancellations versus the year prior, and some 22,000 fewer flight delays. From late June through mid-August, for a period of 50 consecutive days, the

Delta team didn't cancel a single mainline flight. "I really don't think an airline of our size, or even close to our size, has ever run as well as we've run in peak season," Richard Anderson told employees. In 2013, only two much smaller airlines—Alaska Airlines and Hawaiian Airlines, the latter flying from an airport where the weather is always nice and sunny—had better on-time rates.

The operational excellence was a fitting capstone to Delta's remarkable story, a story of how it fell into a state of distress and disrepair in the wake of the 9/11 attacks in 2001—and how it then rebuilt itself into the world's most profitable airline. It did so by merging with Northwest, cutting costs, slashing debt, globalizing its route network, working closely with Air France/KLM, aggressively charging for ancillary services, restraining capacity growth, expanding its New York presence through a slot swap with US Airways, adding seats to its aircraft, investing in three overseas airlines and even buying an oil refinery. It devised a way to simultaneously reward its pilots and right-size its fleet. It restructured its regional operations by selling Mesaba and Compass, closing Comair and buying Pinnacle. It maintained a direct relationship with most of its employees, getting productivity and management flexibility other airlines didn't have. It mastered the art of dynamic flight scheduling by season and day of week. It worked closely with American Express to continue developing SkyMiles into an even bigger cash cow, even while now awarding benefits based on dollars spent rather than just distance flown. And it leveraged its strength in Atlanta, which in 2014 was still the world's busiest airport—and one thoroughly dominated by Delta. More Delta seats departed from Atlanta, in fact, than from its next four biggest hubs—Minneapolis, Detroit, New York JFK and Salt Lake City—combined. No single American or United hub, by contrast, was nearly as important.

Because it was now earning such massive profits, and had so little debt, Delta could share large portions of the bounty with employees, investors and customers. Had it really been only a few years since even business travelers were defecting to AirTran, JetBlue and other rivals, which were offering not just lower fares but often better inflight amenities too? Not anymore. Today, Delta offers lie-flat longhaul premium seats, inflight Wi-Fi, extra-legroom economy seats for loyal customers and others willing to pay more, new airport terminals in New York and Atlanta, renovated lounges, first class cabins on regional jets, customer service via mobile and social media channels, an upgraded website and airport kiosks with ever more functionality. And to make sure the flying public knew Delta was now better than ever, the airline spent heavily on marketing, linking its brand to everything from Apple to the New York Yankees. *Fortune* now ranked Southwest Airlines, Singapore Airlines and Delta as the only airlines among its 50 "most admired companies."

The year 2014 brought more innovation and strategic maneuvering. One example—again a break with industry norms—was Delta's decision to insource its critical information technology, more specifically the 180-odd applications linked to its Deltamatic reservation system and operational control system. Its technology supplier Travelport would still provide tech support, but Delta now owned the intellectual property and assumed responsibility for application development, with plans to be—in Richard Anderson's words—"the first global airline to build a modern passenger service system in house." Ironically, Anderson, while still running Northwest Airlines in the industry's dark days of the early 2000s, had led the negotiation to *sell* the Worldspan reservation system, which Northwest and Delta jointly owned. "We wanted to get it back ever since," he said.

Delta's Asia strategy, meanwhile, was still a work in progress. Its New York operations lost money in 2013, as they had long done. But then, for the first time, they profited in 2014. The airline signed a lucrative new marketing contract with American Express. This time American Express, not Delta, was the one facing rockier business conditions. The specifics of the deal, as always, were secret. But little skill at reading between the lines of public statements was required to conclude that this time, the terms were far more favorable to Delta. Delta applied to form yet another JV, this time with Aeroméxico. It was close to restoring its investment graded credit rating. It began negotiating a new pilot contract. It ordered 25 next-generation Airbus 350-900s, with deliveries due to start in 2017—mostly to replace 747-400s flying to Asia—and 25 Airbus 330neos due to begin arriving in 2019, mostly to replace 767-300s to Europe. It lobbied to open New York's LaGuardia Airport to cross-country flying. And it rebranded its fare offering, marketing international and transcontinental first class seats, for example, as "Delta One" and economy seats as "Delta Comfort Plus," "Main Cabin" or "Basic Economy," that last one a limited-frills offering designed to compete against ultra-LCCs such as Spirit and Frontier, which were attacking Atlanta.

Then something unexpected happened. As late as July 2014, crude oil prices were still hovering above $100 per barrel. Delta and its peers weren't complaining all that much, because even if these prices were high, at least they were stable—and airlines had learned how to match supply with demand to keep fares high enough to profit at almost any price of oil, as long as that price didn't suddenly surge. But then prices began to fall: to $97 in August, $93 in September, $84 in October, $76 in November, $59 in December and just $47 in January 2015, on their way toward $40 later in the year. And this time, unlike when prices tumbled sharply in the second half of 2008, the economy was not in deep recession—on the contrary, it was growing, underpinned by rising employment and now a windfall for American households, who were paying far less to fuel their cars.

The great collapse in oil prices during the second half of 2014 naturally had enormous geopolitical and economic consequences around the globe. And naturally for airlines, cheaper fuel meant greater profits. Delta, well into 2015, couldn't fully enjoy the cheap-fuel windfall because of its heavy hedging. But still, its profits skyrocketed. In 2014's fourth quarter—an off-peak quarter, remember, when Delta historically hoped only to not lose too much money—it earned a $650 million profit, excluding special accounting items. American, which was completely unhedged, was doing even better. All U.S. airlines were basking in their greatest financial performance ever.

It was, in fact, a complete reversal of conditions present in the mid-2000s, when fuel was expensive, domestic demand was weak and international demand was the only safety valve. Now, in the mid-2010s, fuel was cheap, domestic demand was strong and international demand was the only problem area.

And markets outside North America were indeed becoming more problematic. By early 2015, Europe's economy was beginning to show some signs of life, more so in some countries like the U.K. and Spain. But conditions overall were still weak, with the Greek economy again near default. Japan's economy remained largely stagnant too. China's was sharply slowing. So its appetite for raw materials was waning, hurting commodity exporters from South America to Africa to Australia. The long-weak U.S. dollar? It was now a memory. And strengthening dollars rendered dollar-priced fuel more expensive than it otherwise would have been for most airlines outside the U.S. Some with heavy hedging, like Delta's partner Air France/KLM, would hardly see any benefit at all from falling oil prices. The oil-dependent Russian economy, meanwhile, already subject to U.S. and European sanctions because of events in Ukraine, was now suffering its worst crisis since the late 1990s. Brazil, an economic superstar of the 2000s, became an economic basket case of the 2010s, hurt badly by a fall in the price of commodities; who knew a home turf thrashing by Germany in the World Cup would prove the least of its worries? Paris suffered a major terrorist attack, as did other countries including Tunisia, Denmark and Kenya. The ASEAN region was traumatized by not one but two Malaysia Airlines disasters, one a mysterious loss of contact with a plane flying to China, the other a plane shot down by a missile fired from war-torn Ukraine. In the always-turbulent Middle East, an ultra-violent militant group called ISIS emerged a victor of sorts from Syria's bloody civil war, building on its gains to occupy parts of Iraq.

In this world of darkening economies and ever-present tragedies, Delta, like American and United, saw its international revenues weaken. Foreign currency depreciation was one of the chief causes, with tickets sold in euros, yen and Brazilian reals, for example, no longer worth as much. In countries like Japan, meanwhile, cheaper fuel triggered an immediate government-decreed drop in fuel surcharges. So Delta cut its international capacity, ending its wintertime Moscow flights and accelerating retirement of 747s serving Asia.

This international softness didn't worry Delta much, not because of arrogance but because Delta's defenses were more powerful than ever before, even in its earlier glory years. Its size and scale were now massive, and its revenue base was diversified across all major global geographies and buttressed abroad by antitrust-immune JVs. What's more, a full fifth of Delta's revenues now came from sources other than selling tickets—it now minted billions of dollars shipping cargo, maintaining planes for other airlines and charging passengers for checking bags, upgrading their seats and so on.

Even with Air France suffering a debilitating two-week pilot strike in the fall of 2014, Delta still profited in Europe, its most important international region—the

Virgin Atlantic JV, for one thing, was proving a big success, all the more so with London's economy strengthening.

Most importantly, domestic markets were booming. The home economy, to be sure, wasn't problem-free. Unemployment was falling, but wages remained sluggish, and income inequality continued growing. Government finances, meanwhile, were improving but remained burdened by the prospect of skyrocketing pension and health care costs as baby boomers retired. The problem was solvable through benefit cuts or higher taxation, but America's political system was gridlocked over which direction to take. The wars in Iraq and Afghanistan, meanwhile, had cost American taxpayers between $4 trillion and $6 trillion, according to one Harvard University researcher, or roughly a third of the country's gross domestic product. In a way, this money was a huge federal stimulus program, supporting the incomes of many soldiers, suppliers, contractors and American communities with military bases. But this was money the government had borrowed, from Asian governments, most notably, and as such it had created giant debt obligations back when a giant recession loomed—and just as a major demographic shift was taking place.

But long-term risks aside, the U.S. economy was not a major concern for airlines in 2014, and it wasn't likely to threaten the industry's profit renaissance. Government finances were indeed improving rapidly, private sector job growth was strong, inflation and interest rates remained low, oil prices had fallen drastically and the American economy was now considerably larger than it had been before the recession. The global economic boom that U.S. airlines chased in the mid-2000s, when they were eager to avoid turmoil at home, was a thing of the past. Now, foreign airlines were escaping their local problems by eagerly expanding to the U.S.

Case in point: the fast-expanding state-owned airlines of the Arabian Gulf peninsula. In 2014 and early 2015, Emirates began flying to Boston and Chicago while announcing new service to Orlando. Qatar Airways started Miami, Chicago, Dallas-Fort Worth and Philadelphia, with new service planned to Boston, Los Angeles and—yes—Atlanta. Etihad Airways showed up in Los Angeles, San Francisco and Dallas-Fort Worth. What's more, Emirates began flying to New York JFK from Milan, sending shivers down the spines of Delta, American and United, which had worked so hard to consolidate the transatlantic market with their JVs. No airline lobbied harder against this route than Delta, which subsequently joined its rivals American and United in a loud campaign to restrict Gulf carrier expansion. U.S. carriers, Glen Hauenstein sneered, "can't just go out and hire guest workers for two years and if they don't smile at the customers, they get deported."

A low-fare airline called Norwegian was also expanding across the Atlantic, with flights from Scandinavia and London to various U.S. cities, raising the ominous specter of LCCs doing to Delta internationally this decade what they had done to it domestically last decade. At home, Spirit Airlines was earning huge profit margins and expanding rapidly. A small airport near Atlanta was pushing for permission to handle LCC flights, potentially taking traffic from Delta's hub, which, remember, had long enjoyed the considerable advantage of competing against no other nearby airports. Far more significantly, the newly merged American and US Airways, piloted by Doug Parker, got off to a roaring start, earning 2014 operating profit margins not much lower than Delta's. It was still early, of course—post-merger United had gotten off to a strong start too, only to stumble later. Would American stumble, or would it dethrone Delta as America's global airline champion?

In the early months of 2015, Delta and its U.S. airline industry peers, profitable like never before, couldn't help but ask themselves if this was—as had been said about so much else in the broader world—their "new normal." Had the "Three C" reforms—consolidation, capacity cutting and charging for everything—created a structurally reformed business that could stay successful and withstand shocks, even if fuel prices did rebound? Would low oil prices prove an unexpected challenge to the first two "Cs," attracting new startup airlines that would once again fragment the sector, or triggering an unstoppable urge to grow as the variable cost of growth trended toward zero? As 2015 progressed, jet fuel prices continued falling, but—this part was new—airfares had begun falling too. For the moment, fuel prices were winning that race to the bottom, and U.S. airlines were more profitable than ever. But the supply of domestic seats seemed to be outpacing the demand for those seats, and now Delta, American and United could be seen doing something they hadn't had to do in recent years: matching the fares of ultra-discounters like Spirit to fill the most marginal seats. One-way $40 domestic fares on legacy airlines, which had seemed relegated to history, began reappearing in some markets. This could be a perfectly acceptable side effect of cheaper fuel—if, that is, Delta wasn't forced to sell too many $40 tickets, and if fuel prices didn't begin rising again. Were Delta's trials and tribulations of the 2000s a one-off anomaly in an otherwise triumphant history? Or could darkness and despair return?

And if darkness and despair did someday return, might Delta regret something else it was increasingly doing: distancing itself, in more ways than only through its superior profits and operations, from the rest of the industry it was now leading? Delta, upset its U.S. peers weren't doing more to oppose Arabian Gulf airline expansion to the U.S. and were supporting an air traffic control privatization effort Delta opposed, dropped out of its trade group, Airlines for America—an unusual step for a legacy airline anywhere in the world. Delta had already angered Boeing and other U.S.-based exporters by leading the fight against the Export-Import Bank, which facilitated aircraft sales around the world (a practice Delta felt disadvantaged U.S. airlines). Delta lost that fight in late 2015. But now it was angering the broader global aircraft manufacturing and finance community by insisting a giant aircraft price bubble was in the process of bursting—older Boeing 777s, it said, were now available for as little as $10 million. (List prices for new 777s can exceed $300 million.) When manufacturers and financiers—they, to be sure, just as self-interested in high prices as bargain bin-shopping Delta was in low prices—rose to dispute this, Delta provided as evidence its claim that Boeing itself had offered Delta an old 777 for $10 million. This too—apparently revealing aircraft pricing discussions, which are normally shrouded in secrecy—was an unusual step for an airline. Delta wasn't alone among its peers in renegotiating a co-branded credit card deal, but its apparent success at shifting huge sums of revenue back to itself from American Express, the company that had helped save Delta a decade earlier, was a clear signal the airline wouldn't remain deferential forever. Its polygamous partner Alaska Airlines, still the target of Delta network attacks in Seattle, moved ever closer to another partner (and Delta's enemy) American, while Delta's partner Korean Air, which had likewise frustrated Delta's Asia ambitions and which Delta likewise punished, launched a new partnership with American.

American and Delta, meanwhile, took the unusual step of ending a standard interline agreement between the two carriers to, for example, transfer bags for passengers on multi-airline itineraries or reaccommodate passengers from a canceled flight onto the other airline. Delta, in a press release, left nothing to the imagination about which airline had decided to end the deal and why: "In July, for example, American sent passengers to Delta for reaccommodation at a five-to-one ratio. At that rate, the industry agreement was no longer mutually beneficial." Inside jet boarding bridges in Atlanta, advertisements proclaimed to passengers boarding Delta's punctual flights that it was "The On-Time Machine;" a frequent flier with a long memory couldn't help but wonder whether Delta was taunting American, which had prominently used that slogan in a series of its own advertisements in the late 1980s. (American's trademark for the slogan had lapsed in 2002.) By late 2015, Delta's giant mainline operation (that is, the roughly 3,000 daily flights not outsourced to subsidiaries or regional partners) had notched more than 150 days during the year without a cancellation due to mechanical problems. Perhaps even more impressively, it had notched more than 100 days without a single cancellation, anywhere in the world, for any reason—not even for weather, airport worker strikes, political unrest and other factors largely beyond an airline's control. United, American and Southwest, Richard Anderson said in a weekly message to Delta employees, probably didn't have a total of 10 such days combined. And non-mainline flights? Delta was suing its regional flying supplier Republic for messy operations that were due largely, in turn, to a freeze on pilot hiring while Republic fought its pilot union to get the competitive costs Delta and its peers demanded. Delta's competitors, partners and suppliers began whispering that Delta's justifiable pride was perhaps morphing into a more unseemly arrogance. Some surely yearned for Delta to stumble. But these same people were quick to acknowledge Delta was indeed now the envy of the industry. Whether or not Delta's public boasting was advisable—does pride cometh before the fall?—it had earned the right to boast.

Delta had engineered an epic turnaround, among the greatest in American corporate history. After stumbling from the industry's commanding heights to near oblivion, Delta rose from that despair to unprecedented strength. The Delta Air Lines story is one of glory, lost and then found.

Sourcing

The authors have researched, written and formatted this book as a work of journalism. Sources of information and ideas that were not their own, or were not broadly in the public domain, are cited within the text. Except where otherwise noted, airline schedule data—for example, an airline starting or ending flights in a market, or increasing or decreasing seat-mile capacity during a year—is from Diio Mi, an airline data supplier, supplemented with government data. Except in "The Early Years," the primary source of data, where not otherwise noted, was primary research by the authors related to this project as well as to their work producing the *Airline Weekly* newsletter. "The Early Years" relied greatly on information from Delta annual reports dating back to 1943, purchased from the Delta Flight Museum.

Delta, as a company, did not approve, endorse or participate in this project. As will have been apparent to the reader, individuals within the company, who couldn't be named if they are current employees, were generous with their time. To them, and to everyone who contributed knowledge to this project, whether they could be named in the manuscript or not, the authors are extraordinarily grateful.

The reader should not assume that a particular individual told an anecdote to the authors, even if that person was involved in that anecdote, unless the person is clearly quoted as having spoken to the authors. Stories are routinely observed by other people, and people involved in stories routinely recount their experiences to other people. For example, if the authors could corroborate that an idea originated with a certain person—i.e., because several other people independently and clearly recalled that the person thought of the idea—the authors would report that, even if they could not verify it with that person.

The authors have painstakingly attempted to recount events in a fair and accurate manner. Despite those efforts, any project of this scope likely contains errors. The authors apologize in advance for any such errors and—when apprised of them—will correct them in future editions.

Any attempt to individually thank everyone involved in this project would be an exercise in futility: The moment the first copy is printed, the authors would think of yet another person who should have been named—and so they will not attempt to do so. However, to everyone who contributed in any way—from the people who spoke to the authors, both on and off the record, to those who helped put the authors in touch with those people, to those people's family members and staff who helped facilitate the discussions, to friends and family members of the authors who were not only inconvenienced by the project but also offered to supply ideas for the project and/or to read and help edit the book, and whose input made the finished product incalculably better—the authors offer their unconditional, eternal, heartfelt thanks.

About the Authors

Seth Kaplan has been the managing partner of *Airline Weekly* since 2005. Since joining the publication, he has become a globally recognized airline expert and is frequently asked by print and broadcast media to provide perspectives. Within the industry, he's often been a guest speaker and has taught numerous airline economics courses to executives and staff at airlines around the world. Kaplan's role at *Airline Weekly* follows a career in journalism and government. He holds a Master of Public Administration degree from Florida International University and a Bachelor of Arts degree (with a major in journalism) from George Washington University. Kaplan lives in Fort Lauderdale, Florida.

Jay Shabat has been *Airline Weekly*'s publisher ever since he co-founded the company in 2004. His airline experience includes three years as a senior revenue management analyst for US Airways in Virginia and two years as a corporate pricing analyst for Air France in New York City. He has taught numerous airline management courses and consulted for airlines around the world, providing instruction and expertise in airline industry economics, revenue and cost management, network planning and marketing/distribution. Shabat earned a Master of International Affairs degree from Columbia University's School of International and Public Affairs, with concentrations in international finance and economic policy and a regional focus on Europe. He currently lives in Fort Myers, Florida.

Long before all of the above, Kaplan and Shabat were roommates at George Washington University in Washington, D.C. They remain friends to this day.

CPSIA information can be obtained
at www.ICGtesting.com
Printed in the USA
LVOW12s1949170816
500775LV00005B/781/P